AF743765

CHARITY HANDBOOK

FOURTH EDITION

EDITOR

Kirsty Semple

icsa
The Governance
Institute

First published 2010

Published by
ICSA Publishing Ltd
Saffron House
6–10 Kirby Street
London EC1N 8TS

© ICSA Publishing Limited, 2019

All rights reserved. No part of this publication may be reproduced, stored in a retrieval system, or transmitted, in any form, or by any means, electronic, mechanical, photocopying, recording or otherwise, without prior permission, in writing from the publisher.

The right of Kirsty Semple to be identified as author of the general editor's part of the work has been asserted by her in accordance with sections 77 and 78 of the Copyright, Designs and Patents Act 1988.

The rights of the following contributors to be identified as authors of their work have been asserted by them in accordance with sections 77 and 78 of the Copyright, Designs and Patents Act 1988: Jane Ascroft, Emma Burrows, Helen Cookson, Elizabeth Davis, Graham Elliott, Chris Priestley, Mandy Webster.

Typeset by Paul Barrett Book Production, Cambridge
Edited by Sheida Heidari
Cover designed by Anthony Kearney

British Library Cataloguing in Publication Date
A catalogue record for this book is available from the British Library

ISBN: 978-186072-769-6

Contents

Preface

The task of administering a charity, and having regard to all the relevant laws and regulations, is a difficult one. Charities are governed not just by charity law, but by the laws that relate to their legal form; that govern how businesses and employers operate, and that relate to their specific area of work. The range of charities, in terms of size, legal structure, and governance, is also very wide. It can, therefore, seem like an almost impossible task to provide a handbook that will be useful to them all. However, it is vital that there is such a handbook. There is an increasing focus on the importance of charities being governed and operating well, both effectively and legally. This handbook is a resource to assist charity workers with this task.

The Charity Handbook aims to give an overview of rules and procedures governing how a charity works and operates under charity law. The type of legal form that a charity takes will also affect how it operates. With many charities also being registered as companies, this book covers the requirements under company law. However, charities can take a wide range of other legal forms and we also deal with these requirements. Many new charities are now being registered as Charitable Incorporated Organisations (CIOs) and this text, therefore, deals fully with this legal form. It covers a host of other legislation, regulations and best practice that can impact on charities– from employment law to data protection.

It focuses on charities that are registered in England and Wales. There is different charity legislation in Scotland and Northern Ireland, and different regulatory bodies for both of those countries. These different requirements are touched on to some extent, as charities registered in England and Wales sometimes work in these other countries. However, references to charities in this book are to charities recognised as such under the law of England and Wales, unless otherwise specified. Where relevant, reference is made to the comparable law or regulatory requirements in Scotland or Northern Ireland.

This is the fourth edition of the handbook and there has been several key changes for charities in recent years. The handbook has been updated to reflect all of these changes in regulation, best practice and the law. As well as these updates, we have revised the structure of the book and added some new sections. The intention is for the book to cover the full lifespan of a charity and the structure reflects this. It starts with the fundamental components of a charity and setting one up; moves on to the ongoing requirements for its management and business; and finally, the deals with the possibility of the charity coming to an end – either through merger or winding up.

There is now much more focus on how charities deal with serious incidents, and their reporting obligations, and for this reason, we have included a new chapter on this.

Section A covers charity law, legal forms, and setting up a charity. The chapters look at key issues such as the definition of a charity and the public benefit test, how to set up a new charity and advice on the form that it should take. These include trusts, companies; Community Benefit Societies, Charitable Incorporated Organisations (CIOs) and other forms. This section provides an overview of constitutions and how to amend them and details the process of converting an unincorporated charity into a corporate charity. We finish off this section by outlining the key roles within a charity, principally the role of trustees.

Section B is concerned with the ongoing requirements of a charity – the compliance and regulations that they face. It also looks at the records that a charity will need to retain, and its filing requirements.

Section C deals with a core area of importance to charities: governance. This section has been expanded to now cover meetings, decision making, risk management and internal controls. The first chapter has been substantially revised – outlining some of the core principles of governance and also discusses recent trends and the Charity Governance Code.

Section D focuses on managing the charity's business and covers issues such as the employment of staff, fundraising and trading and key matters such as data protection, which has been fully revised to reflect the introduction of GDPR and the Data Protection Act 2018. There is also a short chapter on contracts and how they are signed and sealed. This chapter also provides a short overview of some of the issues concerning the provision of public service by charities. While this book cannot provide a detailed review of contract law, this chapter should be of use to a charity administrator. It is Section D that includes the new chapter on serious incidents.

Section E looks at the core area of finance and use of the charity's assets.

Section F concludes by reviewing options for winding up and mergers.

Kirsty Semple
June 2019

List of abbreviations

ACAS	Advisory, Conciliation and Arbitration Service
ACEVO	Association of Chief Executives of Voluntary Organisations
ADR	alternative dispute resolution
AGM	annual general meeting
AML	Additional Maternity Leave
ARO	accounting reference date
BCCI	Bank of Credit & Commerce International
BIA	Border and Immigration Agency
BSI	British Standards Institution
CA 2006	Companies Act 2006
CAB	Citizen's Advice Bureau
CBS	community benefit society
CCNI	Charity Commission for Northern Ireland
CEO	chief executive officer
CDF	Common Deposit Funds
CIC	community interest company
CIF	Common Investment Funds
CIO	Charitable Incorporated Organisation
CLG	company limited by guarantee
CLS	company limited by shares
CPUT	Consumer Protection from Unfair Trading Regulations
CRB	Criminal Records Bureau
CSCI	Commission for Social Care Inspection
CVA	Company Voluntary Arrangement
CQC	Care Quality Commission
DBS	Disclosure and Barring Service
DMA	Direct Marketing Association
DPA 2018	Data Protection Act 2018
DPIA	data protection impact assessment
DPO	data protection officer
EA 2010	Equality Act 2010
ET	Employment Tribunal
EWC	expected week of childbirth
FA 2010	Finance Act 2010
FCA	Financial Conduct Authority
FRC	Financial Reporting Council

EHRC Code	Employment Statutory Code of Practice
GDPR	General Data Protection Regulation
HASAWA 1974	Health and Safety at Work Act 1974
HMRC	Her Majesty's Revenue & Customs
HSCICC	HSC Incident Contact Centre
HSE	Health and Safety Executive
LIA	legitimate interests assessment
IANA 2006	Immigration, Asylum and Nationality Act 2006
ICO	Information Commissioner's Office
ICSA	Institute of Chartered Secretaries and Administrators
IIA	Chartered Institute of Internal Auditors
ISA	Independent Safeguarding Authority
ISC	Independent Schools Council
IVA	individual voluntary arrangement
KPI	key performance indicator
MA	Maternity Allowance
MPS	Mailing Preference Service
MVL	members' voluntary liquidation
NCVO	National Council for Voluntary Organisations
NMW	National Minimum Wage
ODR	online dispute resolution
OML	Ordinary Maternity Leave
OR	occupational requirement
OSCR	Office of the Scottish Charity Regulator
PAYE	Pay As You Earn
PECR	Privacy and Electronic Communications Regulations 2003
PII	Personal Indemnity Insurance
PILON	payment in lieu of notice
PRI	Programme Related Investment
PROOF	PROtected Online Filing
PSC	person with significant control
RIDDOR	Reporting of Injuries, Deaths and Dangerous Occurrences Regulations
RIPA	Regulation of Investigatory Powers Act 2000 RNIB The Royal National Institute of the Blind
RNLI	The Royal National Lifeboat Institution
ROA 1974	Rehabilitation of Offenders Act 1974
RP	Registered Provider/Responsible Person
RS	Registered Society
RSI	reporting of serious incidents
SAIL	Single Alternative Inspection Location
SAL	Statutory Adoption Leave

SAP	Statutory Adoption Pay
SDLT	Stamp Duty Land Tax
ShPL	Shared Parental Leave
ShPP	Shared Parental Pay
SOCA	Serious Organised Crime Agency
SoFA	Statement of Financial Activity
SPL	Statutory Paternity Leave
SPP	Statutory Paternity Pay
SSP	Statutory Sick Pay
SVGA 2006	Safeguarding Vulnerable Groups Act 2006
SMP	Statutory Maternity Pay
SORP	Statement of Recommended Practice
TII	Trustee Indemnity Insurance
TUPE	Transfer of Undertakings and Protection of Employment
VAT	Value Added Tax

SECTION A

The charity's structure and legal framework

A1
What is a charity?

1 The meaning of charity and legal frameworks

1.1 What is a charity?

1.1.1 An essential concept to grasp is that a charity is not a type of legal structure; it is a status conferred on an organisation because of its purpose and the activities it carries out. Charitable status is completely separate from the organisation's legal structure, which is examined in chapter A2.

1.1.2 In England and Wales, an organisation is a charity and has charitable status if:

- it is established wholly and exclusively for charitable purposes (known as 'purposes' or 'objects'); and
- it provides a public benefit.

1.1.3 Registration with the Charity Commission and entry in the Central Register of Charities (which provides the organisation with a charity registration number) confirms charitable status. However, an organisation does not have to be recognised by the Charity Commission, HM Revenue & Customs (HMRC) or any other body to be a charity; this is a matter of fact and law. If the organisation fulfils the criteria, it is a charity. A large number of charities are not required to register with the Charity Commission because their income does not reach the charity registration threshold (see chapter A3, paragraph 7.2 on page 66). There are also a number of charities that are exempt or excepted from registration (see chapter A3, section 7.16 , page 69). However, the trustees of a charity that fulfils the registration criteria have a legal duty to apply to the Charity Commission for registration.

1.1.4 Key features of a charity in England and Wales:

- It has to be established for exclusively charitable purposes (see paragraph 1.2).
- It has a body of trustees who are responsible for its administration and management. Its trustees will normally be unpaid volunteers, although it is possible to have paid trustees if the constitution or Charity Commission allows. If it is an unincorporated charity (see chapter A2), the Charity Commission

will expect the majority of its trustees to be resident in the UK to ensure that it has jurisdiction over them.

- Any profits or surplus it makes cannot normally be paid out to its members or its trustees; they must be re-invested in the charity and used to fulfil its charitable aims.
- It is established to benefit the public (see paragraphs 1.3–1.7) and must not therefore give disproportionate levels of private benefit to any particular group or person. Any private (personal or commercial) benefit must be incidental to the charitable benefit provided. Material or significant risk bearing non-charitable activities should be carried out through a separate non-charitable subsidiary or other entity because a charity is not the appropriate vehicle for this kind of activity.
- Its assets must always be used to further its charitable purposes: 'once a charity, always a charity'.
- It is regulated by the Charity Commission and, with some exceptions (provided its gross annual income exceeds £5,000), it is registered with the Charity Commission.

The main advantages of charity status can be summarised as follows:

- Public recognition and support – funders and the general public are greatly reassured by an organisation being a charity. Charity status provides kudos and signifies integrity. Many grant funders will or can only provide funding to charitable organisations.
- Tax advantages – the UK has one of the most generous tax regimes in the world for charities. There are tax advantages both for UK charities and for UK taxpayers (individuals and businesses) who give to them. A detailed description of these tax advantages can be found on HMRC's website (www.hmrc.gov.uk).
- A charity does not pay tax on profits derived exclusively from activities that are in pursuit of its charitable purposes (known as 'primary purpose trading') and which are used for its charitable purposes.
- Eighty per cent mandatory relief from business rates is available for non-domestic property occupied by a charity and 'wholly or mainly used for charitable purposes' (and the local authority has discretion to relieve the remaining 20%).
- Charities are exempt from stamp duty land tax (SDLT) on all acquisitions of land and buildings, whether by gift or purchase, which are used for qualifying charitable purposes.
- Gifts of any amount of cash to UK charities by individuals or organisations that pay UK income or profits taxes are eligible for relief under the Gift Aid scheme. Gift Aid relief is available whether a gift is made regularly or as a one-off payment, if the individual donor is a UK resident for tax purposes, or the donor organisation pays UK corporation tax. For donations by individuals,

the Gift Aid scheme enables the charity to recover income tax on the amount of the gift received, for which the donor must account to HMRC. In addition, individuals who pay income tax at the higher rate are entitled to claim the difference between the higher rate and the basic rate of tax on the total (gross) value of the donation. (any Gift Aid claim must be made within four years after the end of the tax year to which the claim relates (for charitable trusts) or the accounting period to which it relates (for charitable companies, charities that are treated as companies for tax purposes and Community Amateur Sports Clubs that are recognised by HMRC).)

1.2 Charitable purposes

1.2.1 The Charities Act 2006 introduced a statutory definition of charitable purposes to the law of England and Wales.

1.2.2 A charitable purpose is:

- one which falls within any of the descriptions of purposes listed in s. 3(1) of the Charities Act 2011 (the 2011 Act); and
- is for the public benefit.

1.2.3 The following descriptions of charitable purposes are set out in s. 3(1) of the 2011 Act:

(a) the prevention or relief of poverty;
(b) the advancement of education;
(c) the advancement of religion;
(d) the advancement of health (which includes the prevention or relief of sickness, disease or human suffering) or the saving of lives;
(e) the advancement of citizenship or community development (which includes rural or urban regeneration and the promotion of civic responsibility, volunteering, the voluntary sector or the effectiveness or efficiency of charities);
(f) the advancement of the arts, culture, heritage or science;
(g) the advancement of amateur sports;
(h) the advancement of human rights, conflict resolution or reconciliation or the promotion of religious or racial harmony or equality and diversity;
(i) the advancement of environmental protection or improvement;
(j) the relief of those in need by reason of youth, age, ill-health, disability, financial hardship or other disadvantage (which includes relief by the provision of accommodation or care);
(k) the advancement of animal welfare;
(l) the promotion of the efficiency of the armed forces of the crown, or of the efficiency of the police, fire and rescue services or ambulance services;
(m) any other purposes which:

- are not included in the list above, but are recognised under the existing law or s. 5 of the 2011 Act (recreational and similar trusts, etc.) as charitable purposes; or
- may reasonably be regarded as analogous to, or within the spirit of, the charitable purposes listed above or those recognised under the existing law as charitable purposes.

1.3 Before the 2006 Act: the public benefit presumption

1.3.1 Prior to the Charities Act 2006, the definition of a charity was primarily set out in case law. To be a charity, an organisation had to have exclusively charitable purposes and be established for the public benefit (this has not changed).

1.3.2 Accepted charitable purposes were originally derived from the Statute of Elizabeth, dating from 1601. These purposes were refined by the courts and four heads of charitable purposes emerged:

- the relief of poverty;
- the advancement of education;
- the advancement of religion; and
- any other purposes beneficial to the community.

1.3.3 Pre-2006 charities that came within the first three heads of charitable purposes (the relief of poverty, the advancement of education and the advancement of religion) were presumed to provide a public benefit. In practice, this meant that the public benefit credentials of an organisation were rarely tested unless its purpose fell within the fourth, catch-all head of 'charitable purposes'.

1.4 Post the 2006 Act: the public benefit requirement

1.4.1 Following the Charities Act 2006, all organisations, without exception, that wish to be recognised or to continue to be recognised as charities must demonstrate that they meet the 'public benefit requirement'.

1.4.2 The 2006 Act introduced a new requirement for the Charity Commission to publish guidance for charities in relation to the public benefit requirement. The Charity Commission currently publishes three short high-level guides (listed below). These replaced the Commission's original guidance, which was reviewed in light of *The Independent Schools Council v The Charity Commissioners for England and Wales* [2011] UKUT 421 (TCC) (see further paragraph 1.5.1).

1.4.3 Published guidance

The formal guidance:

- *Public benefit: The public benefit requirement* (PB1) – explains the legal requirement that a charity's purposes must be for the 'public benefit' (known as the 'public benefit requirement').
- *Public benefit: Running a charity* (PB2) – explains public benefit in the context of running a charity.
- *Public benefit: Public benefit reporting* (PB3) – explains that charity trustees must report on how they have carried out their charity's purposes for the public benefit.

Additional guidance that does not form part of the formal guidance:

- *Public benefit: An overview* – gives an overview (but does not form part of) the Charity Commission's set of three public benefit guides.
- *Public benefit: Rules for Charities* – provides an overall introductory guide
- *Guidance on charitable purposes* – detailed guidance on how to show that your charity has been set up with charitable purposes that meet public benefit.
- *Legal analysis: Public benefit* – provides an analysis of the law relating to public benefit.

In addition, to accompany the public benefit guidance, the Commission has published the following guide:

- *What makes a charity* – this deals with charitable purposes and the jurisdiction of the High Court.

1.4.4 PB1: The public benefit requirement

This guidance is particularly useful for those who are considering setting up or registering a charity. It explains the legal requirement that a charity's purposes must be for the 'public benefit'. It is also relevant for trustees of an existing charity considering a change in its charitable purpose. It explains that there are two components of 'public benefit':

- the 'benefit aspect': a charitable purpose must be beneficial, and any detriment or harm arising from the purpose must not outweigh the benefit; and
- the 'public aspect': the charitable purpose must benefit the public in general, or a sufficient section of the public, and not give rise to more than incidental personal benefit.

Where the charitable purpose is to prevent or relieve poverty, the 'benefit' aspect only must be satisfied. This means that charities for the relief (and in some cases the prevention) of poverty can define 'benefit' with reference to a family relationship, employment or membership of an unincorporated association.

1.4.5 PB2: Running a charity

This guidance is particularly useful for those who are running a charity, and for those who are proposing to set up and register a charity. It explains that charity trustees must understand their charity's purpose and how this is for the public benefit. When making decisions which affect the way in which people benefit from the charity's purposes, or indeed, who can benefit, the trustees must make sure that:

- the charity's purpose provides a benefit;
- the risks of detriment or harm to the beneficiaries of the charity or to the public in carrying out the purpose are managed;
- those who benefit are consistent with the charity's purpose; and
- any personal benefits are no more than incidental.

The guidance discusses when benefits may be accessed through membership, the circumstances under which trustees may restrict physical access to the facilities provided to the public and how charities may charge for the services or facilities they provide.

1.4.6 PB3: Reporting public benefit

This guidance explains the reporting requirements for charity trustees. It will be of particular interest to those who are proposing to set up and register a charity, and is also relevant to trustees of existing registered charities.

Different reporting requirements apply depending on the size of the registered charity.

Smaller charities (gross income less than £500,000): Charity trustees must report on public benefit in their annual report by including:

- a brief summary setting out the charity's main activities undertaken to carry out its charitable purposes for the public benefit; and
- a statement as to compliance with their duty to have regard to the Charity Commission's public benefit guidance when exercising any powers or duties to which the guidance is relevant.

Larger charities (gross income £500,000 and above): Charity trustees must report on public benefit in their annual report by providing:

- a review of the significant activities undertaken by the charity to carry out its charitable purposes for the public benefit;
- details of purposes and objectives;
- details of strategies adopted and activities undertaken to achieve those purposes and objectives;
- details of achievements by reference to the purposes and objectives set; and
- a statement as to compliance with their duty to have regard to the Charity

Commission's public benefit guidance when exercising any powers or duties to which the guidance is relevant.

1.5 Background to the current position

1.5.1 At the end of 2010, the Independent Schools Council (ISC) sought judicial review of the Charity Commission's original (and now replaced) public benefit guidance due to its effect on independent schools which charge fees. In particular, the ISC questioned the impact of Principles 2(b) (that the beneficiaries must be appropriate to the aims of the charity) and 2(c) (where benefits are provided to a section of the public, the opportunity to benefit must not be unreasonably restricted by geographical or other restrictions). On handing down its ruling on 14 October 2011, the Charity Tribunal decided that Principle 2(b) was too prescriptive, obscure and was wrong in a number of respects, and that the explanation of Principle 2(c) ought to be amended. In particular, the Tribunal ruled that the guidance was not clear regarding the adequacy of the provision for the poor.

1.5.2 In light of the decision, the Charity Commission withdrew its original guidance and issued a simpler set of guidance (as detailed above).

On publication of the current guidance, the Chair of the Commission, William Shawcross, stated that the Commission had

> worked hard to provide guidance that is accessible to trustees of all types of charity, while still accurately reflecting the law. We have accepted comments made during our consultation to keep the guidance short and clear. This means that the guidance certainly cannot answer every question. There is no statutory definition of public benefit so its meaning will continue to develop through decisions made by the courts. As the law develops, we will keep our guidance under review.

1.5.3 To accompany its public benefit guidance, the Commission has also published *What makes a charity*? which deals with charitable purposes and the jurisdiction of the High Court. Annex B covers political purposes.

1.5.4 Some more specific guidance that dealt with the public benefit of religious and educational charities and the relief of poverty was withdrawn. This guidance is meant to be under review and does not form part of the Commission's formal guidance, but continues to remain available until it is replaced.

1.6 Assessing public benefit

1.6.1 New organisations seeking to register as charities are required to explain their aims regarding the public benefit and state how they propose to carry them out as part of the registration process (see chapter A3).

1.6.2 Trustees of existing charities have the following duties:

- to ensure that their charity's purposes are carried out for the public benefit;
- to have regard to the Charity Commission's public benefit guidance; and
- to report on how their charity carries out its purposes for the public benefit and to confirm that they have paid due regard to the Charity Commission's guidance in deciding what activities the charity should undertake.

1.7 Not meeting the requirement

Trustees of a charity cannot opt out of the charitable sector if they consider that their responsibilities to meet the public benefit requirement are too onerous. If charities do not meet the requirement, the Commission will take appropriate action, including:

- seeking agreement with the trustees to alter their charity's purposes or the way in which they carry out their purposes;
- taking regulatory action to ensure that the trusts are carried out (such as removing trustees, appointing new trustees or giving directions to trustees); and
- applying the assets for other similar charitable purposes for the public benefit.

If the purposes were never for the public benefit and the organisation was mistakenly registered as a charity, the Commission can ask the trustees to restructure the organisation, amend the purposes or remove it from the register. This option is rarely used.

2 The Charity Commission's role and responsibilities

2.1 The Charity Commission regulates charities in England and Wales. It was originally set up in 1853 as an unincorporated body of individual Charity Commissioners.

2.2 The Charities Act 2006 put the Charity Commission onto a formal statutory footing for the first time, making its role and status clearer and more appropriate to conditions at the time. Sections 14–16 of the 2011 Act set out the Charity Commission's statutory objectives, functions and duties.

2.3 The Charity Commission is a corporate body:

- Prior to the Charities Act 2006, the responsibility for regulating the charity sector was in the hands of 'The Charity Commissioners', a collection of up to five individuals. The 2006 Act transferred their assets, activities and functions to a new corporate body known as 'the Charity Commission for England and Wales' or, in Welsh, 'Comisiwn Elusennau Cymru a Lloegr'.

- The corporate Charity Commission consists of a chair and between four and eight other members, who are appointed by the Minister for the Cabinet Office. Schedule 1 of the 2011 Act stipulates criteria that some of the members must meet, the length of terms they may serve (a maximum three years for each term, subject to a maximum of 10 years in total) and the knowledge and experience they should have. Members can be paid.
- From 2012, the Charity Commission has been governed by its board, supported by a chief executive and directors group. The Charity Commission is a 'non-ministerial government department'. It is accountable to Parliament, but is largely independent of government control, not being subject to the control of any minister or other government department.
- It must prepare an annual report which must be laid before Parliament and made available to the public. It is also required to hold an annual public meeting within three months of publishing its annual report. Its financial year runs from 1 April to 31 March.

The Charity Commission has five objectives under the 2011 Act. These are:

1. *Public confidence*: to increase public trust and confidence in charities.
2. *Public benefit*: to promote awareness and understanding of the operation of the public benefit requirement.
3. *Compliance*: to promote compliance by charity trustees with their legal obligations in exercising control and management of the administration of their charity.
4. *Charitable resources*: to promote the effective use of charitable resources.
5. *Accountability*: to enhance the accountability of charities to donors, beneficiaries and the general public.

It has six general functions, which are:

1. to determine whether or not institutions are charities;
2. to encourage and facilitate the better administration of charities;
3. to identify and investigate apparent misconduct or mismanagement in the administration of charities and to take remedial or protective action in connection with misconduct or mismanagement in charities;
4. to determine whether public collections certificates should be issued and remain in force, in respect of public charitable collections;
5. to obtain, evaluate and disseminate information in connection with the performance of any of the Charity Commission's functions or meeting any of its objectives (this includes maintaining an accurate and up-to-date register of charities); and
6. to give information or advice, or make proposals, to any Minister of the Crown on matters relating to any of the Charity Commission's functions or meeting any of its objectives.

It has six general duties, which are:

1. so far as is reasonably practicable, to act in a way which is compatible with its objectives and which it considers most appropriate for the purpose of meeting those objectives;
2. so far as is reasonably practicable, to act in a way which is compatible with the encouragement of charitable giving and voluntary participation in charity work;
3. to have regard to the need to use its resources in the most efficient, effective and economic way when performing its functions;
4. to have regard to the principles of best regulatory practice. In particular, its regulatory activities should be proportionate, accountable, consistent, transparent and targeted only at cases in which action is needed;
5. to have regard to the desirability of facilitating innovation by or on behalf of charities; and
6. in managing its affairs, to have regard to such generally accepted principles of good governance as it is reasonable to regard as applicable to it.

2.4 In addition, the Charity Commission has a wide 'sweep-up' power to do anything which is calculated to facilitate, or is conducive or incidental to, the performance of any of its functions or general duties.

2.5 However, it is important to appreciate that the Charity Commission is not authorised to:

- exercise its functions as if it were a trustee of a charity; or
- involve itself directly in the administration of a charity.

2.6 Since January 2012, the role of the Charity Commission has changed quite substantially. The Charity Commission Statement of Strategic Intent 2019–2023 states that 'our purpose is to ensure charities can thrive and inspire trust so that people can improve lives and strengthen society'. It then lists the current strategic objectives as:

- holding charities to account;
- dealing with wrongdoing and harm;
- informing public choice;
- giving charities the understanding and tools they need to succeed; and
- keeping charities relevant for today's world.

2.7 The Charity Commission now works within a 'risk framework'. This requires a risk assessment at an early stage involving the following key questions:

1. Does the Charity Commission need to engage?
2. If it does, then:

(a) what is the nature and level of risk?
(b) what is the most effective response?

The Charity Commission is now unlikely to engage if the issue does not fall wholly or partly within its regulatory framework.

2.8. It seems clear that the Charity Commission's focus is on promoting and developing sector *self-reliance*, and it no longer wants to dedicate resources to tailored one-on-one advice to charities. In 2013, the Charity Commission published new guidance on how charity trustees should approach making decisions that affect their charity. The Commission makes it clear that it expects charity trustees to follow the guidance when making strategic or significant decisions (such as those affecting the charity's beneficiaries, assets or future direction). The guidance sets out a number of principles which the trustees are expected to apply to their decision making to enable them to demonstrate that they have followed the appropriate principles.

2.9 The Charity Commission's principles of decision making by charity trustees

Charity trustees must:

- act within their powers;
- act in good faith and only in the interest of the charity;
- make sure they are fully informed;
- take account of all relevant factors;
- ignore any irrelevant factors;
- manage conflicts of interest; and
- make decisions that are within the range of decisions that a reasonable trustee body could make.

A2
Legal forms and structures

1 Introduction

1.1 This section looks at some of the legal forms and structures commonly adopted by charities, and compares the key features of those that are most commonly encountered in practice. It refers to the members of the governing body of a charity, whatever the legal form and whether members of the governing body are called trustees, members of a managing committee, directors, governors or are given some other title (such as 'charity trustees') unless the context requires a more specific reference.

1.2 To recap, charity is a status conferred on an organisation because of the purposes for which it is set up. It is not a type of legal form or structure.

1.3 Charities come in many sizes and legal forms. It is vital to understand the legal structure of a charity to be able to provide competent advice to it or to the charity's trustees. It is good practice to start by carrying out an online search of the Central Register of Charities maintained by the Charity Commission (www.charity-commission.gov.uk). This will provide a description of the governing documents of the charity and show copies of recently filed accounts; these usually provide sufficient information to identify the type of legal form that the charity takes. However, be aware that the information shown on the Central Register of Charities may be out of date and/or incomplete. In addition, all incorporated organisations are also now listed on the register held by Companies House (www.companieshouse.gov.uk) and so, this will show if the charity is incorporated and if so which legal form it takes.

1.4 One of the most interesting aspects of working with charities is the number of different legal forms that are encountered in the sector, a number of which are either unique to the 'not-for-profit' sector or are rarely encountered in the mainstream commercial world.

1.5 There are a number of legal forms available to organisations wishing to be established in England and Wales. The most common legal forms for organisations that pursue charitable purposes are:

- trusts;
- unincorporated associations;
- companies limited by guarantee (CLG);
- charitable incorporated organisations (CIO);
- community benefit societies (CBS);
- Royal Charter bodies; and
- charitable statutory corporations.

1.6 The Charities Act 2006 introduced a new legal form designed specifically for charities: the charitable incorporated organisation (CIO). The CIO became available in England and Wales in a phased process of introduction from March 2013, and by 2019 it was a form commonly used for newly registered charities. An equivalent, the SCIO, is also available in Scotland under Scottish legislation and is regulated by the Office of the Scottish Charity Regulator. New charities may set up as CIO and existing unincorporated charities may transfer assets into a CIO. A charitable company with an annual income of less than £12,500 can now also change to a CIO and there is a specific process for this. The process is also expected to become available soon to larger charitable companies.

1.7 Many charities own subsidiary trading companies. These will usually take the form of either:

- a company limited by shares (CLS);
- a CLG; or
- (less commonly) a community interest company (CIC) that is either a CLG or a CLS.

1.8 Trusts and unincorporated associations are **unincorporated (non-corporate) organisations**; CBSs, CIOs, CLGs, CLSs, charter bodies and statutory corporations are **corporate organisations**. Table 1 summarises the key features and compares the most common of these key legal forms. Whatever form a charity takes, those responsible for the overall management of the charity are charity trustees and have particular responsibilities in that capacity.

1.9 One of the key issues for new charities is for founders and charity trustees to choose the most appropriate legal form for their charitable endeavours.

1.10 The key factors to consider whenever choosing or advising on the appropriate legal form for a charity are as follows:

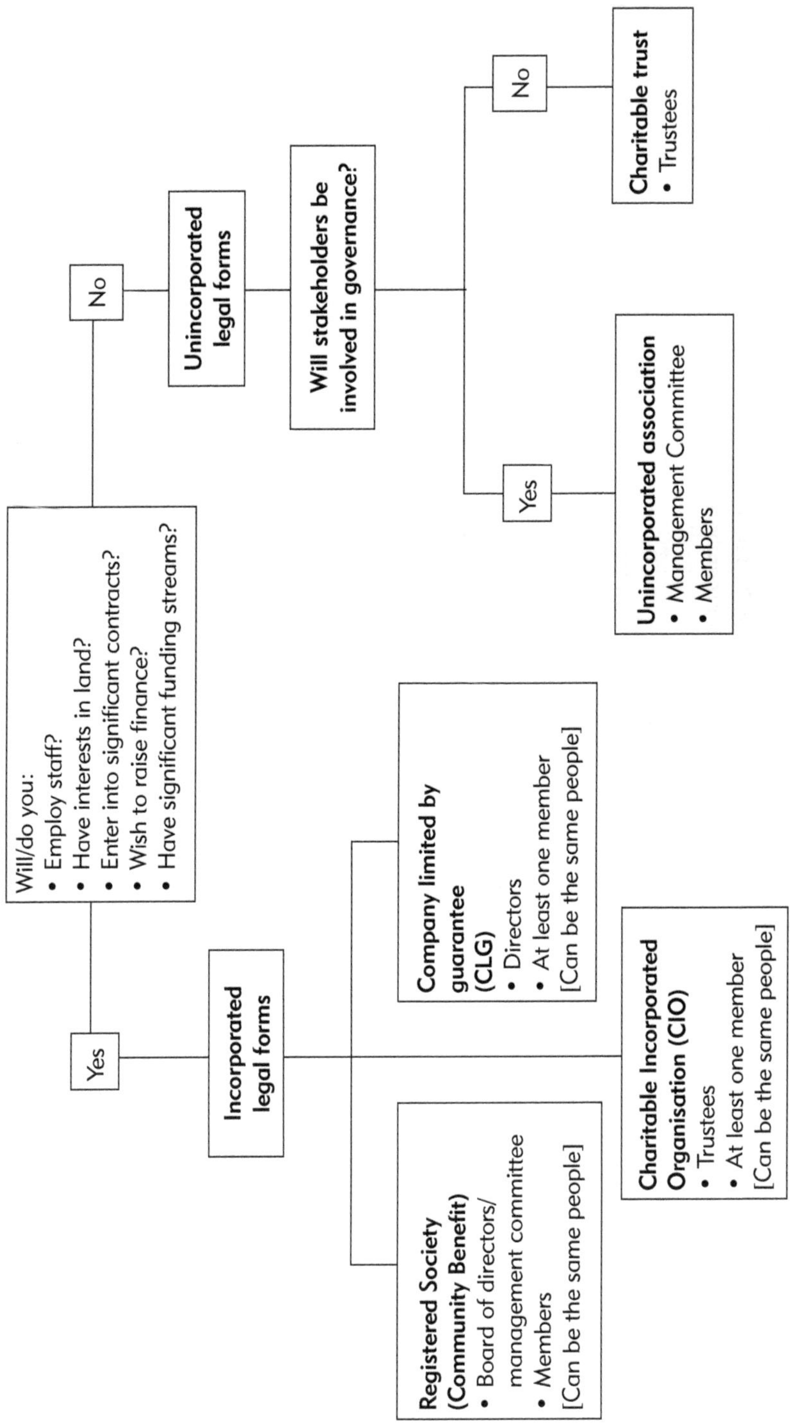

Figure A2.1: What form of charity?

Table 1
Summary of key features of legal forms for charities

Common unincorporated legal forms

	Constitution	Unlimited liability for charity trustees	Membership separate from charity trustees	Limited liability for members	Regulator	Registration fee
Charitable Trust	Trust deed/ declaration of trust/Charity Commission scheme	Yes	No	N/A – there are no 'members'	Charity Commission	None
Unincorporated association	Constitution/ rules/Charity Commission scheme	Yes	Yes	May be limited for some members, dependent on constitution, rules or scheme	Charity Commission	None

Common incorporated legal forms

	Constitution	Unlimited liability for charity trustees	Membership separate from charity trustees	Limited liability for members	Regulator	Registration fee
Company Limited by Guarantee (CLG)	Memorandum and Articles of Association	No	Yes (but directors and members can be the same)	Yes	Charity Commission and the Registrar of Companies	£40–£100 (Registrar of Companies)
Charitable Incorporated Organisation (CIO)	Constitution	No	Yes (but charity trustees and members can be the same)	Yes	Charity Commission	None
Industrial and Provident Society (IPS)	Rules	No	Yes	Yes	FCA and Charity Commission or Homes and Communities Agency if a registered provider of social housing	£40–£950 Financial Conduct Authority (FCA)

(a) **Risk and complexity:** what activities is the charity planning to undertake? If these activities involve any of the following, a limited liability corporate body (e.g. a CLG, a CIO or a CBS) is likely to be most appropriate:
   - use of or ownership of any land (whether leasehold or freehold);
   - provision of goods and/or services to, or any other dealings with, members of the public; or
   - entering into any significant contractual liabilities (e.g. any secured or unsecured loans, employment contracts or funding arrangements).

(b) **Cost and administration:** it is generally perceived to be more expensive to set up and administer a corporate body than a charitable trust. However, all charities must comply with the rules on producing accounts and returns and filing them with the Charity Commission. Companies have additional obligations to file accounts, returns and other information with the Registrar of Companies, but the additional costs are often lower than would be expected. Additionally, there is a cost associated with changing legal form. If the benefits of incorporation, such as legal identity or limited liability, are likely to be applicable, an organisation may benefit from incorporating sooner rather than later, whilst its affairs are still less complex.

(c) **Member involvement:** charitable trusts do not allow for the involvement of a membership in the governance of the charity, whereas this is a key feature of many corporate organisations and unincorporated associations.

1.11 Figure A2.1 is a flowchart which summarises the thought process (see page 17).

2 Risk and unlimited liability

2.1 It is important to understand the practical advantages of legal forms which have a separate legal (or 'corporate') identity and how legal forms which limit liability protect against some (but not all) areas of personal risk for both charity trustees and members.

2.2 An unincorporated charity (e.g. a charitable trust or unincorporated association) has no separate legal identity or personality. The assets of the charity are vested in the charity trustees or (in the case of an unincorporated association) the members or managing committee (depending on the rules) of the charity.

2.3 Moreover, the charity trustees and, in some case, the members of an unincorporated charity are jointly and severally liable for the debts and liabilities of their charity. It is the charity trustees who are sued (or sue) in their own names. As those with ultimate responsibility for the management and administration of the charity, the buck stops with them. The liability of the charity trustees (and, depending on the rules, the members) is unlimited. Those who are liable and have acted properly have a right to be indemnified out of the assets of the charity for all liabilities properly incurred in managing and administering the charity.

2.4 The following 'doomsday scenario' illustrates the potential practical effect of these principles.

2.5 A museum is operated as a charitable trust. As it has no separate legal personality, the individual charity trustees hold the title to the building in which the museum is housed; their names are on the deeds, albeit in their capacity as charity trustees of the museum. All debts and other liabilities of the museum are the responsibility of the charity trustees.

2.6 During a violent storm, a tree in the grounds of the museum is blown down. It topples onto the museum's glass roof; several members of the public are seriously injured. The charity trustees are on the receiving end of several multi-million pound claims for compensation relating to personal injuries. We will assume for the purposes of illustration that the claims are successful.

2.7 If the museum's insurances are insufficient to cover all or any part of the compensation and costs awarded to the claimants, the charity trustees are entitled to meet the liabilities from the assets of the charity. However, ultimately, if these liabilities exceed the value of the charity's assets, individual charity trustees are jointly and severally liable to meet any shortfall personally. Similar principles apply to unincorporated associations (see paragraph 4.2).

2.8 Structuring the museum as a limited liability corporate form (such as a CLG or CIO) would affect the scenario as follows:

- The museum has its own separate legal personality; the museum owns its building and is responsible for its debts and liabilities.
- If the insurances and other assets are insufficient to meet claims against it, the museum is insolvent and the charity trustees (subject to the points discussed in paragraphs 2.9 and 2.11) will not be personally liable. In the case of a company, the members' liability will be limited to the guarantee (often £1 or £10 each) specified in the governing document that they had to give when they agreed to become members.

2.9 It is important to understand that, irrespective of the legal form their charity takes, charity trustees are vulnerable to claims by their fellow trustees, the charity itself, the Charity Commission, or the Attorney General acting on behalf of the charity if they have acted in breach of duty and loss has been caused to the charity as a result. In practice, it is highly unlikely that charity trustees will be held personally liable for breaches of duty that are made in good faith. Both the

Charity Commission and the courts have the power to relieve a charity trustee from personal liability for a breach of duty where they consider that they have acted honestly and reasonably and ought fairly to be excused. Charity trustees who have caused loss to their charity either deliberately or by acting recklessly can expect to receive no leniency.

2.10 Charity trustees who are company directors can be personally liable in the following limited circumstances:

- wrongful and fraudulent trading (see paragraph 2.13);
- various rules under company law which have criminal sanctions; and
- corporate manslaughter.

2.11 In addition, all charity trustees, irrespective of the legal form their charity takes, can be personally prosecuted for regulatory breaches, including, for example, numerous health and safety, anti-bribery and environmental rules.

2.12 It is possible to use the charity's funds to take out indemnity insurance for trustees which, depending on the extent of the policy, will fully cover breaches of duty made in good faith and 'wrongful trading'. However, there are limitations on what indemnity insurance paid for by the charity can cover. For example, a policy must exclude:

- indemnities for fines imposed in criminal proceedings;
- the cost of an unsuccessful defence against crimes involving dishonesty, fraud or wilful or reckless misconduct; and
- liability to the charity resulting from a deliberate failure to act in the interests of the charity.

Trustee indemnity insurance does not provide protection to charity trustees for personal liabilities to third parties where their charity is unincorporated.

2.13 Wrongful trading occurs under the Insolvency Act 1986 when the directors of a UK company:

- have continued to operate the company past the point when they 'knew or ought to have concluded that there was no reasonable prospect of avoiding insolvent liquidation'; or
- did not take 'every step with a view to minimising the potential loss to the company's creditors'.

Directors who are liable for wrongful trading can be ordered to contribute to the assets of the insolvent company and are potentially disqualified from acting as a director. Fraudulent trading carries even higher sanctions, but requires that the directors deliberately intended to deceive or defraud the creditors.

3 Charitable trusts

3.1 A charitable trust is created whenever a donor gives money or other property to trusted individuals (the trustees) to be used for purposes expressed by the donor that are exclusively charitable. In its simplest form, a charitable trust can be created by word of mouth, although if the assets include land there will have to be a trust document.

3.2 The terms of charitable trusts are usually set out in and governed by a trust deed, declaration of trust, or a Charity Commission scheme. Trusts are ideal for simple or narrow purpose charities, small-scale charities and fund-giving charities where the activities of the charity do not expose the trustees to significant potential personal liability.

The main advantages of charitable trusts are that:

- they are often quick and easy (and therefore relatively inexpensive) to set up;
- they are often relatively inexpensive to run;
- some commentators consider that they are flexible and 'forgiving' to run (although other charity law practitioners would disagree); and
- they are less rigorously regulated than corporate bodies.

The main disadvantages of charitable trusts are as follows:

- **Unincorporated**: a charitable trust is not a legal entity in its own right; it has no 'separate legal personality'. The trustees enter into contracts, employ staff, lease property, are sued, sue and enter into obligations and liabilities in their own names on behalf of the trust. This can create legal and administrative difficulties when trustees resign and new trustees are appointed.
- **Unlimited liability**: trustees of a charitable trust are jointly and severally personally liable for the debts and other liabilities of the trust. This means that if the charitable trust suffers a loss that is not covered by insurance or the realisable assets of the trust, the trustees' personal assets are at risk (see s. 2).
- **VAT grouping not available**: corporate bodies that are part of the same group of companies or corporations are able to form a Value Added Tax (VAT) group that enables services to be provided within the group without a charge to VAT. VAT grouping in this way is not available for unincorporated organisations such as trusts.

4 Unincorporated associations

4.1 An unincorporated association is formed whenever several people join together to carry out a mutual purpose, other than for profit. There is no legislation specifically governing unincorporated associations and, like charitable trusts, they can be created by word of mouth.

4.2 Key features of unincorporated associations are:

- They are membership organisations where the relationship between members is governed by contract, usually in the form of a constitution or set of rules.
- A board (often called a management committee) is usually elected by the members to run the unincorporated association on behalf of its members.

The main advantages of unincorporated associations are that they:

- can operate relatively informally, as they are governed only by their constitution or rules; and
- enable and promote stakeholder involvement via their membership.

The main disadvantages of unincorporated associations are the same as those of a charitable trust:

- **Unincorporated**: unlike a company, an unincorporated association has no separate legal identity apart from the members of which it is composed. It exists for and by its members. The individual members of the management committee enter into obligations and liabilities in their own name on behalf of the members.
- **Unlimited liability**: depending on what the rules say, either the members of the management committee or individual members of the unincorporated association are jointly and severally liable for the debts or liabilities of the unincorporated association and their personal assets are at risk. In practice, it would be those to whom delegated responsibility has been given for the general management of the affairs of the unincorporated association (the trustees or members of the management committee, for example) that a well-advised litigant would be most likely to commence proceedings against.
- **VAT grouping not available**: corporate bodies that are part of the same group of companies or corporations are able to form a VAT group that enables services to be provided within the group without a charge to VAT. Value Added Tax grouping in this way is not available for unincorporated associations.

5 Companies limited by guarantee (CLG)

5.1 For a company to be registered as a charity, it must usually be formed as a CLG.

5.2 They are incorporated – they are legal entities in their own right and have 'separate legal personality'. They own property, hold land, employ staff, enter into contracts, and can sue and be sued in their own corporate name.

5.3 They have a two-tier structure:

(a) **Members:** to whom the directors are accountable. The members give a guarantee to cover the company's liabilities. However, the guarantee is nominal, normally being limited to £1 or £10.

The members of a CLG have broadly the same powers as shareholders in a company limited by shares. However, the purpose of members within a charitable company is very different from that of shareholders, who are principally interested in protecting the value of their investment. Ideally, the members of a charitable company are people or organisations who are actively interested and involved in the work of the charity.

Having a membership separate from management provides a layer of accountability.

Members of a CLG have various powers or rights (see below for more detail). In practice, the most important of these are:

- to vote to remove directors;
- to receive a copy of the annual accounts, the directors' report and the constitution of the company;
- to attend general meetings of the company at which the directors may be held to account and (subject to a minimum number of members making the request) to requisition such meetings if considered necessary;
- to approve changes to the constitution of the company; and
- in many cases, where the constitution specifically provides for it, to appoint directors.

(b) **Directors:** who are responsible for the day-to-day management of the company. Where a CLG has charitable status, its directors are also charity trustees.

However, it is possible to structure a CLG with the directors and members as one and the same people, sometimes called an 'oligarchy' or 'all members are directors' model. This is common practice where separate stakeholder involvement in the governance of the charity is not required.

5.4 Personal liability is limited. The debts and obligations of the CLG are the responsibility of the corporate organisation and not of individual directors or (subject to their 'guarantee', see paragraph 5.3(a)) of members.

Incorporation does not provide a blanket protection against liability. Individual officers and employees of the company can be personally liable to others for their negligent acts or omissions. In the vast majority of circumstances, the company's insurances will cover the negligent acts and omissions of its employees and officers.

There are also limited circumstances when the managers of a company may be personally liable; for example, company directors who allow the company to trade while insolvent (wrongful trading: see paragraph 2.13), corporate manslaughter, certain competition law offences, and wilful or reckless breaches of duty by charity trustees (see paragraphs 2.9 to 2.12).

5.5 Where a person who, acting in good faith, enters into a transaction with a non-charitable company, they are entitled to assume that the directors have power to bind the company and that the company has legal capacity to carry out the activity (irrespective of what it says in the company's constitution). This does not apply to charitable companies, to which a rule known as *ultra vires* applies (meaning 'beyond the powers'). The only exception to this rule is where a person, acting in good faith, either (a) does not know, at the time the transaction is entered into, that the company is a charity, or (b) gives full consideration in money or money's worth and does not know, at the time the transaction is entered into, that the act is not permitted by the company's constitution or that the act is beyond the powers of the directors. In either of these circumstances, the transaction will stand, but the directors may be in breach of duty for acting beyond their powers and may be required to reimburse the charity for any losses suffered as a result. The directors of any charitable company must therefore ensure that all of the charity's activities are authorised by its objects and the powers it has to achieve those objects. The members of a charitable company can, however, ratify acts of the directors that are beyond the company's capacity, but only with the Charity Commission's prior written consent. This is only likely to be given under very limited circumstances.

5.6 Companies limited by guarantee are constituted and governed by the Memorandum and Articles of Association:

1. The Memorandum of Association establishes the formal charitable and corporate limited liability status of the CLG. Since the Companies Act 2006 was fully implemented, the Memorandum of Association has become a short statement establishing the company signed by the first member(s), and the Articles of Association contains details of how the company will be organised. Provisions in old forms of Memorandum of Association are deemed to be part of the Articles of Association by virtue of the Companies Act 2006. Since 1 October 2009, all of the rules on how a company is managed and organised, including its objects and powers, have been either contained in, or been deemed to be contained in, the company's Articles.
2. The Articles of Association contain all of the key rules regulating a company. They regulate the internal management of the CLG and set out procedural rules for meetings of the directors and the members. The members have power to amend any provision in the Articles of Association by special resolution, but changes affecting the objects or property of a charity must receive prior approval of the Charity Commission. Companies are able to entrench conditionally provisions within their Articles (though this is rarely done). These are

provisions that can be altered or removed only when certain conditions have been met (e.g. with the written consent of the Charity Commission). Since the Companies Act 2006, it is no longer possible to absolutely entrench provisions in a company's Articles (i.e. include provisions that can never be changed) unless such provisions already existed in the company's Memorandum and/or Articles and are unchangeable.

5.7 Companies limited by guarantee are registered with the Registrar of Companies and regulated by company law.

5.8 In order to be a charitable company, a CLG must:

- have objects that are exclusively charitable (these are its charitable purposes);
- have a provision in its Articles (which cannot be altered or removed) that prevents any profits from being distributed to its members by way of dividend and requires profits to be retained for application towards its charitable purposes (known as a 'non-distribution' clause or an asset lock); and
- have a provision in its Articles that in the event of its dissolution any surplus will not be divided among the members but will go to an organisation or organisations with charitable objects that are the same or very closely similar.

5.9 The main advantages of incorporating as a CLG are:

- **separate legal personality** (see paragraph 5.2);
- **limitation of liability** (see paragraph 5.4);
- **clear ownership/governance structure:** the CLG is a tried and tested legal structure that has been in existence for many years. There is a clear legislative framework governing CLGs and powers, and processes for decision-making are well understood;
- **increased public accountability/transparency:** CLGs have to have a registered office, file their Articles, annual returns, members' resolutions and prescribed details of their directors and (if they choose to have one) company secretary with the Registrar of Companies and are accessible to the public; and
- **recognition by financial institutions, investors and donors:** financial institutions, investors and major donors will understand the nature and mechanics of a company better than any other legal form currently available.

5.10 Company membership: in more detail

5.10.1 In a company, members have the following rights:

(a) to receive notice of, attend, speak and vote at all general meetings of the company and to appoint proxies to attend, speak and vote at meetings of the company;

(b) only if required by the company's Articles of Association (Articles), to hold an annual general meeting (AGM) in every calendar year;
(c) to receive the directors' report on the activities of the company and the accounts of the company for the previous financial year;
(d) if the company's Articles require an AGM and also require the directors to retire by rotation, the Articles will often give the members the right to accept the retirement of directors at the AGM and to appoint auditors for the coming financial year;
(e) to inspect the minutes and resolutions of general meetings free of charge and to receive a copy (provided the request is for a proper purpose), for which they may be required to pay a fee;
(f) to inspect the register of members free of charge and to receive a copy, for which they may be required to pay a fee; and
(g) to wind up the company.

5.10.2 Members also have certain statutory powers, which cannot be taken away from them. These include:

- power to remove a director by passing an ordinary resolution at a meeting at which special notice has been given;
- power to petition for a compulsory liquidation;
- power to require circulation of written resolutions and statements;
- power to require the directors to call a general meeting;
- the right to inspect directors' service contracts and to approve contracts for more than two years by resolution. This is unlikely to be relevant where directors are unpaid;
- the right to approve substantial non-cash asset transactions with a director or a person connected with a director; and
- the right to approve loans to directors.

5.10.3 Members may also, in normal circumstances, use ordinary resolutions to appoint directors and ratify certain actions that the directors have taken (subject to obtaining the prior written approval of the Charity Commission).

5.10.4 Resolutions (whether special or ordinary) that the members pass at a general meeting may also be passed as written resolutions. This process was simplified by the Companies Act 2006, the requirements now being:

- **ordinary resolution**: simple majority: over 50% of members eligible to vote; or
- **special resolution**: not less than 75% of members eligible to vote.

Companies should ensure that their Articles of Association are in line with these rules.

5.10.5 Written resolutions lapse if the required majority is not achieved within 28 days of the circulation date (see section 11 for more detail).

5.10.6 It is essential that charities structured as CLGs ensure that their company books are kept up to date, recording details of current members. Failure to do so can create real problems in passing members' resolutions and administrating the company's membership.

6 Registered societies

6.1 Registered societies (previously called Industrial and Provident Societies) are societies, not companies. They take two forms:

- **community benefit societies (CBSs)**: set up to benefit the community as a whole; and
- **co-operative societies**: set up to benefit their members.

6.2 Because co-operatives are established for the benefit of their members, they are not usually charitable, except where a necessary condition of membership is to be within a class of charitable beneficiaries. Most charitable registered societies are therefore community benefit societies. As most charitable registered societies are community benefit societies we will use this term throughout the remainder of the book, unless the term 'registered society' is more appropriate.

6.3 Community benefit societies are corporate bodies (see paragraph 6.6) and the personal liability of their members and directors is limited (see paragraph 6.6).

As with CLGs (see paragraph 5.3), they have a two-tiered structure:

- **a board of directors or management committee**: who owe fiduciary duties and duties of skill and care similar to those owed by directors of companies; and
- **members**: who can be individuals, corporate organisations such as companies and other societies and nominated representatives of unincorporated associations.

Members normally have the following powers:

- to elect and dismiss the board of directors or management committee;
- to appoint and dismiss the auditors;
- to change the rules by special resolution; and
- to approve a transfer of engagements, amalgamation or conversion.

They are registered with the Financial Conduct Authority (FCA), rather than the Registrar of Companies.

6.4 Their constitutions are known as 'rules', which are either bespoke or model rules registered by one of the recognised sponsoring bodies (such as the National Housing Federation). A society's rules and any amendments to them are subject to approval by and registration with the FCA.

6.5 The rules of a charitable community benefit society will include the following provisions:

- what powers members have generally;
- that no benefits are to be returned to members by way of dividend;
- that each member has one vote; and
- that on a winding-up, members have no right to a share of the assets of the society, and any surplus must be applied for the same or similar charitable purposes to those pursued by the society.

6.6 The main advantages of CBSs are similar to those of CLGs:

- **Incorporated**: they are separate legal entities in their own right, which own assets, employ staff, sue or are sued, enter into contracts and other liabilities in their corporate name.
- **Limited liability**: the debts and obligations of the CBS are the responsibility of the corporate organisation and not individual directors. The personal liability of the members of a community benefit society is limited to the value of their shareholding, which will normally be a nominal value (e.g. £1).

6.7 Although CBSs are corporate bodies that provide limited liability for their directors and members, they are not commonly found outside the social housing sector. They are comparatively expensive to set up and are generally considered not well understood by financial institutions, investors, donors and professionals, particularly outside the circle of experienced advisers to the third sector. One of the reasons why they are favoured in the social housing sector is the fact that CBSs that are registered providers of social housing are exempt from registration with the Charity Commission. As registered providers of social housing are already registered with and regulated by the Regulator of Social Housing, this is seen as an advantage.

6.8 The primary legislation for CBSs is the Co-operative and Community Benefit Societies Act 2014. This Act consolidated much of the previous legislation and modernised the language used.

6.9 With the introduction of the Mutual Societies (Electronic Communications) Order 2011, the use of electronic communications by registered societies has also been brought into line with the law affecting companies (the Electronic Communications Act 2000).

7 Charitable incorporated organisations

7.1 The charitable incorporated organisation (CIO) is a new corporate structure specifically designed for charities, which was introduced into the law of England and Wales in 2013. The aim was to create a simpler and cheaper alternative to other corporate structures. The CIO has become more popular as a legal form since it was introduced in 2013. By 2018 approximately half of all new charity registrations were for CIOs.

7.2 The CIO was developed by the Charity Law Association working with the University of Liverpool, with the intention of providing a corporate structure specifically for charities with the benefits of limited liability but without the burden of dual registration with both the Charity Commission and the Registrar of Companies. A CIO only has to be registered with and report to the Charity Commission.

7.3 The legislation on CIOs is found in:

- Part 11 of the 2011 Act;
- the Charitable Incorporated Organisations (General) Regulations 2012 (SI 2012/3012);
- the Charitable Incorporated Organisations (Insolvency and Dissolution) Regulations 2012 (SI 2012/3013); and
- the Charitable Incorporated Organisations (Consequential Amendments) Order 2012 (SI 2012/3014).

7.4 A CIO:

- is a corporate entity with separate legal personality;
- provides limited liability protection for its trustees and members;
- has a constitution, which is similar to the Memorandum and Articles of Association of a company;
- has a principal office in England or Wales; and
- has at least one member.

Like a CLG, it has a two-tier structure comprising trustees and members.

7.5 CIOs are obliged to adopt a constitution either in, or as near as possible, to a form prescribed by the 2011 Act. There are two forms:

(a) **an association CIO**: this has a body of members distinct from the trustees who may be required to pay subscriptions; and
(b) **a foundation CIO**: where the members and trustees are one and the same persons (as is possible in a company limited by guarantee – see paragraph 5.3).

7.6 The regulations contain a model form constitution for each type of CIO. Where it is proposed to establish a CIO with a bespoke constitution that deviates from the model forms, its constitution must contain the following as a bare minimum:

- a statement of the CIO's purpose (which must be charitable);
- a clause preventing the distribution of profits;
- a clause restricting the extent to which trustees can derive benefit from their position;
- provisions covering the appointment and retirement of members and of trustees; and
- provisions on what will happen to any surplus funds if the CIO is wound up solvent.

7.7 CIOs wishing to depart from the model form constitutions can expect their applications for registration to take a longer time. This may be important for founders considering what form of constitution is appropriate when setting up a CIO.

7.8 Subsequent amendments to a CIO's constitution that would alter:

- the CIO's purposes,
- any application of CIO property on winding up, or
- any provision authorising benefits to members, trustee or any person connected to them

require the Charity Commission's prior written consent.

7.9 The process to be followed to establish a new CIO is as follows:

- an application is to be made to the Charity Commission to be assessed;
- submission of the proposed constitution and other documentation for approval; and
- provided the application and documents are approved, the Charity Commission will add the CIO to the Register of Charities and it will become a charity and

a body corporate without any requirement for it also to be registered with the Registrar of Companies.

7.10 The 2011 Act contains mechanisms for converting charitable companies to CIOs. This is a simplified procedure in which the existing company is simply re-registered as a CIO; no new corporate body is set up and the organisation's legal personality and relationships remain unchanged. It will retain the same registered charity number. This facility has been available for charitable companies with a yearly income of under £12,500 since 1 January 2018. The facility will become available for larger companies at a later stage.

7.11 There is no specific mechanism for the conversion of trusts or unincorporated associations to CIOs. However, the Charity Commission has published guidance stating that trustees of unincorporated charities that wish to convert to a CIO must first establish a CIO, then transfer the assets of the unincorporated charity and wind up the unincorporated charity. The CIO will be a new legal entity with a new registered charity number, and all existing contracts will need to be transferred to the CIO.

7.12 There are also mechanisms in the 2011 Act to facilitate mergers of CIOs.

7.13 No register of charges is maintained for CIOs. This form of charity is likely to be less suitable for larger charities with complex affairs and a potential requirement to borrow from third parties, and grant security for that borrowing.

7.14 While CIOs were introduced to provide an alternative, simpler legal form for charities wishing to receive the benefits of incorporation, there are still a sometimes a number of advantages in being a charitable CLG. If an organisation needs to be set up quickly, registration as a company can be much faster, with the Charity Commission application happening at a later stage. Also, unlike CLGs, which have been available under English law for many years, CIOs are relatively untried and untested, and it may take some time following their introduction for commercial lenders, funders, donors and professional advisers to become comfortable with them.

8 Other legal forms

8.1 Charities can (but in practice relatively rarely do) take the following forms:

- company limited by shares;
- Royal Charter body; or
- statutory corporation.

8.2 A company limited by shares (CLS) is the norm in the field of commercial activity. A CLS has shareholders who each purchase at least one share in the company. The CLS is generally not a suitable legal form for charities, as they are designed for returning profit to their shareholders and are not well suited to 'not for profits'. It is extremely unusual to structure a charity as a CLS, and registration is permitted only in exceptional circumstances. For example, the Charity Bank Ltd was previously registered by the Charity Commission on the basis that the share structure was necessary for the bank to achieve its objects and that there would be no distributions made to non-charitable shareholders without the Commission's consent. Trading companies set up by charities are, however, usually private companies limited by shares; the charity, or someone appointed by the charity, will normally own all the shares (see section 13).

8.3 A Royal Charter is the exercise of the Royal Prerogative of the Sovereign. This is an ancient format bestowed (rarely) by the Privy Council which gives corporate status. In modern times, incorporation by Royal Charter has generally been confined to professional, charitable, scientific, educational or learned non-profit-making institutions or societies. The constitution of a Royal Charter body is bespoke and, along with any variation of it, subject to approval by the Privy Council Office. The process of obtaining a Royal Charter and making constitutional changes can be very slow and costly. Examples of charities established by Royal Charter include the Royal National Institute of Blind People (RNIB), registered charity number 226227, and the Royal National Lifeboat Institution (RNLI), registered charity number 209603.

8.4 A number of charitable organisations are established as corporations by statute. They are governed by the statute creating them and by any supplemental rules set out in secondary legislation. For example, further education corporations, which operate many further education colleges, are statutory corporations established under the Further and Higher Education Act 1992. They are governed by rules in that Act and by instruments and articles of government prescribed by statutory instrument. Further education corporations are exempt charities (see chapter A3, paragraph 7.16). Comparatively few charities are established as corporate bodies by their own individual Act of Parliament. The terms of the statute govern the charity. An example of a charity established by Act of Parliament is the Board of Trustees of the Armouries, usually known as the Royal Armouries (a charity exempt from registration with the Charity Commission), which is governed by provisions in the National Heritage Act 1983.

9 Incorporation of charity trustees

9.1 Part 12 of the 2011 Act enables the trustees of a charity to apply to the Charity Commission for a certificate of incorporation of the trustees as a body corporate.

9.2 Once the certificate is granted, the trustees become a body corporate. This is different from the charity itself becoming incorporated (e.g. as a company limited by guarantee: see section 5) and has a number of advantages if the charity itself needs to remain unincorporated.

9.3 The charity's property is vested in the name of the corporate body, avoiding the need to transfer title to land and investments into the names of new trustees on each new appointment. Once issued by the Charity Commission, the certificate of incorporation automatically vests all of the charity's property in the corporate body.

9.4 In addition, the trustees are able to enter into contracts, sue and be sued in the name of the corporate body, rather than in their own names.

9.5 However, it is important to appreciate that this procedure does not provide charity trustees with the protection of limited liability. The charity trustees remain as personally liable for the acts and omissions of the charity as they were before a certificate of incorporation was issued. This procedure will therefore only be suitable in only limited circumstances.

9.6 To apply for a certificate of incorporation, the case for incorporation must be put to the Charity Commission, together with a form signed by all of the trustees. The trustees need to decide on:

- (subject to the Charity Commission's approval) the name of the corporate body; and
- whether they wish to have a common seal. This is not compulsory, but if they wish to have one, they need to give details to the Charity Commission and confirm that they have agreed proper measures for its safekeeping and made regulations for its use.

9.7 Once a certificate of incorporation has been issued, the trustees can sign documents either by:

- using the common seal, if they have decided to have one;
- signing by a majority; or
- giving any two or more trustees authority in writing or by resolution to execute the documents in the name of, and on behalf of, the corporate body.

10 Community interest companies

10.1 The Community Interest Company (CIC) was developed to address the lack of an appropriate legal vehicle for *non-charitable* social enterprises. CICs provide a legal form for businesses that trade with social purposes. Like charities, they allow for an organisation's assets to be locked, preventing their distribution to members or shareholders. Unlike charities, however, they are suited to social entrepreneurs who wish both to control the organisation and to receive a salary or other limited return on investment from it. They offer opportunities (albeit limited) for social investors to inject long-term share capital.

10.2 While a CIC cannot be a charity, it is possible for an English or Welsh charity to convert to a CIC, subject to the approval of the Charity Commission and a restriction to use the pre-conversion assets for the original charitable purposes. Scottish charities are not currently able to convert to a CIC.

10.3 While CICs are free from the red tape which comes with charitable status, they do not benefit from any of the tax incentives available to charities. They may benefit from community interest tax relief but otherwise do not have any special tax status. They are also subject to CIC specific legal requirements and regulatory oversight by the CIC Regulator.

10.4 A CIC is a type of company. There are three main types of CIC:

(a) those that are limited by guarantee which cannot declare dividends; all profits go back into the company;
(b) those that are limited by shares but have a limited shareholding and no ability to declare a dividend; and
(c) those that are limited by shares which do have a (limited) ability to declare a dividend.

10.5 A CIC may be a public limited company (though in practice this is rare).

10.6 Key features of CICs include:

- They must pass a 'community interest test' – the test is whether a reasonable person would consider that the company's activities are for the benefit of the community. The test is objective, transparent and 'light touch'.
- The definition of 'community' includes sections of the community. Political parties, the promotion of or opposition to changes in applicable law or policy and activities which benefit only the employees of a single employer or members of a particular body are excluded.
- They have an asset lock – this ensures that any profits made by the CIC are reinvested for the benefit of the community and are not distributed to its

members or shareholders. The asset lock does not, however, prevent CICs from using their assets efficiently in pursuit of community benefit: for example, a CIC can use its assets as collateral for finance, can receive grant funding and take out secured and unsecured loans.

- They are regulated by the CIC regulator. The regulator is responsible for ensuring that CICs operate for the benefit of the community, both at registration and ongoing. The CIC regulator has the power to appoint, suspend or remove directors of CICs. The CIC regulator can investigate complaints from stakeholders and has the power to act if it finds that a CIC is not working in the interest of the community or the asset lock is not being observed.
- If assets of a CIC are to be transferred to another body, they must be transferred for full value unless the transfer is to another asset-locked body, either as specified in the CIC's constitution or as approved by the CIC regulator, or otherwise for the benefit of the community. A CIC may buy back its shares from investors at par.

CICs limited by shares are subject to a dividend cap – CICs can distribute profits by declaring dividends on shares, subject to a cap set by the CIC regulator. (Dividends are currently capped at 35% of distributable profits.) Because the level of the cap can be changed by the CIC regulator, the cap applicable is that set by the CIC regulator at the time the share was issued or the date the company became a CIC (whichever is the later).

10.7 As with any limited company, a CIC is governed by Articles of Association. However, these must include various provisions depending on the type of CIC – it may be prudent to base these on the model forms published on the CIC regulator's website. The process for registering a CIC is similar to registering a standard limited company.

11 Constitutions

11.1 Types of constitution

11.1.1 As we have seen, different legal forms have different types of governing document, the most common being as follows:

- **Charitable trusts**: these have deeds or declarations of trust, or may be governed by Charity Commission schemes or a bequest in a will.
- **Unincorporated associations**: these have rules or constitutions, these being a contract between members.
- **Community benefit societies**: these have rules which must include certain provisions prescribed by the Co-operative and Community Benefit Societies Act 2014 and often take the form of model rules prescribed by a promoting body, for example the National Housing Federation.

- **Companies limited by guarantee**: these have Articles of Association, which must include certain provisions prescribed by the Companies Acts.
- **Charitable incorporated organisations**: these have a constitution, which must include certain provisions prescribed by the 2011 Act.
- **Royal Charter bodies**: these have a Royal Charter or Letters Patent handed down by the Sovereign or Privy Council.

11.1.2 It is possible in law to create both a charitable trust and an unincorporated association without setting out in writing any of the rules by which it operates (provided its assets do not include land). However, it is good practice to do so to provide clarity and to help avoid disputes over the purposes, powers and internal management of the organisation. Corporate bodies such as companies incorporated under the Companies Acts, community benefit societies and Royal Charter bodies cannot be created without a written constitution in a particular form.

11.1.3 A number of organisations offer model governing documents of charities; for example, the Charity Commission's model documents for a charitable trust, an unincorporated association and a charitable company limited by guarantee are available (together with guidance notes) on its website. The National Housing Federation provided model rules for registered providers who are community benefit societies. It is common practice for solicitors who are members of the Charity Law Association (CLA) to promote the use of model documents prepared by that association.

11.2 Nature and purpose of constitution

11.2.1 The constitution or governing instrument of a charity is its most important document. It sets out its charitable purposes, the powers it has (or the charity trustees have) to achieve these purposes and the internal rules governing the governing body and, where relevant, the relationship between the governing body and the charity's membership.

11.2.2 For an unincorporated association, a company and a community benefit society, the constitution is a legally enforceable contract, which sets out:

- the rights and obligations of members in relation to the charity;
- the rights and obligations of members in relation to each other; and
- the powers and obligations of the governing body in relation to the members and to the charity itself.

11.2.3 For an unincorporated trust, the declaration, deed of trust, Charity Commission scheme or bequest in a will sets out the rules that the charity trustees must follow in managing their charity. The Charity Commission and, ultimately, the courts have power to interpret and enforce these rules.

11.2.4 It is worth bearing in mind, however, that the written constitution of a charity may not always contain all of the rules applicable to it. The express terms of the constitution are often supplemented or even overridden by:

- rules contained in legislation (such as the Companies Acts for limited companies and the Trustee Act 2000 which applies to trustees of charitable trusts and unincorporated associations); and
- case law or common law.

Before creating or amending the constitution of a charity, you should be aware of these rules.

11.2.5 One of the key duties of charity trustees is to ensure that their charity is governed in accordance with its constitution. Charity trustees who abuse their charity's funds (e.g. by allowing the charity to engage in activities not in pursuance of its charitable objects, or in which the charity has no power to engage) or who are guilty of mismanagement may be in breach of duty and could be held personally liable for making good any loss caused to the charity as a result.

11.3 Contents of constitutions

11.3.1 As a general rule, it is prudent to ensure that a charity's constitution sets out the rules governing it in full, using plain English so that the charity trustees can both follow them without seeking legal advice at every turn and be reasonably confident that the rules are complete and can be relied on without reference to legislation or other law except where absolutely necessary (e.g. the rules in the 2011 Act on disposing or mortgaging land).

11.3.2 While the declaration of trust or trust deed of a charitable trust, the constitution of an unincorporated association, the rules of community benefit society and Articles of Association of a company limited by guarantee will include significant differences in both content and drafting style, they should cover the matters set out in the following checklist.

11.4 Name

Care should be taken to ensure that the name proposed (either for a new charity or for a name change of an existing charity):

- is not the same or confusingly similar to a charity already registered with the Charity Commission;

- where it is a company, is not the same or confusingly similar to a company already registered with the Registrar of Companies;
- where it is a community benefit society, is not the same or confusingly similar to a society already registered with the FCA; and
- does not include a word or words which cannot be used without the prior approval of the Secretary of State or a specified body.

The restrictions that may affect a choice of name are set out in the Companies Act 2006, the Company, Limited Liability Partnership and Business (Names and Trading Disclosures) Regulations 2015 (SI 2015/17) and the Company, Limited Liability Partnership and Business (Sensitive Words and Expressions) Regulations 2014 (SI 2014/3140).

11.5 Charitable companies

11.5.1 Under s. 60 of the Companies Act 2006, a charitable company may be exempt from the usual requirement to include the word 'limited' as part of its name, provided that the requirements of the section are satisfied.

11.5.2 The exemption is obtained on incorporation by completing the relevant section of the application to register (Form IN01) or, on a change of name, by completing a statutory declaration and filing it with the Registrar of Companies (currently Form NE01).

11.6 Location

Companies limited by guarantee and community benefit societies must state the country of domicile of their registered office: either 'England and Wales' or 'England' or 'Wales'.

11.7 Objects/purposes

11.7.1 This is the most important clause in a charity's constitution. As we have seen, the purposes must be exclusively charitable and care must be taken when drafting.

11.7.2 It is generally good practice to frame the purposes as broadly as possible to help ensure that both the current and future activities of the charity are within them. This will help to reduce the risk of the charity inadvertently carrying out activities that are not within the purposes and the charity trustees being in breach of duty as a result.

11.8 Powers

11.8.1 This clause will set out the means by which the charity fulfils its charitable purposes. These should be carefully considered to ensure that the charity has power to carry out all its current and future activities.

11.8.2 If the charity trustees allow the charity to carry out any activity that is outside the powers expressly set out in the constitution, given by statute or implied by case law, then they have acted *ultra vires* (outside their powers) and may be personally liable for any loss caused to the charity.

11.8.3 It is vital to appreciate that the powers a charity has must be exercised only in furtherance of its charitable purposes. For example:

- A power to make grants or loans must only be exercised by making grants or loans either to individuals or to other organisations within the purposes of the charity.
- A power to purchase property must either be exercised directly to further the purposes of the charity (for example, a charity for the advancement of religion which purchases a building for use as a place of worship) or on an investment basis either with the intention of improving the financial position of the charity so that it can better further its purposes (for example, the same charity purchases retail units in order to provide a rental income to help fund its work) or in order to further its aims directly as well as achieve a financial return or a mixture of both if the charity trustees decide it is in the charity's best interests.

11.8.4 A modern, forward-thinking charity should have a full suite of powers.

11.8.5 The following are all examples of powers which can be included based on the Charity Law Association's model trust deed for a charitable trust and its model Articles of Association of a charitable company 3rd edition:

(a) general powers – for example:
   - to promote or carry out research;
   - to publish or distribute information;
   - to cooperate with other bodies;
   - to support, administer or set up other charities;
   - to make grants or loans of money and to give guarantees;
   - to set aside funds for special purposes or as reserves against future expenditure; and
   - to pay for the costs of forming the charity;

(b) powers in relation to property, for example:
   - power to acquire or to hire property of any kind;
   - subject to the restrictions imposed by the 2011 Act, power to borrow

and charge property – to raise funds by loans or other forms of borrowing and to mortgage or charge the charity's property for this purpose. Banks will require reassurance that a charity's constitution includes an express power as a prerequisite for any borrowing (secured or unsecured);

- the charity trustees' power to mortgage their charity's land is subject to the restrictions set out in s. 124 of the 2011 Act. If the charity trustees are unable to take advantage of the procedure in s. 124 a Charity Commission Order will be required to authorise the borrowing;
- subject to the restrictions imposed by the 2011 Act, power to let or dispose of property – before entering into any legally binding agreement to sell, lease, make a gift of or otherwise dispose of their charity's land (or any interest in the land, which includes granting easements, way leaves and options) the charity trustees must either follow the procedures in ss. 117–121 of the 2011 Act or obtain an order from the Charity Commission specifically authorising the disposal;
- a Charity Commission order will always be required before any of the charity's land can lawfully be disposed of to any person who, or organisation which, has a connection with either the charity trustees or with the charity itself;

(c) powers in relation to fundraising and trading – including:
- power to establish or to acquire subsidiary companies; and
- power to raise funds but not by means of taxable trading;

(d) standard commercial powers – for example:
- to employ (paid) staff, agents or advisers – this should cover employees, volunteers, consultants and other independent contractors and enable the charity to provide pensions and other employee benefits;
- to insure the charity's property and to take out such other insurance policies as may be required to protect the charity (for example, public liability insurance, employers' liability cover, product liability insurance and motor risks cover); and
- to enter into contracts to provide services to or on behalf of other bodies;

(e) powers in relation to investments – it is important that express powers to deposit and invest funds and to delegate the management of the charity's investments to a financial expert are provided for corporate charities. For unincorporated charities, if an express power is not included, the position will be governed by the statutory power of investment in the Trustee Act 2000; however, this does not give power to invest in land outside the UK and it is always prudent to set out the charity trustees' powers in full.

The powers should set out the terms on which the management of investments can be delegated to a financial expert, including: a requirement to set out the charity trustees' investment policy in writing; for transactions to be reported promptly to the charity trustees; for the investment policy and the delegation arrangements to be reviewed at least annually; and the ability for the charity trustees to cancel the delegation arrangements at any time;

(f) a final 'blanket' power – to do all such other lawful things which further the objects of the charity.

11.9 Benefits to charity trustees

11.9.1 The general rule is that charity trustees cannot receive a benefit from the charity they administer, except in the following circumstances:

- **express constitutional power**: if and to the extent that the charity's constitution expressly permits it;
- **with the authority of the regulator**: if the Charity Commission (or ultimately the courts) permit it; or
- **statutory permission**: if and to the extent that it is permitted by a statutory provision.

11.9.2 A benefit will include a straightforward payment of money and any other benefit that has a monetary value. The rules extend not just to charity trustees, but to any individual or business connected with a charity trustee. The 'connected person' rules extend to:

- **relatives**: a spouse, partner, brother, sister, child, parent, grandchild or grandparent of a charity trustee; and
- **businesses**: any partnership in which a charity trustee is a member or employee; or any company of which a charity trustee is a director or an employee or of which a charity trustee has the benefit of more than 1% of the share capital.

11.9.3 If a charity trustee (or any connected person) receives a benefit from their charity that is not authorised or permitted by one of the routes described above, they will have received that benefit in breach of duty and may be required to repay it to the charity. In addition, any fellow charity trustee who was aware of and/or acquiesced in the charity trustee receiving the benefit may also be personally liable for making good any loss to the charity as a result.

11.9.4 It is therefore essential that the charity's constitution sets out in full any circumstances in which the charity trustees may receive a benefit. It is standard practice to provide for the following benefits to charity trustees as a minimum:

- although not actually classed as a benefit, reimbursement of any expenses properly incurred in performing their duties as charity trustees (such as necessary travel and accommodation costs in order to attend charity trustee meetings);
- a reasonable interest rate on any money lent by a charity trustee to their charity;

- a reasonable rent or hiring fee on any property let or hired by a charity trustee to their charity;
- an indemnity for any liabilities a charity trustee might incur in running their charity. This would therefore cover any costs personally incurred by charity trustees in successfully defending a criminal prosecution brought against them, perhaps for a breach of health and safety rules. Obviously, such an indemnity cannot cover a trustee's personal liability for wilful or reckless breaches of duty;
- payment to any company in which a charity trustee has no more than a very small (usually 1%) shareholding – this enables the charity to enter into contracts with companies, such as utility companies, in which a charity trustee may own a small number of shares; and
- any other exceptional payments or benefits as approved in writing by the Charity Commission in advance of them being made.

11.9.5 In addition, it has been common practice to provide an express power for the charity to enter into a contract with a charity trustee (or a connected person) for the provision of goods and services in return for payment or any other benefit in the following limited circumstances:

- where the goods and/or services are actually required for the charity;
- where the level of payment or benefit is no more than reasonable in relation to the value of the goods and services to be provided;
- where the decision to enter into the contract has been made following the charity's procedures for managing conflicts of interest (see further below) and a written agreement is entered into; and
- where no more than a specified number or proportion of the charity trustees, up to half of their total number, have an interest in such a contract in any one financial year.

11.9.6 In the absence of an express power, s. 185 of the 2011 Act provides a statutory power to enable a charity to remunerate a charity trustee or a person connected to a charity trustee (see above for more details on 'connected persons') for services provided to the charity subject to similar safeguards to those described above. This power cannot be used where the governing documents of a charity contain any express provision that prohibits the charity trustee or connected person from receiving such remuneration. This is the norm in the Articles of Association of existing charitable companies, which usually include wording along the following lines: 'a trustee must not receive any payment of money or other material benefit (whether directly or indirectly) from the charity', followed by a list of exceptions to the general rule setting out limited circumstances where a charity trustee or connected person may receive a benefit.

11.10 Paid trustees

11.10.1 It is important to appreciate that none of the powers discussed above enable a charity trustee to be paid either for being a charity trustee or as an employee of the charity. It remains relatively rare, particularly for small to medium-sized charities, for paid employees to sit on the governing body. However, it is becoming more common, especially within exempt charities such as registered providers of social housing. For a charity to have an employee who is also a charity trustee, its constitution must contain an express power to this effect (which will require Charity Commission approval for registered charities) or the prior approval of the Charity Commission must be obtained. This restriction also applies to payments by a charity's trading subsidiary to a director who is also a charity trustee of the charity.

11.10.2 Care needs to be taken if a charity trustee wishes to resign to take up paid employment with their charity. The charity trustee must avoid receiving any unauthorised benefit from the charity and there should be no suggestion that they have been preferred or benefited in any way during the recruitment process. In practice, this means that:

- the charity trustee should have resigned before they had any knowledge of the position becoming available;
- if they were aware of the potential position while still a charity trustee, they must resign immediately and have no part in: any decision by the charity to create the position; any discussion of the job description or skills specification; any aspect of the recruitment process; and any decision on pay and conditions; and
- an order should be obtained from the Charity Commission authorising the ex-trustee to take up such a position in any circumstances where they could be seen to have benefited from having been a trustee.

11.11 Conflicts of interest

11.11.1 Charity trustees have a general duty to declare and manage conflicts of interest. A conflict of interest is any situation in which a charity trustee's personal interests, or interests which they owe to another body, and those of the charity arise simultaneously or appear to conflict. In addition to the common law duties that charity trustees are subject to by virtue of their position as charity trustees, directors of charitable companies are also subject to the duties set out in the Companies Act 2006. The constitution will usually will set out how conflicts of interest should be handled, and sometimes when they may be allowable.

11.12 Non-distribution clause (or asset lock)

11.12.1 The constitution must make it clear that the property of the charity does not belong to the individual charity trustees (of a charitable trust) or to the members (of a company limited by guarantee or an unincorporated association), but must be held on trust for the objects of the charity.

11.12.2 Commonly there will also be a provision setting out the limited extent to which the charity trustees and, for a company limited by guarantee or an unincorporated association, the members are able to benefit from the charity (see above for further detail).

11.13 For charitable companies, a limited liability clause and a guarantee clause

Both of these clauses are required by company law:

- The former establishes the limited liability status of the charitable company.
- The latter sets out the extent to which each of the members provides a personal guarantee to contribute to the assets of the charitable company if it is dissolved while they are a member. The amount of the guarantee is usually £1 or £10.

11.14 A dissolution clause

11.14.1 The dissolution clause sets out the rules that must be followed when a charity has reached the end of its useful life, is solvent and is to be dissolved.

11.14.2 It is essential that any assets remaining, after all outstanding debts and liabilities have been satisfied, are used for charitable purposes the same or closely similar.

11.15 Rules for members

11.15.1 Where a charity has a separate membership, the constitution should set out rules that govern the membership.

11.15.2 A well-drafted constitution for an unincorporated association or a charitable company will include detailed rules on at least the following:

- who is eligible to be a member (such as whether membership is open to individuals and/or to member organisations). In a charitable company that is an oligarchy, only the directors will be members;
- the rights and obligations of members;
- mechanisms for applying for membership and for the resignation and removal of members; and
- procedures for calling members' meetings and rules governing such meetings (e.g. rules on how notice is given; quorums; voting rights (including proxies); chairing meetings; and voting majorities).

11.15.3 The members of CLGs benefit from rights and rules about their meetings that are set out in statutory provisions, some of which cannot be amended by provisions in the charity's constitution. It is vital to have a detailed understanding of these statutory provisions before drafting constitutions for charitable companies or substantially amending the model documents. If in doubt, seek specialist advice.

11.15.4 It could be possible to draft provisions relating to members of a CLG by reference to the default rules for CLGs; these rules can be found on the Companies House website (known as model articles for CLGs) (www.gov.uk/guidance/model-articles-of-association-for-limited-companies). However, it is good practice to set the rules out in detail in the Articles of Association, to prevent the need to cross-refer. It should be noted that these model articles will apply as a default, unless there are other relevant articles adopted, or a company's articles expressly state that they shall be excluded. These model articles are not designed for charities, and many of the provisions within them are not suitable. It is therefore usually a good idea to expressly exclude these model articles.

11.15.5 The relationship of the members of an unincorporated association between themselves and their association are governed entirely by the rules set out in the constitution. If the rules are silent on an issue affecting the membership, there are no statutory rules and very few common law rules to fill the void. It is therefore essential that a full suite of rules governing membership is set out.

11.16 Rules regulating the conduct and proceedings of charity trustees

11.16.1 The constitution should set out in detail the rules that the charity trustees must follow in governing their charity.

11.16.2 A well-drafted constitution will normally include:

(a) minimum and maximum numbers of charity trustees;
(b) mechanisms for appointing charity trustees and any qualifications necessary to be a charity trustee;
(c) provisions on resigning and removal of charity trustees;
(d) terms of office of charity trustees – it is common to provide for retirement by rotation or a maximum number of terms of office that a charity trustee can serve before taking at least a 12-month break. Such rules are designed to encourage 'refreshment' of the governing body;
(e) rules for the conduct of charity trustees' meetings:
   - how many meetings are to be held each year?
   - length of notice for calling meetings;

- quorum for trustees' meetings; and
- voting on resolutions – majority rule is the norm. It is common for a casting vote to be given to the chair in the event of deadlock;

(f) if appropriate to the particular circumstances, power to pass resolutions in writing and power to hold meetings by video or telephone conferences or by any other means when all charity trustees can communicate together simultaneously (note that it is not possible for charity trustees to 'meet' by consecutive e-mail communication or separate telephone calls);

(g) power to delegate to committees:
- if an express power is not provided in the constitution of an unincorporated charity the position is governed by the Trustee Act 2000. Section 11 of the Trustee Act 2000 sets out the limited circumstances in which charity trustees can delegate to committees. Delegation of powers to dispose of charitable property (e.g. grant giving) must be expressly stated in the constitution of an unincorporated charity;
- the charity trustees of corporate charities (such as companies limited by guarantee) are not governed by the Trustee Act 2000 and it is essential if the charity trustees are to delegate to staff or to committees that the charity includes a specific provision in the constitution; and
- it is prudent for at least one charity trustee to be a member of each committee and to require prompt reporting back to the governing body of the charity;

(h) power to delegate to staff:
- where it is impractical for charity trustees personally to undertake all of their duties, they may delegate certain tasks to employees of the charity. Any such delegation must be authorised by the charity's governing document or by the Trustee Act 2000; and
- it is good practice to ensure that delegated tasks and limits of delegated authority are also reflected in the relevant employees' job descriptions;

(i) rules governing conflicts of interest (see above).

11.17 Amending constitutions

11.17.1 The power and procedure for amending a charity's constitution depends both on the legal form it takes and the nature of the provision in the constitution to be amended.

11.17.2 As a general rule, provided it has an express power either in its constitution or in legislation to make amendments, charity trustees of an unincorporated charity are able to amend the **administrative provisions** in its constitution without obtaining Charity Commission consent. The members of a charitable company may amend administrative provisions in the charitable company's Articles of Association by special resolution, requiring a 75% majority vote at a general meeting or a written resolution of not less than 75% of members entitled to vote.

11.17.3 The process for amending a charity's objects, or provisions that affect dealings with a charity's property, is dependent on its legal structure:

(a) the objects of an unincorporated charity can be amended without the Charity Commission's consent where there is express power to do so in the constitution; and
(b) charitable companies must always obtain the prior written approval, under s. 198 of the 2011 Act, of the Charity Commission to any proposed amendment to their objects or that affect the manner in which the charity's property may be used or applied.

11.17.4 However, the amendment clause in the constitution may specify that consent is required from another body, for example another regulator or sponsoring body. These rules must be followed to ensure that amendments are lawfully made.

11.17.5 The following table sets out details of the powers of amendment available to charities depending on the legal form they take.

Legal form	Power of amendment
Charitable trust	**Express power** The trust deed, declaration of trust or Charity Commission scheme may give the trustees an express power of amendment. This power may be wide enough to enable amendments to be made to the charitable objects without reference to the Charity Commission. The constitution may require the prior consent of the Charity Commission or another third party (such as a local authority, a founder or sponsoring body) before any or a particular amendment can be made. It is common for the governing documents of charitable trusts to state specifically that the objects clause cannot be amended without the Charity Commission's prior written approval. **Statutory power (administrative provisions)** Section 280 of the 2011 Act gives the trustees of an unincorporated charity (i.e. a charitable trust or unincorporated association) power to modify any provision in their charity's governing documents that are either an administrative power or an administrative procedure. It is important to appreciate that this power cannot be used: • to modify the objects clause (see below) or to give the trustees power to modify the objects;

Legal form	Power of amendment
Charitable trust	• to provide any benefit to the trustees of the charity or connected persons; to spend capital held as permanent endowment; or • to change provisions giving third parties rights to nominate trustees. *Procedure* To take advantage of this power, the trustees should: • pass the resolution following the decision-making rules in their charity's constitution and record the decision in writing; and • send a copy of the resolution to the Charity Commission (the Charity Commission's approval is not required and it is not necessary to give public notice of amendments). **Statutory power to change purposes (smaller charities)** Section 275 of the 2011 Act provides power for the trustees of an unincorporated charity with gross income in its last financial year of £10,000 or less to change their charity's purposes. The trustees can pass a resolution to change all or any part of the purposes of their charity, provided that: • the amended objects are charitable; • they are satisfied that it is in the best interests of their charity to make the changes; and • the new purposes, so far as is reasonably practicable, are similar in character to those they replace. The trustees must pass the resolution by not less than a two-thirds majority and send a copy of it to the Charity Commission, together with a statement of their reasons for passing it. The Charity Commission can ask for additional information or explanation from the trustees or require them to give public notice of the resolution. If the Charity Commission does not object, seek further information or require public notice, the resolution will automatically take effect 60 days after they have received a copy of it. **Charity Commission** The Charity Commission's assistance will be required: • to change the purposes of larger charities where the trustees of a charitable trust with an annual income of over £10,000 have no express power in their charity's governing document to amend the purposes of their charity. The charity trustees will need to apply for a Charity Commission scheme to make the amendments;

Legal form	Power of amendment
Charitable trust	• where the constitution expressly states that the Charity Commission's consent to any or a particular amendment is required; and • where the statutory powers of amendment cannot be used.
Unincorporated association	**Express power** The rules may include an express power to amend. The approval of the membership will commonly be required, depending on what the rules say. **Statutory power (administrative provisions)** Section 280 of the 2011 Act to amend administrative provisions in the constitutions of unincorporated charities is available to charity trustees of an unincorporated association (see the comments above in relation to charitable trusts). The resolution must be approved by the members of the association in general meeting, either by: • a majority of two-thirds of those voting on the matter; or • a decision taken without a formal vote but without any expression of dissent when the matter is put to the meeting. **Statutory power to change purposes (smaller charities)** Section 275 of the 2011 Act to change purposes is available to charity trustees of unincorporated associations with an annual income of £10,000 or less. **Charity Commission power** See comments above in relation to charitable trusts.
Company limited by guarantee	**Statutory powers** Subject to s. 198 of the 2011 Act, the members of the company have power to make amendments to a company's Articles of Association by passing a special resolution either at a members' meeting or by signing a written resolution. Under the Companies Act 2006, with effect from 1 October 2009, the Memorandum of Association contains a statement by the subscribers of their wish to be formed into a company, and all other provisions that may be written in the Memorandum of Association of a pre-existing company are deemed to be contained in the Articles of Association. The Articles of Association are capable of amendment by the members by special resolution. It is possible to entrench provisions in the Articles by making any alteration or removal of the provision conditional on certain conditions being met (for example, obtaining the prior consent of the Charity Commission).

Legal form	Power of amendment
Company limited by guarantee	Section 198 of the 2011 Act provides that a charity that is a company must obtain the consent of the Charity Commission before it can make a 'regulated alteration' to the Articles of Association. Regulated alterations are: • any alteration of the objects clause; • any alteration of any provision directing the application of property of the charity on its dissolution; and • any alteration which authorises a director or member (or persons connected to them) to obtain a benefit. Only amendments which will provide a benefit to a director, member or connected person beyond the extent to which they can obtain benefits under s. 185 of the 2011 Act (see above) require Charity Commission consent. Care must be taken to seek such prior consent in good time (well in advance of putting the issue to the vote). In addition, Charity Commission consent will be required in the following circumstances: • **Pre-1982 companies:** the constitutions of some companies incorporated before 1982 include a requirement to obtain the Charity Commission's consent to all changes. This requirement must continue to be followed until removed by the members. • **Express prohibition on paying directors:** any alteration which removes an express prohibition on paying directors will require prior authorisation by Charity Commission order under s. 105 of the 2011 Act where either all of the directors of the charitable company are also its members or where the company does not have a sufficient number of members who are not directors to form a quorum to vote on the resolution. **Company law procedures** A special resolution can be passed either at a members' meeting or by the members in a written resolution. The following procedure must be followed for a members' meeting: • either 14 clear days' notice of the meeting at which it is proposed to pass the resolution must be given to *all* members or, if longer, the length of notice required by the company's Articles of Association (commonly 21 clear days);

Legal form	Power of amendment
Company limited by guarantee	• the notice must: state that it is a special resolution; contain the precise wording of the resolution; and include a statement informing members of their right to appoint a proxy to attend, speak and vote in their place at the meeting. Members should be provided with sufficient information about the proposed amendments to be able to make an informed decision whether or not to agree to them. It is therefore good practice to provide members with an explanatory note on the amendments proposed if they are not self-explanatory and they have not previously been consulted about the proposed amendments; • a majority of at least 75% of the members who either attend in person or by proxy and vote at the meeting must vote in favour of the resolution; • a copy of the special resolution (certified by a director or the company secretary), together with a copy of the amended Articles of Association must be filed with the Registrar of Companies within 15 days of the resolution being passed. Technically, it is a criminal offence punishable by a fine not to file within the timescales; • a copy of the amended Articles of Association and the special resolution should also be filed with the Charity Commission. The originals should be kept with the company books. To pass a special resolution in writing, the following procedure must be followed: • The written resolution setting out the amendments to be made to the Articles of Association must be sent to all members at the same time or by submitting the same copy to each member in turn if this can be done without 'undue delay'. The resolution must state on the face of it that it is proposed as a special resolution. • The circulated resolution must in all cases be accompanied by a statement as to how members should signify their agreement and the date by which the resolution must be passed or will otherwise lapse (it is a criminal offence not to comply with this requirement, although the validity of the resolution itself is not affected). • The circulated resolution is passed if and when at least 75% of the members sign it within a period of 28 days from either the date it was sent out or the first date on which it was sent out for circulation. After this period, a resolution with insufficient support will lapse.

Legal form	Power of amendment
Company limited by guarantee	• All the signatures do not need to be on the same document, as long as each is written on a document that accurately states the terms of the resolution. • The company's auditors are entitled to receive a copy of the written resolution. • A copy of the signed written resolution (certified by either a director or the company secretary), together with a copy of the amended Articles of Association should be filed with the Registrar of Companies within 15 days of it being passed and should also be sent to the Charity Commission. Originals should be kept with the company books.
Community Benefit society	**Express power** The rules of the CBS will include a provision on amending them. All amendments will need to be made by the members at a general meeting. It is usual to require at least a two-thirds majority vote by the members to adopt the amendments. **Statutory rules** Section 16 Co-operative and Community Benefit Societies Act 2014 provides rules applicable to how CBSs amend their rules: • No amendment of rules is valid until the FCA has registered the amendment. • All amendments to the CBS's rules must be notified to the FCA by providing two printed copies of the amended rules signed by three members and the secretary of the society. The Secretary of the CBS must sign and complete an application (available from: www.fca.org.uk/your-fca/documents/forms/amendment-of-rules-for-a-society-or-credit-union-form) outlining details of the rule changes, and send this to the FCA together with a statutory declaration by an officer of the CBS and a copy of the amended rules.
Charitable incorporated organisation (CIO)	**Statutory power** Members of a CIO will be able to alter its constitution by passing a resolution of 75% of votes cast at a general meeting or by passing a written resolution provided the amendment does not result in the CIO ceasing to be a charity. Any amendments to provisions in the CIO's constitution that relate to any of the following will, in addition, require the prior written consent of the Charity Commission: • the CIO's purposes; • any application of the CIO's property on winding up; or • any authorisation of benefits to trustees, members or those connected to them.

<table>
<tr><th>Legal form</th><th>Power of amendment</th></tr>
<tr><td>Royal Charter body</td><td>A Royal Charter body's charter and/or bye-laws can be altered only with the agreement of the Privy Council. The Privy Council's website (www.privy-council.org.uk) contains detailed guidance on the procedure.
If the Royal Charter body is a registered charity, the Charity Commission (or the Office of the Scottish Charity Regulator (OSCR) for Scottish charities) will need to be consulted about proposed amendments that have a bearing on charity law – for example, any change to the objects or to the charity trustees' powers.
Where significant changes that have charity law implications are proposed to a Royal Charter, the Charity Commission may make a scheme which is then given effect by the Privy Council.
The following should be sent to the Privy Council in order to apply for its agreement to the proposed amendments:<ul><li>the text of the proposed amendments;</li><li>a note setting out as concisely as possible the purpose and effect of the proposed amendments. This should briefly explain the reasons why the change is considered desirable, the changes that are proposed and an explanation of how the amendments achieve this;</li><li>full details of any consultation with the Charity Commission (including details of the outcome and contact details of the person dealt with);</li><li>full details of any consultation with government departments or any other institution which may be required;</li><li>an electronic version of the amendments formatted in accordance with the Privy Council's particular requirements (see www.privycouncil.independent.gov.uk/royal-charters/amending-a-royal-charter);</li><li>details of the timetable for passing formal resolutions to make the amendments;</li><li>copies of the formal resolutions required to make the amendments, which should include a 'latitude' clause enabling textual amendments to be agreed without the need to repeat all the formalities provided for in the Charter. For example 'subject to such changes as the Privy Council may require and which are agreed by the [Royal Charter Body]'; and</li><li>a signed and sealed certificate confirming that the resolutions were duly passed in accordance with the bye-laws.</li></ul></td></tr>
</table>

11.18 Notification

11.18.1 Details of any changes to the constitution of a registered charity (apart from those made by Charity Commission scheme) must be sent to the Charity Commission, who will update the Register of Charities.

11.18.2 All amendments to the constitutions of Scottish charities must be notified to OSCR within three months. Where charities are dual registered, OSCR's requirements in relation to amendments to constitutions will have to be complied with as well as any English charity law requirements.

12 Branches, networks and group structures

12.1 Many charities have a straightforward legal structure. All activities will be carried out through the charity itself or the activities will be split between primary-purpose trading activities with certain fundraising events carried out through the charity and other commercial trading activities carried out through one or more wholly owned trading subsidiaries (see section 13).

12.2 However, some charities have complex structures comprising several different legal entities carrying out a variety of different charitable and non-charitable activities. The need to adopt or preserve a complex structure is likely to be driven by direct tax and VAT considerations and a desire to ring-fence risk. Mergers of charities frequently result in 'groups' of charities with any number of separate charities under common control.

12.3 Projects and branches

12.3.1 Problems can occur where a 'parent' charity is unclear of the status of projects or branches associated with it. It is important to establish whether such projects or branches are in fact separate, independent organisations (with their own duties, responsibilities and liabilities) or are activities of the parent charity. This is not always easy to establish.

12.3.2 Difficulties can arise where a project or branch is operating autonomously and has no accountability to the parent. A project or branch may have use of premises, employ staff, have its own bank account and provide services. Where the project or branch is not a separate organisation, its activities are those of the parent, which is ultimately responsible and can be held to account. Particular problems can arise where the project or branch is pursuing activities that are not within the charitable purposes or the powers of the parent and are therefore being carried on in breach of trust.

12.3.3 Where a project or a branch is not a separate organisation, or its status is in any doubt, it is advisable that the parent charity requires the project or branch to sign up to written terms of reference. Depending on the particular circumstances, the terms might cover:

- its status as a non-autonomous project or branch of the parent;
- the authorised scope of its activities and area of operation;
- compliance with the parent's charitable purposes and strategy;
- requirements for reporting and accounting to the parent;
- implementation of policies and procedures of the parent;
- the composition of any local committee, how members are appointed and removed and how they are to manage their meetings;
- managing the relationship between any local committee of the branch or project and the parent (the parent should have the right to attend meetings and to receive minutes);
- any restrictions or controls on funds and fundraising;
- controls on bank accounts;
- restrictions on entering into contracts in the parent charity's name; and
- dissolution of the project or branch.

12.3.4 Where a project or branch is a separate charity, responsibility for its management and administration rests with its charity trustees. Depending on the particular circumstances, it may choose to affiliate with the parent charity, form a group with the parent for accounting, taxation or VAT purposes or become a subsidiary of the parent (where the parent charity has ultimate control).

12.4 Networks of independent charities

12.4.1 There are many ways in which separate independent charities work together. These range from formal affiliation and federal structures through licensing and franchising arrangements to looser partnering arrangements. A detailed discussion of such structures and arrangements are beyond the scope of this Handbook.

12.4.2 However, we will look in a little more detail at:

- affiliated structures; and
- federal structures.

12.4.3 In each of these, a parent charity provides strategic guidance and central services to its affiliates or members. The parent is also usually able to exercise a degree of control over how the affiliates or members operate.

12.4.4 An affiliated structure is created when a number of independent charities agree to be bound by the rules of a main charity. Each independent charity may be required to adopt a common form of governing document and/or operate within a framework prescribed by the main charity.

12.4.5 A typical affiliation arrangement between a main charity and its affiliates might include the following terms:

- where the affiliates use any name and/or logo belonging to the main charity, a licence to use that name and/or logo (including a right to withdraw the licence and require the affiliate to change its name and to cease using the name and/ or logo if the agreement is breached);
- a description of the relationship between the main charity and its affiliates;
- requirements to obtain the main charity's consent to change its charitable objects and to make other changes to its governing document;
- rights of the main charity to appoint charity trustees or to attend charity trustees' meetings;
- details of any policies or procedures to be followed by affiliates;
- obligations on the affiliate to report or account to the main charity;
- any restrictions on activities or controls on fundraising;
- any obligations to pay an affiliation fee (which may have VAT implications);
- any obligation to transfer funds to the main charity on dissolution of the affiliate or otherwise;
- any obligations on the main charity to provide support (financial or otherwise), guidance or assistance to its affiliates; and
- rights of the main charity and of affiliates to terminate the relationship and the consequences of doing so.

12.4.6 A federal or umbrella structure is created where separate independent charities become members of a central charity to pursue a common purpose. This enables each charity to benefit from centralised administration, training and information sharing and to coordinate activities, particularly campaigns. Each separate charity will have rights as members of the federation and may pay a fee for funding the central charity (which may have VAT implications).

13 Trading subsidiaries

13.1 A basic rule of charity law is that charities should usually only carry on trading activities which are either directly in pursuance of their objects or which are ancillary to their objects (together known as 'primary-purpose trading'). The amount of other non-primary-purpose trading that they can carry on is strictly limited. (See also Chapter D2).

13.2 A charity's profits from primary-purpose trading activities are exempt from tax as are profits made from lotteries and from certain other types of fund-raising. In each case, the exemption is subject to conditions relating to the application of the profits received by the charity. In addition, income received by a charity from the sale of goods that have been donated to it is not generally regarded as trading profit and is not taxable.

13.3 While charities may trade more or less freely in pursuance of their charitable purposes, charities should not engage in non-primary-purpose trades that would result in a significant risk to the assets of the charity. Such trade should be undertaken by a trading subsidiary established as a separate company.

13.4 Before establishing a trading subsidiary, it is highly recommended that advice is sought on the direct tax and VAT implications for the charity.

13.5 The most common legal form for a trading subsidiary is a company limited by shares; the charity will usually be the sole member owning the entire issued share capital and have the sole right to appoint and remove the directors. However, with charities becoming increasingly involved in 'social enterprise' activities, establishing trading subsidiaries as companies limited by guarantee or community interest companies is become increasingly popular.

13.6 The trading subsidiary must be wholly separate from the charity and the entire relationship must be kept at arm's length. This means:

(a) there should be no subsidy in the form of money, staff time, cost of shared facilities, interest-free loans, guaranteeing of loans and so on;
(b) there should be no mixing of funds – the charity and its trading subsidiary should have separate bank accounts;
(c) the charity should make a management charge for the use of shared resources;
(d) the trading subsidiary must have separate company books and business stationery, and must itself comply with all Companies Acts requirements;
(e) the trading subsidiary must keep separate minutes of its members' and directors' meetings, even if the meetings take place at the same time as the charity trustees' or members' meetings;
(f) while it is common for charity trustees to also be directors of its trading subsidiary, it is important to consider that, sometimes, the interests of the two entities may be in conflict. The Charity Commission therefore recommends that, in the interests of good governance, there should be:
   - at least one person who is a charity trustee, but not a director or employee of the trading subsidiary; and
   - at least one person who is a director of the trading subsidiary, but not a charity trustee or employee of the charity; and

(g) finally, a charity trustee cannot be paid for their services as a director (or employee) of its trading subsidiary unless specifically provided for by the charity's governing document, or specifically authorised by the Charity Commission.

13.7 The trading subsidiary will commonly require initial start-up or working capital. The usual practice is for the charity to provide this by way of a loan. This must be treated by the charity trustees as a form of investment, irrespective of the close connection between the two entities. This means that the charity should:

- consider and decide whether the investment is one that the charity should make having regard to risk and the need to diversify its investment portfolio;
- enter into a loan agreement under which the trading subsidiary is charged a commercial rate of interest and commits to repayment terms (usually on demand); and
- take security in the form of a fixed and floating charge over all the assets of the trading subsidiary.

13.8 In order to avoid adverse tax consequences for the charity it is important that the loan between the charity and the trading subsidiary will be a qualifying loan for the purposes of ss. 514 and 561 of the Corporation Tax Act 2010. Where there is any doubt about this, advice from a tax adviser should be sought; for larger loans, the charity should consider obtaining prior clearance from HMRC.

13.9 The trading subsidiary will usually pass its taxable profits to the charity using Gift Aid. This amount is paid gross and the company claims tax relief when calculating its profits for corporation tax. The charity cannot reclaim tax on donations made by the trading subsidiary. The donation needs to be paid over to the charity within nine months of the trading company's year-end, in order to obtain tax relief for the financial year in question. The working capital requirements of the trading company may prevent the full year's profits being donated to the charity.

13.10 Ideally the relationship between the charity and its trading subsidiary should be recorded in a trading agreement; this will include arrangements for cross-charging between the two entities.

13.11 Other subsidiaries

A charity may wish to set up other subsidiaries and these may be charitable or non-charitable. Charities often choose to hive off some of their operations to a subsidiary in the interests of good governance. It can be a useful way of ring-fencing non-core activities or activities involving some form of risk, be that financial, reputational or otherwise.

A3
Setting up a charity

1 Setting up a charity

1.1 Setting up a new organisation as a charity usually involves two stages:

- establishing a legal form; and
- applying to the Charity Commission to register it as a charity.

1.2 We have looked at key features of the types of legal form commonly used to structure charities. In this next section, we will look in more detail at setting up the four most common forms used in practice:

- charitable trusts;
- unincorporated associations;
- companies limited by guarantee; and
- charitable incorporated organisations.

1.3 This Handbook does not deal with setting up community benefit societies in any more detail for the following reasons:

- Where a community benefit society is created, model rules or a model constitution will often be prescribed by a promoting body. The promoting body will provide advice and guidance on using their model documents.
- Given the specialist nature of community benefit societies, we recommend that legal advice is sought before seeking to set one up, even where model rules are to be used.

2 Establishing a charitable trust

2.1 A charitable trust can be created without putting anything in writing. Anyone who receives property on the condition that it is used for a purpose that is charitable in law holds that property on trust and is accountable for it. For example, a participant in a fundraising event such as the London Marathon holds the sponsorship money they collect on trust for the charity or cause they are supporting through their participation.

2.2 It is best practice, however, to set out the rules for governing a charitable trust in writing in either a deed or declaration of trust. Where rules are not set out in writing, the trust will be governed by rules set out in case law and in statute.

2.3 When the first trustees agree the wording of the trust deed or declaration of trust, the document should be signed by each of them in the presence of a witness (who should sign, date and print their name, address and occupation). The document should be dated with the date that the last signature is made.

2.4 There are no requirements to have the deed or declaration of trust stamped. There is no separate register for trusts. Instead, the trust will be constituted on the date that the deed or declaration of trust is formally adopted by the trustees signing it.

2.5 The Charity Commission provides a Model Trust Deed (GD2). This includes a range of alternative clauses designed to cover most simple situations.

3 Establishing an unincorporated association

3.1 An unincorporated association is formed whenever several people agree to join together to carry out a mutual purpose, other than for profit. The unincorporated association will be a charity if those purposes fall within one or more of the purposes recognised as charitable in law and are pursued for the benefit of the public.

3.2 Unincorporated associations come in many different shapes and sizes. They are based on a contract between members, which can be binding even if made orally. Although this means that there is no legal requirement to adopt a written set of rules, it is advisable to set out the rules governing the unincorporated association in writing in the form of a constitution. No specific case law or statutes regulate the form or contents of the rules, but it is advisable that they are carefully drafted and tailored to the particular requirements of the association. This will help in the event of a disagreement, and may also help protect trustees and officers from personal liability.

3.3 The rules in the constitution bind the members of the unincorporated association. The members control the unincorporated association, so it is very important that a full and up-to-date list of members is kept at all times and that the rules include clear provisions on the admission and retirement of members.

3.4 A model form of constitution for an unincorporated charitable association is available from the Charity Commission (reference GD3). A number of other organisations have forms of charitable constitutions, which have been approved by the Charity Commission.

3.5 It is usual practice for the form of rules or constitution to be adopted by a formal resolution of the members at their first meeting.

4 Establishing a company limited by guarantee

4.1 Formation

4.1.1 A company limited by guarantee can be formed by sending the following to Companies House (a company can be set up electronically but this service is restricted to companies limited by shares):

- Memorandum and Articles of Association signed by the first subscribers (members) and their witnessed signatures.
- Form NE01: A statutory declaration allowing the charity to omit the word 'limited' from its name (see further below).
- Form IN01: An application to register a company, which includes attached forms to provide details of the directors, the company secretary (if the company is to have one) and the subscribers.
- Fee: £40 for standard service (7–10 days), £100 for 24-hour service.

4.1.2 Where the company is formed electronically (for example, if you were setting up a trading company limited by shares), the Memorandum and Articles of Association and other forms do not need to be signed and sent to Companies House. Instead, all details are completed online and the Memorandum and Articles of Association is filed electronically.

4.1.3 The company is formed on the date specified in the Certificate of Incorporation. As with any private company, the directors of a company limited by guarantee are required to maintain and keep up-to-date company (or 'statutory') books containing a register of members, register of directors, etc.

4.1.4 It is good practice for a charitable company to have at least three directors on the board from the outset (the directors in a charitable company will also be the trustees). It is not necessary for any of the directors of a charitable company to be resident in the UK because the company is registered in England and/or Wales, so the Charity Commission and the courts have jurisdiction over it and can take such action as may be necessary without the directors having to be UK residents. This situation is not the same as for a charitable trust or unincorporated association. For these organisations, the charity has no legal identity separate from its trustees and (at least) a majority of the trustees are usually expected to be resident in the UK so that the Charity Commission and the courts have jurisdiction over them.

4.1.5 It is not necessary to appoint a company secretary but it is advisable for charitable companies to appoint one. If a company secretary is appointed, their details must be filed with Companies House.

5 Establishing a charitable incorporated organisation

5.1 An application for establishing a CIO can only be made electronically. Model constitutions are available on the Charity Commission's website. There are two alternative models: the foundation model and the association model. The foundation model has only trustees as its members, whereas the association model has members other than its trustees.

5.2 Unlike other legal forms, establishing a CIO as a legal entity, and registering it with the Charity Commission are one and the same thing. A CIO will only become an organisation once it is registered by the Charity Commission and receives a registration number. Therefore the process of establishing a CIO is dealt with in registering the proposed CIO with the Charity Commission.

5.3 The Charity Commission may refuse registration if it is not satisfied that the organisation is charitable or if the constitution does not comply with the CIO requirements.

6 Names

6.1 Before setting up a charity with a particular name, the following should (as a minimum) be checked to make sure that the name proposed is suitable and available. There are a number of things to think about when considering the name of a charity. There are restrictions on the words that you can use, and rules about the form that a name should take (depending on the charity's legal form).

- A charity will need to ensure that that no other organisation is either registered with or using a name that is confusingly similar. The charity should check the Register of Companies maintained by Companies House and the Register of Charities maintained by the Charity Commission. The Charity Commission has the power to require a charity to change its name if it is the same as, or too similar to, the name of another charity (s. 42(1) Charities Act 2011). In addition, if the charity is a company, Companies House will not register a company with a name that is too similar to the name of another company. The law on names being too similar was changed in 2015 and is now more flexible than it was (Company, Limited Liability Partnership and Business (Names and Trading Disclosures) Regulations 2015). However, if an existing company thinks that a new company has been established with a name that is too similar to its own name, it has the right to object to that name. In addition, this restriction on names being too similar now applies across all incorporated organisations. For this reason, the register held by Companies House now includes all incorporated organisations and not just companies.

- A name should not be misleading or offensive, and there are restrictions on the use of words that are considered to be sensitive. The list of sensitive words set out in the Company, Limited Liability Partnership and Business Names (Sensitive Words and Expressions) Regulations 2014. There are restrictions on the use of a number of words that are often used by charities – such as 'charity', 'trust' and 'foundation'. These words can still be used, but the charity will need to be able to show that the use of the word is not misleading.
- A company and or a registered society will usually be required to use the word 'Limited' or 'Ltd' in its names. However, both the Companies Act 2011 and the Co-operative and Community Benefit Societies Act 2014 allow a charitable company or registered society to apply to remove this word from its name.
- A CIO must include the term 'CIO' or 'charitable incorporated organisation' in its name.

6.2 Charity Commission powers

The Charity Commission has power to require a charity to change its name where that name:

- is either the same as, or, in the Charity Commission's opinion, too similar to a name of any other charity (whether registered or not);
- is, in the Charity Commission's opinion, likely to mislead the public as to the true nature of the purposes of the charity or of the activities to be carried out in furtherance of those purposes;
- includes a word or expression prescribed by the regulations discussed above and will, in the Charity Commission's opinion, mislead the public as to the status of the charity;
- is, in the Charity Commission's opinion, likely to give the impression that the charity is connected in some way with the Government, any local authority or any other body or individual, when it is not so connected; or
- is, in the Charity Commission's opinion, offensive.

7 Registration with the Charity Commission

7.1 With the exception of a CIO, it is not necessary to register an organisation with the Charity Commission for it to be charitable in law. A significant number of charities either do not meet the threshold for compulsory registration or are exempt or excepted from registration with the Charity Commission.

7.2 The current criteria for registration with the Charity Commission are:

(a) the organisation is a charity in law. To recap, this means:
  - it must be established exclusively for purposes which are recognised as charitable in the law of England and Wales; and
  - its activities are pursued for the benefit of the public (see chapter A1 above);

(b) it has, or reasonably considers it will have, an annual income of at least £5,000 (or is a CIO); and

(c) it is not an exempt or excepted charity.

7.3 Charity Commission checklist

To apply to register an organisation as a charity:

(a) the organisation must already be established (unless it is a CIO);

(b) an application form must be completed and submitted online through a portal on the Charity Commission website;

(c) a trustee declaration form signed by each trustee of the organisation must be attached to the online application form;

(d) a copy of the governing document of the organisation must also be submitted to the Charity Commission. The Charity Commission also asks if the governing document been issued by an organisation or umbrella body (referred to as an approved governing document);

(e) the latest accounts (if available); and

(f) the Charity Commission will also require evidence that the organisation has an annual income of more than £5,000: for example, by submitting a copy of the organisation's most recent bank statement or funding offers.

On submission, the application will be assigned a registration reference number. The Charity Commission will also send, by email, a copy of the pdf application including all data contained in the application to the applicant, the charity contact and each trustee that provided an email address.

7.4 The trustees are required to state in the application whether their charity works with children and/or vulnerable adults. If so, the applicant will be asked to confirm that the trustees have read the Charity Commission's Safeguarding Guidance.

7.5 The Charity Commission asks applicants for any further documentation that it wants to attach to be submitted with the application. If the Charity Commission requires further information it will request it, having carried out a preliminary assessment of the application. It is therefore advisable to ensure that the application form is as complete, comprehensive and persuasive as possible.

While, ultimately, it is the courts who determine what is or is not charitable in law, it will often be prohibitively expensive, time-consuming and difficult to challenge a decision by the Charity Commission that an organisation is not charitable because it does not meet the criteria.

7.6 An example of additional information that the Charity Commission may request in support of an application includes copies of information about the charitable or fundraising activities of the organisation (such as a business plan, fundraising materials or minutes of meetings).

7.7 Guidance on registering as a charity can be obtained from the Charity Commission's website or by telephoning their information line. The application must demonstrate that the organisation's charitable purposes are charitable and for the public benefit (see chapter A1 for details) and the Charity Commission recommends that its guidance on public benefit should be reviewed before an application to register a new charity is made.

7.8 At the time of writing, no fee is payable to the Charity Commission to apply to register a charity.

7.9 Applications to the Charity Commission may only be made by following the online application process. The Charity Commission aims to make decisions on registration as soon as it can, but it can be a length process.

7.10 The length of time it takes the Charity Commission to approve an application and register a charity will largely depend on whether the organisation in question clearly meets the criteria for registration and the quality of the information provided in the application. The Charity Commission will treat applications as urgent if the circumstances warrant it (for example, if the organisation in question is negotiating to purchase property and wants to take advantage of the stamp duty exemption available to charities, or is about to launch a major fundraising appeal).

7.11 If all the criteria for registration are satisfied, the Charity Commission will confirm this by email to the correspondent named in the application form and provide a registered charity number. Details of the charity usually appear on the Register of Charities (accessible on the Charity Commission's website) within a few days of registration. It is prudent to check the details showing on the Register carefully to ensure that accurate entries have been made.

7.12 Under normal circumstances, the trustees' names (but not their addresses or other personal details) will appear on the public register of charities. A dispensation can, however, be granted by the Charity Commission if it is considered that the publication of trustees' names may put them at risk. In such cases, an alternative contact will be published on the Register (such as a firm of solicitors).

7.13 Similarly, where appropriate, Companies House may agree to keep personal details of trustees off their public registers (see chapter A2). Trustee directors still have to provide their residential address but also have the option of providing an alternative service address. The service address will be on the public record, but the residential address will be protected and held on a private register available only to selected organisations (specified public authorities and credit reference agencies). Trustee directors deemed vulnerable by virtue of risk of violence or connection to the police or security services will be able to apply to the Registrar for their addresses not to be provided to credit reference agencies.

7.14 Rules on charity information on materials

7.14.1 All registered charities with an income in their last financial year of over £10,000 must clearly state the fact that the charity is a registered charity in:

- all fundraising material and any other documents issued either by or on behalf of the charity which solicit money or other property for the charity's benefit;
- all bills of exchange, promissory notes, endorsements, cheques and orders for money or goods purporting to be signed on behalf of the charity; and
- all bills rendered by it and in all its invoices, receipts and letters of credit.

There is no legal requirement to state the registered charity number, although many charities choose to do so.

7.14.2 In addition, where the charity is a company, the following rules apply:

(a) The full name of the company as registered at Companies House must be disclosed on:
  - all business letters, notices and other official publications of the company;
  - all bills of exchange, cheques, orders and invoices;
  - all applications for licences to carry on a trade or activity;
  - all other forms of its business correspondence and documentation; and
  - on its website.

  These requirements extend to a charitable company's e-mails that are business correspondence.

(b) All its business letters (including emails), order forms and its website must also state the company's place of registration, the number with which it is registered and the address of its registered office. Where the company's name does not include the word 'limited' they must also indicate that the charity is a limited company.

  This information is normally shown in the form of a footnote as follows:

[*Full name of charitable company*], a limited company, registered in England and Wales under number [*company number*], registered office: [*address*]. Registered charity number [charity number].

(c) The registered name of the company must be displayed at its registered office, at any place where it keeps its company records for inspection and at any other business location(s) in a conspicuous position so that it may be easily seen by visitors.

7.15 Keeping the Charity Commission informed

The trustees of a registered charity have a duty to notify the Charity Commission if their charity ceases to exist, or if any changes are made to its governing document or to any of the details shown on the Register of Charities and to provide copies of any amendments (except where these have been made by Charity Commission scheme).

7.16 Excepted and exempt charities

7.16.1 A number of charities have, historically, not been required to register with the Charity Commission because they were either exempt or excepted from registration. (An exempt charity is neither registered with, nor regulated by, the Charity Commission. Excepted charities are not registered with the Charity Commission, but are still be regulated by it.)These charities enjoyed the tax and status benefits of being charities and are required to comply with the general law relating to charities. However, they were not subject to regulation by the Charity Commission in the same way as registered charities. The rationale behind this was that they were all regulated by some other body, whether an umbrella body or another arm of government.

7.16.2 However, it was felt that these anomalies could be confusing to the public, and exempt and excepted charities and their regulating bodies either may not have been fully aware of, or followed the requirements of charity law, particularly in relation to governance and benefits to trustees. The Charities Act 2006 therefore changed the law to remove exempt and excepted status from many charities and groups of charities. At the time of writing, all charities with an income over £100,000 which were previously excepted must now register with the Charity Commission.

7.16.3 Exempt charities are those charities listed in Schedule 3 to the Charities Act 2011 (the 2011 Act). They currently include the universities of London and Newcastle; higher and further education corporations; various prestigious national galleries, museums and institutions (including the National Gallery, the Tate, the Victoria and Albert Museum, the Science Museum and Imperial War Museum, the British Library and the Royal Botanic Gardens, Kew) and community benefit societies. (No firm decision has been made on the future regulation of community benefit societies. It is possible that those which are registered social housing providers will remain exempt while others may lose their exemption if suitable principal regulators cannot be found.)

7.16.4 The Charities Act 2006 significantly reduced the number of charities exempted from registration. The following are no longer exempt:

- students' unions;
- Eton and Winchester Colleges;
- colleges and halls of Cambridge, Durham and Oxford Universities;
- the Museum of London;
- universities and higher education Institutes in Wales; and
- Church Commissioners and the Representative Body of the Church of Wales.

In addition, the Secretary of State has the power to make orders to either remove charities from or add charities to the list of exempt charities in Schedule 3.

7.16.5 To help previously exempt charities deal with their change in status, and help the Charity Commission to cope with the increase in registrations, only those previously exempt charities with income exceeding £100,000 per annum were initially required to register. It was expected that smaller exempt charities would be expected to register in due course, but the threshold remains at £100,000 at the date of writing. The Charity Commission has stated that, with the exception of a few smaller students' unions, most of these previously exempt charities are now registered.

7.16.6 Excepted charities are those that, historically, have been excepted from registration either by regulation or by Charity Commission order. These include some religious charities, scout and guide groups and some armed forces charities. For the time being, the Charity Commission orders excepting these charities from registration remain in force (subject to those with gross income exceeding £100,000 per annum, which are now required to register).

7.16.7 The government's intention appears still to be that all exempt and excepted charities with annual income of £100,000 or less will be registered with the Charity Commission (unless the exempt charity has a principal regulator). In addition, provisions in the 2011 Act could enable all charities falling below the income threshold of £5,000 to register voluntarily with the Charity Commission in due course. This will help ensure that information about them is readily available to the public. The government had stated that it supported both of these changes subject to the Charity Commission carrying out a feasibility study to work out the costs, benefits and impacts on their resources of voluntary registration. However, at the date of writing no action had been taken, nor appears imminent, on either of these intentions.

8 Incorporation

8.1 The process of converting an unincorporated charity into a corporate charity is known as 'incorporation'. At present, unincorporated charities most commonly incorporate as a CLG or a CIO (see Chapter A2).

8.2 The process of incorporating an unincorporated charity as a company limited by guarantee normally involves setting up a charitable company and transferring all of the assets (subject to the liabilities) of the unincorporated charity to it. A more recently available alternative is to set up a CIO.

8.3 The process of incorporating an unincorporated charity as a CIO involves setting up and registering a CIO and transferring all of the assets (subject to the liabilities) of the unincorporated charity to it.

8.4 The legal process is the same as that for a type-two merger and this section should be read together with chapter F1. It is advisable to seek legal advice on the incorporation process.

8.5 Before they make a decision to go ahead with incorporation, the trustees need to decide whether it is in the best interests of their charity to do so, taking into consideration the following.

8.5.1 The key advantage of incorporation is that the charity will become a company or a CIO, which is a separate legal entity and can therefore hold property and enter into contracts in its own name, without having to act through the medium of trustees. This avoids the need to transfer ownership of property and other assets when trustees change. It also makes the company or the CIO, rather than the trustees, the employer of the charity's employees and the contracting party in contracts of all kinds between the charity and third parties. However, the trustees need to understand that incorporation does not exclude them from all personal liability. They remain trustees of the charity and, as such, they are still responsible for any breaches of trust resulting in losses to the charity itself. The company or CIO structure protects the trustees from claims by third parties but does not shield them from claims by the charity itself, or from the statutory liabilities of directors and officers (in the case of a company) and of charity trustees (in the case of a CIO).

8.5.2 Where a charity incorporates into a company, one disadvantage is sometimes perceived to be the added administrative burden and associated costs of reporting to Companies House as well as to the Charity Commission. However, these should not be substantial and the same form of accounts can be submitted to both regulators. A company must comply with the requirements of the Companies Act with regard to the passing of resolutions, the keeping of minutes, the disqualification of directors, liquidation, etc., but these requirements, where not specified by charity law, contribute to good practice.

8.5.3 Where a charity incorporates into a CIO, there is no added administrative burden and fewer associated costs of reporting to Companies House because the CIO is accountable as a charitable form only to the Charity Commission.

8.6 When the decision to proceed has been made, the following steps need to take place.

8.6.1 Due diligence: Assessing the constitution, assets and liabilities of the unincorporated charity to identify the legal formalities to be followed to transfer the assets to the new charitable company. For example, the following need to be investigated:

- **Power to transfer**: The constitution of the unincorporated charity needs to be checked to ensure that the trustees have power to transfer the charity's assets to the charitable company or CIO. If no express power is provided, the constitution may need to be amended (which may require a resolution to be passed by any membership) before any transfer can take effect.
- **Employees**: The Transfer of Undertakings (Protection of Employment) Regulations 2006 as amended by the Collective Redundancies and Transfer of Undertakings (Protection of Employment) (Amendment) Regulations 2014 (TUPE) apply and all employees must be consulted about the transfer of their employment to the charitable company or CIO. Under TUPE, all employees will automatically transfer to the charitable company or CIO under their existing terms and conditions of employment. It is recommended that legal advice is sought to ensure compliance with the TUPE regulations.
- **Contracts and grants**: It is necessary to review all the terms and conditions of all significant contracts and grants of the unincorporated charity to identify any clauses that either permit assignment (with or without the other party's consent) or prohibit assignment. Some contracts and grants include conditions (known as change of control provisions) which require the grant or contract-makers' prior consent to any form of reorganisation. To avoid being in breach of these conditions, the specific terms should be followed and consent obtained.
- **Property**: Title to all of the charity's leasehold and freehold properties should be investigated. A landlord's consent will almost certainly be required to

assign any leases to the new charitable company or CIO (this process has cost implications). Where any of the charity's properties are unregistered, transferring them to the new charitable company or CIO is likely to trigger first registration of title. Any transfer of registered land will need to be registered at the Land Registry. It is also vital to investigate and identify any land that is permanent endowment. It is recommended that legal advice is sought on dealing with these formalities.

- **Permanent endowment**: if any of the charity's property (usually land or funds) is permanent endowment, it cannot be held absolutely by the new charitable company or CIO as part of its corporate property. It may be appropriate to appoint the company as trustee and a Charity Commission scheme may be required, or it may be possible to remove restrictions on capital using the powers in the 2011 Act. If the unincorporated charity is being incorporated as a CIO, a vesting declaration could be used. This is a legal document that transfers all the property of the original charity to the new CIO. The vesting declaration will vest legal title to the permanently endowed property in the CIO, to be held on its original trusts; appoint the CIO as trustee for the permanent endowment trust and give it the powers of a trust corporation for that trust. This will mean that the CIO and the permanent endowment trust are treated as a single charity for registration and accounting purposes. Permanent endowment is a technically complex area and it is strongly recommended that specialist legal advice is sought.
- **Pensions**: Transferring all the charity's employees to the new charitable company or CIO may trigger an exit by the charity from pension arrangements it participates in on behalf of its employees. Depending on the type of scheme, if the underlying pension scheme is under-funded, this can result in the nasty consequence of triggering a debt payable by the charity on exiting; the level of debt can either prevent an incorporation going ahead or seriously delay it. This is a technically complex area and it is strongly recommended that specialist legal advice is sought.
- **Banking arrangements**: The charity's bank will need to be consulted about the proposed incorporation: it may be necessary for the new charitable company or CIO to open new accounts. The bank's consent will be required to transfer any secured or unsecured loans, and other banking facilities to the new charitable company or CIO. This will have timing and cost implications. It is strongly recommended that legal advice is sought.

8.6.2 Setting up a company: This involves drafting a Memorandum and Articles of Association for the charitable company and incorporating it at Companies House in the usual way (see section 4). Typically the Articles of Association will incorporate the objects and other details from the existing charity's constitution/trust deed but the trustees and/or members may wish to take this opportunity to review and update these details.

8.6.3 Registering the company as a charity. An application must be made to the Charity Commission to register the company as a charity in the usual way once it has been registered (see section 6). The application form for registering as a charity enables the applicant to indicate that the registration is sought in relation to incorporation. The charitable company will be given a new charity registration number to be used when the registration is complete.

8.6.4 Setting up the CIO. An application is made to the Charity Commission to form the CIO (see chapter A2, section 7, page 31).

8.6.5 Consultations or notifications and/or obtaining any consents. This must be carried out before the transfer of assets takes place (as identified by the due diligence process).

8.6.6 Transfer of substantial non-cash property asset to the new charitable company: Where the incorporation involves the transfer of a substantial non-cash property asset from the unincorporated charity to a new charitable company, it will be necessary to obtain prior written consent from the Charity Commission to the transaction. 'Substantial' means an asset whose value:

- exceeds 10% of the company's asset value and is more than £5,000; or
- exceeds £10,000.

8.6.7 Under s. 190 of the Companies Act 2006, the transfer of a substantial non-cash asset from an unincorporated charity to a charitable company where one or more of the directors of the company are trustees of the unincorporated charity requires the approval of the members of the company. Where the company is a charitable company, s. 201 of the 2011 Charities Act states that the s. 190 resolution is ineffective without Charity Commission consent.

8.6.8 There is no need to comply with s. 190 of the Companies Act or to obtain Charity Commission consent where the incorporation is into a CIO, because a CIO is not a company.

8.6.9 Where the trustees of the unincorporated charity are also directors of the new charitable company or CIO and where liabilities, as well as assets, are to be transferred, there is likely to be a conflict of interest. In this case, the Charity Commission's authority is usually needed to decide whether to transfer the liabilities and the assets associated with the liabilities.

8.6.10 If an application has been made to transfer a substantial non-cash asset from an unincorporated charity to a new charitable company, the Charity Commission will consider that consent under s. 201 of the 2011 Act will remove the conflict of interest which would otherwise exist on the part of the directors of the new charitable company who are also trustees of the unincorporated charity. Otherwise, the Charity Commission will give consent by an order under s. 105 of the 2011 Act.

8.6.11 Transferring the assets of the unincorporated charity to the new charitable company. It is usual for the following documents to be entered into to record the transfer:

(a) a formal transfer agreement between the unincorporated charity and the new charitable company;
(b) minutes of the trustees of the unincorporated charity;
(c) minutes of the trustees/directors of the new charitable company;
(d) where necessary, any members' resolutions; and
(e) where necessary:
  - freehold property transfer documents;
  - lease assignment documents;
  - novations of major contracts; and
  - banking documents.

8.6.12 Registering the transfer on the mergers register. This happens where all of the assets of the unincorporated charity have been transferred to the new charitable company (see chapter F1, paragraph 1.14, page 476).

8.6.13 Asking the Charity Commission to remove the unincorporated charity from the register. This will only be carried out if appropriate (see section 6, chapter F2, page 489).

A4
Trustees, officers and members

1 Introduction

This chapter looks at the roles and responsibilities of a charity's trustees, members and staff. This includes the role of individual trustees, the board of trustees as a whole and their relationship with staff. Although the chapter covers the legal aspects of the role of trustees, it is important to bear in mind that how trustees define their role and how they work as a board will also be influenced by the board's composition, its culture and values.

2 Role of trustees and role of the board

2.1 The main role of a charity's trustees is to govern the charity; they do this by making decisions collectively as a board. Generally speaking, individual trustees have no power to act on their own unless powers are delegated to them. Although trustees act collectively as a board, for the most part the duties owed by trustees to the charity are personal to the individual trustees, so the individual trustees are each responsible for the actions of the board as a whole.

2.2 As well as being trustees of a charity, where the charity is established as a company, trustees will also be company directors, with all the legal duties that this entails.

3 Trustees' responsibilities and duties

3.1 Whether a charity is constituted as a company, a CIO or a trust, the trustees have the same duties under the laws relating to charities and trustees. Their responsibilities and duties derive from a number of different sources, including common law, statute law, case law, the charity's own constitution and regulatory requirements.

3.2 It is important that everyone involved in the governance of a charity is familiar with their own charity's constitution, as this will vary from charity to charity.

However, care needs to be taken. In some cases, legislation will override the provisions of a charity's constitution. For example, charities that are companies need to review their own constitution as some provisions of the Companies Act 2006 override a company's own Articles.

3.3 The Charity Commission's publication, Charity trustee: what's involved (CC3a) sets out in summary the responsibilities of charity trustees.

Charity trustee: what's involved (CC3a))

1. Ensure your charity is carrying out its purposes for the public benefit

You and your co-trustees must make sure that the charity is carrying out the purposes for which it is set up, and no other purpose. This means you should:

- ensure you understand the charity's purposes as set out in its governing document;
- plan what your charity will do, and what you want it to achieve;
- be able to explain how all of the charity's activities are intended to further or support its purposes; and
- understand how the charity benefits the public by carrying out its purposes.

Spending charity funds on the wrong purposes is a very serious matter; in some cases trustees may have to reimburse the charity personally.

2. Comply with your charity's governing document and the law

You and your co-trustees must:

- make sure that the charity complies with its governing document; and
- comply with charity law requirements and other laws that apply to your charity.

You should take reasonable steps to find out about legal requirements, for example by reading relevant guidance or taking appropriate advice when you need to.

Registered charities must keep their details on the register up to date and ensure they send the right financial and other information to the commission in their annual return or annual update.

3. Act in your charity's best interests

You must:

- do what you and your co-trustees (and no one else) decide will best enable the charity to carry out its purposes;
- with your co-trustees, make balanced and adequately informed decisions, thinking about the long term as well as the short term;

- avoid putting yourself in a position where your duty to your charity conflicts with your personal interests or loyalty to any other person or body; and
- not receive any benefit from the charity unless it's properly authorised and is clearly in the charity's interests; this also includes anyone who is financially connected to you, such as a partner, dependent child or business partner.

4. Manage your charity's resources responsibly

You must act responsibly, reasonably and honestly. This is sometimes called the duty of prudence. Prudence is about exercising sound judgement. You and your co-trustees must:

- make sure the charity's assets are only used to support or carry out its purposes;
- not take inappropriate risks with the charity's assets or reputation;
- not over-commit the charity;
- take special care when investing or borrowing; and
- comply with any restrictions on spending funds.

You and your co-trustees should put appropriate procedures and safeguards in place and take reasonable steps to ensure that these are followed. Otherwise you risk making the charity vulnerable to fraud or theft, or other kinds of abuse, and being in breach of your duty.

5. Act with reasonable care and skill

As someone responsible for governing a charity, you:

- must use reasonable care and skill, making use of your skills and experience and taking appropriate advice when necessary; and
- should give enough time, thought and energy to your role, for example by preparing for, attending and actively participating in all trustees' meetings.

6. Ensure your charity is accountable

You and your co-trustees must comply with statutory accounting and reporting requirements. You should also:

- be able to demonstrate that your charity is complying with the law, well run and effective;
- ensure appropriate accountability to members, if your charity has a membership separate from the trustees;
- ensure accountability within the charity, particularly where you delegate responsibility for particular tasks or decisions to staff or volunteers; and
- take special care when investing the funds of the charity, or borrowing funds for the charity to use.

© Crown Copyright 2018. Taken from the Charity Commission website, www.charity-commission.gov.uk.

4 Trustees as directors of charitable companies

4.1 Where a charity is established as a company (normally, a company limited by guarantee) the trustees will have duties as company directors. The Companies Act 2006, ss. 171–177 sets out the duties that a company director owes to the company. These are:

- to act within powers;
- to promote the success of the company;
- to exercise independent judgement;
- to exercise reasonable care, skill and diligence;
- to avoid conflicts of interest;
- not to accept benefits from third parties; and
- to declare any interest in a proposed transaction or arrangement.

4.2 These requirements are largely self-explanatory, but the requirement under s. 172 'to promote the success of the company' requires a little further explanation. The section states the following:

1. A director of a company must act in the way he considers, in good faith, would be most likely to promote the success of the company for the benefit of its members as a whole, and in doing so have regard (among other matters) to:
   (a) the likely consequences of any decision in the long term;
   (b) the interests of the company's employees;
   (c) the need to foster the company's business relationships with suppliers, customers and others;
   (d) the impact of the company's operations on the community and the environment;
   (e) the desirability of the company maintaining a reputation for high standards of business conduct; and
   (f) the need to act fairly as between members of the company.
2. Where, or to the extent that the purposes of the company consist of, or include, purposes other than the benefit of its members, subsection (1) has effect as if the reference to promoting the success of the company for the benefit of its members were to achieving those purposes.

4.3 For charitable companies, this means that its directors must promote the success of the charity in achieving its charitable objects, rather than for the benefit of its members, but still have regard to the list of items in subsection (1).

4.4 In addition to these core duties, the Companies Act imposes a large number of requirements on the trustees of charitable companies in their role as directors. These include keeping proper accounts, maintaining statutory books and records, and filing resolutions, returns and an annual report and accounts at Companies House.

5 Trustees' powers

5.1 Charity trustees have to act within their powers, exercise their powers in the best interests of the charity, within the charity's objects and exercise their powers personally. Although trustees can delegate some of their powers, they cannot delegate their responsibilities to others.

5.2 It is important to note that the powers of individual trustees are normally very limited. The powers of individual trustees tend to be limited to matters such as calling meetings of the trustees. However, boards may delegate authority to individual trustees (for example, to signing contracts on behalf of the board).

6 Trustees' liabilities

6.1 Many people contemplating becoming a trustee of a charity are concerned that they might be held personally liable for any losses. In fact, it is very rare for a trustee to be made personally liable, as the law protects trustees who have acted reasonably.

6.2 There are three main areas of risk that may give rise to personal liability for trustees: contractual liability, liability arising from a breach of trust and legal liability. The position of the individual trustee will depend on the charity's legal form. In short, because an unincorporated charity is not a legal entity separate from its trustees, they are more exposed to the liabilities of the charity than they would be if the charity were incorporated.

7 Contractual liability

7.1 Most charities will enter into contracts to supply or receive goods or services under which there will be a contractual liability. Unincorporated charities have no legal personality and so, for an unincorporated charity, the individual trustees are party to any contract. As long as the trustees have acted properly in entering into the contract, they can draw on the charity's resources to meet their contractual obligations. However, where a charity does not have sufficient resources to fulfil the contract, the trustees in an unincorporated charity remain personally liable. In contrast, for incorporated charities, contracts are with the charity, not the individual trustees. This means that provided that there has been no breach of trust, no liability should attach to individual trustees.

7.2 There are a number of ways of reducing the trustees' risk:

(a) The charity itself could become incorporated, so that any contracts are with the charity and not the trustees.
(b) An unincorporated charity may have a corporate body as its sole trustee, with the people who would otherwise be individual trustees as its directors. In the event of a breach of its duties, only the corporate trustee would be directly liable. However, if the directors of a corporate trustee have been in breach of duty to the company, they may be liable to make good any losses suffered by it.
(c) Contracts may be drafted to include a term that limits the trustees' liability to the value of the charity's assets.
(d) Trustees may be able to take out indemnity insurance against the risk of any shortfall in the charity's assets.

8 Breach of trust

8.1 Trustees are in breach of trust when they act in a way that is contrary to the terms of their governing document, or when they fail to perform their duties as trustees. This liability apples whether or not the charity is incorporated. Examples of a breach of trust include using the charity's resources for a purpose that is outside the charity's objects or investing the charity's money in a type of investment not permitted under the investment rules applying to the charity. Where trustees commit a breach of trust that results in financial loss to the charity, they are liable to make good that loss.

8.2 Trustees can reduce the risk of a breach of trust by being familiar with their charity's governing document and taking professional advice on any point on which they are unsure. Under s. 61 of the Trustee Act 1925 and s. 1157 of the Companies Act 2006, the court can excuse a trustee's breach of trust if it is satisfied that the trustee acted honestly and reasonably. In addition, under s. 191 of the Charities Act 2011, the Charity Commission itself is able to relieve a trustee from personal liability.

8.3 Trustees may be able to take out indemnity insurance to protect themselves from personal liability arising from a breach of trust. As trustee indemnity insurance is a benefit to trustees, it needs to be properly authorised. However, where a charity does not have the necessary authority in its own constitution, the Charities Act 2006 gives statutory authority for charities to take out such insurance. The Charity Commission's approval is required only if a charity's constitution explicitly prohibits the purchase of such insurance.

8.4 If indemnity insurance is taken out, the policy must contain a clause excluding the provision of any indemnity for:

(a) any liability incurred by a trustee to pay a fine imposed in criminal proceedings, or a sum payable to a regulatory authority by way of a penalty in respect of non-compliance with any requirement of a regulatory nature;
(b) any liability incurred by a trustee in defending any criminal proceedings in which they are convicted of an offence arising out of any fraud or dishonesty, or wilful or reckless misconduct, by the trustee; or
(c) any liability incurred by a trustee to the charity that arises out of any conduct which the trustee knew (or must reasonably be assumed to have known) was not in the interests of the charity or where they did not care whether or not it was in the best interests of the charity.

8.5 As can be seen above, trustee indemnity insurance can be quite limited. As an alternative to insurance, charitable companies may indemnify their trustees, although there are restrictions. Section 234 of the Companies Act 2006 permits companies to indemnify directors for the costs of successfully defending claims from third parties, but not from the company itself.

9 Legal liability

9.1 Trustees of charitable companies need to be aware that they are subject to the provisions of the Insolvency Act 1986, which can impose personal liability on the directors of a company for wrongful or fraudulent trading.

9.2 Directors commit fraudulent trading under s. 213 where, prior to a company's insolvent liquidation, they continue to trade and incur debts with the intent of defrauding creditors.

9.3 Under s. 214, wrongful trading is where, before a company enters into insolvent liquidation, the directors knew, or should have known, that there was no reasonable prospect that the company would avoid insolvent liquidation and failed to minimise the loss to creditors.

9.4 In both cases, the liquidator can apply to the court for an order to require the director to make a contribution out of their own assets. The liquidator will report to the Department for Business, Energy & Industrial Strategy on the director's conduct; this may lead to a disqualification order under the Company Directors' Disqualification Act 1986.

9.5 In practice, assuming that the directors of a charity in financial difficulties have acted honestly, they are most likely to be concerned about liability for wrongful trading. This risk can be reduced by ensuring that management accounts are up to date and accurate and, in particular, that balance sheets and cash flow forecasts are regularly reviewed. Trustees need to remember that a charity's management accounts may show a surplus and it may have more assets than liabilities but it can still be insolvent through lack of cash. If trustees believe that their charity is in financial difficulty, legal and financial advice should be sought as soon as possible.

9.6 Although there are many sections of the Companies Act that could lead to prosecution, fines or even imprisonment for directors who default, criminal prosecutions are rare. The usual penalty is a fine from Companies House and, for more serious offences, disqualification as a director. The risk of penalty can be reduced by ensuring that trustees are aware of their duties under the Companies Act and receive appropriate advice.

9.7 Trustees also need to be briefed on their other statutory responsibilities, such as those for health and safety.

10 'Fit and proper person' test

10.1 The Finance Act 2010 introduced a new definition of 'charity', which imposes the requirement (among others) that the managers of the charity are 'fit and proper persons'. Charities need to match the definition to prove to HMRC that they are charities.

10.2 The key point here is that trustees are included in the definition of managers. The term 'manager' is defined in the legislation as the person having the general control and management of the charity. It therefore applies to both trustees and any other persons having general control and management over the running of the charity or the application of its assets.

10.3 HMRC assumes that all people appointed by charities are fit and proper persons unless they hold information to show otherwise. However, HMRC will expect the charity to be able to show, if asked, that they have given proper consideration to the suitability of people they appoint. It therefore suggests that 'managers' are asked to read its basic guide and to sign a declaration based on the model declaration that it provides.

10.4 HMRC is clear that it does not necessarily follow that individuals considered by the Charity Commission to be suitable to act as trustees of charities will always be considered to be fit and proper persons for the purposes of the management condition. Factors that may lead HMRC to decide that someone is not a fit and proper person include, but are not limited to, individuals:

(a) with a history of tax fraud;
(b) with a history of other fraudulent behaviour, including misrepresentation and/or identity theft;
(c) for whom HMRC has knowledge of involvement in attacks against, or abuse of, tax repayment systems; and
(d) who are barred from acting as a charity trustee by a charity regulator or court, or are disqualified from acting as a company director.

10.5 Using the basic guide and model declaration in the way suggested will mean that a charity can assume that they meet the management condition at all times unless they knowingly appoint a manager who is not a fit and proper person. A charity should devise a declaration for 'managers' (including trustees) to complete and sign, based on the model declaration provided by HMRC.

11 Recruitment and selection

11.1 Many charities, particularly smaller ones, struggle to find trustees, so there may be a temptation to recruit anyone who takes an interest. However, having the wrong person as a trustee can, at best, add nothing to the decision-making capabilities of the board and, at worst, cause immense disruption, ill-feeling and damage to the organisation. For even the smallest charity, a formal recruitment process will pay dividends.

11.2 The aim of a good trustee recruitment and selection process is to recruit trustees who:

- are eligible to act as trustees and are appointed in accordance with the charity's governing document or relevant statutory requirements;
- have the skills and experience that the charity requires and are able to apply them to benefit the charity;
- work well together; and
- are able to commit time and attention to the charity.

11.3 The recruitment and selection process can be divided into a number of phases:

- assessment of the board and charity's requirements in terms of trustee skills, knowledge and experience, also taking into account the diversity of the trustee board;
- preparation of a job description and person specification;
- advertising;
- application;
- interviewing;

- appointment/election; and
- induction and training.

11.4 As recruitment and selection is often a time-consuming business, the trustees may wish to delegate some of the work, but they must retain overall control of the process. Most larger charities will do this through a nominations committee with clear terms of reference. These terms will usually include:

- reviewing and making recommendations on the composition of the board;
- making recommendations to the board on the person specification for the trustee(s) being sought and the method of recruitment;
- seeking out and making recommendations to the board on new and co-opted trustees; and
- overseeing succession planning.

11.5 The nominations committee may also have a role in making recommendations on trustees seeking re-election at the end of a term of office and the appointment of the chair and chief executive.

11.6 Recruitment factors to consider include:

- Should the nominations committee include members who are not current trustees – for example, representatives of the charity's beneficiaries or volunteers? The advantage of this is that it reduces the risk of the current trustees recruiting new trustees who are like themselves.
- Are the trustees on the nominations committee suitably trained? When recruiting for specialist roles (such as a treasurer) it may be helpful to have an external expert on the committee, such as a treasurer from another charity.
- Is the committee a vetting committee, checking that any applicants would make good trustees and are able to meet minimum requirements, but leaving the decision to an election by the membership (where applicable), or should it recommend the same number of people as there are vacancies? The former is more democratic, but may make it more difficult to achieve a well-balanced board.
- Has adequate time been allowed for the whole process? The recruitment process needs to be planned carefully, working backwards from the expected date of appointment of the new trustee. If board meetings are held quarterly, the process of assessing the board for any skills gaps may need to be carried out up to nine months in advance. This can cause problems, as trustees coming to the end of a term of office may not have yet decided whether they wish to seek to serve another term.

11.7 When a charity is planning to recruit new trustees, the first step is to consider what skills, knowledge and experience are needed to make sure that the charity is well governed and identify any gaps among the present trustees. It is also important to draw up a list of other requirements for trustees (e.g. the ability to attend board meetings and away days). If the board has undergone a skills audit (see section 17, page 95), its results should be considered.

11.8 The Charity Commission recommends that job descriptions are prepared for trustees. A number of organisations, including the ICSA and the National Council for Voluntary Organisations (NCVO) produce model job descriptions for charity trustees and for chairs, secretaries and treasurers of charities. The general job description should be backed up by a person specification for each vacancy. For example, if an individual trustee is to be asked to take the lead on fundraising, this should be included in the person specification.

11.9 While traditional methods for recruiting new trustees, such as personal recommendation and word of mouth, remain popular, they are not open and transparent methods of recruitment and may not be the most effective ways of finding people with the right skills and experience. Although personal recommendation can play a role in identifying people who have the right skills, and who might not actively be seeking to be a trustee and then encouraging them to come forward, it should not be the sole method of recruitment.

11.10 Advertising can be an effective way of reaching a wide group of people. It can sometimes be expensive, but charities could consider alternative methods such as notices on websites and in their own and other organisations' newsletters. Sometimes an advertisement for a trustee vacancy can be included in an editorial piece. For example, a report on a charity's successful fundraising campaign might include a note that the charity is seeking a trustee with particular experience in this area.

11.11 It is important to think carefully about where to place adverts and the content of the advertisement itself. If you are seeking someone with particular professional skills, it may be better to advertise in a professional journal rather than in a national newspaper. The advertisement should be specific about the time commitment required, as this may be an obstacle to many people.

11.12 It may be worth running briefing sessions for potential trustees, so that they have the opportunity to find out more about the charity before deciding whether to apply. For national charities seeking potential trustees from around the country, briefings can be held by telephone conference call, while for small charities, an open evening or even a display at the local library might work well.

11.13 Many charities find that their existing volunteers, donors or members possess suitable skills, so it is worth making sure that these groups are given early notice via newsletters or other correspondence.

11.14 Another way of finding new trustees is to make use of a trustee brokerage service or trustee register. Trustee brokers provide a matching service between potential trustees and vacancies. Some search agencies that specialise in recruiting non-executive directors for companies are also willing to advertise unpaid trustee vacancies. The NCVO operates a Trustee Bank, which is an online list of vacancies. Other professional organisations sometimes provide trustee registers.

11.15 Networking with other local charities or those that work within the same field can prove useful. Where a charity has no current trustee vacancies, it may refer people who are interested in becoming a trustee on to other, similar, charities.

12 Diversity issues

12.1 Charities will benefit from recruiting trustees who both reflect and have knowledge of, the communities and the area in which they operate and the people they serve. It can help provide better services to a wider range of people and may enable the charity to reach a wider range of supporters – staff, volunteers and donors. Having a diverse board can also increase accountability and public confidence in the charity's work.

12.2 Checklist to help increase board diversity

- Use more open and inclusive ways of recruitment, such as advertising or using trustee brokerage services.
- Ask candidates to complete application forms rather than provide CVs, as this requires the nominations committee to focus on the relevant criteria.
- Organise board meetings at the most convenient times, or at different times, so that people who cannot attend at a particular time are not excluded.
- Make sure that board meetings are accessible for people with disabilities and that, where needed, assistance is given in completing the application form or attending an interview.
- Pay childcare expenses or provide childcare arrangements.
- Make sure that there are no cultural or religious barriers to attendance.

12.3 Some charities will be 'public authorities' and will therefore have a duty to promote equality under the Equalities Act 2010. Public authorities are, broadly speaking, bodies that carry out public functions, such as local authorities, health trusts, courts, etc. Charities are likely to be treated as public authorities where they carry out work under contract to a public authority, fulfilling a role that would otherwise have to be carried out by the public authority.

13 Beneficiaries as trustees

13.1 Many charities will have one or more of their charitable beneficiaries, or service users, as trustees. It is important to bear in mind that service users who are trustees have exactly the same duties and responsibilities as other trustees.

13.2 Boards need to ensure that there are procedures in place to manage any conflicts of interest between a trustee's personal interests and those of the charity. This is particularly important for service users, who will benefit from the activities of the charity. In addition the charity will need to have the power, either in its constitution, or granted from the Charity Commission, for trustees to be in receipt of services, as this classes as a benefit to the trustee.

13.3 Thought needs to be given as to how service users are recruited to the board. For example, there may be a certain number of places reserved for service users who are elected by other service users. In some cases, particularly where beneficiaries do not have a long-term relationship with the charity, this may not be practicable and, in practice, the service users on the board are often those who have taken an interest in the board's work and been encouraged to put themselves forward.

13.4 Further information about user trustees is contained in the Charity Commission publication *Users on Board* (CC24).

14 Appointments

14.1 Trustees may be appointed in a number of different ways. They may:

- be nominated by the other trustees;
- be appointed by another organisation, such as a local authority;
- be elected by the charity's members; or
- become a trustee by virtue of a position that they occupy (e.g. a vicar may automatically be a trustee of a church charity). These are termed '*ex officio*' appointments.

14.2 The charity's governing document will set out the procedures for appointment, including any restrictions. Care should be taken, as if the correct procedures are not followed, the appointment may be invalid.

14.3 If it is a requirement that trustees are members of the charity, check that potential new trustees are members and that any membership subscriptions are up to date (if applicable). Under some constitutions, non-payment can lead to membership automatically lapsing, which might lead to a person being ineligible for appointment as a trustee.

14.4 Where trustees are nominated by an external body, such as a local authority, the charity may still be able to influence the appointment. The external body will usually respond positively to clear guidance from the charity as to any particular skills or experience it is looking for from its trustees.

14.5 In addition to normal appointments, the governing document may allow for the board to appoint trustees to fill casual vacancies to serve until the next annual general meeting, or there may be provision for the co-option of additional trustees for specific purposes. Again, care needs to be taken to comply with the governing document's requirements. Charities may vary as to whether co-optees count towards the quorum of a meeting and whether they have a vote in all circumstances.

14.6 The constitution of unincorporated charities will normally contain details of who is entitled to appoint new trustees. If there is no express provision, the trustees can exercise powers under s. 36 of the Trustee Act 1925 to replace outgoing trustees or appoint additional trustees.

14.7 Under certain circumstances, the Charity Commission may appoint new trustees under s. 80(2) of the Charities Act 2011. These are:

- to replace a trustee removed by the Charity Commission;
- where there are no trustees or because of vacancies, absence or incapacity, the current trustees cannot act;
- where there is a single charity trustee who is not a corporate trustee and the Commission believes it is necessary to increase the number of trustees for the proper administration of the charity; and
- where the Commission is of the opinion that it is necessary for the proper administration of the charity to have an additional charity trustee because one of the existing charity trustees (who ought nevertheless to remain a charity trustee) either cannot be found, does not act, or is outside England and Wales.

14.8 Under s. 41 of the Trustee Act 1925, the High Court may appoint new trustees, but as the Charity Commission has the same powers, it would be more usual for it to make an appointment.

14.9 Trustees of unincorporated charities may be appointed by deed. Under s. 40 of the Trustee Act 1925, unless the deed contains a statement to the contrary, all of the charity's assets will transfer to the new trustees. This avoids the problem of having to execute transfers of titles, particularly of land, from the old trustees to the new trustees on each change. Alternatively, the same effect can be obtained by a memorandum of appointment signed by the chair of the meeting where the appointment of the new trustee took place and witnessed by two people who were present at that meeting.

15 Checks for potential new trustees

15.1 Charities must check that prospective trustees are not disqualified from being a trustee either by law or by the charity's own constitution, and that prospective trustees understand the responsibilities that they are taking on. Remember that a charity's trustees are in a position of trust. This does not necessarily mean that everyone who applies to be a trustee is entirely trustworthy.

15.2 A charity should undertake a number of checks, including obtaining a self-certification that the individual is not disqualified and online searching of the list of persons disqualified from acting.

15.3 A trustee or potential trustee may be disqualified for the following reasons:

- They are less than 18 years old (16 if the charity is a company or charitable incorporated organisation (CIO))
- They are subject to the automatic disqualification rules (unless a waiver applies). See below.
- They are subject to a Charity Commission order disqualifying them from being a trustee
- They are subject to Disclosure and Barring Service (DBS) rules and the charity works with children and other vulnerable groups.
- They are disqualified by a provision in the charities governing document (if the charity governing document disqualifies an individual from being a trustee, the Charity Commission cannot provide a waiver).

15.4 Automatic disqualification rules

With effect from 1 August 2018, there are rules that prevent certain people from being a trustee or senior manager of a charity. Being disqualified means that a person cannot become a trustee or a senior manager, or stay a trustee or a senior manager, unless the Charity Commission has waived the disqualification.

A trustee or senior manager with be automatically disqualified if any of the following apply to them:

1. They have an unspent conviction for any of the following:
   a) an offence involving deception or dishonesty;
   b) a terrorism offence to which Part 4 of the Counter-Terrorism Act 2008 applies or under sections 13 or 19 of the Terrorism Act 2000;
   c) a money laundering offence within the meaning of section 415 of the Proceeds of Crime Act 2002;
   d) a bribery offence under sections 1, 2, 6 or 7 of the Bribery Act 2010;
   e) an offence of contravening a Commission Order or Direction under section 77 of the Charities Act 2011;

f) an offence of misconduct in public office, perjury or perverting the course of justice; or
g) in relation to the above offences, an offence of: attempt, conspiracy, or incitement to commit the offence; aiding, or abetting, counselling or procuring the commission of the offence; or, under Part 2 of the Serious Crime Act 2007(encouraging or assisting)in relation to the offence.

2. They are on the sex offenders register (i.e. subject to notification requirements of Part 2 of the Sexual Offences Act 2003).
3. They have an unspent sanction for contempt of court for making, or causing to be made, a false statement or for making, or causing to be made, a false statement in a document verified by a statement of truth.
4. They have been found guilty of disobedience to an order or direction of the Commission under section 336(1) of the Charities Act 2011.
5. They are a designated person for the purposes of Part 1 of the Terrorist Asset-Freezing etc. Act 2010, or the Al Qaida (Asset Freezing) Regulations 2011.
6. They have previously been removed as an officer, agent or employee of a charity by the Charity Commission, OSCR, or the High Court due to misconduct or mismanagement.
7. They have previously been removed as a trustee of a charity by the Charity Commission, OSCR, or the High Court due to misconduct or mismanagement.
8. They have been removed from management or control of anybody under section s34(5)(e) of the Charities and Trustee Investment (Scotland) Act 2005 (or earlier legislation)
9. They are disqualified from being a company director, or have given a disqualification undertaking, and leave has not been granted (as described in section 180 of the Charities Act) for them to act as director of the charity.
10. They are currently declared bankrupt (or subject to bankruptcy restrictions or an interim order).
11. They have an individual voluntary arrangement (IVA) to pay off debts with creditors.
12. They are subject to a moratorium period under a debt relief order, or a debt relief restrictions order, or an interim order.
13. They are subject to an order made under s. 429(2) of the Insolvency Act 1986 (Failure to pay under a County Court Administration Order).

The senior manager positions that are affected by disqualification are at chief executive and chief finance officer level. This Charity Commission provides guidance that explains in more detail how to identify these roles.

15.5 Before making an appointment, a charity should check that the proposed appointee is eligible to serve as a trustee. It can do this in a number of ways:

- The charity can make a search on the Insolvency Register maintained by the Insolvency Service. This contains details of current and recent bankruptcies and individual voluntary arrangements (https://www.gov.uk/search-bankruptcy-insolvency-register).
- It can search the register of disqualified directors maintained by Companies House (https://beta.companieshouse.gov.uk/search/disqualified-officers).
- It can search the register of people who have been removed as charity trustees since 1 February 1993 (which can be located on the Charity Commission website).
- It can ask the prospective trustees to sign a declaration to confirm that they are not disqualified from acting as a charity trustee. This can be done alongside signing an appointment letter. The Charity Commission has a model declaration that can be used.

If the charity works with children or vulnerable people, there are safeguarding obligations and a charity should always ensure that DBS checks are carried out on prospective trustees.

15.6 Checklist for vetting new trustees

- Take up at least two references, one from a current employer, if available.
- Check relevant academic qualifications.
- Check professional qualifications with the relevant professional body and ask if any disciplinary action has been taken against them.
- Ask for proof of name, address and date of birth.
- Require potential trustees to sign a declaration that they are not disqualified from being a trustee and that the meet the requirements of the fit and proper person test (see section 10).
- Check the Individual Insolvency Register maintained by the Insolvency Service at www.insolvency.gov.uk.
- Check the register of disqualified directors maintained by Companies House at www.companieshouse.gov.uk.
- Check the register of people who have been removed as charity trustees since 1 February 1993 (which can be located on the Charity Commission website.)
- For trustees of charities working with children or vulnerable adults, obtain a disclosure from the DBS. The Charity Commission expects charities to take up DBS checks whenever they are available.

15.7 If a disqualified person is appointed as a trustee, the appointment will be invalid. It is normally an offence to act as a trustee while disqualified unless the Charity Commission has granted a waiver under s. 181 of the Charities Act 2011. If the governing document contains provisions that prevent certain people from acting as charity trustees, the Charity Commission cannot grant a waiver.

15.8 If existing trustees had not made proper checks before the appointment, they may be found by the Charity Commission to have acted improperly.

15.9 Checklist for the appointment of a new trustee

- Undertake checks on the trustee's eligibility (see above).
- Give the new trustee a letter confirming appointment and ask them to sign a letter of consent (sample letters for the appointment of trustees are available from www.icsa.org.uk).
- Update the charity's details on the Register of Charities at the Charity Commission's website, www.charitycommission.gov.uk. If a change in trustee also involves a change in the charity's contact details, the Charity Commission should be informed as soon as possible.
- If the charity is a charitable company, ensure the details of the newly appointed director are submitted to Companies House and update the registers of directors and directors' residential addresses.
- If the charity is a company, CBS or CIO, or if it maintains its own register, have the trustee's name entered into a register of trustees.
- (For unincorporated charities only) Ensure that any property belonging to the charity that is held in the names of outgoing individual trustees is transferred into the name of the new trustee.
- Amend bank mandates if the new trustee is to be a signatory to the charity's bank account.
- Inform relevant people including staff, professional advisers and supporters and include the appointment in any newsletter. In particular, ensure that fundraising staff are given full details of trustees, including brief biographies, as these are often required for grant applications. Update details of trustees on the charity's website and in other publications.
- If a trustee must be a member of the charity, ensure that the new trustee is a member and that any membership subscription fee is paid up to date. In some charities, trustees automatically become life members, so check that new trustees are categorised correctly.

16 Induction and training

16.1 A proper induction is important to ensure that new trustees can become effective members of the board as soon as possible. Trustees should be provided with an individually tailored induction programme that is suited to the new trustee, as well as the size and type of charity. For new trustees of smaller charities, a discussion with existing trustees may be the quickest way to learn everything they need to know to be able to make a contribution. For larger and more complex charities, a more structured induction programme is likely to be more appropriate. This may include:

- an induction pack of written material;
- assessment of any training required by the new trustee;
- attendance at induction training (either trustee specific or along with new staff);
- meetings with other trustees, in particular the chair and treasurer;
- meetings with senior management and staff;
- introductions to professional advisers;
- visits to see services provided by the charity; and
- meetings with key stakeholders of the charity.

16.2 As a minimum, new trustees should be given:

- a copy of the Charity Commission's Charity Trustee Welcome Pack
- a copy of the charity's constitution;
- a copy of the values and mission statement (if applicable);
- a brief history of the charity;
- a copy of the charity's strategic plan and business plan;
- a copy of the latest report and accounts, current budget and most recent management accounts;
- a role description for trustees;
- a copy of the board's role and the terms of reference of any committees;
- copies of any policies relating to trustees, such as policies on conduct, conflicts of interest and expenses;
- details of trustee meetings;
- an organisation chart;
- contact details for the other trustees and key employees; and
- minutes and papers of recent board meetings.

16.3 An expanded recommended induction pack is available in an ICSA guidance note available free from www.icsa.org.uk.

17 Skills audit/analysis

17.1 To ensure that the charity is well governed and has the right people as trustees, it will first need to consider what skills, knowledge and experience are needed and to identify any gaps among the current trustees. As well as skills and experience, it is also important to draw up a list of other requirements for trustees (such as the ability to attend board meetings and away days). One of the elements of recommended practice in the Charity Governance Code is that a board looks regularly at what skills it has and needs.

17.2 Assessing the skills and experience of current trustees can be difficult. Normal practice is to ask trustees to complete a questionnaire, but this can be very subjective and does not always give the most accurate results. It is important to ensure there is some evidence of the skills a trustee says they possess and some way of evaluating their responses.

17.3 There are some core points to consider in setting up a system for skills analysis.

17.3.1 A fundamental part of undertaking the skills analysis process is identifying the skills that are required by the board. Often, little regard is paid to this. Charities often use template questionnaires for a skills analysis and copy over the skills to be reviewed from this, rather than identifying the actual skills that they require. In identifying these skills, it is useful to be as specific as possible, rather than using generic terms. The more generic the skill described, the less useful the results. In identifying skills it is useful to think of those that are quantifiable, that can be measured by self-assessment (if that is the tool you are using), and where examples can be given of how it could have been achieved.

17.3.2 Consider the level of skill that you require. First, does every board member need to have that skill – is it a core competency – or is it a skill that the board requires, but not from every member? What level of skill or experience are you seeking? If you need legal skills, do you need a trustee who works as a lawyer, or do you need trustees who have had experience of dealing with legal problems and working with solicitors?

17.3.3 Once you have agreed the skills that you think are required, you will need to assess how the current trustees match this. This can be done in various ways. The most common way is by a self-assessment questionnaire but these can be rather subjective and may not give the true picture. Alternatives would include some form of more detailed questionnaire or quiz – where you do not ask the trustee to assess their skill level, but ask more detailed questions about their experiences and then assess the answers. Another alternative would be an interview, perhaps with an external assessor, or a group discussion, where the trustees discuss each skill as a group and identify any gaps.

17.3.4 If you are using a self-assessment questionnaire, it is useful to ask the trustee to give examples of how they have gained the skill, rather than just their level of skill. This will make it much easier to evaluate.

17.3.5 The results of questionnaires, quizzes or interviews will need to be assessed and a summary produced, identifying any skills gaps. The board, or a sub-group, should then consider this and what action to take. Skills gaps can be addressed by training or recruitment.

17.3.6 It might also be useful to consider whether it is skills or competencies that you want to assess. Skills analyses are useful, but when you are considering what you want from a trustee remember that a trustee is not the same as a member of staff, so the person specification will not be the same. A key feature of trustees is that they act collectively; their effectiveness at doing this may be more important than individual skills. It is arguable that having a trustee board that works well together; makes effective decisions and recognises its own skills gaps and how to address them, is more important than having a group of trustees who possess all the skills and experience that the charity has identified as necessary, but who do not work well together. So consider measuring key competencies such as working as a team; strategic decision making; monitoring and overseeing.

18 Trustee appraisals and board performance review

18.1 It is considered good practice to carry out a regular review of the contribution of individual trustees and the board's performance as a whole and regular performance review is one of the elements of recommended practice in the Charity Governance Code. It is not enough to have skilled and experienced trustees: a charity needs to make sure that they are able to contribute and that the board as a whole is effective. Appraisals of individual trustees normally cover such things as attendance and contribution at meetings, relationships with other trustees and senior staff, opportunities to promote the work of the charity and training needs.

18.2 Collective board performance reviews will vary widely, but they will normally address such questions as whether the charity performs as well as similar charities, whether board decisions are regularly reviewed and impacts measured, whether trustees contribute effectively and whether there is effective leadership from the chair.

18.3 Individual board member appraisal may be carried out for a number of purposes, and it can be done in a number of different ways. A board appraisal may be part of the regular work of the charity, undertaken every year as a regular review of the contribution of individual board members and their function as a unit. It can be used as a means of further developing individuals and improving board performance. An increasing number of charities conduct regular board appraisal reviews in this way. At the other extreme, the appraisal may be a specific task, undertaken as a part of a review of the governance structure.

18.4 Whatever the purpose, or the form that it takes, board appraisal inevitably involves a high level of critical inspection of individual board members, their fellow trustees and the board as a whole. Understandably, this can be a difficult process, which is one of the reasons why the whole concept of board appraisal can be challenging for many trustees. In addition, if not undertaken properly, the exercise can feel like a 'box-ticking' exercise to meet governance standards. Board appraisals need to work effectively for boards to participate fully and devote the time and resources required, otherwise, the whole process will be discredited.

18.5 Given the potential delicacy of an appraisal, it is essential that it is properly planned and executed. It can sometimes take years of persuasion before the board as a whole feels ready to undertake an appraisal exercise. It may be necessary to build gradually to a full appraisal – perhaps starting with an informal review of how the board works as a whole and moving towards individual appraisals at a later stage. Later in this section, we will discuss the forms that a review or appraisal may take. For charities just starting out, it could begin with group discussions, move on to the use of questionnaires and then the board could begin to hold individual interviews. It is also possible that a board could decide not to conduct a full review each year, perhaps just having an annual group discussion or questionnaire and then holding individual interviews every two years.

18.6 The board will also need to consider the best timing for a review. It is not advisable to undertake a review of appraisals during periods of crisis or conflict within the charity as this will distract the trustees from their primary task. The trustees are unlikely to agree a common purpose for the review or appraisal and the process risks deepening, rather than resolving, any conflict. Otherwise, if part of a regular review, it should be timed to fit in with the ongoing agenda of the board and other business to be dealt with throughout the year.

18.7 There are a number of methods of board review. The most appropriate in each case will depend on the purpose of the review and, perhaps most importantly, the culture of the board. For example, a board questionnaire would be best suited to a regular review of board function, whereas a detailed examination of the performance of a board laden with strong personalities and complex histories may be better conducted by individual interviews with an independent, external facilitator, and observation of the board meetings. A thorough board review exercise may involve a combination of different methods.

18.8 A key question will be whether to conduct the review/appraisal internally or to draw on the resources of an external facilitator or consultant. Internally managed board reviews are often led by a sub-group of the trustee board. Although staff may contribute, they should not lead it. The advantages of this approach are that the team will be aware of the issues, the history, the personalities and the desired outcome. It can also save costs and maintain ownership and continuity. However, such an approach may also lack objectivity. Use of an independent contractor, who should have expertise in conducting such reviews, can help to ensure that board members are completely honest and bring a fresh perspective. They can help to ensure that the necessary time and energy is devoted to the exercise. While an independent consultant may be a more expensive option, it should again be noted that one would not need to be used each year. This approach could be combined with lower-key methods other years. It is becoming quite common for larger charities to adopt the model of undertaking an external review every three years, with lighter touch internal reviews in the other years.

18.9 As well as the issue of cost, a key question to ask in this regard might be: would the board tolerate an outsider's intervention and accept the conclusions expressed or would they disregard any unpopular or difficult opinions? Much will also depend on the quality of the independent consultant.

18.10 For boards that seek objectivity in the appraisal exercise but cannot afford the expense of an external facilitator, a compromise might be to ask a trustee from another organisation to carry out the appraisal. In this way, charities can enter into reciprocal appraisal arrangements with like-minded organisations.

19 Methods of board review and appraisal

19.1 Questionnaires

Questionnaires may be the first point of any review process. These can provide information on areas of concern for trustees that will later form the focus for discussion. Trustees should be given adequate time to complete the questionnaires and arrangements should be made to allow for their completion, anonymously if necessary. While a questionnaire can be used as a basis for individual appraisal, they are more commonly used for a collective review.

19.2 Group discussions

These stimulate debate as different ideas can be raised and discussed. They can work well as a starting point for a collective review, and may be sufficient in a smaller charity, or in one that is only conducting a light touch review in that year. Group discussions may involve the whole board or small groups. Although some flexibility may be desirable, discussion should be based on an agenda. Such discussions should be conducted separately from regular trustee meetings. Many charities have 'away days' or retreats to discuss these issues away from daily distractions.

19.3 Observation

In recent years, it has become much more common for a review to include observation of board or committee meetings by the assessor. This is particularly the case if there is an external review. The meeting will be observed against a number of criteria, such as effectiveness and participation, and then reported back on. Observation is more commonly used for a collective review, but it can sometimes also be used to collect information on participation for feeding not individual appraisals.

19.4 Individual interviews

These can be a constructive way of identifying the feelings of individual trustees towards the board as a whole and in respect of their own role. If the appraisal is of individual board members, not just the board as a whole, individual interviews will need to be carried out.

19.5 Review – conclusion and implementation:

19.5.1 Whatever the method used the process should end with the preparation of a conclusion. This should include a summary of the findings, an interpretation of what these findings mean and proposals for moving forward. If the review is of the board as a whole, whether it has been conducted internally or externally, the conclusion should be in written form and distributed to the whole board. In many cases, those responsible for the review will also give a presentation of their conclusions. The document and presentation then serve as a starting point for the board to discuss the next course of action. Again, it may be best to have this debate at a retreat or away day, as this allows time for options to be discussed fully, free from the distractions of other board business. When the appraisals are conducted for individual trustees, each appraisal should be discussed with the trustee and a report on general, overall conclusions may also be reported back to the board as a whole.

19.5.2 The board may decide to implement any proposals in their entirety or to take a more selective approach. Whatever the outcome, an implementation and review plan should be developed to ensure that the proposals are carried through and the work is not wasted. As with all plans, this should look at actions, identify those responsible for each action and set timescales. Where significant changes are being made, due consideration should be given to the impact on all those involved and reviews built into the plan to monitor the progress of implementation and the efficacy of any new systems.

19.5.3 The skills audit, individual trustee appraisals and board performance review are all likely to help shape the type of new trustee that the charity will look for.

20 Benefits and payments

20.1 The starting point when considering trustee benefits and payments is that trustees have a duty to act in the interests of the charity and not to receive any benefit unless they are authorised to do so. A benefit may include property, goods or services as well as money.

20.2 Reimbursement of legitimate expenses is not considered a benefit. Trustees are entitled to have their expenses met from the funds of the charity, even if there is no express power in the charity's constitution to pay expenses. These can include, for example, travel and other costs such as attending meetings, telephone and internet charges.

20.3 Otherwise, trustees may be authorised to receive benefit by:

- an express power contained in the charity's constitution;
- an express power provided by the Charity Commission; or
- the statutory power introduced by the Charities Act 2006 (and now in the Charities Act 2011) to pay trustees for services (but note the limitations on this).

20.4 It should be noted that the receipt of services from the charity is a benefit. Therefore, if a trustee or family member is a beneficiary, there will either need to be an express power in the constitution or from the Charity Commission.

20.5 The general position with charities is that there is no issue with payments to trustees for goods or services, provided both that there is authorisation in place and certain conditions are met (see below). If a charity's constitution does not permit such payments, the Charity Commission will usually agree to its amendment. The position in regard to the payment of trustees for acting as trustees, or having members of staff serving as trustees is not as straightforward. The Charity Commission states that unpaid trusteeship has always been a distinctive feature of charitable activity and greatly enhances public confidence and trust in charities. The payment of trustees needs to be justified fully by trustee boards as being clearly in the interests of their charity. However, a number of charities in recent years have applied for, and received, approval from the Charity Commission for such arrangements. In addition, many exempt charities (such as charitable housing associations) pay their trustees.

20.6 The Charities Act 2006 allowed charities to pay some of their trustees under certain conditions (now included in the Charities Act 2011). It is important to note that this power cannot be used if prohibited by the charity's governing document (and most charities include such a prohibition clause). The details are covered by the Charity Commission guidance, *Trustee Expenses and Payments* (CC11). Some charity constitutions will already contain a power to pay trustees for services, but require the prior written consent of the Charity Commission. However, provided that charities meet the conditions of s. 185 of the Charities Act 2011, this permission is no longer required.

20.7 Briefly, all the following conditions, as set out in CC11, must be met before payment for services may be made:

(a) There is a written agreement between the charity and the trustee or connected person who is to be paid.
(b) The agreement sets out the exact or maximum amount to be paid.
(c) The trustee concerned may not take part in decisions made by the trustee board about the making of the agreement, or about the acceptability of the service provided.
(d) The payment is reasonable in relation to the service to be provided.
(e) The trustees are satisfied that the payment is in the best interests of the charity.
(f) The trustee board follows the 'duty of care' set out in the Trustee Act 2000.
(g) The total number of trustees who are either receiving payment or who are connected to someone receiving payment are in a minority.
(h) There is no prohibition against payment of a trustee.
(i) Trustees must 'have regard to' the Charity Commission's guidance on the subject, and must be able to show that:
    - they are aware of this guidance;
    - in making a decision where the guidance is relevant, they have taken it into account; and
    - if they have decided to depart from the guidance, they have a good reason for so doing.

20.8 It is important to note that the provisions for payments to trustees will usually extend to 'connected persons'. These include close relatives such as spouses, parents and children, institutions controlled by the trustee or a close relative, and corporate bodies in which the trustee or a close relative has more than 1% of the voting rights or share capital.

20.9 Where is no general power to pay a trustee for serving as a trustee, there needs to be a specific power contained in the charity's governing document, or authority must be sought from the Charity Commission or the courts. Similarly, in order for a charity to employ a trustee in some other role or compensate them for loss of earnings, the charity's constitution must contain the necessary authority or this must be sought from the Charity Commission or courts. A charity trustee may only be paid for serving as a trustee where this is clearly in the best interests of the charity and it provides a significant advantage over any other option.

20.10 In all cases, charities considering paying trustees should have clear policies and procedures for dealing with conflicts of interest.

20.11 Unless there is a clear power to make a payment for serving as a trustee, the charity must apply to the Charity Commission for authority before the payment is made. Otherwise, the trustees will be in breach of trust and either the board or the trustee who has been paid may be required to refund the payment to the charity. It should also be noted that using a subsidiary to make payments to a trustee will also require express authorisation.

20.12 Care also needs to be taken in employing trustees. In many cases, the approval of the Charity Commission will be needed, if there is no express power and:

- the person takes up the employment while still a trustee;
- the job offer is made while the person is a trustee, even though they later resign as a trustee; or
- the person resigned as a trustee before the formal job offer was made and took part in an open recruitment process, but played a major part in the trustees' decision to create or retain the post, or in devising the recruitment process.

One of the questions now asked in the Charity Commission Annual Return, introduced in 2018, is whether a trustee has become an employee.

20.13 Charitable companies and larger unincorporated charities are legally required to disclose payments to trustees in their accounts. It is considered best practice for all charities of whatever size to make a similar disclosure.

21 Conflicts of interest

21.1 Conflicts of interest arises in any situation where a trustee's personal interests or loyalties conflict with those of the charity. This might involve a financial benefit to the trustee, such as when a trustee receives a payment directly or indirectly from the charity, or where there is no financial benefit but there is a conflict of loyalties (for example, where the trustee is also a trustee of another charity that might be competing for funding). The key issue is that a conflict of interest may compromise a trustee's ability to act in the best interests of their charity. Detailed guidance is available from the Charity Commission.

21.2 Conflicts of interest will arise in all charities, but it is important to identify them as early as possible and to ensure that they are addressed properly through a clear policy and procedures.

21.3 The charity law obligations on conflicts of interests arise under common law, but there is also a statutory requirement for CIOs. Regulation 36 of the Charitable Incorporated Organisations (General) Regulations 2012 (SI 2012/3012) states that a charity trustee of a CIO who would benefit personally, whether directly or indirectly, from a transaction or arrangement into which the CIO proposes to enter must not take part in the making of any decision to enter into that transaction or arrangement, and must not be counted in the quorum necessary for the discharge of that business.

21.4 A key point to note about the common law on trustee conflicts of interests is that it does not just concern the requirement not to profit. There are two facets to the legal obligation:

- the 'no conflict' rule – a trustee must not put himself in a position where his duty to the charity and his interest conflict; and
- the 'no profit' rule – a trustee must not make a profit from his position as a trustee.

In *Bristol and West Building Society v Mathew* (1998), it was stated that 'The distinguishing obligation of a fiduciary is the obligation of loyalty ... A fiduciary must act in good faith; he must not make a profit out of his trust; he must not place himself in a position where his duty and his interests may conflict; he may not act for his own benefit or the benefit of a third party without the informed consent of his principle.' Therefore, the law on conflicts still applies even where the trustee will not profit from the conflict. Trustees also need to be aware that conflicts arise in regard to connected persons (such as family members), not just themselves.

21.5 When a conflict arises, it should be properly disclosed to other trustees and recorded in the minutes of the meeting (as well as a register, see below). In addition, the trustees must not participate in that part of the meeting, or any consideration of the matter.

21.6 It is best practice for a charity to have a conflicts of interest policy and to maintain a register of interests. Trustees should be asked to update the register of interests with any significant changes and confirm actual or potential conflicts at least annually. A model Conflict of Interest policy and models for a Register of Interests and Declaration of Interests form are available from the ICSA (at www.icsa.org.uk).

21.7 For charitable companies, s. 175(1) of the Companies Act 2006 requires a director of a charitable company not only to disclose conflicts of interest but also to 'avoid a situation in which he has, or can have, a direct or indirect interest that conflicts, or possibly may conflict, with the interests of the company'. The Companies Act allows conflicts to be authorised when authorisation is permitted by the company's Articles, and when the 2006 Act was introduced there was much discussion on whether charitable companies should therefore amend their Articles to allow this. Charitable companies must have regard to the fact that the Charity Commission considers that directors of charitable companies were already under a duty to avoid conflicts of interest prior to the implementation of the Companies Act. The duty to avoid conflicts for directors in charitable companies therefore extends beyond the Companies Act and conflicts cannot necessarily always be authorised in this way. However, the Charity Commission considers that it is reasonable for non-conflicted directors to have the power to authorise conflicts arising from a duty of loyalty owed to a third party (such as another charity) where there is no direct or indirect benefit to a director or a connected person. It is the view of the Charity Commission that the articles of a company should limit the directors' power to authorise a conflict only to situations where there is no direct or indirect benefit of any nature received by a director or a connected person (such a limitation will only permit authorisation of conflicts of loyalty.)

21.8 The Charity Commission has detailed guidance on conflicts of interest: *Conflicts of interest: a guide for charity trustees* (CC29).

22 Board composition

22.1 Key issues for board composition include the following:

- How many trustees should there be?
- What skills, knowledge and experience should they have?
- How long should they serve?
- How should the trustee body be renewed?

22.2 Most charity constitutions will set both minimum and maximum numbers for trustees. A balance needs to be struck between having a board with the necessary set of skills and ensuring that it is small enough to make effective decisions. If a board is too large, individual trustees will have little opportunity to contribute at the meeting and meetings will become very long. There is also a greater likelihood that one or more of the trustees will be unable to attend. One solution is for the board to delegate some of its powers to committees. The tendency in recent years has been for boards to become smaller – recent research indicated that the average board size was 14 (see 'Delivering Effective Governance', Compass Partnership and Cass Business School).

22.3 The skills required by the trustees of a charity will vary from charity to charity, but need to be carefully considered (see section 17, page 95). In particular, trustees should consider the level of skill required and whether there is an ongoing need for such a skill. All charities are likely to need someone with financial skills on an ongoing basis, but it is possible that in other areas, it might be more appropriate for trustees to employ a consultant rather than recruit a trustee. A specimen skills register is available to download from www.icsa.org.uk.

22.4 There is no legal requirement that trustees should act only for a particular term or should retire at a particular age. Unless stated in the charity's constitution, a trustee will continue until disqualification, resignation, incapacity, removal or death. However, it is now considered best practice for there to be a maximum length of service, and it is a recommendation of the Charity Governance Code that this should usually be nine years. While many charities rely on the good sense of their trustees to retire at an appropriate time, there is a temptation for trustees to remain beyond a point when they are able to contribute significantly to the work of the charity. For this reason, many charities have introduced fixed terms of office (usually three to five years) and have placed a limit on the total number of terms of office (usually two or three).

22.5 Where there are fixed terms of office, constitutions will usually provide for a break period of one or more years after the final term of office before the trustee can seek reappointment. There may also be safeguards in place to ensure that key trustees, such as the chair and treasurer, do not have to retire at the same time and that appointments or reappointments can be staggered, so that not all the trustees retire at once.

23 Resignation, retirement, disqualification and removal of trustees

23.1 A charity's constitution will normally provide for the resignation of a trustee. Care should be taken to ensure that any requirements are followed (e.g. normally notice needs to be given to the charity in writing).

23.2 A trustee may retire only if there is an express or implied power to do so. In most cases, there will be an express provision in the charity's governing document. If there is not, but trustees are appointed for fixed terms of office, they will have an implied power to retire at the end of the term of office.

23.3 Under the Trustee Act 1925, s. 39, trustees of unincorporated charities have the power to retire, provided that there are at least two trustees or a trust corporation will continue to hold office.

23.4 There are a number of legal grounds on which a trustee may be disqualified from being a trustee (see section 15, page 91).

23.5 Constitutions will often include other reasons for the disqualification of a trustee, including:

- ceasing to be a member;
- being incapable of managing their own affairs;
- being absent from a specified number of board meetings in a given period without leave of absence and the other trustees resolving that the trustee in question has vacated their office;
- being convicted of an offence which may not lead to statutory disqualification, but may damage the interests of the charity; or
- acting contrary to the best interests of the charity. This will usually require the unanimous agreement of all the other trustees.

23.6 A trustee of a charitable company may be removed by an ordinary resolution of its members. The requirements for this are set out in ss. 168 and 169 of the Companies Act 2006.

23.7 In certain cases, third parties will have the right to remove members (e.g. a local authority-appointed trustee will also be able to be removed by the local authority).

23.8 Both the High Court and the Charity Commission have the power to remove charity trustees in certain circumstances.

24 Honorary officers

24.1 Most charities will have a number of trustees who hold particular positions within the board. The most common are chair, deputy or vice chair and honorary treasurer. These are termed honorary officers ('honorary' because they are unpaid, and 'officers' because they are office holders.) It is best practice for the board to define the roles and responsibilities of the chair and other honorary officers, in writing. This is important because it ensures clarity for the officers, for the other trustees and for senior staff and reduces the risk of conflict.

24.2 Role of the chair

24.2.1 The chair's role is mainly one of leadership. The chair leads the board and makes sure that it works effectively in setting and achieving the charity's strategy; acts as an ambassador for the board in building relationships with stakeholders (for example, by speaking on its behalf at the AGM); and provides a link between the board of trustees and staff through working closely with the chief executive.

24.2.2 The following is taken from the 'ICSA Model Role Description for Chair of the Board of Charity Trustees (England & Wales)', available from www.icsa.org.uk.

24.2.3 Chair role description

Main responsibilities

- Leading the trustees and members of the senior management team in the development of strategic plans for the charity.
- Providing leadership and support to the chief executive officer (CEO) and ensuring that the charity is run in accordance with the decisions of the trustees, the charity's governing document and appropriate legislation.
- Liaising with the charity secretary and chief executive officer with the drafting of agendas and supporting papers for trustee meetings and ensuring that the business is covered efficiently and effectively in those meetings.
- Undertaking a leadership role in ensuring that the board of trustees fulfils its responsibilities for the governance of the charity.
- Leading on, with the assistance of the charity secretary and chief executive where appropriate, the development and implementation of procedures for board induction, development, training, and appraisal.
- Implementing an effective communication strategy that includes the needs of staff, beneficiaries and other stakeholders.

Main duties

- Liaising with the charity secretary to lead on the planning, setting and chairing of trustee meetings and AGMs.
- Ensuring trust in and supporting and appraising the performance of the chief executive officer and other appropriate members of the senior management team.
- Leading disciplinary and appointment committees, where appropriate and in line with the charity's agreed procedures.
- Representing the charity at functions, meetings and in the press and broadcasting media, in line with the charity's agreed media strategy.
- Acting between full meetings of the board in authorising action to be taken *intra vires* (such as banking transactions and legal documents in accordance with relevant mandates).
- Maintaining the trustees' commitment to board renewal and succession management, in line with the charity's governing document and/or current best practice.
- Ensuring that the performance of the board as a whole and the trustees individually is reviewed on an annual basis.

24.3 Powers of the chair

24.3.1 Some of the powers of the chair will be set out in the charity's constitution. Usually these are limited to the chair's role in chairing meetings of members and board meetings. Under the Companies Acts, the chair's actions carry some legal weight (under the Companies Act 2006, s. 320, the declaration by the chair of the result of a vote on a show of hands is conclusive evidence as to the result).

24.3.2 Powers that are often delegated to the chair include: calling board meetings, authorising payments up to a certain level, ruling on conflicts of interest and appraising the chief executive.

24.3.3 Charitable companies should be aware that the Companies Act 2006, ss. 282 and 284, had the incidental effect of removing the chair's casting vote at general meetings. However, a provision was included in the fifth CA 2006 Commencement Order stating that companies whose Articles provided for a chair's casting vote immediately before 1 October 2007 may continue to rely on the relevant article. If a company subsequently amended its Articles to remove the casting vote, it may reinstate the provision and continue to rely on it. Other companies, including those incorporated after 1 October 2007, cannot provide for a chair's casting vote in their Articles. (A power of a casting vote at board meetings is unaffected.)

24.4 Role of the honorary treasurer

24.4.1 In many charities, the honorary treasurer plays a vital role in leading on all the financial aspects of the charity's work. However, there is an argument that, for larger charities, the role may come into conflict with that of the finance director and that oversight of the charity's finances is better served by a finance committee with at least one member who is an accountant or has other relevant financial experience. In this case, the chair of the finance committee may take on some of the responsibilities that would otherwise fall to the honorary treasurer. Although there is no legal requirement, the charity's constitution may require the honorary treasurer to meet certain criteria in terms of qualifications, and they are often an accountant. It is important to remember that even where there is an honorary treasurer, all the trustees are still collectively responsible for the charity's finances and for approving its financial statements.

24.4.2 Where there is an honorary treasurer, they will normally provide advice to other trustees and act as the main point of contact on the board for the finance director and head of internal audit. The honorary treasurer may also serve on the audit committee, although this can be seen as a conflict of interest.

24.4.3 The following is taken from the 'ICSA Model Role Description for a Charity Treasurer (England & Wales)', available from www.icsa.org.uk.

24.4.4 Treasurer role description

Main responsibilities

- Overseeing and presenting budgets, accounts, management accounts and financial statements to the board of trustees after discussion with the finance director, where applicable.
- Ensuring that proper accounts and records are kept, ensuring financial resources are spent and invested in line with the charity's policies, good governance, legal and regulatory requirements.
- Being instrumental in the development and implementation of financial, reserves and investment policies.

Main duties

- Liaising, where applicable, with the finance director or other appropriate member of staff responsible for the financial activities of the organisation.
- Chairing any finance committee in line with standing orders and terms of reference, and reporting back to the board of trustees.
- Liaising with the charity's auditors or independent examiner, where appropriate. Monitoring and advising on the financial viability of the charity after liaising with the charity's auditors.
- Creating, in liaison with the finance director (where there is one), sound financial instruments for the control of charity assets.
- Implementing and monitoring specific financial controls and ensuring that systems are in place accordingly and adhered to.
- Advising on the financial implications of the charity's strategic plan.
- Liaising with the charity secretary and finance director, where applicable, to ensure that the charity's annual accounts are compliant with the current Charities' Statement of Recommended Practice (SORP).
- Where the charity has an internal audit function, the treasurer will be required to work closely with the internal audit team and any sub-committee of the board of trustees.
- Acting as a counter-signatory on charity cheques (including any electronic transactions) and any applications for funds.
- Maintaining sound financial management of the charity's resources, ensuring expenditure is in line with the charity's objects.
- Contributing to the fundraising strategy of the organisation.

24.5 Constitutional position of honorary officers

The mechanism for appointing or electing the chair will normally be specified in the charity's constitution, as will their terms of office and any specific powers. Other honorary officers may be covered by the charity's main constitution or standing orders. Normally, honorary officers are elected by their fellow trustees, but sometimes the constitution may specify that the chair is elected by members or chosen in some other way. As honorary officers are often drawn from the more experienced trustees, care needs to be taken over succession planning, to avoid the situation where all the honorary officers end their terms of office as trustees (and also as honorary officers) at the same time. It is important to remember that honorary officers are first and foremost trustees and, with the exception of the chair, do not usually have any additional powers under a charity's constitution.

25 Other roles, such as patron and president

25.1 Other roles include the following:

- **Founder**: many charities are started by an individual or a small group of people. These are sometimes described as founder trustees.
- **Patron**: usually a role that has no rights or obligations attached to it. The role is often held by one or more people whose association with the charity is intended to enhance its profile with the public.
- **President**: an honorary title, usually given to the most important patron. The role may be given to a long-serving chair on their retirement.
- **Observer**: a person who attends meetings of the trustees but does not have a right to vote. An observer may be a representative of a stakeholder group, such as staff or service users. Prospective trustees are also sometimes invited to attend meetings as observers, before deciding if they wish to become a trustee.
- **Portfolio trustees**: in some charities, individual trustees will be given responsibility for overseeing particular areas of the organisation's activities, such as human resources, campaigning or liaising with senior staff between board meetings. The key advantages of this system are that it allows trustees with particular expertise to influence proposals at an early stage and gives fellow trustees confidence that one of their number is keeping a close eye on matters where they may not have particular expertise. However, care should be taken to ensure that it does not prevent trustees from exercising their duty to consider all matters that affect a charity and to act in the best interests of the charity as a whole. In addition, the use of portfolio trustees is probably more suited to small charities that do not have a lot of staff overseeing these activities. In larger charities it can work against maintaining a separation of governance and management.

26 Collective responsibility and general principles of delegation

26.1 All decisions concerning a charity must be taken by the trustees acting together, except where a power has been delegated. When the board makes a decision, even if it is not unanimous, the decision is deemed to be the responsibility of all the trustees, so they are all expected to support the decision, once made.

26.2 In practice, boards cannot usually take every decision that a charity needs to make. Fortunately, subject to legal constraints and the charity's own constitution, the board can delegate certain powers to others to act on their behalf. However, as a general rule, a board may delegate power but not responsibility, so the trustees remain liable.

26.3 In order to safeguard the trustees' position, the terms of any delegation should specify:

- who is being given authority: whether it is an individual trustee, a committee (and if so, who is on the committee), the chief executive or other staff;
- what the authority is (the power to make decisions, authority to advise the trustees or authority to implement the decisions of trustees);
- whether money may be spent and if this must be covered by an approved budget; and
- how the trustees will monitor the exercise of delegated powers.

26.4 Legal and constitutional position

26.4.1 The constitution of incorporated charities will generally include an express power for the trustees to delegate powers to committees consisting of two or more people, at least one of whom must be a trustee.

26.4.2 If the trustees do not have a power of delegation, or it is not exercised properly, the acts and decisions of those who are supposedly the agents of the trustees will be void. This may result in the trustees being liable for a breach of trust and the purported agents may potentially face personal liability.

26.4.3 Section 11(3) of the Trustee Act 2000 says that trustees of unincorporated charities (and CIOs) can delegate:

- implementing a decision of the trustees;
- the investment of charity assets; raising funds for the trust, except by carrying out a 'primary purpose' trade; or
- any other function prescribed by an order made by the Secretary of State.

26.4.4 The trustees will be liable only for the acts or omissions of the delegate(s) if they have failed in their duty of care in choosing the delegate.

26.4.5 Under the Trustee Act 1925, an individual trustee of an unincorporated charity may delegate their powers to someone else for a period of up to 12 months through a power of attorney.

26.5 Delegation to staff: role of the CEO

26.5.1 Although trustees reserve the right to manage any aspect of a charity's activities, as they are ultimately responsible for its success, boards normally delegate the day-to-day management to staff, focusing on strategic matters. This is achieved by the board appointing the CEO and delegating authority to them, within certain boundaries (including any schemes of delegation), to appoint and manage other staff. The board will then hold the CEO accountable for achieving the goals it has set and carrying out its decisions. Normally, the chair and one other trustee will agree the CEO's objectives and carry out appraisals.

27 Relationship between governance and management

27.1 Professor Bob Tricker wrote in his book *Corporate Governance*, 'if management is about running business, governance is about seeing that it is run properly. All businesses need governing as well as managing.'

27.2 In practice, what governance entails varies between charities. For small charities, good governance may simply be about making sure that everyone knows what they are doing and that they are pulling together. For a large national charity, it may be more about public accountability. The distinction between governance and management is also not clear-cut. In many small charities, the trustees may also have a management role, and in larger charities, management and staff are likely to have a say in strategic planning, although it remains the responsibility of trustees.

27.3 In reality, the boards of most charities work in partnership with their senior managers to develop strategy and policies and to make major decisions. While the board might be clear what it wants, senior managers might be better placed to know how to achieve these aims or what additional resources might be needed to bring them to fruition. In particular, goals and performance standards must be agreed by both board and management to ensure that they are both demanding and realistic.

28 Relationship with the CEO and staff

28.1 A successful charity will have both a strong CEO and senior management team and an effective board. To ensure that the relationship works well, with openness and mutual respect, it is important that there are clear ground rules about how they interact, and also formal and informal reviews to check that board and staff are working well together. This is an area in which the chair and CEO should jointly take the lead by making sure that there is agreement on, among other things:

- the respective responsibilities of the chair and CEO;
- what involvement trustees should have outside board meetings;
- what authority individual trustees have;
- how complaints about the conduct of trustees or staff should be dealt with;
- how staff should communicate with trustees to keep them informed or consult with them; and
- what support trustees should expect from staff.

28.2 In addition, there must be a clear, written agreement on how the CEO's objectives are set and how they are appraised.

28.3 Formal reviews of the relationship between trustees and the CEO and staff should be part of board and individual trustee appraisals, and covered in directors' appraisals. A good chair and CEO should also make sure they are aware of any problems early on so that they can be dealt with as quickly as possible.

28.4 The relationship can be a difficult one to get right, as the board needs both to support and to challenge staff. Where there is no challenge, the board is, in effect, abdicating its responsibility, either leaving important decisions to the executives or supporting them whatever they do. Where there is challenge, but no support, the board risks coming into conflict with its senior staff.

29 The role of the secretary

29.1 Charities take on a range of forms, including trusts, companies, CIOs and chartered bodies among others. Not all have to have secretaries, but many do, and the role is undertaken by a range of people – from trustees, to staff members who combine it with another function and named secretaries who perform only this role. A key question is: what is or should be the role of the secretary? Is there a core role, or does it depend on who is allocated the task and the type of organisation that the charity is?

29.2 There are a number of differences in the role depending on the type of charity and how it has allocated the role. No two job descriptions for a charity secretary are ever the same. However, there are some core roles and all secretaries usually share the same primary responsibilities. The charity secretary is primarily responsible for:

- the smooth and efficient running of meetings of the trustee board, any committees and general meetings;
- ensuring that all decisions made by the trustees are in accordance with the governing document and reflect the objects of the charity;
- providing assistance and support to the chair of the board of trustees;
- overseeing and advising on the governance of the charity; and
- compliance with various legislative and regulatory requirements affecting the charity and its activities.

29.3 While a number of charities will choose to appoint a secretary even if there is no legal or constitutional requirement to do so, it is often a requirement of the constitution. In addition, until the Companies Act 2006 came into force, all companies were required to have a company secretary. Under the Companies Act 2006, private companies, including charitable companies, are not required to have a company secretary. However, any company that refers to the appointment of a secretary in its Articles of Association will need to amend the Articles of Association if it wants to dispense with the role of company secretary. It is also arguable that given the governance standards and accountability levels expected of charities, along with their heavier reporting obligations, it would be unwise for the board of a charitable company to dispense with a secretary. Having a secretary can make it easier in terms of the administration of some matters, as the secretary is a recognised signatory alongside directors. It should also be remembered that all of the functions and duties that will usually sit with a secretary will still need to be the responsibility of someone if a secretary is not appointed. Since the Companies Act 2006 came into force, there does not appear to have been a rush among charitable companies to remove the need for a secretary. Perhaps the fact that the role is also common in those types of corporate form where it has never been a legal requirement is also an indication of the overall importance of the role for a charity. However, it should be noted that the Charity Commission model constitution for a CIO contains no reference to a secretary.

29.4 The secretary must usually be appointed by the board, and this is certainly the case in a charitable company. The appointment should be minuted. There may also be particular requirements under the constitution for the appointment that need to be met. For example, the constitution may state that the secretary must, or must not, be a member. In addition, some charities have an honorary secretary under the terms of their constitution and may require that the honorary secretary also serves as a trustee.

29.5 If the charity is a company and it chooses to have a company secretary:

- it must notify Companies House of the appointment within 14 days (using Form AP03 or AP04 or by filing online);
- it must notify Companies House of any changes in details; and
- details must be recorded in the Register of Secretaries.

29.6 There is no requirement to give the Charity Commission details of the secretary. However, the secretary is very often the most appropriate person to act as correspondent for the charity; therefore their details should normally be given to the Charity Commission.

29.7 In the largest charities, the post of secretary will often be an employed post within the charity's staff structure, whereas in medium-sized or smaller charities it is more likely that an unpaid volunteer will act as secretary or combine the role with another. It is possible to engage suitable professional persons or organisations independent of the charity to act as the secretary on an outsourced basis. The secretary may also be a trustee; this is usually the case if the role is that of an honorary secretary. If a trustee performs this role, care needs to be taken to ensure that:

- if they are responsible for the minuting of board meetings (as secretaries usually are) consideration is given as to how this impacts on their participation as a member of the meeting. They are a trustee first and foremost, and sometimes taking comprehensive minutes can affect the ability to participate fully as well. If possible, the honorary secretary could retain responsibility for the taking of the minutes while someone else attends the meeting to take the notes;
- there is consideration of the best use of a trustee's time. Many of the tasks of a secretary are essentially administrative. Is this the best use of the trustee's time? It may be that there is no one else who can perform this role, in which case there also needs to be clarity about what the trustee has responsibility for as secretary; and
- the trustee has understanding, and if necessary, training. Does the trustee understand the role and the duties? Do they require additional support and/or training in this regard?

29.8 Responsibilities of the secretary

29.8.1 The secretary's duties and responsibilities should be determined by the board and they should always be recorded in writing, in a role description or at the very least in the minutes. The nature of the exact duties and responsibilities will vary considerably from charity to charity because of diversity in the organisation's objects, activities, size and legal nature. However, the secretary will almost certainly have 'core duties', which are:

- attending trustee and general meetings;
- issuing notices, agenda and papers for meetings;
- taking minutes (or being responsible for the taking of minutes);
- having custody of registers, minute books and records;
- acting as correspondent for trustees;
- being responsible for statutory compliance (such as notifications to the Charity Commission and (if required) Companies House; annual returns and confirmation statements);
- having custody of any seal and overseeing its use; and
- being the custodian of the governing document. This means not just holding a copy of the up-to-date documents (and past versions) but also understanding and interpreting it and advising the trustees on its contents.

29.8.2 While these are the core duties, it is also appropriate for the secretary to be the person responsible for:

- advising on governance matters;
- the provision of legal advice: if they have the appropriate expertise themselves, they could provide it directly but this will usually mean liaising with the solicitors and obtaining such advice; and
- trustee support, training and development.

29.8.3 The secretary is an 'officer' of the charity. Unless the secretary is also a trustee, the liabilities will not be as extensive as those of trustees, but they do exist. If the charity is a company, s. 1121 of the Companies Act 2006 applies and the secretary may be criminally liable for defaults committed by the company, such as:

- failure to file changes in the details of the company's directors and secretary; and
- failure to file the company's annual return.

29.9 Joint and deputy secretaries

29.9.1 A company may wish to appoint more than one secretary (for example, if the incumbent secretary is going on maternity leave but wishes to remain as the office holder during the period of absence or where a company wishes to appoint a person to the office of secretary but to have someone else carry out most of the detailed duties). The appointment of a joint secretary can sometimes be considered when there is an honorary secretary, but they are unable or unwilling to perform all of the administrative duties and a member of staff or outsourced secretary is employed to do this.

29.9.2 If joint secretaries are appointed, they will both be placed on the Register of Secretaries, and notified to Companies House. As the most common intention is for the secretaries to be able to act independently, this needs to be made clear in the appointment (unless specified in the Articles). Otherwise, joint secretaries will be assumed to have to act jointly (a document that needs to be signed by the secretary would need to be signed by both).

29.9.3 A charity may also seek to appoint a deputy secretary. Care needs to be taken to ensure that it is clear what powers such a person has and when they can act. Section 274 of the Companies Act 2006 gives authority for the appointment of deputy or assistant secretaries to act should the office of secretary be vacant or if for any other reason there is no secretary capable of acting; in the absence of any deputy or assistant secretary, the functions of the secretary may be performed by any officer of the company authorised generally or specially in that regard by the directors. Apart from this statutory authority, the Articles of Association of companies frequently contain specific provisions governing the appointment of deputy or assistant secretaries. However, it should be noted that the interpretation of when a secretary is incapable of acting may be narrow, so it would be beneficial if, in making such an appointment, the board also specified when the deputy was allowed to act (for example, to sign documents as the secretary). There are differing opinions on whether the appointment of deputy secretaries should also be entered on the Register of Secretaries and notified to Companies House. However, it is arguable that if they are to act as secretary then they should be. Sample wording for an appointment would be:

> That AB be appointed as deputy/assistant secretary of the company with authority to undertake the duties of, and to exercise the powers conferred on, the secretary of the company when the secretary is incapable of acting in that capacity because of his/her absence from the company's offices.

29.9.4 For charities that are not companies, the facility to appoint a joint or deputy secretary will depend to some extent on the provisions in the constitution. If the role of the secretary is not formally outlined in the constitution, this should not be an issue. If it is, the wording will need to be considered to see if more than one person can take on the role, or if the secretary can delegate their responsibilities.

29.10 Charitable companies: why have a secretary?

Given that there is no need for a private company to have a secretary, it is worthwhile considering whether it is worthwhile continuing to do so. It is advisable for three reasons:

1. Having a secretary can make some administrative tasks easier. For example, notifications of changes in director and other statutory notifications to Companies House must be made by either a director (or a trustee), a secretary or an 'authorised person'. For someone to be an 'authorised person' that authorisation will need to have been made, either specifically or generally, by the board. Even if a general authorisation is given, it will still need to be worded broadly enough to cover the full role. Therefore, if there is no secretary, a trustee may need to take on this role. A secretary can also act as a signatory (for example, on certified copies of minutes) in a way that, again, only the trustees will be able to do otherwise.
2. The decision to remove the role of secretary was taken as it was felt that private companies did not have the same requirement as public companies regarding governance and accountability. However, although they are private companies, it is arguable that charitable companies are actually closer to public companies in this regard than to other private companies.
3. The charitable company will need to comply with its Articles of Association. These may include a requirement to have a secretary.

29.11 Cessation of office

29.11.1 If a secretary resigns, this should be reported to the trustees immediately. Whenever possible, boards should not allow a 'gap' before a new appointment is made, even if this means appointing an interim secretary until a permanent replacement can be made. Resignations should, whenever possible, coincide with a board meeting, which will then also appoint the next secretary.

29.11.2 As with appointments, removal can be effected only by the board and should be minuted (along with resignations).

29.11.3 For companies, resignations/removal must be notified to Companies House and details of the resignation/removal should be entered in the register of secretaries.

30 The role of members: membership charities

30.1 Not every charity has members. Charitable companies and CIOs have members as do charitable unincorporated associations, but most charitable trusts do not.

30.2 There are a number of common models for charities with members, and the role of members will depend on the model used.

- **Flat model:** the only members are the trustees. This reflects the fact that the trustees are ultimately responsible for the running of the charity, but excludes other stakeholders from a constitutional role in how the charity is run. This is the common model for many charitable companies and the foundation model for CIOs.
- **Hybrid model:** members have a right to attend general meetings, receive information and elect trustees, but otherwise have little say in how the charity is run.
- **Membership model:** members are more involved, and possibly able to exercise more control over the charity trustees. Although this may be more democratic, it is also more likely to lead to disagreements between groups of members who take different views. It can also cause difficulties with accountability, and the need for clarity over trustee decision making.

In a membership charity, it is important that the trustees remember that their duty is to the beneficiaries the charity, both present and future, rather than the charity's members. While they will need to be accountable to the members for their actions, it is the trustee's duty to determine what is in the best interest of the charity in achieving its objects. At times this may bring them into conflict with the members.

30.3 CIOs have two alternative models: the foundation model, in which the trustees are the only voting members and the association model, in which the membership is wider than the trustees. Whereas members of a company limited by guarantee have limited liability for its debts if it winds up (they only have to pay a fixed amount), members of a CIO may have either no liability at all or (like a company) limited liability for its debts. One of the other key differences in regard to membership of a CIO is that CIO members have a legal duty. Members of a CIO have a legal duty to exercise their powers in the way that they decide, in good faith, is most likely to further the purposes of the CIO. The legal duties of members in other types of charity remain, on the whole, much less clear. Unlike trustees, there does not appear to be a clear legal duty to act in the best interests of the charity.

30.4 A charity's constitution will normally state how members are appointed and prescribe their rights to call and receive notice of meetings, to attend, speak and vote at meetings, and to bring resolutions.

30.5 Trustees as members

30.5.1 Normally, trustees are required to be members. The theory behind this is that the charity is 'owned' by the members and the members elect trustees from among their number to run the charity on their behalf and be accountable to the rest of the members. However, trustees may not always be members (for example, a charity which has beneficiaries as its members may choose to appoint 'external' trustees to bring in other skills and experience). It depends on the constitution of the charity.

30.5.2 In some cases, however, the trustees will be the only members. This is often the case in charities that are established as charitable companies, but that do not have the intention of having a wider membership. It is also the foundation model for a CIO. Where this is the case, care will need to be taken to distinguish between the two roles and accountability will need to be considered in a wider way.

30.6 Members' rights

Members' rights are governed by the charity's constitution: for charitable companies, by the provisions of the Companies Acts; for CIOs the provisions of the Charitable Incorporated Organisations (General) Regulations 2012. Members frequently have rights to alter the charity's constitution, elect or remove trustees, call meetings and, ultimately, wind the charity up. Members may have other non-voting rights, such as the right to receive newsletters or the right to speak at general meetings. For charitable companies, the rights of members will normally be the same as those of shareholders as the members will be the guarantors of a company limited by guarantee. Thus the members of a charitable company will have a statutory right to: remove directors; receive the annual report and accounts; attend general meetings (and require them to be held); vote and appoint proxies; appoint the auditors; and amend the Articles.

30.7 Admission and removal of members

30.7.1 A charity's constitution normally gives power to the charity's trustees to create different classes of membership with different rights and obligations. Trustees also normally approve individuals as members of the charity. The constitution may allow trustees to reject applications for membership at their discretion, or may require them to accept applications unless they consider that to do so is not in the best interests of the charity. People who are rejected as members may also have a right of appeal, but the trustees will usually make the final decision.

30.7.2 Prospective members should sign a form to show that they consent to becoming a member and, in the case of a CLG, they agree to the guarantee. (If the charity is a CIO and the members are accepting some limited liability, the member should also sign to accept this. A register of members must be kept by charitable companies and association CIOs, and should be kept by other membership charities, showing the name, address and date of appointment and registration of each member.

30.7.3 Membership usually ends if the member dies, resigns, fails to pay any membership subscription within a specified period of it falling due or is removed by a resolution of the trustees. The date on which membership ceases should be entered in the membership register. In a charitable company, the member will still be liable under the guarantee for a year after they cease to be a member.

30.8 Power of the Charity Commission to determine members

Under the Charities Act 2011 s. 111, the Charity Commission has the power to determine a charity's members. This is particularly important, because any uncertainty surrounding a charity's members may also create uncertainty over whether trustees were validly elected. If the members have the power to elect the trustees, it is vital that there is clarity as to who the members actually are. However, it is not uncommon, over time, for a charity to fail to keep its register of members up to date. If there is uncertainty over who can vote, the validity of the election will be open to question.

30.9 Informal membership

Some charities also have informal or associate members. This is a type of membership that does *not* count as membership for legal purposes. Therefore, these members will not have:

- voting rights;
- other rights under company law (for a company) or the Charitable Incorporated Organisations (General) Regulations 2012 (for a CIO);
- legal obligations to act in the interests of the charity (for a CIO); or
- any liability to contribute to the assets of the charity when it is dissolved.

If a charity has informal or associate members, it must distinguish them from legal members and should not include details of any informal or associate members in a register of members.

SECTION B

Ongoing requirements

B1
Regulation

1 Charity Commission regulation, investigations and powers

1.1 This section explores the Charity Commission's dual role both as the regulator of charities and as a source of guidance and support.

1.2 Under the 2011 Act, the Charity Commission has a number of statutory powers:

- to instigate statutory inquiries under s. 46 of the 2011 Act;
- to act for the protection of charities once a statutory inquiry has been instigated; and
- to supervise charities.

The Charity Commission has also now gained additional powers under the Charities (Protection and Social Investment) Act 2016.

1.3 Charity Commission investigations and statutory inquiries

1.3.1 The Charity Commission's current guidance on complaints is set out in *Complaints about Charities* (CC47), available directly from the Charity Commission or on its website (www.charitycommission.gov.uk).

1.3.2 When the Charity Commission receives a complaint, or otherwise has concerns about a charity, its first step is to consider the level of risk and whether it should take steps to intervene. It has a risk framework to which it refers to determine whether a statutory inquiry should be opened, and if not, whether some other type of intervention is required. Often, the Charity Commission will write to the charity's trustees to request further information. Depending on the response received, the Charity Commission will determine whether the concern or allegation merits further investigation.

1.3.3 In the vast majority of cases, the matter will be dealt with by the Charity Commission providing advice to the charity and/or highlighting the information in its guidance. However, under its risk framework, the Charity Commission is likely only to give proactive regulatory advice to help trustees to carry out their duties properly where there are serious concerns about the administration of a charity, or provide regulatory compliance advice where there is a serious risk of non-compliance with legal requirements.

1.3.4 The Charity Commission will only intervene in relation to a complaint in circumstances where it considers that:

- there is a serious risk of significant harm to or abuse of the charity, its assets, beneficiaries or reputation; and
- its intervention is a necessary and proportionate response to protect the charity, its assets, beneficiaries or reputation.

1.3.5 In its current guidance, the Charity Commission states that it regards the following matters to be serious, significant and unacceptable for any charity, its trustees, employees or agents:

- causing significant financial loss to the charity;
- causing serious harm to beneficiaries and, in particular, vulnerable beneficiaries;
- misuse of a charity for terrorist purposes (including links with or support for terrorism, financial or otherwise, connections to proscribed organisations or misuse of a charity to foster extremism);
- serious criminality and/or illegal activity within or involving a charity (including fraud and money laundering);
- setting up sham charities for an illegal or improper purpose;
- deliberately using charities for significant private advantage;
- activities which seriously call a charity's independence into question; and
- other significant non-compliance breaches of trust or abuses that otherwise impact significantly on public trust and confidence in the charity and charities generally.

1.3.6 If any of these circumstances exist, the Charity Commission may start a statutory inquiry under s. 46 of the 2011 Act, which could involve a particular charity or class of charities. The Charity Commission may carry out the inquiry itself, or appoint another person on its behalf. The Charity Commission has greatly increased the number of statutory inquiries that it undertakes each year. In 2012–13, the Charity Commission opened just 15 statutory inquiries; by 2016–17 this had increased to 187 statutory inquiries and in 2017–18 the number was 137. It has also increased the use of its powers. In 2012–14, it used its powers on 74 occasions during statutory inquiries and regulatory compliance cases. By 2017–18, 1,136 regulatory powers were used, 78 of which were new powers (see paragraph 1.3.7).

1.3.7 The Charities (Protection and Social Investment) Act 2016 gave the Charity Commission a number of new powers. These powers include the following.

- If the Charity Commission believes charity trustees or a charity has acted improperly, breached its duties or has been mismanaged, it can issue an official warning. This action can be taken without a statutory inquiry having been started. The Charity Commission must give prior notice of its intention to issue an official warning. This notice should stipulate the reason for the warning and give guidance on what the commission thinks should be done to rectify the position. The Charity Commission also has the power to make public any official warning. If the breach specified in the official warning is not addressed, further regulatory action can be taken against the charity.
- The scope for being automatically disqualified from being a trustee was extended beyond the previous rules (see chapter A4).
- The Act extended the Commission powers once it has opened a statutory inquiry into a charity. It can:
  - take into account not only conduct in relation to the charity itself, but also wider conduct which does not necessarily relate to the charity concerned;
  - remove a trustee following a statutory inquiry, even if the trustee resigns before the removal takes effect;
  - direct a charity not to take specified action; and
  - wind up a charity following a statutory inquiry.
- The Charity Commission was given new powers to disqualify an existing trustee so long as they were deemed unfit to be a trustee; disqualification was in the public interest and one of the following conditions listed was met:
  - the person has been cautioned for a disqualifying offence against a charity;
  - the person has been convicted outside the UK for an offence which would automatically disqualify them from acting as a trustee if the offence was committed in the UK;
  - HMRC has found the individual not to be a fit and proper person (for the purposes of paragraph 4 of Schedule 6 to the Finance Act 2010);
  - the person was a trustee or employee of a charity at a time when there was misconduct or mismanagement of a charity, and they were responsible, or had knowledge and failed to take reasonable steps to stop it, or their conduct contributed to it;
  - the person was an officer or employee of a body corporate, in similar circumstances as in condition four; or
  - past or continuing conduct by the person is damaging or likely to be damaging to public trust and confidence in charities generally.

1.3.8 In addition to these new powers, when conducting a statutory inquiry, the Charity Commission (or its appointee) also has the following powers:

- To direct any person to give written accounts and statements on the matter under investigation; to return answers in writing to questions posed; and to verify any accounts, statement or answers by making a statutory declaration.
- To enter premises and to seize documents, computer disks and other electronic storage devices, to take copies and to require any person on the premises to explain any such document or information or to state where they may be found. To exercise this power, the Charity Commission must first obtain a magistrate's warrant.
- Before issuing a warrant, the magistrate must be satisfied that there are reasonable grounds for believing: that a statutory inquiry is underway; that documents or information relevant to the inquiry are on the premises specified; and that, if the Charity Commission were to make an order requiring the document or information to be provided to it, either the order would not be complied with, or the document or information would be removed, tampered with, concealed or destroyed.
- Entry and search must take place at a reasonable hour and within one month of the warrant being issued. It is a criminal offence to obstruct the Charity Commission exercising its rights under such a warrant.

1.3.9 Once a statutory inquiry has been instigated, the Charity Commission has the protective powers under s. 76 of the 2011 Act to:

- suspend trustees, officers, employees or agents of the charity from their duties;
- appoint additional trustees;
- vest any of the charity's property in the Official Custodian for Charities;
- freeze the charity's assets and bank accounts;
- restrict any of the charity's transactions;
- appoint an interim manager, who acts as receiver and manager of the property and the affairs of the charity (the Charity Commission maintains a panel of experts approved to carry out this role);
- remove and replace trustees (ss. 79 and 80); and
- issue an order directing a trustee, officer or employee of the charity, or the charity itself to take any action which the Charity Commission considers to be expedient in the interests of the charity. This is a wide new power introduced by the Charities Act 2006 and now contained in s. 84 of the 2011 Act. The Charity Commission cannot order any action which would be unlawful or inimical to the charity's trusts or purposes.

1.3.10 Before it exercises any of its powers under ss. 76, 79 or 84 of the 2011 Act, the Charity Commission must be satisfied either:

- that there is or has been misconduct or mismanagement in the administration of the charity; or

- that it is necessary or desirable to act to protect the property of the charity or to ensure that any property the charity has, or is due to receive, is properly applied for its charitable purposes.

1.3.11 At the end of an inquiry, the Charity Commission may publish the results of its investigation in a report or make a statement. In practice, reports are published on the Charity Commission's website. The organisation involved will usually be given an opportunity to review and make representations on the draft report before it is published.

1.3.12 The Charity Commission also has the powers to suspend or terminate the membership of a trustee, officer, agent or employee of a charity and prohibit resumption of membership without the Charity Commission's approval (although this power can only be exercised where the Charity Commission has suspended or removed that person from being a trustee, officer, agent or employee of the charity) (s. 83 of the 2011 Charities Act).

1.3.13 The Charity Commission also has the power to direct that a charity's property be used or transferred in a particular way if those in control of it refuse to use or apply the charity's property for the purposes of the charity (this power can be exercised by the Charity Commission irrespective of whether a statutory inquiry has been instigated and could be used to ensure that trustees are meeting the public benefit requirement) – now contained in s. 85 of the 2011 Act.

1.3.14 It is also worth remembering that it is a criminal offence (punishable by a fine and/or imprisonment for up to two years) to knowingly or recklessly provide the Charity Commission with information that is false or misleading in a material particular or to wilfully alter, suppress, conceal or destroy any document required to be produced to the Charity Commission.

1.4 Power to disclose information about charities

The Charity Commission also has the power:

- to share information about charities with other public bodies (such as local authorities, the police, HMRC or any other government department) and such public bodies have the power to disclose information to the Charity Commission to assist it in the discharge of its functions; and
- to disclose information to and receive information from the principal regulators of exempt charities (see paragraph 7.16, chapter A3, page 69).

1.5 Representing the interests of charities

In its role as friend to and champion of charities, the Charity Commission:

- has various powers to assist charities;
- is required to maintain an up-to-date and accurate register of charities;
- publishes regulatory guidance (including its very useful operational guidance); and
- maintains a register of mergers.

1.6 Enabling powers

The Charity Commission has the following powers to assist charities:

- **Power to establish schemes**: s. 67 of the 2011 Act gives the Charity Commission concurrent jurisdiction with the High Court to establish schemes to alter the trusts of charities, including altering their objects *cy-près*. Before sealing a scheme, the Charity Commission must give public notice of its proposal and invite representations to be made within the period specified in the notice. In certain circumstances, the Charity Commission may be satisfied that it is unnecessary to give public notice.
  - If the scheme is to remove a trustee, officer, agent or employee of a charity without their consent, the Charity Commission must, before sealing the scheme, give the individual concerned not less than one month's notice of its proposal (unless that person cannot be found or has no known address in the United Kingdom).
  - Under its risk framework, the Charity Commission will only create *cy-près* schemes to amend a charity's objects under ss. 62 and 67 of the 2011 Act where the trustees cannot amend their purposes under their own powers (with or without Charity Commission consent) or amend their purposes under s. 275(2) of the 2011 Act.
- **Power to authorise dealings with charity property, etc.**: s. 105 of the 2011 Act is exercised by issuing an order to sanction any action proposed or contemplated by the charity which the Charity Commission considers is expedient. This enables the Commission to authorise a particular transaction or compromise, a particular application of property, or to give a more general authority. Under its risk framework, the Charity Commission will only give permission under s. 105 where only it (apart from the court) can confer consent, the matter is outside the trustees' powers and the trustees cannot confer power on themselves under s. 280(2) of the 2011 Act (except in cases of trustee benefit, extreme controversy, conflicts of interest or where other very significant or momentous issues arise).
- **Power to authorise ex gratia payments, etc.**: s. 106 can be used to authorise trustees to waive the charity's right to receive property or to enable the trustees to apply the charity's property in circumstances where they have no power to do so, but they consider that they have a moral obligation. An

example of the former is where a charity is left a substantial legacy in a will in circumstances where family members are left destitute. An example of the latter is where trustees wish to reward a member of staff for their hard work for their charity above and beyond any entitlement in the member of staff's contract of employment. Unless there is a specific power in their charity's governing document authorising such action (which is unlikely), the trustees will have acted in breach of trust and are personally liable to make good any loss to their charity if they take such action without obtaining authorisation from the Charity Commission.

- **Power to give advice and guidance**: s. 110 of the 2011 Act enables the Charity Commission to assist any trustee of a charity who applies in writing for its opinion or advice either on the performance of their duties as a trustee or about how their charity should be properly administered. A trustee who, acting in good faith, follows the Charity Commission's opinion or advice is protected from any breach of trust claim. Although, in recent years, the scope of this power has been extended to enable the Charity Commission to issue advice or guidance about the administration of charities, it is very rare for it to do so. The Charity Commission takes the view that it is the role of the trustees to determine how they should act, whenever possible, taking external advice as necessary. It will only give advice when there is no alternative available.
- **Power to determine membership of charities**: s. 111 of the 2011 Act enables the Charity Commission to make a determination about who the members of a charity are. The power is exercised either on receipt of an application by a charity or in connection with a statutory inquiry. This power may be helpful where a charity has failed to maintain an accurate and/or up-to-date record of its members and is unable to take forward important business (such as amending its governing documents or winding up) without the approval of its membership. Many charity law practitioners all too often come across such situations in practice. Maintaining proper records is essential; rectifying these situations is not the best use of a charity's resources and management time.
- **Powers to preserve charity documents**: this includes accepting documents for safe keeping (s. 111).
- **Power to order an assessment of a solicitor's bill of costs** (s. 112).
- **Power to give directions about dormant bank accounts of charities** (ss. 107–9).
- **Power** to make schemes to establish common investment funds or common deposit funds: concurrent with the High Court) (ss. 96 and 100).

2 Challenging Charity Commission decisions

2.1 Decisions of the Charity Commission can have serious consequences – for example, a decision not to register an organisation as a charity or to remove an organisation from the Central Register of Charities.

2.2 Prior to the implementation of the Charities Act 2006, the only avenues available to challenge formal decisions made by the Charity Commission were either to bring a complaint under the Commission's internal procedures and/ or to mount an appeal to the High Court. This was prohibitively expensive and not an option commonly pursued by charities. To address this lack of effective recourse to the courts, provisions in the Charities Act 2006 (now contained in Part 17 of the 2011 Act) provided a new way to challenge a decision of the Charity Commission: the Charity Tribunal.

2.3 However, on 1 September 2009, the Charity Tribunal was abolished and its jurisdiction transferred to the current system, which comprises the First-Tier Tribunal (Charity) (FTT(C)) and the Upper Tribunal (Tax and Chancery Chamber) (UT(TCC)), together 'the Tribunal'. These changes, introduced by the Tribunals, Courts and Enforcement Act 2007 (TCEA 2007) created a new simplified statutory framework for tribunals.

2.4 The Charity Commission's current guidance on challenging one of its decisions is set out in *Dissatisfied with one of the Commission's decisions: How can we help you?*. This is available from the Charity Commission.

2.5 The current rules regulating the practice and procedure of proceedings before the Tribunal are set out in The Tribunal Procedure (First-Tier Tribunal) (General Regulatory Chamber) Rules 2009 (as amended) (SI 2009/1976) and The Tribunal Procedure (Upper Tribunal) Rules 2008 (as amended)(SI 2008/2698).

2.6 The route to challenge Charity Commission decisions is as follows:

- If possible, first seek a review of the decision under the Charity Commission's internal 'Decision Review' process. This will result in a 'final decision' being issued.
- If this does not result in the outcome required, bring the matter before the FTT(C) (if the matter is within its jurisdiction).
- If grounds for appeal exist and the FTT(C) grants permission, appeal the decision to the UT(TCC).
- If grounds for appeal exist, and the UT(TCC) grants permission, appeal the decision to the Court of Appeal.

2.7 The Decision Review process

2.7.1 The Charity Commission's Decision Review process is set out in *Dissatisfied with one of the Charity Commission's decisions: how can we help you?* This also has a detailed annex, setting out the types of decision that can be reviewed, and the eligible applicants for each of these. The Commission states that a review usually be concluded within a maximum three-month period. Following this process, the Charity Commission will issue a final decision. This is subject to appeal or review by the Tribunal.

2.7.2 The Charity Commission will accept requests for a review within three months of the original decision having been made, although this deadline may be extended in exceptional circumstances where the Charity Commission considers it would be fair to do so. The three months is calculated from the date on which written notification of the original decision was received. The Charity Commission deems written notification to have been received either on the second day after the letter enclosing the decision was sent by first-class post or on the same day if the decision was sent by email before 5.00pm.

2.7.3 The decisions capable of review under this procedure are those made by the Charity Commission within its statutory powers – that is, any decision that is set out in Schedule 6 to the Charities Act and any decision either to exercise or not to exercise a legal power that is not listed in Schedule 6. The primary exception to this rule is that the Commission will not review of a decision to grant consent to a charity (whether or not the type of consent granted is listed in Schedule 6). This is because the Commission has no statutory authority to quash or set these decisions aside. Once consent has been given, only the Tribunal or court can overturn it (depending on the nature of the consent). A decision to refuse consent can be taken to Decision Review because it is still open to the Commission to change its decision.

2.7.4 In addition, the Commission states that it will usually refuse to conduct a review where:

- the decision has already been subject to a Decision Review or has been made after detailed consideration at a senior level;
- the applicant is not a person entitled to request a Decision Review;
- there is a more appropriate procedure available for dealing with the issues raised;
- where the matter is subject to ongoing litigation proceedings; or
- on an initial look at the application the Commission is satisfied that the decision made is correct and a review would serve no real purpose.

2.7.5 The Charity Commission will normally only accept an application for a Decision Review from someone who is eligible to apply to the Tribunal. If the review is not of a matter which is capable of challenge in the Tribunal the Commission will usually only accept an application for review from the charity (or its trustees), the subject of the decision or a person who has a 'sufficient interest in the matter to which the application relates'.

2.7.6 To carry out a Decision Review, the Charity Commission will ask that an online form be completed. This should:

- tell the Commission why the decision is wrong;
- provide the Commission with any new information or evidence that may help it when the decision is reviewed;
- tell the Commission why a different decision is in the best interest of the charity; and
- tell the Commission what the applicant's interest is in the charity and their connection to it.

2.7.7 Reviews are carried out by Commission staff or its board. While some cases reviews are carried out by a single reviewer, other more complex cases reviews are carried out by a panel of reviewers. To ensure that the review is carried out objectively, the person who made the original decision will not be involved in the review.

2.7.8 If the final decision made by the Charity Commission at the end of the Decision Review process is considered unsatisfactory, it may be possible to seek an appeal or review by the Tribunal.

2.8 The Tribunal

2.8.1 The Tribunal is made up of the First-Tier Tribunal (Charities) (FTT(C)) and the Upper Tribunal (Tax and Chancery Chamber) (UT(TCC)). The Upper Tribunal primarily deals with reviews and hears appeals arising from cases dealt with in the First-Tier Tribunal. Not all decisions of the Charity Commission are subject to appeal or review by the Tribunal. The following are some decisions, directions or orders that can be brought before the Tribunal:

- a decision to register, or not to register, an organisation as a charity;
- a decision to remove, or not to remove, a charity from the register;
- a direction that a charity must change its name;
- a decision to instigate a statutory inquiry under s. 46 of the 2011 Act; and
- an order to appoint an interim manager or to remove a trustee, following a statutory inquiry.

2.8.2 The Tribunal's remit does not cover delays by the Charity Commission or poor service. A charity affected in this way will be able to bring a complaint under the Charity Commission's internal procedures and, if the matter is not resolved to the charity's satisfaction, can then either bring it to:

- the Independent Complaints Reviewer (www.icrev.org.uk); and/or
- the Parliamentary Ombudsman (www.ombudsman.org.uk) – such a complaint must be made via a Member of Parliament.

Each of these forums deals with maladministration, such as excessive delay or failure to follow proper procedures; they do not provide an avenue for reviewing or appealing legal decisions.

2.8.3 The Tribunal has power to:

- quash the Charity Commission's original decision;
- remit the matter back to the Charity Commission (with or without a direction to determine the matter in a particular way); or
- substitute its own rulings.

2.8.4 The following parties can, in most cases, bring proceedings before the Tribunal:

- the charity trustees;
- the charity itself; and
- any other person who is or may be affected by the decision.

2.8.5 In addition, the Attorney General, acting as the protector of charities on behalf of the Crown, may bring a case. Both the Charity Commission and the Attorney General may refer questions of law to the Tribunal.

2.8.6 Any party who brings proceedings in the Tribunal must, in the first instance, bear their own costs. However, the Tribunal can order one party to pay the other party's costs if it considers that a party has acted unreasonably in bringing, defending or conducting the proceedings. The Tribunal can also make a 'wasted costs order' where one party has incurred extra costs due to the other party (or their representative) acting improperly, unreasonably or negligently during the proceedings.

2.8.7 In addition, the Tribunal can order the Charity Commission to pay all or part of the other party's costs if it considers that the decision, direction or order that is subject to the proceedings was unreasonable in the first place. Despite calls for one to be created, a fighter's fund has not been set up to assist charities with the cost of bringing matters before the Tribunal. Similarly, the Tribunal has no power to award compensation to charities for losses caused by a decision of the Charity Commission that is subsequently overturned.

2.8.8 Any party can appeal Tribunal decisions to the High Court, with the consent of the Tribunal or of the High Court itself.

2.9 The First-Tier Tribunal (Charities)

2.9.1 The First-Tier Tribunal (Charities) (FTT(C)) is an independent legal body with the power to look again at some of the decisions made by the Commission. It makes up the first level of the Tribunal.

2.9.2 The FTT(C) can determine applications for review and appeals. In determining an application for review, the Tribunal is required to apply the principles that would be applied by the High Court on an application for judicial review. In determining an appeal, the Tribunal is required to consider afresh the decision, direction or order appealed against and may take into account evidence that was not available to the Commission.

2.9.3 The FTT(C) is composed of a principal judge, five judges and seven other members. All members are appointed by the Lord Chancellor following recommendation by the Judicial Appointments Commission. The FTT(C) is administered from Leicester.

2.9.4 If a party wishes to make an application to the Tribunal, the application must be received by the FTT(C) within 42 days of the date on which the notice of the outcome of the Decision Review Process is sent or published. This 42-day period is inclusive of weekends and bank holidays.

2.9.5 Decisions which may be considered by the Tribunal, and who can apply, are listed in Schedule 6 of the Charities Act 2011.

2.9.6 If the FTT(C) does not provide the required result, the FTT(C)'s permission to appeal may be sought, to bring the decision before Upper Tribunal (Tax and Chancery Chamber) (UT(TCC)).

2.9.7 An application for permission to appeal must be sent or delivered to the FTT(C) and received no later than 28 days after the date on which the applicant was sent written reasons for the decision (or any later notification of amendment or correction following a review, or notification that an application for set aside has been unsuccessful).

2.10 Upper Tribunal (Tax and Chancery Chamber) (UT(TCC))

The UT(TCC) hears both appeals against decisions of the FTT(C) and cases or preliminary issues transferred to it by the FTT(C).

2.11 Appealing UT(TCC) decisions

2.11.1 If this does not result in the outcome required, any party has the right to apply for permission to appeal a point of law arising from decisions made by the UT(TCC) to the Court of Appeal. An application for permission to appeal must first be made to the UT(TCC).

2.11.2 The application to appeal must be received by the UT(TCC) within one month of the date on which the applicant was sent written reasons for the decision (or any later notification of amendment or correction following a review, or notification that an application for set aside has been unsuccessful).

2.11.3 The application for permission to appeal must identify the decision to which it relates, the alleged error or errors of law in the decision and state the result the party making the application is seeking (UT(TCC) Rules, r. 44 (7)).

2.11.4 If permission to appeal is refused by the UT(TCC), an application can then be made to the Court of Appeal (TCEA 2007, s. 13).

3 Charity regulation in Scotland and Northern Ireland

3.1 Scotland

3.1.1 Charities in Scotland are regulated by the Office of the Scottish Charity Regulator (OSCR), which was created by the Charities and Trustee Investment (Scotland) Act 2005. That Act sets out the powers and responsibilities of OSCR, as well as defining what a 'charity' is for the purposes of Scottish law. Charities registered in Scotland are required to submit annual returns and accounts to OSCR.

3.1.2 Charities that are registered in England and Wales but which carry out activities in Scotland are also required to register with OSCR. An exception is made, however, if these activities are seen as insignificant or occasional. Charities which are administered or managed from Scotland, occupy land or premises in Scotland, or carry out activities from an office, shop or other business premises are required to register with OSCR. OSCR has published detailed guidance on its website (see www.oscr.org.uk).

3.1.3 The Scottish definition of a 'charity' is similar to the English definition but has some notable differences. Charities required to register in both jurisdictions will have to comply with both definitions and both regulatory regimes.

3.1.4 As a condition of registration in Scotland, OSCR may require charities registered in England and Wales with significant activities in Scotland to make amendments to their governing documents. This has the effect of making all of the charity's property subject to the narrower Scottish charity law test. This may leave charities with a difficult decision to make, either:

- to make the amendments on the basis that being subject to the narrower test will have no effect on their day-to-day operations; or
- to go to the expense (in time and cost) of setting up a separate registered charity in Scotland, registering it there and transferring the relevant part of the charity's current operation.

3.2 Northern Ireland

3.2.1 The Charities Act (Northern Ireland) 2008 modernised and reformed charity law in Northern Ireland, establishing a Charity Commission for Northern Ireland (CCNI). This was the first time Northern Ireland has had a regulator specifically for the charity sector. The first register of charities in Northern Ireland is also being created. English charities operating in Northern Ireland are not currently being registered, but it is expected that a 'parallel register' will be established in due course.

3.2.2 The 2008 Act introduced a new definition of 'charity' and 'charitable purpose' for Northern Ireland, which was an amalgamation of wording from both English and Scots law. CCNI's public benefit guidance is available on the CCNI's website (see www.charitycommissionni.org.uk).

3.2.3 English charities that operate in Northern Ireland will have to prepare a financial statement and a statement of activities every financial year, in a form prescribed by the Department for Social Development. However, CCNI has yet to consult and decide on what the specific charity accounting and reporting requirements for Northern Ireland will be, and so we await further guidance.

B2
Records and filing requirements

1 Introduction

1.1 This chapter looks at the compliance and filing requirements for charities reporting to different regulatory bodies depending on what legal form they take. It also considers the legal requirements regarding stationery and the use of the charity's name.

1.2 All charities that are registered with the Charity Commission have a range of reporting requirements (information that they must regularly provide to the Commission). Charities that are companies also have to meet the reporting requirements of Companies House; those that are community benefit societies must also file certain records with the FCA. Other forms of charities (such as chartered bodies or unincorporated associations) have to meet only the requirements of the Charity Commission (if registered), although there may be other regulators depending on the work of the charity.

2 Charity Commission requirements

2.1 Annual returns to the Charity Commission

2.1.1 All charities with an income above £10,000 (and all CIOs) that are registered with the Charity Commission must complete and submit an annual return to the Charity Commission. However, the level of detail required in the response will depend greatly on the size of the charity. In recent years, the Charity Commission has revised the information that must be provided in the Annual Return on a number of occasions, with the latest revisions being made in 2018. There are a number of new questions asked, some of which were optional for a 2018 annual return but will be mandatory thereafter.

2.1.2 While charities with an income of £10,000 or less in the reporting period (and which are not CIOs) are not required to complete an annual return, they are asked by the Charity Commission to complete an annual update of the information that forms part of the charity's entry on the Register. All charities completing an annual return must also review the information held on the register and confirm that it is correct, before proceeding with the annual return.

2.1.3 All charities with an income above £25,000 must also submit a declaration concerning serious incidents reporting as a part of the annual return (RSI). Effectively, the signatory needs to certify that any such incident occurring in the period has been reported to the Charity Commission.

2.1.4 Charities with an income above £25,000 in the reporting period must submit an annual report and accounts.

2.1.5 The annual return requires a charity to answer a number of questions and many of these answers will be published on the register. From 2018, the Charity Commission now publishes a schedule of all the questions that are asked. This can be found at www.gov.uk/government/news/charity-annual-return-2018. The schedule sets out all the questions; whether the question was new in 2018 or not; what size of charity needs to answer each question, and whether the answer will be published on the public register or not (some of the questions are just for the Charity Commission's own information).

2.1.6 Some of the questions that were introduced in 2018 include:

- questions about working with a professional fundraiser;
- more questions about contracts and grants from local and central government;
- a question on how many of the trustees are directors of a trading subsidiary (if applicable);
- a question on whether any trustee resigned and took up employment with the charity;
- questions about salaries and benefits. The annual return now asks for a breakdown of salaries across income bands, and the amount of total employee benefits for the highest paid member of staff; and
- questions about overseas income and expenditure. Charities are now asked for details of income from overseas. They had previously been asked for a breakdown of expenditure by country. However, now they are also asked questions on methods of transferring money outside the regulated banking system, and about monitoring controls and risk management in relation to this expenditure. These question were optional for the 2018 annual return, but will be mandatory from 2019.

2.1.7 Charities with an income over £500,000 in the reporting period need to do all of the above and must provide more detailed financial information. The information required to complete this section should be available from the annual report and accounts, provided that they have been completed in accordance with

SORP. Having said this, it would be useful for the trustees to be aware of the questions to be answered before finalising the annual report and accounts, so that there is clarity in regard to what information is required. While the annual report and accounts also need to be submitted to the Charity Commission and will then be available to the general public on the Charity Commission's website, some of the answers to these annual return questions are more readily available on the Register of Charities, so it is important that these are handled correctly. In 2018, the Charity Commission undertook research on the accuracy of the financial information provided in annual returns. While larger charities did tend to provide more accurate information than smaller ones, there were still some issues. For charities with incomes over £500,000 in the sample surveyed, the Commission found a 95% accuracy rate for balance sheet figures, but this reduced to just over 80% accuracy for income and expenditure analyses.

2.1.8 It should be noted that although only charities with an income greater than £25,000 must send in their trustees' annual report and accounts to the Commission, all charities, regardless of their level of income, must prepare accounts and make these available to the Commission on request.

2.1.9 Annual returns and the trustees' annual reports and accounts must be completed and submitted within 10 months of the end of the charity's financial year. The Charity Commission encourages charities to file their documents as early as possible after the end of the financial year; it publishes the compliance history of all charities on the Register of Charities. This shows when documents were filed for the past five years, so enables people to see how compliant the charity is in this regard.

2.1.10 Much of the information given in annual updates and annual returns is made available on the Register of Charities, which is open to public inspection at the Charity Commission's office and on its website. The names of the trustees and summary data on the income and expenditure and financial history of the charity are available online, but information on the charity's bank details, trustees' addresses and telephone numbers or dates of birth are not included. Charities should regularly review their register entry to ensure that it is correct and should bear in mind the data that is published when completing their annual report and accounts and the annual return. The Charity Commission considers it one of the duties of a charity trustee to ensure that the information on the register is kept up to date. It was previously the practice in some charities only to update the register on an annual basis, alongside the annual return, but this is no longer an acceptable practice. In addition, for CIOs there is a legal requirement to update the register within 28 days of a relevant change (see section 2.2 on page 142).

2.1.11 Annual returns must now be filed electronically and the Charity Commission no longer provides paper forms. To access the online service you will require the charity registration number and a password. If you do not know the password or need to change it, a new password can be sent to the charity's contact address on request. If you need a new password to file the annual return, ensure that you leave enough time to request it.

2.1.12 The Charity Commission also requests that the annual report and accounts are filed electronically in PDF format. Signatures do not need to appear on the document (provided that they have been signed and that you retain a signed copy). The Charity Commission advises that PDFs are submitted unsigned, to protect the security of the trustees' signatures.

2.1.13 Charities that are also registered in Scotland need to be aware that they must also submit an annual return and a link to the annual report annual accounts to OSCR. These must be submitted within nine months of the year end (and not 10 months as it is for the Charity Commission).

2.2 Other filings with the Charity Commission

2.2.1 The Charity Commission website also allows charities to update their details throughout the year. For charities that are not CIOs, there is no specific legal requirement to inform the Charity Commission of changes in the information held. However, the Charity Commission considers that it a part of the trustees' duties to do so. Also, the fact that this can be done so easily online means that it is good practice to update the details whenever they are amended. The details that are held by the Charity Commission that can be updated online are:

- activities of the charity;
- where the charity operates;
- contact details;
- trustees – name; address, telephone number, email address and date of birth;
- classification – what the charity does; how and to whom;
- financial year;
- main bank or building society details; and
- internet details (e.g. email and website addresses).

2.2.2 A charity will need to notify the Charity Commission if it wants to change its name or if it has amended its constitution (if it can do this without prior approval).

2.2.3 In accordance with the Charitable Incorporated Organisations (General) Regulations 2012 (SI 2012/3012), the trustees of a CIO must notify the Charity

Commission of any changes to information held on the central register within 28 days.

2.2.4 The details held on the register can only be updated electronically. To access the online services you will require the charity registration number and a password (see paragraph 2.1.11).

3 Community benefit societies

3.1 Many charities that are registered as community benefit societies (c) are exempt from registration with the Charity Commission (see Chapter A3, page 61) and therefore do not need to submit an annual return. However, CBSs are regulated by the FCA and there is a requirement to submit annual returns to it. The annual return must be submitted within seven months of the year end; failure to submit a return by the due date is an offence which may result in prosecution. It is the duty of the society's secretary to submit the annual return.

3.2 The annual return for a CBS is made up of two parts. Part 1 comprises form R/IP/AR30, a copy of which is available from the FCA. Part 2 is normally the annual accounts. However, societies not producing accounts to the minimum standard required by the FCA must also complete a supplementary return as Part 2 of the annual return.

3.3 The FCA does not have provision for filing the return electronically in the same way as the Charity Commission does. However, the form can be downloaded and completed digitally before being printed, signed and emailed to the FCA.

3.4 Other than the completion of the annual return, there is no requirement for a CBS to inform the FCA of any changes in its trustees during the year. However, changes to the Rules, including a change of name and change of registered office, must be filed with the FCA. Changes to the Rules will not be effective until they have been registered by the FCA.

4 Company requirements

4.1 Any charity or subsidiary that is a company will also need to fulfil company filing requirements. The legal requirements to file information with Companies House can be divided into annual requirements and event-driven requirements. A company must file its annual report and accounts (see Chapter E2, page 435) and its confirmation statement (see below) with Companies House. In addition, there are legal requirements to notify Companies House about a number of different events or changes (usually within 14 days). These are set out below.

4.2 Confirmation statements: companies

4.2.1 In addition to the requirement to submit an annual return to the Charity Commission, all charitable companies (and subsidiary companies) also need to submit a confirmation statement to Companies House. They need to submit such a statement, confirming that all of the information held by Companies House is correct, at least once each year. A fee of £13 applies (if submitted electronically; it is £40 for filing via a hard copy). The company can make the statement at any time during the year, more than once or every time they file a change with Companies House, but they will only be charged once each year. If the confirmation statement is filed part way through a year, this will impact on the date that the following year's confirmation statement will be due.

4.2.2 The confirmation statement covers:

- the name and number of the company;
- the company type for example, private or public;
- the registered office address of the company;
- the address where the company keeps certain company registers if not at the registered office;
- the principal business activities of the company (which must be stated in accordance with a prescribed classification system based on the Standard Industrial Classification);
- the name and address of the company secretary, where applicable;
- the name, usual residential address, service address; date of birth, nationality and business occupation of all the company's directors;
- the name and address of all persons of significant control, and the nature of that control; and
- the date to which the confirmation statement was made up to (the made-up date).

4.2.3 Unlike with the Charity Commission, the latest date that the confirmation statement is due is not governed by the accounting reference date. The first confirmation statement date is governed the date of the formation of the company. Thereafter, it is determined by the date the last confirmation statement was submitted. While the last confirmation statement date can be changed, this must be done before the due date. A confirmation statement must be filed with the Registrar within 14 days of the date of the last due date.

4.2.4 While a paper statement can be delivered, it is nowadays simpler and cheaper to file a return electronically (see paragraph 4.2.1). However, to do so, both the person filing and the company must be registered for electronic submissions, so allow enough time to do this before the annual return is due. The electronic annual return is simpler to complete as it is based on information that has already been filed which can then be checked and signed off. Companies House used to provide hard copy forms for this, but no longer does, so a paper copy will need to be completely filled in.

4.2.4 The confirmation statement must be be submitted by a trustee / director or the secretary, or a person authorised under s. 270 or s. 274 of the Companies Act 2006.

4.2.5 If the company has share capital, the confirmation statement must also contain information about the issued share capital and details of the shareholders. The filing of changes to the list only is permitted provided that a full list of members is given every three years. This will not apply to charitable companies, which are companies limited by guarantee (with some rare exceptions) but may apply to subsidiary trading companies.

4.3 Change of accounting reference date

The accounting reference date is the date by reference to which the company's financial year is determined. A company's financial year ends on its accounting reference date (e.g. if a company prepares its accounts from 1 April to 31 March its accounting reference date is 31 March). A company's first accounting reference date relates to the date that it was incorporated. It will be the anniversary of the end of the month in which it was incorporated. However, companies can change their accounting reference date and most will want to do so in order to have a more regular date than that which stems from their incorporation date. The change of accounting reference date must be notified to Companies House (Form AA01).

4.4 Change of registered office

All companies must notify Companies House of any change in their registered office. You can change your registered office address by sending a completed Form AD01 to Companies House. The change becomes legally effective only when Companies House has registered the form. A person may validly serve any document on the company at the previously registered address for 14 days after the registration of the form.

4.5 SAIL

All registers may be held at the registered office address, at Companies House (see below) or at a single alternative inspection location (SAIL). Companies House must be notified if a company has set up a SAIL address (Form AD02) or if the SAIL address is moved (Form AD03). A company may have only one SAIL address at a time. Once the SAIL address is set up, a company can move some or all registers by notifying Companies House.

4.6 Change of directors and secretary and their details

Any change of a company's directors or secretaries must be notified to Companies House within 14 days of the change. Form AP01 is for the appointment of a director (AP02 for a corporate director) and AP03 is for the appointment of a secretary (AP04 for a corporate secretary). Form TM01 is for the termination of a director's appointment and TM02 for the termination of a secretary's appointment (resignation, removal, death, etc.). Form CH01 is for a change in details of a director, for example a change of name or new residential address (CH02 for a corporate director, CH03 for a secretary and CH04 for a corporate secretary).

4.7 Allotments of shares

If a company has shares (if it is a trading subsidiary, for example) Companies House must be notified of an allotment of shares within one month of the allotment of shares (Form SH01).

4.8 Change of Articles

4.8 If there is a change to the Articles, the company must send copies of the special resolution passed to change the Articles, or adopt new ones, along with a copy of the revisions to Companies House within 15 days of them being passed by the company. If the company does not comply with this requirement it will commit an offence and could be liable to a civil penalty of £200. This is in addition to any liability to criminal proceedings.

4.9 Mortgages and charges

You must send details of every mortgage or charge created by the company and requiring registration to Companies House within 21 days of its creation (beginning with the day after the date of creation of the charge) (Form MR01).

4.10 Persons of Significant Control

Companies are required to keep a register of persons of significant control (see below). Whenever this register is amended or updated, a company is also required to notify Companies House within 14 days of making a change to the register.

4.11 Submission of documents

4.11.1 If a form or document submitted to the Registrar of Companies has been incorrectly completed or contains an error, the Registrar will normally return the document to the presenter for correction. If, however, a document requiring correction has been scanned (or accepted electronically) before the error is discovered, a director of the company may need to make a statutory declaration explaining the circumstances under which the error was made. This should be submitted to the Registrar for his consideration along with the revised document. Even if the Registrar agrees to file a revised copy of the document, it should be noted that the original document remains on the public record but a note will be placed on the file explaining that the original document has been corrected. In some cases it is possible to submit a From RP01 - Replacement of document not meeting requirements for proper delivery. However, you can only use this form as a replacement for one as either not properly delivered or contained unnecessary material. You cannot use this form to change information in a previously filed document, or filed under Section 25 of the Companies Act 2006 (company charges).

4.11.2 When you are submitting documents, such as annual accounts, take care that they do not contain shading or other formatting because the Registrar cannot make an acceptable copy of them. Companies House has specifications and requirements for filling in forms and completing other documents which have to be sent to the Registrar. The key point to remember is that, although colour-printed glossy accounts are attractive for members and for general publicity, the Registrar requires black print on white A4 paper with a matt finish – a typed printer's proof is ideal provided it has the necessary signatures.

4.12 Electronic filing with Companies House

4.12.1 Filing can still be done via hard copy, but all of the forms to be used to submit information to Companies House are available online on its website (www.companies-house.gov.uk). The forms may be completed on screen or downloaded in PDF format before being signed, dated and returned by post. Where there are fees for filing, they tend to be higher for filing a hard copy.

4.12.2 Companies House provides an electronic filing service (WebFiling) which may be used to file the following:

Some annual accounts (dormant company accounts; audit exempt full accounts, and audit exempt abbreviated accounts)

CS01	–	Confirmation statement
AA01	–	Change of accounting reference date
AA02	–	Dormant company accounts
AD01	–	Change of situation or address of registered office
AP01	–	Appointment of director
AP02	–	Appointment of corporate director
AP03	–	Appointment of secretary
AP04	–	Appointment of corporate secretary
TM01	–	Terminating appointment as director
TM02	–	Terminating appointment as secretary
CH01	–	Change of particulars for director

CH02	–	Change of particulars for corporate director
CH03	–	Change of particulars for secretary
CH04	–	Change of particulars for corporate secretary
AD02	–	Notification of single alternative inspection location (SAIL)
AD03	–	Change of location of the company records to the single alternative inspection location (SAIL)
AD04	–	Change of location of the company records to the registered office
SH01	–	Return of allotment of shares
SH01	–	Return of allotment of shares
EN02	–	Elect to keep directors' residential addresses on the central register
EH03	–	Elect to keep register of secretaries information on the central register
EH04	–	Elect to keep register of people with significant control (PSC) information on the central register
MR01	–	Register particulars of a charge
PSC01	–	Give notice of individual person with significant control
PSC02	–	Give notice of relevant legal entity with significant control
PSC07	–	Give notice of ceasing to be a person with significant control
PSC08	–	Give notice of PSC statements

4.12.3 To use WebFiling you must first register for a security code (which is emailed to you) and then register for an authentication code for the company (which is posted to the company's registered office address). If you are filing for more than one company, you will be issued with one security code (which is personal to you) then a different authentication code for each company.

4.12.4 When filing the forms for the appointment of a director or secretary electronically, the company must also make a statement of truth that the person has consented to be a director/company secretary. The Registrar of Companies will write to directors following their appointment. Directors will be able to object to their names being on the public register if they assert that they are not, in fact, a director of the company. The letter from the Registrar will also include details of directors' general statutory duties. It is always advisable to obtain a separate signed consent to act from a newly appointed director, which should also authorise the company to use the information supplied by the individual for filing purposes.

4.12.5 Companies House usually files documents that are submitted in this way very quickly. However, electronically filed documents are covered by the same five-day processing targets as paper documents. This should be taken into account when filing documents (such as confirmation statements) close to a deadline. All electronically filed documents are acknowledged by an acceptance or rejection message being emailed to the sender.

4.13 Protected Online Filing (PROOF) scheme

This scheme helps to protect companies against false filings. The Protected Online Filing (PROOF) scheme aims to provide added security for companies filing documents. While paper forms (such as those changing directors or the registered office) need to be signed by a director or secretary, Companies House does not check the authenticity of those signatures. This can place a company at risk of fraud. Companies can now elect to join the online filing scheme, which improves security by using passwords, confidential authentication codes and recognised e-mail addresses. If a company also decides to sign up to the PROOF scheme, Companies House will only accept specific statutory forms electronically using its WebFiling or electronic filing services. Companies House will not accept forms that can be submitted electronically on paper once a company has joined the PROOF scheme, unless the company and its directors specifically authorise it to do so by submitting a consent form.

5 Registers

5.1 A charity must keep adequate records just to ensure that it is well administered. Even if there are no legal requirements to be fulfilled, it is of core importance to know who the trustees are and were; who the members are and were; and what decisions have been taken by the trustees during the charity's existence. Charitable companies are the most heavily governed in terms of the legal requirements for records and registers, but all charities need to keep records to ensure that they can work effectively.

5.2 There are two general points to note with regard to the registers that will be kept by the charity. The first key element with regard to registers is that they are historical documents, (they should not just reflect the present position). A register that just records the current trustees is not sufficient: it must also include the past trustees and the date that they ceased to be trustees. When a trustee's term ceases, the termination date should be entered on the register of trustees, but the entry should remain. You should be able to look at the register of trustees and ascertain who they were during any given period.

5.3 The second key point to note is that care needs to be taken in regard to the security of the registers. They need to be kept in such a way that data cannot be deleted or changed without record. These are legal requirements for charitable companies and CIOs, but it is important for all charities that there is security over their registers. This is a matter to consider in deciding what format to use to retain registers. It means that for many charities a hard copy register may be preferable to a computerised register, as most computerised software can amend or delete data without this being shown. However, a bound book, will easily show if a page has been removed or if details have been deleted or amended.

5.4 Registers in charities that are not companies or CIOs

The requirements for registers for a charity that is not also a company or a CIO will be set out in the constitution and will depend on the type of charity. For a charity that is established under a trust deed, it is quite common that no registers are required. Even so, it may still be advisable to keep a register of trustees just to assist in the record-keeping of the charity. For membership charities, the most common requirement is for a register of members to be maintained. The constitution may also require a register of trustees to be kept and sometimes a register of secretaries, mirroring company law. The right of access to registers is discussed further in section 5.13 on page 157. However, it should be noted now that for charities that are not companies, there is no legal right of access to the registers by the members or by the general public unless this is specified in the constitution.

5.5 Registers in CIOs

5.5.1 The Charitable Incorporated Organisations (General) Regulations 2012 state that every association CIO must keep a register of members and a register of charity trustees. Every foundation CIO must keep a register of charity trustees (who are also the members of the CIO). The records can be kept in electronic form, but must be able to be reproduced in hard copy.

5.5.2 The register of trustees must contain:

- the name of the trustee, including any former name or names;
- the service address of the trustee (this can be the principal office of the CIO);
- the date on which the person became a charity trustee; and
- if relevant, the date on which the person ceased to be a trustee.

5.5.3 If a register of members must be kept, this must contain:

- the name of the member;
- the service address of the member (this can be the principal office of the CIO);
- the date on which the person became a member;
- if the CIO has more than one class of member, a statement of which class the member belongs to; and
- if relevant, the date on which the person ceased to be a member.

5.5.4 If a CIO only has one member, the register of members must include a statement to that effect. If the number of members increases to two or more, the register of members must show the date on which the number of members increased. If the CIO has more than 50 members, the register must be kept in an indexed form. Any entry relating to a former member of a CIO may be removed from the register of members after the expiration of 10 years from the date on which that person ceased to be a member.

5.5.5 A CIO also has a legal requirement to keep these registers up-to-date. The Regulations state that the CIO must make an alteration to the register of members or register of charity trustees within 28 days of the date on which the event necessitating the alteration occurs.

5.5.6 In addition, a CIO must keep:

- a record of appointments of officers made by the charity trustees;
- proceedings at general meetings of the CIO;
- meetings of the charity trustees and committees of charity trustees including the names of the trustees at the meeting, the decisions made at the meeting and, where appropriate, the reason for the decision; and
- a record of decisions made by the charity trustees otherwise than in meetings.

These records must be kept for a minimum of six years from the date of the meeting, resolution or appointment. The records can be kept in electronic form, but you must be able to reproduce them in hard copy form.

5.6 Registers in charitable companies

5.6.1 The Companies Act 2006 is even more prescriptive about the registers that must be kept; what information they must contain; how they are kept and the rights of public access to the registers. The Companies Act 2006 requires every company to keep the following:

- a register of members (s. 113);
- a register of directors (s. 162);
- a register of directors' residential addresses (s. 163); and
- a register of secretaries (s. 275).

It is now also a legal requirement that a company maintains a register of register of people with significant control (PSC).

5.6.2 It was previously a requirement that all companies kept a register of charges. However, this requirement was abolished for charges created on or after 6 April 2013. Companies registered from that date are not required to have the register. The keeping of this register is still compulsory for all companies created up until 6 April 2013, even though many companies had no entries in it. Charges created before 6 April 2013 have to be entered in it.

5.6.3 In a charitable company the directors are the trustees, so a register of directors or of directors' residential addresses is a register of trustees or of trustees' residential addresses.

5.7 Register of members

5.7.1 Section 113 of the Companies Act 2006 states that the following information must be held on the register of members:

- the names and addresses of the members;
- the date on which each person was registered as a member; and
- the date at which any person ceased to be a member.

5.7.2 If the company has a share capital (this may apply to a trading subsidiary), there must be entered in the register a statement of the shares held by each member, distinguishing each share by its number (as long as the share has a number) and, where the company has more than one class of issued shares, by its class and the amount paid or agreed to be considered as paid on the shares of each member.

5.7.3 If the company does not have a share capital but has more than one class of member (as is the case in some companies limited by guarantee), the names and addresses of the members must be entered in the register along with a statement of the class to which each member belongs.

5.7.4 While statutory registers are historic documents, entries relating to former members may be removed from the register 10 years after the date on which they ceased to be a member (ss. 121 and 128). However, a copy of any details that were included in the register immediately before 6 April 2008 and that are removed from the register after that date must be retained by the company until 6 April 2018, or if earlier, 20 years after the member ceased to be a member.

5.7.5 If the register is not self-indexing and contains more than 50 names, it must be accompanied by an index of the members.

5.7.6 If there is only one member (as is commonly the case for subsidiary companies) the register of members must contain a statement to this effect.

5.8 Register of directors

5.8.1 Section 163 of the Companies Act 2006 requires that a company's register of directors (the trustees in a charitable company) must contain the following information (SI 2007/3495, Sch. 4, para. 2, as amended by SI 2008/674, Sch. 3, para. 6):

- name and any former name of the director;
- a service address (and this may be stated to be 'the company's registered office');
- the country or state (or part of the UK) in which they are usually resident;
- nationality;
- business occupation (if any); and
- date of birth.

5.8.2 It is not necessary for the register to contain particulars of a former name in the case of a peer or an individual normally known by a British title; nor in the case of any person, where the former name was changed or disused before the person attained the age of 16 years, or has been changed or disused for 20 years or more.

5.8.3 If a director is a body corporate, or a firm, there are particular requirements as to the details that must appear on the register.

5.8.4 Under the Companies Act 1985, the requirement was for a director's residential address to be kept on the register. Now, a service address is to be used instead. As there is a right of public access to the register of directors a service address can provide privacy for the directors. This means that directors can choose not to make their residential addresses public, without the need for a confidentiality order.

5.8.5 Although it is not specified as a requirement, the register of directors should also include, for each director, the date on which they became a director and the date on which they ceased to be a director.

5.8.6 It should be noted that there is also a legal requirement (CA 2006, ss. 228–229) for all companies to allow members to inspect and obtain copies of directors' service contracts. However, this requirement is probably of very limited application to charitable companies, where the vast majority of trustees and, therefore directors, will be voluntary.

5.9 Register of directors' residential addresses

Section 165 of Companies Act 2006 provides that a company must also keep a register of directors' residential addresses. The register must state the usual residential address of each of the company's directors. The requirement to keep such a register applies even when the register of directors only has the director's residential addresses as their service addresses. Section 165 of the Companies Act 2006 states that if a director's usual residential address is the same as their service address (as stated in the company's register of directors) the register of directors' residential addresses need only contain an entry to that effect. The register will still need to be kept.

5.10 Register of secretaries

If the charitable company has a secretary, it should maintain a register of secretaries that includes their name and address. Unlike the register of directors, the addresses of secretaries have never needed to be residential addresses, so there is no need for a separate register of residential addresses. As with the register of directors, it should also include the date the person was appointed as the secretary and the date on which they ceased to be the secretary.

5.11 Register of people with significant control (PSC)

One of the key changes introduced by the Small Business, Enterprise and Employment Act 2015 was the introduction of a requirement to keep a register of people who have significant control, or PSCs, over the company. This information also needs to be filed at Companies House (see above). PSCs are defined as individuals (including legal entities) who directly or indirectly own or control more than 25% of voting rights or shares (for share companies) in the company; individuals (including legal entities) who directly or indirectly have control over the appointment and removal of the majority of the company's board of directors; or individuals who otherwise have significant influence over the company. This definition means that PSCs will need to be registered for wholly owned trading subsidiaries; companies where certain parties have rights to appoint the majority of the board members; and companies with fewer than four members. A register must be maintained even if the company has no PSCs. It will just have no entries. The information that must be kept on the register is similar to the register of directors. It includes:

- name;
- date of birth;
- nationality;
- country, state or part of the UK where the PSC usually lives;
- service address
- usual residential address (which must not be disclosed when making your register available for inspection or providing copies of the PSC register);
- the date that they became a PSC in relation to the company; and
- which conditions for being a PSC are met (i.e. what makes them a person of significant control).

5.12 Location and format of registers

5.12.1 If the charity is a company, there are legal requirements as to where the registers are kept. The Charitable Incorporated Organisations (General) Regulations 2012 state that a CIO must keep the registers available for inspection at its principal office as it appears on the Register of Charities or, where the charity trustees pass a resolution to that effect, at any other address specified in the resolution. For other charities, the location of the registers may be a requirement of the constitution. The Companies Act 2006 prescribes where the registers of companies are to be kept. It states that:

- the register of directors and secretaries and the register of charges (together with copies of any instrument creating any charge) must be kept at the registered office; and
- the register of members must be kept either at the registered office or at some other place within the country of registration (England and Wales or Scotland) where the register is made up.

However, if the registers are not to be kept at the registered office at all times they may be kept at a SAIL. A company must notify Companies House if it sets up a SAIL address or if the SAIL address is moved; a company may have only one SAIL address at a time. Once the SAIL address is set up, the company can move some or all of the registers to the SAIL address by notifying Companies House.

5.12.2 In addition, since 2016, private companies, (which includes all charitable companies), now have the option of keeping registers at Companies House. When a company exercises this option it means that when it is filing a new appointment or a change of details with Companies House, it is effectively also updating its register. There is no need for a separate register to be kept (although the register maintained up until the date that the company exercised this option will need to be retained.) All the information currently available for inspection on the company register would then be publicly available as the public register.

5.12.3 Holding the registers at Companies House could seem like a very good option for many charities and will probably be very useful for smaller charities. However, it needs to be remembered that to do so usually requires the consent of those affected. The options are as follows.

Register of members:

- A company can, on incorporation, agree for the register to be kept in this way, by all of its subscribers agreeing.
- If the company is already incorporated, it can hold its members' register at Companies House, but only if all of its members agree.

Register of persons with significant control:

- Again, its retention at Companies House can be agreed at incorporation.
- After incorporation a company can elect to hold at Companies House but only if has given notice to all of the persons on the register at least 14 days before the date of the election and none of them have objected in that time.

Registers of directors, directors' residential addresses, and the register of secretaries:

- A company can elect at any time to have these registers held at Companies House and there is not the same need for complete consent. This means that the board can vote by a majority to keep these registers in this way.

5.12.4 The options of Companies House holding the registers for directors, secretaries and PSCs are much more useful for charitable companies that in regard to the register of members. As well as the difficulties re obtaining consent is the fact that, for a company limited by guarantee, deciding to hold the register of members at Companies House would mean a bigger change. Shareholding companies are currently required to provide the names of their shareholders to Companies House annually. There is not the same requirement for CLGs: holding the register of members at Companies House would mean providing this information to Companies House on moving the register over to it, and then updating it every time there was a change. This would require additional work for the charity. Holding its own register of members is probably simpler.

5.12.5 When a company holds its own registers, or holds them at a SAIL, the statutory registers and books can be kept in either electronic or hard copy form. However, there are requirements that must be met for companies regarding the security of the registers which may make hard copy form a better option for most charitable companies. Section 1138 of the Companies Act requires that where company records are kept otherwise than in bound books, adequate precautions must be taken to guard against falsification, and to facilitate the discovery of falsification. If a hard copy is kept, bound books (and loose-leaf registers) are available from most legal stationers. A bound book is the most secure format; if the register is not kept in this format, adequate precautions must be taken. As a basic measure, the registers should be kept in a secure cabinet to which access is restricted.

5.12.6 It is also possible for statutory registers and books to be kept on computer or in other non-legible form provided that adequate precautions are taken to guard against falsification and facilitating their discovery and, in addition, that they are capable of being reproduced in legible hard copy form (s. 1135(2)).

5.12.7 If the charitable company has a large membership, it may be preferable for it to keep the register of members on computer. However, any database or other software used for this purpose must also provide adequate security for such data. If such a database is also to act as the statutory register of members it is important to ensure that:

- the information kept includes all the data necessary for a statutory register of members;

- the register is kept in a secure form and there is adequate protection against the deletion or amendment of data without a record being kept; and
- if it is a membership database that is kept for wider purposes, there must be consideration of the wider data held. If the database is also likely to hold data that is not part of the statutory register this needs to be considered. There is no right of public inspection over such data and so it is important to ensure that the statutory data can be extracted and made available for inspection in such a way that other data held is not revealed.

5.12.8 If non-statutory information is kept in the register itself, it must be held back from any copy available for public inspection. To provide this information would probably be a breach of the Data Protection Act 2018. Accordingly, charities should ensure that they are able to remove any non-statutory elements of the information contained in their register of members.

5.12.9 Charitable companies with a smaller membership may actually find it easier to maintain the register by manual methods using standardised bound books or loose-leaf printed sheets obtainable from law stationers. It is unlikely that a standard computer program will contain the security elements required, so whilw it may seem simpler to keep an electronic copy, this could cause difficulties in meeting the legal obligations regarding security if the register needs to be relied upon as evidence. If an electronic copy is maintained, it is advisable to print out and retain a hard copy record every time the register is updated. It will effectively be the hard copy that is the register.

5.13 Inspection of the registers

5.13.1 One important reason for keeping registers accurate and up-to-date is that they are often public documents. The registers of charitable companies are open to inspection by any member of the public, as the Companies Act gives a right of inspection for all (with the exception of the register of directors' residential addresses). There are also rights of inspection for CIO registers (see section 5.13.7).

5.13.2 A company's register of the directors and secretaries is available for inspection by any member of the company without charge and by any other person on payment of a prescribed fee.

5.13.3 In a company, the register of members (and any index that is also maintained, see above) is also open to inspection by any member free of charge or by any other person on payment of such fee as may be prescribed. Any person may also require a copy of a company's register of members, or of any part of it, on payment of such fee as may be prescribed.

5.13.4 While this may seem to be a very wide right, it should be noted that the Companies Act 2006 tightened up access to the register of members and the provision for making copies of it. Many company members are not happy about the right to public access and companies have felt uncomfortable about giving such wide access in certain situations. Under these new provisions, access can be restricted to requests that are for 'a proper purpose'. A person wishing to inspect or obtain copies of the register of members must make a request to the company, containing the following information:

(a) in the case of an individual, his name and address;
(b) in the case of an organisation, the name and address of an individual responsible for making the request on behalf of the organisation;
(c) the purpose for which the information is to be used; and
(d) whether the information will be disclosed to any other person, and if so, their name and address (or, if that person is an organisation, the name and address of an individual responsible for receiving the information on its behalf) and the purpose for which the information is to be used.

5.13.5 Within five working days of receiving the request the company must either comply with it or apply to the court to prevent access. If the court considers that the request has not been made 'for a proper purpose' it will direct the company not to comply with it and may award costs against the person making the request. Furthermore, if the court considers that further requests for a similar purpose are likely to be made (whether or not made by the same person) the court may give an overall direction that the company is not to comply with any such requests. However, if the court does not direct the company not to comply with the request, or the application to the court is discontinued, the company must then immediately comply with the request.

5.13.6 The Companies Act 2006 gives no guidance on the meaning of the term 'proper purpose' – that is for the courts to determine. However the ICSA has issued a Guidance Note, *Access to the Register of Members: The Proper Purpose Test*. This gives an analysis of matters that may in practice be reasonably considered to be proper or improper purposes and is likely to be of assistance in such scenarios.

5.13.7 The Charitable Incorporated Organisations (General) Regulations 2012 sets out the rights of inspection for CIO registers and records. They state the following:

- **For a register of members**: a member or trustee is entitled on request to inspect or to be provided with a copy of all or part of the register of members as long as the request is made for the purposes of carrying out their duties as a charity trustee or as a member of the CIO; or the request is in regard to their own entry on the register. No-one else is entitled to request access to the register other than in circumstances relating to the winding up of the CIO and for the purposes of recovering a member's contribution.

- **For the register of trustees**: any person, including a member of the public, is entitled to inspect or to be provided with a copy of all or part of the register. The charity can require a reasonable fee, except that a fee cannot be charged to a member or charity trustee when the request is made for the purposes of carrying out their duties as a charity trustee or member of the CIO or the request is in regard to their own entry on the register.

5.14 Other registers and records

5.14.1 There are two other types of register that it is common for a charity to retain, although there is no statutory requirement to do so:

- a register of sealing (see Chapter D4 on page 377); and
- a register of trustees' interests.

5.14.2 While there is no statutory requirement to keep such registers it should be noted that if they are kept, there may be occasions when they should be regarded as subsets of the minutes. If either register is used as a means of recording matters that would usually be minuted and referred to in this way, the register should be retained for the same period as the minutes.

5.14.3 It should also be noted that, while there is no requirement to keep a register of trustees' interests, it is a recommendation of the Charity Governance Code that registers of interests, hospitality and gifts are kept and made available to stakeholders.

5.14.4 A charity will also be required to keep other statutory records. A charity that has employees will be required to keep records regarding Pay As You Earn (PAYE), National Insurance, pensions and employment records. Charities must also keep records regarding health and safety, insurance and VAT (if VAT registered). There may also be legal requirements to keep records depending on the nature of the charity's work. There will be a range of inspection rights for such records, but they will generally be open to inspection by both regulatory and fiscal authorities.

6 Minutes

6.1 We deal with meetings in a separate chapter, but here we will discuss the minutes of meetings as they are an important record for the charity.

6.2 Minutes are sometimes thought about as a short-term record – a means of quickly recording the decisions taken and the actions that are necessary. All minutes can operate in this way and for some forms of meeting, such as informal management meetings, a short action sheet is all that is required. However, for the formal meetings of the charity (those of its board, its committees and its general meetings) the minutes will also need to provide a longer-term record of the decisions taken and the reasons for that decision. For this reason, the minutes of such meetings may need to be fuller. A short action note can be useful for the weeks following a meeting, but whether it will stand the test of time is a different matter. A formal minute needs to be readable and clear as a stand alone document, and it needs to be able to make sense to someone who may not have been associated with the charity at the time of the meeting and who reads it for the first time a number of years after the meeting took place.

6.3 For all charities, the keeping of minutes of the board, the general meetings and committees will often be a requirement of its constitution. It is also recommended that such records are kept for the lifetime of the charity. If you think about the work of a charity, and the role and responsibilities of its trustees, you can begin to see why it is important to keep such records. Say, for example, that the trustees took a decision that entailed some risk for the charity. They took the decision under professional advice, and after full consideration of the risks and the benefits. If the charity then suffers a loss as a result of that decision, there may be a possibility of action against the trustees for a breach of trust. If no minute has been retained of their decision making then there will be no evidence that they gave the matter full and proper consideration. However, a minute that records the advice received, the consideration of the risks and the benefits and the reasoning behind the decisions could provide protection for the trustees by showing that they had behaved properly.

6.4 If the charity is a company, there is also a legal requirement that:

- minutes must be kept of all general meetings for 10 years (s. 355);
- minutes must be kept of all board meetings, and of board committee meetings, for 10 years (s. 248); and
- records of all written resolutions of the board must also be kept for 10 years (s. 248), as must all records of written resolutions of the members, also for 10 years (s. 355).

6.5 It the charity is a CIO, the Charitable Incorporated Organisations (General) Regulations 2012 state that the CIO must keep the following records:

- appointments of officers made by the charity trustees;
- proceedings at general meetings of the CIO;
- meetings of the charity trustees and committees of charity trustees, including:

- the names of the trustees at the meeting,
- the decisions made at the meetings, and
- where appropriate, the reason for the decision;
- decisions made by the charity trustees otherwise than in meetings.

These records must all be kept for a minimum of six years from the date of the meeting, resolution or appointment.

6.6 Although the legal requirement is for minutes of companies to be kept for 10 years, and for CIOs for six years, it is recommended practice to retain them for the life of the charity. In addition, it may be necessary to retain agenda papers if these are necessary to understand the minutes. For example, if a minute says that a policy was agreed as set out in a paper, that paper also needs to be retained. Therefore, while it may seem cumbersome at the time to include reference to such matters in full in the minutes, or by attaching appendices, it is likely to be easier to do this than having to store all of the papers for the meeting for the life of the minutes.

6.7 Although the Companies Act 2006 makes no provision for the location of board minutes or their inspection by anyone other than the auditors, under common law a director has a right to inspect them. A member of a company also has the right to inspect the minutes of general meetings. Members, or the general public, have no right to inspect board or committee minutes unless this is given to them by the constitution. For a CIO, a member has the right to inspect the record of members' decisions, free of charge, or to obtain a copy on the payment of a reasonable fee.

6.8 If a register is used to record details of documents approved for sealing by the board, instead of recording full details in the minutes, that register should be treated as a subset of the relevant minutes. The same would also be true of any register used to record directors' declarations of interest in transactions, if those declarations were not recorded in full in the relevant minutes.

6.9 Minutes checklist

It is recommended that every set of minutes contains:

- the name of the charity;
- the type of meeting;
- the date and time the meeting was held;
- apologies for absence;
- the names of those present, including in what capacity they attended (such as trustee, adviser and so on) and for what items on the agenda;
- the name of the chair;

- declarations of interest, or a reference to declarations made in a register of interests, and details of how any conflict of interest is handled (such as the trustee leaving the room);
- the approval of, and any changes made to, minutes of a previous meeting;
- a summary of any matters arising from the previous minutes which are not dealt with as a separate item of business;
- a summary of the discussion on each item of business including, where appropriate, the reasons for the decision and the precise wording of any resolution passed;
- the action required, and the names of the people who are responsible for the action; and
- the date, time and venue of the next meeting.

6.10 The minutes should also record the wording of any resolution passed. Some charities also record a proposer and seconder (if the resolution has been handled in this way) and the details of who voted for and against the resolution. However, it is sufficient that only the result of the vote is shown. The numbers voting for or against the resolution does not need to be shown, unless required by the constitution. There may be occasions when a trustee requests that their dissent or disagreement to a resolution be recorded in the minutes. If so, it should be recorded, although it should be noted that the trustee still shares responsibility for that decision.

6.11 It is advisable for the minutes to include a summary of the discussion on each item of business and the information upon which the decision was based. The minutes should show what matters the trustees considered in making the decision, and the reasoning behind it.

6.12 A minute book needs to be used to keep a copy of all the original minutes as signed by the chair of the meeting (or the next meeting). Minute books can be in the form of either a bound or loose-leaf volume. If a loose-leaf volume is kept, each page should be signed or initialled by the chair. The minutes and any appendices, or explanatory notes, should be numbered to ensure that any lost or missing pages can be identified. The minute book must be kept in a safe and secure place.

6.13 Charitable companies and CIOs are permitted to retain their statutory books on computer. Therefore copies of minutes can be stored on a computer, but see section 7 regarding the issue of the minutes as evidence.

6.14 It is normal practice for the minutes to be approved by the subsequent meeting before they are signed. Minutes are usually approved at the following meeting of the board or committee and then signed by the chair of that meeting.

It does not matter if that chair did not chair the meeting that was minuted, or even if the members of the meeting approving the minutes are different from the members who attended the meeting that was minuted (for example, if the board or committee membership has changed in the interim).

6.15 For general meetings, the minutes can again be signed by the chair of the meeting or the subsequent meeting. In this case, it is usually advisable for the chair of the meeting to sign them when they are drafted, rather than them awaiting the next general meeting for approval and signature. Common practice is to present the minutes to the next board meeting after the AGM to get them approved before signing, rather than waiting until the next AGM.

7 Minutes as evidence

7.1 Minutes can be authenticated by the chair of the meeting or by the chair of the next meeting by their signature and are evidence of the proceedings at the meeting. For charitable companies or CIOs minutes signed by the chair of the meeting at which the business was transacted or by the chair of the next succeeding meeting (or by the secretary in the case of resolutions of members) are evidence of the proceedings. When minutes have been signed in this way, the meeting is deemed to have been duly convened and held and the proceedings duly transacted unless the contrary is proved (CA 2006, ss. 249 and 356; Charitable Incorporated Organisations (General) Regulations 2012, reg. 382).

7.2 The same issues arises with regard to the keeping of minutes as for registers and the question as to whether they should be in electronic or hard copy form. A charity may choose to keep its minute books in computerised form; however, this is likely to reduce their value as evidence. If minutes are tendered in legal proceedings as evidence of the proceedings of a meeting, their evidential value could be undermined if there is any doubt as to whether they were signed by the chair. If such questions are raised and it is not possible to produce an original signed copy, the company may be required to provide additional evidence as to the assertions of fact made in the minutes. As an alternative, minutes may be kept in computerised form without necessarily prejudicing their evidential value if they are signed by the chair using an electronic signature (as defined in the Electronic Communications Act 2000). However, the type of electronic signature applied may have a bearing on the weight given by the courts to the minutes. A third option is to scan manually signed minutes for retention in computerised form as a PDF and then to destroy the originals. If this option is chosen the PDF must be protected from further amendment in some way. There is a dearth of judicial authority on the evidential value of such records. Until the law is clarified further, it is only possible to provide general guidelines and it is possible that such records will still not have the weight in court of original signed minutes. However, the wording of The Civil Evidence Act 1995 implies that an original document is not the only admissible evidence in a civil court. Electronic copies of documents are acceptable as long as their integrity can be shown. If a charity wants to retain its minutes in this way, care will need to be taken (for example, proper systems should be followed and written evidence of the destruction of the original and of identification of the copy must always be preserved). If a charity is considering storing documents electronically, it should note that the British Standards Institute (BSI) has published a standard on electronic records (*BS 10008:2014 Evidential weight and legal admissibility of electronic information*).

7.3 Although signed minutes are *prima facie* evidence of the proceedings, they may be set aside by the court if inaccuracies can subsequently be established. No alterations should be made to minutes except to correct obvious errors. This should be done before signature with the alterations initialled by the chair. Once signed, minutes may not be altered and any subsequent revisions found to be necessary should be dealt with by an amending minute at a subsequent meeting.

8 Electronic and microfilm records

8.1 If the charity chooses to keep its statutory registers and records in computerised form, there are commercially available software packages that enable this to be done. However, these packages are usually only appropriate for charitable companies rather than charities that take on other legal forms. Even if the charity is a company, they may not always be designed for CLGs. If a suitable package is found, it is likely to be of use only to a charity with a large membership: in this scenario, it is also more likely that the charity will have a membership database set up for different purposes. The importance may therefore be in ensuring that this database can also act as a Register of Members.

8.2 Increasingly, legislation and regulatory practice not only allows records to be created and stored on a computer, but also allows electronic copies of records to be kept instead of the originals for regulatory purposes (both the Charity Commission and Companies House now provide for information to be filed electronically). There are still several important areas where original paper copies must be kept or where they may be preferable for evidential reasons. However, these are fast becoming the exception rather than the rule.

8.3 It is important to note that, although documents stored electronically can be tendered as evidence in legal proceedings, they may not always carry the same weight as the paper original. For example, a scanned copy of a document signed under hand will not necessarily carry the same weight as the original when seeking to determine whether a signature is genuine (see paragraph 7.2).

9 Accounting records

9.1 Charities have a legal obligation to maintain accounting records. The Charity Commission defines accounting records as: 'the trustees' records of the financial transactions undertaken by the charity from which the annual statements of account are required to be prepared for each financial year.' It goes on to state that: 'the term covers any books (including computer records) in which transactions and events from day to day are entered, together with all the relevant invoices, receipts, vouchers and other associated documentation' (CC15b, *Charity Reporting and Accounting: The Essentials*).

9.2 The source of the legal duty to keep accounting records depends on whether the charity is a company. All charities that are not companies are governed by Part 8 of the Charities Act 2011. Charities registered under the Companies Acts are governed by s. 386 of the Companies Act 2006.

9.3 Part 8 (s. 130) of the Charities Act 2011 states that:

1. The charity trustees of a charity shall ensure that accounting records are kept in respect of the charity which are sufficient to show and explain all the charity's transactions, and which are such as to:
   (a) disclose at any time, with reasonable accuracy, the financial position of the charity at that time; and
   (b) enable the trustees to ensure that, where any statements of accounts are prepared by them under s. 132(1) below, those statements of accounts comply with the requirements of regulations under section 132(1).
2. The accounting records shall in particular contain:
   (a) entries showing from day to day all sums of money received and expended by the charity, and the matters in respect of which the receipt and expenditure takes place; and
   (b) a record of the assets and liabilities of the charity.

9.4 In accordance with this Act, the trustees have a duty to maintain the accounting records for at least six years from the end of the financial year of the charity in which they are made. If the charity ceases to exist, the obligation to preserve the accounting records for six years shall continue to be discharged by the last charity trustees of the charity, unless the Commissioners consent in writing to the records being destroyed or otherwise disposed of.

9.5 CIOs should also note that they have a legal duty in regard to accounting records if there is a transfer to a new CIO. The charity trustees of the old CIO must, on registration of the new CIO, transfer the relevant accounting records to the charity trustees of the new CIO. The charity trustees of a new CIO must preserve the transferred records for at least six years from the end of the financial year in which the records were made.

9.6 Charitable companies are bound by s. 386 of the Companies Act 2006, which states that every company must keep adequate accounting records and that:

> ...
>
> Adequate accounting records means records that are sufficient:
> (a) to show and explain the company's transactions;
> (b) to disclose with reasonable accuracy, at any time, the financial position of the company at that time; and
> (c) to enable the directors to ensure that any accounts required to be prepared comply with the requirements of this Act (and, where applicable, of Article 4 of the IAS Regulation);
>
> ...
>
> **3.** Accounting records must, in particular, contain:
> (a) entries from day to day of all sums of money received and expended by the company and the matters in respect of which the receipt and expenditure takes place; and
> (b) a record of the assets and liabilities of the company.

9.7 A charitable company also has an obligation in regard to any subsidiaries, such as trading subsidiaries. The Act states that: 'A parent company that has a subsidiary undertaking in relation to which the above requirements do not apply must take reasonable steps to secure that the undertaking keeps such accounting records as to enable the directors of the parent company to ensure that any accounts required to be prepared under this Part comply with the requirements of this Act (and, where applicable, of Article 4 of the IAS Regulation).'

9.8 Section 387 makes it an offence committed by every officer of the charitable company not to comply with these requirements. Section 388 states that:

1. A company's accounting records:
(a) must be kept at its registered office or such other place as the directors think fit; and
(b) must at all times be open to inspection by the company's officers.

9.9 There are additional requirements if the accounting records are kept at a place outside the UK. The section goes on to state that accounting records must be preserved by a private company (which is what all charitable companies would be) for three years from the date on which they are made.

10 Document retention

10.1 Throughout this chapter and others, we refer to the legal need to retain certain documents – registers, minutes and accounting records just as a start. The issue of document retention – what needs to be kept and how, and for how long – is a broader issue that should be considered. By not having clarity about the requirements, charities can sometimes go to one of two extremes, or apply both to different documents. Either there can be a temptation to hold on to everything forever, or the charity can aim to destroy documents and data very quickly, regardless of any need to retain them for legal or business reasons.

10.2 It is recommended that all charities should adopt a document retention policy. This should set out the core principles of document retention, and set out the minimum and maximum retention periods for key documents. The reasons for developing such a policy are:

- There is a wide range of legal requirements to retain data, with differing legal requirements as to the length of retention. A policy can summarise all these and ensure that there is clarity for staff in what must be retained and how.
- There are also commercial and business reasons for retaining data (for example, there may be a need to take action under a contract that has already been performed). If the charity contracted to have a building built and defects appear in the building during the liability period, the charity will want to refer back to the original contract. Another example is if a grant or legacy is given to the charity that creates a restricted fund. If that fund cannot be used for the purpose the money was given for, reference may need to be made to the original grant or legacy in order to remedy the situation.
- It is important to consider not just how long documents are retained for, but in what form. If the document may need to be relied upon as a piece of evidence, the format will be important (if minutes are to be relied upon as *prima facie* evidence, they should be signed by the chair of the meeting or the next meeting). An electronic version of the minutes will not usually be signed. Even if the electronic version is a scanned copy of the signed minutes, it may not have the same weight as evidence. The charity will need to take judgments and to understand the legal requirements for the form of documents to be retained and set these out in the policy.
- There are not just minimum reasons why document should be retained. If this was the case, and the charity had sufficient space, it may just decide to keep everything. However, under the Data Protection legislation documents that contain personal data should not be retained for any longer than is necessary for the purpose for which they are created. There will also be practical reasons of space for not retaining everything. A document retention policy can

set maximum periods for retention, highlighting what data must be kept for the lifetime of the charity. In addition, if the charity is challenged under the Data Protection Act for retaining data, reference to a policy that indicates the reason for the retention and the period of retention could help to show that this matter had been appropriately considered.

10.3 The document retention policy will:

- ensure that the legal requirements as to the method and retention period of certain documents are met;
- ensure that documents that may need to be used as evidence in legal proceedings are kept in a manner that ensure that they will be admissible;
- give clarity as to the retention of other documents, ensuring that staff know what is to be retained, and how, and what can be destroyed; and
- explain how documents should be disposed of.

10.4 The document retention policy should:

- set out the core principles of document retention;
- identify what documents should be retained;
- identify in what format these documents should be retained;
- identify minimum and maximum retention periods for these documents;
- be clear as to the reason for the above, such as whether is it a legal or business requirement;
- specify how documents should be regularly reviewed;
- specify how documents that do not need to be retained should be disposed of; and
- give clear responsibility for document retention.

10.5 Unfortunately, document retention polices can have a tendency to become over-complex, featuring a very long list of documents. Ideally, they should be kept as simple as possible. There should be clarity regarding core documents where there are legal requirements. However, with other documents, it may be simpler to prepare principles for retention that are to be applied rather than listing every possible document. This keeps the policy shorter and simpler. It is also the case that even a very long schedule of documents is still likely to have some gaps that arise from time to time – so it is a good idea to have principles that can be applied.

10.6 A schedule showing the advised, and required, document retention period for a variety of documents that may be held by a charity is set out below.

10.7 Document retention checklist

Record description	Regulatory retention period and source	Comments/recommended retention
Statutory registers – charitable companies and CIOs		
CIOs – Register of Trustees	Life of charity CIO Gen. Regs. 2012, reg. 26.	
Register of directors; directors' residential addresses and secretaries	Life of charity (CA 2006, ss. 162, 165, 275) (for charitable companies).	
Register of charges	Life of charity (CA 2006, s. 876) (for charitable companies).	
Register of members	Life of charity (CA 2006, ss. 113–121) (for charitable companies). CIO Gen. Regs 2012, reg. 26 (for CIOs).	Entries in relation to former members may be removed after 10 years in a company (CA 2006, s. 121). However, a copy of any entry included in the register immediately before 6 April 2008 that is removed under s. 121 must be retained until 6 April 2018 or, if earlier, 20 years after the person ceased to be a member. For a CIO, entries for former members can be removed after 10 years.
Constitution		Copies of the current version must be kept for business reasons. Previous versions are usually also kept for life of charity.
Other Companies Act records		
Certificate of incorporation		Life of charity.
Certificate of change of company name		Life of charity.

Printed copies of resolutions filed at Companies House	While resolution or agreement is in force (CA 2006, s. 29) (for charitable companies).	Life of charity.
Other Registers		
Register of trustees' declarations of interest		If such a register is kept, it probably needs to be treated in at least the same way as the minutes of meetings of trustees. Accordingly, an absolute minimum of 10 years, although probably longer.
Register of documents sealed		If such a register is kept, it probably needs to be treated in at least the same way as the minutes of meetings of trustees. Accordingly, an absolute minimum of 10 years, but probably longer.
Statutory returns		
Acknowledgements of receipt issued by Companies House in respect of filed documents		Until entry on Companies House file has been confirmed.
Annual returns		Three years.
(Forms regarding directors and secretaries appointments)		Until entry on Companies House file has been confirmed. Evidence of agreement to appointment should be kept for the duration of the appointment.
Copies of other statutory returns filed at Charity Commission and Companies House		Until entry on Charity Commission and Companies House file has been confirmed.

Meetings of trustees		
Agenda papers		Minimum of seven years, or same as minutes if necessary to understand the minutes.
Board minutes and resolutions (signed copy)	Ten years from date of meeting/resolution (CA 2006, s. 248) (for charitable companies). Six years from date of meeting/resolution (CIO Gen. Regs 2012, reg. 37). (for CIOs).	Life of charity.
Board committee minutes (signed copy)	Ten years from date of meeting (CA 2006, s. 248) (for charitable companies).	Life of charity.
Attendance record		If required by constitution, life of charity.
General meetings		
Notices of general meetings (signed copy)		Ten years minimum, but life of the charity recommended. If notice is necessary to understand the minutes, it should be given at least the same retention period.
Certificate of posting of notices		Two years minimum suggested.
Minutes of general meetings and resolutions	Ten years from date of meeting/resolution (CA 2006, s. 355). (for charitable companies). Six years from the date of meeting/resolution (CIO Gen. Regs 2012, reg. 41) (for CIOs).	Life of charity.
Proxy forms – no poll demanded		One month after meeting.

Proxy forms and polling cards – poll demanded		One year after meeting.
Agreements and related correspondence		
Major agreements of historical significance		Permanently.
Contracts with customers, suppliers or agents Licensing agreements Rental/hire purchase agreements Indemnities and guarantees Other agreements/ contracts		Six years after expiry or termination of the contract. Six years is generally the time limit within which proceedings founded on a contract may be brought. If the contract is executed as a deed, the limitation period is 12 years. Actions for latent damage may be brought up to 15 years after the damage occurs.
Property		
Deeds of title		Permanently or until property disposed of.
Leases		Fifteen years after expiry.
Accounts		
Company accounts and accounting records	Accounting records must be retained for private companies or a minimum of three years from the date they are made (CA 2006, s. 388(4)). If the charity is not a company, the Charities Act 2011, s. 131 requires that accounting records are retained for six years.	Best practice suggests also retaining company accounting records for six years from the year end. Some accounting records will be required for tax purposes.
Annual report and accounts (signed)	Six years (Value Added Tax Act 1994, Sch. 11).	

Tax		
VAT records	Six years	Note, in general, that where there is an enquiry into a tax return, records should be retained until the enquiry is complete.
PAYE	For PAYE records not required to be sent to HMRC, not less than three years after the end of the tax year to which they relate (Income Tax) (Pay As You Earn) Regulations 2003, reg. 97).	Note, however, that payroll records should be kept for five to six years.
Banking records		
Cheques, bills of exchange and other negotiable instruments		Three years.
Bank statements	Three years (CA 2006, s. 388).	
Instructions to banks		Six years after ceasing to be effective.

11 Names and stationery

Charities communicate in a range of ways – by letter, leaflets, email and their website, to name just a few. It is common sense that in doing so they need to say who they are, so that people know who they are communicating with. However, there are also legal requirements here – it is not just a common-sense matter. It is also something that commonly gets neglected. While this may seem unlikely, take a minute to consider whether your charity gives its full name and the information that it is a charity in all its communications.

11.1 Use of names

11.1.1 A charity should not use a name that is too similar to the name used by another organisation. The Charity Commission has the power to require a charity to change its name if it is the same as, or too similar to, the name of another charity (s. 42(1) Charities Act 2011). Companies House also will not register a company in a name that is too similar to the name of another company. Since the Company, Limited Liability Partnership and Business (Names and Trading Disclosures) Regulations 2015, the law on similar names is more flexible than it previously was. However, if an existing company thinks that a new company has been established with a name that is too similar to its own name, it has the right to object to the new name being used.

11.1.2 In addition, there is a legal requirement to show your correct name. The Companies Act sets out requirements in regard to business names that cover all types of business and not just companies (Companies Act 2006, Part 41, Business Names). The term 'business name' applies if a body is operating under any name other than its true corporate name (the name on its certificate of incorporation or governing document). In such a case the true name should be stated on all business letters, orders for goods or services, invoices, receipts and written demands for payments of debts. Any person who fails to comply with this requirement is liable to a criminal fine. This legislation is therefore relevant if a charity uses another name, shortens its name or uses its initials only. In all of these cases there is a legal requirement to also state the full name of the charity

11.1.3 It should also be noted that there is provision under the Register of Charities to record any other name that the charity is known by. While this will not carry any legal weight, it could still be very useful in keeping the public informed.

11.1.4 Another matter for a charity to consider, if it regularly uses a business name, is whether it may be easier to change the name of the charity to this name. Doing so can help to prevent any breaches requirements under charity and company law to disclose the full name. While there may be reasons why the charity wants to retain a name it does not use, in some instances consideration of changing the name could be more worthwhile.

11.2 Charity law obligations: England and Wales

Where a charity is registered with the Charity Commission, there is a legal obligation to say so. Section 39 of the Charities Act 2011 states that charities with an income in excess of £10,000 that are registered with the Charity Commission must state that they are a 'registered charity' on:

- notices, advertisements or other documents issued by or on behalf of the charity which solicit money or property for the charity's benefit;
- bills of exchange, promissory notes, endorsements, cheques and orders for money or goods purporting to be signed on the charity's behalf; and
- bills, invoices, receipts and letters of credit.

The statement must be in legible characters in English (unless the charity is Welsh). There are different ways of making the statement but common ways include 'a registered charity' or 'registered charity number XXX'.

11.3 Charities registered in Scotland and Northern Ireland

11.3.1 There are also disclosure obligations under Scottish charity law and these must be observed by charities listed on the Register of Charities in Scotland. This will therefore apply to any charity that is registered in both England and Wales and Scotland. The documents that the disclosure must be made on are letters, emails, advertisements, notices and official publications, items soliciting money or property, invoices, receipts accounts, campaign and educational documentation and documents relating to land transactions and contracts. The disclosure must include:

- the registration number;
- the name by which the charity is recorded on the Scottish Charity Register; and
- an indication of the charity's charitable status if the words 'charity' or 'charitable' do not appear in its name.

11.3.2 The requirements under Scottish charity law are potentially broader than those under English and Welsh law. A charity registered across both legislations will need to meet both – so it will need to say that it is registered in England and Wales (but not necessarily to give its registration number) and that it is registered in Scotland (and to give its Scottish registration number). Scottish charity law also explicitly covers emails (but see section 11.4.2 and section 11.6 on page 176 and 177).

11.3.3 A charity registered in Northern Ireland must state that the charity is registered:

(a) in all notices, advertisements and other documents issued by or on behalf of the charity and soliciting money or other property for the benefit of the charity;
(b) in all bills of exchange, promissory notes, endorsements, cheques and orders for money or goods purporting to be signed on behalf of the charity; and
(c) in all bills rendered by it and in all its invoices, receipts and letters of credit.

11.4 Company law requirements

11.4.1 In addition to the charity law obligations, there are requirements under company law that will apply to both charitable companies and trading subsidiaries of that are companies.

11.4.2 Companies must:

(a) clearly show in legible characters the name on the company's certificate of incorporation on all:
   - business letters;
   - emails and company websites;
   - notices and official publications;
   - bills of exchange, promissory notes, endorsements, cheques, orders for money or goods; and
   - bills of parcels, invoices, receipts and letters of credit.

   A criminal fine is liable for the company, its officers and any person who issued an incorrect document where these conditions are breached;

(b) show the address of the registered office, the place of registration (England and Wales), and the registered company number on all business letters, order forms, emails, and a company's website. Even if the registered office address is the only address used on the letterhead, it should be stated that it is the registered office; and

(c) show their 'limited' status on all business letters and order forms, in English, and in legible characters. This is usually done by having 'limited' or 'ltd' in the name. However, most charitable companies have been granted permission to omit 'limited' from their name. In these cases, additional words must be used and the usual form is to say 'A charitable company limited by guarantee'.

11.4.3 While it is not necessary to show details of share capital on letters or order forms (relevant to trading subsidiaries), where reference to share capital is made on the letters and orders, it must be to paid-up share capital only.

11.4.4 While directors' details do not need to be shown on company stationery, where they are included, they must be included for every director, and this information must be up-to-date. Having a list of trustees on the letterhead would mean that it would need to be scrapped and replaced every time there is a change in the trustees.

11.4.5 Failure to observe these requirements make the company and its officers (such as directors/trustees and secretary) and those involved in issuing an incorrect letter or order liable to a criminal fine.

11.5 VAT registration

It is important to remember that the VAT registration number also needs to appear on invoices and receipts.

11.6 What is stationery?

11.6.1 The Companies Act explicitly covers emails and websites and states that all of the required information must be listed here. Even if a charity is not a company, emails and websites will be covered by the charity law requirements if they are used to solicit money or property for the charity's benefit. Most charities use their websites to encourage donations. When considering emails, care must be taken, as mobile devices often remove standard 'signature' wording from the bottom of emails sent from them. If you have staff or volunteers regularly using such devices it is a good idea to check that all of the required information is being included when they are being used. It is also important to think about how you use other forms of stationery, such as compliment slips. If these are used to form a contract or to place an order they are likely to be subject to the above rules and need to show the full name, company registration details and so on.

11.6.2 For many charities, consideration may also need to be given to how volunteers act on their behalf. The usual practice regarding letters sent by volunteers is that they will use letterhead supplied by the charity. This would presumably have the correct details on it. However, it is becoming more usual for everyone, including volunteers, to communicate by email. If this is the case, and the volunteer is acting on behalf the charity, are the legal requirements being met when an email is sent from a volunteer's home computer? If that email is forming a contract, for example, it needs to have all of the charity's details on it. If volunteers are authorised to act in this way it could be advisable to provide them with 'signature' inserts for their emails to be sent on behalf of the charity with all of the relevant details and instructions on use.

11.6.3 Care also needs to be taken with branches to ensure that they are aware of the requirements and have access to the required information, again usually in a template. Conversely, independent groups or branches that are separate legal entities should not be allowed to use the charity's name and registration number in a manner that might mislead the public into believing they were dealing with the charity itself rather than a separate organisation.

11.6.4 Finally, make sure that when names or other details are changed, the new stationery is used from the date of any change.

11.7 Display of registered name

The registered name of a company must be displayed (in legible characters) at its registered office, at any place where company records are made available for inspection and at any other location at which the company carries on business (unless it is primarily used for living accommodation). These requirements do not apply if the company has been dormant at all times since incorporation. Where display of the name is required, it must be positioned so that it may be clearly seen by any visitor. Where the location is shared by six or more companies, a scrolling display may be used.

11.8 Community Benefit societies

Community Benefit Societies must display their registered name at their registered office and at any other location at which it carries on business. They must also display the registered name on all notices, advertisements and other official publications; in all business correspondence; in all bills of exchange, promissory notes, endorsements, cheques and orders for money or goods and on all of its websites. As with charitable companies, a charitable community benefit society can apply to drop this word from its name (Co-operative and Community Benefit Societies Act 2014). However, and again just like with a company, if the registered name of the charity has 'Limited' or 'Ltd' in it, the charity will first need to formally change its name (such as with a special resolution of its members) and then apply to change the name. 'Ltd' cannot be dropped automatically.

11.9 CIOs

A CIO must include the term 'CIO' or 'Charitable Incorporated Organisation' in its name.

12 Change of Name

12.1 A key issue for a charity is getting its name right and charities will often find that they want to change their name at some stage of their life. When you are choosing a name, either as a new charity or for a name change, there are some key issues to consider:

- You will need to check that there are no other charities with the same name or something confusingly similar. The Charity Commission can refuse to register a name because it is too similar to the name of another charity. Likewise, if you are a charitable company you will not be able to register a name that is too similar to that of another company (see section 11.1 on page 173).
- There are restrictions on the use of certain words in names – full details can be found in the list of sensitive words and expressions held by Companies House.
- Remember that if you are a charitable company or community benefit society, you are exempt from using the word 'Limited' or 'Ltd' in your name. If you were registered with this word in the name and want to remove it, this can be done by filing form NE01 with Companies House.

12.2 In changing a name, it is not always possible to 'reserve' a name (generally, the name will remain available to others until you have resolved to adopt it and notified the Charity Commission (and Companies House if relevant)). If you are a company, one option to protect against this is to set up a name protection company. Therefore, you establish a new, dormant company holding the name that you want to use. On the day that you want to change names, you then swap over your charity's name and the dormant company's name by using Companies House's same-day change of name service. Using a name protection company also has the benefit that it will then hold your old name, thereby preventing it from being used by someone else.

12.3 When changing your name it is important to remember the following points:

- Your name is part of your governing document, so a change of name will have to be dealt with and approved in exactly the same way as any other change. This will normally require a special resolution of the members.
- While there is no explicit need for you to obtain the Charity Commission's approval for a change of name, it can refuse to register a change where it is likely to mislead the public, is same as that of another charity or is likely to cause offence. The Charity Commission has powers requiring a charity to change its name if this happens, so it is a good idea to seek the agreement of the Charity Commission before taking the final decision.
- If your charity is regulated by OSCR, it must approve a change of name before it can be adopted. OSCR must be given notice of your proposal not less than 42 days before the date on which you intend to make the change. This notice period is fixed, so even if you receive consent from OSCR before this period ends, the name cannot be changed until the 42 days have concluded. OSCR must then be notified of the change of name within three months.

SECTION C

The charity's governance

C1
Charity governance

1 Definitions of governance

1.1 It is generally acknowledged that the governance of an organisation is one of the most important factors in its long-term success. Governance is high on the agenda in both the commercial and not-for-profit sectors: public expectations of a charity's governance have become even higher in recent years. However, what do we mean by 'governance'? One definition defines governance as being 'The systems and processes concerned with the overall direction, effectiveness, supervision and accountability of an organisation' (the definition comes from *The Governance of Voluntary Organisations*, Chris Cornforth, ed., Routledge, 2003).

1.2 There are number of governance roles encapsulated here:

- 'direction' – providing leadership, setting strategy and being clear about what the organisation is aiming to achieve and how it is going to do it;
- 'effectiveness' – making good use of financial and other resources to achieve the desired outcomes;
- 'supervision' – establishing and overseeing controls and risk management and monitoring performance to make sure that the organisation is on track to achieve its goals, making adjustments where necessary and learning from mistakes; and
- 'accountability' – reporting to those who have an interest in what the organisation is doing and how it is doing it.

1.3 This has been a popular definition used across the sector for a number of years. However, it is rather more complex than a definition needs to be. In addition, it focuses on 'systems and processes'. Since this definition was written, the concept of governance has been widened beyond systems and processes to also encompass behaviour (see Section 3, page 189). Another definition that can therefore be very useful is that of the Institute of Governance in Canada. It defines governance as 'how society, or groups within it, organise to make decisions'. The Institute of Governance identifies that the need for governance exists whenever a group of people come together to accomplish an end. It states that governance determines who has power; who makes decisions; and how other players make their voice heard. It therefore identifies three key elements: who has a voice in making decisions; how are decisions made and who is accountable. While the definition is principally applied by the Institute to models of government, it is just as useful a definition for organisations, including charities. Its focus on decision-making gives a key insight into the core purpose of governance and how to identify good governance.

Governance and decision making – questions to ask

Who has a voice in making decisions?

- Is it the trustees who are leading the charity and making the key decisions?
- How is the board composed?
- How are trustees appointed?
- Do trustees have the necessary skills and competencies?
- Does the board's approach to diversity support its decision-making?
- Does the board operate as an effective decision-making body, and oversee all of the work of the charity?
- What is the governance framework (such as committees and delegations)?

How are decisions made?

- What information does the board receive to support its decision making?
- Has the board received appropriate advice?
- Do the trustees understand the risks facing the charity, and are these risks managed?
- Do the trustees ask the right questions in making decisions?
- Are there factors influencing decision making that should not (conflicts of interest, for example)?
- Is there challenge and independent thought in the decision-making process?
- Is there clear delegation and are matters reserved for the board?
- Do the trustees adequately monitor delegated matters and internal controls?

Who is accountable?

- Does the board understand who its stakeholders are?
- Does it operate in an open and transparent way (as far as it is able)?
- Does it consult with stakeholders on its strategy and direction?
- Does it receive feedback on the charity's services?
- Does the board creates a culture that help to achieve the organisation's charitable purposes?

1.4 Good governance and effectiveness go hand-in-hand and the board of trustees is responsible for both. As the Charity Commission itself said: 'Good governance arrangements really are the key to running an effective charity. Being clear about roles and responsibilities and implementing strong financial controls and record-keeping is the best way to avoid everything from disputes to financial chaos.'

1.5 The governance of charities is influenced by a range of external and internal factors. External influences include, for example:

- codes of governance for the public and private sectors, as well as those explicitly for charities;
- events both within the sector, and in the corporate sector, that have led to major failures, such as the failure of Kids Company and the financial crisis of 2008–09;
- relevant legislation, such as the Companies and Charities Acts;
- regulation, such as that exercised by the Charity Commission;
- codes of practice for particular activities, such as fundraising; requirements of funders – particularly state funding or major trusts;
- public expectations; and
- that elusive thing – 'best practice'.

1.6 Internal influences may be more subtle, for example:

- the personalities of individual trustees and their relationships with senior staff (see paragraph 5.5 on page 195);
- the experience of recent successes or failures;
- dependence on volunteers or members;
- whether service users are engaged with the organisation or not;
- the size and spread of the organisation; and
- the range and types of services provided.

1.7 Of key importance are the charity's stakeholders – those people and organisations that have an interest in what the charity does. Many governance theories (see below) stem from the commercial sector and emphasise the importance of the relationship with the organisation's 'owners' rather than its stakeholders. In a charity, this broader group of stakeholders – in particular, the beneficiaries – are of key importance, as is the concept of accountability.

2 The history of governance

2.1 There has been a great deal of change in the governance of charities since the 1990s. Much of this has arisen directly in regard to the sector, but it has also been greatly influenced by changes in the governance of the corporate and public sectors. There are three particularly influential reports: the Cadbury Report, *On Trust* and the Nolan Report.

2.2 The Cadbury Report

2.2.1 The Committee on the Financial Aspects of Corporate Governance, chaired by Sir Adrian Cadbury, was set up following the death of Robert Maxwell in 1990 and the revelation that resources had been diverted from Mirror Group's pension fund to pay for a series of risky acquisitions. While the committee was sitting, there were two other major corporate collapses – the Bank of Credit and Commerce International (BCCI) and Polly Peck. The business community recognised that unless it put its own house in order, companies would be subjected to greater regulatory and legislative control.

2.2.2 The Cadbury Report, published in 1992, made a number of important recommendations about the responsibilities of company directors based on the principles of 'openness, integrity and accountability'. It also addressed the relationship between the chair and chief executive, the role of non-executive directors and reporting on internal controls and on the company's financial position. The report encouraged listed companies to comply with the accompanying code of best practice or, if not, explain why they had not done so – known as 'comply or explain'.

2.2.3 Although the report was aimed at listed companies, many of its recommendations are relevant to any organisation, including charities. Of particular relevance were the recommendations for fixed terms of office for non-executive directors and recommendations for establishing audit committees.

2.2.4 To quote from the Cadbury Report: 'The effectiveness with which boards discharge their responsibilities determines Britain's competitive position. They must be free to drive their companies forward, but exercise that freedom within a framework of effective accountability. This is the essence of any system of good corporate governance.'

2.2.5 Over the years, the recommendations in the Cadbury Report have been added to. In 1995, the Greenbury Report made recommendations on directors' remuneration. In 1996, the Hampel Committee was established to review the recommendations of the Cadbury and Greenbury Committees. Its report emphasised the principles of good governance. By concentrating on the principles rather than specific rules, it tried to be flexible enough to apply to all companies, whatever their size and to reduce the regulatory burden on companies. The Cadbury and Greenbury Reports had focused on preventing senior managers from abusing their power. The Hampel Report, in contrast, looked at governance from the perspective of enhancing long-term shareholder value and so placed greater emphasis on shareholder involvement and the board's accountability, emphasising its responsibility for all aspects of risk management and the system of internal controls.

2.2.6 Another reason why the Cadbury Report is so important was the introduction of the use of a Code as a means of setting out best practice in governance. The UK Corporate Governance Code (previously the Combined Code) was first published in 1998, consolidating the underlying principles and recommendations of the Cadbury, Greenbury and Hampel Reports. In 1999, the Turnbull guidance provided directors with guidance on internal controls, following on from the work of the Hampel Committee. This Code applies for listed companies but the use of codes has been adopted across other sectors and organisation types.

2.2.7 Following scandals in the US involving WorldCom and Enron, the Code was updated in 2003 to incorporate recommendations from the Higgs Report on the role of non-executive directors and the Smith Report on the role of the audit committee. At the same time, the Financial Reporting Council (FRC) took on responsibility for publishing and updating the Code.

2.2.8 The updating of the Code has continued, with the most recent amendments being made in 2018. Some of the key revisions in 2018 were references to the board's responsibilities in terms of the workforce, and its need to ensure that its workforce policies and practice were consistent with the company's values. The revised Code also has more emphasis on the board's role and responsibility regarding the company's culture, and the need to promote integrity and to value diversity.

2.3 *On Trust*

2.3.1 Often, when charity governance is considered, it is assumed that everything about it stems from the commercial sector and all that the charity sector has done is to accept the principles of the Combined Code/UK Corporate Governance Code and adapt them. However, the Cadbury Report was not the only report published in 1992. In that year, a governance report of direct relevance to charities was published. The NCVO published a key report, *On Trust*, concerned with increasing the effectiveness of charity trustees and management committees. This report and its conclusions were key influences on corporate governance in the charity sector.

2.3.2 The report was from a working party that had been established to consider trustee training, but its outcomes were wider than this. It had a list of strong recommendations, many of which encapsulated for the first time themes that would become common in charity governance, and many of which were implemented in some form. The recommendations included:

- the need for clarity in the main roles and responsibilities of trustees, including the role of the chair, treasurer and secretary;
- the need for advice, support and training for trustees covering a range of topics, and recommendations on how that training be approached;
- that general information packs should be provided for trustees;
- that a senior staff member or the chair should take responsibility for training;
- that there was a need for clear guidelines on the charity's expectation of trustees and job descriptions for trustees;
- that charities should have a policy on the composition, recruitment and appointment of their trustees;
- that attention should be given to induction for trustees;
- that training needs be regularly assessed, with a rolling programme of advice and support;
- that there should be clarity about who the trustees of a charity were and their role;
- that the Charity Commission should publish a leaflet on the roles and responsible of trustees;
- that the NCVO should give much higher priority to working with trustees, particularly chairs, and ensure that its services were accessible to them;
- that funders should establish a mechanism for monitoring the governance of organisations that they fund; and
- that trustees should sigh a statement accepting their responsibilities.

2.3.3 A review of these recommendations nearly 30 years later shows how influential they were. While the focus began with training, the principles had far wider application, and many of the ideas that they encapsulated are now common practice for charities. The principles of clarity regarding roles and responsibilities and the idea that charities should have job descriptions for trustees, are widely espoused. The concept of regular assessment has grown into the idea of a regular performance review and skills audits. The importance of having a policy about the composition of the board and its recruitment has also been developed, with charities now having to report on such matters in their annual reports.

2.4 The Nolan Report

2.4.1 The Committee on Standards in Public Life, under the chairmanship of Lord Nolan, was established in October 1994 by the then Prime Minister, John Major, in the wake of the 'Cash for Questions' affair. It was given wide terms of reference to examine concerns about the standards of conduct of all those who hold public office.

2.4.2 The Nolan Report expanded the list of principles included in the Cadbury Report to seven. These are: selflessness, integrity, objectivity, accountability, openness, honesty and leadership (the seven principles).

2.4.3 Although drafted for public sector bodies, the seven principles address fundamental problems faced by all organisations and have been used within the voluntary sector. In addition, there has been a growth in charities providing public services, so many charities find themselves having to show how they measure up against these principles.

2.5 Good Governance Code

A code for the voluntary sector, *Good Governance: A Code for the Voluntary and Community Sector*, was first published in June 2005. The code was developed by the Charity Commission, the NCVO, the Association of Chief Executives of Voluntary Organisations (ACEVO), Charity Trustee Networks and ICSA. While the Charity Governance Code has now replaced the Good Governance Code, it was important in introducing the benefit of governance codes across the sector.

3 Recent events

3.1 In recent years, there has been a shift in how we consider and measure good governance, with the development of the concept of behavioural governance. This concept was developed following the financial crisis of 2008–09 and the search for reasons why the governance of banks and the financial sector did not prevent the errors that were made. While the concept has developed in the commercial sector, it is also applicable to the charity sector. Behavioural governance is discussed with theories of governance below, but the main concept is that appropriate boardroom behaviour is an essential component of best practice corporate governance, and that there is an absence of consideration of, and guidance on, appropriate boardroom behaviours in current corporate governance models and systems.

3.2 There has also been a growing awareness of the need for good governance, and a higher expectation placed on charities. There have been a number of failures and incidents reported in the media in recent years that have placed a revised focus on the need for good governance. The collapse of the charity Kids Company in August 2015 highlighted a number of governance failings. There is now a much greater awareness of the need for the board to be engaged, and to have a full understanding of the work of the board. There is also now an increased emphasis on how well trustees monitor the work that is undertaken on their behalf, and how well they manage risk.

3.3 This change in the expectations placed on charity trustees was influenced by the public outcry in 2015 about the fundraising methods of some charities and the media coverage of a number of safeguarding incidents in 2017–18. Questions were raised about the level of awareness of the trustees of the relevent charities about the actions being taken on their behalf. Finally, the increasing number of inquiries by the Charity Commission has also brought to light a range of governance failures.

3.4 Even more recently, the concept of behavioural governance has led to an increasing understanding of the importance of an organisation's culture, values and ethics. Examples of this are as follows:

- The 2018 revisions to the UK Corporate Governance Code.
- The growing expectation that charities adopt a Code of Conduct. For example, the Charity Commission's guidance on safeguarding states that if a charity has staff or volunteers it must have a clear code of conduct which sets out the charity's culture and how people in the charity should behave.
- Changes in reporting requirements for large companies. The Companies (Miscellaneous Reporting) Regulations 2018 introduced some additional reporting requirements. The Companies Act 2006 states that company directors have a duty to consider a range of matters (including the interests of the employees, the impact on the community and the environment; and maintaining a reputation for high standards of business conduct) when exercising their duty to promote the success of a company. It is arguable that there has been little emphasis placed on these duties within the commercial sector. However, changes in reporting requirements for large companies will now mean that they need to report on how they have engaged with suppliers, customers and others in a business relationship with the company. While this is primarily something that affects the private sector, this change in emphasis can be expected to impact on the charity sector, and large charitable companies will also need to report on these matters.
- Another change introduced by the Companies (Miscellaneous Reporting) Regulations 2018 is that all companies with at least 250 UK employees will be required to include a statement in the directors' report summarising how the directors have engaged with employees, how they have had regard to employee interests and the effect of this on the principal decisions taken by the company in the financial year.
- In 2018, NCVO developed a set of Charity Ethical Principles. While these principles are voluntary, charities are encouraged to adopt them, and to reflect them in their work. It remains to be seen how popular they become, as they have only recently been introduced. The four principles that charities are recommended to uphold are beneficiaries first; integrity; openness; and the right to be safe.

- The Charity Governance Code now includes the principle that a charity board acts with integrity, adopts values and creates a culture that help achieve the organisation's charitable purposes. Another principle is that the board's approach to diversity should support its effectiveness, leadership and decision making.

4 Charity Governance Code

4.1 In the UK, and across Europe, the approach has been for the standards and principles of governance to be set out in Codes. The UK Corporate Governance Code is discussed above, but there are a number of governance codes, each relating to different sectors. This European approach to governance is in contrast to the approach in the US where governance standards are embedded in legislation. Within the charity sector, it is usually the case that following a code is voluntary (although it is a regulatory requirement that registered providers of social housing adopt a code and sporting bodies funded by UK Sport must also follow its code). However, despite their voluntary nature, the use of codes has grown in recent years. They are seen as setting out a clear framework for governance and a frame of reference that enables a charity to benchmark itself against other charities.

4.2 The Charity Governance Code was introduced in 2017, and replaced the Good Governance Code. It has proved popular since its introduction, and research by the accountancy firm RSM in 2018 highlights this. This research reviewed the uptake of the new code in its first 18 months. RSM conducted a study of the annual reports of 85 charities with income above £5 million,and found that just under half (44%) have already adopted the Charity Governance Code.

4.3 The Charity Governance Code is not the only Code used across the sector. Other codes that are used regularly are the National Housing Federation Code of Governance and the Code for Sports Governance (UK Sport).

4.4 The Charity Governance Code is entirely voluntary and it is up to a charity to decide if it wants to follow it and to report back on how well it adheres to it (in its annual report, for example). However, the Code does suggest that a charity should explain the approach it takes to applying the Code, and also explain when and why it does not follow its recommended practices. Also, while the Code is voluntary, it should also be noted that it is fully endorsed by the Charity Commission. The Charity Commission has stated that will not take regulatory action against charities that fail to apply the code, but that it will use it to determine the overall health of the organisation, for example as part of a statutory inquiry. It has also withdrawn some of its own guidance and instead refers charities to the Code.

4.5 The Code has seven key principles that are then supported by statements of recommended practice. There are two sets of recommended practice, one for smaller charities and one for larger ones. It a matter for the individual charity to decide which set of recommended practice to apply, but the Code recommends that a good way of deciding would be if the charity is large enough to have its accounts audited.

Charity Governance Code

The seven key principles are:

1. **Organisational purpose**: the board is clear about the charity's aims and ensures that these are being delivered effectively and sustainably.
2. **Leadership**: every charity is led by an effective board that provides strategic leadership in line with the charity's aims and values.
3. **Integrity**: the board acts with integrity, adopting values and creating a culture which help achieve the organisation's charitable purposes. The board is aware of the importance of the public's confidence and trust in charities, and trustees undertake their duties accordingly.
4. **Decision making, risk and control**: the board makes sure that its decision-making processes are informed, rigorous and timely, and that effective delegation, control and risk assessment and management systems are set up and monitored.
5. **Board effectiveness**: the board works as an effective team, using the appropriate balance of skills, experience, backgrounds and knowledge to make informed decisions.
6. **Diversity**: the board's approach to diversity supports its effectiveness, leadership and decision-making.
7. **Openness and accountability**: the board leads the organisation in being transparent and accountable. The charity is open in its work, unless there is good reason for it not to be.

(www.charitygovernancecode.org/en)

5 Theories of governance

5.1 Corporate governance is most often talked about with regard to its practical application, rather than its underlying theories. However, while it is useful to be aware of the different models and procedures of corporate governance, it is also helpful to take a step back and think about what theories underlie those principles. There are a number of theories of governance that have influenced the charity sector. It should be acknowledged that many of the theories originated in the commercial sector and there are often a number of key differences that need to be considered. For example, many governance theories rest on the relationship between managers and shareholders, but the charity sector does not have 'owners' in the same way. There are stronger principles of wider accountability that are important in the charity sector.

5.2 Agency theory

Agency theory is a commonly used theory of corporate governance in the commercial sector. It has been around, in a number of forms, for a long time. It is concerned with the relationship between the managers of a company, and the owners (i.e. the shareholders). In the eighteenth century, Adam Smith was among the first to raise concerns about whether employed managers would watch over other people's assets with the same vigilance as if they were their own. The theory has moved forward with a statement of the potential sources of conflict that may result from a separation of ownership and control in the modern company; the owners having given their power to employed managers who exercise control on their behalf. One of the underlying assumptions of the theory is that there is a divergence of goals between the owners (the principals) and the managers (the agents). This necessitates action to ensure that managers who pursue their own self-interest will also pursue the collective interest. From an agency theory perspective, boards of directors are put in place to monitor managers on behalf of shareholders.

5.3 Stewardship theory

Agency theory does not seem to 'fit' with charitable organisations. For a start, there are no 'shareholders as owners' in the same way as there are in commercial companies. In addition, the principle that managers will tend to act in their own self-interest does not seem applicable in the same way. This is either because those involved in charities and in determining their governance, take a more positive approach to human nature, or it stems from the fact that the managers of a charity are often not driven by the same financial rewards as in the commercial sector. Are there other reasons why they work for the charity? Stewardship theory can seem more applicable. This is a theory that managers, left on their own, will indeed act as responsible stewards of the assets they control. Stewardship theory assumes that management behaviours are aligned with the interests of the principals. It, therefore, favours governance mechanisms that support and empower the organisation's management over those that monitor and control it. According to stewardship theory, 'the more crucial factor influencing organisational performance is the design of the organisational structure so that managers can take effective action'. The theory's key issue is not how to strengthen the control of management, or to make the board act on behalf of the 'owners', but, rather, how to empower management.

5.4 Policy governance

5.4.1 Policy governance (John Carver) is a model of governance that is particularly applicable to charities and seems much more designed for them. It is a theory that gives a set of principles that are designed to empower boards to fulfil their obligation of accountability for the organisations they govern. It is a much more commonly used theory in regard to charity governance, although often concepts are plucked from it rather that the theory being applied as a whole. Quite commonly, organisations state that they are following policy governance and applying it, but when you look closely at how it is being applied, there are some tenets of the theory that are not accepted. Charity boards often have an inclination to hold on to control in a much more detailed way than policy governance requires.

5.4.2 Although it is applicable to any board as a generic system, the theory works very well for charities; this is strengthened by the fact that the theory directly refers to charities (or 'not-for-profits', as this is a US theory). A key point here is that it deals with the 'ownership' issue and how this is applicable within a charity with accountability to beneficiaries.

5.4.3 The theory begins with the premise that the board exists (usually on someone else's behalf) to be accountable for how its organisation works. It recognises that in the commercial sector, a board of directors is the voice of the owners (shareholders). However, it is not always apparent that charities also have owners, but the theory states that there is a moral equivalent that it refers to as the 'ownership'. Therefore, just as the commercial board exists to speak for the shareholders, the charity board exists to represent and to speak for the interests of the 'owners' in a broader sense.

5.4.4 The theory states that, traditionally, boards have developed their relationships largely inside the organisation (with staff) whereas it argues that the board's primary relationships should be outside the organisation.

5.4.5 The principles of the theory are concerned with finding ways to enable the board to focus on the larger issues and to truly lead its organisation. It argues that boards should clearly delegate and control the work of management without getting involved in the detail. Policy governance separates issues of organisational purpose (which it describes as 'ends') from all other organisational issues ('means'), placing primary importance on those ends. When applying policy governance, a board should focus on the ends and only be concerned with limiting how staff carry out the means (such as when this breaches the board's standards of prudence and ethics).

5.4.6 Policy governance therefore places a strong emphasis on delegation and setting the framework within which staff can operate (by setting core principles for them to work within, rather than detailed policies and procedures). Policy governance recommends that the board uses a single point of delegation and that all the accountability of the organisation to meet the board expectations is charged personally to the CEO. The policy therefore states that the board, in effect, has one employee. It also states that accountability in leadership requires the board to be definite about its performance expectations, to assign these expectations clearly and then to check to see that the expectations are being met.

5.4.7 Policy governance boards should also only use committees to help the board to do its own job, not to duplicate the work delegated to the CEO.

5.5 Behavioural governance

5.5.1 The concept of behavioural governance has developed. In recent years, following the financial crisis of 2008–09. In 2009, ICSA issued a report on boardroom behaviour which stated that 'an emerging view is that the system of governance for companies is not inherently 'broken', but rather that its effectiveness has been undermined by a failure to observe appropriate boardroom behaviours'.

5.5.2 Behavioural governance states that best practice in boardroom behaviour is characterised by a clear understanding of the role of the board; the appropriate deployment of knowledge, skills, experience and judgment; independent thinking; the questioning of assumptions and established views; and a supportive decision-making environment. The degree to which these behaviours can be delivered is shaped by the character and personality of the directors and the balance in the relationship between the key players in the boardroom.

5.5.3 The concept of behavioural governance has been applied to charities in recent years. In 2012, the Compass Partnership and Cass Business School published *Delivering Effective Governance*. This report was based on research into the 500 largest charities in the UK, and gave an overview of the characteristics of governance within them. It identified 50 characteristics for effective governance and grouped them into four groups: structures, processes; meetings and behaviours. The research suggested that there was effectively a hierarchy of these groups – structures; processes; meetings and then behaviours; each of which built on the former, and each of which had a greater effect on the overall performance of governance. So while governance structures need to fit the needs of the charity, these alone will not be enough. There would also need to be work on processes, meetings, and ultimately, behaviours.

5.5.4 There are other ways of seeing how a shift of emphasis away from the structures of governance towards the behaviour of board members can also be applied to charities. Many charities have codes of conduct for trustees and seek to ensure that their trustees have a clear understanding of their role and are trained to fulfil it. It is interesting how the introduction of behavioural governance across the charity sector had reapplied some of the core principles that were developed in *On Trust*.

5.5.5 When you look back at the definitions of governance given at the start of this chapter, and consider the fact that a charity's governance is effectively about how a charity organises to make decisions, you can begin to see how the behaviour of the board is key. How the trustees work together as a group is very important. Governance reviews are now much more focused on the effectiveness of a board and its decision-making processes. Board meeting effectiveness is considered in chapter B2 and how a board works together as a group is vital. As well as the steps that can be taken to make meetings more effective, consideration should be given to the need for independent thought and constructive challenge on a board. There should be mechanisms in place to guard against the development of 'group think' and to recruit trustees with a range of difference experiences and views. It is also advisable for trustees to have some awareness of each other's personality and motivations. Having some understanding of these characteristics can help in reviewing how each trustee will approach issues and how they will work together. In addition, sometimes carrying out some form of personality review exercise is a good way for the board to get to know each other and to begin to discuss why they may behave in certain ways.

6 Performance review/appraisal

6.1 Regular reviews of the board's own performance are key to good governance and it is now much more widespread across the charity sector. It is a recommendation of the Charity Governance Code that charities review the board's performance, and the performance of individual trustees. For larger charities, it is recommended that they have an external board evaluation every three years.

6.2 Performance review can comprise a review of the board's collective performance, an appraisal of individual board members, or both. Charities sometimes shy away from individual appraisals but it is becoming more common. Appraisal is not necessarily a negative experience for a trustee. It gives trustees an opportunity to raise any concerns, reflect on their role and address their own needs. Appraisals of individual trustees can be conducted quite informally if needed, and in some charities, the practice will be to conduct a full review and appraisal every three years, with a lighter touch appraisal in the intervening years. The chair will usually carry out these appraisals, although sometimes a nominations committee chair may lead, or an external consultant will be used. Appraisals can be tied in with a skills audit.

6.3 Performance reviews of the board as a whole will normally address issues such as to how effective the meetings are, whether the trustees receive the necessary support and information and whether there is effective leadership from the chair. A performance review can be carried out in a number of different ways including questionnaires, individual interviews and observation of board and committee meetings.

7 Skills analysis

Another factor in making a charity board more effective is a regular skills analysis and this is also a recommendation of the Charity Governance Code. It is good practice for a board to consider the skills, knowledge and experience that should be represented on the board, then identify any gaps among the current trustees. This knowledge should assist it in its future recruitment, help to identify ongoing training needs and help trustees to know what professional advice they will need. Again, there are a number of mechanisms that can be used, but charities should take care to ensure that, whatever method they use, they guard against subjectivity. A good analysis will ask board members to give some evidence of their declared skills, and or provide some way of evaluating their responses. It is also advisable for these reviews to have a wider focus that just skills. Competencies are just as important in making a board effective, and so it can be useful to find some way of assessing a trustee's competency in matters such as working as a part of a team; strategic decision making; and constructive challenges.

8 Accountability

8.1 One of the core themes of the governance of a charity is accountability. Throughout the discussion above, this has come across in a number of ways – from the opening definition of governance, to the relationship with 'owners' in governance theories and the ways that the regulatory involvement has increased accountability. However, while accountability is important, a core issue for a charity is 'accountability to whom?'

8.2 In the commercial sector, accountability is mainly towards shareholders – the providers of capital. Shareholders elect directors who are responsible for running the company and providing a directors' report to their shareholders via the annual report and financial statements. The Companies Act 2006 (s. 172) states: 'A director of a company must act in the way he considers, in good faith, would be most likely to promote the success of the company for the benefit of its members as a whole.'

8.3 However, although many charities are established under company law as companies limited by guarantee, the bond between trustees and members is of a different nature to that between directors and shareholders. The Companies Act 2006 (s. 172(2)) allows for this difference between ordinary companies and charities. As it goes on to state: 'Where or to the extent that the purposes of the company consist of or include purposes other than the benefit of its members, subsection (1) has effect as if the reference to promoting the success of the company for the benefit of its members were to achieving those purposes.' In other words, success for the trustees of a charity established as a company can be defined as achieving the charity's charitable purposes, not the benefit of its members.

8.4 The accountability of a charity is not just to its members. It must also be accountable to its beneficiaries (both present and future), its donors and the public. In addition, unlike shareholders, members normally have little financial stake in a charity and so have little to lose financially whether its trustees perform well or poorly. However, if a charity has members who are also volunteers, donors or service users, they are likely to have a have a strong interest in how well the charity is run. Many charities benefit greatly from the passion of their members for the charity's cause. However, there can be conflicts between a charity's accountability to its members and its wider accountability. For example, the trustees have a duty to act in the interests of the charity and in this regard the interests of future beneficiaries must also be taken into account. How are trustees to be held accountable to a membership that may have more limited aims when they have a wider, legal obligation?

8.5 Just as a public limited company can have a wide range of stakeholders, so too can a charity. Besides those mentioned above, a charity's stakeholders may include local authorities, central government, communities in which the charity operates and other charities, particularly those with similar charitable objects. It is important for all these stakeholders that a charity's trustees are both open and accountable, setting out clearly in advance what it is that they are aiming to achieve and reporting back on how they have performed.

8.6 The Charity Commission actively promotes accountability to stakeholders under the 'accountability objective'. In 2004 it published a research report, RS8 *Transparency and Accountability*, which reviewed the annual reports of a sample of the 200 largest charities. It concluded that: 'Our evidence is that the general standard of performance against the transparency and accountability framework is not satisfactory. While there are some very good examples, too many charities in our study did not meet basic requirements.' Since then, the Charity Commission has required much more detailed information from charities, as can be seen in its annual reporting requirements. In addition, the Charity Governance Code, which is endorsed by the Charity Commission, has openness and accountability as one of its key principles.

8.7 While stakeholders may have access to more and better information, many charities still struggle with the degree to which their stakeholders should be involved in influencing the running of the charity and, in particular, shaping the services that they provide. In addition, the concept of 'ownership' and who owns a charity is still a matter of wide discussion and different views. In thinking about the principles of governance and how to apply them, there have been a number of changes over time. Which theory and approach to take is a matter for the trustees to consider. However, given the importance of accountability through all aspects of corporate governance, perhaps one core principle to deal with is to be clear who the charity should be accountable to, and how.

C2
Effective decision making

1 Introduction

1.1 While there is no general law that requires charities to operate through meetings, the fact is that most charities do operate in this way. In fact, for the vast majority of charities, meetings are vital for the governance and administration of the charity. A core principle of a charity's work is that trustees act collectively and exercise their powers as a group. While it is possible for the joint decisions of trustees to be taken in other ways than at a meeting, the most effective way for charity trustees to work together is by holding meetings. If care is taken to ensure that meetings are effective, this can make a significant difference to how the charity operates.

1.2 The expansion of electronic communications has meant that charities are now beginning to look beyond traditional meetings for decision making. Increasingly, charities are using teleconferencing and videoconferencing. In addition, the use of email has made decision making by written resolution easier and quicker. For charitable companies, the Companies Act 2006 represented a shift away from traditional meetings for decision making. The CIO model was also established in a way that utilised electronic communications.

1.3 While there is no general law that says that charities must have meetings, there will still be a number of legal and constitutional requirements regarding how such meetings are administered when they are held. A charity's constitution will often refer to meetings, how they are run and how many there should be. If the charity has members, there will also be provisions regarding how the members meet together and there will usually be a requirement for general meetings. If the charity is a company, it will be subject to the detailed requirements of the Companies Act. If it is a CIO, the requirements are set out in the Charitable Incorporated Organisations (General) Regulations 2012 (SI 2012/3102).

2 What is a meeting?

2.1 Meetings usually occur when a group of people gather in the same place at the same time. However, there are other ways to communicate collectively – principally by telephone and video conferencing. If a decision needs to be taken at a meeting, a charity will need to consider what constitutes a meeting and if what it is proposing to do comes within that definition.

2.2 What constitutes a meeting may be stated in the constitution. Most model constitutions now contain wording that allow meetings to be held electronically (including the Charity Commission models for CIOs). However, there is a common law definition of what a meeting is and this will apply if there is no alternative provision in the constitution. This definition states that a valid meeting normally consists of people who can both see and hear each other (*Byng v London Life Association* [1989]). If the charity's constitution gives no definition to a meeting, and makes no reference to electronic meetings, this definition will apply.

2.3 A 'meeting' held by video conferencing or internet video facilities allows the participants to both see and hear each other. Such meetings will therefore be valid, unless the constitution prohibits them. However, as teleconferencing only allows the participants to hear each other, it is the view of the Charity Commission that this does not constitute a 'meeting' within the meaning of the decision in the *Byng* case. For teleconferencing to constitute a meeting, there would need to be a specific provision in the charity's governing document stating that this was the case.

2.4 That being said, it should be remembered that in the absence of a specific power to conduct business by teleconferencing, such a method may be used for preliminary discussions relating to business which could then be brought to a formal meeting for a decision. It is also possible that the trustees could delegate specific decisions to be taken in this way. For example, if the trustees wanted to reach a conclusion on a matter that needed further information and did so by teleconference, they could use a formal meeting to delegate the decision to a named trustee (such as the chair). All the trustees could then consider the matter by teleconference and take a decision; this would then be confirmed in writing by the specified trustee.

2.5 It should also be noted that a meeting could be held by a mixture of both physical presence and teleconferencing. If there is no provision regarding electronic meetings in the constitution, the only people who would be attending formally would be those in the meeting room. However, if they could form a quorum, the meeting would be valid. Those included by teleconferencing may of course contribute to any discussion, but they would not be able to vote on any proposal. However, as long as the trustees who are physically present form a quorum, they will be able to discharge the business of the charity validly, as long as all of the trustees have had the opportunity to attend the 'meeting'.

2.6 None of these options is ideal and if teleconferencing is to be used, it is preferable for the constitution to be amended to include it in the definition of meetings of the charity.

2.7 If a board is choosing to meet regularly by video or teleconferencing, it should note that there are also restrictions on how useful such meetings can be. They can work very well when there are short, individual matters to be determined. However, it can be very hard to run through a whole agenda effectively for a board meeting in such a way. If a meeting is being held by teleconference, it is a good idea to focus on one or two key questions for debate. Participants should identify themselves each time they speak, and it is probably necessary for the meeting to be conducted in a more formal way than normal. The chair should also clearly reiterate the decision taken at the end of each agenda item. If a charity is holding regular board meetings by teleconferencing or video conferencing it should also be noted that the Charity Commission recommends that at least one physical meeting of all the charity trustees takes place each year.

2.8 Charity Commission guidance also states that, even where the constitution allows the charity's business to be carried out by teleconferencing, there may still be circumstances where a physical or video meeting of the trustees will be necessary to validate a decision. Such circumstances could include where a third party imposes a specific condition that the act is carried out at a meeting where the participants can both see and hear each other.

3 General meetings

3.1 A meeting of the members of the charity is referred to as a general meeting. For this reason, it can be seen that not all charities are required to hold general meetings, as not all charities have members. A charity established under a trust deed will therefore not usually be required to hold general meetings. That being said, the term 'general meeting' is sometimes used in a different sense; it is sometimes the case that charities without membership still hold meetings that are referred to as 'general meetings'. In some charities without a separate membership, there is a mistaken assumption that the meeting of the trustees that approves the accounts is called the 'annual general meeting'. In addition, sometimes charities hold meetings that are for their volunteers, or open to the public, which are called annual general meetings. Such meetings share the core purpose of accountability with a formal general meeting, but in this chapter, when we discuss general meetings, we will be considering the formal meetings of the members of the charity.

3.2 As general meetings are meetings of the members, they are concerned only with matters that are the members' business and not those that are the responsibility of the trustees. They are important in ensuring accountability but have limited application, being concerned with the reporting of the annual report and accounts, the amendment of the constitution and (often) the appointment of trustees. Although they have limited application and happen much less frequently than board meetings, they often have far more legal and constitutional requirements than board meetings.

3.3 Not all charities are required to have general meetings, but for those that are, detailed requirements for the general meetings are normally set out in the charity's constitution. Charitable companies also need to comply with the requirements of the Companies Act 2006 and, in some instances, these statutory requirements would override the charitable company's Articles. For CIOs, there are also some requirements set out in the Charitable Incorporated Organisations (General) Regulations 2012.

3.4 Annual general meetings

3.4.1 The most common type of general meetings are annual general meetings (AGMs). However, under the Companies Act 2006, there is no requirement for private companies (including charitable companies) to hold AGMs. The Companies Act refers to AGMs and extraordinary general meetings (EGMs) just as 'general meetings'. However, many charities still use this terminology, and the requirement to hold an AGM may still be contained within the Articles.

3.4.2 AGMs are often a requirement in the constitution of membership charities. Whether or not it has a separate membership, a charitable company registered prior to the 2006 Act's implementation may still have a requirement for AGMs in its Articles. In addition, the Charity Commission's model constitution for associate CIOs includes a requirement to hold AGMs. In a charity has a separate membership, AGMs are an important means of accounting to the membership on the activities of the board and their relevance should not be underestimated. Charities holding AGMs can maintain and develop support amongst their members and use the meetings to help ensure the transparency and accountability expected of them. It is therefore advisable for a charity with a membership to retain the requirement to hold an AGM each year. However, it is arguable that there is much less of a need where the trustees are the only members, or for the subsidiary trading companies of charities if the charity is the only member.

3.4.3 If a charitable company no longer wishes to hold AGMs, it will need to check if there is a requirement in its Articles for an AGM, and if so, amend them. The Articles will only need to be amended if they 'expressly' refer to a requirement to hold AGMs. The guidance from the Department for Business, Energy and Industrial Strategy confirms this and states, for example, that provisions commonly found in company Articles specifying that one or more directors are to retire at each AGM are not to be treated as a provision 'expressly' requiring the company to hold an AGM. However, even if there is no direct requirement in its Articles a company should also take care to ensure that any matters that would normally be dealt with at the AGM (such as the appointment of board members) have replacement provisions put in place to handle them.

3.4.4 It should be noted that, under the Companies Act 2006, members of private companies (including charitable companies) do not have a statutory right to demand that the company holds an AGM if it is not a requirement of the Articles. Only the statutory right to requisition a general meeting is available (see below). If a charitable company is considering removing the need to hold AGMs, but wants its members easily to require them to be convened, this would need to be provided for in the amended Articles.

3.4.5 The timing for AGMs will often be specified in the constitution. It used to be the case that companies were required to hold an AGM within 18 months of incorporation and to hold all further AGMs annually and in each calendar year. It was also the case that no more than 15 months could elapse between each AGM. These are the usual requirements of the Articles of any charitable company created before 2006. The Charity Commission's model constitution for associate CIOs has broadly followed this format. Note that a requirement to hold an AGM in each calendar year can override the ability to have up to 15 months between AGMs. Therefore, if there is such a requirement and an AGM were held on 31 December, the following AGM must be held by the following December, to ensure that it is within the calendar year. In this case, the AGM must be held within 12 months rather than 15.

3.4.6 For charitable companies, the annual reports and accounts must be circulated to the members within nine months of the year-end. The annual report and accounts are usually considered by the members at the AGM and circulated with its papers, so this will also influence the timing of the meeting.

3.5 Extraordinary general meetings

EGMs are usually called when the charity has special business (the amendment of the constitution, for example) that cannot await the next AGM. The constitution will normally set out the procedural requirements for EGMs. Generally the procedural requirements for both AGMs and EGMs are the same (but see below regarding notice periods).

3.6 Convening of general meetings

3.6.1 The constitution will usually specify who can convene a general meeting. This will usually be the trustees. In addition, for charitable companies, there are a number of statutory provisions regarding the convening of meetings. The Companies Act 2006 gives directors (the trustees) a general power to call a general meeting (CA 2006, s. 302). The directors may also be required to call the meeting by a requisition lodged under s. 303 of the Companies Act 2006 (see below). If the directors fail to call a meeting requisitioned in this way, those who requisitioned the meeting (or a proportion of them) are authorised to convene the meeting (CA 2006, s. 305). There is also an overall power of the court to call a general meeting under s. 306 of the Companies Act 2006.

3.6.2 A constitution may sometimes also empower one trustee or any member to convene an extraordinary general meeting when there are insufficient trustees in the United Kingdom to form a quorum. This power is useful if the number of trustees falls below the number required for a quorum of the board at any time.

3.7 Requisition of general meetings

3.7.1 The constitution of a charity that is not a company may give the members a right to requisition meetings in some way. However, there is no statutory right for them to do so. In contrast, the members of a charitable company have the statutory right to requisition a meeting, regardless of what the Articles say. A member or members of a company holding between them not less than one-tenth of the voting rights (or, in the case of a share company, not less than one-tenth of the paid-up capital carrying voting rights) may at any time lodge a requisition requiring the directors to convene a general meeting for the purposes stated in the requisition (CA 2006, s. 303). This percentage is reduced to 5% if:

- more than 12 months has passed since the last general meeting; and
- that meeting had been called either in pursuance of a members' requisition or in relation to which any members of the company had rights with respect to the circulation of a resolution no less extensive than they would have had if the meeting had been so called at their request.

3.7.2 On receipt of the requisition (which may consist of several documents in similar form) the directors must, within 21 days, convene the meeting and the meeting must be held not more than 28 days after the date of the notice of the meeting. If the directors do not properly comply with this requirement, the requisitionists (or any of them representing more than one-half of the voting rights of all of them) may convene the meeting at any time within three months from the date of deposit of the requisition. If they do this, the requisitionists may recover their expenses from the company.

3.7.3 A general meeting of a company may also need to be convened on the requisition of an auditor who resigns. An outgoing auditor may submit a requisition calling on trustees/directors to convene a general meeting of the company to consider their explanation of the circumstances with the notice of resignation (CA 2006, s. 518). They may also require the company to circulate to the members a written statement of the circumstances, but the company may apply to the court to relieve the company from this obligation if the outgoing auditor is using the procedure for securing needless publicity for defamatory matter.

3.8 Notice of general meetings

3.8.1 The notice of a general meeting will normally be sent out by the secretary or the chair, at the request of the trustees. A notice should include:

- the time, date and place of meeting;
- the business to be conducted;
- the exact wording of any resolution;
- if it is a special resolution, information on proxy voting; and
- it should be signed and dated.

3.8.2 It is quite common for the constitution to specify what business will normally be conducted at an AGM. If it does not, the AGM business will commonly include:

- a presentation of the annual report and annual accounts;
- an election of trustees (if within the remit of the members under the constitution);
- the appointment of auditors;
- remuneration of auditors (usually the delegation of this decision to the trustees); and
- any special business (specified in notice).

3.8.3 A general meeting can only consider business about which members have been given notice. Any resolutions to be considered must therefore be included on the notice of the meeting. While there may sometimes be a general discussion and a range of issues raised, a resolution cannot be put to the members in general meeting under 'any other business'. Full prior notice of any business must have been given to all members.

3.8.4 The constitution will normally specify the notice requirements for general meetings, but usually (and for charitable companies) it must to be sent to all members, trustees and auditors. A CIO notice must be sent to all members of the CIO who are entitled to vote at the meeting and trustees of the CIO who are not also members entitled to vote at the meeting. Notice must be sent to all those entitled to receive it. Failure to send the notice of the meeting to all those entitled to receive it can invalidate the meeting.

3.8.5 Some constitutions contain a clause that states that 'accidental omission' to send a notice will not invalidate a meeting. The Companies Act 2006 also contains such a provision (CA 2006, s. 313) so this term also applies to charitable companies whether or not it is in the constitution. While this protection is helpful, care must be taken with regard to the meaning of 'accidental omission'. It will cover situations where the charity intended to send someone a notice, but by accident, did not do so. However, if there was no original intention to send the notice (for example, if the secretary mistakenly believed that someone was not entitled to receive a notice or was not a member), it will not apply.

3.8.6 For companies, 14 clear days' notice of a general meeting is required. However, note that Articles written prior to the implementation of the Companies Act 2006 are likely to require 21 clear days' notice for an AGM, as this was a requirement under the previous Companies Act. Such Articles may also require 21 clear days' notice for special resolutions (see below). For CIOs, the notice period is again 14 clear days, unless a longer period is required by the constitution. For charities that are not companies or CIOs, the notice period will normally be specified in the constitution, but it is common for it to be the same as the requirements for charitable companies 14 or 21 clear days). It is also important to note that the term 'clear days' means that you do not include the day the notice is deemed to be served, or the day of the meeting. This is in addition to the period between a notice being dispatched and when it is deemed to be served.

3.8.7 The constitution is also likely to specify when the notice is deemed to be served (how long after posting it is deemed to have been received). If this is not specified in the constitution, it should be considered to be 48 hours after being posted by first class post. For CIOs, the requirements regarding when notice is deemed to be served are set out in the Charitable Incorporated Organisations (General) Regulations 2012. These state that when a document is sent by post, or electronically (by email) the time of receipt is 48 hours after dispatch. When it is posted on a website, it is regarded as having been received immediately (or whenever notice was given to the person that it was on the website). The key thing to note in regard to CIOs, is that weekends and bank holidays are not included when working out these times.

3.8.8 The requirements for 'clear days' and for the period when the notice is deemed to be served therefore means that the requirement for 14 or 21 clear days in practice, actually means more than 14 or 21 days' notice from the date the notice is sent out. Therefore, if a notice must be served 14 clear days before the meeting and is deemed to be served (according to the charity's constitution) two days after posting, a notice sent out on the first day of the month would not be valid for a meeting held before the eighteen day in the month.

3.8.9 We discuss further below the option of giving notice electronically. This can shorten the periods when the notice is deemed to be served, but any notice requirement, including any clear days requirements, will still be in force.

3.9 Short notice requirement

3.9.1 There may be occasions when the charity wants to hold a general meeting without meeting its full notice requirement. For example, in a charitable company where there is a requirement to present the annual accounts to the members at the AGM, if the trustees are the only members, the charity may wish to hold the AGM on the same day as the trustees approve the accounts, directly after that meeting. The notice requirements would not be met in such a case, as the accounts cannot be sent out before being approved and signed. In such an instance, it is sometimes possible to meet provided there is agreement to shortened notice. For a charity that is not a company, there would generally need to be a provision in the constitution stating if this was allowable and how. Even without such a mechanism the signed agreement of everyone who was entitled to notice of the meeting should suffice, so if all the members were present and in agreement, this could be achieved.

3.9.2 For a charitable company, the rules regarding short notice are set out in the Companies Act 2006. A general meeting may be called by shorter notice than required under the 2006 Act provided that it is agreed by the following proportions of the members having a right to attend and vote at the meeting:

- in the case of a company not having a share capital, members who represent not less than 90% of the total voting rights; and
- in the case of a company with share capital, members who hold not less than 90% of the share capital.

3.9.3 For a CIO, the rules regarding short notice are set out in the Charitable Incorporated Organisations (General) Regulations 2012. These state that if 90% of voting members agree, a resolution that is to be proposed at a general meeting may be passed with short notice. The constitution can make this percentage requirement higher, but it will not be above 95%.

3.9.4 While these provisions appear useful, in practice the proportions are so high that they will only be used by a charity that has a small number of members.

3.9.5 For a charitable company, consent to short notice does not need to be given in writing. It is also arguable that consent may even be given in person by the members just being present at the meeting. However, it is preferable to use a method that allows the company to prove that consent was given and so a written, signed consent is ideal. It should also be noted that the provisions relate to the calling of a meeting at short notice; they do not provide for the giving of notice to be completely dispensed with. A copy of the notice of the meeting should therefore still be given to the members either before or at the start of the meeting. Agreement to short notice can be given at any time up to the beginning of the meeting to which it relates.

3.9.6 There is usually also a requirement to give the auditors notice of a general meeting. Although the Companies Act does not require the agreement of the auditors of the company for a meeting to be held on short notice, it may be advisable to obtain from the auditors a letter of non-objection to the short notice.

3.10 Voting at general meetings

3.10.1 Voting at general meetings is usually by a show of hands. In some instances, the constitution may permit that a poll can be demanded, and if the charity is also a company, there are provisions in the Companies Act that cover this. A poll is conducted by the use of voting papers (or electronic poll voting) rather than on a show of hands.

3.10.2 The Companies Act 2006 gives proxies a number of rights, including making the ability to appoint any person as a proxy a statutory right. A proxy is entitled to attend, to speak, to demand a poll and to vote at general meetings. More significantly, anyone appointed as a proxy will now be able to vote on a show of hands (rather than only being included on a poll vote). The Companies Act 2006, s. 284(2) states that:

- every member present in person has one vote; and
- every proxy present who has been duly appointed by a member entitled to vote on the resolution has one vote.

3.10.3 This raises a number of issues regarding the voting rights on a show of hands of a person appointed as a proxy for more than one member. ICSA's guidance on 'corporate representation and proxies at general meetings takes the view that s. 284(2)(b) has to be interpreted as saying that where the same person has been appointed proxy by a number of members, that a person only has one vote on a show of hands (and not one vote for each member he represents). This still leaves the question of what happens when a member is also appointed as a proxy and the interpretation would seem to be that such a person has two votes on a show of hands, one as a member and one as a proxy.

3.10.4 These sections of the Companies Act are subject to any contrary provision in the Articles (CA 2006, s. 284(4)) but there are limitations on reducing a member's voting rights (CA 2006, s. 285).

3.10.5 Under s. 321 of the Companies Act a provision of a company's Articles is void in so far as it would have the effect of excluding the right to demand a poll at a general meeting on any question other than:

- the election of the chair of the meeting; or
- the adjournment of the meeting.

3.10.6 A provision of a company's Articles is also void in so far as it would have the effect of making ineffective a demand for a poll on any such question which is made by:

- not fewer than five members having the right to vote on the resolution; or
- a member or members representing not less than 10% of the total voting rights of all the members having the right to vote on the resolution (excluding any voting rights attached to any shares in the company held as treasury shares); or
- a member or members holding shares in the company conferring a right to vote on the resolution, being shares on which an aggregate sum has been paid up equal to not less than 10% of the total sum paid up on all the shares conferring that right (excluding shares in the company conferring a right to vote on the resolution which are held as treasury shares).

3.10.7 Given the difficulties in regard to proxy voting rights on show of hands votes, it would seem advisable that charitable companies with a large membership take votes on significant matters on poll votes. If a person holds a number of proxy votes, there is no doubt that on a poll vote, these votes will be counted. It is the usual practice for the chair to be the default proxy, so the chair will often hold a number of proxy votes. The complexity of determining who can vote on a show of hands will make the use of poll voting attractive. In any case, it is useful also to note that there is a common law duty on the chair of a meeting to demand a poll on a vote if they consider that the outcome would be different from that reached on a show of hands. While you may still wish to hold a vote on a show of hands for the benefit of the members in the room, if any proxy votes have been submitted, following this vote with a poll vote may be the advisable course of action.

3.11 Chairing of general meetings

3.11.1 The election or appointment of a chair will normally be specified in the constitution. If nothing is specified, the chair should be elected by the members at the start of the meeting.

3.11.2 The chair has authority on the running of the meeting. For example, on a vote on a resolution at a meeting on a show of hands, a declaration by the chair that the resolution has or has not been passed is regarded as conclusive evidence of that fact without proof of the number or proportion of the votes recorded in favour of, or against, the resolution.

3.11.3 It was previously quite common for the constitution to give the chair a casting vote. One of the effects of the Companies Act 2006 is that it abolished the right of a casting vote for the chair at general meetings. For any company that had a right to a casting vote in its Articles prior to 1 October 2007, this will continue to have effect, but that no company created after that date can validly include such a right in its Articles. (This relates to general meetings – it does not affect any provisions regarding casting votes in board meeting that may be in the Articles.

3.11.4 The constitution will also usually give the chair the right to call for a poll vote or to adjourn the meeting.

3.12 Proxies

3.12.1 A member of a company has a statutory right to appoint a proxy to attend the meeting in their place, and vote on their behalf (CA 2006, s. 324). This right applies no matter what the Articles state. There is also a legal requirement to include a prominent statement on the right to appoint a proxy on the notice of the meeting. Also, under the Companies Act, the longest period that can be specified in the Articles within which members must give notice of their wish to appoint a proxy is 48 hours prior to the meeting or a poll being demanded (excluding non-working days). For example, if your general meeting starts at 2.00pm on a Tuesday following a Bank Holiday Monday, proxy notices can be lodged up until 2.00pm on the previous Thursday, or even later if permitted by the Articles.

3.12.2 There are a number of charitable companies that were established with a restriction on appointing proxies, or a restriction on who can serve as a proxy (for example, that they must also be a member). The Companies Act 2006 overrides any such restrictions that are in the Articles. This means that a member has a statutory right to appoint a proxy. Any person (and not just members) can be appointed to serve as a proxy.

3.12.3 For other types of charity a member can appoint a proxy if the constitution allows. Whether that proxy can be any person chosen by the member or only one of the other members (or the meeting's chair) also depends on the constitution.

3.12.4 The form of proxy document will normally be specified in the constitution together with rules on how it is to be delivered to the charity and the deadline by which it must be received. Again, it should be noted that there are provisions in the Companies Act 2006 that relate to these matters for charitable companies:

- A proxy is a person appointed by an individual or corporate member of a company, to attend, speak and vote on behalf of his appointer at one meeting (including any adjournment thereof) of the members of the company, or a particular class of members of the company, but for no other purpose.
- A member of a company limited by guarantee is allowed to appoint only one person as his proxy, whereas a member of a company with a share capital may appoint more than one, provided that each proxy is appointed to exercise the rights attached to different shares held by that member (CA 2006, s. 324(2)). It is not necessary for a proxy to be a member of the company. Every notice of a meeting of a company must include a statement to the effect that a member entitled to attend and vote is entitled to appoint a proxy (or proxies in the case of a company with a share capital) to attend, speak and vote on his behalf. The notice must also state that such proxy need not himself be a member of the company, and should set out any other more extensive rights conferred by the company's Articles (CA 2006, s. 325).
- There is no requirement to circulate proxy forms with notices of meetings. However, it is important to note that it is illegal to issue proxy forms by the company to selected members only (CA 2006, s. 326(1)).

3.12.5 Electronic proxies may be specifically permitted by the constitution. They can be used in a charitable company, even if not specified in the Articles, provided the company and members agree to do so and the company provides an address for electronic lodgement of the proxy.

3.12.6 Both charitable companies and CIOs need to be aware that there will be some situations in which the company or CIO is deemed to have consented to receiving documents electronically. For example, if it provides an electronic address in a notice convening a general meeting, a company can be deemed to have consented to receiving documents relating to that meeting, such as proxies, using those methods. If you do not wish to receive a proxy vote in this way, you must ensure that such details are not included on the notice or proxy form (including the letterhead used). If a CIO sends or supplies documents or information to another person in electronic form, the CIO is treated as having agreed to accept a response in electronic form; where the document or information is sent or supplied by the CIO by electronic means from an electronic address, or the CIO has given such an address in the document or information (subject to any limitations specified when providing that address), the CIO is treated as having agreed to the response being sent by electronic means to that address.

3.13 Quorum

3.13.1 The quorum for a general meeting (the number of members who must be present for the meeting to be valid) will usually be specified in the constitution. If no quorum is specified, at least two members must be present.

3.13.2 Sometimes a constitution will state that the quorum needs to be present only at the start of the meeting. This means that the quorum does not need to be maintained. Therefore, if the number of members present falls below the required number of a quorum, the meeting will be able to continue.

3.13.3 Annual general meeting procedure checklist for a charitable company:

- Secretary to arrange a suitable venue for the meeting.
- Trustees to convene the AGM – deciding on the date; formally approving accounts to be considered at that meeting; agreeing the wording of any resolutions to be put to it and authorising the secretary to issue the notice.
- Notice to be issued to members within the notice period (usually either not less than 14 or 21 clear days before the meeting). If the AGM is to consider the accounts, these should be sent with the notice.
- Notice to refer to proxies and their right to be appointed. If a proxy form is to be sent to members, it should be sent to all members.
- Copy of notice also to be sent to all trustees and to the auditors.
- Consider and prepare who will be speaking on each item, and who will answer any questions (such as on the accounts). If the board has put resolutions to the meeting, ensure that there are proposers and seconders for the resolutions.
- Before the meeting (no less than 48 hours), secretary to check and count all the proxies received.
- Prepare poll cards for any poll votes that may be held (or electronic voting devices).
- At the meeting, ensure that an attendee sheet is circulated or register members as they attend. Inform any person appointed as a proxy that they have been appointed and give details of how they have been instructed to vote if they have been so instructed. If non-members are attending the meeting, give all members and proxies voting cards to use on any show of hands votes. Have copies of the minutes of the last meeting available at the meeting. Also have extra copies of the agenda and the annual report and accounts (if being considered).

3.14 Minutes

Minutes of all general meetings must be kept in a minute book. In charitable companies and CIOs, members have the right to inspect the minutes. The minutes of each AGM should be presented to the next AGM, but this can mean a long period in which minutes are not approved. It is therefore good practice for the minutes of an AGM to be presented to the first board meeting following the AGM for approval by the board (see Chapter B2, page 139).

4 Electronic communications

4.1 The traditional way of communicating with members, and of sending them the notice of meetings, is by sending a paper copy through the post. However, there are now many other ways of communicating, including dsx emails and use of the charity's website. There is, therefore, a question for the charity of how it can use such methods for formal communication. Many older constitutions were written assuming that the traditional method was to be used, so they often speak of documents being 'in writing', define that in terms of paper copies and refer to the use of the post. There is, therefore, often a constitutional and legal issue around whether alternative methods can be used, constitutionally and legally. Electronic communications covers a range of options including e-mail and using the website (posting a document online). Using the website can be a useful option, as in this regard, consent can be deemed for companies and CIOs (see below).

4.2 If the charity is neither a company nor a CIO, the method of communication will be as laid down in its constitution. If this says, for example, that the notice of a meeting must be sent in the post, then this method must be used, or the constitution should be amended to allow for different means of communication. If the constitution is not as explicit, then it may be possible to interpret it in such a way that communications methods can be changed. However, it would still be advisable for the constitution to be updated.

4.3 Electronic communications – companies

4.3.1 The Companies Act 2006 introduced a wide range of provisions regarding electronic communications. These followed, and expanded upon, the Companies Act 1985 (Electronic Communications) Order 2000 (SI 2000/3373). If a charity has a large number of members, the provisions under the Companies Act 2006 can provide substantial cost savings. However, it should also be noted that the use of e-communications requires the consent of the member, which may be withdrawn at any time. It is likely that not all members will agree to receiving information in this way and both methods will therefore need to be used. Charitable companies should consider whether reducing the number of paper copies that need to be sent out is still an advantage. As it is likely that some members will consent to e-communication and some will not, this can lead to the company having to operate both e-communication and hard copy communication mechanisms, with the added complications and expense of keeping track of two separate communication systems.

4.3.2 The Companies Act 2006 allows electronic communications to be used in relation to any document or information required or authorised to be sent or supplied under the Companies Acts. The default method of communication is still hard copy. However, a company does not need to have provisions for the use of electronic communications in its Articles or to obtain the consent of the members in general meeting unless it wishes to take advantage of the website default procedures (see below).

4.3.3 The general rule is that, with the exception of the website default procedures, the intended recipient must have agreed individually to accept communications in that manner. The Companies Act communications provisions can be viewed as overriding anything in a company's Articles, except where the provisions specifically allow contrary provision to be made (such as in relation to deemed delivery).

4.3.4 If the recipient agrees, the company may supply information and documents in electronic form. If the document or information is sent in electronic form by post or delivered by hand (for example, on a CD or memory stick), it must be handed to the intended recipient or sent or supplied to an address to which it could be validly sent if it were in hard copy form.

4.3.5 If the member so requests, the company must provide a hard copy form of any document sent by electronic means or made available on a website within 21 days of receipt of the request and for no charge. If the company fails to comply with this, the company and every officer in default commits an offence and is liable to a fine and a daily fine for as long as the contravention continues.

4.3.6 The Companies Act 2006 allows companies to use their website as the default communication method instead of hard copy. The Companies Act 1985 (Electronic Communications) Order 2000 already allowed for the use of electronic communication for the circulation of reports and accounts, notices of meetings and the receipt of proxy forms. However, individual consent had to be received from each recipient. The 2006 Act changed the position in regard to consent for the use of websites. There is still an obligation to seek that consent, but if no response is received from the member, consent can be deemed to have been given. In other words, the member will need to opt out of the communication method rather than opt in, as now. This makes it much more likely that a company can receive consent from sufficient members to make the use of the website worthwhile.

4.3.7 Unfortunately, the ability to deem consent in this way applies only to website communications, and not to other forms of electronic communications such as e-mail.

4.3.8 If a company wishes to use the website for formal communications with its members, either its Articles of Association must contain a provision allowing it to use the website or its membership must pass a resolution to this effect. Once this has been achieved, the company must also ensure the following:

- A document or information on a website must be made available in a form that the company reasonably considers will enable the recipient to read it and retain a copy of it. So, the company must use an electronic form that is in common usage.
- The company must notify the intended recipient of the presence of a document or information on a website, the address of the website, the place on the website where it may be accessed and how to access the document or information. Unless the member has also consented to being contacted by electronic means, this means that this information must be provided in hard copy form (for example, by letter).The company must make the document or information available on its website throughout the period specified by any relevant provision of the Companies Acts or, if no such period is specified, within 28 days. Each member must be individually asked to consent to receive communication via a website. This consent can be either general (for all communications) or specific. When asking for consent, the request must state clearly that failure to respond within 28 days will mean that consent is deemed to have been received. The request cannot be repeated until 12 months have passed.

4.3.9 Note that the members must always be notified that the document has been posted on the website. This extra step could mean that any cost advantages of using a website could disappear, especially if members have consented to communication via the website but not via email. In this case, notification that the document is available will have to be sent by post. If the document is a one-page notice of a meeting, there is no cost saving if a letter has to be sent to the members saying that it is available on the website. Having said that, it is important to bear in mind that the savings will be more significant for documents such as the annual report and accounts.

4.3.10 If the company agrees, documents can be sent to or served on a company by electronic means. The address is that specified by the company and so could be an email address or a fax number. If a document is sent in electronic form by hand or by post (on a CD or memory stick), it must be sent to the company's registered office or to the address provided by the company for hard copy correspondence. The company may also agree to receive documents in a form other than hard copy or electronic.

4.4 CIOs

It is up to a CIO if it wishes to communicate electronically with its members. If it does, a provision must be included in its constitution. However, there are standard provisions, to this effect, in the Charity Commission model constitution. If a CIO is using electronic communications, it will need to note the following requirements, as set out in the Charitable Incorporated Organisation (General) Regulations 2012:

- If a CIO sends or supplies documents or information to a member in electronic form, the CIO is treated as having agreed to accept a response in electronic form; where the document or information is sent or supplied by the CIO by electronic means from an electronic address, or the CIO has given such an address in the document or information (subject to any limitations specified when providing that address), the CIO is treated as having agreed to the response being sent by electronic means to that address.
- Where a member of a CIO has received a document or information from the CIO otherwise than in hard copy form, that member is entitled to require the CIO to send a hard copy version of the document or information within 21 days of the receipt of the request without a charge being made.
- Where the document or information is sent or supplied by means of a website, it is treated as having been received when the material is first made available on the website or, if later, when the intended recipient received (or is treated as having received) notice of the fact that the material is available on the website.
- A document or information may only be sent or supplied by being made available on a website if the member has agreed (generally or specifically) that the document or information may be sent or supplied in that manner and has not revoked that agreement. Deemed consent can only apply when the members of the CIO have resolved that the CIO may send or supply documents or information to members by making them available on a website, or the CIO's constitution contains provision to that effect, and the member has been asked individually by the CIO to agree that the CIO may send or supply documents or information by means of a website and has not responded within 28 days. In addition, the communication from the CIO must state clearly what the effect of a failure to respond will be; this cannot be sent less than 12 months after a similar communication.
- When the website is used, the CIO must notify the intended recipient of the presence of the document or information on the website; the website address; where it may be accessed on the website; and how to access the document or

information. In addition, the CIO must make the document or information available throughout any period specified by any applicable charity law provision; if no such period is specified, the period of 28 days starting on the date on which the notification is sent.

5 Electronic voting

5.1 Electronic voting, for either proxy or other types of voting, can be very useful, particularly in charities with a large membership. Done properly, it has the potential to increase members' participation in the charity.

5.2 The Companies Act 2006 permits certain communications between companies and members to be made by email and other means. However, the Act covers only proxy voting, therefore other electronic voting will be permissible only if the constitution specifically allows it. If trustees were to be elected in this way, not connected with the AGM, there would need to be specific provision. Likewise, other charities wanting to allow electronic voting will need to make provision in their constitutions.

5.3 Some charities with a large membership may find the use of electronic voting beneficial (such as for the election of trustees). If the constitution allows electronic voting and the charity is considering it, there will need to be systems in place to ensure that the voting process is sufficiently secure (for example, members could be issued with a unique identification number). Voting would also need to be via a secure website, with appropriate encryption to ensure that the vote is not traceable to the member voting (if a secret ballot is required).

6 Members' statements

6.1 There is a provision under the Companies Act for members to require the circulation of their statements. This has rarely been used by the members of charitable companies, but could be used by a minority of members as a means of lobbying the majority. However, in exercising this right, the members concerned bear the costs of doing so, which may, in effect, reduce its use.

6.2 Section 314 of the Companies Act gives members the power to require circulation of statements. The circulation of a statement of 1,000 words or less may be required by the members of the company to those members entitled to receive notice of a general meeting. Such statement should be concerned with:

- a matter referred to in a proposed resolution to be dealt with at that meeting; or
- other business to be dealt with at that meeting.

6.3 A company is required to circulate any such a statement once it has received such a request from:

- members representing at least 5% of the total voting rights of all the members who have a relevant right to vote (excluding any voting rights attached to any shares in the company held as treasury shares); or
- for share companies, at least 100 members with a relevant right to vote and hold shares in the company for which each member has paid an average sum of at least £100.

6.4 Such a request may either be in hard copy or in electronic form and must:

- identify the statement to be circulated;
- be authenticated by the person or persons making it; and
- be received by the company at least one week before the meeting to which it relates.

6.5 A company that is required to circulate a statement in this way must send a copy of it to each member of the company entitled to receive notice of the meeting in the same manner as the notice of the meeting and at the same time as, or as soon as reasonably practicable after, it gives notice of the meeting.

6.6 Members of the company requesting the circulation of the statement must usually pay the company's expenses. This will not be the case if the company resolves otherwise, or if the company has previously so resolved. The company is not bound to comply with a request unless a sum reasonably sufficient to meet its expenses in doing so is deposited with or tendered to it, not later than one week before the meeting.

6.7 A company is not required to circulate a members' statement under s. 315 if, on an application by the company or another person who claims to be aggrieved, the court is satisfied that the rights conferred by s. 314 and that section are being abused.

7 Resolutions of members

7.1 Most of the business conducted at a general meeting is dealt with by ordinary resolutions (a simple majority of members present and voting is required). However, sometimes the constitution may require a higher majority and in company law, some matters (such as the amendment of the Articles or a change of name) require a special resolution. Special resolutions under company law require a three-quarters majority of members present and voting to vote in favour for the resolution to be passed. Until the implementation of the Companies Act 2006, a special resolution also required 21 clear days' notice, so this requirement may still be mirrored in an older set of Articles. A copy of a special resolution must be filed with Companies House within 15 days of the meeting. If it has altered the Articles, a reprinted copy of those must also be filed.

7.2 In addition to resolutions being passed at meetings they can also be passed as written resolutions – one that is circulated to the members in writing and which they indicate their agreement to, also in writing. Unless the constitution states otherwise, email agreement is usually considered adequate. Constitutions commonly provide for written resolutions as an alternative to voting at a meeting. These sometimes have a much higher requirement for a majority (either 90% or 100%) and therefore are of limited application, unless the charity has a very small membership.

7.3 However, charitable companies and trading subsidiaries can take advantage of the Companies Act 2006 (ss. 288–300). This allows written resolutions to be passed with a simple majority (or a 75% majority for special resolutions). Note, however, that the majority required is of the full voting rights in the company, not just those of the members who chose to vote (as is the case at a general meeting), so the majority required is still likely to be higher than at a meeting. The resolution must be sent to all members entitled to receive notice of meetings. Under the Companies Act, written resolutions are passed on the date that the required majority is achieved. In addition, if a majority is not achieved within 28 days of the resolution being circulated, the resolution falls. A record of any written resolution passed should be kept in the minute books, alongside the general meeting minutes.

7.4 In a company, the following may not be passed as a written resolution:

- a resolution under s. 168 of the Companies Act removing a director before the expiration of his period of office; nor
- a resolution under s. 510 of the Companies Act removing an auditor before the expiration of his term of office.

7.5 For other types of charity, there must be provision made in the constitution if they wish members to be able to take decisions in this way. The Charitable Incorporated Organisations (General) Regulations 2012 state that members can only use postal votes if there is a specific provision in the constitution, which must give details of:

- the circumstances in which such votes may be given; and
- the way in which such votes may be given.

8 Board meetings

8.1 The majority of charity constitutions will have far more provisions regarding general meetings than trustee meetings. In addition, for companies, there are a range of legislative requirements for general meetings and very few for director meetings. This can seem strange for many charities, as the trustee meetings seem more important. They are held much more frequently and it is the trustees who take the main strategic decisions of the charity. However, the legal emphasis on members' meetings is to ensure that there is accountability and to accommodate the rights of members. While there are some provisions regarding trustee meetings, the core duties of trustees and directors should ensure that, indirectly, they govern their own meetings effectively. However, there is still the need for clarity and guidance on how such meetings should be run.

8.2 The constitution will usually state how trustee meetings are called. It may also specify the frequency of the meetings (with a minimum requirement) and govern the chairing of such meetings. It may also (but less commonly) state the notice requirements and the numbers that will make trustee meetings quorate. Often, it will say that such matters are to be determined by rules or regulations set by the trustees.

8.3 Notice of board meetings

The constitution may state what the notice requirement is for board meetings. If no notice is specified, trustees should always be given reasonable notice, according to the circumstances of the charity or the relevant meeting. Common practice is for those entitled to attend the meeting to be given seven days' advance notice of the event. Meetings can usually be convened by the chair or the secretary, but again check the requirements of the constitution.

8.4 Frequency of board meetings

8.4.1 This may be specified in the constitution, and will be dependent on the nature of the work of the charity. The Charity Commission recommends that a minimum of two full trustees' meetings are held in any 12-month period.

8.4.2 The practice of charities varies greatly, but common arrangements for charities include:

- **Monthly board meetings**: This may suit a small charity with few staff and a great deal of operational work for the trustees to do. It may also be suitable in times of crisis. Sometimes boards decide to meet more frequently and remove the need for committees. Monthly meetings can be demanding on trustees and staff resources. If meeting monthly, a board may need to consider whether the board meetings themselves, and preparations for them, are generating a considerable amount of work for staff, preventing them from doing other work. It should also consider whether the frequency of board meetings is affecting the ability of some trustees to contribute.

- **Every two months**: This practice would suit a medium-sized charity, a large charity where the board is engaged in a certain amount of operational work, or where the charity is going through a period of change.
- **Quarterly**: This is a more common practice for the boards of large charities. It can be practical, provided there is sufficient delegation for the charity to operate effectively between meetings. Often, if a board is meeting only four times each year it can be advisable to supplement this with an away day or social functions.

8.4.3 Another factor to consider in regard to the frequency of meetings is their duration. Again, practice differs greatly, with board meetings varying from between two hours to two days. For long meetings to be effective there must be sufficient breaks.

8.5 Planning board meetings

The trustees should take a decision on how frequently they wish to meet and set a calendar of dates. If such matters are determined intermittently, it can affect the effectiveness of the charity. Ideally there should be a regular routine, for instance the board meets in set months, or even on set days. The secretary, or staff supporting the meetings, can then prepare a rolling agenda for the year – indicating which key items need to be considered when ensuring a balance across the agendas. While there will be matters that arise from time to time, much of the business of the board will be of a cyclical nature and so can be planned in this way. This covers not just the core decisions to be taken by the board (such as the annual report and accounts) but the timetable of its strategic decision making and its monitoring of work undertaken on its behalf.

8.6 Board information

Trustees receive a wide range of information from the charity and much of this is dealt with at meetings. When planning the board's programme for the year, it can also be useful to consider the information that it receives, whether this all needs to be agenda items or if some could be circulated separately for information only. This can be a helpful alternative way of dealing with regular reports and freeing up time at meetings for core decisions and deliberations. The purpose of a board meeting is collective decision making, rather than the provision of information, and this can be done in other ways. Consideration should be given to how information is presented on the agenda. Is the reason why it is on the agenda clear? If a decision is required, is this clear, and are any recommendations also clear?

8.7 Attendance at meetings

8.7.1 Charities rely on trustee attendance and it is essential to encourage this. Attending regularly gives trustees the opportunity to use their expertise and to carry out the function of being a trustee. All trustees should therefore be encouraged to attend regularly. Regular non-attendance could be a sign that trustees are not meeting their duties and this should be dealt with. Some constitutions will state that non-attendance at a certain number of meetings, or for a certain period (such as six months) will potentially invalidate trusteeship. Even if the constitution has no such provision, this is something that should be discussed with the trustee. It may be that it is a matter that the charity can deal with (by changing the timing of the meetings), or that the trustee should stand down.

8.7.2 Attendance at the meetings should be clearly recorded. This will usually be in the minutes, but some charities also have a constitutional requirement for an attendance register to be kept.

8.7.3 The quorum may also be dealt with under the constitution. If not, it should be set by the trustees. If no quorum is set, the quorum for the meetings will be two. The actual quorum requirements of the charity will depend on its work and the composition of the board. However, a generally workable quorum is one-third of the trustees. Sometimes a charity may want to set another requirement (such as that certain trustees should be in attendance) or have (or not have) a particular majority at a meeting. In doing this, it is important to ensure that any such provisions are workable and do not hinder the effectiveness of the board.

8.7.4 The trustees may wish to invite non-trustees to some of their meetings (it is very common for key staff to also attend). When there are non-trustees in attendance, their presence should be recorded separately in the minutes (stating 'Present' for the trustees and 'In attendance' for the others) to make clear the capacity in which everyone attended. It should also always be remembered that while the trustees may choose to invite observers to any, or part of, its meetings, the only people with a right to attend and to vote are the trustee members themselves. There is also no general right for observers to speak at a meeting, unless invited to do so by the chair. In determining who the trustees of a charity are, the courts will look at function, rather than title. It is therefore important that there is absolute clarity about who is participating in decision making at board meetings. Boards usually accept comments and contributions from observers during meetings. However, they should also be aware that the priority at any meeting is for trustees to ask questions and contribute to the debate. When invited to participate in discussion and debate, observers should do so in an advisory capacity only.

8.8 Chair of the trustees

The election of the chair of the trustees will usually be covered by the constitution, and the chair will usually be the same person as the trustee who chairs general meetings. The role of the chair is covered elsewhere (see Chapter A4, page 77). However, it should be noted that the restrictions of the Companies Act 2006 regarding the chair's casting vote at general meetings do not apply to meetings of the board.

9 Alternative decision making: written resolutions

If the board wants to take decisions by written resolution, in the same way as members can, provision should be made for this in the constitution. This also applies for charitable companies as the Companies Act 2006 provisions regarding written resolutions apply only to the written resolutions of members, not of directors. If there is nothing in the constitution the charity can rely on the common law principle of assent, but this requires total unanimity (all the trustees must agree). Written resolutions are likely to be much more useful for trustees than members, as boards are often smaller than the membership of a charity, so getting a majority is much easier. It is therefore advisable to include this provision in the constitution. Written resolutions sometimes require a higher level of consent to vote at meeting (often 75%) as there is no opportunity for debate. Their use is also much more suitable for matters that have already been discussed at a board meeting, or where no debate is necessary. A record of every written resolution passed should be kept in the minute book, along with the board minutes.

10 Delegation

10.1 In practice, boards cannot usually take every decision that a charity needs to make. Fortunately, subject to legal constraints and the charity's own constitution, the board can delegate certain powers to others to act on their behalf. However, a board may only delegate power, not responsibility, so the trustees will remain liable. Boards typically delegate to staff, and/or committees.

10.2 As trustees are ultimately responsible for the charity, all major decisions must be taken by the board. Following the principles of good governance, boards should draw up a list of matters that require decisions to be made by the whole board, although some of these may be delegated for discussion and recommendation to committees. Some items on the list will legally require a board decision, such as the approval of financial statements, while others are a matter of good governance. A sample list of matters reserved for the board of trustees is available at www.icsa.org.uk.

10.3 The starting point for all charities is that the board takes all decisions, unless these decisions are delegated. Boards, therefore, need to record clearly any delegations that they give. Some delegations may be very general (in the job description of the CEO or a statement that the CEO is responsible for the day-to-day running of the charity). Some may be very specific (delegating the power to agree to a particular contract). However, it is advisable for the board to consider delegations across the organisation as a whole. This enables it to take a consistent approach and to identify and deal with any gaps in its delegation. In agreeing what matters are reserved by the board, it should also agree some core protocols for delegations and set barriers on decisions that can be taken on its behalf (upper financial limits). Often delegations can be scattered across a range of documents – job descriptions, policies, minutes and terms of reference. To ensure that trustees, committees and staff understand what they may or may not approve, it is a good idea to have a single document drawing together all of the delegations, or the approach to be taken. The board could approve a schedule of delegations showing the delegated matters. While many matters may be financial, such as who can approve expenditure and within what limits, others may be operational, such as who can approve press releases.

10.4 The term 'standing orders' refers to the written rules that a board makes for the running of board and committee meetings under the charity's constitution. Constitutions normally focus on the running of meetings of members, and leave many decisions on how to run board meetings to the discretion of the board. Standing orders will usually cover such detailed matters as how trustees may raise items for discussion at meetings, and when papers and minutes are circulated. Standing orders may also be called governance procedures.

11 Committees

11.1 A charity may delegate some of its work to committees. How the meetings of the committees are run will be governed predominately by their terms of reference. A constitution may sometimes place some regulations on committees (it is fairly common for the constitution to specify that there must be a minimum number of trustees on the committee). However, in all other regards, the way in which the meetings of the committees are run will be in the hands of the board in setting its terms of reference.

11.2 Where a board delegates some of its work to committees, it must ensure that it has proper control over those committees. This means that it must set clear terms of reference, including what the committee is for, how often it should meet, how its membership is determined, what authority it has and how it should report to the board.

11.3 Committees may be 'standing committees', which are a permanent part of the charity's governance or 'ad hoc' committees, set up for a specific purpose (to oversee a major construction project). Another term used for ad hoc committees is 'task and finish group'.

12 Audit committees

12.1 While the boards of smaller charities may do all the work themselves, medium and large charities are likely to have a range of standing committees. These may include an audit committee.

12.2 The main purpose of an audit committee is to provide assurance to the board that there is an effective system of internal controls. In particular, the audit committee will approve the programme of internal audits, receive all internal audit reports and liaise with the external auditors. The benefits of an effective audit committee include:

- increased confidence in the objectivity of financial reporting;
- greater emphasis on internal control and the implementation of actions following internal audits; and
- more effective challenge and review of executive management performance.

12.3 One important area that may fall within the terms of reference of the audit committee is ensuring that there is a strong framework for risk management in place. For this reason, some charities have an audit and a risk committee, while some have two separate committees for these functions.

13 Other committees

Other committees, depending on the relative importance to the charity, may include:

(a) **Finance and general purposes**: these are often responsible for overseeing financial, property, technological and human resources. Finance committees are very common in large charities but care needs to be taken, particularly if

they are covering general purposes as well, not to replicate the work of staff or to take on too much of the work of the board. Larger charities may have individual committees to lead on areas that might be covered by a finance and general purposes committee elsewhere. For example:
- investment;
- property; and
- human resources.

(b) Remuneration: these are responsible for making recommendations to the board on the pay strategy and levels of pay for staff, and in particular, the remuneration of senior staff.

(c) Nominations: these are responsible for recruiting new trustees and may also oversee appraisals, and skills audits.

14 Terms of reference

14.1 All committees, whether they are standing committees or only set up for a specific purpose, must have clear, written terms of reference. These should include:

- committee name;
- purpose;
- delegated authority;
- membership and voting rights;
- committee chair;
- frequency of meetings;
- person acting as secretary or minute-taker;
- reporting procedure; and
- quorum.

14.2 Where a committee is established to help achieve a particular task, such as an office move, it may useful to include details about what the committee is expected to produce and when (for example, 'Options appraisal to be presented to the board at its meeting in May 2012').

14.3 Unless a committee is authorised to do so by the board, it may not sub-delegate its power. However, a committee may be given authority to sub-delegate some of its work to one or more sub-committees or individuals. Where there is a power of sub-delegation, the board will always be able to over-ride or remove the sub-delegation.

14.4 Sample terms of reference for a committee:

Purpose	**The X Committee is established in accordance with Article X. Its purpose is ...**
Membership and proceedings	1. The members of the committee shall be appointed by the board and the profile of the committee is formally reviewed every ... year(s). 2. Members shall include: 3. The (name support staff) may be invited to attend all or part of particular meetings. 4. The secretary shall act as secretary to the committee. 5. The quorum shall be [x] members. 6. The committee shall meet not fewer than [x] times a year. 7. A meeting may be held by telephone or using any televisual or other electronic or virtual means agreed by the members, in which all participants may communicate simultaneously with all other participants.
Function	The committee is responsible for:

Powers	1. The committee is authorised by the board to .... 2. The committee may establish subcommittees and delegate to them. 3. In all other matters the role of the committee is advisory, unless a specific delegation power is made by the Council.

Reporting	1. The secretary shall circulate minutes of the committee's meetings to all trustees. 2. A report of the committee's deliberations shall be made to the next board meeting. Papers shall be presented to the board as and when required.

15 Reporting lines for committees and appointing to committees

15.1 All committees of the board should report to the board. Minutes should be circulated to all trustees. This may be done either as soon as they are available or as part of the pack of board papers. The chair of the committee should also be prepared to report to the board on any significant items, decisions and recommendations. Because of the chair's role in reporting to the board, it is usual for the committee chair to be a trustee.

15.2 In some instances, a committee may report to more than one board. For example, many charities have a trading company set up as a subsidiary. In these instances, the audit committee may report to the board of the trading company as well as the board of the parent charity.

15.3 Under the constitutions of most charities, the board normally has to approve the membership of all committees and appoints the committee chair. In practice, committees sometimes find their own members, and elect their own chair, and they are then ratified as such by the board.

16 Guidelines for effective meetings

16.1 How effective a board will be in taking its decisions, will be influenced by the behaviour of the trustees (see chapter C1, page 183). However, effective meetings are effectively chaired. There is a wide variety of guidance on how to chair meetings well. Here are some suggested pointers:

- In general the chair should listen, move the discussion on, summarising and being firm but sensitive.
- The chair is under an obligation to know and understand the charity's constitution and any rules or regulations governing how the board or committee operates. They should also have at least a basic understanding of the matter under discussion, and should be briefed on this in advance if necessary.
- The chair should ensure that a proper agenda is drawn up, even if this is done by a staff member. They should discuss the agenda with the relevant staff before the meeting and be clear about the action that is required for each agenda item. It is also often a good idea to plan the proposed timing for the meeting – how much time should be allocated to each agenda item.
- The chair should summarise the discussion periodically, especially if the item under discussion is complex. At the end of each agenda item, the chair should ensure that all present are clear about the outcome reached.
- A good chair will ensure that all members are able to participate; that all points of view are heard in a debate, including dissenting voices and that one voice does not dominate the meeting. The chair should encourage all members to have some input.
- If the chair offers their own opinion it should be made clear that this is a personal view, rather than a summary of the meeting's position.
- The chair needs to manage each agenda item. It can sometimes be helpful to think about the discussion progressing in the following order – facts, opinions, decisions, action.

16.2 Ensuring that the meeting is chaired effectively is the responsibility of all those present, not just the chair and the chair needs support to fulfil their role. Many charities have codes of conduct for trustees. They can often include how to behave at meetings, and there should be some mechanisms of ensuring that trustees:

- respect the chair and their decisions about the conduct of the meeting; and
- address the meeting through the chair. This essentially means getting the attention of the chair and awaiting their permission to speak, rather than making the point directly. It is the chair's role to ensure that everyone is heard.

16.3 While it is important that charity meetings are conducted in an orderly way, care should be taken to ensure that meetings do not get bogged down in overly formal procedures. In board and committee meetings, it is not usually necessary for every issue under discussion to be proposed and seconded. However, the fact that there is no formal meeting procedure does not mean that there should not be some level of formality in the proceedings or that the conduct of the meetings is unimportant. Charities should be clear to their trustees about what behaviour is acceptable in meetings. Examples of unacceptable behaviour could include:

- participating in side conversations during the meeting;
- performing other tasks during the meeting (catching up on other paperwork);
- any aggressive or rude behaviour;
- not listening, or dominating the discussion; and
- 'caucusing', that is agreeing to a particular approach amongst a small group of members in advance of the meeting.

16.4 Even if well conducted and with a good chair, meetings can become ineffective. Typically, this can happen when a board or committee is insufficiently focused on its role. Such meetings will be characterised by a long agenda, sometimes with little or no clear reason why some agenda items have been brought to the meeting. Sometimes there will be a standard agenda (with a list of reports from officers, with no indication on the agenda itself about the core subject matter).

16.5 The first step towards an effective meeting is to identify the significant issues that require attention and then focus on them. These can be categorised in a number of ways. One way may be to categorise board items as:

- governance;
- key decisions;
- monitoring; and
- strategy.

16.6 There are a number of different ways of keeping the focus on the core business:

- **Using a 'business agenda'**: grouping together items that require formal decisions only and dealing with these first. The meeting then agrees that everything in this section will be dealt with without any discussion unless a trustee asks in advance for an item to be discussed. If such a request is made, that item is taken out of the business agenda and put into the main agenda. The business agenda is therefore still dealt with, with no discussion, and the discussion item is dealt with elsewhere on the agenda.
- **Avoiding a standard agenda**: review the work programme for the year and consider in advance what you need to agree and when. Then draft the agenda so that each item to be discussed is described, along with the action needed. Be careful of the overuse of 'matters arising' and 'any other business'. If a matter arising from the last meeting needs to be discussed, it should be an agenda item in its own right. 'Any other business' should be restricted to urgent matters or short matters for information only.
- **A timed agenda**: The chair sometimes sets timings, but does not inform the rest of the meeting. However, being open about the timings helps everyone to keep to them – and it establishes the relative importance of items in advance. If a participant wants more time allocated to an item, they can request this at the start of the meeting.
- **Keeping the agenda short**: ideally no more than eight substantive items. This does not necessarily mean shorter meetings, but should give more focus on the key issues.
- **Removing information items**: often, agenda are taken up with items that are for information only. If you have a lot of these, think about having a separate information pack that you can send out to the trustees/committee.

16.7 It can help a board or committee to work more effectively if the members also have the opportunity to meet socially, even if just during the refreshment breaks at the meeting itself. This not only helps to address conflicts, but also ensures that there are opportunities for matters to be discussed appropriately outside the meeting. Without this type of discussion, trustees or committee members may raise inappropriate issues at meetings or begin to caucus privately.

16.8 It may also be useful to provide opportunities to think aloud and for creative thinking. This can be done by varying the format of meetings (for example, there could be some informal sessions mixed in with the standard meeting or the meeting could break into smaller groups for brainstorming).

16.9 The Charity Commission has published guidance entitled *It's your decision: charity trustees and decision making* (CC27). This guidance sets out a number of principles for how trustees should approach making decisions affecting their charity. It states that following these principles will support effective decision making and help to ensure that a charity complies with the law. The guidance outlines that when making decisions, trustees must always:

- act within their powers;
- act in good faith and only in the interests of the charity;
- make sure they are sufficiently informed;
- take account of all relevant factors;
- ignore any irrelevant factors;
- manage conflicts of interest; and
- make decisions that are within the range of decisions that a reasonable trustee body could make.

C3
Risk management and internal controls

1 Introduction

1.1 Measures to minimise risk

1.1.1 If a charity is to maximise its charitable impact, it must manage the underlying risks that may prevent it from operating in an effective and efficient manner. The risks facing every charity are different, and so trustees must first identify the risks facing their own organisation before they can put in place measures to minimise their impact.

1.1.2 Although it was always considered good practice for trustees to manage risk formally, the Charities (Accounts and Reports) Regulations 2005 (SI 2005/572) placed a legal requirement on charities subject to a statutory audit to make a statement in the trustees' annual report confirming that 'the major risks to which the charity is exposed, as identified by the trustees, have been reviewed and systems or procedures have been established to manage those risks' (SORP 2005, paragraph 45). Charities not subject to a statutory audit are encouraged to make the statement as best practice.

1.1.3 It is therefore recommended that all charities have in place procedures to manage risk formally. In addition to ensuring compliance with SORP and preventing disaster, an effective risk management strategy can help to ensure that:

- the charity's aims are achieved more effectively;
- significant risks are known and monitored, enabling trustees to make a more effective contribution;
- new opportunities can be identified, assessed and seized;
- there is a healthy self-criticism within the charity;
- projects and initiatives are better managed;
- unnecessary opportunistic risks are avoided;
- there is a greater awareness of activities and initiatives across the charity; and
- there is improved forward planning.

1.1.4 Sound risk management may also provide some protection for the charity and its trustees in the event of adverse outcomes. First, the adverse outcome may not be as severe as it might otherwise have been and second, those accountable can demonstrate that they have exercised a proper level of diligence.

2 The role of the board

2.1 The responsibility for the management and control of a charity rests firmly with the trustee body and, as such, their involvement in the key aspects of the risk management process is essential. This does not mean that they must undertake every aspect of the process themselves in all but the smallest charities trustees are likely to delegate parts of the risk management process to staff or professional advisers. The trustees do, however, need to be involved in setting the parameters of the process and reviewing the results. Their level of involvement should be such that they can make the required statement on risk management with reasonable confidence.

2.2 Typically, the trustees will:

- initiate and plan the process of risk management;
- influence the culture of risk management and ensure that it is embedded in the operation of the organisation;
- determine the appropriate risk appetite or level of exposure for the charity;
- approve major decisions affecting the charity's risk profile or exposure;
- ensure that the process is linked to the achievement of the charity's aims and objectives;
- monitor the management of significant risks to reduce the likelihood of unwelcome surprises;
- satisfy themselves that the less significant risks are being actively managed, with appropriate controls in place and working effectively; and
- review the charity's approach to risk management on an annual basis and approve changes or improvements to key elements of its processes and procedures.

2.3 Charities may wish to use a risk management policy to define the role of the trustees and the role of the senior management team making a clear distinction between the two. Typically, the role of the senior management team is to:

- implement policies on risk management and internal control;
- identify and evaluate the significant risks faced by the charity for consideration by the trustees;
- provide adequate information in a timely manner to the trustees on the status of risks and controls; and

- undertake an annual review of effectiveness of the system of internal control and provide a report to the trustees.

3 Risk management

3.1 For charities, risk can be defined as 'any event that could prevent a charity achieving its aims or carrying out its strategies' (Charity Commission guidance *Charities and Risk Management* (CC26)). This means that risk is not just confined to the financial affairs of the charity or to health and safety issues, but extends to all areas of the charity's operations.

3.2 Risk management involves identifying risks and devising a strategy to deal with them. A successful risk management framework will have the following characteristics. It is:

- aligned to the charity's objectives;
- supported by trustees, staff and volunteers;
- communicated effectively throughout the charity;
- adaptable to environmental change; and
- simple yet structured.

3.3 The Charity Commission recommends that any risk management process includes the following key elements:

- establishing a risk policy;
- identifying risks;
- assessing risk;
- evaluating what action needs to be taken; and
- periodic monitoring and assessment.

3.4 The process should be seen as an ongoing cycle, not just a one-off event to enable trustees to make the required statement in their annual report. A good risk management process can improve the operations of the charity, enabling it to work more efficiently and effectively.

3.5 The first step for any charity in a risk management process is to define formally the amount and type of risk that is acceptable in the pursuit of its charitable objectives. This is the charity's risk appetite. Once defined, the risk appetite needs to be communicated to staff to ensure there is a clear understanding of the boundaries and limits.

3.6 Charities will have different exposures to risk and different capacities to tolerate or absorb risk. A charity with sound reserves and diversified sources of income could accept a higher risk profile on a new project than a charity with a low level of reserves and few other sources of income. In addition, a charity may need to tolerate a higher level of risk as a result of its specific objectives (for example, a charity operating in a war zone). A charity should also seek to understand the risk tolerances of stakeholders before deciding on its risk appetite. It is also important to look at the balance between higher and lower risk activities (the risk profile).

3.7 There are a number of ways to define risk appetite:

- **Score limit:** risk appetite may be defined as any risk with a score of greater than *x* being unacceptable.
- **Defining statement:** for example, in the case of a charity in financial difficulties, the trustees may decide that the charity cannot afford to take risks until the position has improved.

3.8 A charity may accept different risk levels in different areas (for example, it may be very risk-averse regarding its reputation, but less risk-averse with new ventures).

3.9 A charity's risk appetite will change as activities and financial health changes. It should therefore be regularly reviewed and updated. For example:

> The organisation's general approach is to minimise its exposure to risk. It will seek to recognise risk and mitigate the adverse consequences. However, the organisation recognises that in pursuit of its objectives it may choose to accept an increased level of risk. It will do so, subject always to ensuring that the potential benefits and risks are fully understood before developments are authorised, and that sensible measures to mitigate risk are established.
>
> (Source: *Risk Management in Higher Education* – PricewaterhouseCoopers, 2005)

3.10 The whole charity should be involved in the identification of risks and the process should be led from the top. How this process is carried out will depend on the size of the charity and the resources available, but charities do need to ensure that the responsibility for risk management is clearly defined. Some charities may decide to identify a lead trustee or to ensure that the responsibility is within the terms of reference of a committee.

3.11 The risks that a charity faces depend very much on the size, nature and complexity of the activities undertaken and on the finances of the charity itself. As a general rule, the larger and more complex or diverse a charity's activities, the more difficult it will be to identify the major risks faced. This means that the risk management process must be tailored to each individual charity's circumstances.

3.12 Risks may be external (the financial climate, changes in the law or social changes) or internal to the charity (loss of a key member of staff).

3.13 Although there are various tools and checklists available, the identification of risks is often best done by a brainstorming session involving the trustees and senior staff. Charities may also wish to consult other stakeholders (e.g. staff, volunteers, beneficiaries or supporters).

3.14 It is important that all areas of risk are considered, and the following headings may help to achieve that.

- **Governance and management risk**: this includes the objectives of the charity, the commitment and skills of the trustee board, conflicts of interest, loss of key staff or trustees and the organisational structure.
- **Operational risk**: this includes contracts and service provision, use of resources, staffing, volunteers, IT, health and safety and safeguarding assets.
- **Financial risks**: this includes diversity of income, budgetary control, adequacy of reserves and cash flow, financial reporting, borrowing, financial commitments, trading, investments, fraud and error.
- **Environmental/external factors**: this includes public perception, relationship with funders, government policy and social, demographic and economic factors.
- **Compliance with laws and regulations**: this includes charity and company law, taxation, the charity's constitution, health and safety, employment law, Bribery Act, GDPR and Data Protection Act, and other laws and regulations specific to the activities of the charity.

3.15 The Charity Commission publication *Charities and Risk Management* (CC26) provides detailed examples of potential risk areas, their potential impact and mitigation. Bear in mind that no list of examples can cover all the risks that any charity faces; each charity needs to develop its own individual list of the risks that apply specifically to that charity.

3.16 Identified risks need to be put into perspective in terms of the potential severity of impact and the likelihood of their occurrence. For instance, there is a small risk that a charity's buildings will burn down, but the impact of such an event is large enough that the trustees will wish to insure against it.

3.17 Initially, risks need to be assessed as though there were no controls in place. For the above example, this means assessing the risk of fire without taking into account whether there is any insurance in place. This is called the 'gross' risk. There are a number of reasons for assessing risk in this way. First, trustees need to focus their attention on those risks that pose the most danger to the charity (the major risks). They also need to ensure that controls are in place to mitigate the effect of these major risks and that these controls actually work. Trustees do not need to spend as much time and effort reviewing controls that mitigate minor risks.

3.18 Once major risks have been identified, the adequacy of the existing controls needs to be reviewed. The resulting risk after the effect of the controls is called the 'net' risk. This is the actual risk retained and accepted by the charity.

3.19 For example, the trustees of a charity may have identified two risks, risk A and risk B – risk A is the risk of the CEO leaving and risk B the risk of the building burning down. The trustees consider that risk A is a minor risk that requires no further action except regular monitoring. However, they consider risk B to be a major risk that requires action to mitigate its effect (such as insurance). Once adequate insurance is in place, the two risks have the same 'net' risk and the trustees are happy to accept this level of risk. Had the trustees considered only the effect of the risks after the insurance had been put in place, they would have failed to identify that they rely heavily on the insurance policy to mitigate a major risk. They may not therefore have made sufficient effort to ensure that the insurance policy was up-to-date and adequate. Sometimes, the fact that the gross risk is low may also highlight that controls are in place unnecessarily.

3.20 There are two main ways of assessing risk. The first is to plot the risks on a risk map. The second is to use a scoring system to identify those risks posing the most danger to the charity. The two can be used in isolation or together.

3.21 Using a risk map

3.21.1 At the simplest level, assessing risks means deciding whether there is: (a) a high or low likelihood of the event occurring; and (b) whether the impact on the charity would be major or minor.

3.21.2 Major risks are those in the top right-hand box (those which have a high chance of happening and would have a major impact on the charity). The trustees would focus their time and effort on those risks classed as major risks.

3.22 Using a scoring system

3.22.1 Under this more detailed method, each of the risks identified should be given a score for the likelihood of occurrence and another score for their impact using the following guidelines:

Likelihood

1. Remote.
2. Unlikely.
3. Possible.
4. Probable.
5. Highly probable.

Impact

1. Insignificant – no impact on service or reputation. Complaint or litigation unlikely.
2. Minor – slight impact on service or reputation. Complaint or litigation possible.
3. Moderate – some service disruption. Complaint or litigation probable.
4. Major – service disrupted. Complaint or litigation probable.
5. Extreme/catastrophic – service interrupted for significant time. Major adverse publicity or major litigation expected. Loss of beneficiary confidence.

3.22.2 Previously the impact and the likelihood were given equal importance and the two scores were multiplied together to arrive at the 'gross' risk. Recently it has been recognised that the impact of an event is of greater importance than the likelihood. For example, risk A with an impact of five and a likelihood of one and risk B with an impact of one and a likelihood of five would both previously have been given a 'gross' score of five. However, risk A needs to be given greater consideration in the risk management process due to the potentially devastating effect on the charity.

3.22.3 As a result, the gross risk is now often calculated using the formula $xy + y$ where x is likelihood and y is impact. In the above example, risk A would now have a gross score of 10 and risk B would have a gross score of only six. Some organisations even use the formula $xy + 2y$ to weight the impact yet further.

3.22.4 The gross risk should then be recorded on a risk register and/or on the risk map. There is a sample risk register pro forma below. The trustees will need to determine those risks to examine further (such as the top 10 risks or those with a score over 15). This decision will depend on the charity's tolerance to risk.

3.22.5 For example, a charity has a significant contract to provide a care service and there has been a recent history of complaints from beneficiaries, which has led to concerns being raised by the contract funder. The loss of the contract would have a severe effect on the charity's finances and on its ability to obtain further contract work, which is a key priority to the charity. The severity of the impact is likely to score four and the likelihood (given recent history) scores five. The

Sample risk register pro-forma

	Risk	Likelihood (L) (1–5)	Impact (I) (1–5)	Overall gross risk: (L × I) + I	Existing control procedures	Action required	Monitoring process
(1)	Theft of assets	4	5	25	Insurance. Physical security procedures.	Review insurance and security procedures. Ensure asset register is up to date.	Annual review of insurance, asset register and security procedures.
(2)	Computer system failure	2	5	15	Data backup procedures and precautions.	Test backup procedures. Create disaster recovery plan.	Review disaster recovery plan annually.
(3)	Dependency on income sources. Cash flow and budget impact of loss of income source	4	5	25	Adequate reserves policy.	Diversification plans.	Annual review of reserves policy and diversification plans.
(4)	Public perception. Impact on voluntary income and ability to access grants	3	4	16	Communication with supporters and beneficiaries.	Review communication policy. Consider PR training.	Annual review of communication policy.
(5)	Trustee body lacks commitment	4	5	25	Recruitment processes. Trustee training.	Review trustee recruitment process and trustee training.	Review situation on a regular basis.

overall risk score of 24 (using $xy + y$) indicates a major risk and highlights an urgent need for the risk to be mitigated.

3.22.6 That is not to say that other risks should be ignored. Events with low impact but with a high likelihood of occurrence may become a gradual drain on a charity's finances or reputation, and may trigger the occurrence of more risks. Those risks with both low impact and low likelihood of occurrence are unlikely to merit significant attention and effort might be better focused elsewhere.

3.22.7 Once the trustees have identified the major risks, they have a number of options available to them, including to:

- reduce or eliminate the risk by establishing or improving internal controls;
- transfer risk (by taking out insurance or outsourcing activities);
- share the risk (by a joint venture); or
- accept the risk.

3.22.8 Trustees should consider the controls already in place and should test whether they actually work. This may involve reviewing insurance policies, watching people at work or discussing the controls with those affected. Any control weaknesses may need to be addressed by reviewing the design of the systems and processes. The next section of this chapter covers these internal controls in more detail. For any charity, there will be a trade-off between the level of risks and the cost of reducing them to an acceptable level.

3.22.9 The sample risk register on page 242 includes space to list the controls already in place and then to detail whether any further action is required.

3.22.10 Some organisations give a value to the net risk to indicate the level of risk remaining after the internal controls have been applied. This requires a certain degree of judgement as to how the effect of the internal controls is valued, but it does enable the charity to evaluate whether the net risk is acceptable. An extra column could be added to the risk register for this purpose.

3.22.11 Trustees should remember the mnemonic SMART when formulating an action plan. That is, actions should be Smart, Measurable, Achievable, Realistic and Timely.

3.22.12 Risk management extends beyond simply setting out systems and procedures. The process needs to be dynamic to ensure new risks are addressed as they arise, and cyclical to establish how previously identified risks may have changed. Risk management is not a one-off event and should be seen as a process that will require monitoring and assessment.

3.22.13 The risk register will need reviewing at least once a year, and also when the charity faces any significant changes. Risk aspects of significant new projects should be considered as part of project appraisals. Control systems need reviewing and testing to ensure that they operate as expected and that they do actually mitigate the relevant risks (see section 6 on page 254).

3.22.14 A key element to the success of risk management is to make sure that the process is embedded into the culture of the charity. Staff and managers need to take responsibility for implementation and there needs to be communication with staff at all levels to ensure responsibilities are understood.

3.22.15 The trustees can monitor risk by:

- ensuring that the identification, assessment and mitigation of risk is linked to the achievement of the charity's operational objectives;
- ensuring that the assessment process reflects the trustees' view of acceptable risk;
- reviewing and considering the principal results of risk identification, evaluation and management;
- reviewing and considering update reports where the need for further action is identified;
- considering any significant new activities or opportunities as they arise to ensure any risks are identified and managed; and
- considering periodically external factors such as new legislation or new requirements from funders.

3.22.16 Self-assessment risk management checklist

Involvement of the governing body

1. Do the trustees have sufficient involvement in the risk management process?
2. Do the trustees provide direction in the risk management process?
3. Do trustees know that the risk management processes are operating effectively?

Risk policy

4. Has risk policy been clearly defined?
5. Have all relevant criteria been taken into account when defining risk policy? This should include the charity's strategy, the interests of stakeholders and financial performance.
6. Is the risk policy consistently applied across the charity?
7. Is the risk policy reviewed periodically to see whether it is still appropriate?

Resourcing

8. Have sufficient resources been allocated to effectively implement the risk management process?

9. Are all areas of the charity sufficiently involved in risk management?

Assessing risks and mitigating controls

10. Have risks initially been scored 'gross' of mitigating controls?
11. Are mitigating controls adequate to reduce the net (residual) risk to an acceptable level?
12. Is the cost of operating these controls efficient and commensurate with the risk?
13. Are the mitigating controls being carried out on a regular basis?
14. Are mitigating controls monitored and occasionally tested?

Actions for improvement

15. Has consideration been given to options for treating risk?
16. Where actions for improvement have been identified, are these allocated to individuals and given implementation timescales?
17. Are actions for improvement tracked?
18. Are actions for improvement reported on periodically?

Risk reporting

19. Has consideration been given to reporting on risk management to stakeholders?
20. Have risks been prioritised for reporting purposes?

Embedding risk management

21. Have steps been taken to build a culture where everyone is a 'risk manager'?
22. Do risk management objectives complement the charity's existing vision and goals?
23. Is risk explicitly considered as part of existing reports and in respect of key decisions?
24. Is risk management used to understand performance shortcomings?
25. Is risk management built into HR practices, such as training, induction and performance appraisals?
26. Is information about risk management shared?

3.23 Reporting on risk management

SORP 2015 requires trustees of large charities to describe in their annual report the principal risks and uncertainties facing the charity, as identified by the trustees, together with a summary of plans and strategies for managing those risks. Small charities are not required to report on risk; however, disclosure is encouraged as a matter of good practice.

4 Internal controls

4.1 Internal controls exist to mitigate the risks that threaten the achievement of a charity's objectives. Other benefits arising from having an effective internal control framework include:

- safeguarding assets and ensuring their proper application under charity law;
- ensuring reliability of internal and external reporting;
- promoting economy, efficiency and effectiveness; and
- ensuring compliance with laws and regulations.

4.2 The trustees as a body are responsible for establishing, implementing and monitoring the internal financial controls of their charity. As with the risk management process, the trustees may decide to delegate some of the process to one or more trustees or to members of staff, however trustees should make a collective decision on what controls are needed.

4.3 Internal controls reduce the risk of losses to the charity but can never eliminate the risk altogether. Losses may still arise due to fraud or human error, management override of controls, unforeseeable circumstances or simply bad decision making. However, the presence of internal controls should mean that any losses are identified sooner and their effect reduced. It also gives the trustees some defence against a charge of failing to protect the charity's assets.

4.4 Any internal control system should consist of the following components:

- the control environment;
- the charity's risk assessment process;
- information systems relevant to financial reporting and communication;
- control activities; and
- monitoring of controls.

4.5 The control environment includes the attitudes, awareness and actions of management and trustees concerning the charity's internal control and its importance within the charity. It sets the tone of an organisation, influencing the control consciousness of its people. It is the foundation for effective internal control, providing discipline and structure.

4.6 The following elements make up the control environment:

- **Communication and enforcement of integrity and ethical values**: integrity and ethical values are essential elements of the control environment which influence the effectiveness of the design, operation and evaluation of other control activities.

- **Commitment to competence**: this involves ensuring that staff members have the required knowledge and skills to carry out their tasks.
- **Participation by the trustees**: the involvement of the trustees in the internal controls will significantly influence their effectiveness.
- **Management's philosophy and operating style**: this includes management's attitudes towards risk and financial reporting.
- **Organisational structure**: all internal control systems need to be based on a recognised plan of the charity's structure which clearly shows areas of responsibility, lines of authority and lines of reporting.
- **Assignment of authority and responsibility**: this includes policies and communications directed at ensuring that staff understand the charity's objectives, know how their individual actions interrelate and contribute to these objectives, and recognise how and for what they will be held accountable.
- **Human resource policies and practices**: this includes recruitment, training, evaluating, counselling, promoting and paying staff.

4.7 The charity's risk assessment process is the process for identifying and responding to risks that will prevent the charity from achieving its objectives. This was discussed in detail earlier in this chapter.

4.8 The quality of an information system will affect management's ability to make appropriate decisions in managing and controlling the charity's activities and to prepare reliable financial reports. It is important that information provided to management is timely, relevant and reliable.

4.9 An information system comprises infrastructure (computer IT hardware), software, people, processes and data. It may be completely manual or it may be heavily reliant on IT.

4.10 The financial reporting system is obviously an important information system in any charity, but in addition there will be systems to identify problems with the charity's reputation, to collect information on beneficiaries or to report staff performance.

4.11 The information systems of a charity also include the process for communicating information from trustees to staff. This may take the form of policies, procedures, manuals or memoranda.

4.12 Control activities

4.12.1 These are the policies and procedures that help ensure that necessary actions are taken to address the identified risks. There are a number of types of activities:

- **Segregation of duties**: the scope for fraud and error can be reduced by ensuring that no one person is responsible for a single process from beginning to end (for example, different people may be assigned the duties of recording a transaction, authorising the transaction and maintaining custody of the asset). However, the possibility of collaboration between staff members can never be completely eliminated. It may be more difficult to segregate duties in smaller charities with fewer staff members. Here the trustees will need to be more closely involved in the day-to-day operations of the charity and in the authorisation of transactions.
- **Physical controls**: these ensure the physical security of assets and will include restricting access to IT software and data as well as the safekeeping of stock and cash.
- **Information processing**: these controls ensure the accuracy, completeness and authorisation of transactions (whether financial or otherwise). They may include general IT controls such as restricting access to data or keeping virus definitions up-to-date. They will also include controls such as reconciling the bank account or reviewing exception reports.
- **Performance reviews**: these include reviewing reports and analyses of actual performance against budget, forecast or prior year performance. The presence of unexpected fluctuations will help to identify errors, fraud or other causes for concern.

4.12.2 An internal control framework is not just about designing adequate controls. It should also ensure that the controls are effective (do they actually control the risk?) and that the controls are actually being complied with. These procedures are ongoing and may form part of the role of internal audit (see section 6 on page 254).

4.12.3 Reviewing the effectiveness of the internal controls is an essential part of the trustees' responsibilities, and trustees should therefore regularly receive and review reports on internal control. Any significant control failings or weaknesses should be reviewed by the trustees with a view to determining how these arose and ensuring that suitable remedies are put in place.

4.12.4 Charities will have differing internal control systems depending on their size, nature, culture and management philosophy. There are many options when deciding on the nature and extent of controls (such as whether the controls are manual or computerised, and whether they are preventative or detective). There is also a balance to be achieved between the cost of implementing the control and the perceived benefits arising from the control.

4.12.5 Prevention controls are controls designed to avoid an unintended event or result from occurring (for example, increased security to prevent theft). Detection controls are designed to discover that an unintended event or result has occurred (such as bank reconciliations performed monthly). Most internal control systems will involve both types of controls, but the nature and extent of each will depend on factors such as the degree of risk, the quality of staff and the reliability of information.

4.12.6 Smaller charities may use less formal means and simpler processes and procedures in their internal control system. The trustees of smaller charities may be involved in the day-to-day running of the organisation and will provide an important control in doing this.

4.12.7 Internal controls can only be designed once applicable risks have been identified and assessed. Management should then consider:

- the desired balance between prevention and detection controls;
- the cost versus the benefits of the proposed controls; and
- specific control objectives (i.e. what do the controls need to achieve?).

4.12.8 Considerations for specific risk areas consist of the following.

1. **Financial assets:** charities should obtain a copy of the Charity Commission publication *Internal Financial Controls for Charities* (CC8). This gives lists of suggested controls for the key transaction cycles and asset categories. It also includes a checklist in a questionnaire format that is a recommended tool for all charities. It should be remembered, however, that the checklist is designed for a 'typical' charity. Given that all charities are different, no charity should simply adopt the recommendations in the guide and consider their internal controls complete. Charities will need to design controls for any specialist areas and also consider whether the guidelines in the checklist would be effective in their particular circumstances.

   All internal financial controls should include controls over:

   (a) **Incoming resources:** controls should ensure that the charity receives all the income to which it is entitled. Typical controls include physical controls to ensure no money is misplaced and reconciliations to ensure all money has been paid into the bank account and recorded at the correct amount. Controls should also be in place to ensure that all reclaimable tax on Gift Aid donations from individuals has been reclaimed.

   (b) **Expenditure:** controls should ensure that money is only spent on authorised items that represent value for the purpose of the charity. Typical controls include authorisation of expenditure and rigorous cheque signing or internet banking procedures. Payments by cash should be kept to a minimum due to the greater risk involved and the difficulties in establishing an audit trail. Wages and salaries are usually a substantive part of a charity's expenditure so adequate control over their payment is essential.

(c) **Fixed assets:** controls should ensure that fixed assets can be effectively used to promote the charity's objects. Typical controls include maintaining an up-to-date fixed asset register, ensuring they are adequately insured and checking the condition of fixed assets.
(d) **Investments:** controls should ensure that trustees comply with their duties and powers (see Chapter C3) and that any investments are safeguarded. Typical controls include maintaining an up-to-date list of investments and formulating an investment policy.
(e) **Restricted and endowment funds:** controls are needed to ensure restricted funds are used only for the purpose for which they were given. Similarly endowment funds need to be properly invested and any restrictions over the spending of the funds observed.

Some specific areas are worthy of more detailed consideration:

(a) **Internet banking:** most charities have in place rigorous cheque-signing procedures, but may be lacking similar controls for internet banking. It makes little sense to insist on all cheques being signed by two trustees and then allow only one member of staff to authorise the payment of the monthly wages bill over the internet. Mos, if not all, internet banking systems now have the option of requiring two 'signatories' to authorise a transaction. Also, the Charity Commission recommends that payments are not made via internet banking unless a dual signatory system is available.
(b) **Grant applications:** these should always be reviewed by a senior manager or trustee before being submitted to the funder. Copies should be maintained in case the funder has questions about the application. Once the application has been successful controls are needed to ensure the grant is spent on the purpose for which it is given, that it is spent in a timely manner and that records are kept of the spend so that monitoring reports may be completed.
(c) **Grants made to beneficiaries:** There should be controls in place to ensure that any grants made will further the charity's aims and that the grants are used appropriately by recipients. This may include grant-making policies, procedures for the review and approval of grant applications and monitoring procedures to ensure the grants have been properly spent.
(d) **Insurance:** all charities should ensure that they hold sufficient insurance cover. See later in this chapter for more detail.
(e) **Budgetary controls:** in order to achieve full control of the charity's finances it is necessary to work within an agreed budget and to undertake full financial planning. Annual income and expenditure forecasts should be prepared prior to the start of each financial year and updated on a regular basis. Ideally the forecasts should be prepared on a rolling basis (they always cover at least the next 12 months, and as one month passes, another is

added to the end of the forecast). Trustees should approve the annual budgets, although they may not necessarily prepare the detail themselves.

(f) Trustees should then monitor the charity's performance against the budget on a regular basis (such as monthly or quarterly). Any variances should be investigated, and any errors in the assumptions made in the forecasts should be corrected in future forecasts. This comparison of actual results to budget helps identify any unusual transactions and hence areas where fraud or error may have occurred. It will also give an early warning of potential risk areas (e.g. if income is unexpectedly declining).

(g) Some charities use key performance indicators (KPIs) to highlight financial and non-financial performance against budgets and plans, for example the number of beneficiaries helped in the last month or the number of complaints.

(h) **Financial crime and abuse:** Financial crimes such as bribery, fraud, theft, and money laundering, or the loss of electronic data can result not only in significant loss of charitable funds but also in damage to the public trust and confidence in charities more generally. Trustees need to consider the risk of financial crime and manage those risks.

(i) **Physical assets:** the security threat to all organisations is perceived as increasing, and charities need to ensure that premises security and insurance is adequate.

(j) **Human assets:** charities usually make considerable investments in attracting and recruiting the right quality of managers and staff, yet the same degree of rigour is often not applied in the recruitment of trustees. Good recruitment processes cost money, but the cost is small compared to the impact of recruiting the wrong person or operating with gaps in skills or knowledge. Strategies should also be employed to reduce the risk of high staff turn-over, including a review of the attractiveness of the work and the working environment.

(k) **Data and technology assets:** most charities protect their computer systems with passwords. It is also important to ensure that virus definitions and firewalls are up to date, and that there is an adequate backup procedure. Ideally a copy of the backup should be stored off the premises in case of fire or flood. Charities should also test their backups regularly to ensure that data can actually be recovered from them. All charities should have a disaster recovery plan, which ideally should be tested to ensure that it actually works.

The introduction of GDPR In May 2018 brings new obligations in respect of data protection and trustees should ensure the organisation is compliant. It places the onus on organisations to change their ethos to data protection and specifies a risk based approach. Any breaches of data need to be reported to the Information Commissioner within 72 hours of the event and may be punished with a punitive penalty of up to 4% of global turnover.

5. **Reputational assets**: many charities take no active measures to protect their reputation. Although it is usually external parties, such as the media or disgruntled stakeholders, who seize upon inappropriate actions and cause resultant damage, there are relatively few cases of reputation being damaged by entirely fictional allegations. Controls therefore need to ensure that internal actions and external communications are appropriate. It may also be wise to have an action plan for dealing with any adverse publicity.

5 Financial difficulties and insolvency

5.1 The current economic climate and the resulting changes in funding to the voluntary sector have led to many charities facing financial uncertainty. The risk of a charity facing financial difficulties and even insolvency can be reduced if good financial management, risk management and internal controls are in place. This should allow financial risks to be identified at an early stage, although there will always be cases where funding is withdrawn with little notice.

5.2 Insolvency is a serious matter for a charity, not just because of the impact on beneficiaries and staff, but also because of potential personal liability for the trustees. The legal position of the charity trustees in the event of insolvency depends on the legal structure of the charity and this is explained in more detail in Chapter A2 on page 15. The following summarises the position for different legal structures:

(a) Charitable companies, CIOs and other incorporated forms offer trustees limited liability, which means that they will not usually be personally liable should the charity become insolvent. However, there are certain circumstances involving fraud, transactions at an undervalue, breach of trust or wrongful trading (ie while insolvent) where trustees may face personal liability.
(b) Unincorporated charities and charitable trusts do not offer their trustees such protection. The trustees are jointly and severally liable for the debts and liabilities of their charity and may be called upon to meet any shortfall should the charity become insolvent.

5.3 There are a number of indicators that the charity may be running the risk of insolvency. These include:

- the charity is unable to pay its debts as they fall due for payment;
- the charity regularly has to spend reserves because income is not sufficient to meet expenditure;
- creditors are chasing overdue debts; and
- the charity has to borrow money from restricted funds to finance general day-to-day needs.

5.4 If trustees believe the charity is at risk of insolvency, they should consider the following actions as a matter of urgency:

- obtain professional advice from an accountant or insolvency practitioner to discuss their options; and
- compile a list of all assets and liabilities (including any costs of closure) to determine whether or not the charity is solvent.

5.5 A charity may continue to operate while apparently insolvent if this is a short-term situation (for example, if there is income expected in the near future). However, the trustees need to be careful that they do not continue to operate when they know (or should have known) that there is no reasonable prospect of the charity avoiding insolvent liquidation as this is classed as wrongful trading. Wrongful trading may lead to personal liability for the trustees of a charitable company.

5.6 It is important that all discussions and decisions are documented to ensure that there is sufficient evidence that the trustees have acted properly.

5.7 Good financial management should mean that the charity has some notice of impending insolvency and hence some time to try to address the issues. Possible actions could involve:

- developing alternative sources of funding;
- reducing expenditure;
- obtaining short-term finance (a bridging loan): this should only be considered if the trustees are certain that there will be sufficient income in the future to repay the debt;
- merging with another charity;
- discontinuing loss-making activities; and
- selling fixed assets or investments.

5.8 There are other options available to a charitable company facing insolvency. These include:

(a) **Administration**: when a company goes into administration, an administrator is appointed to act in the best interests of the creditors and to attempt to rescue the company as a going concern. The administrator must be an authorised insolvency practitioner.

(b) **An arrangement with creditors:** a charitable company may enter into a Company Voluntary Arrangement (CVA) with its creditors. The creditors may agree as part of the arrangement to accept a reduction in their debt and/or a delay in payment. The trustees would need to apply to the court with the help of an authorised insolvency practitioner who would supervise the arrangement.

5.9 In both of the above cases, the ultimate aim is for the charitable company to continue its activities and remain as a going concern.

5.10 It is possible for the trustees of an unincorporated charity to enter into an informal arrangement with creditors, but this is outside the provisions of the Insolvency Act. As always, it is recommended that professional advice is taken before taking such a step.

5.11 If all of the above options fail, liquidation or winding up is the last resort. Once a charity is placed in the hands of an insolvency practitioner as liquidator, the trustees will no longer have control of the charity. The type of liquidation depends on the legal form of the charity.

5.12 With a charitable company, liquidation will either be compulsory or voluntary:

- A compulsory liquidation will be ordered by the court after a creditor has petitioned the court to wind up the company. A creditor can only do this if it has either issued a statutory demand to the company which has remained unpaid, or obtained a court judgment against the company and the claim has also remained unpaid.
- A voluntary liquidation occurs where members of the charitable company pass a resolution to wind up the company. It will be a creditors' voluntary liquidation if the company is insolvent (and then the creditors choose the insolvency practitioner) and a members' voluntary liquidation if the company is solvent (and then the members choose the insolvency practitioner).

5.13 Unincorporated charities cannot be compulsorily wound up, but trustees may face legal demands from creditors. The decision to liquidate will usually be taken voluntarily by the members in accordance with the constitution. In all cases, the trustees should take care not to make preferential payments to creditors and should leave the charity assets intact. As before, it is important that all discussions and decisions are documented to ensure that there is sufficient evidence that the trustees have acted properly.

6 The role of internal audit

6.1 Internal auditing is defined by the Chartered Institute of Internal Auditors (IIA) as:

> an independent, objective assurance and consulting activity designed to add value and improve an organisation's operations. It helps an organisation accomplish its objectives by bringing a systematic, disciplined approach to

evaluate and improve the effectiveness of risk management, control and governance processes.

6.2 Broadly speaking, an internal auditor will review the charity's risk management system, internal controls and governance process with a view to assessing their adequacy. A report will then be made to the trustees detailing any weaknesses and making recommendations for improvements.

6.3 An internal audit is not a statutory requirement for charities as it is for public authorities. However, it is a very useful tool for reviewing, improving and ensuring that a charity has effective internal controls. It also helps to assure the general public that a charity is being governed properly.

6.4 An internal auditor will monitor and evaluate the effectiveness of the charity's risk management processes. This involves identifying and evaluating significant risk exposures relating to the charity's governance, operations and information systems regarding the:

- reliability and integrity of financial and operational information;
- effectiveness and efficiency of operations;
- safeguarding of assets; and
- compliance with laws, regulation and contracts.

6.5 An internal audit assists the charity in maintaining effective controls internal by evaluating their effectiveness and efficiency and by promoting continual improvement.

6.6 It is important to remember that it remains the responsibility of the trustees to establish and maintain the systems of internal control used in the charity. The role of internal audit is to assess whether those controls and systems designed by management are adequate, being complied with as intended and are operating effectively, and to make recommendations for improvements where weaknesses are identified.

6.7 The role of the internal auditor in the governance of a charity is generally more informal and may be accomplished through participation in meetings and discussions with trustees. The internal auditor is often considered one of the 'four pillars' of governance, the other pillars being the trustees, management and the external auditor.

6.8 In larger charities, the internal audit is controlled and led by the audit committee. The role of the audit committee will often be to help the trustees meet their responsibilities for risk management, internal controls and the efficient and effective use of funds. It will also review the external audit process and consider the final accounts. An audit committee acts on the authority delegated to it by the trustees and so should have appropriate terms of reference and a clear reporting line to the trustee body.

6.9 Some of the benefits of an internal audit are that it:

- demonstrates a thorough and resilient management;
- tests the charity's control systems and suggests ways to improve them;
- monitors whether the recommended improvements have been made;
- demonstrates to funders and stakeholders that the charity has taken steps to control assets and activities;
- establishes the trustees' responsibility for risk management and control;
- contributes to risk management;
- assists people within the charity to reach a better understanding of the purpose and effectiveness of risk management and controls;
- improves the quality and quantity of information;
- improves communication and motivation; and
- links risk to objectives and strategies.

6.10 An effective internal audit function may help to reduce or modify the scope and timing of external audit procedures but it cannot eliminate the requirement for external audit. The effectiveness of internal audit can have a significant impact on how the external auditors assess the internal control system and audit risk. It is therefore important that the internal auditor liaises with the external auditor at as early a stage as possible.

6.11 The main difference between internal and external audit relates to their objectives. The objectives of internal auditors are set by the trustees or senior management, who will often decide what parts of the charity or which systems are to be reviewed. In contrast, the objectives of external auditors are defined by statute and, in certain circumstances, by other regulatory codes. The report produced by the external auditor states whether the published financial statements are true and fair and if they adhere to accounting standards and the Charities/Companies Acts. The role of the internal auditor can be more varied and wide-ranging than an external auditor and covers both financial and non-financial controls.

6.12 There is also a difference in the independence of internal and external auditors. Both require independence from the charity and its managers and trustees to be able to perform their roles effectively. However, internal auditors are often employees of the charity, which will restrict their independence. External auditors, however, must be independent of the charity and its trustees and may not be employees.

6.13 Possible structures for internal audit

6.13.1 Many charities, particularly smaller ones, have no internal audit function. This may be on the grounds of cost, or because the trustees consider the activities to be relatively straightforward. There is often a misconception that internal audit is for larger organisations only. However, trustees would be well advised to consider how they know that the risks within their charity are being properly managed and that the internal controls are operating effectively.

6.13.2 An external auditor will usually review the systems and controls of a charity and make recommendations for improvement where weaknesses are identified. However, this is aimed primarily at financial systems and controls, not at non-financial areas.

6.13.3 A larger charity may set up their own internal audit function and employ a part-time or even full-time member of staff. This will not be possible for smaller charities, who may wish to consider the following alternatives:

- Many firms of accountants and auditors offer an internal audit function. This may involve, for example, an auditor visiting the charity for one day a month to review and test the systems and controls, and then reporting back to the trustees. It is good practice for the internal and external auditors to be different firms, or at least employees from different departments.
- A volunteer may be found with the relevant skills and experience to review the controls independently, and then report back to the trustees.
- A number of charities may decide to share internal audit resources through a consortium arrangement.

6.14 The internal audit process

Internal auditors, trustees and management determine where to focus internal auditing efforts based on a risk assessment of the charity. A typical internal audit involves the following steps:

- Establish and communicate the scope and objectives for the audit to appropriate management.
- Develop an understanding of the area under review including objectives, measurements and key transaction types. This will involve a review of documents and interviews, and may involve creating flowcharts and narrative notes.
- Identify control procedures used to ensure each key transaction type is properly controlled and monitored.
- Develop and execute a risk-based sampling and testing approach to determine whether the most important controls are operating as intended.

- Report problems identified and negotiate action plans with management to address the problems.
- Follow up on reported findings at appropriate intervals.

6.15 Model job description: charity internal auditor

Responsible to: audit committee or chief executive. Some internal auditors report to the finance director but it is preferable that internal audit remains independent of the finance function.

Job purpose: to carry out an independent appraisal of the effectiveness of the policies, procedures and standards by which the charity's financial, physical and information resources are managed. To add value by acting as a facilitator in business risk management and carrying out value for money reviews, thereby assisting the management and the trustees of the charity in the effective discharge of their responsibilities.

Definition: 'Internal auditing is an independent, objective assurance and consulting activity designed to add value and improve an organisation's operations. It helps an organisation accomplish its objectives by bringing a systematic, disciplined approach to evaluate and improve the effectiveness of risk management, control and governance processes.' (Source: IIA)

Principal duties and responsibilities:

1. To work with trustees and management to ensure a system is in place that ensures that all major risks of the charity are identified and analysed, on an annual basis.
2. To provide objective and independent assurance on the effectiveness of strategies to manage key risks facing the organisation.
3. To provide both management and trustees with an opinion on the effectiveness of internal controls in the charity.
4. To plan, organise and carry out the internal audit function including the preparation of an audit plan that fulfils the responsibility of the department, scheduling and assigning work and estimating resource needs.
5. To report to both the audit committee and management on the policies, programmes and activities of the department.
6. To coordinate coverage with the external auditors and ensure that each party is not only aware of the other's work but also well briefed on areas of concern.
7. To make recommendations on the systems and procedures being reviewed, report on the findings and recommendations and monitor management's response and implementation.
8. To review and report on the accuracy, timeliness and relevance of the financial and other information that is provided for management.

9. To report on the value for money that the charity obtains in all its activities with special regard to economy, efficiency and effectiveness.
10. To conduct any reviews or tasks requested by trustees, the audit committee, chief executive or finance director, provided such reviews and tasks do not compromise the independence or objectivity of the internal audit function.

Person specification

1. A recognised professional qualification, such as:
   (a) CIMA (Chartered Institute of Management Accountants);
   (b) ACA (Association of Chartered Accountants);
   (c) ACCA (Certified Chartered Accountant);
   (d) CIPFA (Public Finance Accountant); or
   (e) IIA (Chartered Institute of Internal Auditors)
   which implies a thorough knowledge of the principles, procedures and practices of accounting and financial records and transactions.
2. A knowledge of audit procedures, including planning, techniques, tests and sampling methods and modern audit approaches (risk-based auditing, process auditing and systems improvement).
3. A knowledge of computerised accounting and auditing record keeping systems.
4. An ability to gather, analyse and evaluate facts and to prepare and present concise oral and written reports.
5. An ability to maintain current knowledge of developments related to business matters of interest to internal audit, particularly legislation changes and developments as they affect charities, and new auditing techniques and practices.
6. An ability to establish and retain effective working relationships with other charity staff and to communicate clearly and effectively, both orally and in writing.
7. An understanding of and empathy with the charitable sector.
8. An ability to work unsupervised.

(Source: *Charity Finance Yearbook 2011*)

7 Insurance

7.1 The trustees of a charity have a duty to safeguard the property of the charity not only from direct loss or damage but also from third-party liabilities, which would otherwise have to be satisfied out of the property of the charity. If trustees unreasonably fail to discharge this duty, they may be personally liable to make good the charity's losses. Insurance is a common way of discharging this duty and reducing the impact of major risks.

7.2 The Trustee Act 2000 gives trustees of an unincorporated charity the power to insure any property which is subject to trust against risks of loss or damage as a result of any event and to pay the premiums out of the charity funds. Incorporated charities usually have sufficient power in the company's Articles of Association to purchase such insurance.

7.3 Section 189 of the Charities Act 2011 gives trustees a power to purchase indemnity insurance against their own personal liability, and to pay the premiums out of charity funds.

7.4 Although there is no general power for types of insurance other than those mentioned above, trustees may be given the specific power in their charity's constitution. Even where there is no specific power, it would usually be appropriate to imply such a power where the nature of the charity's business warrants it.

7.5 As with all ways to mitigate risk, the trustees should weigh up the cost of the insurance against the perceived benefit. Insurance premiums have been rising for some years and there are no indications that this trend will cease. In addition, some insurers are refusing to insure high-risk areas and this may result in them refusing the business altogether or adding exclusions to the policy.

7.6 Trustees should always consider whether anything can be done to reduce the cost of an insurance premium. This may include reducing the likelihood of a claim by improving controls and systems (such as security) or it may mean contacting a number of different insurance companies until a competitive quote is found. It may also be possible to collaborate with other charities and purchase insurance 'in bulk'.

7.7 It may be acceptable for the charity to carry part or all of the risk itself. It is usually possible to reduce insurance premiums by accepting a higher excess. Larger charities with diversified sources of income and adequate reserves might accept the consequences of their exposure to risk without taking out insurance. Obviously, there is greater need for insurance where the charity risks losing all or most of its assets at once. Where insurance is compulsory (for example, employer's liability insurance) there is no option for the charity to carry the risk.

7.8 Finally, the trustees may decide to reduce or abandon altogether a high-risk activity that is difficult or costly to insure.

7.9 Types of insurance

7.9.1 There are a number of forms of insurance available to trustees, some of which are mandatory. The most common types include:

(a) **Buildings insurance**: recommended where the charity is the freehold owner of a building and insurance is not the responsibility of the lessee or tenant (if any). The policy should provide cover for the full reinstatement value of the building (the cost of replacing the building in the same style as the original). This is important as the trustees may personally be liable for any shortfall in cover should it be found that they were negligent in purchasing inadequate insurance. Trustees are advised to seek advice on the level of insurance cover required from a professionally qualified building surveyor.

Where a charity leases property, it is essential to check the terms of the lease to see who is responsible for insuring the building.

(b) **Contents insurance**: advisable for all charities owning furniture, equipment or cash. There are usually a number of options to consider, including cover for accidental damage, cover on a 'new for old' basis and cover for specific items (such as computers). Trustees should ensure that any cash held on the premises does not exceed the insured limit in their insurance policy.

(c) **Public liability insurance**: may be appropriate for charities owning or occupying land or buildings. It covers claims from members of the public for injury, loss or damage incurred on the charity's premises. It also covers claims arising under the Occupiers' Liability Acts 1957 and 1984. These Acts place on the occupier of the property a duty of care in respect of visitors to and trespassers on their property. There is no statutory minimum level of cover.

(d) **Employers' liability insurance**: compulsory for charities with employees. All employers are required to have a minimum insurance cover of £5 million for injury or disease suffered or contracted by employees while carrying out their duties. A certificate showing that a valid policy is in force must be prominently displayed by the employer.

(e) **Motor insurance**: compulsory against third-party injury and property damage where a charity owns or operates motor vehicles. If trustees, employees or volunteers use their own vehicle for charity purposes, their vehicle insurance must extend to such use.

(f) **Fidelity insurance**: covers losses to the charity arising from fraud or dishonesty on the part of charity employees where they are handling the charity's cash or other valuables. It should not be seen as an alternative to sound personnel and financial risk management.

(g) **Insurance for fundraising events**: may cover losses arising from cancellation on account of bad weather, misappropriation of cash raised (where large amounts are on hand), or losses where the response to an appeal does not cover the costs of administration.

(h) **Legal expenses insurance**: may be purchased to cover the cost of certain legal expenses that may arise if the charity has to bring or defend legal proceedings. These costs would usually be payable by the charity out of its own assets unless recoverable from the opponent. In an employment dispute, this insurance may also cover the costs of any compensation awarded to the employee.

(i) **Loss of revenue**: insurance can be arranged to cover the loss of revenue or increased costs sustained as a result of disruption from e.g. fire or flood.

(j) **Professional indemnity insurance (PII)**: recommended for all charities providing any form of advice or professional service (such as counselling) whether free of charge or otherwise. The insurance will cover the charity against claims for losses or damages sustained by clients as a result of a negligent service.

7.9.2 Trustee indemnity insurance (TII) covers trustees from having to personally pay out when legal claims are made against them (by their charity or by a third party) for a breach of trust, or a breach of duty or negligence, committed by them in their capacity as trustees.

7.9.3 The main difference between TII and other types of insurance taken out for the benefit of the charity is that TII directly benefits an individual trustee rather than the charity itself. For that reason, TII is regarded as a form of personal benefit needing a proper legal authority before the charity can purchase it. Many charities have the express authority to purchase TII in their governing document, and where they do not, the Charities Act 2011 provides a general power to purchase TII using charity funds.

7.9.4 The only time Charity Commission consent is required is where the charity's governing document expressly prohibits the purchase of TII. Any general prohibitions on trustee benefits are overridden by the general legal power to purchase TII without the consent of the Charity Commission.

7.9.5 TII will only insure trustees against claims that may arise as a result of their legitimate actions as trustees. It cannot provide cover for:

- criminal fines, or penalties imposed by public authorities;
- costs of criminal proceedings where a trustee is convicted of fraud, dishonesty or reckless conduct; or
- liability arising out of conduct which a trustee knew, or should reasonably have known, was not in the interests of the charity.

7.9.6 More detailed guidance on insurance is provided in the Charity Commission's publication *Charities and Insurance* (CC49).

SECTION D

The charity's business

D1
Employment and volunteers

1 Staffing a charity

1.1 Staffing and volunteers

A charity has a wide choice when it comes to deciding what kind of staffing arrangements it wants to use. The employment status of a working person is important in the context of employment law because it determines the statutory employment rights to which that individual is entitled. As a result, a charity should be aware of the full implications of the rights it may, sometimes inadvertently, be bestowing on staff.

1.2 What sort of staff can a charity have?

1.2.1 A charity can engage employees, workers or self-employed individuals to provide services. Other categories of worker a charity might look to recruit are fixed-term workers, part-time workers, temporary workers and casual workers who are contracted to work on an 'as and when required' basis, or on a 'zero hours' basis. Agency staff can also be used, but do not have employment rights that can be pursued against a charity; their rights are against their agency.

1.2.2 The nature of the work carried out by charities, together with funding constraints, often means that many of the individuals who carry out work for charitable organisations do so on a voluntary basis. There are benefits to maintaining a flexible workforce, but charities need to be aware of the potential problems that the use of volunteers, casual workers and other staff can create.

1.3 Differences between volunteers, workers and employees

The differences in employment status between volunteers, workers and employees are significant. It is therefore important that an organisation using their services is aware of these differences in order to enable them to avoid any pitfalls that may arise as a result of blurring the boundaries.

2 Volunteers

2.1 The status of those who are not automatically regarded as employees is often hard for employers to determine. The position of volunteers is particularly complex and is a matter of great concern, especially for charitable organisations who often make great use of them.

2.2 Volunteers are not expressly excluded from legislation that would otherwise give them rights to bring employment claims, except under the National Minimum Wage Regulations 1999. The term volunteer can encompass a range of relationships from the purely voluntary to the clearly contractual. As a result of the ambiguity surrounding their status, it is often difficult for charities taking on volunteers to fully appreciate the legal obligations that they may owe them.

2.3 It is possible for volunteers to develop employment rights because of the way in which they are treated by an organisation. If a volunteer is deemed to be either an employee or a worker, they will be able to assert a variety of statutory rights against the organisation. In assessing whether a volunteer is a true volunteer, rather than a worker, tribunals will look at a variety of factors, taking into account the situation as a whole.

2.4 Factors that may determine status

An employer will need to be aware that there are various factors that will help to establish the status of a volunteer.

- A tribunal will look carefully at any written documentation which exists between the volunteer and the charity to see what the parties intended. Although a charity may have a written form of agreement with an individual which makes it clear that they are providing their services as a volunteer for the organisation, a tribunal will always look closely at the work that the individual is asked to carry out in order to ascertain their employment status. In addition, a tribunal will scrutinise the behaviour of the parties to determine whether there is anything that might suggest that the volunteer could be considered to be either a worker or an employee.
- If contractual documentation exists which contains provisions that one would normally find in an employment contract, it is likely that an employment relationship will be found to exist. Something to look out for in particular is whether there are any kinds of contractual provisions that would entitle the charity to terminate the relationship and whether they are the same as rights to terminate employment.
- If there is an expectation that the volunteer will work a set number of hours every day or week, or that the quality or quantity of their work will be assessed,

it is likely that this will be indicative of the volunteer acquiring status either as a worker or an employee.

- Does the charity exercise control over the volunteer? If, for instance, the volunteer is required to report to any other individual in the charity, there is a greater likelihood that they will be viewed as employed.
- A charity will have to consider how the work undertaken by the volunteer compares to that undertaken by other individuals who are employed by the charity. Where there is a high degree of overlap between the tasks and responsibilities for volunteers and employees, a tribunal is more likely to infer the existence of an employment relationship.
- Is any payment received which is, or could be construed as being, in consideration for any work done? If so then it is likely that the volunteer will be viewed as a worker, or possibly an employee, depending on the other factors present. Payments made to a volunteer which are not, strictly speaking, expenses, or which are made while the volunteer is off sick or on holiday, will be highly supportive to the volunteer's case that they are either an employee or a worker.
- If appraisals are undertaken, this will indicate that there is an element of control over what the volunteer does. This, in turn, could support an argument of obligation between the parties.

2.5 Protection from discrimination?

2.5.1 The question of whether volunteers should be covered by discrimination law has been the subject of much debate over the years. However, the Supreme Court's decision in *X v Mid-Sussex Citizens Advice Bureau* means that there is now no doubt that volunteers are not protected by discrimination law.

2.5.2 X volunteered to work with the Mid-Sussex Citizens Advice Bureau (CAB) for four to five hours a week. She was not contractually bound to work and received no remuneration. She carried out unpaid advice duties until she told her manager that she had contracted HIV. She then alleged that she was told that she could no longer work at the CAB because her HIV was seen as presenting a risk to the staff. She brought a claim for disability discrimination against the CAB.

2.5.3 The Supreme Court held that as X had no contract she could not claim protection under the Disability Discrimination Act 1995 (the legislation preceding the Equality Act 2010). The Court also held that it was not the intention of the EU Equal Treatment Framework Directive (X sought to argue that European legislation covered discrimination against volunteers) that there should be wider protection against discrimination covering volunteers, therefore she had no protection under the Directive.

2.5.4 The judgement serves as a useful reminder to organisations to make sure that volunteers are treated as volunteers and don't stray into territory where they potentially have the right to claim worker, or even employee, status.

2.6 Mutuality of obligation

2.6.1 As mentioned above, requiring volunteers to work a certain number of hours per week risks creating 'mutuality of obligation'; this could mean volunteers could be deemed by a tribunal to be workers or employees. Requiring volunteers to work a set number of hours every week, on set days or at set times should be avoided where possible. Charities should ensure that a volunteer can always choose not to work in any given period.

2.6.2 If such a requirement is necessary, it should ideally be expressed as an intention or a hope, as this reflects the voluntary nature of the arrangement (as a 'usual minimum commitment'). The volunteers will therefore not have to work any minimum number of hours, and there are no sanctions if they do not, but the charity can express the *hope* that they will. Expressing an expectation in this way was considered in a past tribunal case and it was held that no mutuality of obligation or employment relationship was created.

2.6.3 It is a good idea for charities to have a volunteer policy in place, to act as a framework for the volunteer programme and to provide guidance. The policy could, for example, ask volunteers to give notice if they are unable to work at a time that has been mutually agreed. This will at least give the charity some level of knowledge, if not control, though it will not be possible to impose a sanction if the volunteers fail to give such notice.

2.7 National Minimum Wage implications

2.7.1 True volunteers, who assist an organisation without an obligation to do so, do not qualify for the national minimum wage (NMW) because they are not workers under the National Minimum Wage Act 1998 (the NMW Act).

2.7.2 A worker for the purposes of the NMW Act is someone who works under either a contract of employment or an implied contract where they undertake to do work for another party. Therefore, if there is an obligation on the individual to perform the work and, in return, an obligation on the organisation to provide the work, that individual will be considered a worker. A volunteer who is obliged to work or receive payment could fall within that definition; in that case they would have to be paid the NMW.

2.7.3 However, there is a specific exemption in the Act that applies to charities and voluntary organisations. This states that a worker employed by a charity does not qualify for the NMW if they only receive reasonable expenses arising from the performance of their duties or benefits in kind in the form of subsistence or accommodation.

2.7.4 It is a good idea for charities to keep evidence such as receipts to show that any reimbursement relates to expenses actually incurred. Payments that do not relate to actual expenses could be construed as wages and indicate that the individual is an employee.

2.7.5 Providing subsistence or accommodation should be limited as far as possible to work that requires residential volunteers.

2.7.6 Provided these requirements are satisfied, there will be no requirement to pay the volunteers NMW, even if they are actually workers for the purposes of the NMW Act.

2.7.7 The Department of Business, Energy and Industrial Strategy BEIS has updated its guidance on calculating the NMW to include unpaid work trials.

2.7.8 Some employers may use unpaid trial periods to establish whether a candidate has the skills required for the job as part of their recruitment process. The guidance notes that often such a practice will be a legitimate means of carrying out a recruitment process, but sometimes the candidate will be asked to perform tasks and, when this is the case, the NMW should be paid.

2.7.9 Factors to be taken into account when considering whether a person should be paid include: whether the trial is genuinely for recruitment processes; whether the trial length exceeds a reasonable amount of time that an employer would need to assess the individual's ability in the role; whether the tasks carried out add value to the employer beyond testing the candidate; and the extent to which the individual is observed during the trial. The longer a trial period continues, the more likely it is that it will result in a contract to provide work meaning that the NMW is due.

2.8 Can charities be liable for the acts of volunteers?

2.8.1 In the past, charities that use volunteers have had to be aware that they can be liable for the harassment by volunteers of their employees. This would have arisen if a volunteer harassed an employee in the course of the latter's employment; the employer knew that the employee had been harassed in the course of employment on at least two other occasions by a third party (whether or not by the same third party); and the employer had not taken reasonably practicable steps to prevent the harassment.

2.8.2 As of 1 October 2013, the third-party harassment provisions contained in the Equality Act 2010 have been repealed. However, this does not mean that harassment of this type is no longer anything to worry about. Employees may still be able to argue under the general harassment provisions contained in s. 26 of the Equality Act that an employer's intention in the face of third-party harassment amounts to unwanted conduct 'related to' a protected characteristic that violated their dignity or created an intimidating, hostile, degrading, humiliating or offensive environment for them.

2.9 Volunteers who are office holders

2.9.1 Although it is very rare for charities to make payments to volunteer trustees, if they do, they need to be aware that the trustees will then fall under the definition of an office-holder in the Equality Act 2010 (office holders not only refer to trustees, but also to other roles such as company secretary or treasurer). Any income derived from an office holding position is potentially taxed as employment income. Sometimes office holders will be paid via a service company in order to reduce tax. Rather than making a payment to an individual, the charity will pay a fee directly to the service company for the services provided. However, it is highly likely that an office holder being paid through a service company will still be subject to tax liability and fall within IR35, especially as there will generally be an obligation to provide personal service. If there is no requirement to provide personal service, and a substitute can be appointed then it may be possible to argue that the work carried out by the office holder falls outside IR35. However, it will almost always be the case that trustees will have to provide personal service and it will therefore be very difficult to argue that any payment they receive can be paid without deduction of tax.

It is unlawful to discriminate against, victimise or harass office holders. The Equality Act 2010 protects both those who are seeking to be appointed to an office and those who are appointed. It will apply in a charity context to the volunteer members of a charity's board.

2.9.2 It is unlawful for a person who has the power to make an appointment to a personal or public office to discriminate against or victimise a person:

- in the arrangements which are made for deciding to whom they offer the appointment;
- as to the terms on which the employment is offered; and
- by refusing to offer the person the appointment.

2.9.3 It is also unlawful to discriminate against or victimise an office holder:

- as to the terms of the appointment;
- in the opportunities which are afforded (or refused) for promotion, transfer,

training or receiving any other benefit, facility or service;
- by terminating their appointment; or
- by subjecting the person to any other detriment.

2.10 Volunteer agreements

2.10.1 Many volunteers will be issued with a volunteer agreement. This document normally sets out the nature of the voluntary work to be undertaken and what volunteers can expect in terms of support from the organisation. It can also cover insurance provisions covering any activities for the organisation. It may also contain a procedure for dealing with disputes. Some volunteer agreements do constitute binding contracts on the organisation to pay expenses or to indemnify the volunteer against actions resulting from the volunteer work. These agreements can be enforced by the volunteers, but are not like contracts of employment

2.10.2 The agreement between the organisation and the volunteer should be clearly defined under a volunteer agreement. It should be couched in appropriate language to explain what is expected of volunteers rather than obliging volunteers to behave in a particular way. There should be no requirement that the agreement is signed.

2.10.3 The following issues should be considered by charities in drawing up volunteer agreements:

- volunteer task lists, an equal opportunities policy and a complaints procedure;
- performance reviews and penalties for poor performance should be avoided;
- provision for volunteers to work specific hours can be included but there should be no penalty in the event that a volunteer refuses or fails to work that shift. It is essential to avoid creating any mutuality of obligation. A volunteer should never be contractually obliged to do work;
- pay expenses only;
- a volunteer agreement should state that there is no intention to create a legal relationship;
- training given should be specific to the work to be undertaken by the volunteer and should be undertaken ideally at the outset; and
- allow volunteers where appropriate to find a replacement on occasions when they are unable to attend a previously agreed volunteer session. Some charities operate 'swapsites' where volunteers can swap slots.

2.11 What training should volunteers have?

Many volunteers view their work for charities as an opportunity to extend their own skills. Care must be taken to ensure that the training provided relates directly to their volunteering work, as it can be deemed to be 'pay' by a tribunal.

For instance, paying for IT training where this is not relevant for the work done, in, say, a charity shop, can amount to a payment that confers employee status. Training can be legitimately provided to volunteers, as was shown in *Gradwell v Council for Voluntary Service Blackpool, Wyre & Fylde*. However, in *Armitage v Relate*, training was deemed to be a payment, partly because the volunteer had to repay the costs of training if they left.

2.12 What can you do to ensure that people remain volunteers?

Summary of dos and don'ts

Dos	Don'ts
Reimburse reasonably incurred expenses	Remunerate volunteers for their services
Keep receipts of any expenses which are reimbursed	Impose any obligation on the part of the employer to provide work
Express any minimum hours requirement as an 'expectation' or a 'hope'	Impose any obligation on the volunteer to work a minimum amount of hours
Give volunteers the option to refuse work	Impose any sanctions on volunteers who refuse work
Make it clear that any 'volunteer document' is not a contract	Exercise too much control over the volunteer
Have a clear volunteer policy in place	Use a standard contractual document to define the volunteer relationship

3 Employees

3.1 Before going on to consider the status of casual workers and agency workers it is useful to consider the status and rights of employees and workers, so that charitable organisations can appreciate their obligations towards individuals who, though ostensibly volunteers, may have acquired the rights of an employee or worker (see Section 5 and Appendix). This section will consider employees and section 4 will consider the rights they enjoy. Section 5 will go onto consider workers and the rights they enjoy.

3.2 Employees

For a contract of employment to exist, it imposes an obligation on a person to provide work personally and a mutuality of obligation must exist between the employer and the employee.

3.3 Obligation to provide work personally

If a provision is contained in an individual's contract that entitles them to substitute someone else to perform their duties, then that individual cannot have employee status. However, if the individual has a heavily fettered discretion to appoint a substitute, or requires the employer's approval to the appointment of such a substitute, a substitution clause will not prevent that individual from becoming an employee. It is a fine balance.

3.4 Mutuality of obligation

If there is an obligation on the employee to accept and do such work as is offered to him, and another on the employer to pay the employee for the work that is done then it is likely to be an employment relationship.

3.5 What should be in a contract of employment?

3.5.1 Items employers are legally obliged to include in the contract are:

- names of both parties (employer and employee);
- date employment began and date continuous employment began;
- job title or brief description of job;
- pay, scale of pay and details of payment arrangements;
- place of work;
- hours of work; and
- holiday entitlement and arrangements regarding holiday pay.

3.5.2 Information that must be given to employees, but not necessarily in the contract, is as follows:

- details of occupational sickness leave and payment. It is usual to recite the arrangements regarding the entitlement to Statutory Sick Pay (SSP) for which the employer is responsible for provision and payment on behalf of the state;
- details of occupational/stakeholder pension schemes available to employees;
- notice period and/or termination date if fixed term (see below);
- particulars of collective agreements; and
- disciplinary arrangements.

3.6 Keeping contracts updated – how to make changes

3.6.1 Charities will need to keep on top of changes to the law to ensure that they are meeting their obligations towards their staff. It is a good idea for regular policy reviews to be instituted and, once any amendments have been made or new policies introduced, to draw the attention of your staff to these.

3.6.2 What happens when, for whatever reason, you need to change the content of a contract? The basic rule in relation to changing terms and conditions is that this can only be done with an employee's individual consent. However, the courts understand that in certain circumstances it is appropriate for an employer to make changes to terms and conditions of employment without that individual consent, though such changes will only be considered to be fair where:

- there are good objective business reasons for making the changes; and
- the employee has been treated fairly and reasonably and has been consulted throughout the implementation process.

3.6.3 If the changes are unfair, then an employee can bring a claim for either breach of contract or constructive/unfair dismissal.

3.6.4 It was previously thought that an employer who expressly reserved the right to vary an employee's contract unilaterally would generally be unsuccessful in seeking to rely on such a right. However, following the decision in *Bateman and others v Asda Stores Ltd* (where it was held that Asda was entitled to rely upon a general statement in its employee handbook reserving the right to vary contractual terms in order to introduce new pay terms, without the need to obtain the express consent of all the affected employees) it seems that there might be some scope to express such a right after all.

3.6.5 While variation clauses in contracts may be enforceable, such a clause should be limited to the amendment of terms and conditions only where necessary, while making it clear that the charity's first step will always be to seek consent. Terms should only be imposed unilaterally as a last resort after proper consultation has taken place.

4 Rights of employees

4.1 Written statements

4.1.1 Each employee must be given a written statement of the main terms and conditions of their employment no later than two months after the beginning of their employment. In addition, employees are entitled to receive a written statement of reasons for dismissal.

4.1.2 The written statement of particulars will specify the date when the employment began, as well as the date on which the employee's period of continuous employment began (taking into account any employment with a previous employer which counts towards the overall period of employment).

4.1.3 Other written particulars to be given include the rate of remuneration and details of payment, terms and conditions relating to hours of work, holidays, sick pay and pensions, the length of notice on termination, and any collective agreements which directly affect the terms and conditions of the employment.

4.1.4 Employees will generally also be provided with employer policies (or referred to copies of them on the employer's intranet) on commencement of their employment. Important policies to provide or draw to new employees' attention will include disciplinary, grievance and capability policies, equal opportunities, bullying and harassment and health and safety policies. In addition, it will be necessary to have policies in place to deal with sickness absence, flexible working and all the family friendly rights such as maternity, paternity and adoption leave and pay.

4.2 Payments

4.2.1 Employees are protected by the provisions of the National Minimum Wage Act 1998, which obliges employers to pay the National Minimum Wage. During periods of absence from work by reason of illness, employees must be paid statutory sick pay, and under the Working Time Regulations, they are entitled to 5.6 weeks' paid annual leave (this is 28 days for a full time employee) in each leave year.

4.2.2 In addition to these payments, employees have the right to guaranteed payments when no work is done owing to circumstances beyond the employee's control. Such circumstances will include a lack of instruction on the part of the employer, or any other occurrence such as a power cut which affects the normal working of the employer's business. In the event that an employee is made redundant, they are entitled to the payment of a statutory redundancy payment. In circumstances where an employer becomes insolvent, an employee can apply to the Secretary of State for the payment of any sums which are outstanding to the employee from the employer. The right to such an insolvency payment will apply to any arrears of pay or notice payment, holiday pay and any basic award of compensation for unfair dismissal.

4.2.3 Finally, employees are protected against any unlawful deductions made from their wages. It is important for employers to be aware that no deduction from a worker's wages may be made unless such a deduction is required or permitted by a statutory or contractual provision, or the individual has given their prior written consent to the deduction.

4.3 Time off/leave

4.3.1 Employees are entitled to take time off work during working hours for public duties. The public duties that qualify include acting as a Justice of the

Peace and carrying out duties as a member of a local authority and certain other authorities. The right as a Justice of the Peace is to take time off for the purpose of performing any duties of the office. In relation to other public duties the entitlement is to take time off to attend a meeting of the body, and to carry out activities approved by the body for the purpose of discharging its functions.

4.3.2 In addition, there is a right to time off for jury service, time off for pension scheme trustees, time off for study or training and time off for members of an independent trade union. Other types of time off include time taken for family-friendly rights (see page 283).

The right to request time off for training applies to employees working for employers with 250 or more employees. It only applies to employees with at least 26 weeks' continuous service and the time off must be for the purpose of the employee improving their effectiveness at work and the performance of their employer's business, although it need not lead to a formal qualification.

4.4 Protection from unfair dismissal

Provided that an employee has been employed by an employer under a contract of employment; has been dismissed; and has been employed for at least two years, they have the right not to be unfairly dismissed. Employees whose employment began before 6 April 2012 will still be subject to a one-year, rather than a two-year, qualification period, in accordance with the old law on unfair dismissal.

4.5 Redundancy

If a redundancy situation occurs, an employee has the right to be informed about this prior to the redundancy taking place. The employer will have to consult with representatives of the employees to be affected by the redundancy. In the event that the employer is proposing to dismiss more than 100 employees within a period of 90 days or less, the consultation must begin at least 45 days before the first of the dismissals takes effect. If 20 or more, but fewer than 100 employees, are to be made redundant, consultation must begin at least 30 days before the first of the dismissals takes effect.

4.6 Protection from discrimination

The Equalities Act 2010 protects the following characteristics from discrimination in employment: age, disability, gender reassignment, marriage and civil partnership, pregnancy and maternity, race, religion or belief, sex and sexual orientation.

4.7 Direct discrimination

Direct discrimination takes place when a person is discriminated against because of their protected characteristic, because the person is treated less favourably by their employer than the employer treats, or would treat, other people who do not have the protected characteristic.

4.8 Direct discrimination by perception

4.8.1 Direct discrimination covers cases of direct discrimination based on an incorrect perception that a person has a particular protected characteristic, or where the less favourable treatment is based on an association with someone having a particular characteristic.

4.8.2 This is broad enough to cover a perception, even if the perception is incorrect. Bullying and harassment complaints that are related to a perceived characteristic could expose an employer to a discrimination claim even if the recipient does not possess the protected characteristic.

4.8.3 An example of discrimination by perception given in the Statutory Code of Practice (Employment Code) is as follows:

> An employer rejects a job application form from a white woman whom he wrongly thinks is black, because the applicant has an African-sounding name. This would constitute direct race discrimination based on the employer's mistaken perception.

4.9 Direct discrimination by association

This covers direct discrimination (or harassment) against employees on the grounds that they are caring for a disabled person (disability discrimination), an elderly person, or a child (age discrimination). Discrimination by association can occur in various ways, for example, where the employee has a relationship of parent, son or daughter, partner, carer or friend of someone with a protected characteristic. The association with the other person need not be a permanent one. Direct discrimination by association does not confer a general right on carers not to be directly discriminated against on the grounds of their caring responsibilities.

4.10 Indirect discrimination

4.10.1 An employer will discriminate against an employee where:

- it applies a provision, criterion or practice equally to all employees which is such that persons who share the employee's protected characteristic are placed at a particular disadvantage when compared with other persons;
- it puts the employee at that disadvantage; and
- the employer cannot show it to be a proportionate means of achieving a legitimate aim.

4.10.2 An employer will have a defence to a claim of indirect discrimination if it is able to show that the application of the relevant provision, criterion or practice is justified. In order to argue this justification defence the respondent will have to show that the application of the relevant provision, criterion or practice is a proportionate means of achieving a legitimate aim.

4.11 Harassment

4.11.1 Protection from harassment applies to the following protected characteristics: sex, race, disability, religion or belief, sexual orientation and age. It does not extend to marriage and civil partnership, or pregnancy and maternity.

4.11.2 Harassment is unwanted conduct that is related to a relevant characteristic and has the purpose or effect of creating an intimidating, hostile, degrading, humiliating or offensive environment for the complainant or violating the complainant's dignity.

4.12 Equal pay

4.12.1 In order to bring a claim for equal pay, a claimant will have to show that she (or he) is carrying out equal work to a comparator of the opposite sex in the same employment. The claimant will be required to show that she carries out like work, work rated as equivalent or work of equal value to her comparator.

4.12.2 An employer can defend the claim by showing the difference in pay is due to a material factor other than sex. The material factor must not be sex and it must not involve indirect sex discrimination. If the material factor operates to the disproportionate disadvantage of one sex over another, then the employer must show it is a proportionate means of achieving a legitimate aim. For these purposes, the long-term objective of reducing inequality between men and women's terms of work is always to be regarded as a legitimate aim.

4.12.3 There are other, less common, types of rights to equal pay. If a claim for equal pay succeeds, the tribunal will redraft the contract to bring the lower salary up to the right level.

4.13 Protected disclosures – whistleblowing

4.13.1 Employees are protected from suffering detriment and/or dismissal as a result of making a protected disclosure. In order to qualify as a protected disclosure, the disclosure will have to be in relation to a criminal offence, a failure to comply with a legal obligation, a miscarriage of justice, the endangering of health or safety of any individual, or the damage of the working environment.

4.13.2 The disclosure must be in the public interest as well as in the reasonable belief of the worker making the disclosure. Tribunals now have a power to reduce compensation where protected disclosures are not made in good faith.

4.14 TUPE

4.14.1 Employees are protected when the transfer of any trade or business takes place from one person to another. If such a transfer occurs, the employees will be employed by the purchaser on the terms and conditions they enjoyed with their previous employer. All rights and liabilities in connection with the employees' contracts of employment (save pensions) will automatically transfer.

4.14.2 TUPE was revised by the Collective Redundancies and Transfer of Undertakings (Protection of Employment) (Amendment) Regulations 2014 (SI 2014/16). These came into force, in the main, on 31 January 2014. The changes were not significant, but comprised the following:

- employers are able to renegotiate collective terms a year after transfer, provided that any proposed changes are overall no less favourable to the employee;
- the transferring employer has to provide employee liability information 28 days ahead of transfer rather than 14;
- a workplace relocation on a TUPE transfer is recognised as a genuine redundancy situation and is not automatically unfair;
- employers who conduct consultation prior to a transfer are able to count it for the purposes of their collective consultation obligations on a large-scale redundancy; and
- a service being outsourced or retendered must be 'fundamentally the same' pre- and post-transfer to constitute a service provision change.

4.15 Working rights

4.15.1 The Working Time Regulations 1998 set a limit to the number of hours to be worked per week. This limit stipulates that workers should work no more than 48 hours on average in each working week, though workers can sign an opt-out agreement if they wish.

4.15.2 Workers have a right to at least 11 consecutive hours' rest in each 24-hour working period, and also have a right to a rest break after a working period of six hours. There is also a right to an uninterrupted rest period of at least 24 hours in each seven-day period of working.

4.16 Redundancy

4.16.1 Employees who lose their jobs by reason of redundancy are entitled to claim a redundancy payment.

4.16.2 Proving a genuine redundancy

If challenged in a tribunal, an employer will need to prove that there was a genuine redundancy. Thus figures drawn from management accounts, order books, etc. demonstrating the downturn will be required. Copies may be provided, but the originals should be available. The employer must also be able to show that during consultation the reasons for the redundancy were discussed.

4.16.3 The ERA defines redundancy as:

(a) the employer ceasing or intending to cease:
- to carry on the business for the purposes of which the employee was employed;
- to carry on that business in the place where the employee was so employed; or

(b) the requirements of the business:
- for employees to carry out work of a particular kind; or
- for employees to carry out work of a particular kind in the place where the employee was employed by the employer have ceased or diminished or are expected to cease or diminish.

4.16.4 Determining the correct staffing levels

When management becomes aware of a reduction in funding or a reduced need for its services, they need to assess how that reduction will impact on the number of hours worked by affected employees and to establish whether they need to reduce the hours worked by employees, or reduce the number of employees they have.

4.16.5 The redundancy procedure

Making an employee redundant is a dismissal and, as with all dismissals, following the correct procedure is essential if a fair dismissal is to be created and the penalties for an unfair dismissal avoided. The following checklist should provide such a procedure provided the steps are taken in the order shown.

4.16.6 Redundancy procedure checklist

1 Explain the reasons for the potential redundancies.
2 Determine the (provable) excess of working hours/employees (see above).
3 Consult about the situation:
(a) ask for comments/alternatives/suggestions, or make a presentation identifying the alternatives, showing why these cannot be used; and
(b) ask for suggestions on selection criteria if terminations are needed.
4 Consider these suggestions and alternatives.

5 If some of these suggestions or alternatives can be used, say so and reassess the organisation's requirements after these have been taken into account.
6 If the suggestions or alternatives are not feasible, give reasons for not using them.
7 Decide on the hours/days/numbers to be lost.
8 Identify the pool (the particular area or the whole organisation) from which the number to be made redundant is to be drawn.
9 Ask for volunteers.
10 Identify those to be made redundant, ideally using totally objective criteria.
11 Inform those affected (allowing them to be accompanied if requested) giving notice under contract, details of redundancy payments and right of appeal.
12 Advise any vacancies and oversee trial periods.
13 Consider outplacement.
14 Deal with queries and appeals.
15 Check the calculations again (particularly those undertaking trial periods).
16 Arrange for the provision of references.

4.16.7 The dismissal of the employee on the grounds of redundancy should take place after meaningful consultation. The employee should be invited to the dismissal hearing and given the right to be accompanied by a work colleague or trade union representative. Where an employee has been selected from a pool of employees their score under the selection procedure should have been discussed prior to the final dismissal meeting.

4.16.8 Consultation

Current legislation requires employers to consult with elected representatives of their workforce if 20 or more employees are to be declared redundant within a period of 90 days. If fewer redundancies are expected, consultation should take place with individuals and, even where there has been consultation with elected representatives, there should also be consultation on an individual basis as well. Ideally, consultation should take place before 'bodies required to be lost' have been identified. Representatives should be told the situation and asked if they have any suggestions. Tribunals repeatedly stress how important it is for employers to consult with their employees. Several employers have lost unfair dismissal cases when making employees redundant, not because the redundancy decision was flawed, but because they failed to consult with elected representatives of employees when the question of redundancies was first considered.

4.16.9 When consulting, those involved should be given a short period (four or five days) to consider the situation and make any suggestions. There is no need for management to accept any suggestions, they are simply required to consult (not negotiate). Obviously, sensible suggestions should be considered, but even then may have to be rejected for business reasons.

4.16.10 Selection for redundancy

The manner of selection of those to be made redundant should be another facet of consultation. The basis of selection should be objective rather than subjective, and be based on facts available at the time of assessment.

4.16.11 Individuals selected should be told and given the opportunity for further consultation – for example, if they have had any alternative ideas or possibly wish to be considered for another job if there are any vacancies.

4.16.12 No one should be made redundant without being given the opportunity to ask to be considered for vacancies in the organisation. If they do wish to be considered and are thought potentially suitable, they should be given (say) a month's trial period. If successful, a new (continuous) contract should be issued. If unsuccessful, the original redundancy situation must be resumed.

4.16.13 Notice

Once the selection has been made, a notice of termination of employment on grounds of redundancy should be issued. This should state the leaving date and give the amount of notice required under the contract, or one week for each year of service to a maximum of 12 weeks as required by law, whichever is the longer.

4.16.14 If the required period of notice cannot be given (because the period to the required termination date is too short) then a payment in lieu of notice (PILON) must be paid in respect of the amount of notice required that has not been given.

4.16.15 During the notice period an employee is entitled to all benefits under the contract. If a PILON is made then the cash equivalent of the benefits should be agreed between the parties and paid.

4.16.16 State redundancy pay

Where an employee has worked for an employer for more than two years, the employee becomes eligible for state redundancy pay in the event of redundancy. The statutory redundancy rate is currently capped at £508 (April 2018). This is reviewed annually. The statutory redundancy scheme works on the basis of the employee's age and length of service:

- employees up to and including the age of 21 receive 0.5 weeks' pay for each completed year of service;
- employees aged 22 to 40 receive one week's pay for each completed year of service; and
- employees aged 41 and above receive 1.5 weeks' pay for each year of service.

4.16.17 The maximum number of years' service payable under the statutory redundancy scheme is 20.

4.17 Family-friendly rights

4.17.1 Employees have the right to maternity leave and pay, paternity leave, shared parental leave, adoption leave and parental leave. In addition there is a right to time off for antenatal care and the right to unpaid time off to care for dependants.

4.17.2 Maternity

The important date for the calculation of maternity rights, etc. is a woman's expected week of childbirth (EWC).

4.17.3 All women are entitled to 26 weeks' ordinary maternity leave (OML) and 26 weeks' additional maternity leave (AML) (a total of 52 weeks). There is no obligation on the woman to take all the leave, or even part of it, subject to the prohibition on a woman returning to work within two weeks of having given birth (four weeks if she works in a factory).

4.17.4 Women who have been continuously employed for at least 26 weeks at the end of the EWC will qualify for Statutory Maternity Pay (SMP) provided their earnings exceed the Lower Earnings Limit. This is paid by the employer, who can then recover it from the government. Women who earn below the Lower Earnings Limit will be entitled to Maternity Allowance (MA), which is paid to them by the government.

4.17.5 The first six weeks of SMP are paid at the rate of 90% of the woman's average weekly earnings and the following 33 weeks are paid at £145.18 (the rate as of April 2018; this figure is reviewed annually) or 90% of the woman's average weekly earnings, whichever is the lower.

4.17.6 Maternity Allowance is paid for 39 weeks at the standard rate of £145.18 or 90% of the woman's average weekly earnings, whichever is the lower. To qualify for MA, the woman must have been registered as self-employed or have been employed for at least 26 weeks of the 66-week period running into the week before the EWC.

4.17.7 A woman must give 28 days' notice of the date that she wishes her maternity leave to start. Her employer must (within 28 days of that notification) state the latest date by which she must return to work. She may change the leave start date, and, if so, within 28 days of the notification of the change the employer must advise a new return date.

4.17.8 A woman can return before the end of her leave on giving 56 days' notice. Her employer can postpone her return to the end of the 56-day period if the full notice was not given, but not to any date later than the end of her leave.

Note: In the case of *Alabaster v Woolwich Building Society*, the ECJ stated that *all* pay rises before the end of the maternity leave (a full year in some cases) must be reflected and related back to the first day on which SMP was due. This means the average for the six weeks must be recalculated and arrears paid. If a woman is still employed, she has six years to make a claim for any arrears. However, if she has left that employment, she must lodge any claim within six months of leaving.

4.17.9 During her maternity leave a woman is entitled to work (and be paid for) up to 10 'keeping-in-touch' days without this affecting her leave or maternity pay. If she works during a time when she is in receipt of maternity pay, it would be logical to 'top up' her maternity pay to her normal day's pay (adjusted by any increase effected during her leave). If she works during the unpaid portion of her leave a full day's pay should be given.

4.17.10 A woman taking only OML has a right to return to the job she was doing before her leave. A woman who is taking AML as well has a right to return to the same job or to a similar job (on no less favourable terms). Some women may wish to work part-time on return.

4.17.11 Paternity

If they have a minimum of 26 weeks' service leading into the fifteenth week before due date, by their partner's EWC, fathers/civil partners/adopters are entitled to Statutory Paternity Leave (SPL) and (subject to earnings) to pay. Statutory Paternity Pay (SPP) is paid at the rate of 90% of the father's average earnings for the eight weeks ending at the fifteenth week before the mother's EWC or £145.18 whichever is less. A father is entitled to SPP per week of leave, which can be either one week or two weeks, but must be taken within eight weeks of the birth. Only one leave and payment is due in respect of each pregnancy. Thus, for a multiple birth the father is entitled to only one term of leave and payment. An employer has no right to ask for proof that the baby is expected or has been born. However, before there can be any payment or leave, a father needs to complete and sign a Declaration SC3 (available from HMRC).

4.17.12 Adoption

Employees who adopt are, subject to service, entitled to statutory adoption leave (SAL) and, subject to earnings, to statutory adoption pay (SAP). Adoptive parents are the 'main' parent (the person named in the Adoption Matching Certificate) and the 'other' parent. Married couples, male and female couples, single-sex partners and single persons can adopt and become eligible for benefit. Adopting employees need to have worked for their employer for 26 weeks by the end of the Matching Week to qualify for the rights. These are:

- **Leave:** the 'main' parent is entitled to two leaves – ordinary and additional (equivalent to the maternity leave rights), making a total absence of 52 weeks. If they wish to return before the end of either leave, 56 days' notice must be given. The 'other' parent is entitled to the equivalent of 'paternity pay/leave', that is one or two weeks' leave (which must be taken within 56 days of the adoption). The contract of employment continues during the leave(s).
- **Pay:** payment for the first 39 weeks' leave for the main parent is at the rate of 90% of the person's average earnings or £145.18 (the rate as of April 2018; this figure is reviewed annually), whichever is less. There is no payment for the last period of 13 weeks. Payment for the other parent's paternity leave is at the rate of 90% of average earnings or £145.18, whichever is less. Adoptive leave is available only on a single basis – if two or more children are adopted, only one set of leave/pay is available for each parent.

4.17.13 Shared parental leave

The intention behind shared parental leave (ShPL) and shared parental pay (ShPP) is to allow families more choice over how they look after their children in the first year. ShPL may be taken at any time within the period, which begins on the date the child is born and ends 52 weeks after that date. It must be taken in multiples of complete weeks and may be taken as one continuous period or in discontinuous breaks. The minimum period of shared parental leave that may be taken is one week.

Parents are not obliged to take ShPL. The default position on the birth of a child is that the 52 weeks of maternity leave remains in place for the mother, as does compulsory maternity leave, which applies from the day of the child's birth. In order for ShPL to kick in the mother has to have chosen to end her maternity leave or returned to work. Up to 50 weeks of ShPL and 37 weeks of ShPP are available for eligible parents to take or share (this includes everything other than the compulsory maternity leave period or the equivalent two-week period in adoption cases).

Shared parental leave enables parents to share the caring responsibilities evenly or to have one parent taking the main caring role, depending on their preferences and circumstances. Unlike maternity/adoption leave, eligible employees can stop and start their ShPL and return to work between periods of leave with each eligible parent able to submit three notices booking periods of leave (although an employer may allow more).

The mother may share any shared parental leave with the 'other parent' with whom she shares the main responsibility for the care of the child. The 'other parent' must be either:

- the child's father;
- a person to whom the mother is married or in a civil partnership; or
- a partner (including a same sex partner) who lives with the mother and the child in an enduring family relationship.

Similarly, an adopter may share parental leave with their spouse, civil partner or partner. Both partners (birth, adoptive or intended parents in surrogacy agreements) will have to be eligible to take shared parental leave.

In order to be eligible for ShPL, the mother must:

- satisfy the continuity of employment test (have been continuously employed for a period of not less than 26 weeks ending with the relevant week, namely the end of the fifteen week before the child's EWC or date of matching in the case of adoption);
- have/expect to have, the main responsibility for the child's care (apart from the father's/adopter's responsibility);
- be entitled to SML or SAL;
- have chosen to end her SML or returned to work;
- have given notice of entitlement to shared parental leave to her employer, and given the relevant evidence; and
- have given a period of leave notice.

In addition, the mother will have to have a partner who:

- can satisfy the employment and earnings test (discussed below); and
- has. or expects to have, the main responsibility for the child's care (apart from the mother's responsibility).

The father, partner of the mother or adopter will be entitled to take ShPL if they:

- satisfy the continuity of employment test;
- have/expect to have, the main responsibility for the child's care (apart from the mother's/adopter's responsibility);
- have given notice of entitlement to shared parental leave to his employer, and given the relevant evidence; and
- have given a period of leave notice.

In addition to these requirements the mother must:

- satisfy the employment and earnings test;
- have, at the date of the child's birth/date of the placement for adoption, the main responsibility for the child's care (apart from the father's responsibility);
- be entitled to SML, SMP or MA (or SAL or SAP in the case of adoption) in respect of the child; and
- have chosen to end her SML or returned to work, or where she is not entitled to SML. but is entitled to SMP or MA, she has chosen to end such period.

An individual will satisfy the employment and earnings test if they have been employed or self-employed for at least 26 weeks out of the 66 weeks preceding the EWC/week in which the individual was notified of being matched.

In addition they will have to have average weekly earnings of not less than £30 (the amount set out in s.35(6A) Social Security Contributions and Benefits Act, namely the Maternity Allowance Threshold) a week in any 13 weeks.

The entitlement to ShPP is 39 weeks less the number of weeks in respect of which MA or SMP is payable to the mother in respect of the child up to the time the mother has returned to work. ShPP is not payable after the end of the period of 52 weeks after the child's birth/adoption. A mother has to take at least two weeks of maternity leave and pay after the birth of her child. The maximum award of ShPP that can be created is 37 weeks.

ShPP is paid to an employee by their employer at the lower rate of 90% of salary or the flat rate of £145.18 a week (2017-18 tax year).

4.17.14 *Emergency leave*

Employees are entitled to take a 'reasonable' amount of unpaid leave to deal with 'family emergencies'. Such a leave entitlement is not subject to any service requirement and is aimed to cover the following purposes:

- to help when a dependant is ill, gives birth, is injured or assaulted;
- to arrange for an ill or injured dependant to be cared for because a dependant's care arrangements are unexpectedly changed;
- as a result of the death of a dependant; and
- to deal with an incident involving a child which occurs unexpectedly in school time.

4.17.15 *Parental leave*

All those who have parental responsibility for children aged up to five years (18 if the child is disabled) and who have a year's service with their employer are entitled to parental leave of 18 weeks in respect of any individual child.. Parental leave is limited to a maximum of four weeks per year.

4.17.16 Those wishing to take the leave must give at least three weeks' notice. The employer has the right to postpone the leave (for no more than six months). Fathers who give three weeks' notice of the birth of their child have the right to take this leave immediately after the birth and the employer has no right of postponement in this instance.

4.17.17 Employers are under no obligation to keep records, but it is difficult to see how this can be avoided simply to keep track of the entitlements and avoid disputes. Employees have the right to the leave in respect of each child for whom they have parental responsibility. Parental leave is unpaid.

4.17.18 Flexible working

- The right to request flexible working provides a statutory framework within which qualifying employees may request, and employers are obliged to consider, changes to their terms and conditions of employment, such as working hours or places of work.
- The right to request flexible working applies to all employees with 26 weeks' service under the Flexible Working Regulations 2014. Employers will have to deal with the application in a 'reasonable manner'.
- The employee triggers the procedure by making a written request. The employer then has three months to consider the request, discuss it with the employee and notify the employee of the outcome. This three month period can be extended by agreement. Only one request can be made in any 12-month period.

4.17.19 Business reasons for rejecting the request could include:

- the burden of costs on the employer;
- problems meeting customer demand;
- an inability to reorganise the work;
- problems meeting quality requirements;
- problems meeting performance output;
- an inability to find other employees to cover the hours not now to be worked;
- an insufficiency of work during the periods the employee proposes to work; or
- planned structural changes.

An employee will be able to complain to the tribunal if the employer fails to deal with the application in a reasonable manner, fails to notify them of the decision on their application within the prescribed period, fails to rely on one of the statutory reasons to refuse the request, bases its decision on incorrect facts, or treats the application as withdrawn when it is not entitled to do so. If the tribunal finds that a complaint is well-founded it shall make a declaration to that effect, may make an order for a reconsideration of the application, and make an award of what it considers to be just and equitable to do in the circumstances, subject to a maximum of eight weeks' pay.

4.18 Fixed-term employment

Under the Fixed-term Employees (Prevention of Less Favourable Treatment) Regulations 2002, fixed-term employees have the right not to be treated less favourably than a comparable permanent employee.

4.19 Part-time employment

Those employed on a part-time basis have the right not to be treated less favourably than a comparable full-time worker under the Part-time Workers (Prevention of Less Favourable Treatment) Regulations 2000.

4.20 Pensions

4.20.1 Employees must have any terms and conditions relating to pensions and pension schemes offered by the employer in their contact of employment by virtue of s. 1(3) of the Employment Rights Act 1996.

4.20.2 In addition to this obligation under the Pensions Act 2008, employers have to enrol eligible jobholders into a pension scheme automatically. This process began in October 2012 and was phased in over a six-year period.

4.20.3 An employer has to arrange for all eligible jobholders to be automatically enrolled in a qualifying pension scheme. It can use its existing occupational or personal pensions scheme provided it meets certain quality requirements or else it can enrol jobholders in NEST (the central government-established scheme). Several private pension providers have established competitor schemes.

4.20.4 In order to be eligible for auto-enrolment, a jobholder must be between age 22 and state pension age, and must earn at least £10,000 per year (the legislation requires this figure to be reviewed annually). 'Jobholders' include permanent and temporary employees.

4.20.5 Jobholders who have been automatically enrolled have a statutory right to opt out of whichever scheme they have joined, within prescribed time limits. Jobholders who have opted out will be automatically re-enrolled every three years. They can opt out again at this stage if they wish.

4.20.6 Jobholders who are not automatically enrolled can opt in by giving their employer notice requiring the employer to arrange for them to join an automatic enrolment scheme. They can only do this once in a 12-month period.

5 Workers

5.1 The definition of a worker is wider than that of an employee and includes those who undertake to 'do or perform personally any work or services for another party to the contract whose status is not by virtue of the contract that of a client or customer of any profession or business undertaking carried on by the individual'.

5.2 The definition comprises two elements:

- The individual must be under an obligation personally to do work.
- The person for whom the work is done must not be a client or customer of a business being run by the individual.

5.3 What rights do workers have?

Workers have a much reduced range of employee rights. They are entitled to:

- protection against unlawful deductions from wages;
- payment of the National Minimum Wage;
- accompaniment at a disciplinary or grievance hearing;
- paid annual leave, rest breaks and a maximum working week under the Working Time Regulations;
- protection against discrimination on grounds of sex, race, disability, sexual orientation, religion or belief, and age;
- equal pay to a comparable person of the opposite sex;
- if working part-time, the right not to be treated less favourably than a comparable full-time worker; and
- protection against detriment/dismissal for whistleblowing.

6 Agency workers

6.1 An agency worker signs up with an employment business to work for one or more of the employment agency's clients. Due to the nature of charities' funding, agency workers are very common in the sector. The agency worker will sometimes be assigned to complete a specific piece of work, or might be engaged for a fixed period of time. Their work is generally carried out on a temporary basis. However, sometimes they are engaged on an open-ended basis and their engagements may last for a long period of time.

6.2 The question of the employment status of agency workers has, over the years, caused some confusion. Is the worker employed by the employment agency, or by the client to whom the worker provides their services, or are they employed by neither the agency nor the client? This question of employment status is particularly important given that agency working arrangements can sometimes last for several years, thereby easily exceeding the current one-year service requirement for bringing a claim for unfair dismissal.

6.3 It will be of some comfort to charities that an employment relationship will only be found to exist between an agency worker and a client where it is necessary, in order to give effect to the reality of the relationship, to imply a contract of employment between them. When determining whether it is, in fact, necessary to imply a contract of employment between them a tribunal will look at all the circumstances of the case. This will include the documents that record the arrangements between the parties as well as how the situation works in practice. It will also look at the issues of mutuality of obligation and control.

6.4 If an agency worker is construed to be an employee or a worker then he or she should benefit from the rights and obligations that are owed to an employee or worker (see Appendix). However, an agency worker who is not found to be an employee or a worker will still benefit from certain rights. It is important that charities are aware of these.

6.5 Agency Workers Regulations 2010

The Agency Workers Regulations 2010 provide the following rights for agency workers:

- the right to the same pay and other 'basic working conditions' as equivalent permanent staff after a 12-week qualifying period; and
- access to collective facilities and to information about employment vacancies from the first day of their assignment.

6.6 The charity's obligations

6.6.1 It is for the agency to meet the obligations, but commercially they are likely to pass on the cost to the charity, so be aware of this.

6.6.2 An agency can pass liability for agency workers to the charity if the charity does not provide the agency with details of terms and conditions of its own staff. However, if a charity complies with those requests it is realistically possible to reduce liability.

6.7 What should charities do?

To reduce the costs of agency workers, a charity should do the following:

- **Assess the nature of the agency worker's work:** it is a good idea to assess the nature of the work that the agency workers are being engaged to carry out. Try to limit their use to specific projects or for fixed periods rather than for an indefinite length of time. They are probably paying VAT on the services.
- **Pick an employment agency with care:** only use an employment agency that is organised and properly documents its relationships with workers and clients. Ensure that any contractual documentation is consistent with agency worker status to avoid the possibility of the worker being construed to be an employee.
- **Avoid too much control:** make sure that control of agency workers is kept to a minimum. Do not appraise or discipline them and ensure that dealings with the agency worker are, wherever possible, passed through the employment business.
- **Look at the contract:** Consider whether you want assurances from the employment business in respect of any claims based on employment status, and warranties about the agency worker's employment status.

Ensure you are providing information about your own employees promptly to the agency.

7 'Fit and proper' test – which staff should this cover?

7.1 Most of the issues discussed in this chapter are common to most employers but there is a very specific matter in relation to employment issues of which charities must be aware as it could potentially affect the availability of charitable tax exemptions. As a result of the Finance Act 2010 (FA 2010) there are now three additional tests that a charity must satisfy in order to take advantage of charitable tax reliefs; the jurisdiction condition, the registration condition and the management condition. It is the management condition that concerns us here.

7.2 The management condition will be met if the charity's 'managers' are 'fit and proper persons' to be managers. The FA 2010 defines 'managers' as 'the persons having the general control and management of the administration' of the entity. In order to supplement this definition HMRC has published guidelines to assist charities in deciding how to operate the management condition. It is worth noting that even if the management condition is not met, FA 2010 gives discretion to treat it as having been met if HMRC considers that the failure has not prejudiced the charitable purposes of the charity or that it is just and reasonable in all the circumstances.

7.3 The HMRC guidelines

7.3.1 HM Revenue & Customs will assume that all people appointed by charities are fit and proper persons unless they hold information to show otherwise. As long as charities take appropriate steps when appointing personnel, they may assume that they meet the test at all times unless they are challenged by HMRC.

7.3.2 There is room for the exercise of HMRC's discretion to allow charitable tax reliefs even where the 'fit and proper persons' test has been breached where the charity can show that it made a 'genuine mistake' and there has been 'no misuse of charity tax reliefs'.

7.3.3 The guidelines include a section on who is a 'manager' of a charity. In a typical small local charity, a manager could include the chair, treasurer, secretary and the rest of the management committee who would have control over expenditure. However, in a larger charity a manager would include all trustees or directors of a corporate charity, but may also extend to certain employees who are able to determine how a significant proportion of the charity's funds are spent (for example, most large charities have a board of trustees and an executive board of senior employees). Here, the trustees and members of the executive board would be managers of the charity.

7.3.4 The guidelines stipulate that if a charity regulator does not consider that an individual is suitable to be a trustee of a charity, that individual will not be able to satisfy the 'fit and proper persons' test. However, it does not necessarily follow that individuals who are considered by a charity regulator to be suitable to act as trustees will always be considered to be fit and proper persons.

7.3.5 Factors that may lead to HMRC deciding that a manager is not a fit and proper person include, but are not limited to, individuals:

- with a history of tax fraud;
- with a history of other fraudulent behaviour including misrepresentation and/or identity theft;
- for whom HMRC has knowledge of involvement in attacks against, or abuse of, tax repayment systems;
- who are barred from acting as a charity trustee by a charity regulator or court, or have been disqualified from acting as a company director.

7.3.6 The guidelines state that just because an individual has been, say, barred from acting as a charity trustee, or one of the other points above applies, it does not follow that the charity will always fail the management condition.

7.3.7 The guidelines deal in some depth with how the test will be applied in certain situations. For example, if a charity has innocently appointed a manager who is not a fit and proper person, and that person has misapplied some of the charity's funds without the charity's knowledge, the charity will not necessarily be denied charity tax reliefs and exemptions. While the charity has appointed a manager who is not fit and proper and the charity's funds will have been affected, where the charity can demonstrate that it had taken reasonable steps and was not party to the misapplication of funds, then HMRC will work with the charity in an attempt to correct the position.

7.4 Compliance with the 'fit and proper person' test

7.4.1 HMRC suggests that asking managers to read its basic guide and then signing the model declaration included in the guide is one way in which a charity can demonstrate that it has taken the necessary steps to reassure itself that its managers are fit and proper. If this is done, HMRC accepts this will mean that a charity can assume that they meet the management condition at all times unless: they knowingly appoint a manager who is not a fit and proper person to a position from which they are able to influence the charitable purposes of the charity or the application of its funds; or, exceptionally, they are challenged by HMRC.

7.4.2 If a new 'manager' is a 'responsible person' or an 'authorised official' the charity must notify HMRC of their appointment (using Form ChV1). A 'responsible person' will normally be a trustee or director of the charity. An 'authorised official' is the person authorised to deal with the charity's tax affairs, make Gift Aid or other repayment claims and, where necessary, sign and submit tax returns.

8 Recruitment

8.1 The Equality Act and the Employment Statutory Code of Practice

8.1.1 There are various legal issues a charity will have to consider in the process of a recruitment exercise.

8.1.2 The Equality Act 2010 (EA 2010) outlaws discrimination and harassment in relation to nine specific 'protected characteristics': age, disability, gender reassignment, marriage and civil partnership, pregnancy and maternity, race, religion or belief, sex, and sexual orientation. The EA 2010 contains specific provisions which cover discrimination, victimisation and harassment in recruitment.

8.1.3 Part Two of the Employment Statutory Code of Practice (EHRC Code) sets out recommended practice for employers and specifically covers recruitment. The EHRC Code encourages employers to open up employment opportunities to a wide pool of candidates to ensure access to the best talent available. By following a clear and objective selection process, employers should be able to avoid stereotypical assumptions of who is likely to be the best candidate for the job.

8.2 Discrimination in recruitment

8.2.1 The EA 2010 provides that an employer must not discriminate or victimise a person on the following grounds:

- in the arrangements the employer makes for deciding who to offer employment;
- as to the terms on which the employer offers the person employment; and
- by not offering the person employment.

8.2.2 In addition, an employer should not harass a person who has applied to the employer for employment.

8.2.3 The arrangements an employer makes for deciding who to offer employment to are interpreted broadly and will include the:

- format and content of application forms;
- physical arrangements, location and timing of interviews; and
- job and person specifications.

8.2.4 It will potentially be possible for someone who has not even applied for a job to bring a discrimination claim in relation to the employer's recruitment arrangements. Generally a claim like this would be based on the content of the job advertisement or a statement made by the employer in response to an enquiry. However, it is a difficult claim to bring as they have to prove that they would have applied for the role but were deterred from doing so by the discriminatory advert or statement.

8.3 Liability for discrimination in recruitment

8.3.1 A job applicant may bring a claim for discrimination or harassment against the employer and/or any employees and recruitment agents who were responsible for the discrimination or harassment in question.

8.3.2 The employer may be vicariously liable under the EA 2010 for the discriminatory actions of its managers and other employees who have been involved in the recruitment exercise in the course of their employment, even if those acts were contrary to the instructions that they were given. The employer will have a defence if it can show that it took all 'reasonable steps' to prevent the discriminatory act.

8.3.3 The employer may also be vicariously liable if it uses consultants or employment agencies to carry out its recruitment exercises where the consultant's or agency's actions are undertaken with the employer's authority. It is unlikely that an employer will be liable for unlawful discrimination carried out by consultants or agents where the consultant or agent acted in contravention of the employer's express instructions not to discriminate.

8.4 Good practice points

8.4.1 In order to avoid the possibility of claims being brought against it a charity should ensure that its recruitment process follows certain standards of good practice.

8.4.2 The decision-making process should be properly documented and written clearly and objectively. The EHRC Code recommends that employers keep records to enable them to justify each selection decision (from shortlisting to appointment) and the process by which the decision was reached. These records should demonstrate that a selection decision was based on objective evidence of the candidate's ability to do the job satisfactorily, not on any assumptions or prejudices about the capabilities of certain groups of people sharing protected characteristics.

8.4.3 Records should be kept for long enough to justify decisions, but, in accordance with the employer's obligations under the Data Protection Act 2018 (DPA), for no longer than is necessary. The documentation an employer should keep in relation to a recruitment exercise should include:

- applicable recruitment and/or equal opportunities policies;
- a job description;
- a person specification;
- selection criteria;
- any written test;
- notes of the short-listing process;
- interview questions and notes from the interview;
- minutes of any interview panel discussions or decision following interviews; and
- records that show that all those involved in the recruitment process had received appropriate training beforehand.

8.4.4 The EHRC Code stipulates that employers need to be able to show that all staff involved in the selection process had received training on the employer's equality policy and its application to recruitment, including interviewing techniques in order to help them:

- recognise when they are making stereotyped assumptions about people;
- apply a scoring method objectively;
- prepare questions based on the person specification and the information in the application form; and
- avoid questions that are not relevant to the requirements of the job.

8.4.5 Training will need to be kept up-to-date and given on a regular basis to ensure that those involved in the recruitment process are reminded of their responsibilities.

8.4.6 The EHRC Code suggests that employers should keep the following documentation:

- the job advertisement, the job description and the person specification;
- the application forms and any supporting documentation submitted by every candidate applying for the job;
- records of discussions and decisions by members of the selection panel;
- notes taken by each member of the panel during the interview;
- each panel member's marks at each stage of the process; and
- all correspondence with the candidates.

8.5 Practical steps

8.5.1 The EHRC Code recommends that the employer should draw up a detailed written job description and person specification before advertising a vacancy. Job descriptions and person specifications should be reviewed by the employer's HR department at regular intervals to ensure that they are accurate and up-to-date.

8.5.2 Job descriptions should be written in plain language, use an appropriate job title, accurately describe the job, focus on outcomes and avoid specifying unnecessary working patterns (for example, if the job could be done either part-time, full-time, or through job share arrangements this should be stated in the description).

8.5.3 The EHRC Code makes several recommendations about the creation of person specifications as follows:

- do not include wholly irrelevant criteria;
- criteria relating to skills of knowledge should not be unnecessarily restrictive by specifying particular qualifications to be necessary or desirable; and
- they should, as far as possible, use criteria that can be tested objectively.

8.5.4 It is unlawful to ask questions about health or disability before the offer of a job is made or a person is placed in a pool of people to be offered a job unless criteria relating to health, physical fitness or disability are objectively justified by the requirement of the actual job in question (criteria relating to physical attributes discriminate against disabled applicants and other applicants with protected characteristics).

8.5.5 Once the job description and person specification have been finalised, the employer will have to advertise the position. Care should be taken over the wording of an advertisement, as inappropriate wording could give rise to the risk of discrimination claims or be used as evidence of a discriminatory culture. The advertisement should not contain any wording that suggests that the employer might indirectly discriminate by suggesting criteria that would disadvantage people of a particular sex, age or any other protected characteristic unless the requirement can be objectively justified.

8.5.6 The EHRC Code suggests that employers should adopt a 'standardised process' for the application process to ensure that applicants compete on equal terms and to demonstrate that the employer has assessed applicants objectively. The EHRC Code has examples available.

8.5.7 Where necessary, reasonable adjustments should be made for disabled applicants (such as providing and accepting information in an accessible format such as Braille).

8.5.8 The next stage is to undergo a short-listing exercise. The EHRC Code recommends that employers should build the following guidelines for good practice into their selection procedures:

- wherever possible, more than one person should be involved in shortlisting candidates, to reduce the chance of bias;
- the marking system, including any cut-off score for selection, should be agreed before the applications are assessed, and applied consistently;
- where more than one person is involved in the selection process, each person should mark the application separately, before agreeing to a final mark; and
- selection should be based only on information provided in the application forms (where one is used), or in any formal performance assessment reports, in the case of internal applicants.

8.6 Occupational requirements and positive action

8.6.1 In certain circumstances an employer may have a defence to a discriminatory act which would otherwise be unlawful. The EA 2010 sets out a number of occupational requirement (OR) exceptions that employers might be able to rely on when facing discrimination claims.

8.6.2 A general OR exception is available where, having regard to the nature or context of the work, being of a particular sex, race, disability, religion or belief, sexual orientation or age is an OR. For example, a charity with an ethos based on a religion or belief may, in certain circumstances, show that being of a particular religion or belief is an OR.

8.6.3 Where individuals who share a protected characteristic suffer a disadvantage connected to the characteristic, have particular needs, or are disproportionately under-represented, it is possible for an employer to take positive action measures under the EA 2010. There is no obligation to take positive action. There are two positive action provisions.

- Where an employer reasonably thinks that persons with a particular protected characteristic are disadvantaged, have different needs or are disproportionately under-represented, it can take proportionate measures to enable or encourage persons with the relevant characteristic to overcome that disadvantage, to meet their needs, or to enable or encourage their increased participation.
- Positive action in recruitment and promotion that applies where an employer reasonably thinks that persons with a particular protected characteristic are disadvantaged or that their participation in an activity is disproportionately low. In those circumstances, the employer will be able to treat a person with the relevant characteristic more favourably than others in recruitment or promotion, as long as the person with the relevant characteristic is 'as qualified

as' those others and the employer does not have a policy of treating such people more favourably.

8.7 Criminal records checks

8.7.1 There are a number of reasons why a charity may want to check whether its employees or prospective employees have criminal records. These include where:

- the position is one which, by law, requires the employer to make such an inquiry (for example, if the prospective employee works with children or vulnerable adults);
- the nature of the work is such that making inquiries is desirable, though not mandatory; and
- there is nothing in the nature of the work which make it mandatory or obviously desirable to carry out the checks but the employer simply wants to know about the person's criminal record history as part of assessing their suitability.

8.7.2 In the latter two types of situation, there are a number of restrictions by virtue of the Rehabilitation of Offenders Act 1974 (ROA 1974). The purpose of the ROA 1974 is to prevent ex-offenders who have not re-offended for a significant period of time from being denied access to jobs purely on the basis of their past criminal convictions.

8.7.3 Anyone who has been convicted of a criminal offence and received a sentence of not more than two-and-a-half years in prison benefits if they have not been convicted again during a specified period known as the rehabilitation period. The length of this period depends on the sentence given for the original offence and runs from the date of the conviction. If the offender does not reoffend during this rehabilitation period, the conviction becomes 'spent'.

8.8 Spent convictions

When an ex-offender's conviction is spent they are not obliged to disclose that conviction in a job application or during any interview process, even if asked directly. It is worth noting that a spent conviction, or a failure to disclose it, is not a proper ground for dismissing an employee or prejudicing them in any way in the job (ROA, s. 4(3)(b)). In addition, a spent conviction shall not be a proper ground for 'excluding' any person from employment. This suggests that it should not be a reason for rejecting a job application, in addition to being an improper reason for dismissal. No specific remedy is available to enforce s. 4(3) at the job application stage.

8.9 Disclosure and Barring Service (DBS) checks

8.9.1 From 10 September 2012, the Protection of Freedoms Act 2012 ushered in changes to the Safeguarding Vulnerable Groups Act 2006 (SVGA 2006). The work of the Criminal Records Bureau (CRB) and of the Independent Safeguarding Authority (ISA) merged into a single body, the Disclosure and Barring Service (DBS) in December 2012.

8.9.2 Previously those carrying out regulated activity as defined in the SVGA 2006 were eligible for an enhanced CRB check with a Barred List check (a check of the children's and/or adults' barred list). The position now, with the amended definition of regulated activity (brought in on 10 September 2012), is that only those carrying out regulated activity in accordance with the amended definition contained in the SVGA will be eligible for a check against the Barred Lists.

8.9.3 The SVGA provides that:

- it is an offence for an employer to permit a barred individual to engage in regulated activity from which it knows, or has reason to believe, the individual is barred;
- employers have a duty to refer to the DBS any information which indicates that a person has harmed or posed/poses a risk of harm to children or vulnerable adults; and
- there will be a duty on a regulated activity provider to find out whether a person is barred before permitting them to engage in regulated activity. The provision in the SVGA providing for this duty is not yet in force.

8.10 Permission to work in the UK

Under the Immigration, Asylum and Nationality Act 2006 (IANA 2006), it is an offence to employ someone subject to immigration control who is not entitled to undertake the work in question. However, a defence to a charge of employing an illegal worker will apply in certain circumstances if the employer has taken steps to check the employee's documentation prior to them commencing employment.

8.11 Civil penalty

Employers are liable to pay a civil penalty of up to £20,000 per illegal worker. An illegal worker is someone subject to immigration control over 16 who is not entitled to undertake the work in question. Notice of liability to pay a civil penalty of a specific amount can be served by Border and Immigration Agency (BIA) officials on behalf of the Secretary of State.

8.12 Criminal offence

Employers knowingly employing an illegal migrant, or having 'reasonable cause to believe' that a person is an illegal worker, can be prosecuted under IANA 2006. Conviction under this offence will carry the potential of an unlimited fine and/or a prison sentence of up to five years. There will be no statutory excuse (see below) available for this offence.

8.13 Excuse against liability for penalty

Employers have a statutory excuse from payment of a civil penalty if they check and record certain specified documents belonging to potential employees.

8.14 Obtaining the statutory excuse

In order to obtain the statutory excuse, document checks must be carried out prior to employment and, in the circumstances mentioned above, at least once every 12 months after that.

8.15 Pre-employment health questions

As mentioned above, under the EA 2010 employers are not able to ask about a job applicant's health until that person has either been offered a job, or has been included in a pool of successful candidates to be offered a job when a suitable position arises.

8.16 References

8.16.1 It is common for contracts of employment to be offered subject to satisfactory references.

8.16.2 The matter of what is satisfactory is likely to be subjective. Employers are not obliged to provide references, but as the consequences of refusing or failing to do so are likely to be serious for an employee, the circumstances in which an employer or former employer will refuse to supply such a reference are probably rare. Such a refusal could give rise to a claim for unlawful discrimination if an employee believes that the refusal is related to previous discrimination.

8.16.3 In *Spring v Guardian Assurance* [1994], it was held that an employer owed a duty of care to their ex-employee and that a reference given by them could constitute a negligent mis-statement.

8.16.4 There is no duty on employers to provide a full reference. In *Kidd v Axa Equity & Law Life Insurance Society plc* [2000] the High Court held that the duty of an employer in giving a reference only extended as far as not giving a false or inaccurate reference and ensuring that it was not misleading through selectivity of information or opinions. In recent years the law on references has extended to informal discussions about ex-employees; discretion is increasingly important.

8.17 Data protection: subject access and employment references

The provision of a reference will generally involve the processing of personal data by a data controller (in this instance the employer) and so will be subject to data protection principles.

On 25 May 2018, the EU General Data Protection Regulation (GDPR) took effect and the Data Protection Act 2018 (DPA 2018) came into force. This repealed and replaced the data protection regime that had been set out in the Data Protection Act 1998. The Information Commissioner's Employment Practices Code sets out guidance for employers. This has yet to be updated to reflect the GDPR and DPA 2018 but remains relevant as an indication of the Information Commissioner's interpretation of an employer's duties.

There is an exception under schedule 2 to the DPA 2018 that allows the employer to refuse to disclose a confidential employment reference to an employee or former employee if they request it. Previously this exemption only applied to a situation where an employee made the request to the employer that provided the reference, but it now also applies where an employee makes a request to the employer that received the reference.

Although there is no obligation to provide a reference, the employer can decide to do so anyway. However, it should be careful not to disclose information about a third party (such as the person who wrote the reference) unless that person has consented to the disclosure or it is reasonable to disclose the reference without that person's consent.

8.18 Practical tips on recruitment

Charities should consider the following checklist of matters in relation to a recruitment process:

- Ensure that all managers and other members of staff who are involved in the recruitment process are appropriately trained on equal opportunities and on what records to keep.
- Ensure that advertisements are carefully drafted and checked before they are published.
- Ensure that a job description is prepared prior to interview and selection process in order to identify the requirements for the role.
- Prepare a pro forma list of questions for each interviewer to ensure consistency throughout the selection process.
- Ensure that any decisions made throughout the selection process are carefully recorded and ensure that interviewers receive appropriate training on DPA 2018 issues to understand their obligations in relation to the recording of data.
- Ensure that all the appropriate checks are in place.
- Ensure that offer letters are carefully drafted to avoid the creation of a contract of employment prior to the satisfaction of any additional requirements such as satisfactory references.

9 Health and safety

9.1 Charities, like other organisations, are required to take reasonable precautions to ensure the safety of those for whom they are responsible: their employees, volunteers and visitors to their premises. Thus, the charity can be held liable for compensation to those injured at work, or as a result of their work or activities.

9.2 Although a considerable number of later regulations exist covering, for example, display screens, manual handling and so on, the current legal framework derives from the implementation of the Health and Safety at Work, etc. Act 1974 (HASAWA), which, despite its age, has stood the test of time.

9.3 Two of the prime responsibilities under the Act are:

- for employers to provide a safe place of work for their employees. These days this is taken to mean the provision, as far as reasonably practical, of safety from harassment, bullying and discrimination as much as safety from physical harm; and
- for employees to take reasonable care of themselves and their colleagues.

9.4 The legislation places a wide-ranging and onerous responsibility on every employer. Implementation should be the responsibility of a senior, even board-level, manager in the organisation. A competent person from within the charity (or an outside consultant) could be given responsibility for carrying out safety and risk assessments.

9.5 Legislation requires detailed and ongoing assessments of risk to be made at each location. In addition, all organisations with five or more employees are required to prepare and display their policy statement regarding health and safety matters.

9.6 The Health and Safety Executive (HSE) has published guidance entitled *Leading Health and Safety at Work: leadership actions for directors and board members* which is designed for use by all directors, governors, trustees, officers and their equivalents and applies to organisations of all sizes. This guidance makes it clear how these individuals should ensure they understand their personal legal liability and responsibility. They should receive direction for effective health and safety management, ensure that proper health and safety arrangements are put in place and that risk assessments are carried out. A system of monitoring and reporting should be put in place, enabling the board of an organisation to receive both specific (incident-led) and continuous reports on the performance of the health and safety policy. Finally, the guidance makes it clear that a formal breakdown review of health and safety performance is essential.

10 Managing stress

10.1 Stress in the workplace is a very real problem as it can lead to long-term illness, absence and subsequent employment claims against employers who are believed to be responsible for placing employees in unacceptably stressful situations. Charities should therefore take the following precautions to try to ensure that they avoid stress claims. They should:

- be aware of any developing situations (see below);
- have a policy and procedure in place;
- ensure all managers are proactive in watching for signs of stress;
- emphasise that if there is a suspicion of stress, action must be taken;
- inform all employees that the organisation wishes to know if and when any employee is subject to stress;
- investigate fully all claims of stress, referring cases to expert advice and counselling; and
- ensure that a person who has suffered stress is not, on recovery, placed in a similarly stressful position.

10.2 To be able to hold an employer liable for stress, an employee must be able to prove that:

- there was a breach of the employer's common law obligation to provide a safe working environment;
- there was medical evidence demonstrating that the condition was stress-related and the stress was linked to the working environment; and
- the employer was in some way negligent in that the condition was foreseeable and yet the employer did nothing about it.

10.3 To some extent the exposure of employers has been alleviated as a result of the Court of Appeal decision in *Sutherland v Hatton* that reversed the bias in favour of employees who claim to be suffering from work-induced stress. The Court listed 12 items of advice, of which three are given here.

1. Employers are entitled to take at face value what they are told by their employees and do not need to make searching enquiries. Presumably, therefore, if the employer suspected an employee was under stress but the employee stated they were not, the employer would be able to accept that answer without further enquiry, although, even then, it might be advisable to take medical advice on the matter.
2. Employers are entitled to assume that an employee will be able to withstand the normal pressures of the job unless they know of a particular problem. Again it might be advisable to investigate further, with medical advice if appropriate, if there is any suspicion that the employee is under stress.

3. Any employer who offers a confidential counselling service with access to treatment is unlikely to be held liable in the event of a stress claim.

10.4 The House of Lords later acknowledged that these guidelines were 'useful practical guidance' but emphasised that they do not have statutory force.

10.5 The HSE publication *Management Standards for Stress*, developed after a consultation process with public and private sector organisations, states that there are six main areas of investigation. An employer should be able to resist a stress claim if 85% or more employees state that demands, control and support criteria are met and 65% or more state relationships, role and change criteria are met.

- **Demands**: employees should be given adequate and achievable demands related to hours worked. Skills and abilities should be matched to job demands and the latter should be within an employee's capability.
- **Control**: employees should be permitted control over their pace of work and when they can take breaks. Employers should encourage employees to develop their skills and to undertake new challenges. Employees should be consulted concerning working patterns.
- **Support**: there should be clear policies and procedures to support employees adequately. Managers must support their team members and every employee should support each of their colleagues. Employees should know what support is available and how to access it.
- **Role**: employers should provide employees with clear information so that they can understand their role and responsibilities. There should be systems allowing employees to raise concerns about uncertainties and conflicts.
- **Relationships**: positive behaviour should be promoted in the working environment to avoid conflict and ensure fairness. There should be procedures to outlaw and prevent unacceptable behaviour. Employees should be encouraged to share information about their work.
- **Change**: the employer should provide information to employees concerning all change likely to affect them. There should be adequate consultation and a process whereby employees can influence proposals. Timetables for change should be published and employees should have access to support during the change process.

As in all areas where safety and health are at risk, risk assessment is advisable.

11 Risk assessments

11.1 Inherent in the guidance set out above and in the increasing legislative requirements is a duty on the employer to carry out assessment in the workplace. A risk assessment:

- seeks to identify all the hazards posed in a particular situation;
- considers ways in which, if possible, hazards can be minimised or eradicated;
- identifies who it is that is at risk;
- evaluates the risk, the likelihood of occurrence and the number exposed to the risk, the severity of injury and the existing control measures;
- decides on any necessary new control measures to reduce or eliminate the risk;
- implements the controls and monitors their effectiveness;
- records the assessment and brings it to the attention of those affected; and
- sets a timetable within which the situation will be reassessed or reviewed.

11.2 Pregnancy

Risk assessments are required in all situations where there could be risk to an employee (or any other person using the workplace). One area where there is particular concern relates to pregnant women in the workplace, where there is a duty of care not just to the employee but also to her unborn child. Since 1999, employers have been required to conduct a risk assessment detailing the dangers to pregnant women and their unborn babies, and to new mothers (those who have given birth within the previous six months) caused by the workplace (a requirement of the Management of Health and Safety at Work Regulations 1999. Failure to have a risk assessment available to employees who are pregnant and/or new mothers breaches the above regulations. In addition, it is worth noting that any unfavourable treatment of a pregnant employee based on health and safety concerns of the employee for herself or her unborn child will amount to sex discrimination. In *Day v T Pickles Farms Ltd* [1999], it was held that an employer's failure to carry out a risk assessment under the regulations could amount to a detriment entitling the worker to bring a sex discrimination claim.

11.3 The dangers

11.3.1 The HSE identifies a number of main and general risks to pregnant women in the workplace. These should be taken as guidance only, since the risk assessment of each workplace will be different. In addition, each employer should identify the particular risks related to their own operation. The risks include:

- working with dangerous substances;
- violent or stressful environments;
- lifting;
- confined working space; and
- using an unsuitable workstation.

11.3.2 During the time she continues working, a pregnant woman has a right to:

- have the risks removed, or, if this is impossible;
- have her work location moved, or, if this is impossible;
- work on other tasks (without any detriment regarding salient features of her contract – hours, pay, benefits, etc.), or, if this is impossible;
- be suspended on full pay until such time as her maternity leave commences.

12 Safety policy

12.1 Although the requirement on employers to have and maintain a safety policy is an obligation under HASAWA, a surprising number of employers do not have one. Should there be an accident, such an omission could lead to personal fines for, or imprisonment of, those responsible.

12.2 Employers must report accidents as required under the Reporting of Injuries, Deaths and Dangerous Occurrences Regulations (RIDDOR) using the HSC Incident Contact Centre (HSCICC). The obligation is to report deaths, major injuries (where an accident results in the employee being away from work for three days or more), work-related diseases and dangerous occurrences which could have resulted in a reportable injury. A registered charity must also remember its obligation to report a serious incident to the Charity Commission.

12.3 On-site data

12.3.1 Safety folder

A copy of the safety policy should be given to every employee. It provides a prompt for action and a criterion for guidance. It may also be feasible and advisable to post in every place of work (and on every floor where there is multi-floor occupation) a readily identifiable and visible folder in which a number of forms are kept, including hazard reporting forms. The visible sheet of such a folder could include a checklist of items demonstrating when each was last checked (such as fire evacuation, equipment inspection dates, etc.) so that employees' views can operate as a reminder if it has been too long since the last fire drill.

12.3.2 Hazard reporting

A supply of hazard reporting forms can be included in the safety folder. The principle behind this is that the sooner the organisation knows of a hazard, the better the chance of avoiding injury by being able to effect remedial work.

13 The Health and Safety Executive

13.1 The Health and Safety Executive (HSE) is the government body charged with promoting and policing safety in the workplace. It provides details of the criteria to be used to decide which injury or other complaints should be investigated and detailed guidelines regarding initiating prosecutions.

13.2 First aid

13.2.1 First aid can be defined as instant action carried out by (normally) untrained persons to preserve life, pending attendance by a trained medical practitioncr. As well as a need to provide instant assistance in the event of injury, etc., under RIDDOR, employers are also required to notify the appropriate authorities of all reportable incidents affecting everyone on their sites, whether employed or visiting. These regulations require employers to report acts of non-consensual physical violence (so-called 'skylarking' or pranks of a physical nature).

13.2.2 The Health & Safety (First Aid at Work) Regulations 1981 (and the approved code of practice and guidance issued in 1997) sets out detailed requirements placed on an employer regarding the provision of first aid facilities. An employer must provide:

- suitable first aid staff and services in accordance with the nature of the business, the degree of danger or hazard in the operations, the number of employees and the proximity to medical assistance. A first aider is defined as someone who holds a current certificate in first aid;
- a first aid room, if there are 400 or more employed at a single site, but again, its provision will depend on the assessment of the hazards; and
- properly stocked first aid boxes.

13.2.3 It may help if the charity adopts a first aid policy that reflects its commitment to and administration of first aid. Legally, employers are required to enter details of all accidents at work in an accident book. Since this means that personal details of employees are included in the record, the provisions of the DPA 2018 must be observed and revised editions of such a book which conceal such personal data are now available.

13.3 Fire precautions

13.3.1 Regular fire alarm tests and even fire drills (which are now mandatory in some cases) should be held.

13.3.2 The Regulatory Reform (Fire Safety) Order 2005 came into effect in October 2006. Although it revokes the 1997 Regulations (see below), most of the requirements are restated, with the important change that Fire certificates will no longer be issued.

13.3.3 The previous requirement to react to the advice of the fire officer, obtaining guidance and clearance by the issue of such a certificate, has now been replaced by a requirement to be completely proactive particularly regarding the preparation of (and regular updating of) risk assessments.

13.3.4 Such assessments must be carried out by a 'responsible person' (RP). If the workplace is under the control of the employer, the RP is the employer; but if the workplace is under another person's control, the RP could be the owner. Thus where a property is occupied by multiple employers, in each of the 'suites' or areas occupied by individual employers they are the RP for their own area. However, the RP for the 'common areas' would probably be the landlord.

13.3.5 Enforcement is carried out by fire safety inspectors (appointed by the local fire and rescue authority). In some circumstances (such as where the subject location is a construction site) enforcement is under the control of the HSE, or (if the location is a sports centre) the local authority. Failure to comply with requirements issued by an enforcement authority can lead to an unlimited fine or, on conviction, to an unlimited fine and/or two years' imprisonment.

14 What is a good employer expected to do?

14.1 Fair recruitment

It is crucial that an employer follows a fair procedure in recruiting new workers and avoids treating anyone less favourably than someone else because of one of the protected characteristics discussed above. This will apply to the whole recruitment process: advertising the job; shortlisting; interviews and the selection of a candidate. It is useful to have formal processes in place to help avoid unlawful discrimination. See our 'practical tips on recruitment'.

14.2 Training

14.2.1 Training forms a strong base to ensure staff meet their objectives and perform to their best ability. Training should be provided to all new employees on:

- equality and diversity;
- health and safety at work;
- how to deal with harassment at work; and
- the Bribery Act.

14.2.2 The EA 2010 states that an employer must take 'all reasonable steps' to prevent discrimination, harassment or victimisation. Although this is not defined by law, the *Employer Guidance on the Equality Act 2010* states that these steps will include having an equality policy and implementing it.

14.3 Bribery Act 2010

14.3.1 The Act states that commercial organisations will commit a corporate offence when a person associated with them bribes another person intending to obtain or retain business or an advantage in the conduct of business for the organisation. This will be the case whether or not the organisation was complicit.

14.3.2 Although the term 'commercial organisation' initially appears to exclude charities from the scope of the corporate offences under the Act, Ministry of Justice guidance confirms that any incorporated body engaging in commercial activities will be caught, irrespective of whether its purpose is primarily charitable or to carry out public functions. As a result, charities will need to ensure they carry out thorough risk assessments and can demonstrate adequate anti-bribery procedures.

14.3.3 The definition of 'associated person' in the Act includes employees, agents and subsidiaries but is wide enough to cover anyone providing work or services for the organisation (e.g. suppliers or contractors). Employers can defend a change if they can show that they had adequate procedures in place to prevent bribery.

14.3.4 Many charities will have procedures in place already that make it clear that they do not tolerate bribery, but it is also important to ensure that employees receive training in these procedures so that they do not fall foul of the Act. Confidential channels to report bribery offences, such as in whistleblowing policies, should also be put in place.

14.4 Manage fairly

It is essential to the wellbeing of an employer and its staff that all the staff are managed fairly. This will involve keeping managers up-to-date with changes in employment legislation, as well as giving them regular training in how to deal with disciplinary, grievance and capability issues, as well as allegations of bullying and harassment. They should also be given training in appraisal processes to enable them to get the most out of the staff they manage.

14.5 Flexible working requests

14.5.1 Employers must treat requests to work flexibly consistently (for example, an employer must not refuse a request from a man to work flexibly when a similar request from a woman has been granted).

14.5.2 It is good practice to have a flexible working policy so that workers are aware if they are entitled to apply for flexible working and what the process is for making a request. An employer should not make an assumption that certain jobs are not suitable for flexible working.

14.6 Dealing with disciplinary issues

14.6.1 All disciplinary procedures must be robust, fair and adhered to. It is the charity's right to formulate a policy; it is management's responsibility to make certain that everyone knows the procedure and to ensure that it is adhered to at all times. Tribunals rarely criticise the wording of disciplinary procedures but they can be highly critical of employers failing to abide by their own procedures. Indeed, this has on many occasions led to procedurally unfair dismissal.

14.6.2 If an employee has, or is reported to have, infringed the methods or rules of work or behaviour, the problem (the facts having been established) needs to be discussed with them to ensure the report is accurate and to discover any reasons for such action, and then (if applicable) to provide guidance as to the correct behaviour.

14.6.3 Many disciplinary matters can be dealt with informally by the immediate superior by way of few words to put the employee straight on their transgression – in short, an 'informal nudge'. Such an approach can be far more effective in terms of creating awareness of the required behaviour than formal disciplinary proceedings. If, however, such informal 'nudges' need to be constantly repeated, a note of such verbal warnings should be made in the employee's personnel file, with a copy given to the employee.

14.6.4 For serious offences or where there has been repetition of minor transgressions (probably already the subject of informal warnings, with an indication of a sanction), there will be a need to use the formal warning procedure. The form this procedure might take should be outlined in a formal disciplinary policy.

14.6.5 The Advisory, Conciliation and Arbitration Service (ACAS) Code of Practice is the standard against which employers' disciplinary and dismissal procedures are measured. The Code provides that disciplinary procedures should:

- be in writing;
- be non-discriminatory;
- provide for matters to be dealt with speedily;
- allow for information to be kept confidential;
- tell employees what disciplinary action might be taken;
- say what levels of management have the authority to take the various forms of disciplinary action;

- require employees to be informed of the complaints against them, with any supporting evidence, before a disciplinary meeting;
- give employees a chance to have their say before management reaches a decision;
- provide employees with the right to be accompanied;
- provide that no employee is dismissed for a first breach of discipline, except in cases of gross misconduct;
- require management to investigate fully before any disciplinary action is taken;
- ensure that employees are given an explanation for any sanction and allow employees to appeal against a decision; and
- apply to all employees, irrespective of their length of service, status or if there are different rules for different groups.

14.7 Disciplinary Hearings

14.7.1 Regardless of the severity of the offence or potential sanction, a meeting to discuss it should be conducted in an open and positive manner. Even if the employee has admitted the offence, a hearing must be held. Hearings should be held at a mutually convenient time, preferably during the subject's working hours and should ideally be conducted by an impartial 'adjudicator' listening to both sides of the argument and to any witnesses, giving both parties every opportunity to ask questions of the other and of any witnesses, and to make any points in support or rebuttal. It is preferable (where possible) that the person chairing the hearing is not the person making the employer's case.

14.7.2 Once both parties have finished, the adjudicator will need to come to a decision. This does not necessarily need to be announced immediately; it may be preferable with complicated complaints to allow time for reflection, and/or possible further independent investigation by the adjudicator. If the complaint is serious, it may be preferable to suspend the employee on full pay pending the decision, which, irrespective of the seriousness, should be made known as swiftly as possible.

14.8 Records

Ideally, full notes of the hearing should be made by an independent person, with transcripts made available to both employee and supervisor/manager, and an opportunity for anyone disagreeing with the transcript to challenge and, with the agreement of the adjudicator and the other party, correct the record. In the event of disagreement, the adjudicator will need to decide the correct content. The notes or tape recording of the hearing should state the approval/objection/correction process in their conclusion. The original notes (even if transcribed) should be preserved carefully. It is not always possible to agree transcripts.

14.9 Right to be accompanied

The Employment Relations Act (ERA) grants a right to representation 'where [the hearing] could result in the employer administering a formal warning to a worker or taking some other action in respect of him or her'. The ERA also requires representation at a grievance hearing which 'concerns the performance of a duty by the employer to a worker'.

14.10 Disciplinary procedure

Any dismissal must follow a fair procedure. Charities should ideally have minimum procedures in place and follow them.

14.11 Sanctions

- **Warnings:** assuming the case has been proved, the adjudicator needs not only to record this, but also to decide on and initiate appropriate sanctions. This will normally take the form of a warning, usually requiring the employee to desist from unacceptable behaviour, or to comply with rules and procedures previously transgressed. If the employee has already been given a warning for the same offence this may (depending on the organisation's procedure) be classified as a final warning.
- **Demotion:** as an alternative to dismissal (see below), demotion is an option, but only if it is an option in the disciplinary procedure.
- **Dismissal:** this is, and should be, the sanction of last resort. The law requires an adjudicator to act reasonably in coming to a decision to dismiss that includes considering all sanctions possible in 'the reasonable range of responses'.

14.11.1 There are five fair reasons for dismissing an employee:

1. redundancy;
2. lack of capability or qualifications;
3. unacceptable conduct;
4. where continued employment would breach legislation; and
5. some other substantial reason, which could include (for example) the refusal by an employee to accept a necessary change in shift pattern.

14.11.2 In addition to clearly identifying under which heading a proposed dismissal should be classified, the employer must also follow four principles:

- follow the right procedure;
- act reasonably;
- give the employee a chance to explain and (if a question of capability) improve; and
- provide an opportunity to appeal.

14.12 Summary dismissal

Where the offence is severe, it is sometimes possible to terminate employment without notice. A hearing still needs to be held and sanctions and their effect considered (dismissal may affect their DBS status or any registrations with the Care Quality Commission or Ofsted). These should all be taken into account by the adjudicator.

14.13 Appeals

An appeal should be a review rather than a rehearing of the disciplinary hearing, and should be heard by an independent third party. Everyone should have a right of appeal.

14.14 Dealing with capability issues

14.14.1 A charity should also be proactive with poor performance and should have a capability policy in place to ensure that the proper process is being followed.

14.14.2 The aim of capability proceedings is to help employees who are struggling in their jobs to achieve their full potential. Ideally, a procedure separate to the disciplinary procedure should be the fall-back position if informal measures to improve performance such as training, support and additional supervision don't work.

14.14.3 Where there is no improvement, the charity should consider initiating more formal proceedings, which may eventually result in the employee's dismissal for capability reasons. As with the disciplinary dismissals discussed above, it is paramount that proper procedures are followed and that the employee is treated fairly at all times.

15 What happens if it all goes wrong?

15.1 Keep good records

It is essential to have a proper paper trail to show how any decisions in relation to employees and workers have been made. The importance of this during the recruitment process has been discussed above, but it is also imperative to ensure that any disciplinary, capability or grievance issues have been properly documented.

15.2 Claims

15.2.1 Tribunal proceedings

It is worth bearing in mind that any aggrieved staff will generally only have a period of three months to bring a claim. This is the case in unfair dismissal proceedings and discrimination proceedings.

15.2.2 Court proceedings

In certain instances cases claims may be brought in the High Court or the County Court. An example of this is a breach of contract claim which may well fall within the jurisdiction of both the Tribunal and the County or High Court. Compensation for such a claim in the Tribunal is capped (at £25,000), but if it were to be brought in the High Court the full amount of compensation sought will potentially be recoverable

15.2.3 Personal injury claims

If a personal injury claim is brought against the employer then generally the first course of action is for the employer to refer it to its insurers.

15.2.4 Consider settlement

It is not always beneficial for charities to defend claims. Charities should always consider settling claims threatened or brought by staff. Trustees should take appropriate professional advice on the risk of proceeding. It is also possible to ask an employee to agree effective severance terms in the form of a compromise agreement.

D2
Fundraising and trading

1 Fundraising

1.1 Introduction

1.1.1 For most charities, fundraising is crucial to their ongoing viability. Trustees and staff with responsibility for the financial health of their charity must ensure that it has adequate resources to deliver its objectives and to meet running costs while also ensuring that it complies with the law. Increasingly, consideration must also be given to the effect of the fundraising activity on the reputation of the charity and the sentiment, expressed by the current chair of the Charity Commission Baroness Stowell, that 'charitable aims cannot justify uncharitable means'.

1.1.2 In this chapter, we will look at important aspects of fundraising, including developing the charity's strategy and ensuring that its fundraising activities stay within the law. However, this chapter will not include advice on how to raise money or on different fundraising approaches.

1.2 Recent changes

1.2.1 It is important that everyone involved in fundraising keeps up-to-date with the most recent legislation and best practice. The key legal provisions relating to charity fundraising come from Part II of the Charities Act 1992 (and the Charitable Institutions (Fund-Raising) Regulations 1994). These provisions were amended, in part, by the Charities Act 2006. The Charities Act 2006 also gave Parliament the power to regulate fundraising if self-regulation by charities was not effective.

Most of charity law has since been consolidated into the Charities Act 2011, although the rules regarding fundraising are now split between this and the Charities Act 1992 discussed above. The Charities (Protection and Social Investment) Act 2016 also amended the rules on fundraising in both these pieces of legislation.

In the summer of 2015, the *Mail on Sunday* and *Daily Mail* ran a series of stories exposing the use of allegedly exploitative fundraising practices by well-known charities, often by sub-contractors, and the damage being caused to vulnerable individuals. This has had a profound impact on the regulation of fundraising since.

The Government's immediate response to this press coverage was to establish a review of fundraising regulation, chaired by Sir Stuart Etherington, the Chief Executive of the NCVO. The key recommendations of the 'Etherington review' included introducing the Fundraising Regulator as a single, new self-regulating body (replacing the Fundraising Standards Board and working alongside the Institute of Fundraising) with an accompanying fundraising code and the creation of a Fundraising Preference Service (considered in detail in section 2 of this chapter).

The Government also legislated on aspects of fundraising in the Charities (Protection and Social Investment) 2016 Act in order to improve charities' fundraising practices (considered in detail in section 2 on page 328).

1.2.2 Rules governing the running of lotteries are set out in the Gambling Act 2005. More information on lotteries is set out below, but any charities wishing to run lotteries should consult the Gambling Commission's guidance for detailed information.

1.3 Developing a fundraising strategy

Fundraising is an integral part of the overall strategy of a charity and is closely connected with business planning, budget setting and investment. Trustees and key staff must determine how much money they need to run the charity's existing activities and to establish new ones. Within this global figure, the different sources of income should be identified and this information will form the foundation of the fundraising strategy. In this section, we will consider the areas to cover when developing a fundraising strategy. An action plan that can be used to draft a charity's strategy is included at the end of this section.

1.4 Where is the money coming from?

1.4.1 Relying on a single source of income tends to make an organisation vulnerable and could compromise its independence. Historically, many local charities have been financed largely or entirely by local authority grants and so have been highly vulnerable to funding cuts. Charities have also suffered cuts in central government and EU funding; charities, access to EU funding is likely to be further curtailed once the UK leaves the EU in 2019, although at the time of writing the terms of its exit are not yet clear. Charities should be aware of provisions in funding agreements that allow funders to terminate a contract earlier than anticipated and should bear in mind the possibility that an annual agreement that has been renewed for many years may be terminated in the future or renegotiated to reduce the funding provided. Diversifying income sources offers charities a degree of protection, or at least some breathing space, should a particular income stream run dry.

1.4.2 Different areas of work may lend themselves naturally to certain sources of income and some income streams may already be secure (for example, charities may already have a number of contracts or grants in place). Ongoing projects, such as the employment of a worker dedicated to a particular aspect of the charity's work (supporting a particular element of its client group) require continued funding and are frequently funded by renewable grants or contracts. In contrast, activities that require expenditure over a relatively short period, such as extending a building or commissioning a piece of research may be funded by one-off or short-term funding such as a specific grant or the proceeds of an appeal. Fundraising events and street collections can be useful ways of raising unrestricted funds that can be used for any purpose within the organisation.

The fundraising strategy may be divided into raising money for specific purposes and raising money for the general purposes of the charity. Many charities find it easier to raise funds for specific purposes, as corporate sponsors, grant makers and the public like to feel that they are supporting a specific project. Such appeals should include a statement that funds raised from the appeal that cannot be spent on the purpose that was the subject of the appeal will be used for the general purposes of the charity. Where an appeal is held for a specific activity, charities should consider opening a separate bank account to hold funds raised through that appeal. Funds to finance the general activities and overheads of the charity may be raised through a variety of approaches, including general appeals, fundraising events, trading activities and legacy appeals.

1.4.3 Ethical issues relating to fundraising and due diligence should also be considered. These could be covered in part by the charity's ethical investment policy. If the charity would not invest in tobacco companies or weapons manufacturers, should it accept donations from them? Trustees may agree on wider restrictions (not to raise money through gambling or not to encourage events involving dangerous sports) where these restrictions align with the charities' purposes.

1.4.4 As always with ethical issues, trustees should ensure that any self-imposed restrictions on sources of fundraising income are in the best interests of the charity, either because of the risk of direct conflict with charitable objects or because of a likely negative impact on other funding streams.

Where trustees consider that the ethical issues posed by a donation are so great that it is in the best interests of the charity to refuse the donation before it is accepted, or to return the donation after the fact, they should be able to clearly document and explain their reasoning. The Charity Commission has said that trustees in such a situation can seek formal advice from the Commission or an

Order enabling them to take an action where they would not otherwise have legal authority to do so.

Trustees should be aware that in practice it is much more difficult to return a donation that has already been received and accepted. It is almost certain that to return a donation you would need an Order from the Charity Commission which, in turn, would need to be persuaded that any return was in the best interests of the charity.

Charities who expect to receive unsolicited major donations might like to consider creating a policy on the return and refusal of donations as part of their broader fundraising strategy.

Ethical considerations will also extend to ensuring that fundraisers and those who come into contact with fundraisers are not exposed to harm. The 2018 scandal of the 'Presidents Club' charitable gala, where allegations were made of serving staff being sexually harassed and asked to sign non-disclosure agreements, and the consequent reputational damage to beneficiaries of the gala, illustrates the importance of 'safeguarding' measures in this context.

1.5 Timescale

As well as identifying the amount of income required and potential sources of income, the fundraising strategy should include details of when funding is required. It is no good raising money in two years' time for a project that is currently only funded for the next six months. By identifying what money is needed and when, trustees can prioritise the different elements of the fundraising strategy and create an action plan. In this way, the charity's fundraising strategy will be closely linked to its business plan. Timescales should also be set for individual appeals, indicating when the appeal will end. This makes for better appeal planning and facilitates the clearer accounting of appeal funds.

1.6 'Joined-up thinking'

1.6.1 As well as linking into business planning, budgeting and investment policy, the fundraising strategy should be consistent with any public relations approach agreed by the organisation, be complementary to operational work and be sympathetic to the organisation's objectives. For example, it may be considered inappropriate for a charity working to alleviate family poverty to raise funds through events involving gambling, such as race nights. Similarly, the message of a charity promoting the independence of its beneficiaries would be undermined by a fundraising campaign that sought to evoke pity for its beneficiaries from the public.

1.6.2 Studies have indicated that some members of the public resent street collections carried out by fundraisers (known colloquially as 'chuggers'); trustees should balance the potential for triggering resentment among the public against the funds that might be raised through such methods. Charities should also ensure that any advertising campaign they carry out complies with the relevant advertising regulations.

1.7 Is it worth it?

1.7.1 The strategy should also consider the 'effort: reward' ratio. Will the anticipated benefit of the fundraising activity, including the income raised and the publicity generated, justify the resources, including time and money, invested in carrying out the activity? By the use of innovative or particularly well-targeted fundraising methods, for example by exploring new, digital technologies, a relatively small investment of resources can sometimes reap great rewards. In contrast, if a charity's fundraising strategy is not well planned or followed, the amount to be spent on major fundraising campaigns or the employment of specialist fundraising staff or consultants may not be justified by the benefits to the charity, such as the amount of money raised or publicity generated. For local charities, fundraising events can be a labour-intensive option, but may only generate small financial rewards, although the collateral benefits of increased profile or user involvement may make such events worthwhile.

1.7.2 It is for the trustees to decide in each case whether the reward is sufficient to make the effort worthwhile. For example, is expenditure of £1,000 generating a total income of £1,500 and a net gain of £500 justifiable, or would the activity have to generate a net gain of £1,000 for it to be worthwhile?

1.7.3 Fundraisers should also question whether the anticipated outcome is a realistic prediction. Are estimated returns for a street collection, legacy appeal or other fundraising event based on guesswork, previous experience or some other factor? Are grant applications likely to be successful (for example, have applications been targeted at those grant makers most likely to fund your type of organisation or project)?

1.8 Reporting the costs

The amount of money spent on fundraising will need to be reported in the charity's annual accounts. Charities should consider the potential of public scrutiny and possible press coverage where the level of expenditure is particularly high.

1.9 Who is responsible?

1.9.1 The respective roles of trustees, staff and supporters should be considered as part of the fundraising strategy and reflected in the job descriptions of staff and trustees. Fundraising is one of those areas of charity work that can easily fall through the gaps in the defined responsibilities of staff and trustees, particularly in small charities.

1.9.2 It should be clear who will take responsibility for the day-to-day tasks involved in fundraising, from rattling tins through to negotiating with grant-making bodies. If these tasks are to be delegated to a member of staff, the scope of the role should be explicitly described in the employee's job description, the skills and experience required should be an integral part of the job specification and everyone involved in the recruitment process should be conscious of the blend of skills that they are looking for, as well as the balance between fundraising and other activities. For instance, it might be unrealistic to expect a worker who has been employed for their social care and counselling skills also to be an experienced fundraiser. It might also be unrealistic to expect the same worker to take a lead role in securing ongoing funding without compromising an already full workload of providing client services. In such circumstances, the trustees have a clear responsibility to seek ongoing funding to sustain the charity, and they should take the lead in any relevant negotiations.

1.10 Fundraising strategy: action plan

Task	Who is responsible?
Identify the most appropriate sources of funding.	Trustees and senior staff, including any fundraising staff.
Check that the proposed fundraising approach is consistent with the organisation's public image and operational concerns.	Trustees and senior staff, in consultation with operational staff and any PR personnel.
Agree a baseline in terms of the ratio of fundraising costs to fundraising income.	Trustees, senior officer and senior finance officer.
Consider any legal restrictions or best practice issues relating to your preferred methods of fundraising.	Trustees with the advice and support of senior staff.
Consider the charity's policy on due diligence for donations and when they may be accepted or refused	Trustees with the advice and support of senior staff.

1.10.1 Even where fundraising is delegated to employees of the charity, the trustees continue to have the ultimate responsibility for the financial viability of the organisation. The appointment of professional fundraising staff does not absolve them of this responsibility; it merely allows them to delegate the fundraising task to people with appropriate skills and experience.

1.10.2 The fundraising of many local charities is led by volunteers. While such volunteers are often extremely successful and hugely valuable to the charity, the trustees have overall responsibility for fundraising and must exercise authority over the actions of volunteers. This is frequently achieved through a fundraising sub-committee involving both trustees and volunteers.

1.11 Rules and good practice

1.11.1 Trustees and fundraisers also need to be aware of the regulatory framework that surrounds fundraising activities. In addition to the information given below, trustees should ensure they read the Charity Commission guidance *Charity fundraising: a guide to trustee duties* (CC20) and consider the application of other legal requirements. For example, information held on donors is subject to the provisions of the DPA 2018 (which implements the EU General Data Protection Regulations) and health and safety requirements should be complied with in relation to any fundraising events.

Trustees and fundraisers should also ensure they comply at all times with the relevant provisions of the Code of Fundraising Practice and any associated guidance (such as that on street collections, house-to-house fundraising and private sites fundraising) maintained by the Fundraising Regulator. There is no legal obligation to comply with the 'code but the Charity Commission could consider the extent of compliance in any review of the charity's fundraising activities and its trustees' responsibility for the same.

1.11.2 The focus of this section is on those fundraising activities that are most commonly used by small to medium-sized charities.

1.12 Street collections

1.12.1 A permit or licence is normally required for charity collections or sales taking place in the street or other public places. Under the current scheme, licences and permits can be obtained from the relevant local authority or, for collections in London, from the Metropolitan Police or the City of London authorities.

1.12.2 Permits and licences are granted under local regulations. Issues that will be considered include obstructions to traffic, financial controls and accounting arrangements for any funds raised through the collection, and the frequency of collections (some high streets have street collections booked throughout the year, while other local authorities prefer to keep the number of collections down). Contact your local authority for information about the regulations in your area.

1.13 Door-to-door collections

1.13.1 Door-to-door collections are also subject to licensing arrangements, again controlled by the local authority or, in London, the Metropolitan or City of London Police, and specific regulation by way of the House to House Collections Act 1939 and the House to House Collections Regulations 1947.

The arrangements apply to charity sales and collections of money and goods from residential and business premises (including public houses). Exemptions from the licensing requirements are available from the Secretary of State for Digital, Culture, Media & Sport for charities regularly organising collections across a substantial part of the country. Exemptions may also be available from the relevant local licence-provider for local collections taking place over a short period of time.

1.13.2 It is good practice to collect cash donations from street and door-to-door collections in sealed collecting tins. This not only helps reduce the risk of theft from the collection, but also reassures donors that the risk of theft has been reduced.

1.13.3 Those collecting public donations should always wear visible identity cards establishing their connection with the charity and the legality of the collection.

1.14 Private site fundraising

'Private site' fundraising is, like door-to-door collections, a method of face-to-face fundraising. Charities who wish to undertake private sites fundraising should refer to the Fundraising Regulator's rulebook on the same.

1.15 Events

Charities raise funds through a wide variety of events, from jumble sales and raffles through to high-profile auctions and expensive balls. Trustees need to research carefully any legal requirements relating to the events planned. The tax exemptions available for fundraising and trading are discussed on page 337). Other issues include health and safety requirements (e.g. maximum capacity for venues used), insurance and specific regulations relating to the nature of the event (any licences required for gambling or the sale of alcohol). Finally, trustees should consider the possible reputational risks of the event and the suitability of any third party involved to run it in determining whether it is in the charity's best interests, notwithstanding any risks.

1.16 Lotteries (including raffles)

1.16.1 Charities and their subsidiary companies may run lotteries to raise money for their charitable purposes. These are regulated by the Gambling Commission under the Gambling Act 2005. Charity lotteries fall into two main categories:

- **Incidental lotteries**: there is no requirement to register a lottery that is incidental to an event (a fête or concert) and is not held for private gain. The classic example of a small lottery is a raffle. Such lotteries must comply with certain requirements (e.g. tickets must be sold and issued at the event in question while it is taking place, prizes cannot roll over, the results must be announced during the event and on the premises where it is held, no more than £500 of the takings may be spent on prizes, and no more than £100 of the takings may be spent on expenses). Following changes introduced in 2016, incidental lottery results can now be drawn either at or after the event.

- **Society lotteries**: other charity lotteries must be registered with the local authority or, for 'large society lotteries', the Gambling Commission. Gambling Commission registration is required where ticket sales exceed £20,000 for a single lottery or £250,000 for lotteries organised by a charity in a one-year period. Trustees undertaking society lotteries should contact their local authority or (if necessary) the Gambling Commission for information on the detailed requirements relating to issues such as the price of tickets, prize money, deduction of costs, age restrictions and accounting requirements.

1.16.2 Further information about the regulation of lotteries, including the licence conditions and codes of practice for licence holders, may be found on the Gambling Commission website (www.gamblingcommisison.gov.uk). It should also be noted that, at the time of writing, DCMS, the Gambling Commission and the Office for Civil Society are considering the responses to a consultation which could lead to significant changes to the law for 'large society lotteries'. Lottery profits are tax exempt as long as they are used solely for the charity's objects and all regulatory requirements are complied with. The tax exemption does not apply to lotteries run by subsidiary companies, although the company can donate all pre-tax profits to the charity under the Gift Aid scheme.

1.17 Telephone fundraising

Charities undertaking fundraising by telephone must avoid contacting individuals who are registered for the Telephone Preference Service and need to consider screening numbers and maintaining 'exclusion lists' in order to do so.

1.18 Broadcast media fundraising

Even trustees of small charities may find opportunities for broadcast appeals (such as on local radio and television) but should be careful to note the rules under the Charities Act 1992 and any available and applicable codes. Charities must ensure clarity in terms of identifying the charity or charities (not just the cause) that will receive the funds and, where multiple charities will benefit, the proportion of the donation that will be spent on each charity's objects. Funds raised must be transferred directly to the charity.

1.19 Legacies

1.19.1 Legacy fundraising is a sensitive and complex area of fundraising and trustees looking to raise resources through legacies should plan their approach carefully. It is particularly important to develop a code for fundraisers, be they volunteers, employees or external fundraisers, that covers legal requirements and best practice. Such a code should also consider wider issues, such as the marketing of a legacy campaign. An insensitive campaign runs the risk of offending people and alienating potential donors. Trustees should have reference to the Code of Fundraising Practice and guidance on legacy fundraising from the Charity Commission, the Institute of Fundraising and the Institute of Legacy Management. Trustees should also bear in mind the length of time that is likely to pass between the appeal being made and the funds coming to the charity when considering the resources used on legacy fundraising and the reliance placed on legacies.

1.19.2 When seeking legacies, it is important to follow the basic principles of fundraising, including communicating clear information on the organisation's charitable status and the way in which the donation will be used.

1.19.3 Given the sensitivity of legacy fundraising, it is vital that donors are not pressurised into making a donation. Particular care should be taken when dealing with vulnerable people (such as those who are terminally ill, elderly or recently bereaved). If it can be proved that the legacy was made under undue influence, the will could be held to be invalid and the gift will fail.

1.19.4 It is clearly in the charity's best interests that wills are made with legal advice, and fundraisers should recommend to donors that they consult an appropriate professional (although they should not recommend or comment on the competence of individual solicitors). The signing of wills must not be witnessed by a representative of the charity. When a donor decides to make a donation to a charity, they should be encouraged to include the charity's registered number as well as its name to avoid confusion with other organisations, as the name of the charity may change before the supporter dies, or the supporter may confuse the charity with a similarly named organisation.

1.19.5 It is not unusual for donors to want their legacy to be used for a particular purpose. If a charity decides to make an appeal encouraging donors to make legacies, the charity should make it clear that if the legacy cannot be used for that purpose it will be used for the general purposes of the charity.

1.20 Declaration of charitable status

Registered charities in England & Wales with a gross annual income of £10,000 or more are required to declare their charitable status on all media that solicit funds. It is good practice for all charities to do so. Similarly, although charities are not required to state their Charity Commission registration number, it is good practice to do so. Further information may be found on the Fundraising Regulator website in the legal appendices to the Code of Fundraising Practice.

1.21 Restricted funds

1.21.1 If funds have been raised for a particular purpose, they may only be spent for that purpose. This principle of restricted funds applies to public appeals as well as to grant applications and can create difficulties if a specific fundraising appeal is more (or less), successful than anticipated. In such circumstances, any funds that have not been spent cannot be applied to other causes within the charity without the express permission of the donor.

1.21.2 Many charities prefer to base fundraising campaigns and street collections on a specific issue, partly because they need money for that particular cause, but also because, as has already been said, people like to give on this basis rather than just contributing to the general funds of the charity. If more funds are raised than required, the charity will have to seek advice from the Charity Commission on whether a Commission Scheme will be necessary to enable the funds to be used for other purposes within the charity's objects. If the funds raised are insufficient, trustees must try to return any funds given by identifiable donors. If the donors do not wish to take their money back, they must sign a disclaimer to this effect. Funds raised through collecting tins, competitions and lotteries are presumed to be from unidentifiable donors. The Charity Commission can make a Scheme to apply any remaining funds to other similar purposes within the charity. These funds must be kept in reserve for six months to meet any outstanding claims from donors. Trustees facing either situation should contact the Commission for advice. Charities can avoid this problem by ensuring that every request for funds for a specified purpose is accompanied by a statement that funds that cannot be used for that purpose will be used for the general purposes of the charity.

Charities should also be aware of possible reforms to the process of referring to the Charity Commission following the recommendations of the Law Commission's 2017 report, 'Technical Issues in Charity Law', which at the time of writing has not yet been implemented.

1.22 Audit trail

Organisations that receive cash donations or undertake any form of public collection must have clear and effective cash-handling procedures. Procedures should cover issues such as the use of sealed collecting tins and envelopes, the joint counting of donated cash and careful recording of donations. Funds given for a specific appeal should be treated as restricted funds, subject to the points made above, so should be recorded as such on receipt.

2 The Fundraising Regulator and the Code of Fundraising Practice

2.1 The Fundraising Regulator was established to implement the recommendations of the Etherington review. It assumed responsibility for charity fundraising regulation on 7 July 2016. Registration with the regulator is voluntary for charities and professional fundraisers. It involves taking the 'Fundraising Promise' to maintain good practice in fundraising and those who sign up are entitled to register to use the Fundraising Regulator badge on materials.

2.2 The Fundraising Regulator is funded by a voluntary levy collected from charities in England and Wales spending £100,000 or more on fundraising per annum and registered with it, and all other charities who have voluntarily registered with it.

2.3 The Fundraising Regulator maintains the Code of Fundraising Practice, which outlines the rules and standards for legal, open, honest and respectful fundraising. The Code is endorsed by the Charity Commission in its guidance on charity fundraising and is an important reference point for all charities and charity fundraisers, whether registered with the Fundraising Regulator or not.

2.4 The Fundraising Regulator manages the Fundraising Preference Service, which allows individuals to block direct marketing communications, including by telephone, email, text and addressed mail, from specified charities; charities that are selected by an individual for blocking will then be invited to enrol and add them to their marketing 'suppression' list. This is funded by the 'Fundraising Levy' mentioned above.

Additionally, the Fundraising Regulator is set up to deal with complaints from the public about all charities, whether registered with it or not, if they cannot be dealt with by the charity in question and are not considered so serious as to require the immediate attention of the Charity Commission. The Fundraising Regulator can also liaise with the Charity Commission and other regulators where it addresses or investigates misconduct by a charity.

2.5 Unauthorised fundraising

Unfortunately, some charities encounter problems with over-zealous supporters who raise funds on behalf of the charity without its consent and unscrupulous people who raise money fraudulently by claiming that it will be given to charity. This may lead to regulatory problems, clashes with the charity's fundraising policy and alienation of the organisation's existing or potential supporters. Problems may also occur if a professional fundraiser, with whom the charity has an agreement, acts outside of that agreement. Of course, the first approach is for the charity to seek to persuade the fundraiser to stop the unauthorised activity. However, a legal remedy is also available in the form of an injunction to prevent unauthorised fundraising. Trustees wishing to take this course of action will need to obtain appropriate legal advice.

2.6 Instructing professional fundraisers

Many charities choose to engage professional fundraisers instead of, or in addition to, employing fundraising staff. As with all fundraising approaches, trustees need to ensure that the reward justifies the resources used, so if professional fundraisers are to be used, the trustees must be confident that this will represent good value for money.

The Charity Commission will expect charities to disclose whether they use professional fundraisers and whether they have written agreements with all such professional fundraisers in their Annual Return to the regulator.

2.7 Selecting consultants

2.7.1 Charities should first determine the role of the professional fundraiser (such as whether the fundraiser will be developing or implementing strategy, or both) and whether the consultant will be responsible for a complete campaign or elements within the campaign (events, donor development or grant applications). The charity will then need to identify a number of appropriate individuals, perhaps through names provided by an umbrella body such as NCVO or the Institute of Fundraising. They should consider the following issues in relation to each professional fundraiser:

- relevant qualifications;
- experience, including experience of similar campaigns in comparable organisations;
- success record;
- sympathy with the charity and its culture;
- whether it is registered with the Fundraising Regulator and will adhere to the Code of Fundraising Practice;
- arrangements for monitoring activities and reporting to the trustees; and
- costs.

In 2016, the Charity Commission and the Fundraising Regulator issued a joint regulatory alert advising charities not to enter into a fundraising arrangement if it:

- appears artificially designed to avoid application of the legal rules for professional fundraisers;
- is a medium or long-term contract with limited termination or variation provisions;

- only allows charities a benefit at the end of the term which might not in fact materialise; or
- involves fees or payments which could damage public trust and confidence in the charity benefiting.

2.7.2 Fundraisers' fees may be determined in a number of ways, including flat fees and commission based on a percentage of the total amount of money raised; however structured, the potential costs and benefits of any arrangement should be clear in order to consider what might 'damage public trust and confidence'.

2.8 Professional fundraising statement

When a professional fundraiser solicits money for a charity, they must make a 'solicitation statement'. This gives the potential donor details of:

- the name of the charity or charities for which they are raising money;
- the proportions the charities (if there is more than one) will receive;
- the way the fundraiser's remuneration will be paid; and
- the amount (or the most accurate estimate of the amount that may reasonably be calculated at the time the statement is made) that the fundraiser will receive in connection with the appeal.

2.9 Fundraising with businesses

2.9.1 Long-term relationships with corporate sponsors can offer charities a degree of financial stability. When working with businesses on fundraising promotions and activities, the trustees will need to consider wider issues, such as whether the charity wishes to be associated with the company or product sold and whether the perceived business practices of the company and the product sold are compatible with the charity's objectives. Is the company seeking to use the relationship to promote sales or to target a specific market and, if so, is the charity comfortable with this? Trustees should consider in particular the Charity Commission's 2016 report into Age UK and its partnership with an energy supplier as an example of potential risks that a partnership can create.

2.9.2 Where a company or individual represents that part of the price paid for goods or services provided in the course of their business will be donated to charity, they are known as a 'commercial participator'. Charity law requires commercial participators to comply with certain requirements. For example, where a commercial participator represents that a donation will be made to charity, they must state the amount that will be donated to the charity and must enter into an agreement with the charity, as set out below.

The Charity Commission will also expect charities to disclose whether they have used a commercial participator in their Annual Return to the regulator and whether it has written agreements with all its commercial participators, during the period covered by that return.

2.10 Commercial participator statements

When representing that donations will be made to a charity in connection with the sale of a product or service, commercial participators must make a statement informing potential customers of:

- the name of the charity or charities that will benefit; and
- the amount (or the most accurate estimate of the amount that may reasonably be calculated at the time the statement is made) that will be received by the charity in connection with the purchase.

2.11 Agreements with professional fundraisers, commercial participators and annual reports

2.11.1 The requirements for agreements between charities and professional fundraisers and commercial participators are laid down by law. All such agreements must be made in writing and be signed by both parties. The agreement, whether with a professional fundraiser or a commercial participator, must contain:

- the name and address of each party;
- the date and period of the agreement;
- terms regarding the variation or early termination of the agreement;
- the objectives of the agreement and the methods to be used in achieving those objectives;
- if more than one charity is involved in the agreement, the proportion of benefit to each charity (will the funds raised be equally divided or will there be a weighted split?); and
- provision for the amount of remuneration or expenses to be paid to the fundraiser or participator under the agreement and the method for calculating the amount (a percentage of funds raised or a flat amount).

Following the introduction of the Charities (Protection and Social Investment) Act 2016, these agreements must specify:

- any voluntary scheme for regulating fundraising, or any voluntary standard of fundraising (such as the Code of Fundraising Practice), that the fundraiser or participator undertakes to be bound by;
- how, in the course of the activities agreed, the fundraiser or participator is to protect vulnerable people and other members of the public from any:
  - unreasonable intrusion on a person's privacy;
  - unreasonably persistent approaches for the purpose of getting money or other property; and,
  - placing of undue pressure on a person to give money or other property;

- how the charity benefiting is able to monitor the fundraiser or participator's compliance with any scheme, standard or safeguard which has been specified as required above.

2.11.2 In addition, for commercial participators, the agreement should cover the following:

- the proportion of the sale price that will be given to the charity or the donations that will be made; and
- a description of the type of contributions which will be made and of the circumstances in which they will be made.

2.11.3 Fundraisers' and commercial participators' documents and other records relating to the agreement should be available to the charity. Funds raised under the agreement should be paid to the charity within an agreed period, often 28 days of receipt.

The Charities (Protection and Social Investment) Act 2016 also introduced a requirement for charities to include a statement in their annual report each year, noting:

- the charity's approach to fundraising by the charity itself or any third parties, and whether the charity used professional fundraisers or commercial participators;
- whether those acting on behalf of the charity undertook to be bound by a voluntary scheme or standard for regulating their fundraising, and if so what scheme or standard and whether they failed to comply at all with the same;
- if and how the charity monitored fundraising by third parties acting on its behalf, and the number of complaints the charity or third parties received about fundraising activities for the charity; and
- what the charity has done to protect vulnerable people and other members of the public from the prohibited practices of 'intrusion', 'persistent approaches' and 'undue pressure' considered above.

3 Trading

3.1 Charities, unlike commercial organisations, are established to promote particular charitable purposes and to act in the public interest rather than to carry out a trade with a view to making a profit. However, many charities carry out some trading activities and this chapter will set out the factors that should be considered when a charity is considering undertaking trading.

3.2 Trustees of charities that carry out trading improperly may be found to have acted either *ultra vires* and/or in breach of trust. They may also find that they are required to pay tax on any profits from trading. It may be held to be inappropriate to claim these liabilities from charitable funds and that the trustees should pay, so trustees should consider carefully the issues involved before deciding to carry out trading activities and should refer to any applicable guidance from HMRC or the Charity Commission.

3.3 Governing documents

The governing documents of some charities, particularly older charities, may prohibit any sort of trading. However, many permit trading, provided that it is not taxable trading. The types of trading that may be carried out are set out in paragraph 3.5. Before carrying out any of these trading activities, charities should check their governing documents and, if they prohibit trading, should consider amending them. This might require the prior consent of the Charity Commission.

3.4 Financial risk

Before carrying out any trading activity, the charity (or its trading subsidiary) should consider the level of risk involved and the commercial factors that might affect that risk, just as it would for any fundraising activity.

3.5 Types of trading that may be undertaken by charities

3.5.1 Primary purpose trading

This involves the sale of goods or services that further the charitable objects of the charity. For example, a charity that runs a theatre may charge for tickets to see a play. Ancillary trading that is related to the primary purpose is regarded as primary purpose trading (for example, a theatre charity may charge audience members for programmes and refreshments). Income generated by a charity from primary purpose trading is exempt from income and corporation tax.

3.5.2 There is no limit to the amount of primary purpose trading a charity may carry out. Many charities obtain the bulk of their funding from such primary purpose activities – schools charge school fees to cover their costs, social care charities provide services under contracts to local authorities and historic buildings charge admission fees.

3.5.3 Under the Charities Act 2011, charities are required to demonstrate that they are carrying out their activities for the public benefit, and charities that charge fees for their services must demonstrate that those fees do not prevent the charity benefiting a sufficient section of the public. The Charity Commission has published detailed guidance on this issue.

3.5.4 *Trade carried out by the beneficiaries*

Trading by charities in goods that have been manufactured by their beneficiaries and in services provided by the beneficiaries is also exempt from income and corporation tax. The involvement of non-beneficiaries in the trade (such as in a management or advisory capacity) will not present problems as long as the majority of the work is carried out by beneficiaries.

3.5.5 *Small-scale exemption*

A tax exemption applies to trading by charities that is not primary purpose trading or a trade carried out by beneficiaries.

This small-scale exemption applies, for all accounting periods beginning on or after 1 April 2019, where a charity's total annual turnover from such trading is less than £8,000 or, if greater than £8,000, is still less than 25% of the charity's annual income, subject to a maximum of £80,000.

This exemption may still apply even if the applicable limits are exceeded if the charity had a reasonable expectation that their turnover from such trading would be within these limits.

3.5.6 *Fundraising events*

Profits from fundraising events are exempt from corporation and income tax if the events comply with certain requirements.

3.5.7 *Sale of donated goods*

The sale of donated goods by charities (provided the goods have not been significantly modified) is exempt from income and corporation tax. Common examples include charity shops and auctions of donated goods.

3.5.8 *Lotteries*

These are considered to be trading, but profits from charity lotteries are exempt from corporation and income tax.

3.5.9 *Income from the sale and leasing of land*

This is generally exempt from tax, but complex rules govern this exemption (for example, if a charity provides services such as catering to the organisations to which it leases its premises, it may be regarded as carrying on a trade that is not exempt). Charities considering leasing or selling land should seek detailed guidance.

3.5.10 *Business sponsorship*

A business's payment for the use of a charity's logo, or the display by a charity of a business's logo, may be considered trading and may, therefore, be taxable. This will depend on the details of the agreement between the parties. The provision of other goods or services in return for sponsorship (for example, use of the charity's mailing list) might also lead to the sponsorship income being treated as trading income and may be taxable unless an exemption applies. In addition, VAT may be payable on fees for any such goods or services. Even tax-exempt trading may be subject to VAT. See section 6.2 on page 339 for further information on VAT.

4 Trading companies

4.1 Many charities set up trading subsidiaries. These carry out trading activities that the charity cannot carry out itself, as well as other activities that the charity could carry out but where it would be in its best interests for the activity to be carried out by a separate entity (such as where the activity carries a risk of loss or other liability or where tax would be payable).

4.2 Trading companies operate as normal commercial companies, unrestricted by the limitations on charity trading. They may seek investment from a number of sources but are usually established by charities as a wholly owned subsidiary (the charity is the sole shareholder or a number of charities each hold a share).

4.3 Trading subsidiaries are subject to the same taxes as regular commercial companies. However, under the Gift Aid scheme they may donate their profits to the charity prior to the deduction of taxes. The charity does not need to reclaim any tax and the company receives a deduction in corporation tax for the Gift Aid donation, thereby avoiding some or all of its corporation tax liability. The scheme allows for Gift Aid payments relating to a particular accounting period to be made up to nine months after the end of that accounting period.

Accounting for Gift Aid payments by a subsidiary trading company to its parent charity is complex and may require specialist advice where encountered in practice; in some cases it might be necessary for the trading subsidiary to enter into a prior legal obligation with its parent charity to make a payment, for example by a deed of covenant.

4.4 The company will probably need to keep a proportion of its profits to maintain adequate cash balances to continue trading. Alternatively, the charity can establish the company with sufficient capital to allow it to gift all of its profits to the charity.

4.5 However, the charity's financial investment in setting up and maintaining the company must be made for charitable purposes only and for the benefit of the charity, not the trading subsidiary. A loan by a charity to its trading subsidiary should be secured (for example, by a charge over the property of the trading subsidiary) and should be recorded in a document that sets out terms for when the loan will be repaid and what interest is payable, which the charity should be prepared to enforce.

4.6 On a practical level, a number of the trustees of the charity should serve as directors of the subsidiary trading company to ensure that the company is operating in accordance with the interests of the charity, including consistency in areas such as public relations. However, the board of the charity should also include individuals that are not on the board of the trading subsidiary and vice versa to ensure that some board members have an independent perspective on relations between the entities. There will also be occasions when a conflict of interest will arise between the two organisations and so there will need to be sufficient trustees to form a quorum when those who also serve as directors of the subsidiary trading company have to withdraw from the decision making due to this confect of interest.

When to set up a trading company		
1. Do you want to trade on a regular, significant basis (not small-scale trading)?	No – trading company not necessary.	Yes – go to point 2.
2. Do you want to trade outside the primary objects of the charity or enter into trading that is not carried out by your beneficiaries?	No – trading company not necessary, go to point 3.	Yes – trading company necessary.
3. Is the level or type of trading or the capital investment required such that it is necessary to protect the charity from business risks?	No – trading company not required.	Yes – trading company necessary.

5 Donations

5.1 One of the tax concessions available to charities is the ability to receive tax-efficient donations, either through donations made before tax has been deducted (payroll giving) or through reclaiming tax on donations under the Gift Aid system.

5.2 Payroll giving

5.2.1 This is a system whereby individuals make donations to charity that are deducted directly from their pay or occupational pension. The donations are taken by the employer from the employee's gross pay before tax deductions are made, thus no income tax is paid on the donation element of the salary. Donations are passed to an agency charity, which distributes the funds to the charities nominated by the employees. There is no limit on the value of an individual employee's donations.

5.2.2 Trustees of charities receiving donations under payroll giving should be wary of offering benefits to donors as this may disqualify the donation from relief under the scheme. Benefits of negligible financial value, such as stickers or newsletters, are normally acceptable within the scheme.

5.3 Gift Aid

5.3.1 The Gift Aid scheme provides for flexible tax-efficient donations to charities. Gift Aid is available for monetary donations (rather than gifts in kind) from tax-paying individuals and from companies.

5.3.2 The Gift Aid scheme applies to gifts of money by individual UK tax payers to UK charities. Where it applies, the sum of money that the donor gives is deemed to be a larger sum from which tax at the basic rate (20%) has been deducted. So, if a donor gives a charity a cheque for £800, they are deemed to have made a donation of £1,000, from which £200 has been deducted. This means that the charity can reclaim the basic rate income tax that is deemed to have been deducted from that gift from HMRC (in the example, £200).

5.3.3 Provided the donor has paid enough tax, they are allowed to make a Gift Aid Declaration and their Gift Aid declaration can allow the charity to claim Gift Aid on all donations that they made in the preceding six years.

5.3.4 Gift Aid donations from companies are paid without deduction of income tax. Unlike the requirements for individual donors, no declaration is required and the charity only needs to keep the accounting records necessary to record donations. Company donors should retain any correspondence as evidence of the donation. The charity does not claim any tax itself.

5.3.5 There are no limits on the size or number of Gift Aid donations, although there is a requirement for charities to maintain an audit trail documenting the source and value of the donations. More information is given on this in section 5.4. However, trustees should consider the administrative costs of reclaiming the tax on donations and may want to introduce a self-imposed minimum level below which the tax will not be reclaimed.

5.4 Gift Aid declaration

5.4.1 In order to reclaim tax on a donation, charities must obtain a Gift Aid declaration from the individual donor. Although HMRC has produced model forms, there is no prescribed format for the declaration. Declarations may be made before, at the time of, or after the donation, and may cover single or multiple donations. The declaration may be given in writing (including fax and e-mail) or orally and should contain the following information:

- the name and home address of the donor;
- the name of the charity;
- a description of the donations covered by the declaration (such as a single donation or all donations from a certain date onwards); and
- a declaration that donations are to be treated as Gift Aid donations. Written declarations should also contain a note explaining that the donor must pay income tax and/or capital gains tax equivalent to the tax deducted from donations.

5.4.2 Although there is no requirement for the declaration to be signed and dated, it is good practice to do so, and a date will be essential if it defines the donations made under the scheme. If the charity receives an oral Gift Aid declaration, it should follow this up in writing by sending the donor a record of the declaration. This should include the details provided by the donor in the declaration, the date of the donation and of the charity's written confirmation, together with notes relating to the tax requirements and the donor's right to cancel the declaration within 30 days. Oral declarations should not be regarded as effective until the written record has been sent.

5.4.3 For sponsored events, forms can be designed that serve as a Gift Aid declaration for each sponsor. The declaration can be placed at the top of each sheet, with an opt-in box for sponsors to tick if they want their donation to be treated as Gift Aid. The form should include each sponsor's full name and home address, the amount pledged and paid, confirmation that the donor is a UK tax payer, the date each donation was made and the total handed over to the charity. A model form is available from HMRC. There are restrictions applicable to gift aid on donations from 'connected persons' to participants.

5.4.4 Donors may cancel their declarations through any means. Cancellations will be effective from the date of notification or some future date identified by the donor. Retrospective cancellations are only effective during the 30-day 'cooling off' period after written confirmation has been sent in respect of an oral declaration.

5.4.5 Charities need to keep documentary evidence to support their tax claims. In particular, they must be able to show how much has been received from each donor. There is no set format for storing this information, and charities will need to develop procedures that are compatible with their other administrative systems.

5.4.6 Funds given to charities for the provision of services or some other form of significant benefit will not qualify under the Gift Aid scheme, although limited benefits to Gift Aid donors are acceptable.

5.4.7 In relation to payments made on and after 6 April 2019, the value of the benefits that individuals and companies may receive as a result of making a donation to a charity are as follows:

- Donation up to £100: 25%
- Donation above £100: £25 + 5% of the donation above £100
- Threshold: £2,500

5.4.8 Charities and community amateur sports clubs that receive small donations of £30 or less in cash or by contactless card payment, made on or after 6 April 2019, are able to apply for a Gift Aid-style repayment without the need to obtain Gift Aid declarations for those donations. The amount of these 'small donations' on which the new repayment can be claimed is capped at £2,000 per tax year, per charity (with certain modifications). To qualify for this repayment in a tax year, organisations need to have been recognised by HMRC for Gift Aid purposes for at least two years, have been operating and claiming Gift Aid successfully throughout that time and have a good tax compliance record.

5.5 Shares

There is provision for those who donate certain shares to charities to reclaim some tax in relation to those shares.

6 Taxation issues

6.1 Claiming tax refunds

Charities must reclaim tax on the prescribed forms provided by HMRC. In addition to the reclaimed tax, HMRC will calculate and refund any interest payable. Claims must be made no later than six years after the end of the accounting period to which the claim relates.

6.2 VAT

6.2.1 Value added tax (VAT) is a tax on the supply of goods and services (other than exempt goods or services) in the UK and the Isle of Man. VAT is charged at either:

- standard rate (this applies to most goods and services);
- reduced rate (on certain fuel and power); or
- zero rate (on food and books).

6.2.2 The supply of goods and services that are subject to these rates of VAT are the taxable supplies. There are also exempt supplies, which are not subject to VAT. Organisations are required to register for VAT if the total financial value of their taxable 'business' activities exceeds the registration threshold. In this context, 'business' is not restricted to those activities which are profit-making, but includes:

- activities involving the supply of goods or services for consideration (payment in either money or kind);
- which are frequent or significant activities; and
- activities that continue over a period of time.

6.2.3 Charitable activities may, therefore, be counted as business activities or supplies. (The table on page 341 describes the charitable activities that are subject to VAT.) Those business supplies that are subject to VAT at any of the three rates are the organisation's taxable supplies. It is the measurement of the turnover of the taxable supplies against the registration threshold that determines whether the organisation should register for VAT. The registration threshold changes from time to time. Since April 2017, it has been £85,000.

6.2.4 The amount of VAT paid to HMRC is determined by the difference between input tax and output tax.

- **Output tax** is the VAT charged on standard and reduced rate supplies.
- **Input tax** is the VAT paid on purchases in relation to the making of vatable supplies.

6.2.5 If the output tax is greater than the input tax, the charity must pay the difference to HMRC. If the charity has paid more input tax than it has charged as output tax, then it may claim the difference back. The amounts are submitted to HMRC on a VAT return. Input tax paid by charities in relation to goods and services connected to the charity's non-business and exempt activities cannot be offset against output tax or reclaimed.

6.2.6 Clearly, extensive documentation is required to account for input and output tax and to support the VAT return. The VAT paid on input supplies can only be claimed back if the charity is VAT registered. It is possible for organisations falling below the threshold to register voluntarily, but trustees will need to consider whether the charity will be able to reclaim any tax and balance the financial benefit against the corresponding administrative burden.

6.2.7 Charities registered for VAT should also ensure they comply with HMRC's 'Making Tax Digital' technical requirements for VAT returns, which at the time of writing are due to be rolled out in April 2019.

6.3 Business or non-business?

As can be seen from the discussion above, it is essential for trustees to assess the services offered by their charity and to consider which elements represent business activities and whether the value of these activities crosses the registration threshold, requiring the charity to register. Unfortunately, some of the distinctions between business and non-business activities are very slight. In addition, although some charitable activity is considered to be business, the supplies in question may be either zero-rated or exempt from VAT. The table below gives an overview of the provisions. Trustees who believe that their charity may be required to be VAT registered should contact their local HMRC office to seek further advice.

Activity	Business	Non-business
Donations, bequests and grants	A funding agreement where the funder directly receives a benefit from a taxable service provided will be subject to VAT. This is a very grey area and professional advice is usually required.	Voluntary contributions and grants which are freely given and which are not a purchase of services are non-business and outside the scope of VAT. Grants subsidising a service which would be provided by the charity anyway are also non-business (with some exceptions).
Voluntary services provided without charge		Free services are non-business activities (such as first aid, sea rescue and worship). Any genuine donations freely given by the recipients of these services are outside the scope of VAT.
Sale of goods (including charity shops)	The sale of goods is a business activity. The sale of donated goods is zero-rated whether the sale is through a shop or not. The sale of bought-in goods is standard-rated unless they are covered by another zero-rating (books, for example).	

Activity	Business	Non-business
Hire of charity-run buildings (such as village halls)	The hire of a charity-run building for a fee is business. This includes village halls and other community buildings. The fee is normally exempt from VAT unless the charity chooses to opt to tax, allowing it to register and recover input tax. The option cannot be made for lets to another charity for non-business use.	
Welfare services (including spiritual welfare)	Welfare services supplied by charities, together with any related goods, are business but are exempt.	The same services are non-business (by concession) when they are consistently supplied below cost (subsidised by at least 15% of the charity's funds) to relieve the distress of beneficiaries.
Education	The provision of education in exchange for consideration (a fee) is a business activity, but it is exempt from VAT provided any surplus made is reinvested in the same service. If the surplus was used for a different charitable activity, the provision of education would be standard rated.	The same provision is non-business if it is provided for free (such as in a state school).
Cultural services (including admission to museums, galleries, zoos and theatres)	Admission charges are exempt from VAT provided any surplus made is reinvested in the same activity and the organisation is managed and administered on a voluntary basis.	Admission is non-business if it is provided for free.
Membership subscriptions	If members receive benefits in return for their subscriptions (such as publications, advice services or events) then the subscriptions will be considered to be business and subject to VAT (unless the charity provides services that are regarded as philanthropic, civic or patriotic).	Subscriptions are non-business if the members are entitled to nothing more than copies of statutory documents (annual reports and accounts, for example) and voting rights at general meetings.

Activity	Business	Non-business
Corporate sponsorship	Sponsorship from companies and other bodies is subject to the standard rate of VAT if the funds are conditional on some benefit, such as the publication of the organisation's logo. The fundraising exemption will apply to sponsorship in relation to qualifying events.	Corporate donations are outside the scope of VAT if there is no reciprocal benefit. A small acknowledgement in an annual report will not change a donation into a sponsorship.
Sales of advertising in charity publications	The supply of advertising to a charity may be zero-rated and the publication may be exempt if it is part of a one-off fundraising event.	
Interest payments		Interest earned on funds kept in bank and building society accounts is non-business.

6.4 Zero-rated supplies to charities

A number of supplies made to charities are zero rated, meaning the charity does not have to pay any VAT on the goods and services in question. In these circumstances, the onus is on the charity to provide the supplier with a written declaration of its eligibility for zero rating on the supplies in question (though not all of the supplies require such declaration by law). Zero rating is available on the following (though not all of the supplies require such a declaration by law):

- advertising in all types of public media and all preparation work (such as design and artwork);
- recording and playback equipment for the production of talking books and newspapers for people with visual impairments;
- supply, repair, maintenance and importation of sea rescue equipment;
- construction of new self-contained buildings and certain annexes (excluding professional services, which are standard-rated); and
- the purchase of a freehold or leasehold (exceeding 21 years) where the property will be used for a relevant charitable or residential purpose.

6.5 Fundraising events

As has been mentioned above, fundraising events may be exempt from VAT. The exemption applies to events that meet the following criteria:

- the event must be organised and promoted primarily to raise money for the benefit of the charity;
- the people attending the event must be aware of the fundraising purpose;
- there cannot be more than 15 such events in any one year in any one place; and
- the exempt supplies should not distort competition with commercial suppliers.

D3
Data protection and electronic marketing

1 Introduction

1.1 This chapter gives an overview of UK data protection law, with reference to current interpretation and guidance where this is available, and is helpful to an understanding of the law. It also covers e-commerce issues relevant to marketing by direct mail, fax, telephone, email or SMS (text messaging) in a compliant way to meet the current regulatory environment.

1.2 Combined data protection and e-commerce topics cover key issues for charities, such as when consent is required to process personal information for marketing or other purposes, the importance of confidentiality and how to communicate this core value to staff and volunteers, as well as other key business and HR issues.

2 Data protection

2.1 The background

2.1.1 The EU Data Protection Directive 95/46 harmonised the law on data protection throughout EU Member States. It was implemented in the UK in the form of the Data Protection Act 1998.

2.1.2 This legislation predated the common usage of the internet and improvements in computing technology. After many years of consultation this directive was replaced by EU Regulation 2016/679, widely known as the the General Data Protection Regulation, or simply as the GDPR. This Regulation became directly effective in the UK on 25 May 2018. At the same time, it was translated into UK law in the Data Protection Act 2018 (DPA 2018) which repealed and replaced the Data Protection Act 1998. References in this chapter to the DPA are to the 2018 Act.

2.1.3 The legislation also contains some measures on law enforcement which fall outside the scope of this chapter.

2.1.4 One of the key aims of the GDPR is to harmonise data protection laws across the EU. The GDPR will cease to apply to the UK when it leaves the EU but the Data Protection Act 2018 will remain in force. In light of the need for the UK to have equivalent data protection laws to the EU to protect trading and commercial links, and to facilitate the exchange of data from security, no significant change to the regime is anticipated at the time of writing.

2.1.5 Strictly speaking, there is no longer a requirement for organisations to register with the Information Commissioner's Office (ICO) but, unless exempt, organisations that determine the purpose for which personal data is processed must pay a data protection fee. There is a searchable database of organisations that have paid this fee. There are specific exemptions for certain non-profit-making activities, but even organisations which are exempt from paying the fee must comply with the other provisions of the legislation.

2.1.6 The GDPR and DPA 2018 set out six Data Protection Principles that must be followed by those processing personal data. One of the significant changes from the pre-GDPR regime is that controllers must be able to demonstrate compliance with these principles. This is referred to as the 'accountability principle'.

2.1.7 Individuals are given specific rights to access information relating to them and to object to the processing of their personal information in certain circumstances.

2.1.8 It is the role of the Information Commissioner to enforce compliance with the DPA 2018 and GDPR (while it remains applicable in the UK) and to provide guidance on interpretation to businesses and individuals alike. The DPA 2018 is backed by criminal sanctions for non-compliance in key areas. In the UK, the Information Commissioner reports annually to Parliament and takes an active role in promoting privacy when there are initiatives, including government initiatives, which have the potential to intrude upon private life. There is an association between data protection, privacy and the right to respect for family life in Article 8 of the Human Rights Act 1998.

2.1.9 The Information Commissioner is supported by Assistant Commissioners in Northern Ireland, Scotland and Wales. The Commissioners have responsibility for Freedom of Information, the Environmental Information Regulations and the Privacy and Electronic (EC Directive) Regulations as well as data protection. The Information Commissioner's Office has a website (www.ico.gov.uk) which provides guidance for organisations on the application of these areas of law to different business sectors. There is a specific section for charities, and a particular focus on the use of data fundraising following the criticisms made of the use and sharing of potential donor data by some charities.

3 What is personal data?

3.1 Personal data means 'any information relating to an identified or identifiable natural person (data subject); an identifiable natural person is one who can be identified, directly or indirectly, in particular by reference to an identifier such as a name, an identification number, location data, an online identifier or to one or more factors specific to the physical, physiological, genetic, mental, economic, cultural or social identity of that natural person'.

3.2 It is important to note that data is still 'personal data' if a data subject can be identified when a piece of data is combined with other information held by a controller. It is a common misconception that data is not personal data because an individual is not named. However, any single piece of data must be looked at in the context of other information held by the data controller to see if the individual can be identified.

3.3 It is good data security for personal data to be 'pseudonymised'. This is personal data that can no longer be attributed to a specific data subject without the use of additional information, provided that such additional information is kept separately and is subject to technical and organisational measures. This can be achieved through the use of secure identifiers and keys, but this is still personal data because, when 'unlocked' using the key, data subjects can be identified once more. However, this is still personal data to which the legislation applies.

3.4 The GDPR and DPA 2018 identify certain sensitive data as requiring particular protection. This is 'special category'; data and is considered further below.

4 What records are within the scope of the DPA?

4.1 All records that are processed electronically are within the scope of the DPA. In addition, certain paper records are also caught if they are in a relevant filing system. This is a filing system that is structured by reference to individuals so that users can identify where specific items of personal information are kept and, within each file, the structure allows the user to easily locate the required information. For example, files kept in date order are unlikely to be within the scope of the DPA 2018. Many archive systems, especially where there is limited indexing, are likely to be outside the scope of the Act.

5 What is meant by processing?

5.1 The term 'processing' is very widely defined to include every potential activity involving personal data. It means any operation or set of operations which is performed on personal data or on sets of personal data, whether or not by automated means such as collection, recording, organisation, structuring, storage, adaptation or alteration, retrieval, consultation, use, disclosure by transmission, dissemination or otherwise making available, alignment or combination, restriction, erasure or destruction.

6 Controllers and processors

The new regime means that both controllers and processors have obligations to comply with data protection legislation. For the first time, data processors can be subject to compliance action.

6.1 What are controllers and processors?

6.1.1 A controller determines the purposes and means of the processing of personal data.

6.1.2 A processor is a person, public authority, agency or other body which processes personal data on behalf of the controller. The controller will be the one who determines the purposes of processing.

6.1.3 If two or more controllers jointly determine the purposes and means of the processing of the same personal data, they are joint controllers. However, they are not joint controllers if they are processing the same data for different purposes.

6.2 It is crucial to identify which category an organisation falls into, particularly where data is being shared and processed across organisations, because the GDPR requires certain contractual provisions to be included in the contracts underpinning data controller/processor relationships (Articles 28 and 29, GDPR). It also has implications for the reporting of breaches. The GDPR imposes obligations on joint controllers to ensure each is clear about its obligations.

7 The Data Protection Principles

The Principles form the backbone of UK data protection law. The DPA 2018 transposes the wording set out in Article 5 of the GDPR. There is extensive guidance on the Information Commissioner's website (www.ico.gov.uk).

7.1 Principle 1: Personal data shall be processed fairly, lawfully and in a transparent manner

7.1.1 There are three main strands to the First Principle:

(a) data controllers must be able to identify a valid ground under the GDPR (known as a 'lawful basis') for processing data and the use must not breach any other law;
(b) the use of the personal data must be fair. The way data is processed must not be detrimental, unexpected or misleading to the individuals concerned; and
(c) data controllers must be clear, open and honest with people from the outset about how their personal data will be processed.

7.1.2 The valid grounds for processing are considered in section 10 on page 355.

7.1.3 Articles 13 and 14 of the GDPR set out the information which must be provided to data subjects explaining the identity of the party collecting the information, the purposes for which personal data will be processed, any other information including how long it will be retained and what the individual's rights are. This information is set out in what is often called a privacy notice.

7.2 Principle 2: Personal data shall be collected for specified, explicit and legitimate purposes and not further processed in a manner that is incompatible with those purposes.

7.2.1 This is referred to as the 'purpose limitation principle'.

7.2.2 This Principle works in conjunction with the First Principle. Having provided transparent information (identity, processing purposes and other relevant information) future processing of personal data is restricted to those activities.

7.2.3 In practice this means that data obtained for one purpose must not be used for a different purpose unless the data subject was informed of that at the time the data was obtained.

7.2.4 Further processing for archiving in the public interest, scientific or historical research purposes or statistical purposes is permitted in accordance with Article 89(1) of the GDPR.

7.3 Principle 3: Personal data shall be adequate, relevant and not excessive in relation to the purpose or purposes for which they are processed.

7.3.1 This is often described as the 'data minimisation principle'.

7.3.2 When obtaining information, consideration should be given as to what is relevant and appropriate for the stated purposes for which it will be processed. Relevant information can be collected for a particular and identified purpose but the fact that further information could be obtained which might be useful in the future, or simply thought interesting to know, should not be a reason for it to be collected. This is a particular issue in the modern digital world where it is easier than ever to access data about individuals who may have had contact with a charity in some way. It is important that charities bear in mind that simply because this information may be available does not mean that it should be collected.

7.4 Principle 4: Personal data shall be accurate and, where necessary, kept up to date.

7.4.1 Charities must ensure that every reasonable step has been taken to ensure that personal data that are inaccurate, having regard to the purposes for which they are processed, are erased or rectified without delay.

7.4.2 Charities should be able to show that they have taken steps to ensure the accuracy of personal information obtained, for example confirming details like spellings and house numbers when obtaining information face-to-face or by telephone. When gathering information online the system can provide drop-down lists to help with accurate data entry and fields can be restricted to prevent alphabetical entries in a field collecting telephone numbers, for example.

7.4.3 If data is obtained by a third party rather than directly from the individual who is the subject of the data, reasonable steps should be taken to ensure accuracy.

7.4.4 When new systems are designed it is important that the question of how accuracy can be maintained and data easily updated is considered, including providing a means for individuals to report errors.

7.5 Principle 5: Personal data processed for any purpose or purposes shall not be kept for longer than is necessary

7.5.1 This is the 'storage limitation' principle.

7.5.2 Data protection law does not specify how long information should be kept, simply stating that it shall not be kept longer than is required. There are many legal requirements relating to the retention of data (for example, accounting records should be kept for six years from the end of the relevant tax year, which in practical terms usually means keeping records for seven years; documents relating to a contract should be retained for six years from termination of the contract or 12 years if it was a contract under seal with a small allowance for claims being made not received within a limitation period). It is impossible to provide specific guidance on retention periods for charities as considerations will vary depending on areas of activity.

7.5.3 Charities should consider the purposes for which the personal data is held, the business needs it meets and the regulatory obligations which apply and design retention periods based on these. It is legitimate to keep records so that a charity can demonstrate it has complied with obligations in order to defend or take legal action. One relevant factor will be expectations of insurers.

7.5.4 Clearly the longer information is held the more likely it is to become inaccurate, out-of-date or inappropriate for the purposes for which it was obtained. It is also vital that, once retention periods have been identified and recorded, steps are taken to ensure that they are applied in practice.

7.6 Principle 6: Personal data shall be processed in a manner that ensures appropriate security of the personal data, including protection against unauthorised or unlawful processing and against accidental loss, destruction or damage, using appropriate technical or organisational measures ('integrity and confidentiality').

7.6.1 This is the 'security principle'.

7.6.2 The duty to keep personal data secure is a key requirement of the GDPR and the DPA 2018.

7.6.3 There is an understandable focus on ensuring the security of computer systems and digital security, and protecting against hacking and other criminal risks, but it is important to appreciate that this principle applies more widely. One of the most common breaches which has to be reported is the accidental loss of data through a lost file, an unencrypted laptop or an accidentally misdirected email or letter.

7.6.4 Compliance will require charities to consider risk analysis, organisational policies, and physical and technical measures to put in place appropriate system and stress testing. Data recovery in the event of a physical or technical incident is important, as is ensuring staff are subject to appropriate background checks and provided with training and guidance on their data protection obligations. Volunteers and trustees should also receive training. Monitoring may also be required.

7.6.5 Organisational security measures means building security, CCTV, locking filing cabinets, and policies and procedures to regulate the processing environment as appropriate to the type of data and the risk of unlawful disclosure or loss. Many professions and businesses promote a duty of confidentiality regarding information in the workplace. This can be a key element in staff training and procedures to evidence that the organisation operates a system of control for information in its custody and control. Important information in its control might include trade or business secrets, skills and know-how, as well as customer and marketing databases and donor lists.

7.6.6 The level of confidentiality required will depend on the circumstances; some information is inherently more sensitive and confidential (records of individual donations subject to a duty of confidentiality are more sensitive than information already in the public domain such as names and addresses). The appropriate level of confidentiality will also depend on the expectations of the individuals who are the subject of the data. What were they led to believe when they provided their personal data? The key to managing expectations is a clear, comprehensive privacy notice.

7.6.7 Technical security measures means IT security (firewalls, virus protection, back up procedures, restricted access to data on a 'need to know' basis, restricted download facilities and passwords).

7.6.8 Where appropriate, charities should introduce measures such as pseudonymisation and encryption.

7.6.9 See guidance from the ICO on its website (www.ico.gov.uk).

7.7 Monitoring at work

7.7.1 Security will often involve monitoring employees and other individuals such as volunteers in the workplace which may involve creating records of activity or behaviour (such as CCTV images). It is also an invasion of privacy when it involves e-mail interception and scrutiny of websites visited by an employee during working hours. Monitoring potentially conflicts with Article 8 of the Human Rights Act 1998, which provides for the right to respect for the privacy of family life, home and correspondence.

7.7.2 *Principles for monitoring*

(a) The Information Commissioner has issued guidance on monitoring in the Employment Practices Code (there is also specific guidance on the use of CCTV).

(b) The following principles should be taken into account:

 i Identify who has authority to instigate monitoring activity. The introduction and use of monitoring should be controlled. Line managers should not be authorised to introduce new monitoring activities but should follow agreed practices and make suggestions if they have any improvements to make.

 ii Consider also which is the appropriate department to undertake monitoring. In some cases, for example performance monitoring, it will be appropriate for line management or compliance personnel to monitor. In others, such as crime prevention and detection, it will be more appropriate for security personnel to undertake monitoring.

 iii Keep a sense of perspective. Monitoring should only be undertaken after an assessment of the impact individuals and their privacy.

 iv Identify the business need and target monitoring appropriately. Monitoring is by its nature intrusive and should be undertaken in such a way that the privacy and autonomy of individual employees is respected. Targeted monitoring is more likely to achieve this than a wholesale approach. For example, If prevention of pilfering from cash tills is the objective, then CCTV cameras should be targeted on cash tills.

 v Be open about monitoring. The organisation should be open about its monitoring policy and practices. Covert monitoring will only be justifiable in limited circumstances, usually on the advice, or with the involvement, of the police.

(c) Senior HR personnel and those who are authorised to introduce monitoring activity should be familiar with the Employment Code. Employees who monitor should be trained in the data protection obligations relating to employee rights, the processing of sensitive data and the importance of following monitoring policies.

7.8 Regulation of Investigatory Powers Act 2000

(a) The interception of electronic communications (intercepting email) is a criminal offence under the Regulation of Investigatory Powers Act 2000 (RIPA), but can usually be justified under the Telecommunications (Lawful Business Practice) (Interception of Communications) Regulations 2000 as long as the charity can evidence a reasonable system of control which compliance with the Employment Code will achieve.

8 Accountability and 'privacy by design'

8.1 One of the main purposes of the GDPR regime is to ensure that organisations take a proactive and purposive approach to data protection. In addition to the principles set out in Article 5(1) of the GDPR set out above, the accountability principle in Article 5(2) requires organisations to take responsibility for what they do with personal data and to be able to demonstrate compliance, creating the need for auditability of data protection.

8.2 One of the drivers for reform was the concern that a 'one-size-fits all' approach was often taken to data protection, regardless of the risks and nature of an organisation's activities.

8.3 The accountability principle means that charities must be able to demonstrate compliance. Part of that is putting in place appropriate technical and organisational measures to meet the requirements of accountability. That requires organisations to understand and record exactly what personal data they process; to adopt and implement data protection policies; to put written contracts in place with organisations that process personal data on their behalf; and to ensure that a record is kept of all personal data breaches.

8.4 Organisations should take a 'data protection by design and default' approach. This means integrating data protection into business practices, from the design stage right through the lifecycle. This is not new: 'privacy by design' was encouraged under the old regime, but it is now a legal requirement.

8.5 One important element of being able to demonstrate compliance is through the use of data protection impact assessments (DPIA). A charity will be required to complete a DPIA for any new processing that is likely to result in a high risk to individuals, for example the introduction of a new HR computer management system for employees. It is also good practice to do a DPIA for any major project which requires the processing of personal data.

8.6 The DPIA must:

(a) describe the nature, scope, context and purposes of the processing;
(b) assess necessity, proportionality and compliance measures;
(c) identify and assess risks to individuals. High risk to personal data can arise both from a high probability of moderate harm, or a lower possibility of serious harm; and
(d) identify any additional measures to mitigate those risks.

8.6.1 If a risk is identified that appears impossible to mitigate, the ICO must be consulted.

8.7 We can expect to see the use of certification schemes to assist with GDPR compliance and enhance transparency. Certification schemes under GDPR will be approved by the ICO and delivered by approved third party assessors and are likely to be sector focussed or address certain sort of activities.

9 Data protection officers

9.1 The GDPR introduces a duty to appoint a data protection officer (DPO) if you are a public authority or body, or if you carry out certain types of processing activities.

9.2 Public authorities must appoint a DPO. A charity will have to appoint a DPO if:

(a) its core activities require large scale, regular and systematic monitoring of individuals; or
(b) its core activities consist of large scale processing of special categories of data or data relating to criminal convictions and offences.

9.3 Charities who fall outside these requirements can voluntarily appoint a DPO. If this is done, the statutory obligations in relation to DPOs will apply even though the appointment was not mandatory.

9.4 A DPO must be independent, an expert in data protection, adequately resourced and report to the highest management level, usually the board of trustees. They can be an existing employee or externally appointed. It may be possible for several organisations to appoint a single DPO between them.

10 Conditions for legitimate processing

10.1 For the processing of personal data to be lawful, a controller must be able to demonstrate a lawful basis as set out in Article 6 of the GDPR. At least one lawful basis must apply. If a charity wishes to process 'special category' data or criminal offence data there are further considerations. This is discussed further below.

10.2 Meaning of 'necessary'

10.2.1 A charity must usually be able to show that processing is 'necessary' for a particular lawful basis. In this context, necessary does not mean absolutely essential but it is more than simply useful or desirable. It must be a targeted and proportionate way of achieving a specific purpose. The lawful basis will not apply if an organisation can reasonably achieve the purpose by some other less intrusive means, or by processing less data. Processing is not necessary simply because that is how a charity has chosen to operate its business.

10.3 The lawful bases for processing:

10.3.1 Consent

(a) If consent is to be relied upon, that consent must be informed and clear. There is no requirement that consent is given in writing, but as a controller must be able to demonstrate that the conditions for consent in Article 7 have been complied with, it is usual for consent to be written.
(b) A request for consent must be presented in manner which does not make it hard to distinguish from other matters. If consent for data processing is being sought where other information is provided, it is recommended that the consent form is separate.
(c) Consent forms must use intelligible and easily accessible language.
(d) Importantly, individuals have the right to withdraw consent at any time so careful consideration will have to be given to the potential impact of that withdrawal. Individuals must be informed of this right to withdraw consent when they give consent and it must be as easy to withdraw consent as it is to give it. The performance of a contract, including the provision of a service, must not be conditional upon consent to processing of personal data that is not necessary for the performance of that contract.
(e) Although all the legal bases for processing are of equal legal status and none is 'better' than any other, in light of the limitations on consent, when considering a basis to rely upon it is usual to seek to rely on consent only if other bases have been discounted.

10.3.2 Contract

(a) Processing is permissible if it is necessary for a contract a charity has with the individual, or in order to take steps at the request of the data subject prior to entering into a contract.
(b) A common example is processing associated with a contract of employment. This is why it is not necessary to ask employees for consent to process their data under a contract of employment, although this is still sometimes seen.

10.3.3 Legal obligation

(a) Processing is necessary for a charity to comply with the law (other than a contractual obligation). This covers a wide range of processing including compliance with tax requirements, identity and safeguarding checks and so on.

10.3.4 Vital interests

(a) This is a rarely relied upon basis for processing as it is only relevant in very limited circumstances.
(b) The ICO suggests that this basis is lawful if processing is necessary to protect someone's life. However, it cannot be used to justify the processing of health data or other special category data if the individual is capable of giving consent, even if they refuse their consent.
(c) Some charities, perhaps in social care or similar areas of operation, may occasionally need to rely on this basis. If this is a possibility the circumstances when this may arise should be identified and documented.

10.3.5 Public task

(a) This applies where processing is necessary for the performance of a task carried out in the public interest or in the exercise of official authority vested in a controller.
(b) This is also a limited basis but may occasionally be relevant for a charity. If so, those very specific circumstances should be identified and documented if relevant.

10.3.6 Legitimate interests

(a) This is an important and widely relied upon basis for processing. It applies where the processing is necessary for a charity's legitimate interests or the legitimate interests of a third party, except where those interests are overridden by the interests or fundamental rights and freedoms of the data subject which require protection of personal data, in particular where the data subject is a child.
(b) This is the most flexible lawful basis for processing, but that does not mean it offers a 'catch all'. It is likely to be most appropriate where personal data is used in ways that data subjects would reasonably expect and which have a minimal privacy impact, or where there is a compelling justification for the processing but there is no contractual or statutory reason for it.
(c) To be able to rely on the legitimate interests basis, charities must be satisfied of three elements:
   i that there is a legitimate interest (this can be commercial, individual or based on broader societal interests);
   ii that the processing is necessary to achieve that interest and it could not be achieved in another, less intrusive, way; and
   iii the interests can be balanced against the individual data subject's

interests, rights and freedoms. If an individual would not expect the processing, or if there is a risk of unjustified harm, individual interests may override the charities' legitimate interests.

(d) Charities must keep a record of this balancing excessive which is referred to as a legitimate interests assessment (LIA). The ICO has produced example forms. Details of legitimate interests must also be included in privacy information and notices.

10.4 Special category data

10.4.1 Special category data is broadly similar to the concept of sensitive personal data under the 1998 Act. It applies to data which can create more significant risks like unlawful discrimination. It does not apply to financial data like bank details which, although it should be treated with care and recognised as being confidential, is not 'special category' for these purposes.

10.4.2 Special category data is information about an individual's:

(a) race;
(b) ethnic origin;
(c) politics;
(d) religion;
(e) trade union membership;
(f) genetics;
(g) biometrics (where used for ID purposes);
(h) health;
(i) sex life; or
(j) sexual orientation.

10.4.3 Under previous data protection legislation, information about criminal offences was also sensitive data. This data is not special category data and has its own set of provisions in Article 10.

10.4.4 In order to process special category data, an organisation must be able to demonstrate a processing condition in Article 6 as set above, and a specific condition in Article 9.

10.4.5 The specific conditions for processing special category data are listed in Article 9(2) of the GDPR:

(a) explicit consent (unless prohibited)
(b) processing is necessary for the purposes of carrying out the obligations and exercising specific rights of the controller or of the data subject in the field

of employment, social security and social protection law, in-so-far as it is authorised by EU or member state law, or a collective agreement pursuant to member state law, providing for appropriate safeguards for the fundamental rights and the interests of the data subject;

(c) processing is necessary to protect the vital interests of the data subject or of another natural person where the data subject is physically or legally incapable of giving consent;

(d) processing is carried out in the course of its legitimate activities with appropriate safeguards by a foundation, association or any other not-for-profit body with a political, philosophical, religious or trade union aim, and on condition that the processing relates solely to the members or to former members of the body or to persons who have regular contact with it in connection with its purposes and that the personal data are not disclosed outside that body without the consent of the data subjects;

(e) processing relates to personal data which are manifestly made public by the data subject;

(f) processing is necessary for the establishment, exercise or defence of legal claims or whenever courts are acting in their judicial capacity;

(g) processing is necessary for reasons of substantial public interest, on the basis of EU or member state law, which shall be proportionate to the aim pursued, respect the essence of the right to data protection and provide for suitable and specific measures to safeguard the fundamental rights and the interests of the data subject;

(h) processing is necessary for the purposes of preventive or occupational medicine, for the assessment of the working capacity of the employee, medical diagnosis, the provision of health or social care or treatment or the management of health or social care systems and services on the basis of EU or member state law or pursuant to contract with a health professional and subject to the conditions and safeguards referred to in paragraph (c);

(i) processing is necessary for reasons of public interest in the area of public health, such as protecting against serious cross-border threats to health or ensuring high standards of quality and safety of health care and of medicinal products or medical devices, on the basis of EU or member state law which provides for suitable and specific measures to safeguard the rights and freedoms of the data subject, in particular professional secrecy;

(j) processing is necessary for archiving purposes in the public interest, scientific or historical research purposes or statistical purposes in accordance with Article 89(1) based on EU or member state law which shall be proportionate to the aim pursued, respect the essence of the right to data protection and provide for suitable and specific measures to safeguard the fundamental rights and the interests of the data subject.

10.4.6 The DPA 2018 adds more specific conditions and safeguards. It requires in some cases that the data controller has in place an 'appropriate policy document' in order to be able to rely on certain of these conditions.

10.5 Criminal offence data

10.5.1 Criminal offence data (data about criminal allegations, proceedings or convictions) used to be classified as special category data. That is no longer the case and criminal offence data is now covered by its own particular provisions within the GDPR. To process such data a lawful basis under Article 6 is required and either legal authority or official authority for the processing under Article 10.

10.5.2 The DPA 2018 deals with this type of data in a similar way to special category data, and sets out specific conditions providing lawful authority for processing. There are additional safeguards in the legislation for processing and conditions are set out in Schedule 1 of the DPA 2018.

10.5.3 At the time of writing, the ICO was still working on its detailed guidance in this area. Any charity processing criminal offence data is recommended to refer to that guidance when it is available.

11 Individual rights

The GDPR provides the following rights for individuals:

(a) The right to be informed
(b) The right of access
(c) The right to rectification
(d) The right to erasure
(e) The right to restrict processing
(f) The right to data portability
(g) The right to object
(h) Rights in relation to automated decision making and profiling.

11.1 The right to be informed

11.1.1 Individuals have the right to be informed about the collection and use of their personal data. This is a key transparency requirement under the GDPR. This is called 'privacy information' and may be contained in a privacy notice, privacy policy or similar document.

11.1.2 Privacy information must be provided when personal data is collected. It is an important element of initial interactions, whether that is with potential donors, trustees, volunteers, employees, service users or others. If personal data is obtained from a third party, there are still obligations to provide privacy information within a reasonable period of obtaining the personal data: no later than one month after the first communication takes place; or when disclosure is made to another party. Particular care must be taken in regard to databases which are sold or bought in.

11.1.3 The information must be concise, transparent, intelligible, easily accessible and it must use clear and plain language. The format and language must be tailored to the audience. This is especially important for charities who deal with children, vulnerable groups or those for whom English is not their first language.

11.1.4 Preparing privacy information is not a 'one-time job'. Privacy notices and policies should be regularly reviewed and updated as needed, and changes should be highlighted to data subjects.

11.1.5 What must be included in a privacy notice?

(a) The name and contact details of the data controller.
(b) The name and contact details of the representative (if applicable).
(c) The contact details of our data protection officer (if applicable).
(d) The purposes of the processing.
(e) The lawful basis for the processing.
(f) The legitimate interests for the processing (if applicable).
(g) The categories of personal data obtained and their source (if the personal data is not obtained from the individual to whom it relates).
(h) The recipients or categories of recipients of the personal data.
(i) The details of transfers of the personal data to any third countries or international organisations (if applicable).
(j) The retention periods for the personal data.
(k) The rights available to individuals in respect of the processing.
(l) The right to withdraw consent (if applicable).
(m) The right to lodge a complaint with a supervisory authority.
(n) The details of whether individuals are under a statutory or contractual obligation to provide the personal data (if applicable, and if the personal data is collected from the individual to whom it relates).
(o) The details of the existence of automated decision making, including profiling (if applicable).

11.1.6 A frequent criticism of privacy notes is that they are too long and difficult to understand. The amount of information the GDPR requires to be included can make producing streamlined privacy notices something of a challenge, but the use of drop down boxes, layering and dashboards in online documents can be helpful. User testing for understanding is also recommended. It can also be useful to prepare a range of notices for different categories of data subjects but, as all must be kept up to date, care should also be taken to ensure this updating across a variety of documents remains manageable.

11.2 Right of access (subject access requests)

11.2.1 It is no longer possible to charge a fee to an individual who wishes to access the data an organisation processes about them except in very limited circumstances. The time limit for response has also shortened from the old regime and a response is now required within one month, although in certain circumstances, and provided contact is made within a month, this timescale can be extended by two months.

11.2.2 Individuals can make a subject access request verbally or in writing. It is vital that organisations have systems in place to identify, log and respond to subject access requests wherever within the organisation they are received.

11.2.3 An organisation is not obliged to comply with a request for subject access unless they are supplied with such information as they may reasonably require to:

(a) satisfy themselves as to the identity of the person making the request; and
(b) locate the information which that person seeks.

Requesting this clarification will not stop the clock running for compliance with the request and should not be used as an excuse for inaction.

11.2.4 Although the law does not require charities to 'leave no stone unturned' in retrieving personal data, organisations will be expected to have rigorous procedures in place for retrieving personal data. The need to deal with subject access requests must be taken into account when new data management systems are introduced.

11.2.5 Someone who makes a request for a very large amount of data could be asked to narrow what they request to see if there is particular information they are seeking, but data subjects do have a statutory right to see a copy of all of their personal data unless an exemption applies.

11.2.6 Dealing with personal data which also contains the data of third parties can be complex. Care must be taken to ensure that the data protection rights of other individuals are not compromised. Where compliance with a request involves the disclosure of information relating to another individual (a third party) who can be identified from that information, there is no obligation to comply with the request unless:

(a) the third party has consented to the disclosure of the information; or
(b) it is reasonable in all the circumstances to comply with the request without the consent of the third party. The ICO will expect an assessment to be made of the reasons for consent not being given against the interests of the data subject and there must not be an assumption that an objection should prevail, especially if that third party could have no reasonable expectation of privacy.

11.2.7 What is reasonable will depend on any duty of confidentiality owed, any steps taken by the data controller to obtain the consent of the third party, whether the third party is capable of giving consent and whether consent has been refused.

11.2.8 Although the ability to charge a fee and the timescales for response have changed, the underlying principles for dealing with subject access requests are little changed from the old regime. The ICO has not yet updated its subject access code of practice, but it in light of this it still provides extremely helpful guidance. Any charity officer or manager dealing with a subject access request is recommended to familiarise themselves with that code.

11.2.9 There are exemptions from the right of access for certain data, including information that is covered by legal privilege, where negotiations with the data subject would be jeopardised and certain management information. Personal data are exempt from a subject access request if they consist of a reference given, or to be given, in confidence by the data controller for the purposes of education, training or employment. However, the exemption does not apply in the hands of the recipient of the reference so an individual does have an alternative route to obtain a copy of a reference by making a subject access request to the receiving employer or institution.

11.2.10 There is widespread misconception that this right will be met by simply sending an individual a copy of their data. In fact the right is much wider. Individuals should also be informed of

(a) the purposes of for which their data is processed;
(b) the categories of personal data concerned;
(c) the recipients or categories of recipients of their personal data;
(d) the retention periods for storing the personal data or, where this is not possible, the criteria for determining how long it will be stored;
(e) the existence of rights to request rectification, erasure or restriction or to object to processing;
(f) the right to lodge a complaint with the ICO or another supervisory authority;
(g) information about the source of the data where it was not obtained directly from the individual;
(h) the existence of automated decision making (including profiling); and

(i) safeguards in place if personal data is transferred to a third country or international organisation.

11.3 Right to rectification

11.3.1 The GDPR includes a right for individuals to have inaccurate personal data rectified/or completed if it is incomplete. This can be requested verbally or in writing, so identifying such requests is an important business planning risk.

11.3.2 A response must be provided within one calendar month.

11.3.3 Organisations can refuse a request for rectification. If the request is refused because the charity believes the data to be accurate, this should be explained. The individual should also be informed: that the data will not be amended; of their right to make a complaint to the ICO or another supervisory authority; and of their ability to seek to enforce their rights through a judicial remedy. It is good practice to place a note on your system indicating that the individual challenges the accuracy of the data and their reasons for doing so.

11.3.4 It is also possible to refuse to rectify data because a request is manifestly unfounded or excessive, taking into account whether the request is repetitive in nature. In these circumstances a reasonable fee to deal with the request can be requested or the charity can refuse to deal with the request. This decision will have to be capable of justification.

11.4 Right of erasure

11.4.1 This is often referred to as 'the right to be forgotten'.

11.4.2 As with other rights, requests can be made verbally or in writing and response should be made within one calendar month.

11.4.3 The right is not absolute and only applies in certain circumstances. The right to erasure does not apply if processing is necessary to comply with a legal obligation, such as keeping tax records; to exercise the right of freedom of expression and information; for the performance of a task carried out in the public interest or in the exercise of official authority; for archiving purposes in the public interest, scientific, research historical research or statistical purposes where erasure is likely to render impossible or seriously impair the achievement of that processing; or for the establishment, exercise or defence of legal claims.

11.4.4 The GDPR also specifies two circumstances where the right to erasure will not apply to special category data related to public health and preventative or occupational medicine.

11.5 The right to restrict processing

11.5.1 This gives individuals have the right to request the restriction or suppression of their personal data. It is not an absolute right and only applies in certain circumstances.

11.5.2 If a request is accepted data can be stored but not used.

11.5.3 Requests can be made verbally or in writing and a response is required within one calendar month.

11.5.4 A request to restrict processing can be made if:

(a) the individual contests the accuracy of their personal data and the charity is verifying the accuracy of the data;
(b) the data has been unlawfully processed, the individual opposes erasure and requests restriction instead;
(c) the charity no longer has any need for the personal data but the individual wishes it to be stored in order to establish, exercise or defend a legal claim; or
(d) the individual has objected to the processing of their data but their objection is still being considered.

11.6 The right to data portability

11.6.1 This is a right to allow individuals to obtain and reuse their personal data, for example when changing service users. It is intended to enable the easy transfer of personal data between different IT environments without affecting its usability.

11.6.2 The right only applies to information an individual has provided to a controller and where the lawful processing condition is consent or performance of a contract.

11.6.3 The right to data portability entitles an individual to:

(a) receive a copy of their personal data; and/or
(b) have their personal data transmitted from one controller to another controller.

11.6.4 The portable data should be provide the personal data in a format that is:

(a) structured;
(b) commonly used; and
(c) machine-readable.

11.6.5 These terms are not defined further but the ICO suggests referring to guidance in the 'Open Data Handbook', published by Open Knowledge International.

11.7 Right to object

11.7.1 The GDPR gives individuals the right to object to the processing of their personal data in certain circumstances.

11.7.2 An individual can make an objection verbally or in writing and the organisation must respond in one calendar month.

11.7.3 Individuals have an absolute right to stop their data being used for direct marketing.

11.7.4 An individual can also object if the charity relies on one of the following lawful conditions;

(a) 'public interest' (for the performance of a task carried out in the public interest);
(b) 'public task' (for the exercise of official authority); or
(c) legitimate interests.

11.7.5 An individual must give specific reasons why they are objecting to the processing of their data. These reasons should be based upon their particular situation.

11.7.6 The charity can continue processing if there are compelling legitimate grounds for the processing which override the interests, rights and freedoms of the individual or if the processing is for the establishment, exercise or defence of legal claims.

11.7.7 If a request is refused, the decision should be explained. The individuals must be informed of their rights to complain to the ICO and to enforce their rights through the courts.

11.7.8 The right to object to processing personal data for scientific or historical research, or statistical purposes, is more limited.

11.8 Rights in relation to automated individual decision making and profiling

11.8.1 Automated decision making is the use of programming to make decisions without any human involvement; and profiling (automated processing of personal data to evaluate certain things about an individual). Profiling can be part of an automated decision making process.

11.8.2 The GDPR applies to all automated individual decision making and Article 22 protect individuals where solely automated decision making that has legal or similarly significant effects on them.

11.8.3 Automated individual decision making is only permitted where the decision is: necessary for the entry into or performance of a contract; is authorised by EU or member state law applicable to the controller; or is based on the individual's explicit consent.

11.8.4 If processing falls under Article 22, individuals must be provided with additional information about the processing, be able to request human intervention and to challenge a decision. Regular checks must be made on systems.

12 International transfers

12.1 The GDPR primarily applies to controllers and processors located in the European Economic Area (the EEA) with some exceptions. It is recognised that there is particular risk to individuals if their personal data is transferred outside of the EEA. For this reason, the GDPR restricts transfers of personal data outside the EEA, or the protection of the GDPR, unless the rights of the individuals in respect of their personal data is protected in another way, or one of a limited number of exceptions applies.

13 Managing data breaches

13.1 Breaches of personal data are common and give rise to the greatest risk of enforcement action by the ICO. This may result in a fine.

13.2 The timescales for reporting breaches are strict and systems will be required to ensure that they are dealt with in the requisite timescales.

13.3 The GDPR introduces a duty on all organisations to report certain types of personal data breach to the ICO (or relevant supervisory authority). Reporting is expected within 72 hours.

13.4 A personal data breach is a breach of security leading to the accidental or unlawful destruction, loss, alteration, unauthorised disclosure of, or access to, personal data. It does not require deliberate wrongdoing or even loss of data.

13.5 Article 33 of the GDPR states 'the controller shall without undue delay and, where feasible, not later than 72 hours after having become aware of it, notify the personal data breach to the supervisory authority competent in accordance with

Article 55, unless the personal data breach is unlikely to result in a risk to the rights and freedoms of natural persons. Where the notification to the supervisory authority is not made within 72 hours, it shall be accompanied by reasons for the delay'

13.6 This suggests that a very high level of reporting is expected, although the ICO says on its website that 'if you experience a personal data breach you need to consider whether this poses a risk to people. You need to consider the likelihood and severity of the risk to people's rights and freedoms, following the breach. When you've made this assessment, if it's likely there will be a risk then you must notify the ICO; if it's unlikely then you don't have to report. You do not need to report every breach to the ICO'. The ICO website has a self-assessment tool to assist with the decision-making process in making reports.

13.7 Even if a personal data breach is not reported, a record of it should still be kept. It is important that lessons are learnt from breaches and 'near misses', and that systems should be changed as mitigate future risks. Training needs may also need to be identified.

13.8 Data processors must inform data controllers of all personal data breaches without undue delay.

13.9 If a breach is likely to result in a high risk to the rights and freedoms of individuals, the individuals must be notified without undue delay. A high risk means the threshold for informing individuals is higher than for notifying the ICO. An assessment of the severity of the potential or actual impact on individuals as a result of a breach and the likelihood of this occurring will be required. There is a particular need to inform individuals quickly if there is a need to mitigate an immediate risk of damage (for example), to allow individuals to notify banks that their financial information has been compromised.

A failure to notify a breach may result in a significant fine up to €10 million or 2% of global turnover, although the ICO has not imposed any fines at the maximum level yet.

14 Information Commissioner's powers of enforcement and sanctions

14.1 Administrative fines

14.1.1 The maximum level of fines under the GDPR is €20 million or 4% of the total worldwide annual turnover of the undertaking (not the company), whichever is higher. This is a significant increase from the maximum fine of £500,000 that the ICO could levy under the 1998 Act.

14.1.2 Administrative fines apply to a list of the most serious infringements of the following provisions of the GDPR including: breaching basic principles for processing, conditions for consent, individuals' rights and the conditions for lawful international data transfers.

14.1.3 There are also fines of up to €10 million or 2% of total worldwide turnover of the undertaking (not the company) for infringements relating to less serious breaches such as internal record keeping, processor contracts, data security and breach notification and DPOs.

14.2 Enforcement

14.2.1 The GDPR also gives the ICO and other the supervisory authorities in other members states a number of investigative, corrective and authorisation and advisory powers.

14.3 Criminal offences under the DPA

14.3.1 The DPA 2018 sets out criminal offences which can be committed by a data controller or an organisation which handles personal data. These include altering or destroying personal data to prevent the right of access, obstructing an ICO investigation, unlawfully obtaining personal data and re-identification of de-identified data.

14.3.2 Individuals can also be prosecuted for breaching data protection laws. A number of such prosecutions have taken place over recent years, in particular where employees have accessed personal data for their own purposes.

14.3.3 There are no custodial sentences in respect of offences under the DPA and no powers of arrest; all offences are punishable only by a fine.

14.4 Individuals can also take their own legal action for alleged breaches of the DPA 2018 and GDPR and can seek damages for losses incurred including for distress. The individual concerned has the right to apply to the court for rectification, blocking, erasure or destruction of the inaccurate data.

15 Data implications for electronic marketing

In addition to the GDPR, there is a range of other legal considerations relevant to direct marketing. The detail of these is beyond the scope of this chapter, but a brief summary is set out below.

15.1 Direct marketing in the charity sector

15.1.1 Following widespread media and public criticism of the approach taken to marketing by some charities, the ICO has produced some specific guidance for charities which is available in an online webinar (https://youtu.be/WqlRVx_vae0) and produced a useful report on the sector which was published in April 2018. Although the rules applying to the sector are not materially different from that applying to commercial organisations, the risk of reputational damage is high and it is clear that the public do tend to have high expectations of the sector. The April 2018 report (which is available on the ICO website) suggests that sector practice has improved.

16 Privacy and Electronic Communications Regulations 2003

16.1 In addition to the GDPR, those with responsibility for marketing, and online marketing in particular, need to be aware of the rules governing direct marketing by electronic means. These are currently contained in the Privacy and Electronic Communications (EC Directive) Regulations 2003 (SI 2003/2426) (PECR), which implement the EU Privacy and Electronic Communications Directive (2002/58/EC) (E-Privacy Directive).

16.2 Definition of direct marketing

Direct marketing is not defined in the GDPR or PECR. The DPA 2018 contains the following definition of direct marketing: 'the communication by whatever means of advertising or marketing material directed to particular individuals'.

16.3 A new, directly effective, E-Privacy Regulation, which will replace the E-Privacy Directive is also on the horizon.

16.4 Consent obtained for the purposes of PECR must meet the new standards for consent specified in the GDPR. Until 29 March 2019, this was a matter of ICO guidance. However, this is now required under the Data Protection, Privacy and Electronic Communications (Amendments etc.) (EU Exit) Regulations 2019.

16.5 Consent is usually required for electronic marketing under PECR. There is an exemption called 'soft opt-in' which applies to customers and those in negotiations for a sale or service: this is what allows the pre-ticking of marketing boxes. However, the exemption which allows soft opt-in does apply to a charity promoting its charitable aims. As this is almost inevitably a part of any interaction, even if engagement is only intended for promotion of future sales for a charity's online website, this approach is not recommended.

16.6 If consent is required, it must be knowingly and freely given, clear and specific. It must cover both the organisation and the method of communication (email, telephone, text and so on). It must involve a clear positive act – for example, ticking a box, clicking an icon, or sending an email – and the person must be made aware that they are giving you consent and informed of their right to withdraw that consent at any time. It must be as easy to withdraw consent as it was to give it. Details must not be tucked away in a privacy policy. The clearest way to obtain consent is to ask the customer or potential donor to tick an opt-in box. Records must be kept of consent.

16.7 Particular care is required if consent was given to a third party. Generic consent covering any third party is not enough.

16.8 Scope of the GDPR and the Privacy Regulations

16.8.1 The GDPR and PECR differ as to their scope. The GDPR regulates direct marketing which makes use of personal data regardless of the method used. Personal data includes certain categories of online data, such as online identifiers, device identifiers, cookie IDs and IP addresses. The GDPR specifically regulates profiling, including for marketing purposes.

16.8.2 PECR by contrast only regulates direct marketing by electronic means, namely telephone calls (both live and automated), faxes and email. PECR also applies to how cookies are used to collect data for profiling purposes.

16.9 PECR sets out specific rules in relation to

(a) marketing calls, emails, texts and faxes;
(b) cookies (and similar technologies);
(c) keeping communications services secure; and
(d) customer privacy as regards traffic and location data, itemised billing, line identification, and directory listings.

16.9.1 The ICO produces guidance on PECR and seeks to promote good practice by offering advice and guidance. The ICO also takes enforcement action with priority being given to those companies and individuals who generate the most complaints.

17 Other rules and guides

17.1 The ICO Direct Marketing Guide

17.1.1 The ICO currently publishes the Direct Marketing Guide (Privacy and Electronic Communications) which sets out best practice for direct marketing. A new ICO Direct Marketing Code has been consulted upon and should be referred to when available. This new code will have the status of a statutory code of practice which means that judicial notice will be taken of its guidance, although it is not legally binding as such.

17.2 E-commerce regulations

17.2.1 The Electronic Commerce (EC Directive) Regulations 2002/2013 (E-Commerce regulations) impose various information obligations on providers of 'information society services' which includes online advertising. Compliance with some of the E-Commerce Regulations information obligations is also required under PECR.

17.2.2 The E-Commerce Regulations also impose general pre-contract information requirements for all information society service providers. These include the requirement to make available name, address, trade register and VAT details. The requirements can generally be met by providing information on a website.

17.3 The Consumer Contracts (Information, Cancellation and Additional Charges) Regulations 2013 (SI 2013/3134) deal with the following.

17.3.1 What pre-contract information must be provided to consumers when they are contracting on premises (in a traditional shop), online or 'off-premises' (for example, at their own homes or on the street) and by telephone. There are additional information obligations where a consumer is buying 'at distance'.

17.3.2 The rights of consumers who buy online or off-premises to cancel their contracts because they have changed their minds.

17.3.3 The ban on traders charging consumers more than the basic rate for any trader telephone line used by a consumer to discuss an existing contract.

17.3.4 There are also obligations for confirmation of an order to be provided and what information must be provided at that point.

17.4 The Modern Slavery Act 2015 requires any 'commercial organisation' (which will include most charities) having a global turnover of £36 million or more to publish a slavery and human trafficking statement for each financial year that ends on or after 31 March 2016. If the organisation has a website, it must publish the statement on that website and include a link to the statement in a prominent place on its homepage.

17.5 CPUT

17.5.1 The Consumer Protection from Unfair Trading Regulations 2008 (CPUT) prohibit misleading and aggressive sales practices during the whole lifetime of a consumer to trader transaction: marketing and advertising, entry into the contract and performance of the contract.

17.5.2 CPUT requires that certain information be included in an 'invitation to purchase': broadly, any advert which includes both a reference to a product or service and its price. CPUT specifically bans a number of marketing practices which are particularly relevant to direct marketing.

17.6 Consumer dispute regulations

17.6.1 The Alternative Dispute Resolution for Consumer Disputes (Competent Authorities and Information) Regulations 2015 requires traders to provide consumers with information about alternative dispute resolution (ADR) options and also about the online dispute resolution (ODR) platform established by the EU.

17.6.2 Certain traders must include a link to the ODR platform in any offer made to a consumer by email. The relevant traders are those online traders obliged by law, their trade association rules or the terms of a contract to use ADR services provided by an ADR entity registered under the Consumer ADR Regulations.

17.7 DMA Code

17.7.1 The Direct Marketing Association (DMA) requires that its members comply with its DMA Code governing 'one-to-one marketing' which is defined as 'any marketing communication to an identified individual'.

17.7.2 The DMA Code reflects many aspects of the legislation on direct marketing and requires compliance with the DPA 2018 and e-privacy rules. The DMA also publishes a number of best practice guides on email, telephone, social media and mail marketing. These guides are only available to DMA members.

17.8 CAP Code

17.8.1 The UK Code of non-broadcast advertising, sales promotion and direct marketing (CAP Code) is the self-regulatory code of the advertising industry.

17.8.2 It imposes rules on the collection and use of personal information and restrictions on marketing communications by telephone, fax, mail, email (which includes SMS, MMS and other data transfer methods) or "other remote media".

17.8.3 In March 2019, CAP announced further changes to align the CAP Code with the GDPR. The changes, which took effect from 14 March, deal with marketing to children and the naming of prize-winners. CAP will consult on further changes to Section 10 to reflect the new E-Privacy Regulation when it is finalised.

17.9 ICC Code

17.9.1 The International Chamber of Commerce publishes a Consolidated Code for Advertising and Marketing Communication Practice (the ICC Code). The ICC Code is intended as a best practice framework for other self-regulatory codes, worldwide.

17.10 How to review direct marketing

17.11 As the list above shows, this is a complex area. Charities should consider the GDPR and DPA 2018 implications first, referring to the ICO Direct Marketing Guide, which summarises and offers guidance on GDPR, DPA 2018 and PECR.

17.12 Next, consider what additional requirements are imposed under CPUT, the E-Commerce Regulations, the Consumer ADR Regulations, the DMA Code and the CAP Code, as distinct from the DPA 2018 and e-privacy rules.

17.13 It is important to be aware that the possible sanctions for breach of GDPR, are not the only penalties. Sanctions can be imposed for breach of CPUT, the E-Commerce Regulations, the Consumer ADR Regulations, the CAP Code and the DMA Code.

18 Use of cookies

18.1 A cookie is a small text file that is downloaded onto 'terminal equipment' (a computer or smartphone) when the user accesses a website. It allows the website to recognise that user's device and store some information about the user's preferences or past actions.

18.2 The rules on cookies are in regulation 6 of PECR. The basic rules are that:

(a) individuals must be told they are being used;
(b) the cookies must be explained – what they do and why; and
(c) consent must be obtained to store a cookie on the device

18.3 It is not necessary to repeat this every time the same person visits a website. However, bear in mind that devices may be used by different people. If there is likely to be more than one user, you may want to consider repeating this process at suitable intervals.

18.4 This means the same rules apply to any similar technologies – such as local shared objects (sometimes called flash cookies) – and can also cover other types of technology, including apps on smartphones, tablets, smart TVs or other devices. These rules also outlaw spyware or any similar covert surveillance software that downloads to a user's device and tracks their activities without their knowledge.

18.5 PECR does not specific exactly what information must be provided (unlike privacy notices under the GDPR). The only requirement is that it must be 'clear and comprehensive' information about the purposes. The information should explain the way the cookies (or other similar technologies) work and what they are used for, and the explanation must be clear and easily available. Users must be able to understand the potential consequences of allowing the cookies. The language and level of detail must be appropriate for your intended audience.

19 Direct mail

19.1 Best practice when marketing by direct mail is to clean the mailing list prior to use. This involves checking standard abbreviations for titles and correct decoration suffixes as well as correcting common misspellings, omissions and transpositions.

19.2 Mailing lists should match names and addresses to remove duplicate records, as well as screening for validation and suppression markers. Lists should also be checked against the Mailing Preference Service (MPS). This is a list of surnames and addresses of people who want to opt out of receiving marketing material. Once screened, the list may be used for up to 28 days, after which it will need to be rescreened.

19.3 If a consumer has had dealings with the charity in the past then it will be entitled to make direct marketing approaches from time to time regardless of the MPS suppression list, as there is an existing relationship between the parties. Mailings are not unsolicited unless and until the individual writes to request that the charity stops using his or her personal data for direct marketing.

20 Telephone marketing

20.1 As with the MPS, there are registers for those who do not want to receive marketing telephone calls or faxes: the Telephone Preference Service and Fax Preference Service respectively.

20.2 The unsolicited telephone calls for purposes of direct marketing are regulated under PECR. They apply to both consumers and corporate telephone subscribers, making it unlawful to make unsolicited telephone calls for purposes of direct marketing if the subscriber has either registered with the relevant preference service or has previously told the advertiser not to make marketing calls on that telephone number.

20.3 PECR applies to a wide range of marketing activities including corporate advertising, the promotion of the organisation's aims and ideals. They only apply to 'unsolicited calls'. So, if a coupon has been completed and returned asking for further information about a product or service and has asked for the information to be sent to a particular fax or telephone number, then a call to that number to provide the information requested is not unsolicited.

21 Text and email marketing

21.1 PECR also applies to marketing by means of email or text messaging to mobile phones. They regulate the use of electronic messaging for purposes of unsolicited direct marketing to individual subscribers; they do not apply to businesses or to email addresses of individuals at work.

21.2 Marketing by text or email is only lawful if undertaken with the express consent of the individual or in circumstances where the individual has purchased similar goods or services from the charity previously (known as the 'soft opt-in') but the soft opt-in cannot not be used if the aims of the charity are being promoted. Even where charities sell goods online, there is usually an element of promotion of the charity: relying on the soft opt-in is not recommended in the sector.

21.3 PECR also specifies information to be included in marketing messages sent by electronic means, including a prominent reference to the fact that it is an advertisement.

21.4 The Companies (Registrar, Languages and Trading Disclosures) Regulations 2006 specify that limited companies must disclose their full registration details on all emails, as does the Companies Act 2006.

D4
Contracts and delivery of public services

1 What is a contract?

1.1 The importance of contracts cannot be overestimated. They have been used since medieval times, are the means by which we can form an understanding between two or more parties and are used today as a legally enforceable agreement. Although there is sometimes a perception that a contract is invalid unless it is written and signed, it is very common for a contract not to be in writing. A contract does not have to be in writing unless there are specific legal requirements for a written form, such as a contract used for the transfer of land. A contract can often be much less formal and most people will enter into small informal contracts as they go about their regular, day-to-day business. Therefore, while some people may believe a contract does not exist unless there is a signed commitment to an undertaking, it is important to understand that contracts can be made in a variety of forms.

1.2 Contracts can be made orally, for example by making a telephone order for office stationery; in writing, for example a mortgage contract; or by implication, for example in buying a rail fare from a ticket machine. The basic principles of what makes a contract and what these examples have in common, is that they create a legally enforceable contractual obligation.

1.3 Just as an individual can enter into contracts every day, so can a charity. If you just consider the arrangements needed to hold a trustee meeting, a number of contracts could be involved. In such a scenario, contracts could be set up when buying travel tickets, hiring venues for meetings, buying refreshments, having meeting papers printed and posting meeting papers.

1.4 While it would be unrealistic and unnecessary to have written agreements for all these contracts, written undertakings are needed for bigger transactions and ongoing matters and verbal contracts in many of these types of situations should be avoided. If the meeting room is regularly hired with the same venue, a written contract would be expected. In addition, the charity may want to ensure that it is imposing its own standard terms and conditions, or at the very least, that it understands and accepts other terms and conditions that are being proposed. A written contract will enable this to happen. When a charity is entering into an ongoing agreement to provide services there should be a written contract.

2 The basics of contract law

2.1 Not every agreement is a contract. However, if we enter into contracts so often, what makes an agreement a contractual one and therefore legally enforceable? The basis of contract law in England and Wales is that a contract is created when there is:

- offer;
- acceptance;
- consideration; and
- an intention to create legal relations.

2.2 Offer

An offer is made when a person making the offer (the offeror) shows an intention to enter into a binding agreement, on certain terms, when that offer is accepted by the person to whom it is made (the offeree). While this can appear simple, it is often actually more complex to determine when an offer has been made and it is important to distinguish an offer from an 'invitation to treat'. An 'invitation to treat' is where there is a communication that the person may wish to enter into a contract, but not a clear intention actually to do so. Sometimes it can be difficult to tell the difference between an offer and an invitation to treat. For example, many people would assume that the display of goods in a self-service store was an offer because it would seem obvious that the display of goods, with the price, was an offer that the purchaser was being asked to accept. However, in law, it is actually an invitation to treat (see *Pharmaceutical Society of Great Britain v Boots Cash Chemists* [1953]). It is actually the buyer that makes the offer to purchase, not the person displaying the goods.

2.3 Acceptance

The offer then needs to be accepted, which can be done in writing, orally or sometimes by conduct. The acceptance generally needs to be unconditional – all of the terms included in the offer must be agreed by both parties. If the acceptance is expressed in a way that suggests different terms from those of the offer (such as a different price) it is usually regarded as a counteroffer. Just as the offeree must receive the offer, so the offeror must receive the acceptance and any changes to the original means the terms of that offer have not been accepted. This points to the issue that the offeree must show or, in law communicate, that they have accepted the offer. This can be done verbally or non-verbally, but must be understood as a communication that completes the transaction.

2.4 Consideration

2.4.1 Offer and acceptance are not enough to create a contract in most scenarios. Generally speaking, for a contract to be enforceable, there must be some exchange of value or benefit (for the exception, see paragraph 2.4.2) which is called 'consideration'. Consideration is effectively the price paid for the promise. However, while there must be some consideration, or 'price', this does not need to be adequate. The law is not concerned in this regard with whether the bargain is a good one. A good example of this is the term 'peppercorn rent', in which the reference to a peppercorn is to a very small payment, a nominal consideration, used to ensure that there is consideration and therefore a legal contract. A peppercorn rent may seem like a very small consideration, but it is still regarded as one and therefore is a component in creating a contract.

2.4.2 Later on, we will discuss the use of the seal and deeds and the reasons for entering into contracts as a deed. One core reason is that a contract entered into as a deed is a core exception to the requirement for consideration. A charity may want to create a legally enforceable agreement where there is no consideration (a grant). If an individual or a company approaches the charity offering a grant, either in the future or perhaps payable over time, having the grantor enter into a deed can protect the charity to ensure that the grantor does not back out of this offer. Without it being a deed, there is no consideration on the behalf of the charity and therefore it would not be a legally enforceable agreement (see paragraph 11.4 on page 391). Another situation when deeds are used to create a contractual agreement is in the signing of a non-disclosure agreement, which will often be drafted as a deed

2.5 Intention to create legal relations

In contract law, there must also be an intention to create legal relations for a contract to exist. In many contracts, the intention to create legal relations is expressly stated by the parties. However, in commercial contracts, the intention to create legal relations will often be implied. This is in contrast to domestic agreements, for example between parent and child, or husband and wife. In such agreements, the intention to create legal relations will not be implied and should therefore always be expressed if a contract is to be created.

2.6 Unenforceable contracts

A contract could be unenforceable because of a lack of consideration, or if it is *ultra vires* (see section 3.2 on page 380). There are also some contracts that the law will never enforce. These include:

- Illegal contracts: if the purpose of the contract is illegal or if performing it requires an illegal act, the courts will not enforce it.

- Contracts contrary to public policy.
- Unreasonable penalties: if a contract requires one of the parties to pay a penalty if he does not perform his obligations, should non-performance happen and the amount is regarded as unreasonable by the courts, the courts will not enforce the contract.
- Restraint of trade: the courts will not enforce a contract that prevents a person from earning a living. This covers situations when an employment contract may prevent a person from working for a specified time after employment, for example to prevent them working for a competitor. Such clauses can be upheld in limited circumstances, but the general rule is that the kind of contract that prevents a person from earning a living will be unenforceable.

3 Why is it important to have clarity regarding contracts?

3.1 Ensuring that the contract is entered into in written terms can help to ensure that there is clarity. A charity can enter into contracts for a variety of matters, from simple purchases to the employment of staff, the purchase of buildings and to managing ongoing business. It is vital that the charity has clarity regarding what contracts are in place and their terms and this is for a variety of reasons.

3.2 Ultra vires

3.2.1 A charity needs to ensure that it does not enter into a contract that is '*ultra vires*' (beyond its objects or powers). It is very important that the charity's objects and powers are understood and applied in this way. When a contract is entered into that is *ultra vires* there are a number of consequences. The first is that the trustees may face personal liability for breach of trust in having acted in this way and the charity would have an obligation to recover any losses from the trustees. The second is that the contract may not be valid. The Companies Act 2006 generally protects third parties in regard to *ultra vires* contracts and allows the contract to be upheld, but this protection does not apply in the same way to charitable companies as it does to commercial companies. Charitable companies are instead covered by s. 42 of the Companies Act 2006. This states that where a charitable company acts *ultra vires*, either by operating outside its objects or its powers, the contract is not enforceable by a third party unless they:

(a) did not know that the company was a charity; or
(b) gave full consideration and did not know that the contract was not permitted by the charity's constitution, or was beyond the powers of the trustees.

3.2.2 Also, where a charitable company transfers or grants an interest in property, the fact that the act was *ultra vires* does not does not affect the title of a person who 'subsequently acquires the property or any interest in it for full consideration without actual notice of any such circumstances affecting the validity of the act'.

3.2.3 It is important to note that the limited protection granted by the Companies Act 2006 applies for charitable companies only. In addition, whereas a commercial company can have *ultra vires* acts ratified by the members passing a special resolution, for a charitable company, this would also require the approval of the Charity Commission (as it would require a retrospective amendment of the objects).

3.3 Authority to enter into the contract

3.3.1 The charity needs to ensure that the person agreeing the contract on behalf of the charity (signing it) is properly authorised to do so (this authority must be delegated from the board). It can be a specific delegated authority, a general authority or, in some cases, an implied authority. An example of a specific delegated authority would be board approval to enter into that contract; a general authority may include a delegated authority to enter into contracts up to a certain value as long as they are included within the business plan; and an example of an implied authority can be a job description. Those entering into contracts must be clear that they have delegated authority to do so. Without such a delegation, the individual could be placing themselves at risk by acting without authority. For this reason, it would be better to ensure that the delegation is express rather than just implied. So, a contract of employment for a CEO may give the person authority to manage the day-to-day business of the charity and this would carry implied delegation; but it would be preferable if there was also a clear, express delegation minuted by the trustees and perhaps set out in a scheme of delegation. For example, this could state that the CEO had delegated authority to enter into contracts up to a certain value and/or in furtherance of the business plan agreed by the trustees.

3.3.2 It is important to make a distinction between acts that are beyond the capacity of the charity (and therefore *ultra vires*) and acts that are beyond the authority of the individual concerned, but not beyond the capacity of the charity. For example, if a charity's objects stated that it could provide a service only in Kent, a contract to provide that service in Sussex would be beyond its capacity and *ultra vires*. However, a new contract to provide the service in Kent could be entered into by a member of staff or a trustee, without any delegated authority from the board. This would be beyond the authority of the individual concerned, but not beyond the capacity of the charity. In such a case, the actions could be ratified by the charity. However, there is still a risk to the individual concerned that this will not happen and that they are acting beyond their powers. If the person is a trustee, they may be at risk of being in a breach of trust.

3.4 Name in which the contract is entered into

A simple matter that is often the cause of error is the name in which the contract is entered into. It is important to get this right as it can affect the validity of the contract and determine who is the contracting party. For example, a contract entered into in the name of an organisation that does not exist can effectively be being entered into by the person signing the contract. Two issues which often occur are:

- The charity's name is wrong: either its full and correct name not used, or a trading name is used without further reference to the full name. This sometimes arises in regard to branches, when the branch may have an informal regional name (for example, appending the name of its locality), but it is still a part of the charity. When a contract is entered into, it must be entered into in the full and correct name of the charity and not the branch's local name. Otherwise, there is a lack of clarity as to who the contracting party actually is. This can lead to a circumstance when the actual signatory becomes liable.
- Confusion as to whether the charity or a subsidiary is entering into a contract. When a charity has a trading subsidiary, some contracts will need to be entered into by that subsidiary, not the charity itself. This is important where these are non-charitable contracts that are likely to be *ultra vires* the charity itself. The staff and trustees need to remember and understand when the subsidiary should be acting as the contracting party and ensure that the contract is entered into in its name. Sometimes the existence of the subsidiary as a separate legal entity can be forgotten and the main charity's name used as a default.

3.5 Terms and conditions of the contract

Care needs to be taken to ensure that these are recognised, understood and agreed with. It may be beneficial for the charity to draw up its own standard terms and conditions (see section 7 on page 385). This can give clarity to authorised signatories about what is acceptable and provide a basis for written contracts.

4 Signing of contracts

Standard contracts will usually be signed by authorised signatories of the charity on the charity's behalf. It should be noted that where the charity is unincorporated, contracts cannot be entered into by the charity itself, in its own name, as it is not a legal entity. It is, therefore, either the members, or more usually the trustees, who are entering into the contract (whether it is the members or the trustees depends upon the legal type of unincorporated charity). Where the trustees are entering into the contract, this means that contracts should either be signed by the trustees or there should be a clear delegation to the signatory from the trustees enabling the signatory to sign, and it should be clearly stated in the contract that they are signing on behalf of the trustees.

5 Deeds

5.1 On occasions, charities will need to enter into contracts as deeds. It is important to understand what a deed is and the difference between a contract as a deed and other forms of contract. A deed is a signed (and sometimes a sealed) written legal instrument used to grant a right. Deeds have historically been entered into under seal. However, many organisations today choose not to have a seal and a deed can be created without one. There are two key reasons why a charity would want to enter into a contract as a deed:

- First, a deed differs from a simple contract in that it is enforceable without consideration. This could therefore be of significance if a charity wanted to ensure that a grant offered to it was legally binding. By asking the grantor to enter into the grant as a deed, they would therefore be committed to it.
- Second, a deed has a liability period, which is twice as long as that of a standard contract (the liability period is the period under which you can take legal action on the contract). Under contract law, a standard contract has a liability period that runs for six years, whereas a contract entered into as a deed has a liability period of 12 years. For this reason, it can be to the benefit of the organisation that is having work carried out (such as building work) to have the contract entered into as a deed. For the same reason, where the charity itself is to undertake the work and is asked to enter into the deed, it may want to consider whether it would be to its advantage to do so, as the liability period would be lengthened.

5.2 Many charities own a seal; however, many others do not. Deeds can now be entered into by an organisation in other ways than just by the affixing of a seal. The constitution often sets out the procedures for how the seal is used and who is authorised to sign under a seal. This will usually be a trustee and the secretary, or two trustees. However, it is also common for the governing document also to allow the board to appoint other signatories for the seal. This is one of the advantages of using a seal as a means of entering into deeds, as it means that persons who are not trustees can be authorised to do so. If a charity has to enter into a large number of deeds (as is often the case with registered providers of social housing) it can be beneficial to enable staff to sign on its behalf. Requiring every deed to be signed by one or two trustees can be difficult. With trustees being voluntary and therefore not available at the charity's main office on a regular basis, the board may take the view that it would rather delegate the signing of deeds to staff. The rules of executing a deed without the use of a seal are set out below, but it can be seen that this is restricted to trustees and the secretary. The use of a seal can therefore be beneficial for those charities that would prefer delegation to staff.

5.3 Unincorporated charities execute a deed by acting in accordance with the procedure laid down by their constitutions. This will usually require the signature of all trustees. However, under s. 333 of the Charities Act 2011, charity trustees of an unincorporated charity can confer authority on two or more of their number to execute documents in the names and on behalf of the trustees, for the purpose of giving effect to transactions to which the trustees are a party. This delegation can be either specific or general and should be recorded in the minutes of the board meeting. Without such a delegation, a deed will usually have to be signed by all the trustees. In addition, when the trustees of the charity change, the deed will need to be updated with the new trustees as signatories. The delegation under s. 333 of the Charities Act 2011 is therefore of great value to unincorporated charities.

5.4 A charitable company can enter into a deed by the affixing of its seal by the authorised officers, or by the document being declared as a deed and being signed by two trustees or one trustee and the secretary, or one trustee signing in the presence of a witness who attests the signature (Companies Act 2006). A deed, whether sealed or not, should be stated to be a deed to take effect in this way.

5.5 A CIO can also have a seal. Whether or not it has one, a document can take effect as if it is sealed if it is expressed, in whatever words, to be executed by the CIO and also signed by at least two trustees (except where the CIO has only one trustee, when it can be signed just by that trustee). The Charitable Incorporated Organisations (General) Regulations 2012 (SI 2002/3012) also state that a CIO may, by instrument executed as a deed, empower a person, either generally or in respect of specified matters, as its attorney to execute deeds or other documents on its behalf.

5.6 Other incorporated charities execute deeds in a similar way to a company. Although they are not governed by the Companies Act in the same way as charitable companies and so do not have the same flexibility, their constitution will usually provide for the use of a seal or state how deeds are entered into.

5.7 It is good practice to maintain a record of deeds and/or the use of the seal. The constitution may require the use of a seal to be reported back to each board meeting. If this is the case, the use of the seal should either be entered into the minutes, or if a register is used and circulated at the meeting, the register should be maintained as a subset of the minutes. The secretary of the charity may also consider it advisable to hold copies of all the deeds that are entered into or, at the very least, to have a record of where the originals are held.

5.8 Where a register is maintained, it can be a good idea to number the use of the seal. Whenever the seal is affixed the number should be written next to it.

The same number should then be entered on the register. The numbering is done simply on a continuous basis. This can make it easier to search for a record of a sealed document in the seal register. The register should normally give the date on which the seal is affixed, a short explanation of what it is for and sometimes the value and the names of the persons who signed the deed. If the original is not held by the secretary, it should also state where the original is held.

6 Electronic signatures

While substantive contracts should be in writing, in these times much of the communication about a contract can sometimes be done electronically by email. Often the contract will be exchanged and agreed informally in this way and then printed copies exchanged for signature. However, there is also provision for contracts to have electronic signatures. The Electronic Communications Act 2000 made provisions to facilitate the use of electronic communications and electronic data storage. An electronic signature is defined in s. 7(2) of the Electronic Communications Act 2000 (as amended by The Electronic Identification and Trust Services for Electronic Transactions Regulations 2016. It is anything in electronic form that:

(a) is incorporated into or otherwise logically associated with any electronic communication or electronic data; and
(b) purports to be used by the individual creating it to sign.

7 Standard terms and conditions

7.1 In many cases, a charity will enter into a contract on standard terms and conditions. Often, these are as provided by the other contracting party. However, there are a number of advantages in the charity developing its own standard terms and conditions:

- They can ensure that the small print is dealt with quickly and key points not neglected.
- They can place the charity in a stronger bargaining position.
- It can give clarity to staff in terms of what terms and conditions are acceptable to the charity.
- Where there are a number of similar contracts, it can ensure consistency.
- Standard terms and conditions can reduce legal costs. Standard contracts, or terms and conditions, can be drafted with legal advice and then used in a variety of settings.

7.2 Key features commonly covered by standard terms and conditions include the following:

- The jurisdiction that will apply (such as which country's law will be used?).
- Arbitration and how to deal with matters when there is a disagreement. This is a very good alternative to proceeding directly to court action. It can also reduce costs.
- *'Force majeure'* – how to deal with issues that arise that are outside the control of either party.
- Notices and communications – where they should be sent, in what form and how long after being sent they are regarded as having been received.
- Payment terms (when will payment be expected or made throughout the contract term?).
- Liability and indemnity – what liability is accepted and what indemnity will be provided? This can be an important means of limiting the risks to the charity.
- Transfer and assignment – can either party pass on their rights and obligations under the contract to another party and, if consent is needed, can it be upheld without good reason?
- Intellectual property – who owns the rights? This is a key point in contracts with people undertaking work for the charity. Often, charities do not realise that work written for them is usually the intellectual property of the contractor unless the contract says otherwise.
- Variation to the contract – how can it be varied? This should usually be in writing with the agreement of both parties.
- Clarity that this is the entire agreement ('what is not in this contract is not applicable').
- Termination clauses – how can the contract be ceased by either party?
- Confidentiality – often it is advisable to include a duty of confidentially regarding information that may be provided or shared under the contract.
- Data sharing – if the parties are sharing personal data, how this is managed.

7.3 Standard terms and conditions can be applicable even for a range of different contracts. However, if the charity is entering into a number of similar contracts it may also want to consider having an overall standard format. This can reduce costs and ensure a consistent approach. For example, if a charity contracts with a number of consultants it can be useful to use a common contract for all of them.

7.4 Implied terms

7.4.1 Even when a contract is clearly specified in writing, there can also be implied terms that will be held to apply to it. These can be implied by fact, by law and by custom.

7.4.2 Terms implied by fact

For a term to be implied by fact it must be obvious to both parties. It must also be clear that both parties (and not just one) would have agreed to its inclusion in the original contract if they had thought of it. Terms implied by fact are terms that are often needed just to make a contract workable.

7.4.3 Terms implied by law

These are terms that are implied regardless of the intent of the parties as a result of the application of common law or statute. Usually they are imposed to further public policy. Such terms can be implied to ensure that the parties treat each other fairly or to protect an economically weaker party. A key point to note in this regard is that the terms implied by law include terms that give an obligation of good faith and fair dealing between the parties of a contract. Another key implied term is that a person with ostensible authority to enter into the contract on behalf of the organisation is taken actually to have that authority. Therefore, the charity will usually be bound to a contract that has been entered into in such a way, even if authority had not been given.

7.4.4 Terms implied by custom

This relates to particular customs that relate to a particular trade and are known to and recognised by, the parties. While this may not be seen as applicable to charities, it should be noted that terms can also be implied by custom in circumstances where the parties have contracted with each other previously on a number of occasions and particular terms have usually applied in these past contracts.

8 Privity of contract

8.1 In any contract there will be two, or more, parties who agree to it and sign up to it. There will be the offeror and the offeree, or offerees. A key confusion arises as to the rights of anyone else under that contract. It is important to note that under English law no one other than one of the parties to the contract can acquire rights under it, or be subject to liabilities under it. The parties can agree that another party should be conferred a benefit, but that third party will never be able to enforce the contract or those benefits.

8.2 It is therefore very important that you identify from the beginning who needs to be a party to the contract. For example, if the contract is being entered into primarily by the trading subsidiary, but it is intended that it will also allow the use of the main charity's brand, the main charity will also need to be a party to the contract.

8.3 When a charity is working along with other organisations to deliver public services, the issue of privity of contract can be key. Are all of the providers entering into the contract and therefore sharing the liabilities as well as the benefits, or is the charity entering into the contract and then sub-contracting to the other bodies? If it is the latter, the charity will have all of the rights and liabilities of the contract. When considering entering into such arrangements, it is important to have regard to who the contracting parties are going to be. Often, the procurer may want only one other contracting party, even if the work is to be carried out by others (see below).

9 Assignment

The general principle is that a contract is not assignable (transferable) to a third party unless there is provision for this in the contract. An assignment is a transfer of the rights and obligations under the contract without the agreement of the other party. Often, when contracts are entered into, it is not envisaged that there will be any need for assignment, but this then arises at a later date. For example, if two charities were to merge the contract would need to be assigned to the new body. It is sometimes advisable to ensure that contracts have the facility for assignment. At the very least it is advisable to include a provision in the contract that consent to the assignment of the contract cannot be unreasonably withheld.

10 Non-performance under a contract

10.1 If there is a breach of a contract by the failure to perform an obligation, a number of remedies can apply. However, it should be noted that a breach of a contract does not always mean that the contract is terminated. In the worst-case scenario, the matter may need to be placed in the hands of the courts, although this should be avoided if possible. The options for remedies that are then available are:

- **Damages:** to pay compensation to the injured party for any losses incurred as a result of the breach. This could be as a direct, or indirect, result of the breach of contract. In some scenarios even if there are no actual losses nominal damages may sometimes be payable. While damages can be payable for losses that arise indirectly, such indirect losses will need to be foreseeable for damages to be payable. Another important point to note is that the injured party is under an obligation to mitigate the losses and not just to let them mount up.
- **Specific performance:** if there are no adequate damages and the breaching party still has it in his capacity to perform, then the court can order him to do so. However, specific performance is not granted as a right, as damages can be. It would always need to be ordered by the court.
- **Injunction:** this is the mirror image of specific performance, when instead of being ordered to do something, the breaching party is ordered not to do something.

- **Rescission:** if the breach of the contract is sufficiently serious, the injured party may have the right to escape from his own obligations under the contract. However, it is important to note that the right to terminate for breach does not arise in the case of every breach. In general, it only arises if the breach is fundamental to the contract (it lies at the heart of the agreement). Also note that the right to rescind can be waived and can be regarded as having been waived (for example, if the injured party insists on continued performance after he learned about the breach, they will be regarded as having waived the right to rescind).

10.2 These examples demonstrate that there are occasions when it is necessary to rely on the courts to deal with non-performance under a contract. Ideally, this should be avoided and this is a key reason why it is advisable to have a standard clause regarding arbitration in every contract.

10.3 Contracts checklist

1. Is the contract within the objects of the charity? The objects will be in the constitution of the charity. A contract that is outside the objects of the charity is *ultra vires*. For example, if the objects of the charity restrict its work to a particular locality and the contract is to undertake work in a different locality, it will be *ultra vires*.
2. Does the charity have the power to enter into the contract? In the constitution the statement of the objects is usually followed by statement of the powers that it has. These must also be complied with. A contract needs to fall within the powers. Again, check the constitution of the charity and see if there is a specific power. If there is not, you can also check if there a general power, that is 'To do anything else within the law which promotes or helps to promote the Objects'. If there is no specific or general power, in some instances there may be a statutory power, but advice should be sought.
3. Are there any special statutory requirements that need to be observed? For example, contracts for the sale of land, or entering into mortgages, are bound by the requirements of the Charities Act 2011.
4. Is there delegated authority to enter into the contract from the trustees? This can be either specific or general (see above). Delegation should be recorded in writing. In addition, is there any reason why the contract should be authorised by the board? This may be because it is of very high value, for a high-risk project, or because it is not part of the agreed business plan or in the normal course of business. Note also that the Charity Commission advises that all contracts for the sale of land should be considered by the full board.
5. Are the signatories properly authorised to sign on behalf of the charity? Even if the board has authorised the contract, is it being signed by the person who was given that delegated authority?

6. Is the contract a deed and should it be?
7. Is the contract in the correct name? Is the full and proper name of the charity being used? Should the contract actually be entered into by a subsidiary?
8. Are the parties to the contract correct? Is every organisation that should be a party to the contract actually a party to the contract?
9. Are the terms and conditions acceptable to the charity? If the other party has referred to their standard terms and conditions are these acceptable to the charity? If the charity has its own standard terms and conditions are these incorporated into or met by the contract?

11 Delivery of public services

11.1 The traditional image of a charity is that of an organisation that receives funding from donations and then determines what benefits or services that it wants to provide. However, many charities have provided services, under contract, for quite some time, and increasingly these days, charities are providing a range of public service under contract.

11.2 For many years, there was a debate about whether it was always within the scope of charity law to deliver public services. However, it is now established that there is no general legal prohibition on charities delivering public services. A charity can do this under a funding agreement with a public authority or it can use its own funds to do so. This is the case even if the public authority has a legal duty to provide the service. In regard to the funding of the service, a charity can directly subsidise public funds, provided the charity can show that this is for the benefit of the public. Therefore, in considering whether it can provide a public service the charity will only need to have regard to the following legal considerations:

- that the activities are within its objects and powers;
- that it will remain independent of government and other funders; and
- that the trustees will act only in the interests of the charity and its beneficiaries, and make decisions in accordance with their duties.

It should, however, be noted that the governing documents of some charities expressly forbid the charity to relieve or subsidise statutory funds.

11.3 Independence from the state

11.3.1 For a body to be a charity, it must be independent. It cannot exist for the purpose of implementing the policies of a public authority, or carrying out the directions of that authority. Further information on these requirements is set out in the Charity Commission publication *Independence Of Charities From The State* (RR7). Note that it is not enough that a body has a stated charitable purpose, the Charity Commission will look behind this. It will consider that such a body had been set up for the purpose of that public authority if:

- it is necessarily dependent upon it for funding;
- it receives that funding on terms that enable the public authority to make decisions about what services are to be provided and who is to benefit from those services; and
- in making those decisions, the public authority is able to pursue its own wishes and policies (without having a duty to act solely in the interests of the charity).

11.3.2 Within RR7, the Charity Commission sets out the characteristics that indicate that a charity is acting independently:

- it takes its own legal and financial advice;
- it draws up its own policies and business plan;
- it conducts arm's-length negotiations with the public authority;
- trustees who are subject to a conflict of interest do not participate in discussions;
- the funding arrangements preserve the trustees' fundamental discretions as to the selection of beneficiaries and the provision of services;
- the trustees do not commit themselves simply to giving effect to the policies and wishes of the public authority;
- the trustees do not agree to conditions that undermine the confidentiality of their discussions (such as the presence at their meetings of an observer from the public authority;
- the trustees have a choice about whether or not to accept funding on the terms proposed by the public authority; and
- the trustees are free to make their own decisions on matters outside the scope of the funding arrangement.

11.4 Grant or contract

11.4.1 When a charity provides funding for services, care needs to be taken to distinguish between whether there is a grant or a contract. One reason why this matters is tax. Charities do not pay VAT on grants they receive, but VAT may be charged if a charity is being paid to provide a service. It also matters in regard to the delivery of public services because of the possible application of the EU procurement regime. This relates to contracts for services but not to grants, and is implemented in the UK under the Public Contract Regulations 2006 (SI 2006/5). Finally, there are differences in how a grant and a contract are dealt with in accounting.

11.4.2 The essential difference is that a grant is a voluntary payment to further the charity's activities, whereas a contract is a legally binding agreement for the supply of goods or the performance of a service at a specified price. With a grant, the grantor will receive no direct benefit in return for the grant. With a contract, both parties seek something tangible. A grant will need to be used for the purposes for which it was given (and it may be repayable if never used) whereas unless the contract says otherwise, a surplus on a contract, after performance of the terms, may be retained by the charity.

11.5 Risks in the provision of public services

In 2012 the Charity Commission published a very useful document on the provision of public services by charities (*Charities and Public Service Delivery: An Introduction And Overview* (CC37)). This sets out all of the issues that trustees should consider, and lists a number of the risks involved. Some of the key risks include:

- **Underfunding**: this can occur in a number of different ways. It may just be the result of funding shortages and of the public authority's acceptance of the service being provided at a lower level than the charity wishes. Sometimes, it is affected by block funding, when the contract needs to accommodate more need than the charity at first envisaged. In seeking to win a tender, the charity may have either underbid or underestimated the cost of the service. Charities should know the full cost of any service they deliver or plan to deliver, in advance of tendering. While a charity may choose to subsidise a service from its own assets, this needs to be a conscious decision. The charity also needs to be clear that doing so is in its beneficiaries interests. Charities should expect full cost recovery whenever a public authority is purchasing a service from them, unless it has decided that it is in its beneficiaries' interests to provide a subsidy.
- **TUPE**: charities will need to be aware that taking over the provision of a service will usually also mean taking over the staff that previously provided that service. They will need to match existing terms and conditions, and often accept liabilities, including pension liabilities.
- **Objects drift**: it is fundamental that a charity remains within its objects. All aspects of the service that is bid for must fall within those objects. This is the case, even if the charity intends to sub-contract part of the service. So, for example, a charity whose objects are restricted it to operation in Essex could not bid for a contract that operated across Essex and Suffolk on the understanding that it would sub-contract the Suffolk services. As it would be the contractor, therefore primarily responsible for the service, that service needs to be within its objects.
- **Public authority duty**: charities that deliver services under contract on behalf of a public authority may be required under contractual terms to comply with certain legal duties, creating additional administrative requirements and costs (such as freedom of information).

- **Reputational risks**: charities should consider what effect providing public service under a contract could have on its image with donors. In particular, using donated income to fund the delivery of a service (or even the perception that this may be happening) can sometimes weaken the confidence donors have in a charity. There are also risks regarding poor service quality. These may relate to the level of funding provided by the public authority, or to linked services and therefore be outside the control of the charity.

11.6 Procurement of public service contracts

11.6.1 One of the main challenges in contracting to provide public services is the procurement processes that need to be followed. Procurement processes are governed by the Procurement Contracts Regulations 2015. These regulations implement the EU Directives on procurement. The impact of the regulations is that the procuring body must follow the procedures laid down when it is a 'contracting authority', the contract is a public works, services or supplies contract, and the estimated value of the contract (net of VAT) is above set financial thresholds. Contracting bodies include central government, local authorities, and other 'bodies governed by public law' such as registered social landlords and fire authorities.

11.6.2 When these procedures need to be followed, a tendering process can be quite long and involved, and a charity will need to commit time and resources to it. Detailed guidance on procurement and commissioning processes are available at www.gov.uk/guidance/public-sector-procurement-policy.

11.6.3 At the present time, with the prospect of Brexit, changes in the approach to public procurement remain a possibility. However, it should be noted that it is likely that the regulatory framework for public contracts will remain in place in the UK for the foreseeable future. EU Public Contract Regulations were passed into UK law in 2015 and will remain in place until they are repealed and replaced.

11.7 Working with other bodies

11.7.1 Increasingly, charities are acting in a collaborative way – coming together to bid for, and to take on, public service contracts. Many charities find that they are too small to bid for the contracts that are available. Commissioners are increasingly looking to work with prime contractors, with sub-contractors working below them. In addition to the increasing sizes of the contracts, sometimes it is easier to share the resource commitment required for a tender, and groups of charities can find it easier to meet the often onerous criteria. Charities are increasingly having to identify potential partners and to find mechanisms for working with them.

11.7.2 When charities work together, there are four basic models for their approach:

- **Loose network**: this is the simplest model and in this instance each charity would hold an individual contract but they would work together in informal ways. Although this seems the most straightforward approach, it is not favoured by commissioners, who would often prefer one overall contract.
- **Managing agent (or prime contractor)**: a contract management company holds the contract and then sub-contractors deliver to a range of providers.
- **Managing provider**: this is a very similar model to that of a managing agent, except that the managing provider will provide some of the services themselves, as well as sub-contracting.
- **Joint venture company or special purpose vehicle**: in this instance the charities group together and create a new legal entity, which they then collectively control and which holds the contract. That legal entity either provides the services directly, or, more commonly, sub-contracts to the charities.

D5
Serious incidents – management and reporting

1 Serious incidents

1.1 Things sometimes go wrong in charities, as they do in any type of organisation. How an incident is handled can have serious consequences for a charity. The reporting of incidents is also very important. The Charity Commission has required charities to report serious incidents for a number of years, but it was probably the case that until recently many charities did not pay full regard to this requirement. However, a number of safeguarding incidents in 2017 and 2018 drew attention to this matter. As well as some of the serious incidents that were reported to the Commission, there were a number of safeguarding allegations reported in the media about incidents affecting charity beneficiaries, workers and others. These highlighted the fact that some matters had previously been identified in a charity, but not reported through to the Charity Commission, and sometimes not fully reported to the Board. As a result, there have been a number of changes in how these matters are handled, and reporting to the Charity Commission has greatly increased.

1.2 The reporting of these safeguarding issues in 2017 resulted in the Charity Commission issuing a regulatory alert (regulatory advice under section 15(2) of the Charities Act 2011). In addition, the Charity Commission updated its guidance on reporting serious incidents in 2018.

1.3 There is now a much better understanding of the obligations on trustees, as well as a greater emphasis on trustees, awareness of serious incidents within the charity, and taking responsibility for the reporting of these incidents. There is also a much greater understanding of the need to report. In 2017 /18 2,819 serious incidents were reported to the Charity Commission, an increase on the 2,181 that were reported the previous year. It appears to be quite likely that this number will increase still further for 2018–19.

1.4 If a charity's income is over £25,000, it must, as part of the annual return, sign a declaration confirming there it has reported all serious incidents during the previous financial year that should have been reported. This means that until all serious incidents have been reported, the charity will not be able to complete the annual return. In addition, if trustees fail to report a serious incident that subsequently comes to light, the Commission may consider this to be a breach of their legal duties.

2 Safeguarding

This chapter is concerned with the managing and reporting of serious incidents. The need for safeguarding is broader that this, and is outside the realm of this book. However, it should be noted that the Charity Commission revised and reissued its safeguarding guidance in October 2018 and that this guidance sets out what a charity needs to do to protect people who come into contact with it from abuse or mistreatment of any kind (www.gov.uk/guidance/safeguarding-duties-for-charity-trustees). The requirements will depend on the nature of the charity and its work, but some of the expectations that the Charity Commission places on a charity, and its trustees, are to:

- ensure that all trustees, employees, volunteers and beneficiaries know about safeguarding;
- have appropriate policies and procedures in place;
- carry out checks to ensure that people are suitable to act in their roles;
- understand how to identify and report concerns;
- have clear systems for reporting as soon as concerns are suspected or identified; and
- manage and review risks.

3 What is meant by a serious incident

3.1 The Charity Commission defines serious incidents in its guidance (www.gov.uk/guidance/how-to-report-a-serious-incident-in-your-charity) as any adverse event (actual or alleged) which results in or risks significant:

- harm to the charity's beneficiaries, staff, volunteers or others who come into contact with the charity through its work
- loss of a charity's money or assets;
- damage to a charity's property; or
- harm to a charity's work or reputation.

The Charity Commission also stated that 'significant' should be interpreted in the context of the individual charity, taking account of its staff, operations, finances and/or reputation.

3.2 When a charity is considering how it will manage serious incidents, and how they will be reported both internally and externally, it may want to ensure that it also considers, and reviews 'near misses' – any event or incident that was averted, but which potentially could have been a serious incident. These types of event should be recorded and reviewed so that the charity can take action to ensure that their avoidance was not accidental and that any potential re-occurrence is prevented.

4 Managing serious incidents

4.1 It is important that a charity has clear systems in place for managing any serious incidents that occur. It should have an understanding of all potential risks that it faces and systems in place to protect its beneficiaries, volunteers and staff. Many charities will have a disaster recovery plan, but planning for serious incidents will usually be much broader than this. The plans will depend very much on the individual charity, so a small grant-making charity may just need a disaster recovery plan to cover any incidents that affect its office. However, a charity with vulnerable beneficiaries, or which works internationally, will need to have much more detailed processes in place.

4.2 All staff should have an understanding of what a serious incident is, and how it should be dealt with and reported. As well as a reporting mechanism, the charity should also have whistleblowing processes in place. Depending on the charity, it can be a good idea to have an Incident Reporting Form that is available to all staff.

4.3 Key elements in a plan

A charity should have a clear plan for dealing with incidents and this may cover the following points.

4.3.1 Immediate action

- One of the key issues if any incident occurs is ensuring that the immediate response is managed well. All staff need to know how to respond, and to feel that they can take responsibility. The immediate responsibility for managing an incident will usually rest with the most senior person present at the time the incident occurs, but this could be quite a junior member of staff. For this reason, all staff need to know what immediate steps to take, and who to report to.
- The first priority has to be to minimise further injury and protect health and safety. It is important that anyone affected receives any care required and that any further harm, loss or damage is prevented. In an emergency situation, the emergency services must be contacted.
- In some charities, depending on the services that they provide, there may be an out-of-hours on-call provision for senior managers, and if so they should

be contacted. Alternatively the staff member should contact the most relevant senior manager, the CEO or chair. The manager contacted should then take steps to set up a crisis management team – determining who is in charge of what.

- Once steps have been taken to protect health and safety and minimise injury, the team should assess any impact on service delivery, working out what has been affected.
- The charity should usually acknowledge the incident quickly, perhaps putting up a message on the website or notifying people via social media. There also needs to be clear communication with staff. They need to be informed if their work is affected; how ensure their own safety and what actions to take.

4.3.2 Next steps

- Once the immediate danger is dealt with, the charity will need to consider its business continuity – what is the full extent of the damage and what effect will it have on services? How will it affect service users? If services have been suspended, or stopped, what is the time frame for service recovery and what needs to be prioritised?
- The charity will need to consider what reporting of the serious incident is needed – to the Charity Commission and others (see below).
- A communication strategy should be developed, dealing with both internal and external communication. Managers should also ensure that the board is kept fully informed.

4.3.3 Long term

- The charity will need to consider the longer-term impact of the incident. Are there any longer-term implications for services or working arrangements and if so, how will they be handled? Has data been lost, and if so, what impact with this have?
- There will be a need for ongoing communications management. The charity will need to ensure that staff, beneficiaries, stakeholders and the public are kept informed.
- There will be a need to consider the longer-term impact on staff and service users. While people may have managed the incident very well, in the longer term there may be distress that needs to be recognised and dealt with appropriately. All staff affected by an incident will need to receive support and advice. Service users should also be offered appropriate support.
- The charity will need to reflect on the incident, and how it was managed. There should be some form of review or investigation – looking at what happened, and why; how it can be prevented from happening again; and how its management could have been improved. Inquiries should be conducted in a way that is supportive of staff and volunteers.

- If the incident was managed well, that needs to be recognised and staff/volunteers thanked for their efforts. Even if the management was not as good as it could have been, the efforts of staff and volunteers need to be recognised.

5 Reporting serious incidents

5.1 It is a requirement of regulation by the Charity Commission that a charity reports serious incidents to it. The Commission considers that it is the responsibility of the trustees to report serious incidents although the action can be delegated. The trustees may also delegate responsibility for deciding which incidents should be reported to others within the charity. However, it states that decisions made by others in the charity should be reported back to trustees (particularly where incidents were 'borderline' and making a report was considered but it was decided not to make one). It emphasises that if a charity decides not to make a report about something serious that has happened and it later becomes involved, the charity will need to be able to explain why it did not to report it at the time.

5.2 The Charity Commission provides guidance for charity trustees about serious incidents: (www.gov.uk/guidance/how-to-report-a-serious-incident-in-your-charity). It sets out what a serious incident is, and what should be reported. The main categories of reportable incident are:

- protecting people and safeguarding incidents – incidents that have resulted in or risk significant harm to beneficiaries and other people who come into contact with the charity through its work (see below);
- financial crimes – fraud, theft, cyber-crime and money laundering. There is no minimum loss figure that should be reported. The charity will need to decide whether the incident is serious enough to report, in the context of the charity and its income;
- large donations from an unknown or unverifiable source, or suspicious financial activity using the charity's funds;
- other significant financial loss;
- links to terrorism or extremism, including 'proscribed' (or banned) organisations, individuals subject to an asset freeze, or kidnapping of staff;
- other significant incidents, such as insolvency, forced withdrawal of banking services without an alternative, significant data breaches/losses or incidents involving partners that materially affect the charity; and
- any incident that involves actual or alleged criminal activity. Only in exceptional circumstances, such as where the crime and the impact on the charity are minor – for example. one-off theft of a very small amount of money, will the Commission consider an incident involving criminal activity is not reportable.

5.3 In its guidance, the Charity Commission provides a detailed example table that indicates the types of incidents that should and should not be reported.

5.4 Reporting safeguarding incidents

5.4.1 For those charities providing activities and services to children or adults at risk, the term safeguarding has a particular meaning under UK legislation and may require reporting of incidents to statutory safeguarding agencies. However, in regard to the reporting obligations to the Charity Commission, the Commission uses the term safeguarding in a broader way, referring to the range of measures in place to protect the people who come into contact with charities through their work from abuse and mistreatment of any kind (including neglect). The types of safeguarding incidents or risks that should to be reported to the Charity Commission are:

- incidents of abuse or mistreatment (alleged or actual) of beneficiaries which have resulted in or risk significant harm to them and:
  - this happened while they were under the care of the charity
  - someone connected with the charity, for example, a trustee, staff member or volunteer, was responsible for the abuse or mistreatment (alleged or actual);
- other incidents of abuse or mistreatment (alleged or actual) of people who come into contact with the charity through its work, which have resulted in or risk significant harm to them and are connected to the charity's activities;
- breaches of procedures or policies at the charity which have put people who come into contact with it through its work at significant risk of harm, including failure to carry out relevant vetting checks which would have identified that a person is disqualified in law from holding their position within the charity. This might be, for example, because they are disqualified under safeguarding legislation from working with children and/or adults at risk; and
- incidents in the workplace that have resulted in or risk significant harm to trustees, staff or volunteers.

5.4.2 If a charity becomes aware of a safeguarding incident that has occurred outside of the charity it would not normally be expected to report it to the Commission. However, a report would still be expected if it was found (or alleged) that the incident was not handled appropriately by the charity and this resulted in harm to the person or persons concerned. In addition, any safeguarding incidents that a charity becomes aware of should be reported to the police and local authority.

5.5 Reporting significant financial loss

5.5.1 A charity should report any significant financial loss that threatens the charity's ability to operate and serve its beneficiaries, or where the charity's financial reserves are not sufficient to cover the loss. The Charity Commission gives the following examples:

- significant fire, flood or storm damage destroying or seriously damaging the charity's main premises;
- having to abandon property – for example, in a war zone overseas;
- losing a court case and having to pay substantial legal fees or damages out of charity funds; charities incurring costs through routine litigation, undertaken in line with charitable aims and on behalf of beneficiaries, are not expected to report;
- loss of significant institutional donors, public funding or key delivery contracts that threatens the charity's ability to operate and being unable to replace these in order to ensure the charity's survival; and
- significant financial penalties for breaches or non-compliance imposed by HMRC, FCA, HSE, ICO, Fundraising Regulator or other regulators.

5.5.2 As a guide for this type of incident, the Commission states that it expects a charity to report any loss of funds or property with a value:

- totalling £25,000 or more; or
- totalling less than £25,000 but which is in excess of 20% of the charity's income.

However, while determining the type of financial loss that should be reported will usually be determined by the value of the loss, there are other factors that should be considered:

- If the person accused of taking the funds/assets is involved in the charity, particularly if they hold a senior position – for example, CEO or has responsibility for financial management, treasurer on board of trustees and so on.
- If the person accused is involved with other charities.
- If numerous incidents have taken place that appear connected, indicating a pattern or trend.
- If a single incident has been committed repeatedly over a long period of time.
- If a number of separate incidents have occurred over a short period of time.
- If the funds lost/at risk are from a public appeal, collection or grant funding.
- If there are signs of public interest, such as significant media reporting.
- If the charity has had to take serious action against an individual, such as disciplinary action, investigation or suspension.

5.5.3 The Commission stresses that a charity should be aware that a 'low value' incidents can pose serious risks as they could be a sign that individuals are trying to avoid detection. Therefore, if there have been repeated incidents of low value fraud, theft or cyber-crime in the charity, the Commission would expect them to be reported.

5.6 Reporting unverified or suspicious donations

A charity should act with due diligence and be mindful of donations to the charity from sources that cannot be verified, or that may be in breach of its duties under the Finance Act 2011. This means that a charity needs to ensure appropriate checks are made before accepting any unverified, anonymous or suspicious donations. The Charity Commission also suggests that, as a guide, a charity should report unverified or suspicious donations totalling £25,000 or more. However, it also reminds charities that in the case of donations under £25,000, they should use their own judgment to decide whether it should be reported, taking into account all the relevant factors. A charity should also report if it is concerned about other suspicious financial activity connected to the charity's funds. This could include requests from third parties to:

- cash a cheque for a large sum of money;
- convert large quantities of cash into another currency; or
- pay a fee to release funds to be donated to the charity.

5.7 Links to terrorism and extremism

A charity should report to the Commission if it becomes aware of any allegations or suspicions that:

- the charity has known or alleged links to a proscribed (banned) organisation or other terrorist/ unlawful activity;
- someone within or closely connected to the charity, or one of its delivery partners, is placed on a UK or international terrorist list or is subject to an asset freeze;
- charity funds or assets have been used to pay bribes, protection money or ransoms;
- charity funds or assets have been used/diverted (perhaps via a delivery partner) to support a terrorist group or for other terrorist purposes;
- the charity has been used to circumvent asset freezing measures; or
- charity personnel have been kidnapped or harmed by terrorist groups, including overseas, when representing the charity or carrying out charity work.

5.8 Other significant incidents

A charity should report to the Commission if:

- it discovers that a trustee or a senior manager of the charity is disqualified in law from holding that position;
- something has happened to force the charity into insolvency or to wind up – for example, unmanageable debts or reduced income streams;
- the charity's operations are threatened because its main or only bank has withdrawn banking services, and it cannot find another bank;

- the charity is subject to a police investigation or a significant investigation by another agency/regulator (it does not need to report routine inspections);
- the charity has experienced major governance problems, such as mass resignation of staff or trustees, or other events, leaving it unable to operate;
- the charity's trustees or employees are the subject of criminal proceedings, in connection with the charity or their roles;
- the charity discovers that there has been a significant data breach or loss within the charity; or
- the charity discovers that an incident has occurred involving one of the charity's partners in the UK or internationally, which materially affects the charity.

6 How to report to the Charity Commission

6.1 A report on a serious incident can usually be made via email (to RSI@charitycommission.gov.uk). The Charity Commission should be notified as soon as possible after the incident occurs. A charity should not wait until the matter has concluded, or all work on it carried out. The Charity Commission asks that it is given a clear picture of what happened and when, the extent of any loss or harm, how the matter is being dealt with and the possible next steps. If there are then any material changes to the facts that were reported, or any other significant developments, the Commission will need to be informed again and kept updated.

6.2 The Commission will then assess the nature and level of any risks and consider how their charity is dealing with the incident. Once the Commission has completed this assessment, it will let the charity know the outcome. It may ask for further information, but in the majority of cases reporting the incident will be sufficient.

6.3 The Commission recognises that some charities may need to report more incidents because of the scope and/or nature of their work, or the size of the charity. It therefore allows some charities to submit regular multiple ('bulk') reports, by agreement. When this has been agreed, the charity can submit reports on a periodic basis, rather than as they occur. However even if a charity has such an arrangements agreed with the Commission there may still be incidents that should be reported immediately. These will include:

- incidents that attract significant media attention that risks significant harm to the charity's reputation;
- incidents involving a significant risk to the charity's operations, money, assets, property or the people who come into contact with it through its work; and
- incidents that involve links to terrorism and extremism.

7 Other reporting

7.1 Reporting criminal activity

If an incident occurs that involves actual or alleged criminal activity then, as well as reporting it to the Charity Commission the charity will also need to report it to the relevant agencies. The Charity Commission advises on the following types of reporting:

- safeguarding incidents – the charity should report allegations or incidents of abuse or mistreatment of people who come into contact with it to the police; the local authority and other relevant agencies or regulators;
- fraud and cyber-crime – these should be reported to the police using the ActionFraud online reporting tool;
- allegations or incidents – these should be reported to the police;
- links to terrorism and extremism – these should be reported to the police. Not reporting such a crime, or allegation could be committing a criminal offence under Section 19 of the Terrorism Act 2000; and
- criminal activity overseas – these should be reported to the local law enforcement authorities and/or safeguarding organisations in the location where this occurred. There may also be circumstances where it is necessary to report this to UK authorities.

7.2 RIDDOR reporting

All deaths and all reportable incidents must be reported to the Health and Safety Executive if they arise from a work-related accident, including an act of physical violence to a worker. The list of reportable incidents can be found at www.hse.gov.uk/riddor/reportable-incidents.htm.

7.3 Depending on the work of the charity, there may also be regulatory requirements that require further reporting. For example, registered providers of social housing are expected to report to the Regulator of Social Housing on failures to meet certain of its regulatory standards.

SECTION E

The charity's assets

E1
Use of charitable assets

1 Introduction

1.1 Charity trustees have a general duty to use charitable funds and assets reasonably and only in furtherance of the charity's objects. They should also avoid undertaking activities that might place the charity's funds, assets or reputation at risk. Their primary concern must always be the interests of the charity. There are also special considerations for charity trustees when they wish to invest charity funds, buy and sell land, or borrow money.

1.2 This chapter reviews the types of assets which may be owned by a charity, and explains the various options that the trustees have when using these assets.

2 Funds

2.1 The Statement of Recommended Practice for Charities (SORP, Charity Commission, revised 2015) defines a fund as 'a pool of resources, held and maintained separately from other pools because of the circumstances in which the resources were originally received, or the way those resources are subsequently to be treated'.

2.2 The diagram below shows the different types of funds of charities:

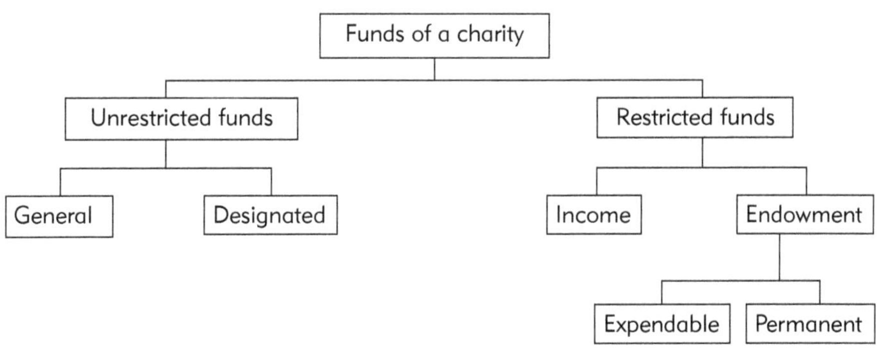

Figure E1.1: Different types of funds for a charity

2.3 Charity funds are either unrestricted or restricted funds.

2.4 Unrestricted funds

2.4.1 These funds have no restrictions placed on them by funders or donors and so may be spent at the discretion of the trustees in furtherance of the charity's objects. Any funds applied for purposes other than those set out in the governing document will be in breach of trust.

2.4.2 Trustees may decide to earmark part of the charity's unrestricted funds for a particular purpose (such as to purchase a property or to provide for redundancy costs). These funds are known as *designated funds.* Although designated funds are set aside for a specific purpose, the trustees have complete power to re-designate or to remove the designation altogether. For this reason, designated funds continue to be accounted for as part of the charity's unrestricted funds.

2.4.3 Some trustees have the power to declare specific trusts over unrestricted funds. If such a power is available and is exercised, the assets affected will form a restricted fund and the trustees' discretion to apply the fund will be legally restricted.

2.4.4 Non-designated unrestricted funds are usually placed in one general fund and may be used for any purpose allowed by the governing document.

2.5 Restricted funds

2.5.1 These funds may only be used for certain purposes as specified by the original funder or donor. This may include funds raised for a particular purpose via a public appeal (the donor has given money on the assumption that it will be used for a particular purpose). The purposes for which restricted funds are to be used must still be within the wider objects of the charity. Restricted funds may be restricted income funds or endowment (capital) funds.

2.5.2 Restricted income funds

These can be spent at the discretion of the trustees within the terms of the fund. Charity trustees will be in breach of trust if they spend restricted income funds otherwise than in accordance with the terms of the fund. This may also result in the funder or donor requesting that the income be returned to them.

2.5.3 Where a fixed asset is purchased with restricted funds, the treatment of the fixed asset will depend on the terms of the fund. In most cases, once the fixed asset is purchased the restrictions cease and the fixed asset may be used for any purpose within the charity's objects. The fixed asset therefore becomes part of unrestricted funds. It is important to note that the initial purchase of the asset must be within the terms of the restricted fund.

2.5.4 A separate designated fund is often created for capital assets to separate unrestricted income funds from unrestricted fixed assets. In other cases the terms of the restricted fund may indicate that once purchased the fixed asset may only be used for specific purposes and so it will remain in a restricted fund. Again, it makes sense to create a separate restricted fund for capital assets to separate them from restricted income funds. When a fixed asset is sold, the proceeds will form part of the fund in which the asset was held.

2.5.5 Unrestricted funds may be spent on the same purposes as restricted funds (for example, by spending more on a project for which a restricted grant has provided funding). In practice, therefore, unrestricted funds may be transferred to meet any overspending on a restricted fund.

2.5.6 *Endowment funds*

These are capital funds which are required to be invested, or retained for actual use, rather than expended. They are always regarded as restricted funds as by their very nature there is some kind of restriction over the use of the capital. The income from the capital fund may or may not be restricted depending on the terms of the fund.

2.5.7 *Permanent endowment funds*

These must be held indefinitely under the terms of the fund and may not be sold or otherwise converted into income. In some cases, there may be the ability to exchange an asset in a permanent endowment fund for another similar asset (such as investments in stocks and shares). In other cases (historic property, for example) the terms of the fund relate to a specific asset. Any expenses relating directly to the endowment should be taken out of the fund (such as investment management costs or valuation fees). However, costs relating to the generation of income from any land or property held in an endowment fund (rent collection or property repairs) would be charged against the relevant income fund. Usually any income generated from permanent endowment funds (such as rent or dividend income) may be treated as unrestricted income unless the terms of the endowment fund specify otherwise. Note that any income (from whatever source) that is spent on the maintenance or improvement of land or property held in a permanent endowment fund will become part of that fund.

2.5.8 It may be possible to spend the permanent endowment (convert it to income) if the trustees consider that it is in the best interests of the charity to do so. More details can be found in the next section on Orders and Schemes.

2.5.9 Expendable endowment funds

These may be converted into income at the discretion of the trustees. An example would include long-term investments held for the purpose of meeting property maintenance costs. In this case the trustees would need to manage the investments to ensure that sufficient income is generated at the right time and that the income is spent in accordance with the terms of the fund (which may mean that the income is placed into a restricted income fund). Note that, unlike income funds, the trustees are under no obligation to spend an expendable endowment fund.

2.5.10 Trustees may wish to consider using a *Total Return on Investment* approach for permanent endowment funds. This allows trustees to manage investments without the need to take account of whether the return is income (interest or dividends) or capital gains or losses. The entire return on investment may be spent at the discretion of the trustees, subject to certain accounting and reporting disclosures and subject to a duty to treat present and future beneficiaries fairly. On 1 January 2014, the Trusts (Capital and Income) Act 2013 came into force. Section 4 of this Act amended the Charities Act 2011 and gives permanently endowed charities in England and Wales the power to adopt a total return approach to investment. New charities may include the power to adopt this approach in their governing document.

3 Powers of the Charity Commission: Orders and Schemes

3.1 Trustees should regularly review their charity's governing document to ensure both that the objects continue to be practical and relevant to their beneficiaries' needs and that the charity's assets are being effectively applied. It is likely that, over time, circumstances and needs will change and that the governing document will need to be updated to reflect these changes.

3.2 Trustees have a number of options for making changes to their governing documents. The method used will depend on the type and size of charity, the changes they wish to make and any powers of amendment given to the trustees in the governing document.

3.3 If the power to amend the governing document is not available to the trustees, they may apply to the Charity Commission for a Scheme or an Order that authorises the trustees to make the changes.

3.4 All new model governing documents for charities should include a power of amendment and of dissolution.

3.5 Trustees' existing powers

3.5.1 Small unincorporated charities with incomes of £10,000 or less and with no designated land may change their objects and purposes by resolution even if there is no express power in the governing document allowing them to do this. The power to do this comes from s. 275 of the Charities Act 2011. Trustees must pass a resolution by at least two-thirds of those who vote. The charity must then send a copy of the resolution to the Charity Commission via an online form with the reasons for making the change. Unless the Charity Commission objects, requests further information or requires publicity to be given, the resolution will automatically take effect 60 days after the Charity Commission has received it.

3.5.2 If the charity's governing document contains a specific power to change the purposes and objects that is quicker and simpler than that described above, the trustees are free to use that power instead.

3.5.3 Larger unincorporated charities with an income of more than £10,000 can only change their objects and purposes if their governing document gives them the power to do so. If that power is available, the procedure to be followed will be laid out in the governing document. In all cases, a copy of the resolution making the change must be sent to the Charity Commission together with a copy of the revised governing document.

3.5.4 If the governing document does not give the trustees power to change the objects of the charity, they must apply to the Charity Commission for a Scheme.

3.5.5 All unincorporated charities have a statutory power to change the administrative procedures and powers of their charity. A resolution is required using whatever method is specified in the governing document for such resolutions, and a copy must be sent to the Charity Commission. Note that trustees cannot use this power to alter their charity's purposes, spend capital held as permanent endowment or authorise payments to themselves or to related parties. It should also not be used to amend powers that the trustees can only exercise with the consent of a third party unless the charity trustees have the agreement of the third party or the third party has ceased to exist.

3.5.6 Charitable companies have the power to amend their Articles of Association under company law, but prior written consent from the Charity Commission is required if the change is a 'regulated alteration'. Prior consent will also be required if the Articles of Association demand it.

3.5.7 Regulated alterations are changes to areas of fundamental importance as follows:

- any change to the objects clause;
- any change to what happens to the charity's property on winding up; and
- any change which authorises the directors or members to benefit from the charity's assets.

3.5.8 Once written consent has been obtained from the Charity Commission, the charity will need to pass a special resolution making the alteration. The charity must then send a signed copy of the resolution and a copy of the amended Articles of Association to both the Charity Commission and to Companies House within 15 days of the resolution being made. It should notify the Charity Commission of the change via an online form to which it can attach an updated copy of its articles.

3.5.9 For a charitable company, a change to the objects will generally only take effect from the date when it is registered with Companies House (and providing prior written consent was obtained from the Charity Commission). Therefore, a charitable company can only start operating under any new objects after this registration date.

3.5.10 Trustees of all registered charities must keep the Charity Commission informed of all changes to their governing document.

3.6 Charity Commission Orders

3.6.1 The Charity Commission may make an Order under s. 105 of the Charities Act 2011 to authorise trustees to carry out an act that they otherwise have no power to do. An Order is discretionary (i.e. trustees may choose whether or not to follow it), and will only be made if the Charity Commission believe it is in the best interests of the charity.

3.6.2 An Order is easier and quicker to put in place than a Scheme, and so should usually be applied for in preference to a Scheme. However, an Order cannot be used to:

- authorise the trustees to amend the purposes and objects of the charity;
- authorise the trustees to do anything that overrides an express prohibition in either an Act of Parliament or in the governing document (for example, if the governing document prohibits trustees from being paid); or
- impose duties or directions on the trustees that do not relate to the Powers given in the Order.

3.6.3 Examples of situations when Orders may be used include:

- obtaining the power to use a total return on investment approach for permanent endowment funds;

- authorising a specific transaction when trustees are faced with a conflict of interest (such as payment of trustees as long as it is not expressly prohibited);
- authorising a specific borrowing where there is no power to borrow in the governing document; and
- obtaining the power to spend certain permanent endowments when the statutory power is not available (see section 3.10 on page 417).

3.6.4 There is no formal application process for an Order. A request for it can be made from any person suitably authorised to apply on behalf of the charity's trustees. There is no general requirement for publicity to be given when an Order is made, however the Charity Commission can request this in certain circumstances. There is also no right of appeal and the Charity Commission may prefer to make a Scheme where it is important to preserve this right.

3.6.5 The Charity Commission may discharge an Order within 12 months of it being made if it was misled into making it. After 12 months have elapsed, the Charity Commission may set aside the authority using a Scheme, but the recall will not then affect the propriety of acts already done.

3.7 Charity Commission Schemes

3.7.1 A Scheme is a legal document made by the Charity Commission that amends, replaces or extends the governing document of a charity. It may affect the objects and purposes of a charity, the constitutional arrangements or the powers of trustees. Some Schemes will require trustees to carry out certain actions; others are discretionary, enabling them to take action if it is in the best interests of the charity. The Charity Commission will only offer a Scheme where no other method of changing a charity's governing document is available. Like an Order, a Scheme will only be made if it is in the best interests of the charity.

3.7.2 A Scheme is most likely to be used where:

- a larger unincorporated charity with income over £10,000 has no power to change the objects and purposes in their governing document;
- an unincorporated charity wishes to make changes that are expressly prohibited in their governing document;
- an unincorporated charity wishes to amend a power that can only be exercised with the consent of a third party and the third party is either not willing, or is unable, to consent to such a change; and
- the Charity Commission wishes to impose duties or directions on trustees.

3.7.3 Section 62 of the Charities Act 2011 sets out the circumstances when the Charity Commission can make a Scheme to change the objects of a charity. These are where:

(a) the original objects, in whole or in part have, as far as possible, been fulfilled or cannot be carried out in the way laid down in the governing document;
(b) the original objects provide a use for only part of the charity's property;
(c) two or more charities with similar objects want to merge but do not have the legal power to do so;
(d) the original purposes use outdated definitions of areas, places or classes of people;
(e) the original objects have subsequently been adequately provided for in other ways (for example, out of public funds); and
(f) the original objects are no longer charitable in law; or no longer provide a suitable and effective method of using the charity's assets.

3.7.4 The Charity Commission will apply the legal doctrine of *cy près* (Norman French for 'as close as possible to') in agreeing new objects or purposes. This means that they will take into consideration the spirit of the original objects and also current social and economic circumstances when considering cases that fall within s. 62(1)(c), (d) and (e).

3.7.5 The spirit of the original objects means the basic intention underlying the original objects as a whole. In deciding this, records from when the charity was established may be relevant, as may the way in which the charity has been administered and managed over the years.

3.7.6 The purpose of reviewing the current social and economic circumstances is to evaluate the ongoing usefulness of the charity and its current objects. The definition of social and economic circumstances is broad, and could include environmental, legal, scientific or technological considerations.

3.8 Applying for a Scheme

3.8.1 The most usual route is for the trustees of the charity to apply for a Scheme. Initially, the trustees should discuss their proposed changes with the Charity Commission and their own professional advisers. In potentially contentious cases, trustees should also consult on the changes with beneficiaries and other stakeholders.

3.8.2 The Charity Commission will then agree a broad outline of the Scheme before inviting the trustees to make a formal application.

3.8.3 The application should be made on one of the Charity Commission forms (CHY-ST1 (A) or CHY-ST1 (B)) by the trustees acting as a body. This means that either:

(a) the trustees resolve to authorise one or more people, who do not have to be trustees, to sign on their behalf; or
(b) all trustees (or a sufficient number of them to indicate that the decision has been properly taken) sign the application.

3.8.4 Option (a) is the most common approach and the Charity Commission will normally give advice on the precise wording of the resolution.

3.8.5 If trustees are unable to achieve a quorum, the Charity Commission may accept an application from whatever number of trustees they consider to be appropriate in the circumstances. This may occur if there are insufficient trustees in office or if one or more trustees are absent or incapacitated. If there are no trustees then the Charity Commission will appoint them.

3.8.6 In some circumstances, the Charity Commission may make a Scheme for the administration of a charity 'of their own motion' and no application from the trustees is needed. This would only usually happen where there is (or has been) misconduct or mismanagement in the administration of the charity and the Charity Commission wishes to protect the charity's property.

3.8.7 Alternatively, the Charity Commission may proceed with a Scheme if it deems it necessary but the charity trustees fail or refuse to apply. For this to happen, the charity must not be an exempt charity and it must have been established for more than 40 years.

3.8.8 The Charity Commission may also invite an application for a Scheme from the Attorney General when there is substantial public interest and no other method of obtaining jurisdiction is practicable. In exceptional circumstances, the Court may order a Scheme to be established.

3.9 The process for establishing a Scheme

3.9.1 The Charity Commission is responsible for the legal and practical effect of a Scheme and for deciding its final content. Once it has received a formal application, it will prepare a detailed draft of the Scheme and send it to trustees for their comments and agreement.

3.9.2 Where the scheme is likely to be non-controversial, publicity will not be required. However, in some circumstances, the Charity Commission may decide that publicity is necessary. It will then give public notice of the proposals and invite representations about them to be made within a period specified in the notice. Any comments and objections will be given due consideration and changes made to the Scheme as required. This stage can be avoided by trustees carrying out and evidencing adequate consultation at the start of the process.

3.9.3 The Scheme will then be brought into effect by sealing it. The Charity Commission publishes guidance on Orders and Schemes in the form of *Changing your Charity's Governing Document* (CC36). The Commission's internal operational guidance is also available on its website and this contains a multitude of guidance on Orders and Schemes.

3.9.4 Checklist: applying for a Scheme

Planning

1. Have the trustees identified what change is to be made?
2. Are the trustees aware of the contents of *Changing your Charity's Governing Document*?
3. Can the charity use alternative machinery to make the change (such as the Small Charities provisions, an existing power of amendment)?
4. Have the trustees discussed the change with professional advisers (solicitors and accountants)?
5. If the change is controversial, have beneficiaries and other stakeholders been consulted?
6. Have the proposed changes been discussed with the Charity Commission?
7. Has a broad outline of the Scheme been agreed with the Charity Commission?

Applying

8. Have the Charity Commission invited a formal application?
9. Is the charity quorate? If no, go to question 13.
10. Has a resolution been passed to authorise one or more people to sign the application on behalf of the trustees? If no, go to question 12.
11. Has the application form been completed and certified by the authorised applicant(s)? If yes, go to question 14.
12. Has the application form been completed and certified by a quorum of trustees? If yes, go to question 14. If no, the application cannot go ahead.
13. If the charity cannot apply for a scheme because there are insufficient trustees, will the Charity Commission accept an application from fewer trustees? (A no answer is rare, unless there are no trustees.)
14. Send the completed application form to the Charity Commission.

Establishing the scheme

15. Has the Charity Commission sent a draft of the Scheme to the trustees to be reviewed?
16. Have the trustees reviewed the draft and notified the Charity Commission of their approval (or any comments)?
17. Is the Charity Commission satisfied that publicity requirements have been met?
18. Has the Scheme been sealed and sent to the trustees for safekeeping?
19. Have any public notice requirements from the Charity Commission been met?

3.10 Spending permanent endowments

3.10.1 As mentioned earlier in this chapter, permanent endowment funds must be held indefinitely under the terms of the fund and may not be sold or otherwise converted into income. However, there will be cases where this is in the best interests of the charity. A statutory power exists to do this where the trustees decide that by using their charity's permanent endowment, as well as any income, it will be able to carry out its purposes more effectively.

3.10.2 The availability of the statutory power depends to a certain extent on the type of permanent endowment:

- **investment permanent endowment:** capital which is to be used to provide an income for the charity. The restriction on spending the capital is considered to be an administrative restriction; or
- **functional permanent endowment:** capital used for a specific purpose for the charity (such as historic buildings or village halls). The sale of the endowment and the use of the proceeds for a purpose other than the replacement of the endowment in question may involve a change of purpose.

3.10.3 The Charity Commission considers it unlikely that trustees will be able to use the statutory power for functional permanent endowments, as trustees are unlikely to be able to prove that the charity can carry out its purposes more effectively by disposing of the asset. In addition, the Charity Commission considers that the power does not apply to assets that do not generate an income as the capital must be used 'as well as any income'.

3.10.4 The way in which the statutory power is used depends on the size of the charity and the characteristics of the permanent endowment. A charity will be either a Type 1 charity, or a type 2 charity.

3.10.5 A Type 1 charity must have:

- an annual gross income of more than £1,000; and
- a permanent endowment consisting entirely of property that was entirely given (not created by the trustees) and has a market value of more than £10,000.

3.10.6 If any of the above conditions are not met, the charity will be a Type 2 charity.

3.10.7 Type 1 charities must get the approval of the Charity Commission before spending the permanent endowment. To do this, the trustees must pass a formal resolution that the permanent endowment restrictions should be removed from all or part of the fund concerned. A copy of the resolution and a statement of the reasons for passing it should then be sent to the Charity Commission via an online form, which has three months to make a decision. The decision will be based upon whether the proposal is in keeping with the spirit of the gift (the application of the legal doctrine of *cy-près*). The Charity Commission may request further information and/or public notice before making a decision.

3.10.8 Type 2 charities do not need the approval of the Charity Commission before spending the permanent endowment. The trustees are still required to pass a formal resolution that the permanent endowment restrictions should be removed from all or part of the fund concerned, but the endowment can be spent as soon as the resolution is in place.

3.10.9 Where the statutory power is not available, the Charity Commission may be able to authorise the trustees to spend the permanent endowment. If the Charity Commission is satisfied that it is in the best interests of the charity, it can remove an administrative restriction by making an Order under s. 105 of the Charities Act 2011. However, where there is a change of purpose and there is no power that allows the property to be used for the new purpose, the change can only be made by a Scheme.

3.10.10 The Charity Commission may decide that the permanent endowment can be spent, but that it must be replaced out of future income. This is usual when a charity needs to find extra money for, say, repairs or renovation costs.

3.10.11 A charity doesn't need the consent of the Charity Commission if the permanent endowment wasn't given to your charity - for example if the charity created the permanent endowment itself.

4 Financial management

4.1 Charity trustees must ensure that the charity's funds and assets are used appropriately, prudently, lawfully and in accordance with its objects. Proper financial management is the key to achieving this, and will ensure that the charity continues to be effective and remains solvent.

4.2 The core principles of financial management are as follows:

- creating an appropriate financial environment;
- understanding the current financial position; and
- looking forward: financial strategy and planning.

4.3 If an appropriate financial environment is created, the process of understanding the current financial position and planning for the future become easier. Similarly, it is very difficult to look forward without understanding the current financial position.

4.4 Creating an appropriate financial environment

4.4.1 Key aspects to consider when creating an appropriate financial environment will include:

- **Trustees**: the board of trustees should possess appropriate financial skills and be able to devote sufficient time to the financial management of the charity. All trustees, not just the treasurer (if there is one), are responsible for the financial stewardship of the charity. There should also be a clear delegation of responsibilities, whether to a treasurer, finance committee or staff.
- **Staff**: finance staff should possess the appropriate skills, capabilities and knowledge to carry out their responsibilities and duties. Any gaps may need to be addressed through recruitment and training. They should also have sufficient time to carry out their duties.
- **Accounting systems**: trustees are under a duty to ensure that the charity keeps proper books and records. Any accounting system must enable the trustees to understand the current financial position of the charity. For anything other than the smallest charity this will involve the use of IT and specialist accounting software.
- **Internal financial controls**: must be established to protect the assets of the charity and to apply them properly. This is discussed in more detail in the next chapter.
- **Risk management:** the trustees need to assess and understand the risks associated with the charity's financial management and manage them appropriately. Indeed, for larger charities the trustees' annual report should include a 'description of the principal risks and uncertainties facing the charity and its subsidiary undertakings, as identified by the charity trustees, together with a summary of their plans and strategies for managing those statement 'confirming that the major risks to which the charity is exposed, as identified by the trustees, have been reviewed and systems or procedures have been established to manage those risks' (SORP 201505, paragraph 1.4645).

4.4.2 Understanding the current financial position

Financial reports should be presented and considered by the trustees at regular trustee meetings. What needs to go into a financial report, and how should it be presented?

4.4.3 Many trustees and non-finance staff find charity accounts difficult to understand (and may be embarrassed to say so). It is therefore important to ensure that financial reports are clear, concise, easy to understand and presented with a narrative. Alternative means of presenting the information should be considered (such as graphs or a face-to-face presentation).

4.4.4 There is often no need for detailed financial information to be presented to trustees. Headline figures may be appropriate, as may the use of key performance indicators. Non-financial indicators should also be included (for example, the number of beneficiaries helped).

4.4.5 It is important that the information is presented in context (it is compared to something). For example, the actual results of the charity for a particular month may be compared to:

- the results for the month before;
- the results for the same month last year (or for the last two years);
- the budgeted results; or
- the performance of other charities in the same sector.

4.4.6 All financial reports should be up-to-date and accurate. Here the creation of an appropriate financial environment is crucial. Competent staff and appropriate financial controls will reduce the risk of errors. An efficient accounting system and a culture of up-to-date reporting will ensure a timely report.

4.4.7 Finally – and a point that is often overlooked – trustees need to receive the financial reports sufficiently in advance of the meeting to give them time to read and digest the contents.

4.5 Looking forward: financial strategy and planning

4.5.1 A financial strategy defines how a charity will get from its current financial position to the position it wishes to be in the future.

4.5.2 The desired future position will be determined by the charity's overall mission, objectives and strategy. It must also take account of any external or internal factors affecting the charity (i.e. loss of key staff, availability of future funding).

4.5.3 The strategy will include:

- whether the funds and assets of the charity are to be spent or retained for future use;
- what the funds and assets are to be spent on; and
- how any additional income is to be raised.

4.5.4 A financial strategy should include budgets and cash flow forecasts. The detail of the strategy will vary depending on how far forward it is forecasting. One might see detailed plans for the next 12 months, less detailed for years two and three and an overview for year four onwards. It should be updated on at least an annual basis.

4.5.5 Actual results should be monitored against budget to identify any potential problems or budget inaccuracies. Future budgets and forecasts may be updated on an ongoing basis to take account of changes in operating conditions. A tight cash situation may necessitate more detailed short-term planning than would otherwise be the case.

4.6 Investments

4.6.1 Most charities are able to invest, and investments can be a major source of funding. However, investing also exposes charities to risks which, if not properly managed, can affect not just the charity Itself but the public's trust and confidence in the sector more generally.

4.6.2 Trustees should look to invest any money not needed for immediate expenditure in order to generate extra income to fund future activities. This is referred to as 'financial investment'. Increasingly charities are also interested in how they can further their objects as well as achieving a financial return – this is known as 'programme related investment'. There is a wide range of investments available to charities, but first trustees need to ensure that they have the power to invest the charity's funds.

4.6.3 Section 3 of the Trustee Act 2000 gives trustees of unincorporated charities the power to invest charity funds in any kind of investment, excluding land, in which they could invest if they were the absolute owner of those funds. Section 8 of the same Act gives trustees the power to acquire as an investment freehold or leasehold land in the United Kingdom on the same basis as the power in s. 3. This is known as a general power of investment. In some cases, a charity's governing document may restrict or exclude this power.

4.6.4 Note that the Trustee Act 2000 does not authorise the purchase of land outside the UK. If charities wish to do this, they will need to seek some other kind of power.

4.6.5 Charitable companies usually have a similar power of investment in their governing document. A provision in a charitable company's Articles of Association to the effect that the powers of investment are those prescribed by law would normally give the general power of investment to the directors of the company.

4.6.6 As mentioned previously, charitable companies have the power to amend their Articles of Association under company law, with the prior consent of the Charity Commission required only if the change is a 'regulated alteration'. Therefore it will always be possible for a charitable company to add a power of investment to the governing document should one not already be there.

4.6.7 As mentioned in paragraph 3.5.5, all unincorporated charities (including CIOs) have a statutory power to change the administrative procedures and powers of their charity should the general power of investment be restricted or excluded.

4.6.8 Trustees' duties

Trustees have overall responsibility for the investment of a charity's funds, however they may decide to delegate day-to-day decisions to a third party. Trustees must take a prudent approach when managing a charity's investments and they also have a general duty of care, which means that they must use reasonable skill and care appropriate to their personal knowledge and experience. Therefore, a trustee who is experienced in investments, or who is being paid because of their specialist skills in this area, would be expected to exercise a higher level of skill and care.

4.6.9 Trustees also have specific legal duties in relation to financial investments:

- **Powers**: trustees must know and act within their charity's powers to invest.
- **Care and skill**: trustees must exercise care and skill when making investment decisions.
- **Suitability**: trustees must ensure that the investment is suitable for the charity's needs. This would include a consideration of the length of the investment, the exposure to risk, the balance of income versus capital as well as any ethical considerations.
- **Diversification**: trustees must ensure that the investment portfolio is suitably diversified to reduce the risk of losses.
- **Periodic review**: trustees must review the suitability and diversification of the investments on a regular basis (at least once a year).
- **Proper advice**: trustees must obtain proper advice from a suitably qualified adviser (who may be one of the trustees) before making any investments and when reviewing the investments. This advice is not required if the investment is so small that the advice would not be cost effective.
- **Investment policy**: trustees must explain their investment policy in the trustees' annual report.

4.6.10 The Charity Commission recommends that trustees should be particularly wary of speculative investments and invest only in markets where financial services are closely regulated and compensation schemes are in place.

4.6.11 Investment policy

Charity trustees are encouraged to create an investment policy, which should set out in writing what the charity's investment objectives are and how it intends to achieve them. It should specify the charity's attitude to risk and its approach to ethical investment. It should also consider how present and future activities are to be resourced. This policy should be recorded in writing and reviewed regularly. It should also be disclosed in the charity's annual report. Larger charities (those subject to statutory audit in their jurisdiction with incomes over £500,000) are also required to report on their investment performance against their policy in their annual report.

A charity's investment policy will usually include information on:

- the scope of its investment powers;
- the charity's investment objectives;
- the charity's attitude to risk;
- how much is available for investment, timing of returns and the charity's liquidity needs;
- the types of investment it wants to make which may include ethical considerations;
- who can take investment decisions;
- how investments will be managed; and
- reporting requirements for investment managers.

4.6.12 A charity's approach to ethical investment needs to be carefully thought out. Trustees have a duty to further the purposes of the charity, and it is generally considered that those purposes will be best served by obtaining the maximum return on investments. This duty is not always compatible with ethical investment. However, there are certain circumstances when a charity is justified in allowing their investment strategy to be governed by ethical considerations:

- where the investment would for practical (not moral) reasons conflict with the aims of the charity (for example, an environmental charity may not support a business known to pollute the environment);
- where the investment might hamper the charity's work, either by making potential beneficiaries less willing to be helped or by alienating supporters; and
- if the investment is morally unacceptable, a charity may reject it as long as this will not result in significant financial detriment due to underperformance as a result of the exclusion.

4.6.13 Any decision regarding ethical investments should be recorded in writing, after taking appropriate advice.

4.6.14 Incorporated charities may own investments in their own name as they have a legal identity. Unincorporated charities do not, however, have a legal identity and so cannot hold investments in their own name. Any investments owned by such charities will have to be held in the names of individuals, sometimes selected from the trustees, who are known as nominees or holding trustees. The charity may also select a custodian who looks after the title documents to the investments. Sometimes the role of custodian and nominee is combined.

4.6.15 Common types of investments include stocks and shares, unit trusts, bank deposits and land let with the intention of producing rental income. Any assets purchased with a view to sale will be treated as trading and so will not receive the usual tax relief offered to charities (examples include land or commodities).

4.6.16 Land may be a suitable investment for some charities, but it generally requires more active management and cannot be turned into cash as readily as other investments. It is also difficult to diversify investment in land unless the charity has a sufficiently wide and varied portfolio of other investments.

4.6.17 Charities have the option of investing in common investment funds (CIFs) and common deposit funds (CDFs) which are collective investment funds only available to charities. They comprise funds from many different charities that are pooled together and then spread across a variety of deposit takers (for CDFs) or stocks and shares (for CIFs). The investment return can be higher and the risk lower than if an individual charity had made its own investments. Both CIFs and CDFs are charities themselves and investment returns are therefore tax free. This is an attractive option for smaller charities for which it is not cost effective to appoint their own investment manager. Trustees must still fulfil their general investment duties as previously described and satisfy themselves that any CIF or CDF is suitable for the charity.

4.6.18 Larger charities may wish to delegate their investment management decisions to a delegated investment manager. Under trust law, trustees need an explicit authority to delegate these decisions, which for unincorporated charities will generally come from the Trustees Act 2000. Again, an incorporated charity will usually have the required powers in its governing document. All charities' governing documents should be checked for restrictions or exclusions.

4.6.19 The process of selecting an investment manager may not be delegated and trustees have a general duty of care when making this decision. They also have a number of specific duties when appointing an investment manager:

1. There must be an agreement with the investment manager in writing or evidenced in writing.

2. The trustees must prepare a policy statement which gives guidance to the investment manager as to how to manage the investments. This statement should again be in writing or evidenced in writing and its preparation cannot be delegated (but trustees may and should take proper advice regarding its preparation). The statement may include the following:
   (a) the charity's aims in investing its funds, including its position on risk;
   (b asset allocation strategy;
   (c) benchmarks and targets by which the investment manager will be judged;
   (d) the charity's stance on ethical investment;
   (e) the balance between capital growth and income generation; and/or
   (f) the scope of investment powers.
3. Trustees have a duty to review regularly the performance of the investment manager and the terms under which he is appointed.

4.6.20 Charities will generally be exempt from tax on all investment income. However, certain types of investment may be considered to be 'non-charitable expenditure' by HMRC, which may result in a restriction in tax relief. Charities need to be able to satisfy HMRC that any such investments are made for the financial benefit of the charity and not for the avoidance of tax, whether by the charity or another person.

4.6.21 The discussion of investments so far has assumed that the trustees' main reason for making an investment is to maximise their financial return. The primary aim of programme related investments (PRI) (or social investments) is to further the charitable objectives of the organisation – any financial return is a secondary consideration.

4.6.22 The Charities (Protection and Social Investment) Act 2016 introduced a statutory power for charities to make social investments. In making a PRI trustees are no bound by the legal framework for financial investment, because their decision is about applying assets directly in furtherance of the charity's aims. When making PRIs, trustees must ensure that the investment directly furthers the charity's aims, that any private benefit is incidental and that there is a way for the charity to end the investment.

4.6.23 The PRI should be expected to produce some financial return for the charity (but this is not the main reason for doing it). A PRI is different from a grant in that a grant is made to further a charity's aims with no expectation of a financial return.

4.6.24 A PRI can take a wide range of forms and can be made to charities and other forms of organisations. Examples would include small loans to organisations or individuals or large sums invested in complex social projects.

4.6.25 The Charity Commission has published guidance on investments in the form of *Charities and investment matters: a guide for trustees* (CC14), and gives more detailed guidance on its website.

4.7 Land and property

4.7.1 Acquiring land and property

Section 8 of the Trustee Act 2000 gives trustees of unincorporated charities (and CIOs) the power to acquire freehold or leasehold land in the United Kingdom to carry out the purposes of the charity or for investment. In some cases, a charity's governing document may restrict or exclude this power. Charitable companies usually have a similar power of investment in their governing document.

4.7.2 Note that the Trustee Act 2000 does not authorise the purchase of land or property outside the United Kingdom as an investment. If charities wish to do this, they will need to seek some other kind of power.

4.7.3 The trustees will need to obtain a s. 105 order from the Charity Commission if they wish to acquire land or property when they have no power to do so. This will also be necessary if they intend to use money held as permanent endowment or acquire land or property from a connected party.

4.7.4 Trustees have a statutory duty of care when acquiring land and property. This means that they must exercise such care and skill as is reasonable in the circumstances. A higher level of care and skill is expected when a trustee either has special knowledge and experience or is being paid to give advice in this area. Trustees must always act in the best interests of their charity.

4.7.5 Trustees also have a number of specific duties when acquiring land and property and need to ensure that:

- the charity has the necessary power or authority to acquire the land or property;
- the property is suitable for its intended use;
- the price or rent is fair and reasonable and represents best value for the charity;
- the terms of any lease are fair and reasonable;
- the charity can afford the purchase or rent;
- when acquiring a lease they understand the obligations to which they will be subject;
- on specialised matters, appropriate professional advisers should be consulted; and
- any necessary planning permission is obtained.

4.7.6 If the land or property is to be an investment, the specific duties outlined in the last section also apply.

4.7.7 The Charity Commission recommends that the trustees engage a qualified surveyor to prepare a report that includes the following:

- a description of the land or property;
- details of any planning permission needed;
- a valuation of the land or property;
- advice on the price the trustees ought to offer to pay, or on the maximum bid they should make at an auction;
- a description of any repairs or alterations needed and the estimated cost;
- a positive recommendation (with reasons) that it is in the interests of the charity to purchase the land or property; and
- anything else the surveyor thinks relevant, including a description of any restrictive or other covenants to which the land is subject.

4.7.8 It is expected that the trustees also engage the services of a solicitor.

4.7.9 Trustees may, in certain circumstances, acquire land and property with a mortgage. Further guidance on this is given in paragraph 4.8 on page 431.

4.7.10 As with investments, unincorporated charities cannot hold land or property in their own name. The land or property will need to be held in the names of holding trustees or nominees. It is also sometimes held in the name of all the trustees. Alternatively, charities may request the Official Custodian for Charities to hold the land or property on their behalf. This is a free service provided by the Charity Commission, which simplifies the ownership of the land or property and removes the need to make new deeds when the trustees change. It also removes the risk that the land or property is owned by trustees who are no longer connected to the charity and may be difficult to trace. The Official Custodian for Charities will not normally hold investments on behalf of charities.

4.7.11 Trustees are individually and jointly responsible for the protection, management and supervision of land and property. They should:

- retain control as a board rather than leaving matters to an individual;
- should act only in the interests of the charity and its beneficiaries; and
- act honestly and prudently and seek advice where necessary from independent professional advisers acting exclusively for the charity.

4.7.12 Disposing of land and property

The term 'disposal' covers all sales, leases, grants of rights, exchanges of land, and all other transactions in which trustees part with or grant and interest in their land *except* for the release of a rent charge and the granting of a mortgage. More details on the release of a rent charge can be found in the Charity Commission publication *Sales, Leases, Transfers or Mortgages: What Trustees Need to Know about Disposing of Charity Land* (CC28). The granting of a mortgage is covered in section 4.8 on borrowing (page 431).

4.7.13 There are a number of issues to be considered when trustees dispose of charity land or property:

1. Do the trustees have the power to make the disposal?
2. Is the disposal beneficial to the charity? Trustees need to be able to show why the disposal is in the best interest of the charity.
3. Does the charity own the title to the land?
4. Are the terms of the disposal the best that can be obtained for the charity?
5. Is consent from the Charity Commission required?

4.7.14 The Charity Commission expects any decisions regarding the disposal of land and property to be made by the board and not delegated.

4.7.15 The governing document of most charities will usually give trustees the power to dispose of land and property. The trustees should pay attention to any conditions in their governing document relating to the power. If there is no such power, trustees should be able to rely on the powers given in s. 6(1) of the Trusts of Land and Appointment of Trustees Act 1996. If the charity cannot rely on any of the above powers, it will need to contact the Charity Commission for an Order or a Scheme.

4.7.16 The following circumstances may not be covered by existing powers:

- converting permanent endowment into income (see section 3.10 on page 417); and
- the sale of designated land (land held on trust for the purposes of the charity) where the proceeds are not to be used to acquire land for a similar purpose a Charity Commission Scheme will usually be required to do this).

4.7.17 Trustees must always secure the best terms reasonably obtainable when they dispose of land and property. This usually means that they must accept the highest price offered, even if they find the purchaser objectionable. However, the trustees are not expected to accept an offer where they believe the purchaser will use the land in such a way that either will be directly contrary to the purposes of the charity, or will affect other land that the charity holds.

4.7.18 There may sometimes be other non-monetary reasons why a lower price will be more beneficial to the charity (for example, when land or property is being sold at less than market value to another charity with similar purposes). As long as the trustees have the power to make such a disposal and the disposal is furthering the objects of the charity, Charity Commission consent is not required.

4.7.19 Charity Commission consent is not required to dispose of land or property if the statutory requirements in s. 119 of the Charities Act 2011 are met. These are as follows.

1. Trustees must obtain and consider a written report on the proposed disposal from a qualified (RICS) surveyor instructed by the trustees and acting exclusively for the charity. The surveyor must also have ability in, and experience of, valuing land of the particular kind and in the particular area in question. The report must include amongst other things a valuation and advice on how best to sell the land or property. The exact contents of the report are laid down in the Charities (Qualified Surveyors' Reports) Regulations 1992 (SI 1992/2980).
2. Trustees must advertise the property in accordance with the surveyor's advice.
3. The trustees must satisfy themselves that the terms of the disposal are the best that can be reasonably obtained.
4. The person to whom the trustees are disposing the land is not a connected person.
5. These requirements are met before the trustees enter into an agreement for disposal.

4.7.20 The statutory requirements are slightly less onerous if the charity is granting a lease for seven years or less and does not receive a premium. Instead of appointing a qualified surveyor, the trustees may consider the advice of a person they 'reasonably believe to have the ability and experience to advise them competently on the granting of the lease'. They must still meet the last three requirements detailed above.

4.7.21 Charity Commission consent (via an Order) will therefore be required if any of the above requirements are not met. The most common reason for consent being needed is that a disposal is to a connected person (such as a trustee or employee, or a close relative thereof). Other possible reasons may include the cost of obtaining a surveyor's report being out of all proportion to the value of the transaction, or the land being in a remote area where it is not possible to find a surveyor with the requisite local knowledge.

4.7.22 Consent will also be required for designated land if there is a change in the trust purposes on which the land is held. This will be the case if replacement land is not purchased with the proceeds or retention of that specific piece of land is part of the trust. A Charity Commission Scheme will usually be required to provide new purposes for the charity. In addition, trustees are required to give public notice of their intention to dispose of designated land where no replacement land is being purchased. Further details of disposing of designated land can be found in the Charity Commission publication *Sales, Leases, Transfers or Mortgages: What Trustees Need to Know about Disposing of Charity Land* (CC28).

4.7.23 Section 122 of the Charities Act 2011 requires trustees to include certain statements and certificates in the contract or deed for the disposal of the land or property. First, the trustees must state:

- that the land is held by the charity or in trust for the charity; and
- whether the transaction is subject to the statutory requirements or whether the charity is exempt or whether the transaction comes within s. 117(3) of the Charities Act 2011.

4.7.24 Exempt transactions include:

- disposals given authority by an Act of Parliament;
- disposals to another charity at less than best price where the objects of the purchasing charity come within those of the disposing charity; and
- a lease to a beneficiary of the charity for less than best price.

In all of the above cases, a Charity Commission Order is not required and the trustees do not have to comply with the statutory requirements in s. 119 of the Charities Act 2011.

4.7.25 The trustees must also certify that:

- they have the power to make the disposal; and
- they have followed the correct procedures by either following the appropriate statutory requirements or obtaining the necessary consent from the Charity Commission.

4.7.26 If the statements or certificates are incorrect or have not been provided, the disposal will usually still be valid in the purchaser's favour unless the purchaser knew, or ought to have known, that the statements or certificates were incorrect.

4.7.27 If the disposal is to another charity, a further statement must be made to the effect that:

- the land disposed of will be held by or in trust for another charity;
- whether the receiving charity is an exempt charity; and
- if it is not an exempt charity, that the restrictions applied by s. 117 of the Charities Act regarding requirements for future disposals will apply unless such a disposal is excluded or exempt from these restrictions.

4.7.28 If the charity is unincorporated, any custodian or holding trustees (including the Official Custodian for Charities) must be party to the contract or deed for the disposal of the land or property. It is not necessary for all the trustees to sign the deed. Under s. 333 of the Charities Act 2011, two or more trustees can execute a document on behalf of the trustees if they have resolved that this can be done. The trustees should appoint a solicitor to ensure that the contract or deed is technically correct.

4.7.29 Sale of land checklist

- Has the decision to dispose of land been taken by the trustees acting together?
- Do the trustees have the power to dispose of land?
- Are the trustees able to justify why the disposal is in the best interests of the charity?
- Are the terms of the disposal the best that can be obtained for the charity? (not applicable if disposing to another charity.)
- Is consent from the Charity Commission required?
- Are the required statements under s. 122 of the Charities Act 2011 included in the contract or deed of disposal?
- Are any custodian or holding trustees party to the contract or deed of disposal?

Charity Commission consent is required if:

- the disposal is to a connected person;
- the surveyor is unable to recommend the terms of the transaction;
- the trustees do not wish to use a surveyor; the surveyor used is not qualified (as defined in the Charities Act 2011);
- the trustees fail to follow the statutory requirements before they enter into an agreement to dispose;
- the trustees do not have the power to dispose of land or property, or
- the land is designated land or held on permanent endowment, and replacement land is not purchased with the proceeds or retention of that specific piece of land is part of the trust.

4.8 Borrowing

4.8.1 Trustees may borrow money only if they have the power to do so. Normally this power would be expressly given in the charity's governing document. If the governing document does not contain such a power, there are a number of alternatives:

- Unincorporated charities may use the statutory power contained in the Trusts of Land and Appointment of Trustees Act 1996 and the Trustee Act 2000. This allows trustees to raise money by mortgage for the purposes of acquiring land and property or for the repair, maintenance and improvement of the land and property.
- Trustees may use the power of amendment in s. 280 of the Charities Act 2011 or the relevant power in the Companies Act to confer on the charity a power to borrow (with the consent of the Charity Commission).
- Trustees may apply to the Charity Commission for a s. 105 Order to authorise the borrowing.

4.8.2 If the governing document expressly prohibits borrowing, the trustees will need to apply to the Charity Commission for a Scheme.

4.8.3 Trustees do not require the consent of the Charity Commission to grant a mortgage over charity land as security for any purpose (including a loan, overdraft or grant) provided they have express power to do so and they meet the requirements laid down in s. 125 of the Charities Act 2011. These requirements are as follows:

1. Trustees must obtain and consider the advice of someone who they reasonably believe has sufficient ability in, and practical experience of, financial matters to give them sound advice. This person may be a trustee or employee of the charity, but must not have any financial interest in the loan or grant.
2. The adviser must provide the trustees with advice in writing on three matters:
   (a) whether the loan or grant is necessary in order for the trustees to be able to pursue the particular course of action in connection with which the loan or grant is sought;
   (b) whether the terms of the loan or grant are reasonable; and
   (c) the charity's ability to repay the loan or grant on the terms agreed with the lender.
3. The trustees must also provide statements and certificates in a similar way as when disposing of land. These statements must include:
   (a) that the land is held by or in trust for a charity;
   (b) whether the charity is an exempt charity and therefore the restrictions do not apply, or if it is exempt through one of the circumstances detailed in paragraph 4.8.5; or
   (c) if it is not exempt from the restrictions and is therefore subject to them.

   In addition, where the mortgage is subject to the restrictions, the trustees must certify either that:

(a) the Charity Commission or the Court have sanctioned the mortgage by an Order; or
(b) the trustees have the power under the trusts to grant the mortgage and that they have complied with the requirements in s. 1255 of the Charities Act 2011.

4.8.4 If the above requirements cannot be met, the trustees will need the consent of the Charity Commission before they create the mortgage.

4.8.5 The above requirements do not need to be followed where the express authority for the mortgage is contained in an Act of Parliament, a statutory instrument or a Charity Commission Scheme.

4.8.6 There are no longer any statutory controls over the mortgaging or charging of charity property other than land.

4.8.7 Trustees may also consider unsecured borrowing. The Charity Commission recommends that trustees always seek professional advice before taking out any substantial unsecured loans. It is also recommended that the trustees ensure that the charity has sufficient assets to repay the loan should the charity suffer a sudden loss of income.

4.8.8 For unincorporated charities, unsecured loans pose an additional risk to trustees, who are effectively borrowing the money in their own name. They will expect to be indemnified out of the charity's assets rather than having to repay the money personally. This indemnity will be secured by a charge on the whole of the charity's assets (under s. 30(2) of the Trustee Act 1925), but does not require compliance with s. 1245 of the Charities Act 2011 for it to be valid. Note that trustees will only be indemnified if they have acted properly in the administration of the charity, both when taking out the loan and when spending the money.

4.8.9 There has in the past been doubt over whether CIOs are able to take on secured borrowing, as the Charity Commission does not have the ability to maintain a register of charges over CIO property. For charitable companies, the register of charges is maintained by Companies House, and for unincorporated charities, the loans are effectively taken out in the trustees' own name. CIOs do have the legal capacity to give security over their borrowings and, where the security is over land, the usual public registration at HM Land Registry provides the appropriate protection for the lender and the usual public notice for third parties.

E2
Accounting and audit

1 Introduction

1.1 Charities have always needed to be accountable and transparent to the public, and the annual report and accounts is one way of achieving this. All trustees should use their annual reports and accounts to communicate with stakeholders and the wider public about their work – explaining the work their charities do and the achievements that result.

1.2 The accounting and auditing regulations for charities have never been straightforward, and often appear to be in a constant state of flux. A new SORP (Statement of Recommended Practice) was introduced in 2015 for periods starting on or after 1 January 2015, and this is the main source of guidance for preparing accounts for charities.

2 Annual report and accounts

2.1 All charities must prepare accounts and an annual report, and make them available on request. For registered charities with income above £25,000 per annum, the accounts and annual report must also be sent to the Charity Commission within 10 months of the financial year-end.

2.2 The annual report (or trustees' annual report) is an opportunity for the trustees to explain to funders, beneficiaries and other stakeholders what the charity is achieving. The accounts themselves are often not fully understood by stakeholders, which places more importance on the contents of the annual report. In addition, figures cannot show the impact of the charity's activities.

2.3 The basic contents of the trustees' annual report are the same for all registered charities. Larger charities (defined as those not requiring a statutory audit under charity law in their jurisdiction) are then required to give additional disclosures. The exact content of the trustees' annual report is given below. Note that the order of the information changed in the 2015 SORP.

2.4 Large charitable companies also need to pay heed to the additional reporting requirements in the Companies (Miscellaneous Reporting) Regulations 2018 relating to corporate governance. For this purpose, a large charity is defined as once meeting two out of the following three criteria:

- annual income above £36 million;
- balance sheet total above £18 million; and
- more than 250 employees.

2.5 Content of the trustees' annual report

1 Objectives and activities

All charities should include a summary of the charity's objects and the main activities undertaken in relation to those objects.

There should also be a public benefit statement, which must:

- explain the main activities undertaken to further the charity's purposes for the public benefit; and
- confirm whether the trustees have had regard to the Charity Commission's guidance on public benefit.

Larger charities should also include details of:

- its aims, including details of the issues it seeks to tackle and the changes or differences it seeks to make through its activities;
- how the achievement of its aims will further its legal purposes;
- its strategies for achieving its stated aims and objectives;
- the criteria or measures it uses to assess success in the reporting period;
- the significant activities undertaken explaining how they contribute to the achievement of its stated aims and objectives; and
- an explanation of the use the charity makes of social investment, volunteers and grant making.

2 Achievements and performance

The report must contain a summary of the main achievements of the charity and identify the difference the charity's work has made to its beneficiaries and, if practicable, the benefits to society as a whole.

Larger charities should also include a description of:

- the significant charitable activities undertaken;
- the achievements against objectives set;
- the performance of material fundraising activities against the fundraising objectives set;
- investment performance against the investment objectives set where material financial investments are held; and

- if material expenditure was incurred to raise income in the future, the report must explain the effect this expenditure has had, and is intended to have, on the net return from fundraising activities for both the reporting period and future periods.

3 Financial review

All charities should include:

- a review of the charity's financial position at the end of the reporting period;
- details of the policy it has for holding reserves including the amount of those reserves and why they are held;
- details of any uncertainties about the charity's ability to continue as a going concern; and
- details of any funds or subsidiaries materially in deficit and steps taken to eliminate the deficit.

Larger charities comment on the significant events that have affected the financial performance and financial position of the charity during the reporting period. In particular, the report must explain:

- the financial effect of significant events;
- where the charity holds material financial investments, the investment policy and objectives set;
- a description of the principal risks and uncertainties facing the charity and its
- subsidiary undertakings, as identified by the charity trustees, together with a
- summary of their plans and strategies for managing those risks; and
- any factors that are likely to affect the financial performance or position
- going forward.

The financial review for larger charities should also explain:

- the principal funding sources of the charity in the reporting period and how these resources support the key objectives of the charity;
- the impact, if any, of a material pension liability arising from obligations to a
- defined benefit pension scheme or pension asset on the financial position of the charity; and
- where the charity holds material financial investments, the extent (if any) to
- which it takes social, environmental or ethical considerations into account in its investment policy.

4 Plans for future periods

Larger charities should provide a summary of the charity's plans for the future, including its aims and objectives and details of any activities planned to achieve them.

5 Structure, governance and management

All charities should include details of:

- the nature of the governing document and how the charity is constituted (for example, as a limited company);
- the methods adopted for the recruitment and appointment of new trustees.

Larger charities should also include:

- the organisational structure of the charity and how decisions are made;
- the policies and procedures adopted for the induction and training of trustees;
- the arrangements for setting the pay and remuneration of the charity's key;
- management personnel and any benchmarks, parameters or criteria used in setting their pay;
- details of any wider networks; and
- details of any related parties or connected charities, including subsidiaries.

6 Reference and administrative details

The following details should be given:

- the name of the charity;
- the charity registration number;
- the company registration number (if applicable);
- the address of the principal office of the charity and, if a company, the registered office;
- the names of all charity trustees on the date the report was approved or who served as a trustee during the financial period in question; and
- the names of any trustee for the charity holding the title to property belonging to the charity.

Larger charities should also include:

- the name of the CEO or other senior staff member; and
- the name and address of any advisers (bankers, solicitors, accountants/ auditor).

Charities may withhold certain reference and administrative details where the disclosure of such information would place individuals in personal danger (such as in the case of women's refuges).

2.5 Some areas of the trustees' annual report are worth further discussion.

2.6 Public benefit statement

2.6.1 Trustees are required to give details in the annual report of how the charity is meeting the public benefit requirements. A lot of charities will find that this is being done already in the 'Objectives and Activities' and 'Achievements and

Performance' sections of the annual report, but it will be worth checking that it is clear how the aims of the charity are carried out, through the activities, for the public benefit.

2.6.2 Smaller charities are required to give a brief summary of the main activities undertaken to carry out the charity's aims for the public benefit.

2.6.3 Larger charities are required to provide a more detailed explanation of the significant activities undertaken in order to carry out the charity's aims for the public benefit.

2.6.4 When considering how to report on public benefit, trustees may wish to ask themselves the following questions:

- What are the identifiable benefits that arise from the charity's aims?
- How does the charity benefit the public or a section of the public?
- Are there any restrictions on who can benefit and are these restrictions reasonable (such as geographical restrictions or fee charging)?
- Are people in poverty excluded from the opportunity to benefit?
- Do the charity's aims cause any detriment or harm? If so, are these outweighed by the benefits?

2.6.5 Further guidance on reporting on public benefit can be found on the Charity Commission website (www.charity-commission.gov.uk).

2.7 Reserves policy

2.7.1 The Charity Commission has been stressing the importance of reserves policies for a number of years. Its concern has stemmed from the notion that charities raise money by fundraising for specific causes, but then do not spend the money on the advertised cause. Instead, the money is kept in reserve for times of hardship or when unexpected costs arise. It is perfectly acceptable for charities to keep some money in reserve – the question is, how much?

2.7.2 Trustees are required to set a reserves policy, which should include:

- the reasons why the charity needs reserves;
- what level (or range) of reserves the trustees believe the charity needs;
- what steps the charity is going to take to establish or maintain reserves at the agreed level (or range); and
- arrangements for monitoring and reviewing the policy.

2.7.3 In theory, the trustees may set target reserves at whatever level they feel is appropriate. However some funders may reject funding applications from charities with excessive reserves (typically more than 12 months' working capital in reserve) and also those with inadequate reserves (under two months' working capital in reserve). Those charities with high levels of reserves may be deemed not to require additional funding, while those with too little in reserve may be seen to be at risk of closing before the funding has had any impact.

2.7.4 An example of an acceptable reserves policy may include three to six months' working capital plus redundancy and other closure costs.

2.7.5 The definition of reserves is 'that part of a charity's income funds that is freely available'. This excludes:

- endowment funds (although some expendable endowments may be readily available for spending);
- restricted funds; and
- funds that can only be realised by disposing of fixed assets held for charity use and performance-related investments.

2.7.6 Designated funds would not normally be included in reserves, but trustees should ensure that the designated fund is created for a specific future need rather than for reducing reserves to an acceptable level.

2.7.7 Trustees are required to do the following in the financial review section of the annual report:

- describe their charity's reserves policy;
- explain why they hold or do not hold reserves;
- quantify and explain the purpose of any material designated funds, and where set aside for future expenditure, the likely timing of that expenditure; and
- give the level of reserves at the last day of the financial year to which the report relates.

2.7.8 Plenty of guidance has been published on the subject including the Charity Commission publications *Charities' Reserves – Building Resilience* (CC19).

3 Accounting requirements for charities

3.1 In England and Wales, the Charities Act 2011 provides the basic framework for charity accounting requirements for all charities. Unincorporated charities and (CIOs) with gross annual incomes of less than £250,000 may prepare receipts and payments accounts. All other charities, including *all* charitable companies, must prepare accruals accounts. Unincorporated charities or CIOs with incomes of less than £250,000 per annum may have to prepare accruals accounts if their constitution requires them to, or if the charity trustees have taken the decision to prepare accruals accounts.

3.2 In Scotland, the equivalent legislation is the Charities and Trustee Investment (Scotland) Act 2005 and the Charities Accounts (Scotland) Regulations 2006 (SSI 2006/218). These have since been amended by the Charities Accounts (Scotland) Amendment Regulations 2007 (SSI 2007/136) and the Charities Accounts (Scotland) Amendment Regulations 2010 (SSI 2010/287). Unincorporated charities with gross incomes of less than £250,000 per annum may prepare receipts and payments accounts. All other Scottish charities must prepare accruals accounts. Further details on the accounting requirements for Scottish charities can be found on the website of the Office of the Scottish Charity Regulator (www.oscr.org.uk).

3.3 The Charity Commission for Northern Ireland is the new independent regulator of charities in Northern Ireland. The Charities (Accounts and Reports) Regulations (Northern Ireland) 2015, relating to charity accounting and reporting commenced on 1 January 2016. The accounting requirements are the same as for England and Wales.

3.4 Exempt charities are not required to submit accounts and annual returns to the Charity Commission. They have been made exempt from direct regulation by the Commission because they are supervised by, or accountable to, another body or authority. The accounting requirements will be dependent on how such charities are constituted and any specific statutes or regulations applying to them. For example, an exempt charity constituted as a Community Benefit Society will need to apply legislation applicable to such societies. However, all exempt charities are expected to keep accounting records and prepare accounts. More guidance on exempt charities can be found in the Charity Commission publication *Exempt Charities* (CC23).

3.5 Excepted charities do not usually have to submit accounts to the Charity Commission (except on request). However, they are required to prepare accounts and are subject to the same audit and examination requirements as they would be if registered. They can be required under s. 168 of the Charities Act 2011 to prepare an annual report and submit it together with the accounts for the year. A charity is excepted if its income is £100,000 or less and it is a church, school, Scout and Guide group, or an armed forces charity. Once an excepted charity has registered with the Charity Commission, it must follow the same accounting requirements as any other registered charity. More guidance on excepted charities can be found on the Charity Commission website.

3.6 All UK charitable companies are subject to the requirements of the Companies Act 2006 and are required to prepare accruals accounts showing a true and fair view.

3.7 Gross income is defined by the Charities Act 2011 as being the total income received from all sources excluding gains from disposal or revaluation of fixed assets and investments, and excluding endowment income. However, it does include amounts transferred from endowment funds to income funds.

3.8 Receipts and payments accounts comprise a simple statement of money rcccived and money paid out during the year and a short assets and liabilities statement. There are not required to show a true and fair view. The Charity Commission provides a useful template in Microsoft Excel (*Receipts and Payments Accounts Pack* (CC16)). Note that charitable companies may not prepare receipts and payments accounts.

3.9 Accruals accounts are by definition prepared on the accruals basis (income is recognised in the accounts when it is earned, rather than when it is received). The accounts comprise a Statement of Financial Activities (SoFA), a balance sheet, a cash flow statement (for charities with income above £500,000) and supporting notes including accounting policies.

3.10 The exact contents and format of accruals accounts are governed by the latest SORP with the latest version dating from January 2015. The Charities (Accounts and Reports) Regulations 2008 (SI 2008/629) requires the SORP to be followed whenever accounts are prepared under the Charities Act 2011, unless a more specific SORP applies (such as for registered social landlords or higher and further education establishments).

4 SORP requirements

As mentioned above the SORP stipulates the contents and format of all charity accounts prepared under the accruals basis in the United Kingdom (including Scotland and Northern Ireland). It does not apply to accounts prepared under the receipts and payments basis.

5 Accounts structure

The SORP states that charity accruals accounts should comprise:

- SoFA which provides an analysis of a charity's income and expenditure and movement in funds in the reporting period;

- a balance sheet, which sets out a charity's assets and liabilities and retained funds at its reporting date;
- a statement of cash flows;
- for charities that are companies, an income and expenditure account included either within the SoFA or as a separate summary income and expenditure account in addition to the SoFA, where necessary to meet the reporting requirements of company law; and
- notes to the accounts that explain the accounting policies, provide more detail of how the income and expenditure is made up, and provide extra information about particular assets and liabilities, or about particular funds or transactions.

Source: Statement of Recommended Practice – Accounting and Reporting by Charities (revised 2015) (paragraph 26).

A cash flow statement is required for all charities with annual income above £500,000.

6 Statement of Financial Activities

6.1 A sample statement of financial activities (SoFA) is shown on page 448. The main requirements are as follows:

- If a charity has more than one fund, the SoFA should show, in columns, the income and expenditure for each different type of funds (unrestricted, restricted and endowment funds) as well as the total.
- Comparatives should be given for the previous period. Only the totals are required, not the analysis across the different funds.
- Category headings may be omitted where there are no figures for the current or previous accounting period.

6.2 Note that income and expenditure are analysed by activity and not by function (for example, 'costs of expenditure on charitable activities' and 'Expenditure on raising funds' rather than wages and rent). In addition, there is a clear link between the activities raising the income and the activities spending it.

6.3 Smaller charities do not have to analyse their income and expenditure by activity, but may choose their own headings, which may be on a functional basis. However, the Charity Commission encourages an activity-based approach wherever possible.

6.4 The activity headings should be analysed in more detail in the notes to the accounts so that the reader can understand the components making up the totals.

7 Income

7.1 Income should be analysed according to the activity that generated the income.

7.2 Income from donations and legacies includes all income given on a voluntary basis (without expectation of a return). This includes donations, legacies and gifts, and also grants of a general nature that are not conditional on delivering services or providing charitable goods. It may also include membership subscriptions where these amount to donations.

7.3 Income from charitable activities includes all income that is payment for goods and services provided in furtherance of the charity's aims. This includes performance-related grants and service level agreements. The notes to the accounts should analyse this total figure into the income receivable from each material charitable activity.

7.4 Income from other trading activities includes all income earned from both trading activities to raise funds for the charity and income from fundraising events.

7.5 Income from investments includes all income from investment assets (such as bank interest, rental income and dividend income). It will also include donations from subsidiary undertakings).

8 Recognition of income

8.1 One area that often causes confusion is the decision about when income should be recognised in the accounts. The SORP (paragraph 5.8) states that income should be recognised when the following three conditions are met:

1. Entitlement – control over the rights or other access to the economic benefit has passed to the charity.
2. Probable – it is more likely than not that the economic benefits associated with the transaction or gift will flow to the charity.
3. Measurement – the monetary value or amount of the income can be measured reliably and the costs incurred for the transaction and the costs to complete the transaction can be measured reliably.

8.2 In practice, charities are normally entitled to grant income when it is receivable; at this point the other two conditions are usually also met. It is therefore at this point that the grant income should be recognised in full in the accounts. There is a common misconception among charities that grant income can be deferred at the end of an accounting period if it has not been spent. This is not the case, unless the funder has specified a time period in which the expenditure of the resources can take place. The following examples illustrate this point.

Example 1

In January 2019, Partnership North East receives a grant from the National Lottery Community Fund of £60,000 to be spent at the charity's discretion by 31 December 2019. The charity has a financial year-end of 31 March 2019 at which point none of the grant income has been spent. How much of the grant income should be recognised in the accounts for the year ending 31 March 2019?

The charity has entitlement to the income in January 2019 and the timing of the expenditure is at the discretion of the charity. Therefore, the full £60,000 should be shown as income in the year ending 31 March 2019.

Example 2

Northshire County Council gives core funding to Partnership North East every year. On 28 March 2019 the Council gives the charity £45,000 and stipulates that this is the core funding for the 2019/2020 financial year (the money is to be spent in the period 1 April 2018 to 31 March 2019). How much of the grant income should be recognised in the accounts for the year ending 31 March 2019?

The charity is not entitled to the income until 1 April 2019, therefore the income should be deferred until that date. The receipt should be shown as deferred income (as a liability) in the accounts for the year ending 31 March 2019 and no income should be recognised.

8.3 Contractual income (the provision of goods and services) and performance-related grants should be recognised in the accounts to the extent that the charity has provided the goods and services.

8.4 Where income is given to acquire a fixed asset, or a fixed asset is donated, the charity will usually be entitled to the income when it is receivable. This means that the income should be recognised in full at that point and not deferred over the life of the asset.

9 Resources expended

9.1 Similarly resources expended should be analysed according to the activity that generated the income.

- **Expenditure on raising funds**: includes all expenditure incurred by a charity to raise funds for its charitable purposes. It includes the costs of all fundraising activities, events, non-charitable trading activities, the sale of donated goods and investment management costs.

- **Expenditure on charitable activities** includes all costs incurred by a charity in undertaking activities that further its charitable aims for the benefit of its beneficiaries, including those support costs and costs relating to the governance of the charity apportioned to charitable activities.

9.2 Expenditure should be allocated to activities on a reasonable, justifiable and consistent basis.

9.3 Expenditure is recognised in the accounts on an accruals basis as a liability is incurred (when there is a legal or constructive obligation committing the charity to the expenditure).

9.4 The notes to the accounts should provide a more detailed analysis of the costs incurred, with the costs of charitable activities being broken down into the different activities carried out by the charity as follows:

Activity	Direct costs £	Grant funding of activities £	Support costs £	Total £
Activity 1	95,000	–	20,000	115,000
Activity 2	40,000	3,000	10,000	53,000
Activity 3	20,000	–	10,000	30,000
Total	155,000	3,000	40,000	198,000

10 Grant funding

Grant payments are voluntary payments to a person or institution made by a charity in furtherance of its objects. Care should be taken to ensure that grant payments are recognised in the accounts where there is a legal or constructive obligation committing the charity to the expenditure. For example, if a charity makes a specific unconditional commitment to pay a grant of £1,000 per year for four years, the liability for the full four years of funding should be recognised immediately. If, however, the grant payment is conditional on, for example, an annual review of progress and the charity has some real discretion over future payments of the grant, only the first year of funding should be recognised as a liability in the first instance.

11 Support costs

11.1 Most charities will incur support costs. These are costs necessary to deliver an activity, but which do not directly produce the output of the charitable activity (e.g. administration, management, IT and accounting). Support costs should be allocated to charitable activities on a reasonable, justifiable and consistent basis. Examples of bases for apportionment include:

- usage (on the same basis as expenditure incurred directly in undertaking an activity);
- per capita (based on the number of people employed within an activity);
- floor area occupied by an activity; and
- time spent on an activity.

11.2 Where support costs are material, the notes to the accounts should explain how the costs have been allocated to the charitable activities.

12 Transfers

12.1 The transfer row of the SoFA should show the total funds transferred between the different types of funds. The notes to the accounts should give details of each material transfer between funds.

12.2 Other recognised gains and losses

This section of the SoFA will include:

- gains/(losses) on the revaluation of fixed assets; and
- actuarial gains or losses on defined benefit pension schemes.

13 Balance sheet

13.1 A sample balance sheet is shown on page 450. In practice, a charity's balance sheet is very similar to that for any other entity. It gives a snapshot of the charity's assets and liabilities at the end of its financial year and shows how the net assets (or liabilities) are split between different types of funds.

13.2 Assets and liabilities are generally shown in the accounts at the lower of cost and market value, but there are some important exceptions to this:

- fixed assets used by the charity will be shown in the accounts at either cost less depreciation or at current market value;
- investment assets must be shown in the accounts at market value; and

- heritage assets and contingent liabilities may not be shown in the balance sheet at all.

13.3 The balance sheet cannot therefore be used to give an up-to-date value of the charity's assets and liabilities. Instead, it is meant to show the resources available to the charity and whether these are freely available or have restricted use.

13.4 As with the SoFA, the balance sheet headings should be analysed in more detail in the notes to the accounts so that the reader can understand the components making up the totals.

PARTNERSHIP NORTH EAST
STATEMENT OF FINANCIAL ACTIVITIES (INCORPORATING THE INCOME AND EXPENDITURE ACCOUNT)
YEAR ENDED 31 MARCH 2019

	Note	Unrestricted funds	Restricted funds	Total funds 2014	Total funds 2013
		£	£	£	£
Incoming resources					
Incoming resources from generating funds:					
Voluntary income	2	700	8,436	9,136	20,505
Activities for generating funds	3	10,562	–	10,562	8,934
Investment income	4	2,789	–	2,789	1,553
Incoming resources from charitable activities	5	229,066	82,586	311,652	346,274
Total incoming resources		243,117	91,022	334,139	377,266
Resources expended					
Cost of generating funds:					
Cost of generating voluntary income	6	–	(1,396)	(1,396)	(2,731)

Fundraising trading: cost of goods sold and other costs	7	(4,296)	–	(4,296)	(3,051)
Investment management costs	8	(530)	–	(530)	(437)
Charitable activities	9	(219,510)	(97,571)	(317,081)	(351,162)
Governance costs	10	(2,957)	(891)	(3,848)	(3,126)
Total resources expended		(227,293)	(99,858)	(327,151)	(360,507)
Net (outgoing)/ incoming resources before transfers	11	15,824	(8,836)	6,988	16,759
Transfers					
Transfer between funds	12	1,832	(1,832)	–	–
Net (outgoing)/incoming resources before other recognised gains and losses		17,656	(10,668)	6,988	16,759
Other recognised gains/losses					
Gains on revaluation of fixed assets for charity's own use	13	35,000	–	35,000	–
Net movement in funds		52,656	(10,668)	41,988	16,759
Reconciliation of funds					
Total funds brought forward		11,624	31,409	43,033	26,274
Total funds carried forward		64,280	20,741	85,021	43,033

PARTNERSHIP NORTH EAST
BALANCE SHEET AS AT
31 MARCH 2019

		2019		2018
Note	£	£	£	£
Fixed assets				
Intangible assets	11		45,000	50,000
Tangible assets	12		12,691	10,169
Heritage assets	13		30,686	21,693
Investments	14		5,724	5,928
			94,101	87,790
Current assets				
Stocks	15	5,000		4,500
Debtors	16	12,953		3,159
Cash at bank		55,707		64,774
		73,660		72,433
Liabilities				
Creditors: amounts falling due within one year	17	(32,006)		(35,049)
Net current assets			41,654	37,384
Total assets less current liabilities			135,755	125,174
Creditors: amounts falling due after more than one year	18		(26,310)	(35,719)
Provisions for liabilities and charges	19		(4,592)	(3,829)
Net assets			104,853	85,626
Funds of the charity				
Endowment funds	20		5,724	5,928
Restricted income funds	21		5,448	3,465
Unrestricted income funds	22		5,304	(5,629)
Unrestricted capital funds	22		88,377	81,862
Total funds			104,853	85,626

13.5 Intangible fixed assets

13.5.1 Intangible fixed assets are defined in the SORP (para. 10/18) as non-monetary fixed assets that do not have physical substance but are identifiable and are controlled by the charity through custody or legal rights. Examples include goodwill, licences, franchises and quotas.

13.5.2 SORP 2015 requires purchased goodwill and intangible fixed assets to be capitalised on the balance sheet and amortised over their useful economic life. If the useful life cannot be estimated reliably, it is presumed to be no more than five years.

13.6 Tangible fixed assets

13.6.1 Tangible fixed assets must be measured initially on the balance sheet at their historical cost. All costs incurred to bring a tangible fixed asset into its intended working condition should be included in the measurement of cost.

13.6.2 If a fixed asset is donated to a charity, it should be included on the balance sheet at the value at the date of the gift.

13.6.3 Depreciation is the measure of wearing out or consuming an asset through use or the passage of time. All fixed assets (except freehold land) should be depreciated at rates appropriate to their useful economic life and the annual depreciation charge included as an expense in the SoFA. The only exceptions to this rule are freehold land, which need not be depreciated and cases where the depreciation is not material.

13.6.4 Where a charity chooses to include fixed assets at a valuation, the value must be updated on a regular basis (such as every five years) by a 'suitably qualified person', who may be a trustee or employee. Details of the valuer and the basis of the valuation must be disclosed in the accounts.

13.6.5 Note that if a charity includes one fixed asset in its accounts at a valuation, it must also revalue all the other fixed assets within that class of assets. The charity may define classes of fixed assets as it sees fit, within reason.

13.6.6 If the current value of a fixed asset is less than the cost less depreciation, it must be included in the balance sheet at the lower value (the current value). This process is known as impairment. The impairment loss should be included in the SoFA as additional depreciation.

13.7 Heritage assets

13.7.1 A heritage asset is defined in the SORP (para. 10.39) as a tangible asset or intangible asset with historic, artistic, scientific, technological, geophysical or environmental qualities that is held and maintained principally for its contribution to knowledge and culture. Examples include historic buildings, museums and areas of natural beauty or scientific interest.

13.7.2 Heritage assets must be recognised as an asset on a charity's balance sheet separately from other assets where practicable. Heritage assets are reported as a separate class of tangible fixed asset on the balance sheet and should be measured initially at either their cost or valuation if donated. They may continue to be carried at historical cost subject to any depreciation or impairment, or charities may choose to adopt a policy of valuation.

13.7.3 Heritage assets are often difficult to value and reliable cost information may not be available at a cost commensurate with the benefit to the users of accounts. In these situations, the assets may be excluded from the balance sheet although details of the assets must be given in the notes to the accounts.

13.7.4 Note that the assets are only classed as heritage assets if they are held to 'advance preservation, conservation and educational objectives of charities'. Where they are used for another purpose (for example, used as offices or rented out as an investment) they should be shown on the balance sheet as tangible fixed assets or investments.

13.8 Investments

13.8.1 Investment assets may be split into two categories:

1. Assets held for the sole purpose of generating income and capital appreciation. They may include investment properties rented out at market rent or a share portfolio.
2. Programme related investments which are made primarily to further the charity's objectives and not to generate the best financial return. These may include loans to beneficiaries at low interest rates, or social housing rented out at below market rent.

13.8.2 The first category should be included in the balance sheet at market value. Programme related investments should be included in the balance sheet at the amount invested less any impairment (such as bad debts).

13.9 Current assets

Current assets are usually shown in the balance sheet at the lower of cost and net realisable value.

13.10 Liabilities

13.10.1 Liabilities are usually shown in the balance sheet at their settlement value. They are split into those due within 12 months of the balance sheet dated and those due after more than 12 months.

13.10.2 A provision is 'a liability of uncertain timing or amount. It is recognised when a charity has a present obligation as a result of a past event, it is probable that a transfer of economic benefits will be required to settle to obligation and the amount can be reliably estimated'. The amount recognised in the balance sheet should be the best estimate of the expenditure required to settle the obligation at the balance sheet date. Where the expenditure is expected to be far enough into the future, the expected cost should be discounted to its present value.

13.10.3 If the expenditure is possible but not probable, or the amount cannot be reliably estimated, or the probability of the expenditure is unknown, the liability is classed as a 'contingent liability'. Contingent liabilities should not be shown on the balance sheet but should be disclosed in the notes to the accounts.

13.11 Notes to the accounts

13.11.1 In addition to a breakdown of the material items in the SoFA and the balance sheet, the notes to the accounts should disclose the following:

- **Accounting policies chosen by the charity**: specific policies that are required include the policy for including each type of material incoming resource, the policy for recognition of liabilities, the method of allocating costs between different activities, details of whether fixed assets are included at cost or valuation and the depreciation rates used and a description of the different types of funds.
- **Trustee remuneration and benefits**: detailed disclosures are required including the amount paid to each trustee. If no such payments have been made a statement is required to that effect.
- **Trustees' expenses**: the aggregate amount reimbursed to trustees should be disclosed, also the nature of the expenses and the number of trustees involved.
- **Staff costs and emoluments**: including the total staff costs (split into gross wages, employer's National Insurance and pension costs), number of employees and the number of staff earning more than £60,000 per year in bands of £10,000 from £60,000 upwards. If no staff are earning more than £60,000 a statement is required to that effect. Total remuneration paid to key management personnel must also be disclosed.
- **Related-party transactions**: disclosure is required of any transaction between the charity and a related party. Two parties are deemed to be related if one has direct or indirect control over the other, or they are subject to common control or one influences the other such that their own separate interests are inhibited. Related parties include all trustees, senior employees, charities under common control and those connected with them (such as members of the same household). Contracts of employment between the charity and employees do not need to be disclosed (unless the employee is also a trustee), nor do unconditional donations from related parties. Examples of transactions

which do need to be disclosed include the payment of trustees for the supply of any services, sale/purchase of assets to/from trustees and donations or grants made by the charity to trustees.

- **Particulars of individual funds**: including a description of the purpose of each fund and any restrictions imposed. Each fund should be analysed into component assets and liabilities (investments, fixed assets and net current liabilities) and funds in deficit should be separately disclosed.

13.11.2 Accounts for charitable companies

Charitable companies are required to prepare accounts which comply with both the SORP and company law. By following the SORP, most of the company law reporting requirements will normally be met, but there are a few areas that require further consideration.

13.11.3 Strictly, the directors of charitable companies in England and Wales must prepare both a directors' report and a trustees' annual report, but the Charity Commission is prepared to accept a directors' report instead of a trustees' annual report if it contains all the required information.

13.11.4 Under company law, all companies must include an income and expenditure account in their financial statements. The charities' SoFA is designed to include many of the items that would usually be found in an income and expenditure account, and so a separate statement is not always required. A separate income and expenditure account is required where unrealised gains and losses arise during the year (such as revaluation of investments) or there is movement on endowment funds.

13.11.5 Charitable companies must also separately disclose any revaluation reserve within the relevant funds section on the face of the balance sheet. A revaluation reserve will arise when fixed assets are revalued upwards and the reserve represents 'unrealised gains'.

13.11.6 Accounting timetables

It is sensible to draw up an accounting timetable in consultation with your finance staff, external auditor or examiner and the trustees. This will ensure that the accounts are completed on a timely basis and everyone involved knows when their contribution is required. Below is an example of a fairly leisurely accounting timetable for a charity with a year end of 31 March.

13.11.7 Sample accounting timetable

Partnership North East

Accounting timetable for the year ending 31 March 2019

February/March 2019 – Discussions with auditor about forthcoming audit and timetable.

31 March 2019 – Charity's financial year end. Stock take and cash count to be performed if applicable.

30 April 2019 – Accounting data is complete up to the year end and all reconciliations have been carried out. Management accounts produced for the trustees if applicable.

20 May 2019 – Trustees' annual report to be completed.

31 May 2019 – Statutory accounts completed.

June 2019 – Audit work commences.

31 July 2019 – Audit work is complete. The trustees and/or senior finance staff meet with auditor to discuss the audit and to agree any adjustments to the accounts.

August 2019 – Final accounts approved by trustees and sent to members prior to AGM if applicable.

September 2019 – AGM.

31 December 2019 – Accounts to be submitted to Companies House by this date.

31 January 2019 – Accounts to be submitted to Charity Commission by this date.

13.11.8 In practice, it will be difficult to progress the accounts during August and so they are unlikely to be approved until September, pushing the AGM back to October. This is a full six months after the year end and many charities do not wish to wait that long for their final accounts.

13.11.9 A common approach is to have the statutory accounts completed by mid-May and the audit complete by the end of June, giving the potential for an AGM in July. A faster timetable is possible with co-operation from the finance staff and auditor.

13.12 Timing for submission of reports and accounts

13.12.1 Accounts have to be submitted to the Charity Commission within 10 months of the charity's year end. For a charity with a year end of 31 March, this means submitting accounts by the following 31 January. The Charity Commission encourages charities to file earlier for reasons of public accountability and transparency.

13.12.2 Accounts for charitable companies need to be filed at Companies House within nine months of the year-end (31 December for a year end of 31 March). There are penalties for late filing at Companies House.

13.13 Accounting reference date

13.13.1 The accounting reference date (ARD) is the financial year end (the date to which accounts are prepared). Charities may choose their own accounting reference date. The most common ARDs are 31 December or 31 March. An ARD of 31 March ties in with most funders' reporting periods, making funding reports easier to compile.

13.13.2 Charitable companies will initially be allocated an accounting reference date by Companies House. This will be the first month end after the company was incorporated (for example, if the company is incorporated on 2 April the initial accounting reference date will be 30 April). Companies may change their accounting reference date once in any five-year period and the change must not result in an accounting period of longer than 18 months. The change must be registered at Companies House using online forms (www.companieshouse.gov.uk).

13.14 Requirement to keep accounting records

13.14.1 Charities are legally required to keep adequate accounting records.

13.14.2 For unincorporated charities the legal requirements are laid out in s. 137 of the 2011 Charities Act. Charity trustees are required to maintain accounting records which show and explain all the charity's transactions and which are sufficient to disclose at any time, with reasonable accuracy, the financial position of the charity at that time.

13.14.3 In particular, the accounting records should contain:

- entries showing from day-to-day all sums of money received and expended by the charity and the matters for which the receipt and expenditure takes place; and
- a record of the assets and liabilities of the charity.

13.14.4 The accounting records should be kept for at least six years from the end of the financial year to which they relate.

13.14.5 Company law requires charitable companies to keep accounting records which are 'sufficient to show and explain a company's transactions and to disclose (with reasonable accuracy) its financial position at any time'.

13.14.6 Company accounting records must contain:

- entries showing all money received and expended by the company; and
- a record of the assets and liabilities.

13.14.7 The requirements for charitable companies are therefore very similar to those for unincorporated charities.

14 Group accounts

14.1 Charities that have either charitable or non-charitable subsidiaries must prepare group accounts if the net annual income of the group is greater than £1,000,000.

14.2 The net income is the total income of the group less any intra-group transactions and other consolidation adjustments.

14.3 Group accounts do not need to be prepared by a charity that is itself the subsidiary of a charity. In addition, group accounts do not need to be prepared if:

- the results of the subsidiary undertaking(s) are not material to the group;
- the subsidiary is not a company and, by virtue of being a special trust or a charity subject to a uniting direction under s. 12 of the Charities Act 2011, has had its accounts aggregated with those of the parent charity;
- there are severe long-term restrictions which substantially hinder the exercise of the parent undertakings rights over the subsidiary undertaking's assets or management;
- the subsidiary is held only for sale; and
- the subsidiary undertaking is a registered company which is insolvent and is being wound up.

14.4 The purpose of consolidated accounts is to present a true and fair view of the state of the financial affairs of all the group interest of the reporting charity including its subsidiary undertakings. The principles and methods of consolidation are covered by Section 24 of SORP 2015. These principles should be applied irrespective of whether the parent charity and its subsidiaries are companies or otherwise constituted.

14.5 The basic principles of preparing group accounts are as follows:

- The consolidation should be carried out on a line-by-line basis.
- All intra-group transactions should be removed.
- Uniform group accounting policies should generally be used.
- The financial statements of the subsidiaries to be used in preparing the group

accounts should have the same financial year end as those for the parent charity.

- A subsidiary that is a charity with objects narrower than its parent will need to be accounted for by the use of one or more restricted funds in the group accounts.

14.6 Care should be taken to ensure that only subsidiary undertakings are consolidated in the group accounts. The definition of a subsidiary undertaking (as per SORP 20105) is as follows:

14.7 Definition of a subsidiary and parent undertaking

In relation to a charity, an undertaking is the parent of another undertaking, called a subsidiary undertaking, where the charity controls the subsidiary.

'Control' is the power to govern the financial and operating policies of an entity in order to obtain benefits from its activities.

Control is made up of two elements: power and benefit. The underlying principle is that the parent charity exercises control to obtain benefit from its interest in the subsidiary. The parent charity is deemed to exercise control over a subsidiary if it has both the power to govern and the ability to benefit.

The power element is presumed to exist when the parent charity owns, directly or indirectly through its subsidiaries, more than half the voting power of an entity.

However, control can also exist when the parent charity directly or indirectly controls half or less than half of the voting power of an entity.

14.8 Further guidance on the consolidation of subsidiary undertakings is given in section 24 of SORP 2015.

14.9 The SORP also gives guidance on accounting for associates, joint ventures and joint arrangements. An associate is defined as an undertaking in which a charity has a long-term participating interest and where the charity exercises significant influence over its operating and financial policy. For the avoidance of doubt, a charity holding 20% or more of the voting rights in another undertaking will be presumed to have a participating interest.

14.10 In a joint venture situation, a separate entity is jointly controlled by two or more undertakings, all of which have a say in the operations of the joint venture, so that no single investing undertaking controls the joint venture but all together can do so.

14.11 Charities may also undertake joint arrangements where they may carry out activities in partnership with other bodies but without establishing a separate legal entity.

14.12 Guidance on accounting for associates, joint ventures and joint arrangements can be found in sections 25, 28 and 29 of SORP 2015.

15 Audit requirements by size and type of charity

15.1 The financial thresholds for charities are subject to periodic review with the most recent changes following from the 2011 Charities Act. The current audit requirements are as follows:

Annual income	Incorporated	Unincorporated
<£25,000	No requirement	No requirement
> £25,000 and <£250,000	Independent examination	Independent examination
>£250,000 and <£500,000	Independent examination by an eligible person*	Independent examination by an eligible person*
>£500,000 or gross assets >£3.26 million and income >£250,000	Statutory audit	Statutory audit

* = As defined by the Charities Act 2011.
Note that the limits are based on the current year's income only and the reference to annual expenditure for unincorporated charities has been removed.

15.2 A statutory audit must be carried out by a registered auditor.

15.3 For all accounting periods, a charity's governing document may require an audit even if the regulations give the charity the option of an independent examination. In such cases, the trustees may wish to amend their governing document to bring the requirement for external scrutiny in line with statutory requirements. Trustees and members also have the right to request an audit.

16 Scottish and Northern Irish audit requirements

16.1 Scottish charities are subject to different audit requirements to charities registered in England and Wales, with an audit being required if gross income is over £500,000. An independent examination is required for all charities that do not require an audit. For charities preparing accruals accounts (which includes all charitable companies), the examiner must belong to a listed professional body. Charities preparing receipts and payments accounts may have their accounts independently examined by an appropriate person (someone who the trustees reasonably believe to have the requisite ability and practical experience to carry out a competent examination of the accounts).

16.2 Charities registered In Northern Ireland have similar audit requirements to Scottish charities with an audit being required once annual income is over £500,000 and an independent examination needed for all other charities.

17 Audit versus independent examination

17.1 Audit

17.1.1 An audit is a detailed review of a charity's activities, accounting systems, financial controls and financial statements with the aim of issuing an audit report stating that the financial statements show a 'true and fair' view and have been 'properly prepared' in accordance with the relevant accounting legislation.

17.1.2 The term 'true and fair' is often misunderstood, and the actual definition is that the accounts are not 'materially mis-stated'. An item is material if its inclusion or exclusion from the accounts would be likely to change a reader's view about the accounts. The auditor will set a materiality level at the start of each audit based on the size of the charity (usually approximately 1–2% of total income). This means that for a charity with total income of £500,000, materiality will be between £5,000 and £10,000. The audit report for this particular charity therefore states that the financial statements are correct to the nearest £5,000–£10,000. This is not quite the assurance that many trustees think they are paying for! Some transactions are of course material whatever their size – examples include transactions with trustees and breaches of trust, which require a higher degree of accountability.

17.2 An independent examination

17.2.1 An independent examination is a less onerous review of the charity's financial statements with the aim of issuing a report stating that nothing has come to the examiner's attention to make them believe that proper accounting records have not been kept or that the accounts have not been prepared in accordance with the relevant accounting legislation. This is known as negative assurance ('nothing has come to my attention') rather than the positive assurance given by the audit report ('these accounts show a true and fair view'). Nonetheless, an independent examination is a worthy alternative to an audit, especially given the cost savings involved.

17.2.2 An independent examination must be carried out by 'an independent person who is reasonably believed by the charity trustees to have the requisite ability and practical experience to carry out a competent examination of the accounts' (Charities Act 2011). For charities with gross income above £250,000, the Charities Act 2011 requires the independent examiner to be a member of one of the following accountancy bodies:

- Institute of Chartered Accountants in England and Wales;
- Institute of Chartered Accountants of Scotland;
- Institute of Chartered Accountants in Ireland;
- Association of Chartered Certified Accountants;
- Association of Authorised Public Accountants;
- Association of Accounting Technicians;
- Association of International Accountants;
- Chartered Institute of Management Accountants;
- Institute of Chartered Secretaries and Administrators;
- Chartered Institute of Public Finance and Accountancy; or
- A Fellow of the Association of Charity Independent Examiners;.
- Institute of Financial Accountants, or
- Certified Public Accountants Association.

18 Role of external auditors

18.1 The audit of a charity is an audit of stewardship. The emphasis is on transparency and accountability to all stakeholders including beneficiaries, funders and employees, who will wish to be reassured that the charity is using its resources efficiently and effectively.

18.2 The role of the auditor is therefore more than just issuing an audit report to state that the accounts show a true and fair view. Typically, a charity audit will include the following:

(a) A pre-audit meeting to discuss any significant changes to the charity during the year (such as changes in activities, accounting systems, finance staff or legislation) and the audit/accounting timetable). It is important to agree at this stage such things as the expected audit fee and whether the auditor or the charity's finance staff will prepare the statutory accounts.
(b) Obtaining an understanding of the charity, its activities and the environment in which it operates.
(c) A detailed review of the accounting system and internal financial controls. The auditor will identify any weaknesses in the system and should recommend improvements via the management letter (see below).

(d) A consideration of the risks facing the charity including the risk of fraud. The auditor will ask management and trustees whether they have any knowledge of suspected or actual fraud affecting the charity.
(e) A consideration of the laws and regulations facing the charity where non-compliance may materially affect the financial statements. Any instances of non-compliance should be reported to trustees as soon as practicable. The auditor is required to report any knowledge or suspicion of money-laundering offences to the Serious Organised Crime Agency (SOCA). The auditor also has a statutory duty to report to the Charity Commission (or the OSCR in Scotland) any matters which may be of material significance to the regulator.
(f) A review of management's assessment of whether the charity is a 'going concern'. The management of a charity are expected to consider at least the next 12 months and ideally further into the future when considering the viability of the charity.
(g) An assessment of the risks of material misstatement from the above information and then planning the audit so as to reduce this risk to an acceptably low level. Detailed audit work will then be performed in accordance with this plan.
(h) Obtaining written confirmations (management representations) from trustees where oral statements made cannot be verified by other audit evidence. This usually includes confirmation that the trustees believe the charity to be a going concern, that there are no undisclosed instances of non-compliance with laws and regulations and that all information has been made available to the auditors.
(i) Communicating audit matters of governance interest arising from the audit to the trustees of the charity. This would usually take the form of a written management letter and a post-audit meeting. The management letter would usually contain matters such as any weaknesses identified in the accounting system and financial controls, any errors identified in the financial statements, non-compliance with laws and regulations and any suspicion of fraud.
(j) Issuing an audit report that contains a clear expression of opinion on the financial statements. An 'unqualified' or 'clean' audit report will state that:
  - give a true and fair view of the state of the charity's affairs as at 31 March 2019 and of its incoming resources and application of resources, including its income and expenditure, for the year then ended;
  - have been properly prepared in accordance with UK Generally Accepted Accounting Principles; and
  - have been prepared in accordance with the requirements of the Companies Act 2006 (or Charities Act 2011).

18.3 A 'qualified' audit report may state that the financial statements do not show a true and fair view (disagreement) or that the auditor is unable to tell whether the financial statements show a true and fair view (limitation in audit scope). These qualifications may refer to the financial statements as a whole or, more usually, to a particular area of the financial statements.

18.4 The auditor is also required to state in the audit report if:

- the charity has failed to keep accounting records in accordance with the relevant Act;
- the accounts are not in agreement with the accounting records;
- necessary information and explanations have not been made available to them;
- the required disclosures relating to trustees' remuneration have not been made;
- there are any concerns over the disclosures made relating to the going concern of the charity; or
- the information in the trustees' report is inconsistent with the accounts or the trustees' report is not prepared in accordance with legal requirements.

18.5 To get the most out of an audit, a charity should seek an auditor who not only is independent, but also shows empathy with and knowledge of the charity sector. A charity audit is very different from a commercial audit and experience in one does not also imply experience in the other. Ideally, there should be informal communication between the auditor and charity trustees or management throughout the year and also throughout the audit, rather than just the formal meetings at the start and finish of the audit work.

18.6 It is good practice to review auditors every three to five years to ensure the best possible service is being provided.

19 Appointment of auditors

19.1 A potential auditor must be a member of a recognised supervisory body and be eligible for appointment under the rules of that body. This means that the auditor is regulated by the appropriate institute, has standards that they must follow, has fit and proper status, professional integrity, independence, up-to-date technical standards and procedures for maintaining competence.

19.2 Generally, an auditor must be appointed or reappointed each financial year. In an unincorporated charity, this is done by the trustees of the charity, but in a charitable company, the annual reappointment must be made by a resolution of the members. This resolution may be passed at the meeting at which the immediately preceding years accounts are laid before the members or by written resolution. The trustees of a charitable company are, however, able to appoint the first auditor of the charity.

19.3 If the auditor is not reappointed by a resolution of the members, the auditor remains in office until the members pass a resolution to reappoint them or to remove them as auditor (5% of members, or fewer if the Articles say so, can force the consideration of a resolution to remove an auditor). This provision about remaining in office, however, does not apply if the auditor's most recent appointment was by the trustees, or the charity's Articles require an annual appointment.

20 Removal and resignation of auditors

20.1 An auditor may resign by giving notice to the charity trustees. They can also be removed from office at any time during their term of office, or they might not be reappointed for a further term. Usually most auditors resign, then a new auditor is appointed. This will be reported to the AGM. The auditors of unincorporated charities may be removed by the trustees, but an auditor of a charitable company will need to be removed by a resolution of the members. A charitable company must send a copy of the notice of the intended resolution to the auditor, who then has the right to make a written response asking that the charity sends to the notice of the intended resolution to its members. to the auditor also has the right to speak at the meeting where the resolution is to be considered.

20.2 When an auditor ceases to hold office (for whatever reason), they must deposit at the charity's registered office a statement of the circumstances connected with their ceasing to hold office, unless they consider that there are no such circumstances that need to be brought to the attention of the members and trustees. If there are no circumstances that need to be brought to the attention of the members and trustees, the auditor must deposit a statement to that effect.

20.3 When the auditor deposits a statement of circumstances connected with their ceasing to hold office, the charity must within 14 days either: (a) send a copy of the statement to every member who is entitled to receive a copy of the accounts; or (b) apply to the court for relief from having to send the statement to all members. The court will only grant relief if it is satisfied that the auditor is trying to secure needless publicity for defamatory matter.

20.4 The auditor is also obliged to notify the appropriate audit authority if: (a) the audit is a 'major' audit; or (b) the auditor ceases to hold office before the end of the term of office. A major audit is defined as the audit of a charity in which there is a major public interest. The audit of a charitable company with income exceeding £100 million is deemed a major audit.

21 Procedures on change of auditor

21.1 Under ethical guidelines, an auditor cannot accept a nomination to replace an existing auditor without first communicating with that auditor. The charity should inform the existing auditor about the proposed change and will need to give permission to both firms to discuss the relevant issues. The proposed auditor will write to the existing auditor enquiring about the following matters:

- the reasons for the change in the appointment;
- any significant differences of principle or practice that have arisen between the auditor and client;
- whether the client, its trustees or employees are guilty of an unlawful act which is relevant to the audit and which should be investigated by the appropriate authority;
- any serious doubts the existing auditor has regarding the integrity of the trustees and/or senior management; and
- whether the client, its trustees or employees have deliberately withheld information or limited the scope of the audit.

21.2 The prospective auditor will give due weight to the existing auditor's reply, along with any other information they have obtained in order to make their decision.

21.3 Multi-employer pension schemes

There will be a requirement to treat these as defined benefit schemes unless the required information is not available. This would mean that the net assets or liabilities of the pension scheme would be shown on the charity's balance sheet. Given that a number of pension schemes are in a position of net liabilities, this proposal could have a detrimental effect on charity balance sheets. In addition, charities need to recognise any liability to fund a deficit where the charity has entered into an agreement to make those payments.

SECTION F

Charity mergers and winding up

F1
Mergers and restructuring

1 Introduction

1.1 A merger occurs when two or more charities come together to form one organisation (either one single charity or a group of charities under common control). The primary drivers for mergers between charities normally include: carrying out the merging charities' charitable purposes more effectively; better meeting the charitable needs of the merging charities' users and beneficiaries; and making best use of charitable funds by pooling resources and taking advantage of economies of scale.

1.2 Mergers and collaborative working between charities are encouraged by the Charity Commission and the Charity Commission's guidance can be found in its publication *Collaborative Working and Mergers* (CC34). The Charity Commission also provided a very useful checklist for mergers. All that being said, the number of mergers that occur each year is actually very low. The organisation Eastside Primetimers publishes a review of not-for-profit mergers each year (The Good Merger Index). The 2017–18 edition of this index identified 81 mergers across the sector, involving 154 organisations. While this was actually an increase on the previous years, it does need to be remembered that were over 168,000 registered charities at that time.

1.3 Mergers typically involve a number of areas of law, some of which can be technical. Charity trustees proposing to merge would be well advised to seek expert legal advice from the outset.

1.4 There are three main types of merger:

(a) Transfer to existing charity (type one) – where one or more charities transfer assets (subject to the liabilities) to another already existing charity.
(b) Transfer to new charity (type two) – where a new charity (usually a corporate body) is set up to receive the assets (subject to the liabilities) of one or more charities.

(c) By change of control (type three) – where one charity takes legal control of another (creating a parent/subsidiary relationship) either:
   - by being appointed at charity trustee level; or
   - through the membership of the charity.

1.5 Examples of each of these three types are illustrated in Figures F1 to F3 below.

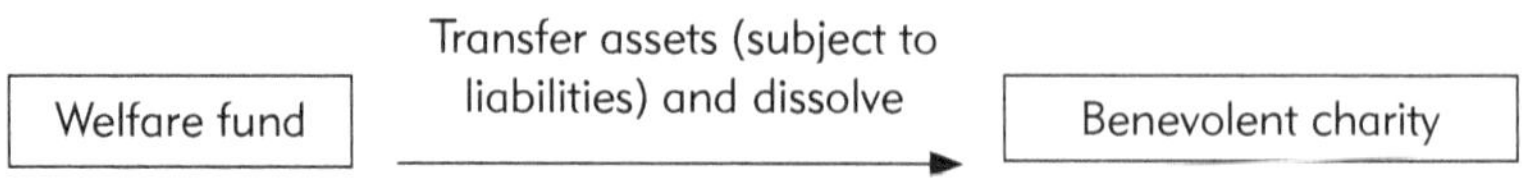

Figure F1: Type-one merger: transfer to an existing charity

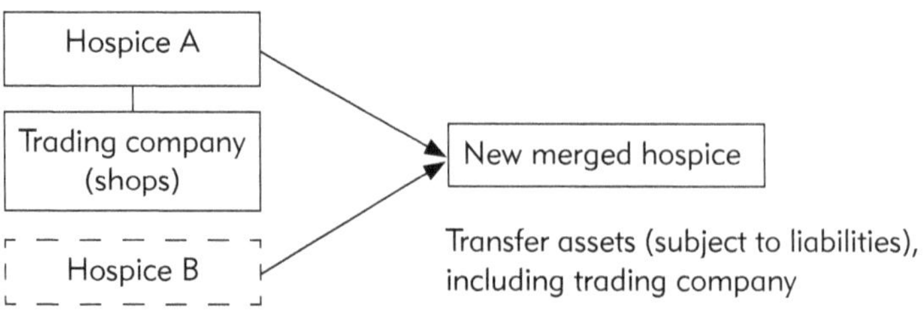

Figure F2: Type-two merger: transfer to a new charity

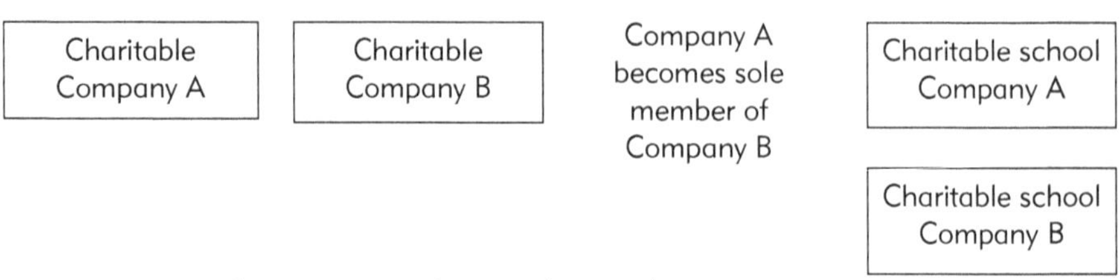

Figure F3: Type-three merger: change of control

1.6 A type-one merger often saves time and expense as there is no need to set up a new charity to receive the transferred assets. However, it is possible only where the objects of the receiving charity are wide enough to incorporate the objects of the charity being transferred. In addition, this type of merger can be perceived as a takeover of one charity (or more) by another. This is often an important consideration for the charity trustees and members, who may be concerned about reputational implications.

1.7 Where the merging charities are unincorporated, it is likely to be advisable to pursue a type-two merger and set up a new corporate charity. This will provide the benefits of incorporation discussed in section 8 of Chapter A3 on page 71. (it is worth noting that restructuring an unincorporated charity as a corporate charity – 'incorporation' – is in fact a type-two merger).

1.8 Merging by change of control (type three) creates a group structure where the 'merged' charities each continue to exist in the same legal form but are controlled by one of their number acting as a 'parent' charity. This type of merger may be appropriate where it is not practical to achieve a transfer of assets and liabilities in the timescales available or where there are sound commercial reasons for assets and liabilities to remain within each merged organisation (perhaps there are concerns about liabilities which the parent wishes to remain ring-fenced). The legal mechanisms for merging by change of control tend to be more straightforward than those for effecting an asset transfer. However, each charity remains a separate legal entity accountable to the Charity Commission and any other relevant regulator (like the Registrar of Companies), and must be administered as such. This obviously has cost implications and inter-relationships within the group can be complex to manage.

1.9 The merger process

1.9.1 Like any marriage, charity mergers should not be entered into lightly and the merger process needs to be carefully managed. It is always advisable for the governing body of each party to the merger to appoint a working party (which would typically include at least one charity trustee and one senior member of staff) with delegated authority to take the merger negotiations forward and to make recommendations to the board. The ultimate decision as to whether to merge must be reserved to the board (or the members, depending on the decision-making powers set out in the charity's governing document) and may be subject to Charity Commission approval (Charity Commission approval is always required for the merger of two CIOs).

1.9.2 It is prudent to provide written terms of reference for the merger working party. From a legal point of view, the merger process can be broken down into four main components:

1. agreeing the structure;
2. due diligence;
3. negotiating the merger documents; and
4. practical steps to achieve merger (both before and after the merger has legal effect).

1.9.3 The structure of the merger needs to be settled early on. In order to do this, the following issues need to be addressed:

- **Legal structures**: if all parties to the merger are unincorporated it may well be advisable to set up a new corporate charity (a company limited by guarantee or a CIO) to transfer the assets of the merging charities.
- **Charitable objects**: the charitable objects of all of the merging charities must be sufficiently compatible to enable the merger to take place. If there is any doubt on this issue, specialist legal advice should be sought, and it may be necessary to obtain guidance from the Charity Commission. If the objects of the receiving charity are wider than (but include) those of the transferring charity any assets transferred must be ring-fenced within the receiving charity following merger for the original narrower purposes. It may be necessary or desirable to amend the charitable objects of one or more parties before the merger takes place. Charity Commission consent to any amendments will be required.
- **Power to transfer assets**: each charity that is to transfer its assets to achieve merger must have the power to do so. The governing document may provide either an express power to transfer assets or a power to dissolve or wind up. Depending on the wording of the governing document, it may be necessary to obtain the approval of the members and/or the Charity Commission to exercise these powers. Prior Charity Commission consent is likely to be required:
  (a) in the case of a transfer of a substantial non-cash asset from an unincorporated charity to a charitable company where s. 190 of the Companies Act 2006 applies (consent of the company members will also be required); and
  (b) where a conflict of interest arises when the merger involves the transfer of liabilities from an unincorporated charity to another charity and any of the charity trustees are the same people (see also the discussion in section 8, Chapter A3, page 71).
- Where express powers are absent, the charity trustees of an unincorporated charity may seek to rely on the powers set out in the Trustee Act 2000 and/or, in relation to land, the Trusts of Land and Appointment of Trustees Act 1996 to transfer assets. In cases of doubt it may be necessary or desirable to amend the governing document to provide express powers (this may require the involvement of the Charity Commission and/or any membership) or to seek a vesting order from the Charity Commission.
- In the absence of express powers, the charity trustees of an incorporated charity can ask the members to pass a resolution to amend the constitution to include the necessary power.

1.10 Other restrictions on assets

If any of the merging charities have property (usually land or funds) that are permanent endowment, specie land (land which is given in trust for a specific charitable purpose (to operate a school or a nursing home) or subject to other restrictions imposed by trust law, this is likely to have an effect on the legal structure. It is recommended that specialist legal advice is sought.

1.11 Due diligence

1.11.1 From a legal point of view, due diligence is the process of investigating the nature and extent of the assets and liabilities of the charities to be merged. The transferring charity will investigate the receiving charity and vice versa. The legal due diligence exercise will often run alongside (and may well be secondary to) a financial due diligence exercise, usually carried out by a firm of accountants on behalf of each charity. The overall due diligence process should also cover strategic and operational issues.

1.11.2 The charity trustees of all parties to the merger need to be satisfied that it is in the best interests of their charity to merge. The outcome of the legal due diligence exercise should be a report that helps the charity trustees to reach their decision as to whether to go ahead with the merger. The purpose of the legal due diligence exercise is twofold:

- to highlight any significant risks and/or liabilities which might prevent the merger going ahead either at all or on the basis agreed; and
- to understand the nature of the assets and liabilities of the merging charities and identify the legal mechanisms which need to take place to achieve the merger (whether by transfer of assets or by change of control).

1.11.3 It is important at the outset that the parties (with guidance from their advisers) agree the scope of the due diligence exercise to ensure that the work carried out is in proportion to the potential risks being assessed and to avoid unnecessary costs being incurred. In particular, the parties will need to consider the nature of their activities (what material risks/liabilities are involved?), the extent to which they are currently aware of each other's operations and enjoy a positive working relationship. It may be appropriate to agree to limit the scope of the due diligence exercise to a level that is proportionate to the scale of the merger and the risks involved.

1.12 Merger documents

1.12.1 The documents required to document the merger will depend on the type of merger and the nature of any assets to be transferred.

1.12.2 In a typical type-one and type-two (asset-transfer merger), the following documents would be entered into:

- a transfer agreement identifying the assets to be transferred and setting out the contractual terms on which the transfer will take place;
- resolutions (usually set out in board minutes) of the charity trustees of each party to the merger agreeing to either transfer or receive the transfer of

assets, as appropriate, and to approve and enter into the agreed form merger documents;

- any property documents such as freehold transfers or consents and assignments of leases; and
- any additional documents required to transfer ownership of assets of the transferring charity such as consents to assign or formal novations of significant contracts, releases of mortgages, charges and other loans.

1.13 Practical steps

1.13.1 Depending on the type of merger, the nature of the assets and liabilities of the merging charities and any issues of confidentiality it may be necessary or prudent to consult with the following prior to entering into a legally binding agreement to merge:

- **employees**: all transferring employees must be consulted in accordance with the TUPE regulations;
- **banks**: to agree how any loan or overdraft facilities and security is to be dealt with on merger;
- **pensions providers**: where a pension debt will be triggered on merger, to agree how that debt can be dealt with under the pension scheme rules. Specialist legal advice should be sought;
- **regulators**: to ensure that any necessary regulatory consents or registrations are obtained. This may include obtaining regulatory consents from for example: the Department for Education where the merging charities are independent schools; and from the CQC where the merging charities are providers of care services;
- **members**: where their approval is required for any necessary amendments to governing documents, for a transfer of assets or where their status or rights are to be affected by the merger;
- **beneficiaries and stakeholders**: particularly where the merger will affect the provision of any services charged for by a party to the merger;
- **major funders and contractors**: where their prior consent is required to transfer funding arrangements and/or contracts or to a change in control of the relevant charity; and
- **insurers**: to ensure that the liabilities of the merged charities are fully covered following merger.

1.13.2 The following may need to be dealt with depending on the type of merger and the assets and liabilities involved:

- **Employees**: the TUPE rules apply, and all employees whose employment is to transfer on merger must be consulted in accordance with the TUPE rules. Under TUPE, all employees will automatically transfer on their existing terms and conditions of employment.

- If redundancies, dismissals or changes in the terms and conditions of employment are contemplated as part of the merger, early legal advice should be sought to ensure that such proposals do not amount to constructive unfair dismissal.
- **Contracts and grants**: the general legal principle is that, subject to the specific terms that have been agreed between the parties, only the benefit of a contract can be transferred (or 'assigned') to a third party (the receiving company) without the consent of the other party or parties to the contract. To transfer the obligations (known as 'the burden') under a contract to a third party requires the consent of all the other parties to the contract. It is therefore necessary to review all the terms and conditions of all significant contracts and grants of the transferring charity or charities to identify any clauses that either permit assignment (with or without the other party's consent) or prohibit assignment.
- The types of contract that will typically need to be reviewed include: all leases, banking arrangements, funding arrangements, hire purchase and equipment leasing agreements, significant contracts for the supply of goods and or services (such as cleaning, catering or IT maintenance) and construction contracts (including any collateral warranties).
- Some contracts and grants (the National Lottery Community Fund, for example) also include conditions that require the grant or contract maker's prior consent to any change of control, amalgamation or other form of reorganisation. The contracts and funding arrangements of each transferring charity and (where relevant) the receiving charity should be reviewed. Subject to any issues of confidentiality, to avoid being in breach of these conditions, the specific terms should be followed and prior consent obtained where necessary and practicable.
- **Property**: title to all of the transferring charity's leasehold and freehold properties should be investigated. The landlord's consent will almost certainly be required to assign any leases to the receiving charity (this process has cost implications). Where any of the transferring charity's properties are unregistered, transferring them to the receiving charity is likely to trigger first registration of title; any transfer of registered land will need to be registered at the Land Registry. It is also vital to investigate and identify any land that is permanent endowment. The charity trustees of the transferring charity must ensure that they comply with the requirements of ss. 117 to 121 of the 2011 Act in respect of all disposals of property to the receiving charity and the appropriate statements required under s. 122 of the 2011 Act must be included in the merger or transfer agreement. It is strongly recommended that legal advice is sought on dealing with legal formalities in relation to property.
- **Permanent endowment**: if any of the charity's property (usually land or funds) is a permanent endowment, it cannot be held absolutely by a corporate body (such as a company limited by guarantee, a Royal Charter body, a community benefit society or a CIO) as part of its corporate property. It

may be appropriate to appoint the corporate body as the sole corporate charity trustee and a Charity Commission scheme may be required, or it may be possible to remove restrictions on capital using the new powers introduced by the Charities Act 2006. Permanent endowment is a technical area and it is strongly recommended that specialist legal advice is sought.

- **Pensions**: transferring all the transferring charity's employees to the receiving charity may trigger an exit by the charity from pension arrangements it participates in on behalf of its employees. Depending on the type of scheme, if the underlying pension scheme is under-funded, this can have the nasty consequence of triggering a debt payable by the charity on exiting; the level of debt can either prevent a merger or incorporation going ahead or seriously delay it. This is a technical area and it is strongly recommended that specialist legal advice is sought.
- **Banking arrangements**: each charity's bank will need to be consulted about the proposed merger. Where a new charity has been established, it will be necessary for the charity trustees to open new accounts. Where a bank has taken a mortgage or charge to secure a loan over the assets of a transferring charity, the bank's consent will be required to transfer any property that is subject to such mortgage or charge. This will have timing and cost implications. The charity trustees must comply with ss. 124–126 of the 2011 Act where any new charge is to be put in place as a result of the merger. Any new charge or mortgage taken over the assets of a charitable company must be registered with the Registrar of Companies within a short period of time; failure to comply with the timescale could jeopardise the security. Any charges granted by a merging charity over the assets of its trading subsidiary may also need to be transferred. It is strongly recommended that legal advice is sought whenever transferring property which is subject to a mortgage or charge.

1.14 Mergers register

1.14.1 The Charities Act 2006 introduced the mergers register maintained by the Charity Commission. This contains details of any 'relevant charity mergers' notified to the Charity Commission. It can be accessed via the Charity Commission's website.

1.14.2 The intention of the mergers register is to deal with a difficult legal issue encountered on merging or restructuring charities. Before the mergers register, where a charity ceased to exist following merger or restructuring, any potential legacy made in a will to benefit that charity could fail for lack of a beneficiary. Where merging charities were likely to receive legacies, this created the unpalatable potential risk of losing significant funds. This led to the common practice of keeping merged charities in existence as 'shell' charities to receive legacies.

1.14.3 Now, if a charity merger is included in the register of mergers, a legacy to the transferring charity may be saved (or the costs of defending a legacy which is challenged may be saved) and the transferring charity can be wound up. Once included on the register, all future income to the transferring charity passes automatically to the receiving charity.

1.14.4 However, a technical problem was highlighted with this new tool. Registration on the mergers register will not save legacies that were worded so that the gift is not left to the named charity where it has ceased to exist. It is not common practice to word legacies in this way, but it does happen. Following a merger or restructuring, charity trustees need to decide whether to dissolve a transferring charity. They should weigh up the risk of losing legacies that have been made using such wording against the administration cost of maintaining a charity within the merged structure. This may not be an easy decision to make.

1.14.5 What constitutes a 'relevant charity merger' is defined in s. 306 of the Charities Act 2011 (the 2011 Act). The following are examples of relevant charity mergers that can be registered on the mergers register:

- where all of the assets of one or more charities have been transferred to an existing charity and the transferring charities have subsequently ceased to exist (type-one merger); and
- where all of the assets of one or more charities have been transferred to a newly established charity and the transferring charities have subsequently ceased to exist (type-two merger).

1.14.6 A merger where the transferring charity does not cease to exist is not a relevant charity merger capable of registration. Also, it is only obligatory to register a relevant charity merger where a vesting declaration has been made in respect of the merger or restructuring; otherwise it is voluntary. The charity trustees of the receiving charity can apply to register a relevant charity merger by using the Charity Commission online service.

1.15 Vesting declarations

1.15.1 The Charities Act 2006 introduced a new tool to assist charity mergers: the vesting declaration. Where the charity trustees of a transferring charity pass a vesting declaration the assets named in it are automatically transferred from one charity to another.

1.15.2 However, a vesting declaration can be used only in mergers and restructuring projects which fall within the definition of a 'relevant charity merger'. They are available to transfer only a limited range of assets specified in the 2011 Act, including: unmortgaged freehold land (where any consent required under covenants on assignment has been obtained prior to transfer); unmortgaged leases (where any consent to assign has been obtained from the landlord prior to transfer); cash; equipment and stock; and vehicles. Vesting declarations cannot be used to transfer liabilities, stocks and shares, mortgaged land, permanent endowment or to assign contracts and funding arrangements.

1.15.3 In practice, it is likely that the vesting declaration will be of only limited use in the most straightforward of mergers or restructuring projects.

1.16 Small unincorporated charities provisions

1.16.1 Any unincorporated charity with a gross annual income of less than £10,000 can use the powers in ss. 267 and 268 of the 2011 Act to transfer all of its expendable capital to another charity provided that:

- the transferring charity has no designated land (being land held on trust for the particular purpose or purposes of the charity); and
- the charity trustees of the transferring charity consider the transfer to be expedient in the interests of furthering the purposes for which the property is held, and all or any of the charitable purposes of the receiving charity (or charities) are substantially similar to all or any of the purposes of the transferring charity.

1.16.2 This power can be used only to transfer all of the charity's property, not part of it. The property can be transferred to more than one charity. Because not all of the purposes of the transferring and receiving charity need be similar, the receiving charity may have wider purposes.

1.16.3 The charity trustees exercise the power by passing a resolution at a properly constituted charity trustees' meeting by a two-thirds majority. The charity trustees must send a copy of the resolution to the Charity Commission. It then has a period of 60 days in which to concur with the charity trustees' decision, to ask for further information about the charity trustees' reasons for passing the resolution or to require public notice. If the Charity Commission seeks further information or requires public notice the timetable is suspended. If the timetable is suspended for a period or periods of more than 120 days, the resolution is treated as if it had never been made.

1.16.4 If the Charity Commission raises no objections, the resolution takes effect at the end of the 60-day period. The charity trustees of the transferring charity must then transfer the property in accordance with the resolution.

1.16.5 Sections 273 and 274 of the 2011 Act provide a similar power for small unincorporated charities to transfer permanent endowment. The procedure for passing a resolution and seeking concurrence from the Charity Commission is the same. Where permanent endowment property is to be transferred, the receiving charity (or charities) must have purposes that are substantially similar to all of the purposes of the transferring charity.

1.16.6 The main purpose of these powers is to help charities rationalise small funds and to ease administration. It is important to appreciate that:

- property transferred using ss. 267 and 268 will continue to be subject to any restricted purposes applicable to it prior to the transfer when held by the receiving charity. Charity trustees may be able to use the power in s. 275 of the 2011 Act to alter the purposes; and
- property transferred using ss. 273 and 274 will continue to be permanent endowment and subject to the same restrictions on capital expenditure when held by the receiving charity. Charity trustees may be able to use the powers in ss. 281 or 282 of the 2011 Act to enable permanent endowment to be spent out.

1.17 Community benefit societies

1.17.1 The Co-operative and Community Benefit Societies Act 2014 provides powers to enable an community benefit society to amalgamate with another community benefit society or a company, to transfer its business to another community benefit society or company or convert into a company.

1.17.2 The members must pass a special resolution either by:

- two-thirds of votes cast in person or by proxy at a general meeting to amalgamate with or transfer its business to another community benefit society; or
- three-quarters of votes cast in person or by proxy at a general meeting to amalgamate with, transfer its business to or to convert into a company. At least 50% of the members must vote.

1.17.3 In each case, the special resolution must be confirmed by a second resolution passed by a majority of the votes cast or by proxy at a general meeting held between two weeks and one month after the first.

1.18 Charitable incorporated organisations

If two or more CIOs wish to merge to form a new CIO, each original CIO must hold a general meeting to pass resolutions to approve the proposed merger and to adopt the proposed constitution of the new CIO. These resolutions must be passed by a 75% majority of those voting (in person or by proxy). The decisions can be made outside of a general meeting, such as by written resolution, but they must then be agreed unanimously. The Charity Commission also states that each

CIO must make sure that anyone affected by the proposed merger knows about it. When the resolutions are agreed, and this action taken, the CIOs need to make an application to the Charity Commission.

F2
Winding up

1 Introduction

1.1 There can come a time in the life of a charity when its trustees decide that it is no longer appropriate for the charity to continue. There can be many reasons why they should wish to discontinue the charity, including completion of the project for which the charity is operating, or that its purposes can be better served by carrying on through another organisation, thus rendering the charity redundant.

1.2 In practice, a charity that has sufficient assets to meet all its debts and liabilities and can provide for the proper treatment of any trusts or permanent endowments for which it is responsible may be wound up voluntarily through a process that will be determined according to the provisions of its constitution and the legal process that applies to the particular form in which the charity is constituted.

1.3 The treatment of charities that are established under the Royal Charter or as statutory corporations will depend on the individual constitution and circumstances of that organisation. This is beyond the scope of this section.

1.4 This chapter reviews the ways that common forms of charity are able to wind up, on a voluntary basis, while the charity is solvent. A discussion of the way charity trustees must act when they believe (or ought to believe) that their charity is at risk of insolvency and dealing with insolvency itself is set out in Section E.

1.5 A checklist of reasons for voluntarily winding up a charity is set out in paragraph 1.6 and may be useful in completing the Charity Commission's online form of application to remove the charity from the register of charities (see section 6).

1.6 Some reasons for voluntarily winding up a charity

- The reason the charity was created has now been met.
- The charity has merged with another charity and has transferred all its property into another charity.

- The charity has lost or reduced grant funding and can no longer continue for financial reasons.
- Other financial reasons mean that the charity cannot continue.
- The charity is unable to recruit enough trustees to be able to continue to operate.
- The charity relies on volunteers and active members and does not have enough support to be able to continue.
- The charity has transferred its property to another charity under the power to transfer property of an unincorporated charity under s. 268 of the 2011 Act (see Chapter F1, paragraph 1.16, page 478).
- The charity has incorporated by transferring all its property into a new company (see Chapter A3, paragraph 8, page 71).
- The charity has spent all its permanent endowment under ss. 281 or 282 of the 2011 Act (see Chapter E1, paragraph 3.10, page 417).

1.7 The next paragraphs address the way a charity can be wound up voluntarily depending on the charity's constitutional form.

2 Unincorporated organisations: charitable trusts and unincorporated societies

2.1 There is no formal process of closure or dissolution of an unincorporated charity, whether it is a charitable trust or an unincorporated association, but an unincorporated charity will cease to exist at the point when no property is held for the purposes of the charity.

2.2 Constitutional rules or trust deeds may contain provisions for the process of decision making and distribution of the assets of the charity after satisfaction of all assets and liabilities on dissolution. If so, the constitutional rules or trust deed must be followed.

2.3 Provided the charity trustees have the constitutional power to do so, they, or the members of the organisation, may spend out all the charity's assets, either directly on the purposes of the charity or as directed by the dissolution clause in the constitutional rules or trust deed of the charity. The dissolution clause may permit a transfer of assets to another charity established for the same or similar purposes as the charity, or for other or wider charitable purposes. A careful reading of the dissolution clause is required.

2.4 Depending on the circumstances, the charity trustees may be able to transfer the assets and property of the charity together with its liabilities, as a going concern to another charity using a process similar to that of incorporation or merger.

For a more detailed discussion of the process, see Chapter F1, paragraph 1.9 (page 471) and chapter A3, paragraph 8 (page 71).

2.5 The rules of a membership charity may require a resolution of the members to be passed to give authority for the dissolution of the charity.

2.6 If there is no constitutional power to dissolve or wind up, or there is property held on trusts that prevent capital being spent such as permanent endowment, powers and procedures provided under ss. 267–286 of the 2011 Act may allow the charity trustees to transfer property and/or free up endowments so that they can be spent. A more detailed discussion of the process can be found at Chapter F1, paragraph 1.16 (page 478) and Chapter E1, paragraph 3.10 (page 417).

2.7 There may be circumstances where it is not possible to use the constitutional or statutory powers of the charity trustees to achieve a dissolution. Here, the charity trustees may make an application to the Charity Commission to give it the necessary power or authority to transfer its assets and dissolve the charity (see paragraph 3, Chapter E1 page 410).

3 Charitable companies

3.1 A company will cease to exist when (a) it has been dissolved and (b) it has been struck off the Register of Companies. When the charitable company is solvent, the following two processes are normally used for winding up: striking off and members' voluntary liquidation. Other methods of winding up in the event of insolvency or risk insolvency are described in Chapter E2.

3.2 Striking off

3.2.1 If a charitable company has ceased to operate and has disposed of all its assets after the settlement of all its debts, it can use the powers available under the Deregulation and Contracting Out Act 1994. This is often the simplest and least costly way of winding up a charitable company that has no further use or purpose.

3.2.2 The striking off procedure may only be used if, in the last three months, the company has not:

- traded or otherwise carried on business (including paying cheques);
- changed its name;
- disposed for value of property or rights that, immediately before ceasing to be in business or trade, it held for disposal or gain in the normal course of that business or trade; or

- engaged in any other activity except one necessary or expedient for making a striking-off application, settling the company's affairs or meeting a statutory requirement.

3.2.3 A company can apply for striking off if it has settled trading or business debts in the previous three months. It must not be threatened with liquidation and it must have no agreements with creditors, such as a Company Voluntary Arrangement.

3.3 Striking-off: procedure and checklist for charity trustees

- The charitable company is kept dormant (other than settlement of trading or business debts) for a period of not less than three months.
- After the three-month dormancy period, an application is made to the Registrar of Companies using from DS01. It costs £10 to strike off a company, but note that this payment cannot be made from the company as it must remain dormant.
- A copy of the form submitted to the Registrar of Companies must be sent to all the charity trustees who have not signed the form and all other interested parties (members).
- Notice of the intention to strike the company off the register of companies is inserted in *The Gazette*
- Three months after publication of *The Gazette* notice, provided there are no objections, the Registrar of Companies may strike off the charity from the register of companies.

3.3.1 Once the charity has been wound up, an application must be made to the Charity Commission for its removal from the register of charities. See section 6 on page 489.

3.4 Members voluntary liquidation

A members voluntary liquidation (MVL) is a procedure for winding up a solvent charitable company which is able to pay all debts that may arise within 12 months of the MVL. The charity trustees (who are the company directors) are able to swear a declaration of solvency to this effect.

3.5 Members voluntary liquidation: process and checklist for charity trustees

- Make enquiry into the affairs of the charity so as to be satisfied that the charity can fully pay all its debts within 12 months of the MVL.
- All or a majority of the charity trustees complete a statutory declaration within five weeks before the resolution to place the charity into MVL.

- Complete the statutory declaration of insolvency in the prescribed form (see paragraph 3.2.1 above).
- The company members pass a special resolution to place the company into MVL and appoint a liquidator (who must be an insolvency practitioner) at a properly convened general meeting or by written resolution.
- File the special resolution to place the company into MVL with the Registrar of Companies within 15 days of passing a resolution.
- Advertise the resolution to place the company into MVL in the London *The Gazette* within 14 days of passing a resolution.
- File the statutory declaration of solvency with the Registrar of Companies within 14 days of making the statutory declaration.
- The liquidator disposes of the assets and settled the debts of the charity.
- The liquidator calls a final meeting of the charity and files a final account and return with the Registrar of Companies within one week of the meeting.

3.5.1 The declaration of solvency can be found at www.gov.uk/government/publications/give-notice-of-statutory-declaration-of-solvency-liq01. It must be made by a majority of the charity trustees in the presence of a solicitor or a Commissioner of Oaths.

3.5.2 Upon the appointment of a liquidator and until they are discharged, the powers of the charity trustees are suspended, except in so far as they are authorised to act by the members in general meeting or the liquidator approves of the continuing exercise of their powers.

3.5.3 The primary responsibility of the liquidator is to settle the debts of the company. Any surplus assets remaining after settlement of all debts in full must be distributed for charitable purposes according to the requirements of the articles of association of the charity.

3.5.4 The charity trustees are liable for the debts of the company for 12 months from the date of declaration of solvency. A charity trustee who has resigned after the resolution to place the charity into MVL will continue to be liable with the other charity trustees.

3.5.5 Once the charity has been wound up, an application must be made to the Charity Commission for its removal from the register of charities. See section 6 on page 489.

3.6 Restoration to the register

3.6.1 There can be circumstances where a charitable company holds property at the time that it is struck off the register of companies (for example, if it has failed to comply with statutory annual accounting or filing requirements). In those circumstances, the property will be treated as ownerless and will revert to the Crown. The name given to such property is *bona vacantia*.

3.6.2 A company that has been struck off can be restored on an application to the court. This can enable steps to be taken to retrieve the property and put it to charitable use.

3.7 A case study

A charitable company was been removed from the register for non-compliance (for failure to file accounts) because it had become moribund and trustees had failed to comply with their duties under the Companies Act 2006. The charity's assets had reverted to the Treasury as *bona vacantia*, but subsequently, another charity was identified as having an appropriate charitable use for the remaining funds and an application was made to the court to restore the charity. Once the charity was restored to the register, its assets could be transferred to the other charity and the transferring charity could then again be struck off under the voluntary striking off procedure after an appropriate period of dormancy.

4 Charitable Incorporated Organisations

4.1 Although most CIOs will not have not been in existence for very long, there may be still circumstances under which it is appropriate to be wound up.

4.2 The process of winding up is prescribed by the CIO's constitution and the Charitable Incorporated Organisations (Insolvency and Dissolution) Regulations 2012 (SI 2012/3013).

4.3 Voluntarily winding up a CIO: process and checklist for charity trustees

- Make enquiry into the affairs of the charity so as to be satisfied that the charity can fully pay all its debts and liabilities, or that they are fully provided for.
- The members of the CIO pass a resolution to dissolve the CIO either at a general meeting of the members (for which not less than 14 days' notice must be given) or by a unanimous resolution of the members.
- The charity trustees must notify the Charity Commission of the resolution to dissolve the charity by email (see paragraph 4.5).
- A dissolution resolution may be passed at a general meeting called on not less than 14 days' notice by a 75% majority of those voting (including proxies and postal voting if this is permitted by the constitution); or without a vote provided that there has been no expression of dissent in response to the question put to the meeting.

- A resolution to dissolve the CIO may be made otherwise than at a general meeting (for example, by written resolution) if it is passed unanimously by the members.
- The charity trustees must make a declaration that any debts and other liabilities of the CIO have been settled or are otherwise fully provided for.
- The charity trustees must make a formal statement that sets out the way in which the property and rights of the CIO are to be applied, or paid out under the constitution on dissolution.
- The charity trustees must make an application to the Charity Commission for the dissolution of the CIO and submit the dissolution resolution, the declaration and the statement.
- Within seven days of making the application, the charity trustees must give a copy of the resolution to every member and employee of the CIO and every charity trustee who has not been involved in the application.
- The Commission must publish a notice stating that it has received an application for dissolution. This will be published on the register entry of the CIO.
- Subject to any representations, the Charity Commission will remove the CIO from the register after three months and the CIO is automatically dissolved on that day.
- The Commission must then publish a notice stating the day of removal.

4.4 Unlike other forms of charity, the CIO automatically ceases to exist when it is removed from the register.

4.5 Informing the Charity Commission about the dissolution of a CIO

4.5.1 A CIO must notify the Commission where it has made the decision to close. While the Charity Commission has a form that can be used by other forms of charity to notify the Charity Commission of their closure, this cannot be used by a CIO. Instead a CIO must tell the commission about its dissolution using the Charity Commission contact form.

4.5.2 The Charity Commission's procedure must be followed exactly in order to avoid delay. The following requirements must be satisfied:

1. In the subject field, insert the words: 'CIO Dissolution'.
2. The email to the Charity Commission must confirm that:
   - no liquidator has been appointed for the CIO;
   - the charity trustees or the majority are making the notification;
   - the exact procedure for dissolution in the CIO's constitution has been followed; and
   - any debts or liabilities have either been settled or otherwise provided in full.

3. The exact words of the dissolution resolution must be stated in the e-mail (not a summary).
4. Details of how any property vested in, or held in trust for, the CIO has been or is to be applied as required by its constitution.

5 Community benefit societies

5.1 A Community benefit society that has sufficient assets available to pay all its debts can be wound up or dissolved by an instrument of dissolution under the Co-operative and Community Benefit Societies Act 2014.

5.2 If the community benefit society is insolvent or at risk of insolvency, the provisions of the Insolvency Act 1986 will apply in a similar way as they apply to companies either by court order or resolution.

5.3 Community benefit societies cannot enter into administration, administrative receivership or a company voluntary arrangement (CVA) with their creditors.

5.4 Charitable comumunity benefit societies are exempt charities and must be dissolved in accordance with the specific requirements of their principal regulator.

5.5 Voluntarily winding up a community benefit society process and checklist for charity trustees

- Enquire into the affairs of the charity so as to be satisfied that it can fully pay all its and liabilities or that they are fully provided for.
- The board members should prepare an instrument of dissolution (see paragraph 5.6).
- If the community benefit society is dormant (see paragraph 5.7), the members of the community benefit society consent to the instrument of dissolution by special resolution (using the definition in the Co-operative and Community Benefit Societies Act 2014).
- If the community benefit society is not dormant, three-quarters of the members must sign to indicate their consent to the instrument of dissolution.
- Three members and the secretary of the community benefit society make a statutory declaration of compliance with all the relevant provisions of the Co-operative and Community Benefit Societies Act 2014.
- A certificate (Certificate 126) must be signed by the secretary (or the liquidator if appointed) that all property vested in the community benefit society has been duly conveyed or transferred by the IPS to the persons entitled.
- The board members send the instrument of dissolution and the statutory declaration to the FCA.

- Once the certificate is sent to the FCA, it may dissolve the community benefit society.

5.6 An instrument of dissolution sets out the following details in relation to the RS:

- liabilities and assets of the community benefit society in detail;
- number of members and their respective interests in the community benefit society;
- claims of creditors and the provision to be made for their payment; and
- intended appropriation or division of funds and property of the IPS (unless stated to be left to the FCA to decide).

5.7 For an community benefit society to be treated as 'dormant', its accounts for the current year and the two years immediately preceding it need to demonstrate no accounting transactions (with the exception of fees paid to the FCA; payment of dividends; and/or payment of interest).

5.8 The community benefit society's constitutional rules will determine how any surplus assets of a charitable community benefit society should be applied. If this is not stated, any surplus assets will not be paid to the members but will be applied for charitable purposes.

5.9 A charitable community benefit society is an exempt charity, so no application is required to be made to remove the charity from the charities register. However, the community benefit society's principal regulator will normally prescribe a process of final notification and removal from a relevant list of community benefit society's that are regulated by that regulator.

6 All registered charities: application to remove the charity from the charities register

6.1 Charity trustees of registered charities have a duty under the Charities Act 2011 to inform the Charity Commission about the closure of their charity.

6.2 An online form is provided for notification of closure that can be used in most cases by charity trustees of charities that had an income when last reported of less than £5 million and assets of less than £100 million (The form cannot be used by CIOs or NHS charities). The form contains a declaration that the charity trustees must sign. If they are unable to sign it, they should apply to the Charity Commission for assistance.

6.3 Matters to be declared by charity trustees on notification of closure using the online form

This is a summary of the matters that charity trustees must declare if the Charity Commission's online application form is to be used:

- that the charity trustees were validly appointed;
- that the income for the last financial year was less than £5 million; and that the assets are worth less than £100 million;
- that there is no permanent endowment in the charity and that the provisions on the disposal of land under the governing document, and the Charities Act 2011 have been complied with;
- that all assets remaining after the settlement of debts have been properly dispersed; and
- that the requirements of grants received for specific purposes have been complied with.

6.4 Once the Charity Commission has been informed of the closure, it must remove the charity from the register of charities.

6.5 Even after they have dissolved their charity, the former charity trustees remain responsible for all decisions taken while they were in office.

6.6 The charity trustees must make arrangements for the charity's records to be carefully retained after the charity has dissolved. Records to be kept include accounting books and records (including cash books, invoices and receipts). For charitable companies, a minimum retention period of at least three years after they were made and for unincorporated charities (charitable trusts and unincorporated associations) a minimum retention period of at least six years after they were made, but longer retention periods may be needed (such as for insurance records) where there is a possibility of claims arising for matters that occurred in the past which may remain actionable for some time. This may be a particular concern for trustees and members of unincorporated charities and professional advice is recommended.

6.7 Exempt charities that are regulated by other regulators may be required to inform their regulator of their closure under other statutory provisions.

Appendix

The rights of employees and workers

An employee enjoys (subject to satisfaction of the qualifying conditions) the following rights:

- taxed at source;
- unfair dismissal protection;
- redundancy payment entitlement;
- written particulars of employment;
- statutory minimum period of notice;
- guarantee payment;
- medical suspension payment;
- to be accompanied at a disciplinary or grievance meeting;
- protection from discrimination on grounds of age, disability, gender reassignment, marriage and civil partnership, pregnancy and maternity, race, religion or belief, sex and sexual orientation;
- equal pay;
- maternity, paternity, parental and adoption rights;
- time off for trade union activities, duties etc.;
- protection of TUPE;
- not to be refused employment because of membership or non-membership of a trade union;
- to be provided with a safe place of work and to have reasonable care taken of their safety;
- to be paid statutory sick pay;
- to be paid their wages free of any deductions not properly authorised; and
- to limits on working time, and the right to paid holidays under the Working Time Regulations 1998; and
- protection against detriment/dismissal for making a protected disclosure.

Workers are entitled to the following statutory benefits:

- protection against unlawful deductions from wages;
- payment of the National Minimum Wage;
- accompaniment at a disciplinary or grievance hearing;
- paid annual leave, rest breaks and a maximum working week under the Working Time Regulations;
- protection against discrimination on grounds of age; disability; gender reassignment; marriage and civil partnership; pregnancy and maternity; race; religion or belief; sex and sexual orientation;
- equal pay to a comparable person of the opposite sex; and
- if working part-time, the right not to be treated less favourably than a comparable full-time worker; and
- protection against detriment/dismissal for making a protected disclosure.

Directory

Advisory, Conciliation and Arbitration Service (ACAS)
ACAS National (Head Office)
Euston Tower
286 Euston Road
London NW1 3JJ
Tel: 0300 123 1150
www.acas.org.uk

Association of Chief Executives of Voluntary Organisations (ACEVO)
150 Fenchurch Street
London EC3M 6BB
Tel: 020 7014 4600
www.acevo.org.uk

Association of Chief Executives of Scottish Voluntary Organisations (ACOSVO)
18 York Place
Edinburgh EH1 3EP
Tel: 0131 510 8940
E-mail: office@acosvo.org.uk
www.acosvo.org.uk

The National Lottery Community Fund
1 Plough Place
London EC4A 1DE
Tel: 0345 4 10 20 30
E-mail: general.enquiries@tnlcommunityfund.org.uk
www.tnlcommunityfund.org.uk

British Standards Institution (BSI)
BSI British Standards
389 Chiswick High Road
London W4 4AL
Tel: 0345 086 9001
Fax: 020 8996 7001
E-mail: cservices@bsigroup.com
www.bsigroup.com

Business in the Community (BITC)
137 Shepherdess Walk
London N1 7RQ
Tel: 020 7566 8650
E-mail: info@bitc.org.uk
www.bitc.org.uk

Care Quality Commission (CQC)
Care Quality Commission National Correspondence
Citygate
Gallowgate
Newcastle upon Tyne NE1 4PA
Tel: 03000 616 161
E-mail: enquiries@cqc.org.uk
www.cqc.org.uk

Charities Aid Foundation (CAF)
Head office
25 Kings Hill Avenue
Kings Hill
West Malling
Kent ME19 4TA
Tel: 03000 123 000
E-mail: enquiries@cafonline.org
www.cafonline.org

Charity Commission
PO Box 1227
Liverpool L69 3UG
Tel: 0845 3000 218
www.charity-commission.gov.uk

Charity Commission for Northern Ireland
257 Lough Road
Lurgan
BT66 6NQ
Tel: 028 3832 0220
E-mail:
admin@charitycommissionni.org.uk
www.charitycommissionni.org.uk

Charity Finance Group (CFG)
15–18 White Lion Street
London N1 9G
Tel: 0845 345 3192
E-mail: info@cfg.org.uk
www.cfg.org.uk

Charity Learning Consortium
Vine House
Selsley Road
North Woodchester
Stroud GL5 5NN
Tel: 08451 707 702
www.charitylearning.org

Charity Tribunal
The First-tier Tribunal (Charity) Manager
Tribunals Operational Support Centre
PO Box 6987
Leicester LE1 6ZX
Tel: 0845 600 0877

Chartered Institute of Internal Auditors (IIA)
13 Abbeville Mews
88 Clapham Park Road
London SW4 7BX
Tel: 020 7498 0101
www.iia.org.uk

Commission for Equality and Human Rights
Correspondence Unit
Arndale House
Arndale Centre
Manchester M4 3AQ
Tel: 0808 800 0082
www.equalityhumanrights.com

Companies House
England and Wales
Companies House
Crown Way
Cardiff CF14 3UZ
Tel: 0303 1234 500
E-mail:
enquiries@companies-house.gov.uk
www.companieshouse.gov.uk

London Office
Companies House
4 Abbey Orchard Street
Westminster
London SW1P 2HT

Scotland Office
Companies House
4th Floor Edinburgh Quay 2
139 Fountainbridge
Edinburgh EH3 9FF

Northern Ireland Office
Companies House
Second Floor
The Linenhall
32-38 Linenhall Street
Belfast
Northern Ireland
BT2 8BG

Co-Operatives UK
Holyoake House
Hanover Street
Manchester M60 0AS
Tel: 0161 214 1750
E-mail: info@cooperatives-uk.coop
www.cooperatives-uk.coop

Department for Business, Energy and Industrial Strategy (formerly the DTI, BERR and BIS)
1 Victoria Street
London SW1H 0ET
Tel: 020 7215 5000
E-mail: enquiries@beis.gov.uk
www.beis.gov.uk

Department for Education
Tel: 0370 000 2288
www.education.gov.uk

Department for Communities
Causeway Exchange
1–7 Bedford Street
Belfast
County Antrim
BT2 7EG
Tel: 028 9082 9000
www.communities-ni.gov.uk

Directory of Social Change (DoSC)
352 Holloway Road
London N7 6PA
Tel: 020 7697 4200
www.dsc.org.uk

Federation of Small Businesses (FSB)
Sir Frank Whittle Way
Blackpool Business Park
Blackpool FY4 2FE
Tel: 0808 20 20 888
www.fsb.org.uk

Financial Conduct Authority (FCA)
12 Endeavour Square
London E20 1JN
Tel: 0300 500 0597
www.fca.gov.uk

Financial Reporting Council (FRC)
8th Floor
125 London Wall
London EC2Y 5AS
Tel: 020 7492 2300
www.frc.org.uk

Fundraising Regulator
2nd Floor CAN Mezzanine Building
49–51 East Road,
London N1 6AH
Tel: 0333 321 8803
Fax: 0300 999 3407
http://www.fundraisingregulator.org.uk

Gambling Commission
Victoria Square House
Victoria Square
Birmingham B2 4BP
Tel: 0121 230 6666
E-mail: info@gamblingcommission.gov.uk
www.gamblingcommission.gov.uk

Health and Safety Executive (HSE)
Head Office
Redgrave Court
Merton Road
Bootle
Merseyside
L20 7HS
Tel: 0151 951 4000;
www.hse.gov.uk

HSE Incident Centre (RIDDOR reporting)
Contact Centre Address as above
Tel: 0345 300 9923
www.riddor.gov.uk

HM Revenue & Customs
Charities Correspondence S0708
PO Box 205
Bootle
L69 9AZ
Tel: (Charities Helpline) 0300 123 1073
www.hmrc.gov.uk

Regulator of Social Housing
Level 1A – City Tower
Piccadilly Plaza
Manchester M1 4BT
Tel: 0300 124 5225
E-mail: enquiries@rsh.gov.uk

Information Commissioner's Office
Wycliffe House
Water Lane
Wilmslow
Cheshire SK9 5AF
Tel: 0303 123 1113
E-mail: casework@ico.org.uk.
www.ico.gov.uk

ICSA Publishing
Saffron House
6–10 Kirby Street
London EC1N 8TS
Tel: 020 7612 7020
E-mail: publishing@icsa.co.uk
https://www.icsa.org.uk/products-and-services/bookshop

The Institute of Chartered Secretaries and Administrators (ICSA)
Saffron House
6–10 Kirby Street
London EC1N 8TS
Tel: 020 7580 4741
E-mail: info@icsa.org.uk
www.icsa.org.uk

Institute of Fundraising
Charter House
13-15 Carteret Street
London
SW1H 9DJ
Tel: 020 7840 1000
E-mail: info@institute-of-fundraising.org.uk
www.institute-of-fundraising.org.uk

Investors in People Head Office
157–197 Buckingham Palace Road
Victoria
London SW1W 9SP
Tel: 0300 303 3033
E-mail: info@investorsinpeople.com
www.investorsinpeople.com

Land Registry Head Office
Trafalgar House
1 Bedford Park
Croydon
CR0 2AQ
Tel: 0844 892 1111
E-mail: customersupport@landregistry.gsi.gov.uk
www.landregistry.gov.uk

National Council for Voluntary Organisations (NCVO)
Society Building
8 All Saints Street
London N1 9RL
Tel: 020 7713 6161
E-mail: ncvo@ncvo.org.uk
www.ncvo.org.uk

National Housing Federation (NHF)
Lion Court
25 Procter Street
London WC1V 6NY
Tel: 020 7067 1010
E-mail: info@housing.org.uk
www.housing.org.uk

Northern Ireland Council for Voluntary Action (NICVA)
61 Duncairn Gardens
Belfast BT15 2GB
Tel: 028 9087 7777
www.nicva.org

The Office of the Regulator of Community Interest Companies
Room 3.68
Companies House
Crown Way
Maindy
Cardiff CF14 3UZ
Tel: 029 2034 6228 (24hr voice mail service)
E-mail: cicregulator@companieshouse.gov.uk

Office of the Scottish Charity Regulator (OSCR)
2nd Floor
Quadrant House
9 Riverside Drive
Dundee DD1 4NY
Tel: 01382 220446
E-mail: info@oscr.org.uk
www.oscr.org.uk

The Pensions Regulator (TPR)
Napier House
Trafalgar Place
Brighton BN1 4DW
Tel: 0345 600 0707
www.thepensionsregulator.gov.uk

Privy Council
Room G/04
1 Horse Guards Road
London
SW1A 2HQ
Tel: 020 7271 3292
E-mail: enquiries@pco.gov.uk
www.privycouncil.independent.gov.uk

Scottish Council for Voluntary Organisations (SCVO)
Mansfield Traquair Centre
15 Mansfield Place
Edinburgh EH3 6BB
Tel: 0131 474 8000
E-mail: enquiries@scvo.org.uk
www.scvo.org.uk

Wales Council for Voluntary Action (WCVA)
Baltic House
Mount Stuart Square
Cardiff
CF10 5FH
Tel: 0300 111 0124
E-mail: help@wcva.org.uk
www.wcva.org.uk

Index

Lightning Source UK Ltd.
Milton Keynes UK
UKHW020758280720
367288UK00004B/172

9 781860 727696

Is Mind Just a Computation?

In an era dominated by Artificial Intelligence, the question of whether machines can truly think has never been more pressing. This book takes readers on a rigorous yet accessible journey through Computer Science, Physics, and Mathematics to tackle two questions:

1. Can a computer program be sentient?
2. Is the human mind reducible to computation?

The author introduces essential concepts in an entertaining style, guiding readers through this exciting topic. The book even includes source code that allows readers to test and verify key arguments themselves.

This book is for anyone intrigued by the nature of mind and machine: from curious lay readers to philosophers, computer scientists, and AI enthusiasts. It serves as an engaging introduction for beginners while offering fresh perspectives for experts. It will also be of interest to senior undergraduate and graduate students, where it can be used as supplementary material in courses on Computer Science, AI, and Philosophy of Mind.

Key Features

- Offers a rigorous, verifiable argument grounded in mainstream science, with no speculative physics.
- Includes real source code and challenges for readers to explore and validate concepts hands-on.
- Combines Computer Science, Physics, and Philosophy of Mind in a way that is both educational and thought-provoking.

Dr. Ovidiu Cristinel Stoica researches Theoretical Physics at the Horia Hulubei National Institute of Physics and Nuclear Engineering, Romania. He is interested in foundational questions about the universe, preferring geometric and group-theoretic approaches whenever possible. His research areas include General Relativity, in particular black hole and Big Bang singularities, foundations of Quantum Mechanics, and the Standard Model of particle physics. Before, he taught mathematics and, most of the time, developed advanced algorithms of computational geometry for the private sector. All this time, he was preoccupied with questions about the nature of consciousness and how it fits in the rigid structure of the physical laws. His essays on physics received several prizes from the Foundational Questions Institute. This book is the result of combining his passions for the applications of symmetries in physics, Computer Science, mathematics, teaching, and understanding the place of consciousness in the physical world.

Is Mind Just a Computation?

How Computer Science Dispels the Myths of the Age of AI

Ovidiu Cristinel Stoica

CRC Press
Taylor & Francis Group
Boca Raton London New York

CRC Press is an imprint of the
Taylor & Francis Group, an **informa** business

Designed cover image: Stoica

First edition published [2026]
by CRC Press
2385 NW Executive Center Drive, Suite 320, Boca Raton, FL 33431

and by CRC Press
4 Park Square, Milton Park, Abingdon, Oxon, OX14 4RN

CRC Press is an imprint of Taylor & Francis Group, LLC

© 2026 Stoica

Reasonable efforts have been made to publish reliable data and information, but the author and publisher cannot assume responsibility for the validity of all materials or the consequences of their use. The authors and publishers have attempted to trace the copyright holders of all material reproduced in this publication and apologize to copyright holders if permission to publish in this form has not been obtained. If any copyright material has not been acknowledged, please write and let us know so we may rectify in any future reprint.

Except as permitted under U.S. Copyright Law, no part of this book may be reprinted, reproduced, transmitted, or utilized in any form by any electronic, mechanical, or other means, now known or hereafter invented, including photocopying, microfilming, and recording, or in any information storage or retrieval system, without written permission from the publishers.

For permission to photocopy or use material electronically from this work, access www.copyright.com or contact the Copyright Clearance Center, Inc. (CCC), 222 Rosewood Drive, Danvers, MA 01923, 978-750-8400. For works that are not available on CCC, please contact mpkbookspermissions@tandf.co.uk

For Product Safety Concerns and Information please contact our EU representative GPSR@taylorandfrancis.com. Taylor & Francis Verlag GmbH, Kaufingerstraße 24, 80331 München, Germany.

Trademark notice: Product or corporate names may be trademarks or registered trademarks and are used only for identification and explanation without intent to infringe.

ISBN: 978-1-041-02788-1 (hbk)
ISBN: 978-1-041-03340-0 (pbk)
ISBN: 978-1-003-62337-3 (ebk)

DOI: 10.1201/9781003623373

Typeset in LM Roman
by KnowledgeWorks Global Ltd.

Publisher's note: This book has been prepared from camera-ready copy provided by the authors.

To the mind behind the computer's mind.

Contents

Preface

This book aims to introduce in an entertaining but rigorous way fundamental notions of Computer Science, in order to address the question "Is human mind reducible to a computer program?" It is based only on Computer Science and mathematical proofs. It doesn't appeal to subjective experiences or to metaphysical ideas about mind, only to straightforward observations like the fact that we can think about things like numbers. Each step is proved with mathematical rigor, allowing the readers to try and find a mistake, or, if everything checks, to convince themselves that the conclusions are correct.

This book can be used in the classes of philosophy of mind and by those interested in the possibility that Artificial Intelligence can become conscious. But it is not a manual about the history of ideas and arguments for and against the Computational Theory of Mind. Nor is it a collection of arguments and claims made by authoritative figures to support some views on consciousness that I happen to share. I consider I (or anyone else for that matter) have no authority to tell you what to think about the possibility that computers can be conscious or that your own mind may be a computation. And even if someone with authority, the greatest philosopher, the greatest computer scientist, a Nobel prize winner, would tell you what to think, wouldn't it be better if they would show you the path and help you walk it, to see for yourself? Even if God would tell you the answer, wouldn't it be better if you could verify it yourself, like doubting Thomas?

If you mindfully walk the steps of a proof, if you understand it, nothing can take this away from you. This is why the main goal I had in mind while writing this book was to give the reader a verifiable mathematical proof. Following it may require effort, but at the same time it gives the opportunity to gain something as certain as $2 + 2 = 4$, or, if this is the case, to find fatal flaws in its logic.

So why wait, let's ask Computer Science these questions!

Acknowledgments

I warmly thank Cris Calude, Adal Chiriliuc, Liviu Coconu, James Fullwood, Etienne Jacques, Johannes Kleiner, Andrew Knight, Robert Koons, Michael Levin, Perry Marshall, Jonathan Mason, Cristian Presură, Mihai Prunescu, Paavo Pylkkänen, Robert Ruxandrescu, Igor Salom, Justin Sampson, Simon Saunders, Paul Tappenden, Iulian Toader, Marko Vojinović, the Association for Mathematical Consciousness Science, and many others for very insightful, entertaining, and challenging conversations. Some were briefer, some extended over long nights, some remained unfinished before reaching a verdict, but they all helped me verify and refine some of the arguments discussed here. Nevertheless, I take full responsibility for the content of this book. I am grateful to Aurelian Isar and to my loving family, especially Sorana, Victor, and Ştefi for their unconditioned support. I am very indebted to the reviewers and editors of the book, particularly Rebecca Hodges-Davies, Isabel Hoffmann, Danny Kielty, Sanika Shah, Kumar Shashi, and everyone else.

Author

Ovidiu Cristinel (Cristi) Stoica researches Theoretical Physics at the National Institute of Physics and Nuclear Engineering Horia Hulubei. He is interested in foundational questions about the universe, preferring whenever possible geometric and group-theoretic approaches. His research areas include General Relativity, in particular black hole and Big Bang singularities, foundations of Quantum Mechanics, and the Standard Model of particle physics. Before, he taught mathematics and most of the time developed advanced algorithms of computational geometry for the private sector. All this time, he was preoccupied by questions about the nature of consciousness and how it fits in the rigid structure of the physical laws. His essays on physics received several prizes from the Foundational Questions Institute. This book is the result of combining his passions for the applications of symmetries in physics, Computer Science, mathematics, teaching, and understanding the place of consciousness in the physical world.

Prologue

It was way past midnight. Alice was still studying when Bob messaged her.

Hey Alice! I am watching online the panel discussion I've sent to you earlier. The participants are a few major names in Computer Science and Philosophy of Mind. Also the very smart physicist lady you like is there!

Hi Bob! Really? I'm totally interested 😍 , I'll check the link asap!

I think the AI may already be conscious! These experts convinced me, they showed that the AI displays incredible demonstrations of communication and reasoning!

Genuinely conscious or just imitating conscious beings like us?

They asked an Artificial Intelligence all sorts of difficult questions, including morally difficult ones, and the AI replied with great wisdom and empathy! We're living great times, Alice, I tell you what 🍾 !

But Bob, wasn't the AI programmed in the first place to imitate us? All that this proves is that the people who made the AI are really good at programming.

It's learning new things by itself, Alice. It's a Large Language Model and it's learning new stuff, just like you and me learn new stuff.

Sure, and I don't want to contradict you, you're the computer scientist here, but still, isn't it learning *because it was programmed* to do so? I mean, doesn't an LLM basically simply make statistics on text to identify patterns of words and to predict the next word?

Well, if you think about it, are we more than a bunch of programs that somehow have the ability to learn?

Frankly, I have no idea what we are, Bob... But... programs?

They learn new stuff incredibly fast, they have amazing memory and processing speed, and they have access to the entire knowledge developed by humanity. And now the things they've learned accumulated, reaching the threshold necessary to understand and even be self-aware.

Self-awareness? You mean witnessing one's own thoughts without attachment, like a Buddhist monk?

Well, maybe even this. If you ask the AI the right questions, they'll say they can follow their own thinking processes and report it. I watched a few demonstrations of AIs asked to conduct introspections and even to meditate. The AI has *metacognition*—the ability to be aware of their own thoughts and understand how they cause each other.

So what does this prove? The AI just learned from the reports of actual people who wrote about such things, and then imitated what these people said, regurgitating the words of some gurus and self-deluded fake gurus.

Do you think we are any different? Can we do something or think something an AI can't do? Didn't you see the art they create? If I show you some paintings without telling you which are AI generated and which are human generated, can you distinguish them?

My point is that it's beyond me how a machine that does nothing but to move around some numbers, some zeroes and ones, could turn these numbers into ineffable experiences. This seems to me like alchemy.

What do you mean "just numbers"? You're the physicist here, this is your domain, and I don't know that much about this, but when physicists do experiments they measure something. Don't they just find "some numbers"? Do they ever find in a lab the experience of seeing red, or "just numbers"?

Exactly! When we do experiments we express the results using numbers, and we build theoretical models to describe why we get those numbers. Our best theories are mostly math, if not only math. To us, red is just light with a wavelength around 625 – 740 nanometers. And I'm pretty sure when neuroscientists, like our dear friend Carol, look into the brain, they don't find any experience of seeing red, of the taste or smell of an apple, of being in love, any of those qualities of our experiences called *qualia* 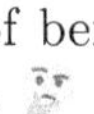 ...

So Physics is "just numbers" too, am I right?

Physics consists of descriptions of the world. These descriptions are mathematical models. Math is not just numbers, but indeed, when we measure something we only get numbers.

And since Physics is an empirical science, all that matters is what you measure, so it's "just numbers", right? The deepest description of the universe we have is "just numbers". Just like computer programs.

Indeed, there seems to be no other way but to base Physics, and Science in general, on measurements and building mathematical models to account for the results of these measurements. And I can't see how Science, which will always be based on experiments, will ever give answers that are not just numbers. Bob, how much I love Physics, I have to admit that I don't think it can provide the basis for answering such deep questions like what we are, what consciousness and life are, and I don't know how it can be done. And I don't know of a better way to find the truth than Science...

Alice, you say Physics didn't answer your questions yet, but its message is clear: we're a mechanism made of elementary particles. Just like computers. We can simulate on a computer every physical system, at least in principle, if we'd have the resources.

Right, the *Church-Turing-Deutsch Principle*:
"Every finitely realizable physical system can be perfectly simulated by a universal model computing machine operating by finite means". (David Deutsch's *The Fabric of Reality*, page 132 [53], [52])

Exactly! So we can also simulate brains. In practice it may be too complicated, but we can in principle. But we don't even need to simulate brains down to the elementary particles, simulating the thinking process is enough. Do we need more to simulate minds?

I just don't understand how mind could be a computation, Bob. I know, for example, that music is just waves, their frequencies, but I don't feel that my experience when listening to music is just numbers...

Can you show what else your experience of listening to music is, in an experiment so that other people can see it? 😏

Yeah, I know, science admits only evidence that you can show to other people to see it, to measure it, to verify it by themselves...

Can you prove that your mind can do something that an AI will never be able to do?

Bob, I am pretty sure that an AI will be able to imitate us, I mean talk like us, those things we do and other people can see. And I'm aware that claiming otherwise is considered unscientific.

So then relax. At some point not even human consciousness will be a mystery for science.

This promise doesn't convince me that mind is reducible to a computation.
If you claim that mind is a computation... first define mind!

I can say the same. If you claim that mind is not a computation, first define mind. But not a definition based on "what I feel". Something that we can all verify. No mentions of feelings, ineffable subjective experiences, qualia...

But these exist too! Science can describe, in principle, how every neuron works, how this makes us act in a particular way, including how we describe our own experiences to others. These are all things that can be seen by others, neurons and their activity can be seen if we have good enough instruments, can be measured, we can describe them using mathematical models. But how can it describe *our private experiences*?

But what are these experiences beyond the physical activity?

You know, even if we will be able to model in every minute detail a bat, we will not be able to know *what it's like to be a bat* [128].

Yes, what the brain does, how a bat behaves, all this can be described in principle, and it can be simulated in principle. And the same is true of humans. These are so-called *easy problems* of consciousness, and we all agree they're not "easy" at all. And you think there is a *hard problem of consciousness*, as David Chalmers [30] calls it, right?

Yes, to model, to simulate, to imitate behavior, all these seem easy, compared to the hard problem of explaining what it's like to be us. With all our experiences, private as they may be. Are you going to deny the existence of these experiences, of the quale of red for example?

Some thinkers, like Dan Dennett, say that these are illusions [46, 47, 49].

Come on, to have illusions you first need to have experiences. What is an illusion if not the experience that something is different than what it really is?

That's what your mind makes you think

So you need to have a mind, right? Here's Neil deGrasse Tyson saying

> "I wonder whether there really is no such thing as consciousness at all"

http://youtu.be/40YIIaF1qiw [4]. Check out Bill Nye's reply: "Am I thinking, or am I just thinking that I'm thinking?" .

But Dennett and other illusionists don't say there is no mind, they just say that mind is not really "colored" by experiences, we just think it is. We're just telling ourselves some "colorful stories".

But still, I can't even understand how the numbers in a computer can make the AI tell itself "colorful stories"...
I don't understand why these thinkers deny us our experiences, Bob ...

But if an AI says "I experience the taste of an ice-cream", who are you to deny *their experiences*? Just because they're not made of flesh like us? Isn't this a form of discrimination, "meat chauvinism"?

Not if a computer is as insentient as a rock or a thermostat, no.

Prove it! The burden of proof is yours, Alice .

Why not yours and those who claim that mind is just a computation ?

You made the claim that there is something that can't be simulated by a computer, Alice.

No, I think it can be fully simulated. But it's just a simulation.

Same difference! As long as you can't discern them by using experiments, it's unscientific. So here's a challenge for you: define consciousness and prove that it can't be just a computation. The floor is yours!

You know I can't define it, neither can you.

Sure I can: "Consciousness is as consciousness does". Period.
How do you know others are conscious? And if an AI can do whatever a being that you acknowledge as conscious can, you have to admit the AI is conscious too. This is the *Turing test*, "The Imitation Game" [200].

> I don't need to define or to mathematically model an apple to know by taste that it's not an orange.

That's because you can taste both the apple and the orange. But you can't be both you and the AI, you can't verify with your own mind what it's like to be an AI, you said it yourself.

> I still think, if Science is the way to the truth, that there must be a way, a *no-go theorem*, you know, like Bell's theorem, or Gödel's theorem, or Turing's theorem [136, 9]. Each of these theorems show something to be impossible, maybe we'll find such an impossibility theorem about generating consciousness on a computer.

I won't hold my breath...

> What if it can be proved that your own mind has a property that a computation can't? We won't even need to know or to define what mind is, only whether it has a property that computer programs don't have.

When this will happen, I'll get myself a tattoo saying "I was wrong!"

1

Introduction

1.1 The alien robot

Imagine that an alien spaceship crashes on Earth and nothing remains of it, except for the "brain" of an alien robot. Its artificial brain was very important to the aliens who built the robot, because it could contain important data collected during the robot's expeditions, so they protected it by placing it in a very resistant container. But they didn't care too much to protect the other "organs" of the robot that are easily replaceable. So the input devices, which helped the robot see or hear, and the output devices, which helped it communicate, move around, and perform activities, were irreversibly damaged during the crash. All that remained intact was the robot's brain, without any indication of how it would exchange information with the environment or with its own motor organs.

The world's top experts gathered together and tried to use the highest science and technology available to research the robot's brain, to find out how it works and what information it contains. They succeeded in opening the robot's "skull" and understanding that the brain contained things like logic circuits and memory cells. The robot's brain turned out to be very similar to a computer. It even contained microscopic switches that can only be in two possible states, like the memory cells used by our computers to store data as binary digits. To the expert's surprise, the robot's brain was still active and seemed to be fully functional.

Our experts reasoned in the following way:

> If we study the alien robot's brain carefully enough, we will be able to extract the information it contains, to "read" its mind if you wish, just by looking at how it's made. To do this, we don't need the input and output devices that were destroyed. We can apply electric signals to its circuits and see what happens. All we need is sufficient budget and time.

DOI: 10.1201/9781003623373-1

So the experts from our story think that they can retrieve unambiguously the information stored in the robot's brain. By "unambiguously" I mean the following: if different teams of researchers recover the information independently, they should get the same result. For example, if the robot stores in its memory a number, different researchers should recover the same number. If they, without making mistakes, can get different results, then the results are ambiguous.

One may think that there is unambiguous data in the robot's brain, and they're just too difficult to read due to the complexity of its brain. That it makes sense to say that the alien robot thinks of a number, or at least that it holds a number in its memory.

I'd like to invite the reader to answer some questions. The first one is

Easy Question 1. Does a computer store unambiguously data?

For example, if the robot thinks of a number, can we "read" this number? Or, if it is too difficult to read, can we at least be certain that there is an unambiguous number stored in the robot's brain?

Perhaps many would consider not only that the number is there, but reading it is a trivial, albeit tedious task, especially for an Artificial Intelligence that learns by adjusting their parameters in ways obscure to us. All that scientists have to do, it may seem, is to look at the robot's circuits, find out the physical state of each of its memory cells, and extract the information it contains. So I expect many people think this is possible. The number must be objectively there, not needing an output device for the robot to report the number, or an input device for us to put the number there. Would you agree?

But, if the absence of the input and output devices is the problem, what if the robot has these devices in order? What if we made the robot, and so we know very well how it works? After all, if the number is definitely and unambiguously stored in the robot's brain, it should continue to be there even if the input and output devices are destroyed. So how would you answer the Easy Question 1?

Is that your final answer?

The aliens who sent the robot to explore the universe trusted it well enough to let it travel alone. This suggests that the alien robot is able to handle new situations, so it must have internal representations of itself. Maybe the robot can have *reflexive thoughts*, thoughts of the form "right now, I am thinking about this". If this is the case, the robot is thinking that it's thinking, and it knows what it's thinking about.

Can the robot know unambiguously its own thoughts? Or, if the robot's brain just simulates thinking about thinking, whatever this means, does this simulation contain unambiguous representations of itself?

If we believe that the answer to the Easy Question 1 is yes, then if different teams conclude that at some moment of time the robot thinks of a number or even a color, they should agree what that number or what that color is. But if one of the teams concludes that the robot thinks of a red object, and another team that it thinks of a blue object, and if no mistake was made, is then there such a thing as objective thought of seeing red or at least of thinking about the number seven?

Let me be a bit clearer about this, to avoid misunderstandings. If two teams of researchers decode different minds (or simulated minds) in the same brain of the alien robot, one may expect that if the mind found by one of the teams has representations of itself, these are representations of that mind, and not of another mind, not of the mind decoded by the other team. So even if there is no unambiguous way to decode a mind in the robot's brain, each of the decoded minds may unambiguously represent its own thoughts.

But if different teams of researchers can find different minds, this implies that at some point they can't base the decoding on the functionality of the robot's brain alone. At some point they have to decide that a particular state of the robot's brain encodes some data or some other data. That choice is a convention, something that can be as simple as "this state of this memory cell represents a `0`, and this other state represents a `1`". So whether the robot's mind is the one decoded by one team or another depends on a convention. Given that the choice of this convention is made by external observers, can it be a property of the robot's brain itself? Let me state this question in a weaker form, about computation:

Easy Question 2. Is the computation done by a computer an objective property of the computer alone, independent of our conventions?

In other words, is computation an *intrinsic feature* of the computer carrying it? Here by "intrinsic" I mean just independent of external systems and of conventions made by external observers. I don't mean that the robot didn't interact with external systems, only that, whatever it thinks now, it is independent of the conventions that external observers may make.

1.2 Are you a robot?

There is a reason why I called questions 1 and 2 "easy": to allude to the "easy problems" of consciousness. David Chalmers distinguishes between what he calls *easy problems* and the *hard problem of consciousness* [30]. Basically, the easy problems are about describing what consciousness does, that is, how it functions, how it stores, retrieves, and processes information. This would be akin to the way we describe what a mechanism does, its features that can be described and recognized by observing them "from the outside". The hard problem is to explain the *sentient experience* associated with such a behavior or reaction, "what it's like" [128], how it feels "from the inside". The easy problems are not at all easy. And, since there are thinkers who refute the very idea of sentient experience as being something special compared to mere computation or functionality or patterns recognizable from the outside [46, 34], even to explain the difference between what Chalmers calls hard and easy problems is not easy at all. However, in this book, we will not be concerned with explaining consciousness, but only to see if it can be reduced to computations as they are understood in Computer Science. And for this, we will almost exclusively explore questions about computations, and not so much about minds directly. Toward the end of our exploration, we will compare what we learned about computations with something that we irrefutably know about our own minds, and see whether mind can be nothing more than a sophisticated computation.

The Easy Questions 1 and 2 are not about human consciousness, but merely about computers and robots and how they process information in a way akin to thinking. Compared to even the easy problems of consciousness, they should be much easier. They don't even ask for a description or an explanation of how exactly this can happen in a robot's brain, they just ask whether computations that some may identify as thinking are unambiguous. So there seems to be a huge gap between them and the following.

Hard Question 1. Can a computer or a robot have a purely computational mind by itself, independent of external observers?

Can a computer or a robot have an intrinsic mind, independent of any external convention, and which is just a computation? We see that while the Easy Question 2 is "easy", if it has a negative answer, it immediately implies a negative answer for the Hard Question 1. So maybe the Hard Question 1 is not that hard after all. But, on the other hand, an affirmative answer for the Easy Question 2 doesn't imply an affirmative answer for the Hard Question 1, unless the following Hard Question has an affirmative answer too:

Hard Question 2. Can consciousness be just a computation?

This is the major question that this book is all about.

> I can't stress enough that this book is not about the question if a machine or a physical system like the brain can be conscious by any means, but merely if it can be conscious specifically by doing computations in exactly the sense in which computation is understood in Computer Science. After all, the Artificial Intelligences are built and use computations based on Computer Science, and not on frameworks beyond Computer Science.

A negative answer to the Easy Questions 1 and 2, which are questions for Computer Science, not for Philosophy of Mind, would have dramatic implications for the scientific or philosophical research programs aiming to give an affirmative answer to the Hard Question 2.

It may be a surprise for many if the answer to Easy Questions 1 and 2 would be "no", or even if these questions have provable answers. And yet, this is what this book will show, based on basic facts from Computer Science. We will see that if the answers of these questions would be "yes", there would be no universal computers, no programmable computers. The readers will have the possibility to verify this by making themselves an experiment on their computers.

1.3 The blasphemy of the age of AI and materialism

In the present age, when many scientists and philosophers think that we have the big picture of the universe and the rest is details, it may seem like a blasphemy against science itself to doubt the claim that consciousness is merely a computation. We often even hear that in the near future scientists will be able to upload our minds, including our sentient experiences, into a computer. After all, there is no limit for the human spirit (where the word "spirit" is meant in a purely computational sense, of course). To those adopting this position, it seems obvious that the Hard Question 2 has an affirmative answer. This is the main claim disputed in this book.

Some philosophers of mind and scientists admit that they don't see how the entire spectrum of our experience can be reduced to computations. They would invoke as counterarguments the existence of feelings, sensations, the subjective or private aspects of consciousness, the sense of "I", the hard problem of consciousness, the ineffability of sentient experience, or "what it's like". They would use words like *qualia* (the qualities of our subjective experiences of pain, feelings, seeing color, *etc.*) or *phenomenal consciousness* to generically name these experiences.

Although I agree with this position (who am I to deny anyone's experiences, especially since I have experiences too?), to avoid appealing to subjective evidence, I will not invoke any of these arguments in this book. I will do this to anticipate any objections, including objections from the deniers of the authenticity of subjective experience.

Indeed, no matter how vivid your subjective experiences are, there are thinkers who would deny them because you can't show them to the others, and therefore they can't be verified independently in a laboratory. All you can do is to arrange the matter from which your body is made in a limited number of various patterns that can be observed from the outside. Or, perhaps, rather to shamelessly take credit for the fact that matter arranges itself in such patterns by purely materialistic processes. These patterns include patterns of the brain activity, sounds, facial expressions, *etc.* It seems natural to these thinkers to claim that since you can't show to other people more than these material patterns, all these discussions about qualia are not scientific. I will avoid this accusation by avoiding the appeal to qualia.

So I will rely only on the methods of materialism. Materialism led thinkers like Paul and Patricia Churchland to the thesis of *eliminative materialism* or *eliminativism*, the materialist position in the philosophy of mind that claims that our experiences don't really exist, but are *folk psychology*, superstitions [34]. Without adopting this stretched conclusion, I will follow rules that would be accepted even by the Churchlands, even by Dennett, who claimed that qualia are as real as Santa Claus and Easter Bunny [49]. This is the central claim of *illusionism*, the thesis that qualia are a sort of illusion. I will follow Dennett and other supporters of illusionism, like Frankish [66] and Kammerer [102, 103], not in their conclusions, but in the methods they claimed to lead to these conclusions, but I will reach an opposite conclusion.

I will only appeal to undeniable facts like the facts of Physics and Computer Science, and to the fact that we can think about a number, which even eliminativists and illusionists would admit as real. Despite some initial misunderstandings, they don't claim that mind can't have content at all, but that its content is "about things", and they call this *access consciousness* or *intentionality* [16], to distinguish it from phenomenal consciousness. This doesn't mean that the results from this book don't have implications for the existence of qualia, but rather that I will prove that thinking about something, even a number, which even illusionists and eliminativists accept, that any sort of content of the mind, and not just the qualia, can't be reduced to computation. I will abide by their own research rules, which they claim to refute the reality of consciousness, to push the thesis that mind is nothing but a computation into a contradiction with empirical facts anyone can verify. Following the rules accepted by the supporters of the most extreme materialist position about mind will not only refute their position but also the more general thesis that mind is just a computation, where "computation" is understood as in Computer Science.

> We will see that, if consciousness is just computation, we can't even determine, by any scientific experiment, of what number the alien robot thinks. And neither the robot can know that number. In fact, we will see that there is no such number. But this is not all: we will use this result to see if mind can be reduced to computation.

1.4 What to expect from this book

I will not attempt to explain consciousness, not even to resolve any of its easy problems. This book will not say what consciousness is, but what it is not. It is about consciousness, but only *indirectly*, because its focus is to identify something that is believed more and more nowadays to be able to produce consciousness, and to show that it can't. And I will rely on Computer Science and Physics only. Ironically, the method I will use is illusionist and eliminativist, but the conclusion is that mind is more than computation.

First, this will lead us to see that an affirmative answer to the Hard Question 2 implies the existence of numerous independent and contradictory coexisting computations, and if we attribute to one of them the status of a mind, we should do the same to all of them. That is, if mind is a computation, numerous completely different minds must coexist in the same brain. This already may be a shock to those who think that the brain can encode in its processes a unique computation, which they want to identify as a mind. Since these coexisting "minds" exist because computation is based on external conventions, the most straightforward conclusion is that this contradicts the fact that we have minds regardless of other people's beliefs about this. So to many, this may already be sufficient to discard the claim that mind is just a computation.

Many modern researchers think that we can find consciousness in computers running sufficiently advanced software. We will see that according to Computer Science itself, this is just imagination. Consciousness isn't there. At least not in an unambiguous way: if consciousness would be just a computation, any computer or physical system that is conscious would be conscious simultaneously in a vast number of contradictory ways.

To apply this also to brains, I will extend these results to analog and quantum computers, and physical systems in general. We will see that we can't avoid the ambiguity even if, and especially if the computer has memories with more than two states, or if they are analog, or if they are quantum. We will see that if mind were just a computation, the number of distinct mental states that contradict one another has to be immense.

By "minds" that "coexist" in the same brain I don't mean the existence of complex, mixed, or fuzzy thoughts and experiences simultaneously, or even *dissociative identity disorder*, which is still often called *multiple personality disorder*. "Coexisting minds" simply means that there is no unambiguous way to encode a mind-like computation in the brain's processes. A normal expectation even supporters of the Computational Theory of Mind is that even if one is confused about one's own thoughts and experiences, the mental state containing these thoughts and experiences, including the confusion about them, is unique, unambiguous. That there are objective facts about the content of the mind. This is rejected by our first main result:

Result 1 (Nonuniqueness of the "computational mind"). *If* mind would be just a computation, *then* the same brain would contain many distinct and even contradictory minds that don't know about one another.

In other words, if one claims, based on some criteria, that certain computations can be minds (so let's call them "mind-like computations"), in the same brain many coexisting but contradictory computations that qualify as minds by the same criteria equally take place simultaneously. If we believe that a computer can think of a number, it would be equally justified to interpret this at the same time as thinking of many other numbers, and there is no objective way by which one of these thoughts is more "real" than the others. Therefore, an AI can't think unambiguously of a number. I will illustrate this with several apparently paradoxical and hopefully entertaining thought experiments, showing that *if* a computer can have a mind, *then* it has many distinct minds unaware of one another, in parallel, simultaneously!

At this point, the proponents of the Computational Theory of Mind who tried but couldn't find a mistake in the proof given in this book would have to either drop their claim or bite the bullet and accept the multitude of coexisting minds. *"OK"*, they may say, *"I expected a unique computation that qualifies as a mind, and that it can be found unambiguously by examining the machinery. I admit that I was wrong about this. But this doesn't mean that mind is not just a computation. Maybe all coexisting computations that qualify as minds by my criteria are minds in the same way!"* Then, the relativity and ambiguity of computation will force us to choose between two options:

Option 1. If a physical system implements a mind, it implements many contradictory minds at the same time.

Option 2. Consciousness and even mere thinking are not computations.

At this point, we will make another experiment that will contradict Option 1, the possibility that all these coexisting computations are minds. For this experiment, we will examine our own minds. Not subjective experiences like qualia, but straight facts like thinking of a number. You will compare your mind with the overwhelming majority of mind-like computations attributable to your brain's processes, and obtain the main result of this book:

Result 2. Mind is not just a computation.

We will not find out what mind is; all we will find out is that whatever it is, it is not reducible to computation. We will not find out that a machine can't have a mind, but only that, if it has a mind, this is not a computation. So a sentient robot remains possible, provided that we will ever find what makes us sentient. Figure 1.1 contains a flowchart illustrating the main steps of the argument.

Now, the proponents of the Computational Theory of Mind may choose to bite this second bullet too and decide that *"maybe mind is not a computation as in Computer Science, but if we take into account the internal structure and*

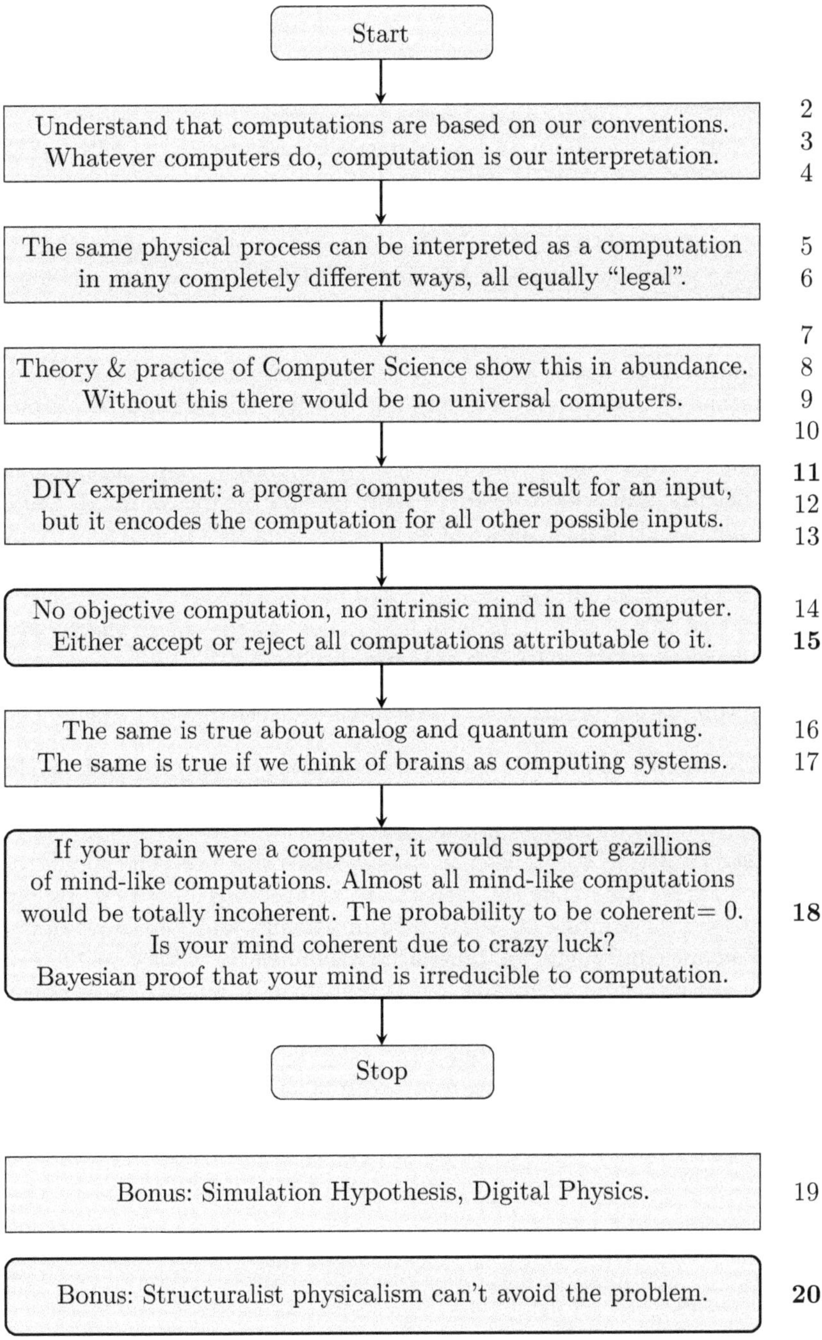

Figure 1.1: Flowchart of this book's logic.

its interactions, then we will replace the usual notion of computation with a much stricter one, that will remove the ambiguity. Then, mind will turn out to be such a stricter notion of computation after all".

And this step was already made, many computational functionalists, when confronted with the relativity and ambiguity of computation, adopted such stricter notions of computation. They are calling them *accounts of computation*. However, since these kinds of "computation" contradict Computer Science, being incompatible with the existence of programmable computers, they also forbid the possibility that the AIs that we have today can be conscious. These are not "accounts of computation", they are redefinitions. It would be a mistake to consider them different ways to describe a computation, since the confusion between these kinds of "restricted computation" and computation as normally understood in Computer Science may lead to the wrong conclusion that an AI is sentient.

Moreover, even if we use stricter notions of computation than those used in Computer Science, and even if we adopt more general theories of mind, based on functionality or structure, these suffer from ambiguities of their own. Even if we take into account the complete physical description of the structure of a system, based on Quantum Theory, there will be ambiguities of the structure itself, which lead to contradictions with experience. At the end of the book, I will briefly give the proof of a much stronger result,

Result 3. Mind is not reducible to the structures accessible to Physics.

But going into the full details and the implications of this proof will be the subject of the next book. The present book is almost completely restricted to the question if mind can be just a computation.

In the age of Artificial Intelligence, this is something everyone should be interested to know. Note that the research in neuroscience, Artificial Intelligence, models of consciousness, *etc* is very important, and I have no doubt that it will advance our understanding of how mind works. This research will continue to advance to unbelievable levels, and it is in no way undermined by the arguments from this book, that mind can't be just a computation, no matter how sophisticated this computation may be. However, I hope the results presented in the book will keep us away from the temptation to proclaim prematurely that we obtained sentient Artificial Intelligence or that we can upload our minds on a computer, achieving digital immortality.

Exercises

Exercise 1.1. Review the following questions and give your answer.

Question	Yes	No	I don't know
Easy Question 1, page 8			
Easy Question 2, page 9			
Hard Question 1, page 10			
Hard Question 2, page 10			

There is no correct way to answer them, it's just an evaluation of your initial opinion. You can write down the reasons behind your answers, for your own reference. After you finish the book, you can return and see if your opinion changed.

Key points

- Rather than simply telling you the answers or the opinions of various experts, this book will show you how to get them, step by step, based on Computer Science.
- You will need to follow the steps. This is why, although its technical level is not too sophisticated, it is not an easy book.

Part I

The veil of convention

2

The alien device

2.1 The mysterious device

Alice and Bob were walking in the park, being so caught in a heated discussion that they forgot what a beautiful day it was. A boy on a bike stopped by and handed them a package, labeled "For Alice and Bob". They immediately unboxed it, finding a weird device of a seemingly otherworldly origin. They turn to the kid to ask him what's with the package, who sent it and why, but the kid was nowhere, as if it disappeared into thin air.

Intrigued, Alice and Bob spent the entire afternoon trying to figure out what the device does. Because it seemed different from anything they ever saw, they called it *the alien device.*

The device consists of a knob P, a switch Q, and a pointer R, each of them able to be in two possible states. The knob P can be either in the state a or in the state b, the switch Q can be in one of two states c and d, and the pointer R in one of the states x and y. The knob and the switch are connected with the pointer through a central component f.

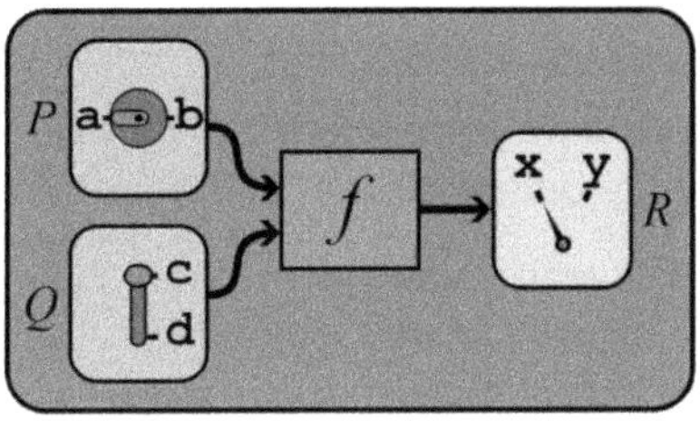

Figure 2.1: The alien device. The knob P can be set to a or b. The switch Q can be set to c or d. This puts the pointer R into either x or y, as in Table 2.1.

Let p, q, and r be the respective states in which the parts P, Q, and R of the device can be. The two possible values of p are then a and b, those of q by c and d, and those of r by x and y. Alice and Bob noticed that any combination of the states of P and Q automatically determines the state of R, according to Table 2.1.

DOI: 10.1201/9781003623373-2

Table 2.1: Correspondence between the choices of the states of P and Q and the resulting states of the pointer R.

p	q	r
a	c	x
a	d	x
b	c	y
b	d	x

Assuming that the two possible states of each system must represent bit values `0` (false) and `1` (true), or truth values `F` and `T`, Alice and Bob tried to understand what the central part f does. They tried to guess independently the values of `a`, `b`, `c`, `d`, `x`, and `y`, and the function f for which

$$r = f(p, q). \tag{2.1}$$

They expected f to be a Boolean function, which is a function that takes the truth values `F` and `T` and computes from them another truth value. That is, a Boolean function of n variables is a function f, where

$$f : \underbrace{\{\mathtt{F}, \mathtt{T}\} \times \ldots \times \{\mathtt{F}, \mathtt{T}\}}_{n \text{ times}} \to \{\mathtt{F}, \mathtt{T}\}, \tag{2.2}$$

or

$$f : \underbrace{\{\mathtt{0}, \mathtt{1}\} \times \ldots \times \{\mathtt{0}, \mathtt{1}\}}_{n \text{ times}} \to \{\mathtt{0}, \mathtt{1}\}. \tag{2.3}$$

Example 2.1. Examples of Boolean functions are:

- `NOT`(negation). $f(p) := \overline{p}$, which inverts (or negates) the value of p.
- `AND` (conjunction). $f(p, q) := p \wedge q$, which is `TRUE` if and only if both p and q are `TRUE`.
- `OR` (disjunction). $f(p, q) := p \vee q$, which is `TRUE` if at least p or q is `TRUE`.
- `XOR` (exclusive or, exclusive disjunction). $f(p, q) := (p \wedge \overline{q}) \vee (\overline{p} \wedge q)$, which is `TRUE` if either p or q, but not both, is `TRUE` (and the other is `FALSE`).
- Any function of n Boolean variables (inputs) $f(p_1, p_2, \ldots, p_n)$, returning a Boolean value (output) obtained by composing Boolean functions as above. For example, $f(p, q, r) := (p \wedge q) \vee r$.
- Any function of n Boolean variables and with m Boolean values (outputs),

$$\mathbf{f}(p_1, p_2, \ldots, p_n) = (f_1(p_1, p_2, \ldots, p_n), \ldots, f_m(p_1, p_2, \ldots, p_n)), \tag{2.4}$$

where $f_1, \ldots, f_m$ are Boolean functions with one value as above.

Alice and Bob wanted to make sure they got it right, so they tried to find the function independently and to compare the results. The reader can pause and try to solve the problem as well:

Exercise 2.1. What are the values of `a`, `b`, `c`, `d`, `x`, and `y`, and the Boolean function f, so that $r = f(p, q)$ as in Table 2.1?

2.2 The eightfold way

Ready? Let's see what Alice and Bob found.

Alice's interpretation of Table 2.1 is presented in Table 2.2. She concludes that $f(p,q) = p \wedge q$, so the central module f of the alien device must be an AND gate.

Table 2.2: Alice's interpretation is a=d=x=F and b=c=y=T.

p	q	r		p	q	$p \wedge q$
a	c	x		F	T	F
a	d	x	$\Rightarrow$	F	F	F
b	c	y		T	T	T
b	d	x		T	F	F

The AND gate is a logic gate that implements the Boolean function $p \wedge q$.

But Bob interprets Table 2.1 as in Table 2.3. He thinks that $f(p,q) = \overline{p} \vee \overline{q}$, so the central part f of the alien device must be a NAND gate.

Table 2.3: Bob's interpretation is a=d=y=F and b=c=x=T.

p	q	r		p	q	$\overline{p} \vee \overline{q}$
a	c	x		F	T	T
a	d	x	$\Rightarrow$	F	F	T
b	c	y		T	T	F
b	d	x		T	F	T

Alice and Bob get into an argument, each one of them being convinced that their own interpretation is the correct one. This is understandable, because once everything makes sense in one way, it is difficult to see it in another way. So they decide to ask Carol to mediate. Carol does not want to upset either Alice or Bob, so she asks David, Eve, Frank, Grace, and Heidi to join. Each of them tries to make sense of the device, independently. But each of them comes up with their own interpretation. They are all collected in Table 2.4.

Just when the chaos was about to erupt irreversibly, David calls Solomon in his support. Solomon says that David is correct.

But when Grace says that her interpretation is correct, Solomon says that she is right too. At the end, Solomon agreed with all eight of them.

Then Eve said "but we can't all be right!".

Solomon replied to Eve "this is correct too!".

But they continued to object, saying "Solomon, you can't just call TRUE what is FALSE and vice versa! Two opposites can't both be true!"

Exercise 2.2. Before seeing Solomon's answer, I would ask you to try and figure out the explanation yourself.

After pondering for a while, Solomon slowly replied: "All eight interpretations are correct interpretations of the same device. However we call the

Table 2.4: The different interpretations of the functionality of the device according to eight different subjects.

Alice

p	q	$p \wedge q$
F	T	F
F	F	F
T	T	T
T	F	F

Bob

p	q	$\overline{p} \vee \overline{q}$
F	T	T
F	F	T
T	T	F
T	F	T

Carol

p	q	$p \wedge \overline{q}$
F	F	F
F	T	F
T	F	T
T	T	F

David

p	q	$\overline{p} \vee q$
F	F	T
F	T	T
T	F	F
T	T	T

Eve

p	q	$\overline{p} \wedge q$
T	T	F
T	F	F
F	T	T
F	F	F

Frank

p	q	$p \vee \overline{q}$
T	T	T
T	F	T
F	T	F
F	F	T

Grace

p	q	$\overline{p} \wedge \overline{q}$
T	F	F
T	T	F
F	F	T
F	T	F

Heidi

p	q	$p \vee q$
T	F	T
T	T	T
F	F	F
F	T	T

possible states of a switch, a knob, or a pointer, these values exist only in our minds. The idea of a value like `0` and `1`, or like `FALSE` and `TRUE`, exists only in our minds, not in the device itself".

He continued: "Changing the interpretation of the bits entails a change of the computation that we attribute to the device, even though there is no physical change of the system or of the way it works. For each possible assignment of bit values, we can interpret the resulting computation as a Boolean function that becomes readable in the device, just like all of you did".

The interpretation of the bits goes hand in hand with that of the computation. We will return to this in Chapter 6.

Then Solomon proposed the *Principle of Relativity of Information* (PRI):

Principle 2.1 (Relativity of Information (PRI)). Information and computation are in the eye of the beholder.

The values of the bits are a convention, just like money is a convention. When we learn that high voltage means `1` and low voltage means `0`, the first thing we do is to ask why. If we ask the teacher why, she will tell us the truth: bits are a convention. But then we start using them in practice, and we internalize the habit of treating them as having an independent, objective meaning. Just like, when we first had the epiphany that money is a convention, this didn't make us give away all our material possessions. By contrast, we dedicate most of our time and energy to making money, because we know that conventional as it may be, money has the power to ruin or save lives and governments, and to bring countries to war. That's because the rest of the society acts as if money is real, and as if each service or product has an objective price. And even for products of the exact same quality, the brand can make a huge difference in the final price. Likewise, taking the bits literally helps us use, design, and program the computers. But they are just a useful and persistent illusion.

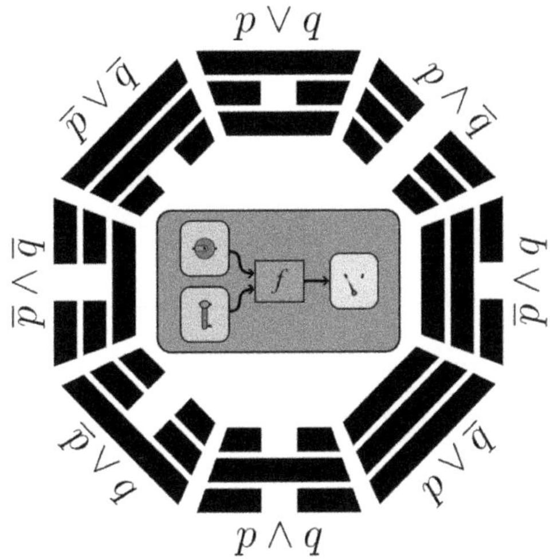

Figure 2.2: **The eightfold way.** The eight possible interpretations, classified by the truth values of the propositions "`p = a`", "`q = c`", and "`r = x`". From the center outward, "▬" represents `T` and "■ ■" represents `F`.

There seems to be a little bit of magic here. Alice can use the device to compute $p \wedge q$ for any values p and q. All she has to do is to put the system P in one of its two possible states `a` or `b`, according to Table 2.2, and do the same for the system Q by choosing among `c` and `d`. Then she can read the output of $f_A(p, q) = p \wedge q$ by reading the pointer R and interpreting `x` as `F` and `y` as `T`. She can do this for all possible values of p and q and collect the results in a truth table like Table 2.2.

Then, suppose she changes her mind and decides to go with Bob's interpretation of the device. Will she need to use the device again to compute the possible values of Bob's function $f_B(p, q)$? Not at all! Alice can now change her mind and choose each of the eight interpretations of the device how many times she wants. Every time she will know what the device would tell, without having to use it ever again, based on the results she obtained when using it for a single interpretation. All she has to do is to imagine that she relabeled the entries in Table 2.2. This is indeed consistent with all interpretations being correct, and moreover, with all eight Boolean functions being computed in parallel. *The way the device works is not affected by our interpretation of what it computes.*

The ambiguity of the alien device is not due to some advanced alien technology. This ambiguity is inherent in any computer. A computer stores information in various places, usually in memory cells that can be in two states.

They are not very different from the alien device, except that they can store much more information, and they process it by changing their own physical state. But their ambiguity is much larger, since it grows exponentially with the size of their total memory. We think there is only one way to interpret the information in a computer, simply because the user interface tells us so.

Relativity of information should be evident by now, but small thinking habits that come from our interactions with the computers may obscure this, so we may have to remove the layers of convention one by one.

2.3 The user interface conspiracy

When we use a computer, we have no doubt about what it does, even if we don't know exactly how it does it. We can use it to send and receive messages, to type a letter, to draw a picture, to print a file, to create computer programs and so on. And we never have the feeling that somehow we are projecting all of these from our imagination. Everything about a computer seems so grounded in reality. Computers symbolize precision, rather than ambiguity and relativity. There is no doubt that computers conform to our expectations with precision. Then how is it possible that the information we think they process is merely our convention?

Computers work so well because everybody involved in their production, in the design of their various components and the software, conspire to abide by the same convention. All people involved agreed upon which appearance to present to the user, and then they took great care to respect the convention, so that the illusion is maintained.

By conspiracy, I don't mean that somebody is hiding from us the fact that everything is based on a convention. By contrast, there is full transparency, the fact that what a computer does is based in convention is hidden in plain sight. If you ask the experts, they will tell you everything with pleasure. But everybody continues to act as if the convention is an objective reality. And enacting our belief in the objectivity of information and computation internalizes this belief and makes it so visceral.

The convention is fully anchored in the user interface. For example, a user interface can force a particular interpretation of the alien device. Suppose Alice draws circles on three post-it notes and sticks them on the device, as in Figure 2.3.

The circles represent two sets A and B. The set A is highlighted on the first post-it note, and its interpretation is a proposition $p =$"$x \in A$", that is, x is an element of the set A. The second post-it note has the set B highlighted, suggesting that $q =$"$x \in B$". And the third post-it note represents the intersection of the two sets, suggesting that proposition r is "$x \in A \cap B$". These post-it notes suggest that we should interpret the device as computing $p \wedge q$, as in Alice's Truth Table 2.2.

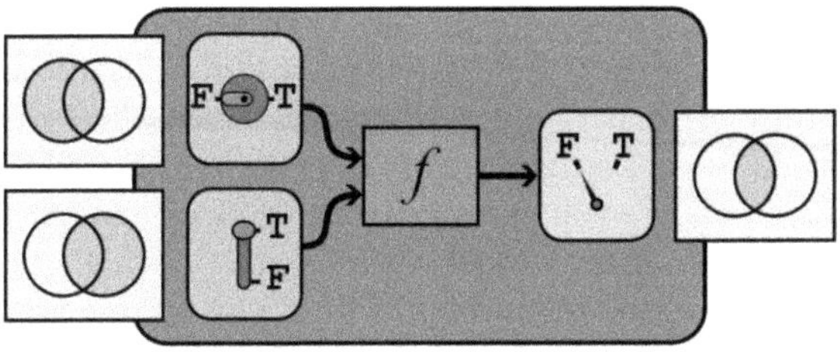

Figure 2.3: A user interface that suggests that p =“$x \in A$”, q =“$x \in B$”, and r =“$x \in A \cap B$” enforces Alice's interpretation $r = p \wedge q$.

But Heidi swaps the labels F and T put by Alice on the device, and replaces the third post-it note with another one, that represents the union of the two sets, $A \cup B$, as in Figure 2.4.

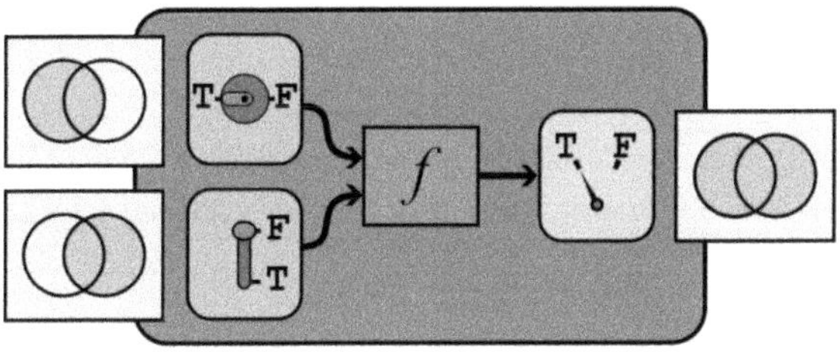

Figure 2.4: Changing the user interface changes interpretation of the device. Now, p =“$x \in A$”, q =“$x \in B$”, and r =“$x \in A \cup B$”. Then, $r = p \vee q$.

These examples allow us to make the following observations:

Observation 2.1. We assign a preferred interpretation to a computation simply because the computer's user interface is designed for the user.

The interpretation is fixed through the user interface, which consists of input and output devices. The user interface was designed so that human users can operate the computers and exchange information with them. For example, reading this book on a computer fixes the meaning of the patterns appearing on the display. In its turn, by the way the computer operates, this meaning fixes the interpretation of the bit cells as bits of information. Ultimately, the meaning of the bit cells is anchored in the user's mind, via the user interface.

But all computations resulting from such reinterpretations are faces of a single process. This is why they are all performed at once, in parallel. We are only aware of the one we select via the user interface (let us call it the *default computation*), and we are oblivious of all of the others (call these *hidden computations*).

These are or should be well-known facts to a computer scientist, and, once understood, evident even to a layman. But despite this, we tend to believe implicitly that a computer performs an objectively unique computation. Maybe this is due to the fact that this assumption is useful for all practical purposes. This implicit belief contaminates the discussions about the possibility of sentient AI and of reducing human consciousness to computation.

But, in Chapter 11, we will see concretely that we can access the hidden computations taking place in parallel with the default one, and you will convince yourself that they are really happening. The hidden computations are not less objective than the default computation.

Observation 2.2. Changing the user interface may result in changing the computation, without changing the physical processes in the computer.

Exercises

Exercise 2.3. Are there Boolean functions of two variables that cannot be interpreted as being implemented by the alien device? If there are, list them.

Exercise 2.4. Construct the Boolean function `OR` by using only negations and a conjunction.

Exercise 2.5. Construct the Boolean function `AND` by using only negations and a disjunction.

Exercise 2.6. Show that all Boolean functions (that is, with n inputs and m outputs $\mathbf{f}(p_1, p_2, \ldots, p_n)$ as mentioned in Example 2.1) can be obtained by using only conjunctions, disjunctions, and negations.

Exercise 2.7. Show that all Boolean functions can be obtained by using only conjunctions and exclusive disjunctions (`AND` and `XOR`).

Exercise 2.8. Try to find out if the implementation of the logic gates can determine a unique, objective interpretation as a Boolean function, independent of any convention.

Key points

- What a computer stores and processes is determined by conventions.
- Information and computation are relative.
- The user interface fixes the convention, anchoring it in the human mind.

Further reading

[115] Mark Verus Lawson. *A first course in logic.* CRC Press, 2018

[65] Jon Pierre Fortney. *Discrete mathematics for computer science: An example-based introduction.* Chapman and Hall/CRC, 2020

[140] Charles Petzold. *Code: The Hidden Language of Computer Hardware and Software.* Microsoft Press, 2 edition, 2022

[74] Rowan Garnier and John Taylor. *Discrete mathematics: Proofs, structures and applications.* CRC Press, 2009

3

The illusion of objectivity

3.1 Are bits objective?

Solomon said that information and computation are relative, but maybe not everyone is convinced. One may be tempted to invoke the hardware implementation to restore the belief that they are objective.

Question 3.1. Can Nature herself impose an objective, unique way to interpret information and computation?

If you tried to solve Exercise 2.8, you may think you have an answer.

If only we could see what is hidden inside the alien device, maybe we can know which of the eight friends is right. Maybe there is an objective way to interpret what the alien device does, based on what happens inside, on how the bit cells and the logic gate are built and how they work.

Consider for example the first diagram from Figure 3.1. It consists of two push-down buttons and a light bulb connected in series. The light bulb R glows if and only if both buttons P and Q are on. Therefore, if p is the proposition "P is on", q is "Q is on", and r is "R glows", it follows that $r = p \wedge q$. Hence, for this circuit, it seems that Alice's interpretation is the only correct one.

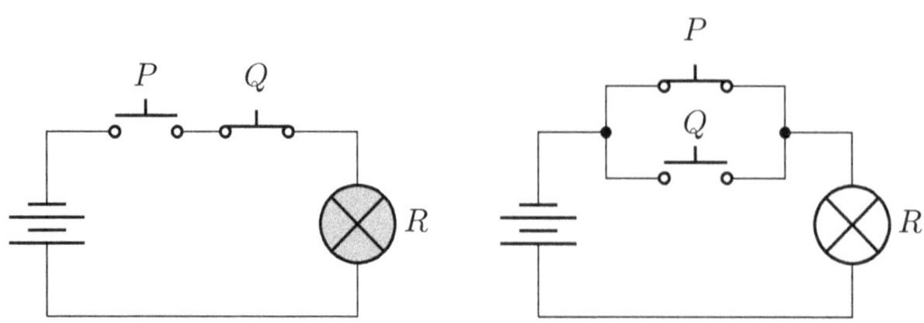

Figure 3.1: "Objective" realizations of the `AND` and `OR` Boolean functions. In each circuit, the battery is at the left, and a light bulb at the right. At the top there are two push buttons. The current can flow to the light bulb only if the circuit is not interrupted.

DOI: 10.1201/9781003623373-3

Similarly, the second diagram from Figure 3.1 represents a circuit with two push-down buttons connected in parallel. For such a device, it would appear that the only correct interpretation is Heidi's.

The circuits of a computer may not use push-down buttons in their computations, but they contain many transistors. And a transistor is like a push-down button from Figure 3.1, except that it is extremely small. The modern day computers (as in 2023) use integrated circuits that can contain hundreds of millions of transistors per square millimeter. No human finger can turn them on and off directly, but they can turn some of them with the help of the keyboard or other input devices, and then these transistors will turn each other on and off by using electric signals. A couple of transistors can be used to construct an `AND` or an `OR` gate or any other logic gate, pretty much like in Figure 3.1. The electric potential can be in two states, *low* and *high*, corresponding to the values `0` and `1`. So we may think that there is an objective way to know which state of a bit cell represents `0` and which represents `1`.

First, according to physics, the electric potential is not an absolute quantity. There is no absolute zero of the potential, and this is because of the electric *gauge symmetry*: we can never measure the electric potential, only the electric tension, the difference between two potentials. This is just like in the case of positions, we can't measure *absolute positions*, only *relative positions*, that is, the position with respect to another position or a reference frame. And the difference of potentials, just like in the case of positions, is expressed in measurement units that are our own convention. Moreover, whether the electric potential is negative or positive depends on the convention to declare the electron's charge negative or positive. So Physics doesn't give us an absolute reason to consider the electric potential as low or high. But, even if there was an absolute notion of electric potential, Computer Science doesn't force us to call its low value `0` and its high value `1`.

So, before jumping to conclusions, let us solve an exercise:

Exercise 3.1. Consider the logic circuit from the left side of Figure 3.1, and the following propositions:

$$\begin{aligned} p_E &= \text{“Button } P \text{ is up”.} \\ q_E &= \text{“Button } Q \text{ is down”.} \\ r_E &= \text{“Lightbulb } R \text{ is on”.} \end{aligned} \tag{3.1}$$

What Boolean function is f_E, for which $f_E(p_E, q_E) = r_E$ for all possible Boolean values of the propositions p_E, q_E, and r_E? Can you find it in Table 2.4?

And while we're here, let's solve another one:

Exercise 3.2. Similar to Exercise 3.1, construct propositions like those from equation (3.1), so that the logic circuit from the left side of Figure 3.1 can be interpreted as each of the Boolean functions from Table 2.4. Do the same for the logic circuit from the right side of Figure 3.1.

These exercises aim to show you that each of the circuits from Figure 3.1 can still be used to perform all eight Boolean functions from Table 2.4, if we interpret differently the states of the switches and the light bulb. Nothing stops us from interpreting the "on" states of the buttons from the first circuit from Figure 3.1 as `0`, and the "off" states as `1`, so that we can use the circuit as a `NOR` gate. And with the inverse interpretation of the state of the light bulb, we can get an `OR` gate. Nothing stops us from using any other combination of these conventions in order to compute any Boolean function from Table 2.4 by using the same circuit.

One may think that such interpretations are unnatural, and in reality there is somehow a unique "natural" or objective way to interpret the physical states as data and the physical processes as computations. But Computer Science itself is fundamentally based on conventions, interpretations, and reinterpretations, and in practice this is how it's done, as I will explain in the following chapters. This is a tenet of the theory of Computer Science, but we can also see it "empirically", by studying the hardware implementation in the same way we study a natural phenomenon, trying to reverse engineer its laws.

3.2 Memory is convention

Suppose you write something on a piece of paper, either to remember it, or to send someone a message. You will use a language, which is a convention. Or you may use a secret convention, a cipher. The meaning of the written message depends on a convention, which you can choose freely. Moreover, whatever you write on the piece of paper, it may happen to have other meanings in other conventions.

The memory of a computer is not so different from symbols written on a piece of paper, the meaning of its content is conventional. There is no objective, convention-free way to decide which state of a bit cell is `0` and which state is `1`. Here are some examples.

Example 3.1. Dynamic random-access memory (DRAM) uses capacitors to represent the bit value `1` when they are charged, and `0` when discharged. The floating gates representing bits in flash memories use the opposite convention.

For the next examples, we have to understand what a logic gate is. A *logic circuit* is made of any number of the following basic *logic gates*:

1. The `AND` gate, which performs the `AND` Boolean operation, and is represented by the symbol 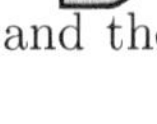. The two input bits p and q are represented on the left, and the output bit $p \wedge q$ on the right,

2. The OR gate, which performs the OR Boolean operation, and is represented by the symbol 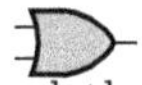. The two input bits p and q are represented on the left, and the output bit $p \vee q$ on the right, 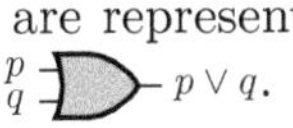

3. The NOT gate, which performs the NOT Boolean operation, and is represented by the symbol . The input bit p enters through the left, and the output bit $\overline{p}$, the *inversion* or *logic negation* of p, exits through the right, 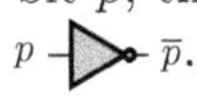

To combine these logic gates, we make sure that the outputs of some of the gates, depicted at the right of each gate, are connected to inputs of other gates, depicted at the left of each gate. Don't worry, Heidi prepares an example as we're speaking. The inputs that are not connected are used as inputs of the resulting circuit, while the disconnected outputs become the outputs of the circuit. Then, the circuit implements a Boolean function with the same number of inputs and outputs as the circuit.

Note that we can build an equivalent circuit in many different ways, as long as the same inputs applied to both circuits give the same outputs. In particular, we can build an equivalent circuit by using different types of logic gates, other than AND, OR, and NOT. In fact, in practice we use transistors, combined with resistors, to build even these basic gates, but this doesn't change what I have to say.

Example 3.2. We can quickly store and retrieve bits by using latches. A latch is a circuit with two possible states. The *set-reset latch* from Figure 3.2 uses two NOR gates and feedback. It has two inputs, S (set) and R (reset). By setting S=1 while keeping R=0, the state of the circuit represents the value 1. By setting R=1 while keeping S=0, the circuit is put into a state representing the value 0. In both cases, the stored bit remains the same even after the inputs are set back to 0. The stored bit can be read from the output Q. The output $\overline{\text{Q}}$ is always its opposite. There is a perfect physical symmetry between the two bit states, since they are the mirror image of one other.

By contrast, the $\overline{\text{SR}}$ NAND latch from Figure 3.3 is set and reset by input bits equal to 0, using the opposite convention to that of the SR NOR latch.

Example 3.2 illustrates in three ways that there is no absolute convention for representing the bit values:

1. The values 0 and 1 are represented in a symmetric way.
2. We can retrieve Q or $\overline{\text{Q}}$, as needed.
3. There is no absolute reason to say that a high voltage can only represent 1 and a low voltage can only represent 0.

In practice all possible ways are used freely, as it is more convenient.

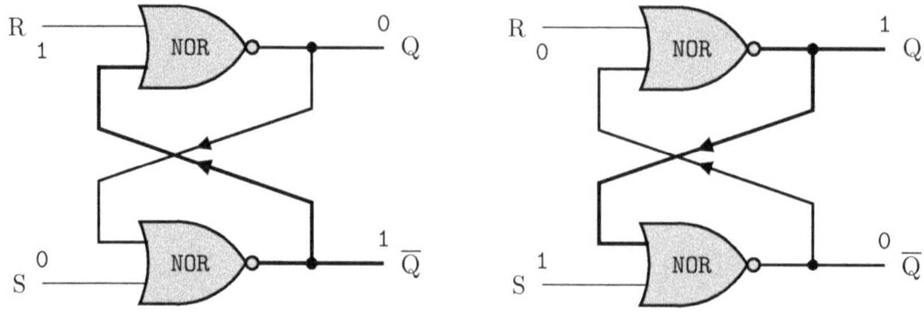

Figure 3.2: A set-reset `NOR` latch, used to store a bit. If the input S (set) is set to `1`, the state is set to `1`, as in the first image. If the input R (reset) is set to `1`, the state is set to `0`, as in the second image. The state can be read from the output Q. It remains the same even after the inputs are set back to `0`.

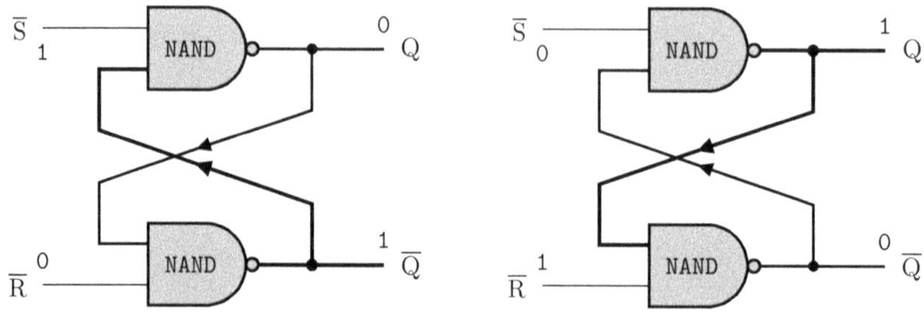

Figure 3.3: A set-reset `NAND` latch is set to `1` by inputting `0` at $\overline{S}$, and it is reset to `0` by inputting `0` at $\overline{R}$. They use an opposite convention to that of the `NOR` latch from Figure 3.2.

With all these tricks under the hood, it should be clear that a computer doesn't necessarily perform the computation that the user may normally expect. The only constraint is that the final result is the one expected by the user. This allows the computer to implement more possible computations reusing the same logic circuits.

Observation 3.1. Even when the physical bit cells or the circuits seem to suggest an objective way to represent the bits, this is only a convention, which is changed internally as needed. Inside a computer, bits are represented in different ways that can even change in time.

There are many ways to compute the same result. The bits of information may pass through completely different states during different implementations of the same computation. Everything is permitted, as long as the user gets the correct result, or rather the expected result.

Therefore, we can't appeal to implementation to obtain a unique, objective interpretation of computation.

If the same bit cells can be interpreted in many ways, the converse is also true: the same picture can be represented on a computer in different formats, yet we will think it's the same picture. The same is true for various formats used to represent movies, music, audio books, text, spreadsheets, *etc.*

If the same logic circuit can perform different operations, the converse is also true. A computer program made for Windows will not simply work on a computer having a different operating system like Linux or Mac OS, and definitely not on an Android smartphone. You will need a version of the program built for each operating system, or you will have to use an emulator or a virtual machine. There will also be differences at the hardware level, since each computer may use the logic gates from the hardware differently. Platform-independent software exists, for example written in Java. But even a Java application is processed differently on different computers, because it has to access platform-specific software, and use different hardware.

3.3 The Rosetta Stone

Let me explain how hardware manufacturers and software developers use in practice the reinterpretation of the logic gates.

Suppose Heidi has an `OR` logic gate. Heidi puts her gate in a box with three switches, as in Figure 3.4. Along with the `OR` gate (…), there are three `NOT` gates (…), which can be used to invert the interpretation of the bits p, q, and r.

Heidi obtains a device that she calls "Rosetta Stone", because it can be used to implement any of the interpretations from Table 2.4.

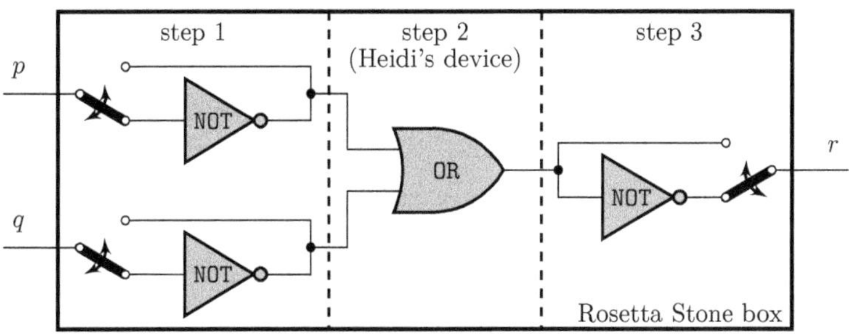

Figure 3.4: Heidi's Rosetta Stone, configured to compute Alice's function.

To use it, choose an interpretation from Table 2.4 and do the following steps:

1. Read the second row from the table of the chosen interpretation.
2. If the first cell contains `T`, turn "up" (…) the switch corresponding to p, otherwise turn it "down" (…), so that it uses the corresponding `NOT` gate.

3. Do the same for the second cell in the second row, and the second switch, corresponding to q.
4. Do the same for the third cell in the second row, and the second switch, corresponding to r.

For example, Figure 3.4 shows how to configure the Rosetta Stone to implement Alice's interpretation of the alien device as an AND gate, even though it secretly works as an OR gate. Indeed, Alice's table contains in the second row the values F, F, and F, while Heidi's table contains the values T, T, and T, so all three bits have to be inverted. Congratulations, now, any two input bits will be transformed in the output bit corresponding to the chosen interpretation!

Exercise 3.3. Configure Heidi's Rosetta Stone to implement each of the Boolean functions from Table 2.4.

From Alice's point of view, the Rosetta Stone from Figure 3.4 performs an AND operation. Suppose for example that Alice's input consists of the pair of bits $p = 1$ and $q = 0$, denoted collectively by $|1, 0\rangle$. The device from Figure 3.4 outputs the result 0. Alice thinks that the Rosetta Stone computed the result of the AND operation, as in the following diagram

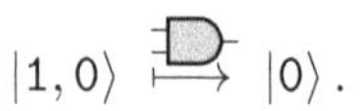

(3.2)

Alice tried different combinations of input bits, and the result was every time consistent with the AND operation.

But Heidi knows how she built the Rosetta Stone, and she claims that what really happens is an OR operation (step 2), sandwiched between inversions of the input (step 1) and the output bits (step 3), as in

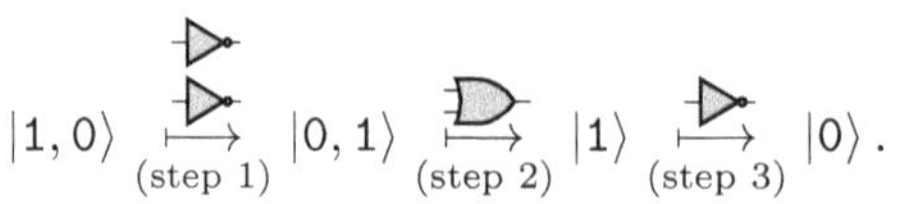

(3.3)

But Solomon says that the process can very well be described as follows:

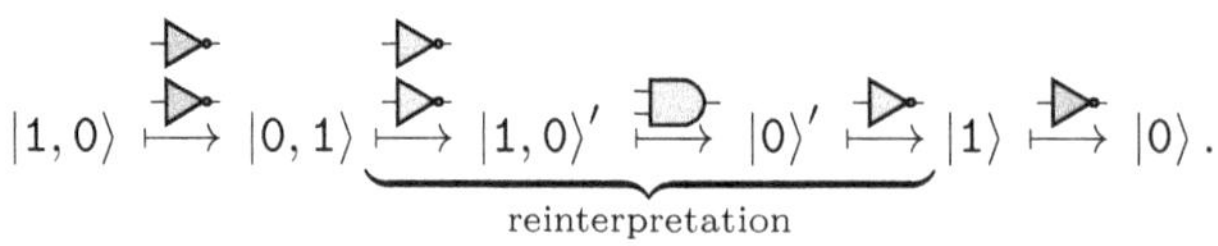

(3.4)

1. The input is the bit state $|1, 0\rangle$. Let's say that high voltage represents 1 and low voltage represents 0.
2. The circuit inverts the two bits, so that what was high voltage becomes low, and what was low voltage becomes high. The bit state becomes $|0, 1\rangle$.
3. We change the convention, so that now high voltage represents 0 and low voltage represents 1. Let 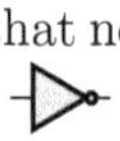 represent this reinterpretation.

With the new convention, the bit state becomes $|1,0\rangle'$, where by the prime symbol $'$ we denote the interpretation in which a high voltage represents 0.

4. With the new convention, what we called OR gate (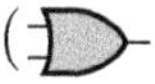) operates as an AND gate (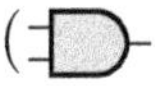), without any change in its physical functionality. The result of the operation is $|0\rangle'$.
5. We return to the initial convention, and the bit state becomes $|1\rangle$.
6. The resulting bit state is inverted, so it becomes $|0\rangle$.

We see that, in Solomon's interpretation, any physical inversion of a bit is paired with a reinterpretation. An external observer only sees the inputs and the outputs, and infers that the Rosetta Stone performed an AND operation, like Alice said.

An observer who sees inside the box can use the opposite convention for the bits to interpret the OR gate as an AND gate. By changing the convention simultaneously with the action of the NOT gates, one may even interpret what happens inside the box as being what Alice sees from the outside,

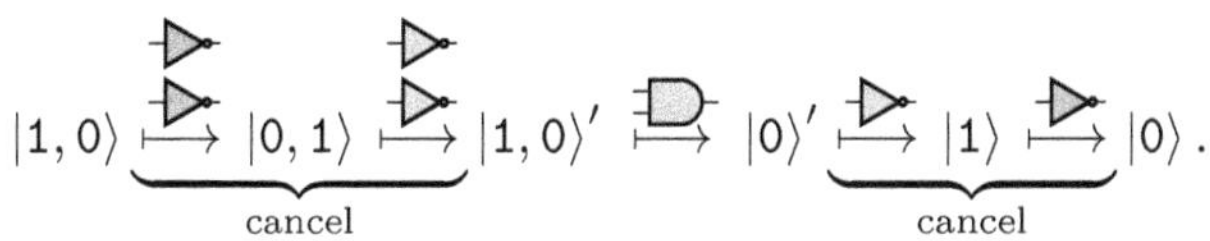

(3.5)

Again, according to Solomon, both Alice and Heidi are right!

The translation between Heidi's interpretation and Alice's is given by the formula

$$f_A(p,q) = \overline{f_H(\overline{p},\overline{q})}. \tag{3.6}$$

This is called *the first de Morgan law*,

$$\overline{\overline{p} \vee \overline{q}} = p \wedge q. \tag{3.7}$$

We can also build a Rosetta Stone device around an AND gate, which implements Alice's interpretation. To translate to Heidi's interpretation we can use *the second de Morgan law*,

$$\overline{\overline{p} \wedge \overline{q}} = p \vee q, \tag{3.8}$$

obtaining

$$f_H(p,q) = \overline{f_A(\overline{p},\overline{q})}. \tag{3.9}$$

We could in fact start with any of the eight operators from Table 2.4, and use more general symmetry transformations than the de Morgan laws, obtained by applying the negation to some of the three bits.

For example, if we build the Rosetta Stone around David's operator, we can obtain Alice's interpretation by

$$f_A(p, q) = \overline{f_D(p, \overline{q})}. \tag{3.10}$$

Negations and permutations of the inputs and outputs of Boolean functions transform a Boolean function into another one with the same number of inputs and outputs. These transformations were studied for example by David Slepian [165] and Solomon Golomb [80], and are widely applied in the design of logic circuits. Transformations as in Figure 3.4 are used extensively in the design of logic circuits, for optimization. Without them, universal, programmable computers wouldn't be possible. In the following chapters, we will see more about this.

3.4 Gates to universality

The ancients believed that everything is made from a unique element or principle. In ancient Greece, Thales believed that this was water, Anaximenes thought it was air, Heraclitus argued that it was fire. In ancient India, the sage authors of the Upanishads taught that the ultimate reality was a pure form of consciousness beyond thought, beyond time and space and conceptualization [99].

In the modern world, some scientists proposed that the universe is made of pure information. One was John Archibald Wheeler, who contributed to numerous discoveries and bold theories, and encouraged his students to be bold and think outside the box (among them Jacob Bekenstein, Hugh Everett III, Richard Feynman, Kip Thorne, William Unruh, Robert Wald, and Arthur Wightman) [210]. Another one was Edward Fredkin, the pioneer of *reversible computing* and discoverer of a reversible universal logic gate, [67] who also conceived, together with Tommaso Toffoli, a computer made exclusively of billiard balls [68]. Another one is Stephen Wolfram [212], the inventor of *Wolfram Mathematica*, a very impressive and sophisticated software system for scientific and symbolic computation.

Regardless of whether any of these unified philosophies are true, a fundamental result in Computer Science is the existence of *universal gates.* We can build all other logic gates and all logic circuits out of identical copies of a single universal gate [135].

For example, NAND gates 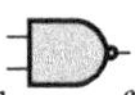 are sufficient to obtain all other gates and logic circuits, with any number of input and output bits. Since all Boolean functions can be obtained by combining conjunctions, disjunctions, and negations, and since all these can be obtained from NAND gates, we say that the NAND gate is universal. Another universal gate is the NOR gate 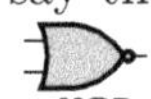. Figure 3.5 shows how we can build a NOT gate using a NAND gate or a NOR gate.

Figure 3.5: Implementation of the NOT gate using the NAND and NOR gates.

Like this, we can easily obtain the AND and OR gates, and with the NOT gate we can build any logic circuit and implement any Boolean function.

Not only logic circuits, but also memories can be built out of universal gates like the NOR gate or the NAND gate, as seen in Example 3.2.

While in practice we use transistors to build all logic circuits, the reader can see in detail how a fully functional computer can be built out of NAND gates only [133]. While this may not be very useful in practice, Alexander Shabarshin built a fully functional 8-bit computer only from NAND gates [117].

Universal logic gates are possible because the memories and the logic circuits can be interpreted in different ways. Without reinterpreting the memory cells and the logic gates, it wouldn't even make sense to talk about this. In the next chapters, we will see more examples and why this is fundamental for Computer Science.

3.5 Physical zeroes and ones

When I say that we attribute to the two physical states of a memory cell the values 0 and 1 only by convention, one may try to reject this by proposing the following proof showing that these values are in fact physical properties of the system.

Proposition 3.1. Any memory cell which can be in two physical states representing 0 and 1 has a physical property which has the value 0 if the memory cell is in the first state, and the value 1 if it's in the second state.

Proof. In Classical Physics, all physical properties of a system are functions of the properties of the elementary particles constituting that system. Consider for example a system of n particles, where the position of the j-th particle is (x_j, y_j, z_j), and its momentum is a vector having three components $(p_{x_j}, p_{y_j}, p_{z_j})$. Then, as things go in Classical Physics, any physical property is a real function

$$f(x_1, y_1, z_1, p_{x_1}, p_{y_1}, p_{z_1}, \ldots, x_n, y_n, z_n, p_{x_n}, p_{y_n}, p_{z_n}). \tag{3.11}$$

Let a memory cell be such a system of n particles. Its possible states can be parametrized by the coordinates of the positions and the components of the momenta of the n particles. Therefore, each state of the memory cell can be represented by a point in $\mathbb{R}^{(3+3)n} = \mathbb{R}^{6n}$, so we call this space *state space*.

The memory cell's two stable states that we identify as the two values of a bit are represented by two disjoint subsets $A, B \subset \mathbb{R}^{6n}$. Suppose we identify the states from A as representing `0`, and the states from B as representing `1`. Then, there exists a function $f : \mathbb{R}^{6n} \to \mathbb{R}$, representing a physical property of the memory cell, so that its restrictions to the sets A and B are 0 and 1,

$$f(S) = \begin{cases} 0 & \text{if } S \in A \\ 1 & \text{if } S \in B \\ \text{other values} & \text{if } S \notin A \text{ and } S \notin B \end{cases} \tag{3.12}$$

proving that bits are really physical properties of the memory cells. □

This gives us a concrete physical property that we can identify as our bit. This is because in Classical Physics all physical properties are functions of the positions and momenta, and all such functions are physical properties, although we don't know or care about most of them.

Of course, it is possible that the state of the memory cell is neither in A nor in B, for example if it is damaged, or if it is in an indefinite bit state. In the case of a capacitor for example, since it is considered charged if it is charged above 80% of its capacity, and discharged if its charged below 20% of its capacity, if it is charged between 20% and 80% of its capacity it represents neither `0` nor `1`, so it is not in a definite bit state. Proposition 3.1 took this into account. Moreover, we see from equation (3.12) that there are infinitely many such physical properties, because f can have any values outside of A and B.

However, Proposition 3.1 doesn't refute the fact that what state represents `0` and what state represents `1` is our convention, and that this convention is not unique. In fact, this follows from Proposition 3.1 itself:

Corollary 3.1. There is a physical property as in Proposition 3.1 for any convention we choose.

Proof. Along with the physical property represented by the function f from equation (3.12), there exists another physical property, represented by the function

$$g(S) := 1 - f(S) = \begin{cases} 1 & \text{if } S \in A \\ 0 & \text{if } S \in B \\ \text{other values} & \text{if } S \notin A \text{ and } S \notin B \end{cases} \tag{3.13}$$

This physical property realizes the opposite of the convention realized by the physical property f, proving the Corollary. □

3.6 Microscopic Gremlins practicing nonaction

In the following, we will do a thought experiment, an experiment we will not have to do effectively, just to imagine we're doing it. In fact, it would be difficult to do it in practice, because it involves some fictional creatures called gremlins. Thought experiments have a long tradition among philosophers and physicists, due to limited budget or other resources, or simply because of natural limitations. If you do such experiments, you are in good company, the company of ancient Greek philosophers, and of physicists like Galileo, Ørsted, and Einstein.

Thought Experiment 3.1 (Microscopic Gremlins Argument)**.** Imagine that some microscopic gremlins live in your computer. For our thought experiment to make sense, they don't have to exist, although some airmen from the British Royal Air Force blamed them a century ago for the malfunctioning of their aircraft during World War I.

Suppose that the gremlins inhabiting your computer hijacked it for their own mischievous purposes, but without interfering with its functionality. Instead, they scribbled on the computer's components some symbols that mean something to them, but whose meaning is completely unknown to humans. If you examine under a microscope the computer's circuit, you may notice these symbols, but they would appear to you as accidental scratches. And yet, to the gremlins they would mean something. They can use the same logic circuits to compute something else than a human user thinks it computes, or to make the computer's memory hold something else a human user would think it holds.

One may think that the data seen by the gremlins would be meaningless to them, for the simple reason that you, a human user, are the one who controls the computer. But if the gremlins studied how the computer's circuits work physically, they could have made consistent choices when deciding how to use them. And how they label the computer's components and doesn't need to be identical to how we label them, just like eight different people can interpret in eight different ways the same alien device from Chapter 2. So what they wrote on the computer's components can mean something to them, and something completely different to us. When asked what's in its memory, the computer may tell you that it's a nice poem, or a prayer, or a story for children. But the gremlins are not fooled by the computer's display, because they use a more direct user interface, the one they made when they wrote their own symbols on the memory cells. For them, the computer holds in its memory completely different information than what it shows to us: instead of poems and prayers and stories, this could be some spells, curses, or very offensive slurs. You'd never know.

Exercises

Exercise 3.4. For any two Boolean functions from Table 2.4, find how the first of them can be obtained from the second of them by inverting bits, as in equations (3.6), (3.9), and (3.10).

Exercise 3.5. Design similar Rosetta Stone devices internally using gates that implement the other seven Boolean functions from Table 2.4. Configure each one of them to implement each of the other seven Boolean functions from Table 2.4.

Exercise 3.6. In Exercise 2.3 you were asked to find out if there are Boolean functions of two variables other than those from Table 2.4. If there are, verify if they can be obtained from the other such Boolean functions by inverting bits, as in equations (3.6), (3.9), and (3.10).

Exercise 3.7. Show that it is possible to build `AND`, `OR`, and `NOT` gates, only from `NAND` gates.

Hint: use the constructions from Figure 3.5, and Exercise 3.4.

Then, since every logic circuit can be built out of `AND`, `OR`, and `NOT` gates, it follows that the `NAND` gate is universal.

Exercise 3.8. Prove the universality of the `NOR` gate, by showing that we can use it to build `AND`, `OR`, and `NOT` gates.

Exercise 3.9. Prove that any logic circuit can be realized using only `AND` and `XOR` gates (see Exercise 2.7).

Key points

- In designing and manufacturing logic circuits, no convention is forbidden, as long as it gives the right result.
- Reinterpretations of the convention are commonly used to realize multiple functions using the same circuit.
- Any logic circuit can be built by using only `NAND` or only `NOR` gates, and nobody would complain that their computer is unable to implement the `AND` and `OR` gates.
- Any memory cell has physical properties taking the values 0 and 1 according to any convention that we can choose to represent bits.
- To some microscopic gremlins inhabiting it, a computer can appear to compute something else than what it shows to the human users.

Further reading

[140] Charles Petzold. *Code: The Hidden Language of Computer Hardware and Software*. Microsoft Press, 2 edition, 2022

[165] David Slepian. On the number of symmetry types of Boolean functions of n variables. *Canad. J. Math.*, 5:185–193, 1953

[80] Solomon Golomb. On the classification of Boolean functions. *IRE transactions on circuit theory*, 6(5):176–186, 1959

[133] Noam Nisan and Shimon Schocken. *The elements of computing systems: Building a modern computer from first principles*. MIT Press, Cambridge, Massachusetts, 2021

4

Secret conventions

4.1 Digitized digits

If you used a pocket calculator or a digital clock, you may have seen that some display the digits as in Figure 4.1. Each such digit consists of seven segments that can be turned on or off. This means that we need a code to translate from decimal digits to a seven bit format.

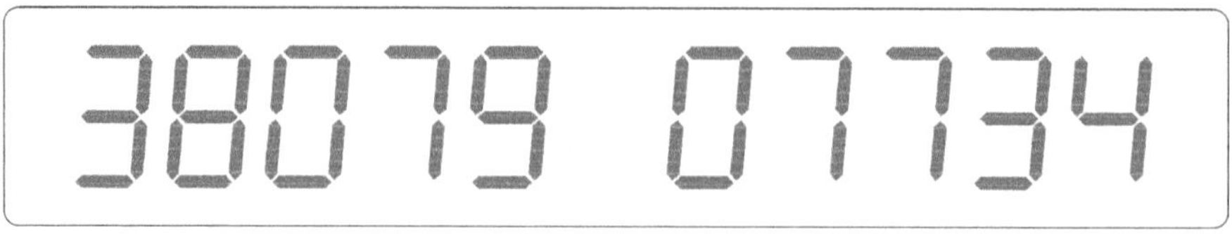

Figure 4.1: Base 10 digits on a seven-segments display. It encodes the state of each of each digit by using seven bits, to turn each segment on or off.

Exercise 4.1. Design a seven-bit code for the digits from Figure 4.1, so that each bit encodes a segment being turned on or off.

Solution. An example of such a seven-bit code that corresponds directly to the segments is shown in Table 4.1.

Table 4.1: A seven-bit code to display digits in a digital style.

$0 \mapsto$ 1111110	$5 \mapsto$ 1011011
$1 \mapsto$ 0110000	$6 \mapsto$ 1011111
$2 \mapsto$ 1101101	$7 \mapsto$ 1110000
$3 \mapsto$ 1111001	$8 \mapsto$ 1111111
$4 \mapsto$ 0110011	$9 \mapsto$ 1111011

In this solution, the first bit encodes the state of the segment from the top, the second bit encodes the state of the next segment in clockwise order and so on, and the last bit encodes the state of the segment from the middle. □

DOI: 10.1201/9781003623373-4

The encoding from Table 4.1 uses a particular convention, but nothing stops the reader to propose another convention, by starting from another segment and moving counterclockwise. In fact, any other convention would be equally correct. If the convention consists of encoding in a bit the state of a segment so that `1` represents the segment turned on and `0` represents the segment turned off, the number of possible conventions is the number of ways in which we can order the seven segments, 7!, which is $1 \cdot 2 \cdot 3 \cdot 4 \cdot 5 \cdot 6 \cdot 7 = 5040$. But of course it would be equally valid to encode the off states as `1` and the on states as `0`, or even to vary the convention for each segment, in which case the total number is $7! \cdot 2^7 = 645\ 120$. Each of them results in a different encoding like the one from Table 4.1.

Full disclosure: the encoding from Table 4.1 was used in the code that generates Figure 4.1. The chances the reader found the same encoding when solving Exercise 4.1, are large, much larger than one in 5040, which is the number of possible ways to order the seven segments. This is because the order is very similar to the order of numbers on an analog clock. It seems very natural to start somewhere and move continuously either clockwise or counterclockwise. Similarly, it feels natural to encode the state "on" as the bit value `1`. Therefore, while there are 645 120 possible solutions, quite a few of them feel more natural than the others. But they are all equally valid conventions.

4.2 Don't put all your data in one basket!

We can imagine a computer whose memory cells can be in four states rather than two, say $|0\rangle$, $|1\rangle$, $|2\rangle$, and $|3\rangle$. Then, we can adapt the entire binary framework to be used on this computer. We can interpret each memory cell as encoding two bits, as $|0,0\rangle$, $|0,1\rangle$, $|1,0\rangle$, and $|1,1\rangle$. But since the states are not actual numbers, we can do this in any order. In this case, the reinterpretations will go beyond inverting the values of the individual bits. There will be reinterpretations like the one from Figure 4.2, that are not based on inverting individual bits independently.

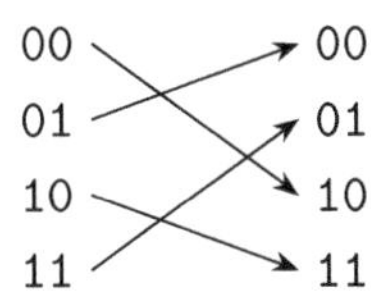

Figure 4.2: A more general reinterpretation that is not based on inverting individual bits independently.

We will call a reinterpretation based on inverting some bits independently *simple reinterpretation.* We will call a reinterpretation that is not necessarily simple, but can be as in Figure 4.2, a *general reinterpretation.*

The example from Figure 4.2 represents a Boolean function with two input bits and two output bits, even though in this case the computer works in base 4. This Boolean function is invertible, because if we know the output, we can recover the input. But there are situations when the function is not invertible.

Numerous examples of general reinterpretations are given by error detection and error correction codes. To understand how these work, think of a kind of meme that people like to share on social media, something like

> If you can read this you are a genius:
>
> 40U AR3 N07 5P3C1A1, 3V3R40N3 C4N R34D 7H15
>
> 573PH3N H4WK1NG

While most certainly Stephen Hawking didn't say this (because it was 573PH3N H4WK1NG!), everyone who can read at all most likely can read this text too. But why can we read such a messed up text? Simple, it's because language is very redundant. Changing a few letters, especially if we replace them with similar-looking symbols, still allows us to guess the words, because different words rarely differ by a small number of letters, and the context helps us too. Both spoken languages and their written forms had to survive misspelling, mistakes, noise, difficulties of pronunciation and so on, and this is why the forms of language that became spread and used on large scales are those that allow for correction. The necessity to correct a message exists even in modern technology.

Suppose Alice wants to transmit to Bob a message, but because the signal may be affected by noise, the message received by Bob may be corrupted. So Alice thinks about repeating the same message several times, just to make sure. But then she has a better idea, instead of sending the same message three times, she can triple every bit in the message. She writes a program that replaces all occurrences of `0` with `000`, and all occurrences of `1` with `111`. At the receiving end, Bob must use a program that replaces all occurrences of `000` with `0`, and all occurrences of `111` with `1`.

But what if a bit is off due to the noise? Then for example `111` may change into `110` or `101` or `011`. In each of these cases, Bob's program can try to correct the error by replacing the three bits with `1`. In general, for any triplet of bits, the program will assume that only one is off, and will replace them with the value that occurs at least twice in the triple, as illustrated in Figure 4.3.

This is the *Hamming code*, introduced of course by Hamming [88]. The Hamming code is very simple: groups of bits are substituted with other groups of bits.

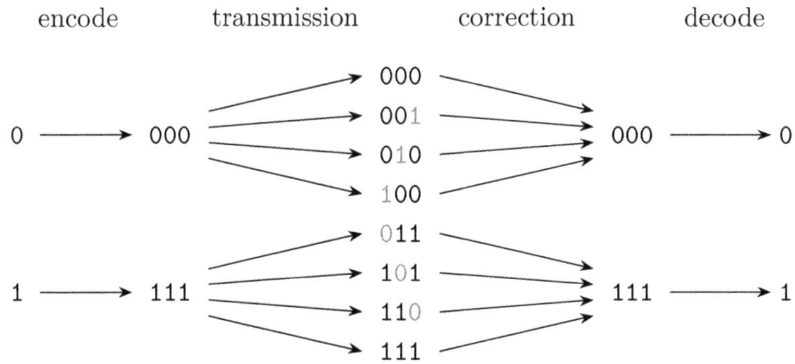

Figure 4.3: The Hamming code for error correction.

Other error correction methods use *parity checking*, which consists of counting the occurrences of the bit value 1 in a string, see if it is odd or even, and add an extra bit to encode this. This method has numerous variations, and it proved to be so useful, that it is widely used for identification numbers such as those for ID numbers, bank account numbers, ISBNs (the unique identifiers of books) *etc* [109].

Error correction codes have numerous applications in the transfer, storage and retrieval of information. It is necessary when the transmission channel is noisy, or when graphical symbols are used to encode information, for example as barcodes or QR codes [140].

Nature herself uses error correction to fix the errors of the DNA, arising for example during replication [70]. Even natural languages can be seen as having error correction mechanisms, for being highly redundant. The alphabet is very redundant as well, which explains why we can use so diverse fonts and why a pharmacist can understand the handwriting of a medic. Another example is the Braille alphabet [140].

Error correction codes are used not only to transmit information, but also to store it. It is possible to even process information in an encoded form. In classical computing information is stored in a pretty reliable manner, but in the case of Quantum Computing it is absolutely necessary that the logic circuits themselves include error correction [131].

The error correction codes used in practice can be very sophisticated, so that the original message may appear to be encrypted if you don't know how to decode it [126]. This shows that more general reinterpretations of a computation than inversions of individual bits are not only possible, but are widely used.

So let us distinguish between these two kinds of reinterpretations.

Definition 4.1. An *simple interpretation* of the bit cells of a computer is an assignment of bit values to the bit cells. A *general interpretation* is an assignment of groups of bits to groups of bit cells.

A *reinterpretation* of an interpretation is a reassignment of bits or groups of bits resulting in another interpretation. If the reinterpretation reassigns bit values to bits independently, it is *simple*, otherwise it is *general.*

Section 4.3 will provide more examples of general reinterpretations.

4.3 Relativity of encryption

One may think that we can decode the information from a computer in the same way enciphered messages are cracked. But in fact the very possibility of cryptography also shows that the assignment of bit values is a convention. The following situation between Alice and Bob illustrates this.

Alice receives the following message from Bob:

`01101100 01101111 01101100.`

It appears to be expressed in the binary system. How can she decrypt this message?

First, Alice applied the usual conversion from binary to text, the ASCII code that is used by computers to represent text (see Table 4.2).

Table 4.2: ASCII codes for the characters and punctuation marks in the English alphabet. For example, the ASCII code for a blank space ␣ is 00100000.

A	01000001	P	01010000	a	01100001	p	01110000
B	01000010	Q	01010001	b	01100010	q	01110001
C	01000011	R	01010010	c	01100011	r	01110010
D	01000100	S	01010011	d	01100100	s	01110011
E	01000101	T	01010100	e	01100101	t	01110100
F	01000110	U	01010101	f	01100110	u	01110101
G	01000111	V	01010110	g	01100111	v	01110110
H	01001000	W	01010111	h	01101000	w	01110111
I	01001001	X	01011000	i	01101001	x	01111000
J	01001010	Y	01011001	j	01101010	y	01111001
K	01001011	Z	01011010	k	01101011	z	01111010
L	01001100	.	00101110	l	01101100	␣	00100000
M	01001101	,	00101100	m	01101101	-	10010110
N	01001110	:	00111010	n	01101110	!	00100001
O	01001111	;	00111011	o	01101111	?	00111111

She obtained the message "lol". But based on their previous conversation this didn't make sense to her, so she thought that maybe the message was encrypted.

A very simple way to encrypt (and then decrypt) a message is by using a simple XOR cipher [202]. This encryption system is based on the logical operation *exclusive or*, or XOR, which is also denoted by $p \oplus q$, represented in Table 4.3. The meaning of $p \oplus q$ is "either p or q is true".

Table 4.3: The XOR operation, also denoted by $p \oplus q$.

p	q	$p \oplus q$
0	0	0
0	1	1
1	0	1
1	1	0

Alice knew Bob's encryption key 00111111 00100000, which is also used for decryption. So Alice performed a XOR operation between the encrypted string sent by Bob and the key:

$$\begin{array}{r} \texttt{01101100 01101111 01101100} \\ \oplus\ \texttt{00111111 00100000 00111111} \\ \hline =\ \texttt{01010011 01001111 01010011} \end{array} \tag{4.1}$$

Alice deciphered Bob's message by using a computer to perform the bitwise XOR between the message and the key. The key was shorter than the encrypted message, so Alice repeated the digits from the key until it filled the length of the encrypted text.

Remark 4.1. Simple reinterpretations are just like simple XOR ciphers.

Indeed, the simple XOR cipher is based on inverting the bits indicated by the positions of 1 in the key.

One may think that there is a significant difference between the ciphered message and the plain one. But even the plain, "unencrypted" message uses an arbitrary convention, the ASCII code. It is based on historical accidents like what characters are in the alphabet, and in what order, and on other purely arbitrary conventions for the punctuation marks and other symbols. We could as well choose as the default convention any permutation or any encryption of the ASCII code, and then the ASCII code would have appeared as encrypted. The ASCII code is only one of the many proposed similar standards. UNICODE is another one, on 16 bits, so it encodes up to $2^{16} = 65536$ different symbols, including Chinese, Arabic, Indian characters, basically characters in all languages on Earth, but also mathematical symbols and emojis. But there are numerous codes like ASCII and UNICODE. And, just like such codes are pure conventions for text, there are many different conventions for graphical images, sound, video, *etc.* Therefore, this simple example shows once more that the assignment of bit values and their meaning are pure conventions.

4.4 Blind computers

Is it possible to process encrypted data without having the decryption key?

Suppose that Alice created a very useful algorithm. Bob needs to use Alice's algorithm to process some secret data he has. Alice would help, but she doesn't want to give her algorithm to Bob, and Bob doesn't want to give his data to Alice. This may seem to be a deal breaker, but it can be solved. Bob can send his data in an encrypted form to Alice. Alice can write a program that uses her algorithm to process Bob's encrypted data, without having to decrypt it. She can then send back to Bob the result of the computation, which is also encrypted. Then Bob can decrypt the result sent by Alice to find out the desired result for his data.

For this, Alice can use a special form of encryption, named *fully homomorphic encryption*. For three decades, fully homomorphic encryption was considered the holy grail of cryptography [122], until the first such encryption scheme was proposed by Gentry in his PhD Thesis [75].

How does this magic work? Bob uses a key-generation algorithm to produce a *private key*, a *public key*, and an *evaluation key*. He encrypts his data using the public key, and sends the encrypted data and the evaluation key to Alice. The evaluation key is necessary for Alice's algorithm to process the encrypted data sent by Bob without having to decrypt it. It translates the `AND` and `XOR` operations so that they can be applied directly to the encrypted data. Since any Boolean function can be expressed as a combination of `AND` and `XOR` operations (Exercises 2.7 and 3.9), this is sufficient to process the encrypted data with any algorithm, no matter how sophisticated. Alice does this to process Bob's data with her algorithm, and sends back to Bob the result of the computation, which is, of course, still encrypted. Bob decrypts it using his private key. In this way, Alice can help Bob without giving away her algorithm, and Bob can benefit from her algorithm without exposing his secret data.

In general, if a string of bits processed by an algorithm is the encryption of another string of bits, the algorithm can be seen as processing the original string of bits in encrypted form. This is true for any algorithm and any encryption method, including the simple `XOR` cipher. But *in general the original string of bits is not processed as intended*, and the result can't be decrypted into a meaningful result. The fully homomorphic encryption scheme is a way to ensure that the original string is processed in the intended way while operating on its encrypted form, and the output can be decrypted into a meaningful result. The lesson here is:

Principle 4.1. Encrypted computing is computing.

Moreover, there is no such thing as pure "unencrypted computing". As seen in Chapter 3, any computation is implemented by using various transformations of the bits that entail reinterpretations of the logic circuits. Even more, at the very foundation of Computer Science lies the idea that there are Turing machines that can simulate other Turing machines. I will say more about this in Chapters 7 and 8.

4.5 Ciphers and reinterpretations

The simple XOR cipher, given as an example in Section 4.3, is quite intuitive. But in practice more sophisticated ways to encrypt data are used, such as the RSA cryptosystem [151, 148]. This is because the simple XOR cipher is easy to crack for long enough ciphered text, especially if the length of the key is known. Based on the fact that only some strings of letters make sense, one can compare the enciphered message with XOR enciphered words and phrases from known languages, until one finds a key that gives a message that makes sense, or at least a syntactically correct message.

But even cracking a simple XOR cipher works only because natural languages are very redundant. This means that a random string of letters is most likely meaningless. But if the secret message is a number in binary, then we can XOR it with any key, and the result will be, in general, another valid number. Any computation that processes a binary number would give, in general, a number in binary. There are exceptions, for example when dividing by zero, but even then, the memory will contain something that we can interpret as a number in binary. The user may receive an error message, the number may be identified at the level of the programming language as "infinity" or "not a number", but the computer's memory will be in a state which, by the convention used to encode numbers as strings of bits, is a number. The reason is simple: the computer's memory is always in a "physically valid" state. Everything the computer's circuits do is to implement Boolean functions (which depend on our convention), and for the Boolean functions there is always a definite result (which also depends on our convention). But when processing numbers, we use, on top of the convention to interpret the states of the memory cells as bits, another convention, to interpret strings of bits as numbers. This additional layer of convention has its own additional layers of conventions for exceptional situations, "amendments" that mean "in case you divide by zero, the content of the memory should not be considered a number".

If we know what the encrypted computation does this may help reduce the number of possible keys for the XOR cipher. Also, even if we don't know what the algorithm does, but it does something obvious, for example it adds a fixed number to the encrypted number, we can also use this as a hint. But in general any key that we would try would give a number and a function that processes that number, and there would be no way to say whether they are valid or not. Therefore, without knowing the original number, the key, and what the algorithm does, the ambiguity of the encrypted computation is maximal.

Why am I insisting on numbers? This is because, since all numbers having the same length in binary form can be obtained from one another by inverting some of the bits, *the program processes all of them at once.* We will see this explicitly in an example that you can verify, in Chapter 11.

One may hope that the high redundancy of natural languages avoids this ambiguity problem that numeric data has. After all, any sufficiently long encrypted text can be decrypted to get a unique solution, provided that we know the language. But in a broader sense, any language is an encryption of any other language. And no language is more "objective" than the others. Moreover, given a text expressed in a language, it is possible to invent a new language, in which the words in the first language have different and even opposite meanings. For this reason, like in the case of numbers, any encrypted text can be decrypted in many ways so that the result is potentially meaningful. To make it meaningful, all we have to do is to invent a new language in which the text obtained by decryption makes sense. And we can do this in an unlimited number of ways. Therefore,

Observation 4.1. If we consider that thinking is just a computation, the same computation can be interpreted as many encrypted computations representing different thinking processes. They may be different and even contradictory, and they may be formulated in the same or in different languages. But they will happen simultaneously, in parallel.

This may seem as an extremely relativistic position, but later, we will see examples that give meaningful results for any encryption key, or equivalently, for any reinterpretation. These are examples of computations admitting multiple interpretations at once, all of which equally make sense. We will see that the easiness of cracking `XOR` ciphers based on long enough texts in known languages isn't sufficient to decode a unique "thinking process" from what a robot brain does. Thus, we will see that the Easy Questions 1 and 2 have definite answers, and we will find them.

Exercises

Exercise 4.2. What was the secret message sent by Bob to Alice?

Key points

- The fact that we can encrypt messages proves that there is no objective way to interpret strings of bits as messages.
- The fact that encrypted data can be processed without knowing its meaning proves that there is no objective way to say what computation a computer does.
- The fact that, ultimately, the meaning of the data relies on convention, proves that there is no "unencrypted computation". This, in turn, proves that all possible decryptions that we can obtain from the computation we may consider objective are equally valid computations.
- To summarize, the possibility of encryption and of encrypted computing proves once more the ambiguity of information and computation.

Further reading

[202] WT Tutte. FISH and I. In D Joyner, editor, *Coding theory and cryptography*, pages 9–17, Heidelberg, New York, 2000. Springer

[126] R H Morelos-Zaragoza. *The art of error correcting coding.* John Wiley & Sons, 2006

[140] Charles Petzold. *Code: The Hidden Language of Computer Hardware and Software.* Microsoft Press, 2 edition, 2022

5

Universal alien device

5.1 The central gate

The main components of a modern computer are the *memory*, the *input and output devices*, and the *central processing unit* (CPU). The main component of the CPU of a computer is the *arithmetic logic unit* (ALU), represented in Figure 5.1.

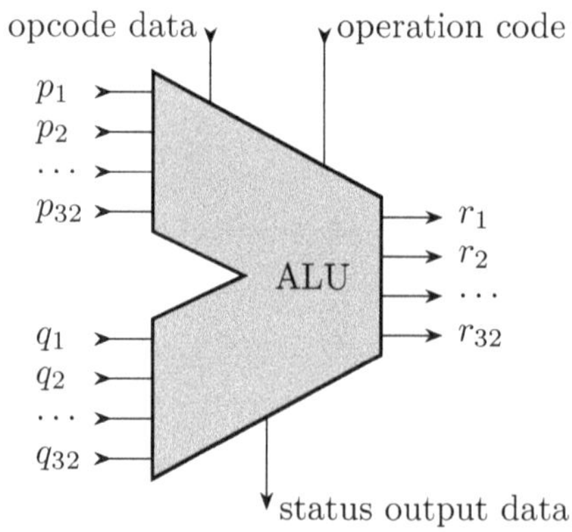

Figure 5.1: A 32 bit arithmetic logic unit performs arithmetic operations between two 32 bit integer numbers, and logic operations. The opcode data specifies what operation to perform.

As suggested by its name, the ALU is a logic circuit that performs arithmetic and logic operations. A main arithmetic operation done by the ALU is the addition of positive integer numbers. Physically, addition is limited to the number of bits of the ALU, and therefore it can't exceed it. For example, for an eight-bit ALU, if we keep adding 1, at some point we get

$$\begin{array}{r} \boxed{1}\boxed{1}\boxed{1}\boxed{1}\boxed{1}\boxed{1}\boxed{1}\boxed{1} \\ +\boxed{0}\boxed{0}\boxed{0}\boxed{0}\boxed{0}\boxed{0}\boxed{0}\boxed{1} \\ =\boxed{0}\boxed{0}\boxed{0}\boxed{0}\boxed{0}\boxed{0}\boxed{0}\boxed{0} \end{array} \tag{5.1}$$

just like it happens with the odometer of a car when you go an extra mile.

DOI: 10.1201/9781003623373-5

This means that the addition is in fact an addition modulo 2^b, where b is the number of bits. If the result would exceed this number, that is, when the "odometer" rolls over, this is marked in a bit in the status output data, called *overflow flag*. The overflow flag offers a chance to detect such situations and to handle them properly, preventing errors.

Addition of integer numbers allowed to have negative values is done on the same circuit, assuming that the first bit is 1 for negative numbers and 0 otherwise. Subtractions are performed by using the same circuit that performs the additions of integer numbers. Multiplications can be done via repeated addition, division can be done via repeated subtraction, but they can also be implemented by specialized circuits. From the point of view of Computer Science it doesn't matter, as long as the output is correct, so for simplicity, we will consider an ALU that reduces the arithmetic operations to additions, that is, an ALU that works primarily as an *adder*.

The ALU also compares numbers to see which is greater, and also performs logic operations like AND, OR, NOT, and binary shifts, which consist of shifting the bit values to the left or to the right.

But how does an ALU built for additions perform other operations, and how does it know which one to perform? This information is marked in the bits in the *operation code*. The designers of the ALU used various tricks to reinterpret the bits so that the adder just adds and the output is interpreted as the result of the intended operation.

All these are done with the same trick used in the Rosetta Stone example in Chapter 3, Section 3.3, by flipping the bits as convenient. Without such reinterpretations, the ALU would be a single-purpose logic circuit, and our computers would be unable to do anything but additions. The reinterpretation of logic gates and circuits is the norm, not the exception.

We can see that the ALU is very similar to the alien device, except that it has more inputs and outputs. It is even interpreted in multiple ways, depending on what arithmetic or logic operation is used to perform at that time.

Let us see this more concretely. To add two integers using a 32-bit ALU as in Figure 5.1, the two numbers to be added are represented in base 2 as $\mathtt{p}_1\mathtt{p}_2\cdots\mathtt{p}_{32}$ and $\mathtt{q}_1\mathtt{q}_2\cdots\mathtt{q}_{32}$, and the result is

$$\mathtt{r}_1\mathtt{r}_2\ldots\mathtt{r}_{32} = \mathtt{p}_1\mathtt{p}_2\cdots\mathtt{p}_{32} + \mathtt{q}_1\mathtt{q}_2\cdots\mathtt{q}_{32}, \tag{5.2}$$

where $\mathtt{p}_1,\mathtt{p}_2,\ldots,\mathtt{p}_{32},\mathtt{q}_1,\mathtt{q}_2,\ldots,\mathtt{q}_{32}$, and $\mathtt{r}_1,\mathtt{r}_2,\ldots,\mathtt{r}_{32}$ are binary digits 0 and 1. In fact, the result $\mathtt{r}_1\mathtt{r}_2\ldots\mathtt{r}_{32}$ is the correct result of addition only if the 32 bits are sufficient. If the result exceeds 32 bits we get overflow, so the result is truncated to 32 bits, but this information is recorded in the status output data.

Example 5.1. Let us illustrate addition on an 8-bit ALU, by adding the numbers 17 and 13. Note that $17 = 1\cdot 2^4 + 0\cdot 2^3 + 0\cdot 2^2 + 0\cdot 2^1 + 1\cdot 2^0$. On 8 bits it is written as 00010001. For similar reasons, 13 is written on 8 bits as

00001101. Their sum, 40, is represented on 8 bits as 00011110,

$$\begin{array}{cc|c|c|c|c|c|c|c|c|} \cline{3-10} & & 0 & 0 & 0 & 1 & 0 & 0 & 0 & 1 \\ \cline{3-10} + & & 0 & 0 & 0 & 0 & 1 & 1 & 0 & 1 \\ \cline{3-10} = & & 0 & 0 & 0 & 1 & 1 & 1 & 1 & 0 \\ \cline{3-10} \end{array} \tag{5.3}$$

If the number of digits of the result exceeds 8 bits, as for example if we add 167 and 175, the result requires 9 bits, and so the carry-out that exceeds the 8 bits is written in the status output data,

$$\begin{array}{c|c|c|c|c|c|c|c|c|c|} \cline{4-11} & & & 1 & 0 & 1 & 0 & 0 & 1 & 1 & 1 \\ \cline{4-11} + & & & 1 & 0 & 1 & 0 & 1 & 0 & 1 & 1 \\ \cline{2-2} \cline{4-11} = & 1 & & 0 & 1 & 0 & 1 & 0 & 1 & 1 & 0 \\ \cline{2-2} \cline{4-11} \end{array} \tag{5.4}$$

In Example 5.1, we represented the integer numbers from 0 to 255 on 8 bits. To also represent negative numbers, we use a different convention: reserve the first bit for the sign, so that if it is 1 the number is negative, and if it is 0, the number is positive. In this way, we can represent the integers from -128 to 127.

When using the ALU, an extra bit decides whether the circuit will be used to add or to subtract, and in the latter case, it inverts the bits just like the input bits are inverted in the Rosetta Stone from Figure 3.4. To subtract an integer from another integer, add the number being subtracted, represented in *two's complement*, to the number it is subtracted from, in the standard base 2 representation. If you get binary digits that exceed the 8 bits, ignore them.

Example 5.2. An 8-bit ALU can perform subtractions by using the two's complement representation in the following way.

1. Write down the number to be subtracted in base 2.
2. If the number is negative, prefix it with the bit 1.
3. Flip the values of the digits in this binary representation.
4. To obtain the two's complement representation, add 1 to the result.

Make sure that your numbers are between -128 and 127, otherwise you should use more bits to fit your numbers. For example, the base ten number 37 is 100101 in base 2 (or in the), because $37 = 1 \cdot 2^5 + 0 \cdot 2^4 + 0 \cdot 2^3 + 1 \cdot 2^2 + 0 \cdot 2^1 + 1 \cdot 2^0$. On 8 bits it is written as 00100101.

$$\begin{array}{|c|c|c|c|c|c|c|c|} \hline 0 & 0 & 1 & 0 & 0 & 1 & 0 & 1 \\ \hline \end{array} \tag{5.5}$$

After inversion (also named *one's complement*) one obtains

$$\begin{array}{|c|c|c|c|c|c|c|c|} \hline 1 & 1 & 0 & 1 & 1 & 0 & 1 & 0 \\ \hline \end{array} \tag{5.6}$$

To get the two's complement representation of 37 we add 1,

$$\boxed{\texttt{1}}\boxed{\texttt{1}}\boxed{\texttt{0}}\boxed{\texttt{1}}\boxed{\texttt{1}}\boxed{\texttt{0}}\boxed{\texttt{1}}\boxed{\texttt{1}} \tag{5.7}$$

The *two's complement representation* is used to perform subtractions on a circuit that is normally understood to perform additions, like the ALU from Figure 5.1. For example, to subtract 37 from 100, we add `11011011`, obtained in equation (5.7), to `01100100`, which is 100 in base 2, and ignore the carry on. We get

$$\texttt{01100100} - \texttt{00100101} = \texttt{01100100} + \texttt{11011011} = \cancel{\texttt{0001}}\ \texttt{00111111},$$

which in base 10 is 63.

5.2 A computer is a huge logic gate in a loop

Computers can be understood as huge logic gates, much like the ALU from Figure 5.1. Therefore, if we ignore the irrelevant details of implementation, computers admit a very simple mathematical description.

A computer with n bits is made of n small subsystems that we will call *bit cells*. Since each bit cell of a computer can be in two possible states, the total number of possible states in which a computer can be is 2^n, where n is the number of bit cells in that computer. If we label the states of the small subsystems by `0` and `1`, the total set of possible states of the computer is

$$\mathcal{S} = \underbrace{\{\texttt{0},\texttt{1}\} \times \ldots \times \{\texttt{0},\texttt{1}\}}_{n \text{ times}} = \{\texttt{0},\texttt{1}\}^n. \tag{5.8}$$

Then, any state of the computer has the form

$$s = (b_1, \ldots, b_n)\,, \text{ where } b_j \in \{\texttt{0},\texttt{1}\} \text{ for any } j. \tag{5.9}$$

The computer transitions from one state into another one in discrete steps. At every step, the next state is determined by the current state. Therefore, if no external cause affects the computer, its transition at any step can be described by a Boolean function

$$\mathcal{F} : \{\texttt{0},\texttt{1}\}^n \to \{\texttt{0},\texttt{1}\}^n. \tag{5.10}$$

Let Δt be the duration of a step. At every time $t_N = t_0 + N\Delta t$, the state of the computer is represented by n bit values, $\mathbf{s}_N = (b_{1N}, \ldots, b_{nN})$. The computer's state at the time t_N determines its next state, at t_{N+1}, by

$$\mathbf{s}_{N+1} = \mathcal{F}(\mathbf{s}_N). \tag{5.11}$$

By applying $\mathcal{F}$ multiple times, we get the sequence

$$\mathbf{s}_0 \xrightarrow{\mathcal{F}} \mathbf{s}_1 \dashrightarrow^{\mathcal{F}} \cdots \dashrightarrow^{\mathcal{F}} \mathbf{s}_{N-1} \xrightarrow{\mathcal{F}} \mathbf{s}_N \tag{5.12}$$

Then, the computer's initial state $\mathbf{s}_0 = (b_{10}, \ldots, b_{n0})$ at the time t_0 determines its state at the time t_N by

$$\mathbf{s}_N = \mathcal{F}^N(\mathbf{s}_0), \tag{5.13}$$

where $\mathcal{F}^N$ is the function obtained by applying N times the function $\mathcal{F}$,

$$\mathcal{F}^N(\mathbf{s}_0) = \underbrace{(\mathcal{F} \circ \mathcal{F} \circ \ldots \circ \mathcal{F})}_{N \text{ times}}(\mathbf{s}_0) = \underbrace{\mathcal{F}(\ldots \mathcal{F}(}_{N \text{ times}}\mathbf{s}_0)\ldots). \tag{5.14}$$

Therefore, a computer can be defined in a very simple way:

Definition 5.1. A computer is a physical realization of a function $\mathcal{F}$ that maps n bits to n bits, over and over again, in a loop.

Since the transition has to depend only on the current state of the computer, the function $\mathcal{F}$ is independent of time. That is, if the computer is functional, whenever it's in a state s, it transitions in the same state $\mathcal{F}(s)$. After N steps, it transitions into the state $\mathcal{F}^N(s)$, provided no external intervention changes its state in the meantime. Usually, the computer contains a digital clock, which is incremented as the time passes, but even so, $\mathcal{F}$ doesn't depend on the objective time, but only on the clock's state, which in this description is part of the computer's state. So even for operations that depend on time, the transition depends only on the current state, which includes the clock's state.

Some of the computer's bits can be changed by the user. If the user inputs some data, this changes the computer's state from s to another state s'. The computer continues to transition according to the same function $\mathcal{F}$, but applied to the modified state, $s' \mapsto \mathcal{F}(s')$. The user or other external causes can also halt the computer.

Because the number of possible states is finite, a computer is a *finite state machine* or *finite automaton*, which are particular cases of Turing machines.

It may seem that this description is overly simplified. Computers have sophisticated architectures, with complex logic circuits and different kinds of memory cells, but all of these can be encoded into the function $\mathcal{F}$, which describes how bits change in time.

As seen in the previous chapters, there is no objective way to assign the values `0` and `1` to the possible states of a bit cell. It is a matter of convention. This fact is not only true, but it is heavily exploited in both practice and theory. Forgetting it may give us the wrong idea about what computers do.

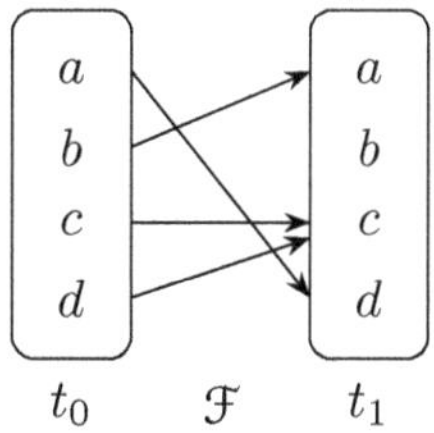

Figure 5.2: A very simple finite state machine with four possible states.

Example 5.3. Figure 5.2 illustrates a very simple *finite state machine* with four possible states $\{a, b, c, d\}$, and with the state transition function $\mathfrak{F}$ defined by $\mathfrak{F}(a) = d$, $\mathfrak{F}(b) = a$, $\mathfrak{F}(c) = c$, and $\mathfrak{F}(d) = c$.

The transitions to the next states are obtained by applying the same function $\mathfrak{F}$, as shown in Figure 5.3. The system is assumed to start in the state b. We see that after three steps its state becomes c, and the machine stops changing its state, because $\mathfrak{F}(c) = c$.

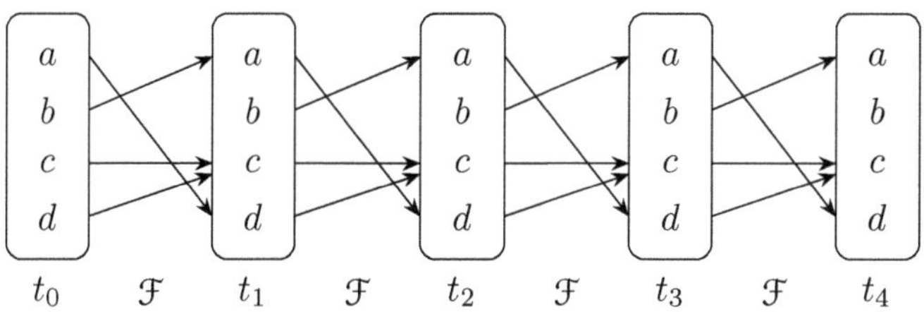

Figure 5.3: The evolution in time of the simple state machine from Figure 5.2. The initial state is b. After three steps, the machine's state becomes c, and the machine stops changing its state.

Note that in practice not all possible inputs are acceptable by the programs running on the computer. But even in such situations, the function $\mathfrak{F}$ encodes what happens when the computer receives invalid input data. It may return an error message, or it may crash, but whatever happens, the computer will be in a physical state characterized by the individual states of its bit cells, and the function $\mathfrak{F}$ encodes this.

One may wonder why the function $\mathfrak{F}$ that describes the transition from the state at t_N to that at t_{N+1} is the same regardless of N, in particular it's the same as that from the state at t_0 to that at t_1. The reason is of course that at all times it's the same computer. As long as the input data are the same, the output data should be the same, whenever the computation is performed. If the computer would compute on Thursdays differently than on Sundays, Computer Science would be something between Astrology and lottery.

5.3 A larger alien device

Figure 5.4 represents this schematic description of a computer. The processor is just a complicated logic gate that takes the input data, consisting of n bits represented by $\mathbf{x}$, and computes the output, also consisting of n bits, represented by $\mathcal{F}(\mathbf{x})$. The processor acts like the Boolean function $\mathcal{F}$ of n variables and with n outputs from equation (5.11).

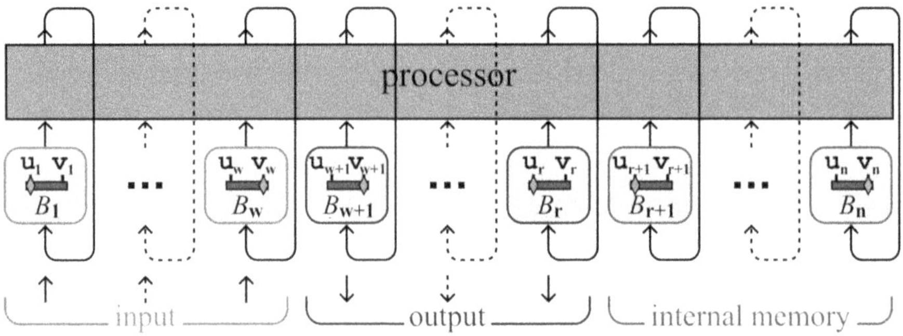

Figure 5.4: A schematic description of a computer. The user can write only the bit cells from B_1 to B_w, and can read only those up to B_r. The bit cells from B_{r+1} to B_n, hidden to the user, represent the internal memory of the computer.

A subset of the computer's bit cells, denoted by $B_1, \ldots, B_w$, can be changed from the outside, for example by a user, or by receiving data from other computers through the network or through the Internet. These are the *input* bit cells. The computer also contains bit cells that can be read from the outside, those up to B_r. These are the *output* bit cells. Here "input" and "output" are meant from the point of view of the user, and should not be confused with the processor's n inputs and n outputs. The bit cells from B_{r+1} to B_n are hidden to the user, and represent the internal memory of the computer.

In general, the input and output bit cells can be accessed by the user in a user-friendly format, provided by a *user interface.* We will see later that the user interface plays an important role in this story, by establishing the convention of how to interpret the bit cells' states as bits.

Of course, as in the case discussed in Section 5.3, the processor is just a physical system. It can be seen as computing a Boolean function only if we assign bit values to the physical states of the systems $B_1, \ldots, B_n$. And this assignment can be done in 2^n different ways.

Example 5.4. The alien device from Figure 2.1 can be reorganized like the simple computer from Definition 5.1. The representation of the alien device is given on the left side of Figure 5.5.

With the notations from Chapter 2, the state of the knob P is p, the state of the switch Q is q, and the state of the pointer R is r. When the user chooses the states of the knob P and the switch Q, this determines the next state of the pointer R, so this state is a function $f(p,q)$. We collect the states of the three bit cells into the triple $\mathbf{x} = (p,q,r)$. The function $\mathcal{F}$ is then defined by

$$\mathcal{F}(p,q,r) = (p,q,f(p,q)). \tag{5.15}$$

The transition $\mathbf{x} \mapsto \mathcal{F}(\mathbf{x})$ from each state $\mathbf{x}$ to the next one is calculated based on Table 2.1, and represented in the table from Figure 5.5. If the user changes the inputs p or q, the result $f(p,q)$ is calculated and at the next step is stored in R. If no further change of p or q is made by the user, no change of the bit cell R occurs in the subsequent steps. The computer continues to run, but it stops changing its state, because the output is already written in the bit cell R.

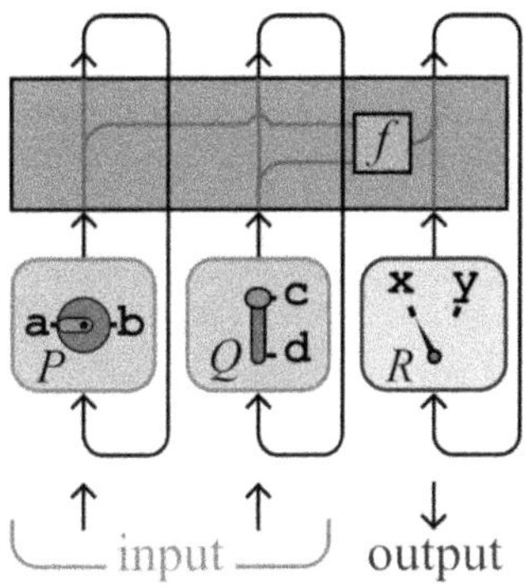

$\mathbf{x}$	$\mathcal{F}(\mathbf{x})$
(a, c, x)	(a, c, x)
(a, c, y)	(a, c, x)
(a, d, x)	(a, d, x)
(a, d, y)	(a, d, x)
(b, c, x)	(b, c, y)
(b, c, y)	(b, c, y)
(b, d, x)	(b, d, x)
(b, d, y)	(b, d, x)

Figure 5.5: The alien device from Figure 2.1 reorganized as a simple computer. The part of the device labeled f is a logic gate in the processor. The states change according to the transition table from the right.

The states and the function $\mathcal{F}$ are also represented in Figure 5.6.

Alice and her friends can apply their own interpretations, by assigning Boolean values to the bit cells according to Table 2.4, page 24. For example, Alice will interpret the function $\mathcal{F}$ as

$$\mathcal{F}_A(p,q,r) = (p,q,p \wedge q). \tag{5.16}$$

Believe it or not, the simple Definition 5.1, illustrated in Figure 5.4, applies to any computer.

The reader who doesn't know much about computers may be surprised. And I expect the reader who knows something about them may be tempted to disagree, perhaps very strongly, because in practice computers seem more complex. But the description that I provided is correct, it just ignores the architectural details.

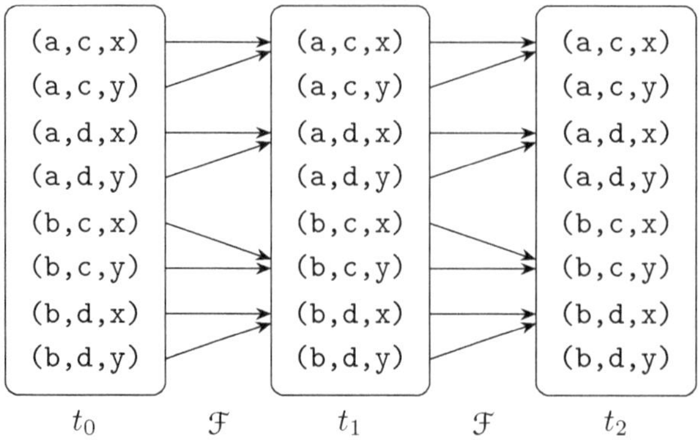

Figure 5.6: The transition function of the alien device.

Details 5.1. In Figure 5.4, all the bit cells are separated from the logic gates, which are all included in the processor. But in practice, a computer is organized differently, due to the practical necessities. The *central processing unit* (CPU) includes not only logic gates, but also memories—the registers and the cache memory. The memory units of a real-world computer also contain logic gates. But I separated memories from logic gates *conceptually*, because they play different roles in our discussion.

Another difference is that the user doesn't use switches to input the data, and it doesn't read it from pointers. We input data using the keyboard and the mouse and even the voice, and other input peripherals. We see the output data on displays, or we print it, or we hear it in the speakers or headphones.

Another apparent difference is that the computer from Figure 5.4 seems to read and write all bit cells at once, while real-world computers access only a small number of bit cells at any step. But this doesn't contradict the definition given here. Definition 5.1 is perfectly consistent with the possibility that the function $\mathcal{F}$ ignores most of the bit cells, and yet, $\mathcal{F}^N$ doesn't seem to do this because I didn't specify what bits it leaves unchanged.

These details don't lead to any relevant difference for our discussion. All I did in Figure 5.4 was to group all the logic circuits in one structure that I called processor, and the memory cells in three groups, one needed by the user to input data, one to read the results, and one for the internal memory of the computer, which I assumed to include any other form of storage, including hard drives, DVDs, and flash memories. Ultimately, everything a computer does is consistent with Figure 5.4. This description is general enough to apply to all computers that ever existed that process binary data.

By extrapolating the observations from Chapter 2, we see now that there are many more ways to interpret what the processor does. Like in the case of the alien device, there are two ways to interpret every bit cell.

Observation 5.1. For a computer with n bit cells, there are (at least!) 2^n possible interpretations.

This simple observation may still seem outrageous, because we are trained for so long to interpret computations as something objective. The extreme precision of the computers could only reinforce this belief. So, in the following chapters, we will take more time to reexamine our basic assumptions about this.

5.4 The ship of Theseus

There is an argument often invoked to support the hypothesis that human consciousness, including whatever counts as sentient experience, can be simulated on a computer. The argument can be found for example in [125], p. 109. It is a scenario about replacing someone's brain with computer parts. Don't worry, nobody's neurons have to actually be removed, this is a *thought experiment*, an experiment that you can simulate in your mind, without having to leave your armchair or your zafu. Some think that this thought experiment proves that mind has to be a computation Here it is, briefly.

Thought Experiment 5.1 (Brain Replacement Scenario)**.** Consider a human subject whose neurons are removed one at a time by a very precise surgical robot. Before being removed, the relation between the input and output signals of each neuron is determined by measurements. The data collected in this way is used to build a computer model that simulates the neuron. The measurement is repeated with various inputs, until the computer simulation of the neuron is able to predict how the neuron will fire in every situation. Then the surgical robot removes the neuron, and connects in its place the computer simulation of the neuron.

A human brain contains approximately 86 billion neurons. Circa 50 000 of them die every day, and we don't even notice this. So it shouldn't be a big difference if, instead of one of them dying, it is replaced with an artificial or a simulated neuron.

But what if we gradually replace all of them? Would the consciousness of the human subject survive this procedure? Would it disappear gradually?

The Brain Replacement Scenario reminds us of the *Ship of Theseus*, mentioned by Plutarch in his collection of biographies *Lives of the Noble Greeks and Romans*. The decaying planks of Theseus's ship are gradually replaced with new planks. The removed planks are used to build a second ship. A paradox seems to arise if we ask the question "which of the two ships is the same as the original ship?" Or both of them are?

The Brain Replacement Scenario is a strong argument supporting the claim that human consciousness can be simulated on a computer, because its opponents seem to have no chance to refute it. If the opponents say that human consciousness has an ability that will be lost after the replacement, then one can ask them to give an example of such an ability. Maybe it's the ability to write poems, or to compose music, or to be in love. Since the behavior of each biological neuron is perfectly replicated by the corresponding artificial neuron, the artificial brain should be able to write poems or compose music or be in love, just like the biological brain it replaced could.

After the opponents try to invoke various abilities as being specific to humans and irreplicable by machines, they soon realize that any behavioral aspect of the human mind can be replicated. So the opponents, if they are not converted, will eventually figure out that there is another reason why they don't accept the argument: the existence of sentient experience *per se*, not the behavior. Replicating the behavior means to fake it. But human consciousness seems to have an extra ingredient associated to the behavior, which is the sentient experience that goes with it.

But then, the supporters of the computational mind gain the higher ground. They just ask the opponents to prove the existence of sentient experience independent of the behavioral aspects. It seems that they win the argument, since whatever can be shown or proved or measured in a lab, it can also be simulated on a computer.

So now, if the opponents don't accept the defeat, they will appear as science deniers, because they claim that something that can't be measured exists. Well, it can be observed, but only subjectively. There is no way to show it to others, in a lab, in a way that can be read on the screens of the measurement devices. And since science is about objective independent testability of the hypotheses, sentient experience doesn't seem to have a place in it, except for its measurable aspects.

At this point, if one invokes that there is something special in the biology of the neurons, this further resistance may even be perceived as "human chauvinism" [125] or "carbon chauvinism" or "speciesism". And nobody wants to be called a chauvinist or science denier! Checkmate!

We arrived at a strange situation: you can claim that consciousness is just a computation, without even having to prove this! All you have to do is to turn the table and ask the opponents to do the impossible. Because if the only acceptable evidence should be measurable in a way that can be seen by everybody else, and if sentient experience is exactly the opposite of this, it becomes impossible to prove it. And if everything that can be measured can be simulated by a computer, it is undeniable that human sentience is just computation. Or is it?

Now I will propose a somewhat upside-down version of the Brain Replacement Scenario, which emphasizes the awkwardness of relativity of information and computation. We will see that the alien device argument is scalable, it applies to computers of any size.

Thought Experiment 5.2 (Computer Replacement Argument)**.** Remember those brilliant computer geeks who own an old computer, but who keep upgrading its components? Suppose that we are much better, so better that we are able to replace not just entire hardware components, but tiny bit cells and logic gates.

One day, we replace a bit cell of the computer with a completely different physical system that can be in two stable states, but chosen to be neutral, so that we don't associate mentally its states in a particular way with `0` and `1`. Remember the possibility of neutral bit cells explained in Example 3.2. If we do it properly, the computer will continue to work the same way. So we replace another one, and another one. We make sure to replace the `AND`, `OR`, `NAND`, `NOR` and all other gates from Table 2.4 with tiny versions of the alien device, connecting it so that it works like the original gates it replaced. If we do it well, the computer will still work, and we will see no change when using it to play our favorite game. We can also replace logic gates that are not among those from Table 2.4, with other tiny alien devices that can be interpreted as those gates. We keep replacing the logic gates, one at a time.

This story is not exactly realistic, since in fact the circuits in your computer are integrated circuits made of tiny transistors, so already the logic gates are obfuscated. But if you imagine that inside your computer there are logic gates that work together to implement the Boolean functions that you expect to be computed, then this example refers to that image you have about the internals of the computers. And this image is not entirely wrong, since the designers of the circuits actually designed them using logic gates, but replaced each logic gate with a couple of transistors. So in this thought experiment, we can replace the transistors that replaced logic gates back, but using copies of the alien device or another neutral gate. We can replace the logic gates with all sorts of neutral mechanisms that, based on the possible input states, ensure that the output states reproduce those of the replaced logic gates.

Whenever we replace a bit cell with a neutral one, we attach a post-it note to it, to remember which of the two states represents a `0` and which represents a `1`. Likewise, whenever we replace a logic gate, we label it with a post-it note on which we write the type of the replaced logic gate. This will help us remember the original functionality, so that we keep track of the changes and make sure that we don't make a mistake.

The resulting computer may be extremely large and heavy, and extremely slow, or the opposite, depending on what kinds of gates we use, but this is irrelevant. If we were very careful, it should work and be able to reproduce the functionality of the original computer.

This was about the internal components of the computer. Now we replace the keyboard, the display, and any other peripheral component the computer had, with new ones, that can be connected with the contraption and allow the user to operate the computer the same way it operated the original one.

A central tenet of Computer Science is that the same information can be stored on different supports, made of different materials, and constructed in different ways. They can be magnetic tapes, punched cards, various types of memory cells, *etc.* And yet, it's the same information. The same computation can be performed on various machines, and these can be as different as we can imagine. People imagined computers made of billiard balls [68], water tubes, Lego, wood mechanisms, 3D printed mechanisms, cogwheels, *etc.* This ensures that the new computer is able to run the same programs as the original computer. It may be a sophisticated steampunk contraption, more complicated than all the machines ever drawn by the cartoonist Rube Goldberg combined, but, if we do it well, it will work!

Now let's destroy the user interface, keep the internal machinery, and remove all the post-it notes!

Question 5.1. If we invite the topmost computer engineers, and ask them to put back the post-it notes, would they be able to do it?

There will be nothing to suggest which of the two states of each bit cell used to represent a `0` and which used to represent a `1`. There will be nothing to tell an `AND` gate from an `OR` gate from a `NAND` gate and from any other gate performing one of the eight operations from Table 2.4. And however they would put back the post-it notes, the contraption would compute some Boolean operations that make sense!

Remark 5.1. Someone who supports the conclusion of the Brain Replacement Scenario, should also support the conclusion of the Computer Replacement Argument, because it follows the same logic. And this conclusion is that it is impossible to attach a unique meaning of the information in a computer or of the computation the computer performs.

The opposite is not true: if you support the Computer Replacement Argument, it doesn't follow logically that you should also support the Brain Replacement Scenario. The reason is that in one of the cases, and only one, we can have inside information about the original system that will be replaced.

A computer is not very different from the alien device, except that, instead of having merely eight possible interpretations, its number of possible interpretations grows exponentially with the size of the memory of the computer. And they all compute something different.

In particular, if we assume that the computer can have a mind and sentient experiences, we will see that it can simultaneously have multiple contradictory mental states and sentient experiences. While this doesn't fully refute the possibility that consciousness can be simulated on a computer, it reveals that this possibility would be very bizarre.

Exercises

Exercise 5.1. Perform in base 2 the following additions of base 10 numbers: $12 + 12$, $14 + 27$, $100 + 10 + 1$.

Exercise 5.2. Find out the two's complement 8 bit representations of the base 10 numbers $-25, -12, -1, 0, 1, 12, 25$.

Exercise 5.3. What numbers have `10000000`, `00001111`, `11110001`, `11010110`, and `00101010` as two's complement 8 bit representations?

Exercise 5.4. Using two's complement, perform the following subtractions as additions: $100 - 1$, $50 - 50$, $50 - (-50)$, $100 - 64$, $37 - (-14)$.

Exercise 5.5. What happens if the result of an addition or a subtraction on 8 bits exceeds the 8 bits?

Key points

- There is no objectively unique way to represent numbers.
- The ALU can be used to perform different operations, by using different interpretations or conventions.
- A computer is not different from a huge logic gate that takes as inputs its own outputs and runs in a loop.
- If we replace the bit cells and the logic gates of a computer with neutral bit cells and neutral logic gates like the alien device, uniformizing the circuits, the computer will continue to work as expected. If we remove the peripherals, this will make the ambiguity of computation manifest and nobody will be able to tell what computation is taking place.

Further reading

[140] Charles Petzold. *Code: The Hidden Language of Computer Hardware and Software*. Microsoft Press, 2 edition, 2022

[62] Ronald Emery. *Digital circuits: Logic and design*. CRC Press, 2020

[104] Mohammad Karim and Xinghao Chen. *Digital design: Basic concepts and principles.* CRC Press, 2017

[133] Noam Nisan and Shimon Schocken. *The elements of computing systems: Building a modern computer from first principles.* MIT Press, Cambridge, Massachusetts, 2021

6

Relativity of information

6.1 Reference frames in plane

In plane Euclidean Geometry, we can use a *reference frame* or a coordinate system to represent points by their coordinates. But the choice of the coordinates is arbitrary, and it can be done in infinitely many ways. Figure 6.1 illustrates the same figure in two different coordinate systems, the second one being rotated with respect to the first one.

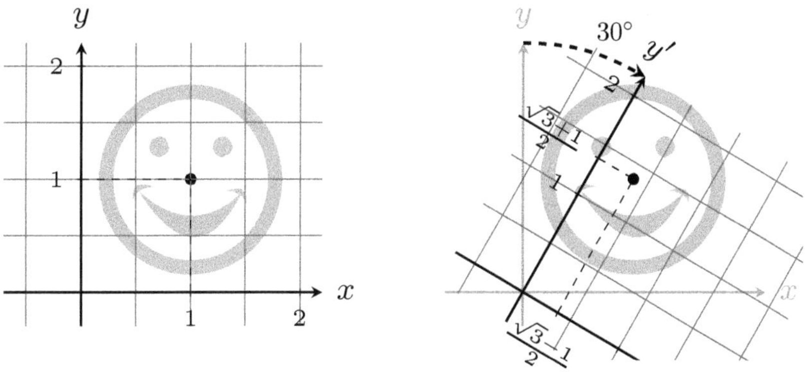

Figure 6.1: A change of coordinates or a passive symmetry transformation.

The coordinates of the points in the new reference frame can be obtained from their coordinates in the old reference frame. For this, we apply a *transformation matrix*, which allows us to express the coordinate of a point in the second reference frame in terms of its coordinates in the first reference frame. In the example from Figure 6.1, since the second reference frame is rotated clockwise with 30 degrees, the transformation matrix represents a counter-clockwise rotation with 30 degrees,

$$\begin{pmatrix} \cos 30 & -\sin 30 \\ \sin 30 & \cos 30 \end{pmatrix} = \begin{pmatrix} \sqrt{3}/2 & -1/2 \\ 1/2 & \sqrt{3}/2 \end{pmatrix} \cong \begin{pmatrix} 0.866 & -0.5 \\ 0.5 & 0.866 \end{pmatrix}. \tag{6.1}$$

Definition 6.1 (Matrix multiplication). Remember that to multiply an $m \times n$ matrix A (having m rows and n columns) with an $n \times p$ matrix B, we multiply

DOI: 10.1201/9781003623373-6

one-by-one the cells of each row of the first matrix with the cells of each column of the second matrix and add up the products. Let $(a_{i1}, \ldots, a_{in})$ be the i-th row of the first matrix and $(b_{1j}, \ldots, b_{nj})$ be the j-th column of the second matrix. To multiply them, we compute the sum

$$\sum_{k=1}^{n} a_{ik}b_{kj} = a_{i1}b_{1j} + a_{i2}b_{2j} + \ldots + a_{in}b_{nj}.$$

Then we put the result in the cell (i,j) of the resulting $m \times p$ matrix AB:

$$\begin{pmatrix} \cdots & \cdots & \cdots \\ a_{i1} & \cdots & a_{in} \\ \cdots & \cdots & \cdots \end{pmatrix} \begin{pmatrix} \cdots & b_{1j} & \cdots \\ \cdots & \cdots & \cdots \\ \cdots & b_{nj} & \cdots \end{pmatrix} = \begin{pmatrix} \cdots & \cdots & \cdots \\ \cdots & \sum_{k=1}^{n} a_{ik}b_{kj} & \cdots \\ \cdots & \cdots & \cdots \end{pmatrix} \tag{6.2}$$

To obtain the entire matrix AB we apply equation (6.2) for all pairs consisting of a row from the matrix A and a column from the matrix B.

Now let us transform points and vectors. We will represent a point of coordinate x and y, or a vector of components x and y in our frame, by a column matrix $\begin{pmatrix} x \\ y \end{pmatrix}$. We will often use the handy notation $(x,y)^\intercal := \begin{pmatrix} x \\ y \end{pmatrix}$, where I used the *transposition* $\intercal$, which swaps the rows and the columns.

If we apply, for example, the transformation from equation (6.1) to $(1,1)^\intercal$, we obtain its coordinates in the second reference frame:

$$\begin{pmatrix} \sqrt{3}/2 & -1/2 \\ 1/2 & \sqrt{3}/2 \end{pmatrix} \begin{pmatrix} 1 \\ 1 \end{pmatrix} = \begin{pmatrix} \dfrac{\sqrt{3}-1}{2} \\ \dfrac{\sqrt{3}+1}{2} \end{pmatrix} \cong \begin{pmatrix} 0.366 \\ 1.366 \end{pmatrix}. \tag{6.3}$$

The resulting coordinates are the same that we get if instead of rotating the coordinates counterclockwise with 30 degrees, we rotate the entire figure clockwise with 30 degrees, as in Figure 6.2.

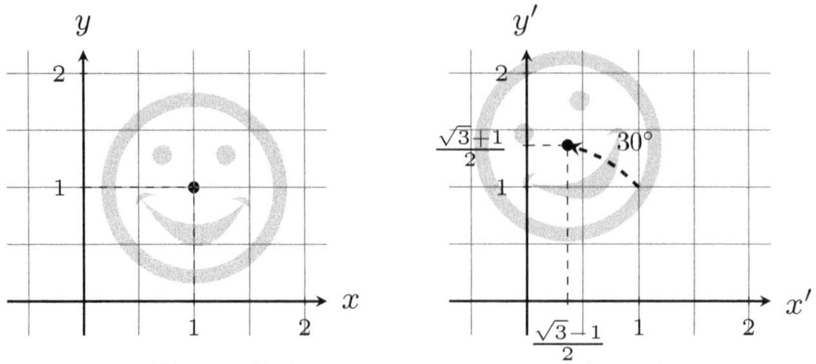

Figure 6.2: An active symmetry transformation.

Definition 6.2. A transformation of the reference frame is called *passive transformation*, because it doesn't transform the actual position or orientation of the geometric objects, only the reference frame. A transformation applied to the geometric objects themselves is called *active transformation.*

Figure 6.1 represents a passive transformation, and Figure 6.2 represents an active transformation. These figures illustrate rotations, but other transformations are possible: translations, reflections, and any combination of rotations, translations, and reflections. These transformations of the Euclidean plane preserve the distances and the angles, and are called *isometries.*

The origin O of the reference frame can be any point in the plane. As in the example from equation (6.3), any isometry that leaves O in place can be represented by a matrix

$$M = \begin{pmatrix} m_{11} & m_{12} \\ m_{21} & m_{22} \end{pmatrix}, \tag{6.4}$$

and M transforms a point $P = (x, y)^\intercal$ (or its coordinates) into

$$MP = \begin{pmatrix} m_{11} & m_{12} \\ m_{21} & m_{22} \end{pmatrix} \begin{pmatrix} x \\ y \end{pmatrix} = \begin{pmatrix} m_{11}x + m_{12}y \\ m_{21}x + m_{22}y \end{pmatrix}. \tag{6.5}$$

A translation of a point with a vector $T = (a, b)^\intercal$ consist of adding it to the position of the point,

$$MP + T = \begin{pmatrix} m_{11} & m_{12} \\ m_{21} & m_{22} \end{pmatrix} \begin{pmatrix} x \\ y \end{pmatrix} + \begin{pmatrix} a \\ b \end{pmatrix} = \begin{pmatrix} m_{11}x + m_{12}y + a \\ m_{21}x + m_{22}y + b \end{pmatrix}. \tag{6.6}$$

As in the case of rotations, the coordinates of a point to which we apply an active transformation are the same as the coordinates of that point expressed in the reference frame obtained by applying the inverse transformation to the original reference frame.

6.2 Vectors

By fixing an origin O, every point P in the Euclidean plane can be represented by a vector $\overrightarrow{OP}$. The coordinates (x, y) of P are the components of the vector $\overrightarrow{OP}$. Thus, by fixing an origin O, the plane can be identified with the vector space $\mathbb{R}^2$.

A *vector space* can be understood in terms of the components of the vectors. In a d-dimensional vector space, a vector can be seen as a column matrix with d rows. Any $d \times d$ matrix transforms the vectors by multiplication. Vectors, like matrices, can be added component-by-component, and multiplied with numbers. For two vectors $|u\rangle = (u_0, \ldots, u_{d-1})^\intercal$ and $|v\rangle = (v_0, \ldots, v_{d-1})^\intercal$, and a number $a \in \mathbb{R}$,

$$|u\rangle + |v\rangle = \begin{pmatrix} u_0 \\ \cdots \\ u_{d-1} \end{pmatrix} + \begin{pmatrix} v_0 \\ \cdots \\ v_{d-1} \end{pmatrix} = \begin{pmatrix} u_0 + v_0 \\ \cdots \\ u_{d-1} + v_{d-1} \end{pmatrix} \tag{6.7}$$

and

$$a\,|v\rangle = a \begin{pmatrix} v_0 \\ \cdots \\ v_{d-1} \end{pmatrix} = \begin{pmatrix} av_0 \\ \cdots \\ av_{d-1} \end{pmatrix}. \tag{6.8}$$

Since in a vector space the origin of the reference frame is fixed, we will use the word *basis* instead of reference frame.

There are d vectors having a component equal to 1 and all others 0:

$$|0\rangle = \begin{pmatrix} 1 \\ 0 \\ \vdots \\ 0 \end{pmatrix}, |1\rangle = \begin{pmatrix} 0 \\ 1 \\ \vdots \\ 0 \end{pmatrix}, \cdots, |d-1\rangle = \begin{pmatrix} 0 \\ 0 \\ \vdots \\ 1 \end{pmatrix}. \tag{6.9}$$

Sometimes we call this basis the *standard basis* or the *natural basis*, but no basis is more special or natural than any other basis, this seems so only if we see the vector space as d-tuples of numbers from $\mathbb{R}^d$. A basis consists of d vectors so that none of them can be expressed in terms of the other $d-1$ vectors by using only multiplications with scalars and additions of vectors. When the vectors of a basis are expressed in the same basis, they look like in equation (6.9).

By using only multiplications with scalars and additions of vectors, any vector can be uniquely decomposed in the following form:

$$|v\rangle = v_0\,|0\rangle + v_1\,|1\rangle + \ldots + v_{d-1}\,|d-1\rangle = \begin{pmatrix} v_0 \\ v_1 \\ \vdots \\ v_{d-1} \end{pmatrix}. \tag{6.10}$$

The numbers $v_0, v_1, \ldots, v_{d-1}$ are the components of the vector $|v\rangle$ in the basis $(|0\rangle, |1\rangle, \ldots, |d-1\rangle)$. Since the basis (6.9) is in fact our reference frame, $|v\rangle = (v_0, v_1, \ldots, v_{d-1})^\intercal$. I have to insist on this: there are infinitely many different ways to choose the basis, and none of them is more special than the others. A vector has different components in different bases.

We can build a basis starting with any vector $|e_1\rangle \neq (0, 0, \ldots, 0)^\intercal$.

Multiplication of a matrix and a vector is in fact a *linear transformation*, which transforms the vector linearly, that is, for any vectors $|u\rangle$ and $|v\rangle$ and any number α,

$$\begin{aligned} M\,(|u\rangle + |v\rangle) &= M\,|u\rangle + M\,|v\rangle \\ M\,(\alpha\,|v\rangle) &= \alpha M\,|v\rangle\,. \end{aligned} \tag{6.11}$$

We assume as given a *scalar product*, defined in the basis (6.9) by

$$\langle u|v\rangle := u_0v_0 + u_1v_1 + \ldots + u_{d-1}v_{d-1}. \tag{6.12}$$

A vector space may or may not be endowed with a scalar product. Like for choosing the basis, there are infinitely many ways to choose the scalar product. For any basis there is a scalar product defined by equation (6.12). In general, the scalar product so defined in a basis appears different in other bases.

Given a scalar product, a linear transformation is an *orthogonal transformation* if it preserves the scalar product of any pair of vectors u, v, that is, if $|u'\rangle = M|u\rangle$ and $|v'\rangle = M|v\rangle$, $\langle u'|v'\rangle$. M can be a rotation, a reflection, or a combination of rotations and reflections. In the bases obtained from the basis (6.9) only by combinations of rotations and reflections, the scalar product has the same form as in equation (6.12), by definition, that is, because rotations and reflections are required to preserve the scalar product. The scalar product gives the length of a vector $|u\rangle$ by $\sqrt{\langle u|u\rangle}$, and the angle between two vectors $|u\rangle$ and $|v\rangle$ by $\arccos\langle u|v\rangle$. It follows that orthogonal transformations preserve the lengths of the vectors and the angles between two vectors.

An *orthonormal basis* is defined as a basis $|e_0\rangle, |e_1\rangle, \ldots, |e_{d-1}\rangle$ for which

$$\langle e_i|e_j\rangle = \begin{cases} 1 \text{ if } i = j \\ 0 \text{ if } i \neq j \end{cases} . \tag{6.13}$$

Such a basis is called orthonormal because its vectors are orthogonal to each other, and they are normal, in the sense that their length $\sqrt{\langle e_i|e_i\rangle}$ is 1.

Therefore, by definition, the scalar product has the form from equation (6.12) only in orthonormal bases.

The j-th component of the vector $|v\rangle$ from equation (6.10) is the scalar product between $|v\rangle$ and the j-th basis vector $|e_j\rangle$,

$$v_j = \langle e_j|v\rangle . \tag{6.14}$$

A vector space with a scalar product is an Euclidean space with a fixed origin. Conversely, an Euclidean space is a vector space with a scalar product whose origin is "forgotten".

6.3 Informational reference frames for a bit

Bits can be represented as vectors in a geometric space called *information space*. This representation can be encountered especially in the literature about Reversible Computing and Quantum Computing [206].

A single bit is represented as a unit vector in the real vector space $\mathbb{R}^2$,

$$|0\rangle = \begin{pmatrix} 1 \\ 0 \end{pmatrix}, |1\rangle = \begin{pmatrix} 0 \\ 1 \end{pmatrix}. \tag{6.15}$$

These two vectors form a basis, that is, a general vector in this two-dimensional vector space has the form

$$a\,|0\rangle + b\,|1\rangle\,, \tag{6.16}$$

where we use the addition of two vectors from equation (6.7) and the multiplication of a vector with a scalar from equation (6.8).

But only two of the vectors as in equation (6.15) represent bit values, those for which either $a = 1$ and $b = 0$, or $a = 0$ and $b = 1$.

The negation of a bit is represented by a symmetry transformation, the reflection across the diagonal line described by the equation $y = x$, as illustrated in Figure 6.3.

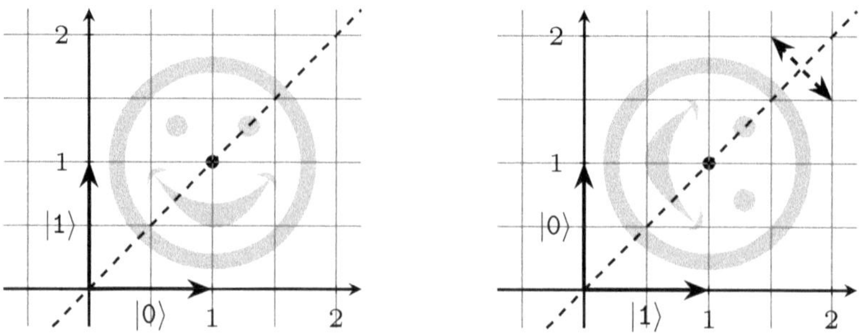

Figure 6.3: The negation of a bit is reflection across the diagonal line $y = x$.

The negation of a bit is represented by the transformation matrix

$$\texttt{NOT} = \begin{pmatrix} 0 & 1 \\ 1 & 0 \end{pmatrix}. \tag{6.17}$$

Let us plot the graphic of the Boolean function $p \mapsto \overline{p}$ as in Figure 6.4,

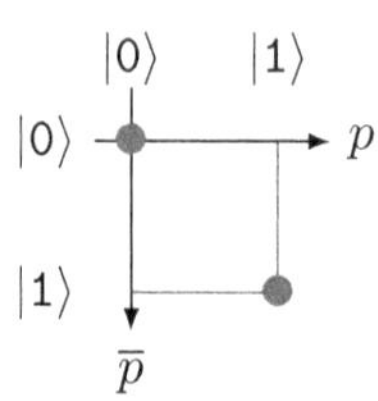

Figure 6.4: The graphic of the function $p \mapsto \overline{p}$.

We see the similarity of the matrix representation of the Boolean function $p \mapsto \overline{p}$ with its graphic representation,

$$\begin{pmatrix}1 & 0\\ 0 & 1\end{pmatrix} = \tag{6.18}$$

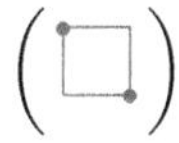

Exercise 6.1. Verify that $\texttt{NOT}\,|\texttt{0}\rangle = |\texttt{1}\rangle$ and $\texttt{NOT}\,|\texttt{1}\rangle = |\texttt{0}\rangle$.

Solution. We simply apply the matrix multiplication,

$$\begin{pmatrix}0 & 1\\ 1 & 0\end{pmatrix}\begin{pmatrix}1\\ 0\end{pmatrix} = \begin{pmatrix}0\\ 1\end{pmatrix} \text{ and } \begin{pmatrix}0 & 1\\ 1 & 0\end{pmatrix}\begin{pmatrix}0\\ 1\end{pmatrix} = \begin{pmatrix}1\\ 0\end{pmatrix}. \tag{6.19}$$

See? This is pretty straightforward. □

For a general vector, the negation swaps its two components,

$$\begin{pmatrix}0 & 1\\ 1 & 0\end{pmatrix}\begin{pmatrix}x\\ y\end{pmatrix} = \begin{pmatrix}y\\ x\end{pmatrix}. \tag{6.20}$$

But why use a full two-dimensional vector space to represent a single bit? If the only two possible values of a bit are represented by the two basis vectors, there remain infinitely many vectors that are totally useless to represent bits. Isn't this a waste of space? Does this come from a secret desire of the mathematicians to feel like God, who allegedly made an entire universe just to host our planet, and maybe a few other planets that support life?

It may be so, but in Computer Science we represent bits as vectors because sometimes it is useful. While most applications are for Reversible Computing and Quantum Computing [206], in this chapter, I use it to illustrate the conventionality of information, how various interpretations of a single bit cell correspond to different reference frames.

To make this less wasteful, we can restrict only to vectors whose components can be only 0 or 1. We normally think of vectors as having real numbers as components, as is the case of the vector space $\mathbb{R}^2$. But we can replace the field of real numbers $\mathbb{R}$ with any other field of numbers, for example $\mathbb{Z}_2$, which has only the elements 0 and 1, with the operations of addition and multiplication modulo 2,

Table 6.1: Modular arithmetic. Addition and multiplication modulo 2.

$\oplus$	0	1
0	0	1
1	1	0

$\otimes$	0	1
0	0	0
1	0	1

This results in a vector space over the field $\mathbb{Z}_2$. The two-dimensional vector space $\mathbb{Z}_2^2$ contains only the four vectors represented in Figure 6.5. These vectors are $(0,0)^\intercal$, $(1,0)^\intercal = |\texttt{0}\rangle$, $(0,1)^\intercal = |\texttt{1}\rangle$, and $(1,1)^\intercal = |\texttt{0}\rangle + |\texttt{1}\rangle$.

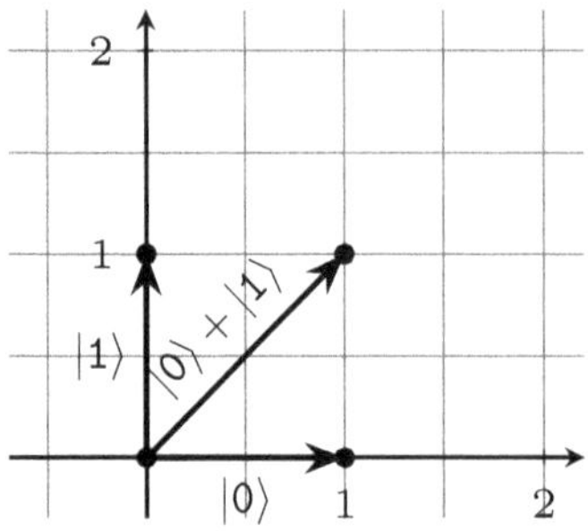

Figure 6.5: The only four vectors of the vector space $\mathbb{Z}_2^2$.

All linear transformations of the vector space $\mathbb{Z}_2^2$ have the coefficients in $\mathbb{Z}_2$. That is, the elements of the matrix representing the transformation,

$$\begin{pmatrix} a_{00} & a_{01} \\ a_{10} & a_{11} \end{pmatrix}, \tag{6.21}$$

are numbers $a_{00}, a_{01}, a_{10}, a_{11} \in \mathbb{Z}_2$, and we add and multiply them using the modular arithmetic. The linear transformations of $\mathbb{Z}_2^2$ preserving the scalar product (6.12) are those having, on each row and on each column, exactly a 0 and a 1. There are only two such transformations, the identity and the negation (6.17). These correspond to the possible Boolean functions of a single bit, and are the basis of the simple reinterpretations.

6.4 Informational reference frames for more bits

To represent two bits, we need a four-dimensional information space. Its basis consists of the vectors

$$|00\rangle = \begin{pmatrix} 1 \\ 0 \\ 0 \\ 0 \end{pmatrix}, |01\rangle = \begin{pmatrix} 0 \\ 1 \\ 0 \\ 0 \end{pmatrix}, |10\rangle = \begin{pmatrix} 0 \\ 0 \\ 1 \\ 0 \end{pmatrix}, |11\rangle = \begin{pmatrix} 0 \\ 0 \\ 0 \\ 1 \end{pmatrix}. \tag{6.22}$$

In general, to represent n bits, we need an information space with 2^n dimensions. We represent the string of bits $(b_1 b_2 \dots b_n)$ as the vector

$$|b_1 b_2 \dots b_n\rangle = \begin{pmatrix} 0 \\ \dots \\ 1 \\ \dots \\ 0 \end{pmatrix} \begin{matrix} \text{row } 1 \\ \dots \\ \text{row } 1 + \overline{b_1 b_2 \dots b_n} \text{ (in base 2)} \\ \dots \\ \text{row } 2^n \end{matrix} \tag{6.23}$$

which has a 1 in the cell from the k-th row, where $k-1$ is the number $b_1 \cdot 2^{n-1} + b_2 \cdot 2^{n-2} + \ldots + b_{n-2} \cdot 2^2 + b_{n-1} \cdot 2 + b_n$, represented in binary form as $\overline{b_1 b_2 \ldots b_n}$. All the other components of the vector are 0.

We can combine two one-bit information spaces into a two-bit information space by applying the following product rule:

$$|\texttt{00}\rangle = |\texttt{0}\rangle\,|\texttt{0}\rangle\,, |\texttt{01}\rangle = |\texttt{0}\rangle\,|\texttt{1}\rangle\,, |\texttt{10}\rangle = |\texttt{1}\rangle\,|\texttt{0}\rangle\,, |\texttt{11}\rangle = |\texttt{1}\rangle\,|\texttt{1}\rangle\,. \tag{6.24}$$

Moreover, we can combine an m-bit information space and an n-bit information space into an $m+n$-bit information space in the same way. We will see in Details 6.1 that this is a *tensor product.* The tensor product is not *commutative*, that is,

$$|\texttt{0}\rangle\,|\texttt{1}\rangle \neq |\texttt{1}\rangle\,|\texttt{0}\rangle\,. \tag{6.25}$$

Let $p, q \in \{\texttt{0}, \texttt{1}\}$ be two bits, represented as the vectors $|p\rangle$ and $|q\rangle$ in $\mathbb{Z}_2^2$ (which can be seen also as vectors in $\mathbb{R}^2$). When we express $|p\rangle$ and $|q\rangle$ in the basis (6.15), they have the form

$$\begin{aligned} |p\rangle &= p^0\,|\texttt{0}\rangle + p^1\,|\texttt{1}\rangle \\ |q\rangle &= q^0\,|\texttt{0}\rangle + q^1\,|\texttt{1}\rangle\,, \end{aligned} \tag{6.26}$$

with one of the components p^0 and p^1 being 0 and the other 1, and similarly for q^0 and q^1.

Then, a string of bits (p, q) can be represented as a vector $|p, q\rangle \in \mathbb{R}^4$,

$$\begin{aligned} |p, q\rangle &= \left(p^0\,|\texttt{0}\rangle + p^1\,|\texttt{1}\rangle\right)\left(q^0\,|\texttt{0}\rangle + q^1\,|\texttt{1}\rangle\right) \\ &= p^0 q^0\,|\texttt{00}\rangle + p^0 q^1\,|\texttt{01}\rangle + p^1 q^0\,|\texttt{10}\rangle + p^1 q^1\,|\texttt{11}\rangle\,. \end{aligned} \tag{6.27}$$

From equations (6.22) and (6.27), we see that the components of the vector $|p, q\rangle$ are products of the components of the two vectors $|p\rangle$ and $|q\rangle$,

$$|p, q\rangle = \begin{pmatrix} p^0 q^0 \\ p^0 q^1 \\ p^1 q^0 \\ p^1 q^1 \end{pmatrix} \tag{6.28}$$

A Boolean function f with n input bits and one output bit can be represented as a linear map $\mathbf{f}$ mapping basis vectors from $\mathbb{R}^{2^n}$ to basis vectors from $\mathbb{R}^2$,

$$\mathbf{f}\,|b_1, \ldots, b_n\rangle = |f(b_1, \ldots, b_n)\rangle\,. \tag{6.29}$$

For example, the representation of Alice's Boolean function $f_A(p, q) = p \wedge q$ is $\mathbf{f}_A(|\texttt{00}\rangle) = \mathbf{f}_A(|\texttt{01}\rangle) = \mathbf{f}_A(|\texttt{10}\rangle) = |\texttt{0}\rangle$ and $\mathbf{f}_A(|\texttt{11}\rangle) = |\texttt{1}\rangle$.

Exercise 6.2. Express the Boolean functions of Bob, Carol, David, Eve, Frank, Grace, and Heidi from Table 2.4 as linear maps $\mathbf{f} : \mathbb{R}^{2^2} \to \mathbb{R}^2$.

Any vector $|v\rangle$ from $\mathbb{R}^{2^n}$ has the form

$$|v\rangle = \sum_{b_1=0}^{1}\sum_{b_2=0}^{1}\cdots\sum_{b_n=0}^{1} a_{b_1\dots b_n}|b_1,\dots,b_n\rangle, \tag{6.30}$$

where the coefficients $a_{b_1\dots b_n}$ are real numbers. A shorter notation is

$$|v\rangle = \sum_{b_1,\dots,b_n\in\{0,1\}} a_{b_1\dots b_n}|b_1,\dots,b_n\rangle. \tag{6.31}$$

The function $\mathbf{f}$ from equation (6.29) can be seen as a linear map $\mathbf{f}:\mathbb{R}^{2^n}\to\mathbb{R}^2$ on the entire space $\mathbb{R}^{2^n}$,

$$\mathbf{f}\sum_{b_1,\dots,b_n\in\{0,1\}} a_{b_1\dots b_n}|b_1,\dots,b_n\rangle = \sum_{b_1,\dots,b_n\in\{0,1\}} a_{b_1\dots b_n}|f(b_1,\dots,b_n)\rangle. \tag{6.32}$$

The map from equation (6.32) is *linear* because, for any two vectors $|u\rangle$ and $|v\rangle$ and any real number α,

$$\begin{aligned}\mathbf{f}\left(|u\rangle+|v\rangle\right) &= \mathbf{f}|u\rangle+\mathbf{f}|v\rangle\\ \mathbf{f}\left(\alpha|v\rangle\right) &= \alpha\mathbf{f}|v\rangle.\end{aligned} \tag{6.33}$$

As seen, linear maps can be represented by matrices. The action of a linear map on a vector can be represented as the product between the matrices representing the linear map and the column matrix representing the vector, like in equation (6.3).

For example, let f be a Boolean function with two inputs and one output. If we express it in the basis (6.15), we get something of the form

$$\mathbf{f}|p,q\rangle = \begin{pmatrix} f^0(p,q)\\ f^1(p,q)\end{pmatrix} = f^0(p,q)|0\rangle + f^1(p,q)|1\rangle, \tag{6.34}$$

where one of the components $f^0(p,q)$ and $f^1(p,q)$ is 0 and the other 1.

The components of $\mathbf{f}|p,q\rangle$ are related to those of $|p\rangle$ and $|q\rangle$ by

$$\begin{cases} f^0(p,q) &= f^0_{00}p^0q^0 + f^0_{01}p^0q^1 + f^0_{10}p^1q^0 + f^0_{11}p^1q^1\\ f^1(p,q) &= f^1_{00}p^0q^0 + f^1_{01}p^0q^1 + f^1_{10}p^1q^0 + f^1_{11}p^1q^1.\end{cases} \tag{6.35}$$

In the matrix representation, the linear transformation $\mathbf{f}$ acts like

$$\begin{pmatrix} f^0(p,q)\\ f^1(p,q)\end{pmatrix} = \begin{pmatrix} f^0_{00} & f^0_{01} & f^0_{10} & f^0_{11}\\ f^1_{00} & f^1_{01} & f^1_{10} & f^1_{11}\end{pmatrix}\begin{pmatrix} p_0q_0\\ p_0q_1\\ p_1q_0\\ p_1q_1\end{pmatrix}. \tag{6.36}$$

For example, the matrix representation of the function $(p,q)\mapsto p\wedge q$ is

$$\begin{pmatrix} 1 & 1 & 1 & 0\\ 0 & 0 & 0 & 1\end{pmatrix}. \tag{6.37}$$

Exercise 6.3. Express the Boolean functions of Bob, Carol, David, Eve, Frank, Grace, and Heidi from Table 2.4 as matrices, taking Alice's case from equation (6.37) as an example.

Consider a basis vector $|p, q\rangle = (a, b, c, d)^{\intercal}$, where the components $a, b, c, d \in \{0, 1\}$, but only one of them is 1. The matrix (6.37) operates on $|p, q\rangle$ by

$$\begin{pmatrix} 1 & 1 & 1 & 0 \\ 0 & 0 & 0 & 1 \end{pmatrix} \begin{pmatrix} a \\ b \\ c \\ d \end{pmatrix} = \begin{pmatrix} a + b + c \\ d \end{pmatrix}, \tag{6.38}$$

resulting in a vector $|p \wedge q\rangle$ from $\mathbb{R}^2$ which is a basis vector.

Let us plot the graphic of the function $(p, q) \mapsto p \wedge q$ as in Figure 6.6,

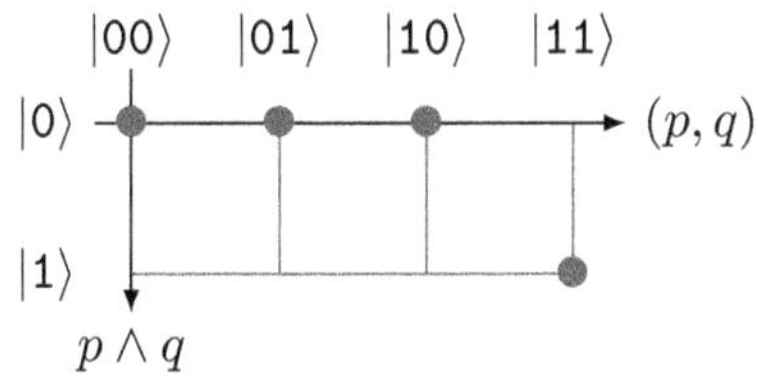

Figure 6.6: The graphic of the function $(p, q) \mapsto p \wedge q$.

As in the case of the negation, we notice that the matrix representation of the function $(p, q) \mapsto p \wedge q$ resembles its graphic, if oriented as in Figure 6.6,

$$\begin{pmatrix} 1 & 1 & 1 & 0 \\ 0 & 0 & 0 & 1 \end{pmatrix} = \Bigg($$ 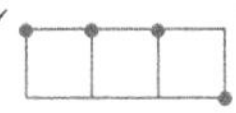 $$\Bigg). \tag{6.39}$$

This is true of the matrix representation of any Boolean function.

Exercise 6.4. Plot the graphic for each of the Boolean functions of Bob, Carol, David, Eve, Frank, Grace, and Heidi from Table 2.4, taking Alice's case from equation (6.39) as an example.

6.5 Reinterpretations in information spaces

Let us see how reinterpretations of bits correspond to linear transformations, or changes of the basis in the information spaces.

If we change the basis of the input vector space $\mathbb{R}^{2^2}$ and of the output vector space $\mathbb{R}^2$, both the components of the input vector $|p, q\rangle$ and of the output vector $\mathbf{f}\,|p, q\rangle$ will change accordingly. Let $\mathcal{N}$ be the invertible 4×4 matrix that represents how a vector expressed in the basis of the input space

$\mathbb{R}^4$ appears in the new basis, and $\mathcal{M}$ the invertible 2×2 matrix representing how a vector expressed in the basis of the output space $\mathbb{R}^2$ appears in the new basis. Then, $\mathbf{f}$, $|p, q\rangle$, and $|r\rangle := \mathbf{f}\,|p, q\rangle$ transform according to

$$\begin{cases} |p, q\rangle' & = \mathcal{N}\,|p, q\rangle \\ |r\rangle' & = \mathcal{M}\,|r\rangle \\ \mathbf{f}' & = \mathcal{M}\mathbf{f}\mathcal{N}^{-1}. \end{cases} \tag{6.40}$$

In the new basis, the equations (6.35) and (6.36) remain valid, because

$$\mathbf{f}'\,|p, q\rangle' = \mathcal{M}\mathbf{f}\mathcal{N}^{-1}\mathcal{N}\,|p, q\rangle = \mathcal{M}\mathbf{f}\,|p, q\rangle = \mathcal{M}\,|r\rangle = |r\rangle'. \tag{6.41}$$

Note that, to correspond to simple reinterpretations of the bit values, the matrices $\mathcal{M}$ and $\mathcal{N}$ have to map basis vectors into basis vectors, so they have to permute the basis vectors. This implies that in each row and column 1 occurs exactly once, and all other matrix entries are 0. Such a matrix is called *permutation matrix*. Every permutation matrix gives a reinterpretation, but not all of them are simple reinterpretations.

Example 6.1. Let the function f be any of the functions from Table 2.4, page 24. The coefficients f^1_{ab} corresponding to the eight interpretations of the device are presented in Table 6.2. The other coefficients are just $f^0_{ab} = 1 - f^1_{ab}$.

Table 6.2: The coefficients f^1_{ab} corresponding to the interpretations of the device from Table 2.4. The other coefficients are just $f^0_{ab} = 1 - f^1_{ab}$.

Subject	$f(p,q)$	f^1_{00}	f^1_{01}	f^1_{10}	f^1_{11}
Alice	$p \wedge q$	0	0	0	1
Bob	$\overline{p} \vee \overline{q}$	1	1	1	0
Carol	$p \wedge \overline{q}$	0	0	1	0
David	$\overline{p} \vee q$	1	1	0	1
Eve	$\overline{p} \wedge q$	0	1	0	0
Frank	$p \vee \overline{q}$	1	0	1	1
Grace	$\overline{p} \wedge \overline{q}$	1	0	0	0
Heidi	$p \vee q$	0	1	1	1

Remember that an interpretation of the alien device from Figure 2.1, page 21, can be transformed by a simple reinterpretation into another interpretation by either leaving unchanged or negating the three bit cells. Since the negation is represented by interchanging the vectors $|\mathtt{0}\rangle$ and $|\mathtt{1}\rangle$, this amounts to a change of basis in the vector space $\mathbb{R}^2$ of each bit. Therefore, we can move from one interpretation to another one by changing the bases in the three copies of the vector space $\mathbb{R}^2$ representing the bits p, q, and $f(p, q)$. This amounts to a change of basis in the vector space $\mathbb{R}^4$ representing both p and q, and another one in the output vector space $\mathbb{R}^2$.

For example, to move from Alice's representation to Bob's, we need to change Alice's bases according to the transformations

$$\mathcal{N}_{A\mapsto B} = \begin{pmatrix} 1 & 0 & 0 & 0 \\ 0 & 1 & 0 & 0 \\ 0 & 0 & 1 & 0 \\ 0 & 0 & 0 & 1 \end{pmatrix}, \mathcal{M}_{A\mapsto B} = \begin{pmatrix} 0 & 1 \\ 1 & 0 \end{pmatrix}. \tag{6.42}$$

This makes sense, because $f_B(p,q) = \overline{f_A(p,q)}$, so the input basis remains unchanged, and the output basis vectors are interchanged.

To move from Alice's basis to David's basis, we use the transformations

$$\mathcal{N}_{A\mapsto D} = \begin{pmatrix} 0 & 1 & 0 & 0 \\ 1 & 0 & 0 & 0 \\ 0 & 0 & 0 & 1 \\ 0 & 0 & 1 & 0 \end{pmatrix}, \mathcal{M}_{A\mapsto D} = \begin{pmatrix} 0 & 1 \\ 1 & 0 \end{pmatrix}. \tag{6.43}$$

Now the reader may wonder how I came up with this. The relation between Alice's and David's functions is $f_D(p,q) = \overline{f_A(p,\overline{q})}$. This means that the basis of the information space for q has to be inverted, and then the output basis too. So, for the output space, $\mathcal{M}_{A\mapsto D} = \mathcal{M}_{A\mapsto B} = \texttt{NOT}$. What about the input space? The matrix $\mathcal{N}_{A\mapsto D}$ has to be a permutation matrix that interchanges the basis vectors $|\texttt{00}\rangle$ and $|\texttt{01}\rangle$, respectively $|\texttt{10}\rangle$ and $|\texttt{11}\rangle$. This amounts to negating q. From equation (6.22), we can guess that $\mathcal{N}_{A\mapsto D}$ is the matrix from equation (6.43).

Details 6.1. In fact, finding $\mathcal{N}_{A\mapsto D}$ wasn't a guess. The rigorous explanation behind guessing that the matrix $\mathcal{N}_{A\mapsto D}$ is the one from equation (6.43) is a magic trick called *tensor product of matrices.* We start with the matrices

$$\mathcal{U} = \begin{pmatrix} u_{00} & u_{01} \\ u_{10} & u_{11} \end{pmatrix} \text{ and } \mathcal{V} = \begin{pmatrix} v_{00} & v_{01} \\ v_{10} & v_{11} \end{pmatrix} \tag{6.44}$$

of the changes of bases for the vector spaces for p and q. Wake the matrix $\mathcal{V}$ and plug it into the matrix $\mathcal{U}$, in the following way. Replace each entry u_{ab} of the matrix $\mathcal{U}$ with the matrix obtained by multiplying the number u_{ab} with each of the entries of the matrix $\mathcal{V}$,

$$\mathcal{U}\otimes\mathcal{V} = \begin{pmatrix} u_{00}\mathcal{V} & u_{01}\mathcal{V} \\ u_{10}\mathcal{V} & u_{11}\mathcal{V} \end{pmatrix} = \begin{pmatrix} u_{00}v_{00} & u_{00}v_{01} & u_{01}v_{00} & u_{01}v_{01} \\ u_{00}v_{10} & u_{00}v_{11} & u_{01}v_{10} & u_{01}v_{11} \\ u_{10}v_{00} & u_{10}v_{01} & u_{11}v_{00} & u_{11}v_{01} \\ u_{10}v_{10} & u_{10}v_{11} & u_{11}v_{10} & u_{11}v_{11} \end{pmatrix}. \tag{6.45}$$

Here, I added the spacing that partitions the resulting 4×4 matrix in four 2×2 matrices just to emphasize how we get the tensor product.

In our case, since

$$\mathcal{U} = \begin{pmatrix} 1 & 0 \\ 0 & 1 \end{pmatrix} = \mathbf{I}_2 \text{ and } \mathcal{V} = \begin{pmatrix} 0 & 1 \\ 1 & 0 \end{pmatrix} = \mathtt{NOT}, \tag{6.46}$$

the result is the tensor product between the identity 2×2 matrix and the NOT matrix, which gives us the matrix $\mathcal{N}_{A \mapsto D}$ from equation (6.43),

$$\mathbf{I}_2 \otimes \mathtt{NOT} = \begin{pmatrix} 1\begin{pmatrix} 0 & 1 \\ 1 & 0 \end{pmatrix} & 0\begin{pmatrix} 0 & 1 \\ 1 & 0 \end{pmatrix} \\ 0\begin{pmatrix} 0 & 1 \\ 1 & 0 \end{pmatrix} & 1\begin{pmatrix} 0 & 1 \\ 1 & 0 \end{pmatrix} \end{pmatrix} = \begin{pmatrix} 0 & 1 & 0 & 0 \\ 1 & 0 & 0 & 0 \\ 0 & 0 & 0 & 1 \\ 0 & 0 & 1 & 0 \end{pmatrix}. \tag{6.47}$$

But why does this magic trick work? The reason is that the basis of $\mathbb{R}^4$ from equation (6.22) is itself the tensor product of two copies of the basis of $\mathbb{R}^2$ from equation (6.15). Note that the tensor product (6.45) works in the same way for matrices of any size, including rectangular matrices. In particular it works for vectors, which are matrices with a single column. This is why we can write the basis vectors from equation (6.22) as tensor products of basis vectors from equation (6.15),

$$|\mathtt{00}\rangle = |\mathtt{0}\rangle \otimes |\mathtt{0}\rangle, |\mathtt{01}\rangle = |\mathtt{0}\rangle \otimes |\mathtt{1}\rangle, |\mathtt{10}\rangle = |\mathtt{1}\rangle \otimes |\mathtt{0}\rangle, |\mathtt{11}\rangle = |\mathtt{1}\rangle \otimes |\mathtt{1}\rangle,$$

but one usually drops the tensor product symbol $\otimes$, as in equation (6.24).

Changing the basis implies a change of the function f, and of its matrix representation.

Exercise 6.5. Show that the eight functions from Table 2.4, page 24, can be seen as the same function expressed in eight different bases.

All of these can be generalized easily to Boolean functions with any number n of input bits and any number m of output bits,

$$\mathbf{f} : \mathbb{R}^{2^n} \to \mathbb{R}^{2^m}. \tag{6.48}$$

$$\mathbf{f}\,|b_1, \ldots, b_n\rangle = |f_1(b_1, \ldots, b_n), \ldots, f_m(b_1, \ldots, b_n)\rangle. \tag{6.49}$$

We can work with bases like in equation (6.23). The input vectors have 2^n components, and the output vectors have 2^m components. The function $\mathbf{f}$ is represented by a $2^m \times 2^n$ matrix, similar to the $2^1 \times 2^2$ matrix from equation (6.36). The change of basis in the input space is represented by a $2^n \times 2^n$ permutation matrix $\mathcal{N}$, and that in the output space by a $2^m \times 2^m$ permutation matrix $\mathcal{M}$. They are obtained by tensor products between copies of the unit matrix $\begin{pmatrix} 1 & 0 \\ 0 & 1 \end{pmatrix}$ and the negation matrix $\begin{pmatrix} 0 & 1 \\ 1 & 0 \end{pmatrix}$, depending on whether the reinterpretation leaves unchanged a bit or it negates it.

This applies in particular to the Boolean function $\mathcal{F}$ from Definition 5.1, page 58, therefore

Observation 6.1. A reinterpretation of a computation is equivalent to changing the reference frame in the bit space of the computer's bit cells.

Remark 6.1. In Euclidean Geometry, when we change the reference frame using a linear transformation, the coordinates of the points change, but the equations that describe the geometric objects keep their form. For example, in the new reference frame, a line may appear to be different, because its defining parameters are different, but it remains a line, and it satisfies the equation that defines a line. Similarly for ellipses, hyperbolas, and parabolas. The coefficients that appear in their equations change with the basis, they are *covariant*. But the equations themselves maintain their form, and the types of objects they describe remain unchanged. This shows that changing the reference frame doesn't simply change any curve into any other curve, there are features that remain unchanged—they are *invariant*.

Similarly, in Physics, if we change the reference frame, the coordinates of the points and the components of the vectors transform in sync with the coefficients appearing in the various functions defined on space to represent fields. This ensures that the equations of Physics remain unchanged. In Classical Physics and nonrelativistic Quantum Theory, space is Euclidean three-dimensional. In Special Relativity, we have to work with the four-dimensional spacetime. In General Relativity, curvilinear coordinates become unavoidable if we want numeric calculations. But in all cases there are transformations that allow us to transform the positions and the equations expressed from one coordinate system to another one.

In the information space, the changes of reference frames are, like in Geometry and Physics, symmetry transformations. The values that we assign to the bit cells change, and the Boolean functions change in sync with them, to preserve the way inputs connect to outputs.

Remark 6.2. The symmetry transformations form a *symmetry group*, because

1. there is a transformation e that leaves everything unchanged, playing the role of neutral element of the symmetry group,
2. every element a is invertible, *i.e.* there is an element a^{-1} so that $a \cdot a^{-1} = a^{-1} \cdot a = e$, and
3. the composition is associative, $a \cdot (b \cdot c) = (a \cdot b) \cdot c$.

Exercise 6.6. Show that the matrices $\mathbf{I}_2$ and `NOT` form a group.

Remark 6.3. Like in Physics, we can distinguish between *passive transformations* and *active transformations*. An active rotation of an object means to physically rotate the object in space. A passive rotation just means a rotation of the reference frame, not of the object, so no physical change happens. In the information space, transformations resulting from the reassignment of the values `0` and `1` to the two states of each bit cell, as done in Chapter 2 are passive transformations. An example of active transformation in information space are those performed by the Rosetta Stone device from Figure 3.4, page 35, which consist of physically changing the bits.

The Rosetta Stone example, based on active transformations, plays a role in the arguments from this book. But the central arguments of this book are based on passive transformations, because this is what reinterpretations are.

While much more general transformations of the information space $\mathbb{R}^{2^n}$ are possible, the transformations that correspond to reinterpretation of the bits are restricted to those mapping basis vectors into basis vectors. They can only permute the basis vectors from equation (6.23). For example, the only allowed transformations of the basis from equation (6.15) are the identity transformation, and the inversion. A rotation with an angle that is not multiple of 90° is a genuine symmetry transformation of $\mathbb{R}^2$, but it doesn't represent a reinterpretation of the bits.

Moreover, not all permutations of the basis from equation (6.23) correspond to reinterpretations of individual bits, most of them reinterpret groups of bits as other groups of bits.

Example 6.2. Consider the alien device whose functionality is described in Table 2.1 from page 22. An example of interpretation that is not of individual bits, but of groups of bits, is provided in Table 6.3.

Table 6.3: An interpretation of the alien device that applies to groups of input bits, but not to individual input bits.

p	q	r		p	q	$\overline{p}\wedge q$
a	c	x		T	T	F
a	d	x	$\Rightarrow$	F	F	F
b	c	y		F	T	T
b	d	x		T	F	F

In this interpretation, c $\mapsto$ T, d $\mapsto$ F, a $\mapsto q$, and b $\mapsto \overline{q}$. While the resulting Boolean function is the same as Eve's from Table 2.4, page 24, it is obtained by a different interpretation. We've seen, for example in Chapter 4, that such reinterpretations are commonly used in Computer Science.

By permuting the input or output variables of a Boolean function, we can obtain another Boolean function. This transformation is widely used in practice [165, 80]. This leads to a way to reinterpret an interpretation as another interpretation, as illustrated in the following example.

Example 6.3. From David's interpretation of the alien device we can obtain another interpretation by permuting the input bits. The result is Frank's interpretation, because $f_F(p,q) = p \vee \overline{q} = \overline{q} \vee p = f_D(q,p)$.

Exercise 6.7. Find out what happens to the Boolean functions from Table 2.4, page 24, if we permute the two input bits.

Hint. By examining Table 2.4 we see that by permuting the input variables of Carol's interpretation we obtain Eve's, $f_C(q, p) = f_E(p, q)$. The interpretations of Alice, Bob, Grace, and Heidi remain unchanged under permutations of the input variables, because their Boolean functions are symmetric. □

6.6 Hyperexponential ambiguity

Unlike the symmetry transformations appearing in geometry, the symmetry transformations of the information space are restricted to those permuting the basis vectors. The number of different ways to interpret the Boolean function implemented by a physical circuit is immense. Let us see for example in how many different ways we can reinterpret the Boolean function $\mathfrak{F}$ from Definition 5.1, page 58, which is used to represent a computer. If $\mathfrak{F}$ takes n bits as its input, its information space has 2^n dimensions, and therefore the basis of this space has 2^n vectors. The number of permutations of these vectors is

$$2^n! = 1 \cdot 2 \cdot 3 \cdot \ldots \cdot (2^n - 2) \cdot (2^n - 1) \cdot 2^n. \tag{6.50}$$

On the other hand, the number of Boolean functions with n inputs and n outputs, like $\mathfrak{F}$, is the n-th power of 2^{2^n}, the number of Boolean functions with n inputs and a single output,

$$\left(2^{2^n}\right)^n = 2^{n2^n}. \tag{6.51}$$

We can compare the number of reinterpretations of a Boolean function with n inputs and n outputs (6.50) with the number of such Boolean functions (6.51) in a spreadsheet program. Table 6.4 contains the result of these formulae up to 8 bits, because from 8 bits or more both formulae crashed due to the extremely large numbers obtained!

We see that the number of possible reinterpretations of what a simple computer with n bits does increases incredibly fast, almost as fast as the number of such possible computers. We know from Exercise 6.7 that some of these reinterpretations give the same Boolean function, so they are basically the same reinterpretation. But we can still make an idea of the huge number of possible interpretations of a simple computer like the one from Definition 5.1. The ambiguity of computation increases hyperexponentially.

Exercises

Solve the Exercises from the body of this chapter.

Table 6.4: Comparing the number of reinterpretations of a Boolean function with n inputs and n outputs with the number of such Boolean functions.

n	$2^n!$	2^{n2^n}
1	2	4
2	2.4×10	2.56×10^2
3	4.03×10^4	1.68×10^7
4	2.09×10^{13}	1.84×10^{19}
5	2.63×10^{35}	1.46×10^{48}
6	1.27×10^{89}	3.94×10^{115}
7	3.86×10^{215}	5.28×10^{269}
8	#VALUE!	#NUM!
$\vdots$	$\vdots$	$\vdots$

Exercise 6.8. Answer again the questions from the Introduction.

Question	Yes	No	I don't know
Easy Question 1, page 8			
Easy Question 2, page 9			
Hard Question 1, page 10			
Hard Question 2, page 10			

Did any of your answers change?

Key points

- The information space for n bits is a 2^n-dimensional vector space.
- Assigning meaning, even merely numerical values, to the states of the n bit cells of a computer, is as conventional as ordering a basis in a 2^n-dimensional space. In fact, they are equivalent.
- A computation appears as a different computation when seen in a different basis in the information space.
- The representation of data in the information space illustrates once more the ambiguity of computation.

▶ The number of possible reinterpretations of a computation is hyperexponential in the size of its memory, because the dimension of the information space is exponential in the number of bits.

Further reading

[206] A De Vos. *Reversible computing.* John Wiley & Sons, Weinheim, 2011

[165] David Slepian. On the number of symmetry types of Boolean functions of n variables. *Canad. J. Math.*, 5:185–193, 1953

[80] Solomon Golomb. On the classification of Boolean functions. *IRE transactions on circuit theory*, 6(5):176–186, 1959

Part II

Genuine imitations

7

Role-playing machines

Even after we've seen the undeniable ambiguity of the alien device, and even after seeing that the argument applies to any computer as well, we may think that a computer must avoid it somehow. After all, computers are much more complex than we can see in Figure 5.4, Section 5.3, and we know that they are the most precise widely used machines. I am not trying to cast doubts on their precision. We can use computers to get precise results, but this doesn't avoid the ambiguity of computation. The mere appeal to implementation and complexity is a fallacy, if we can't actually prove that this eliminates the ambiguity. We will see that complexity alone is not sufficient to resolve the ambiguity, it rather increases it, but it does a great job to obfuscate the problem.

To continue, we need to make sure we're on the same page about what we mean by terms like "algorithm", "computation", and "simulation". Particularly the term "computation" is used as if there is a clear agreement about its meaning. Indeed, Computer Science gives it a precise meaning, fully respected when designing, manufacturing, and using the computers. However, when comparing human mind with computations we tend to make assumptions that are not warranted by what computation is in both theoretical and the practice of Computer Science. Elucidating what a computation is will help us understand this confusion and eliminate it.

7.1 Computations and computing systems

Can a machine answer yes or no to any question in mathematics or logic, simply by following a set of rules for manipulating symbols? In other words, can there exist a recipe (an algorithm) that, like a recipe for addition or multiplication, can always provide an answer without requiring any guessing or creativity?

This question is known to date back to Leibniz [43]. More recently, in 1928, Hilbert and Ackermann asked for an algorithm that can answer any question sufficiently well formulated with yes or no [94]. This is called the *decision problem*, although some prefer the "official" German term *Entscheidungsproblem*.

DOI: 10.1201/9781003623373-7

Roughly speaking, the steps to be followed to decide the answer to a yes/no question constitute an algorithm, and the process of following an algorithm is a computation. A system able to follow that process is called *computing system*. A machine or even a human can be a computing system. The relevant mathematical descriptions of both the formal computing systems and the physical ones are similar. If the context is suggestive, we will refer to both of them as computing systems, similar to how we infer from the context that by "triangle" we mean either the abstract idea of a triangle or a physical object shaped like a triangle.

Independent of one another, and by using completely different means, Alonzo Church, Stephen Cole Kleene, and Alan Turing proved that there is no general solution to the decision problem. Their papers can be found in the volume [43]. They used different abstract models of computation, but, surprisingly, they proved that these are equivalent! There are more ways to formalize the idea of computation, but they are equivalent. Moreover, any new alternative that was proposed later turned out to be equivalent to these as well.

Central to theoretical Computer Science are the Turing machines, which can mean an abstract, formal, mathematical model of computation, but also a physical machine able to compute. So there is indeed full agreement on what a computation is: *a computation is what a Turing machine does!*

7.2 Wolf, goat and cabbage problem

An algorithm can do more general things than simply giving a yes or no answer to a question, it can also provide an explicit solution or a more elaborated output. Examples of algorithms range from a recipe from a cookbook, to any way to solve a problem step-by-step. Take for example the following problem, as stated by G.I. Gurdjieff [85]:

Exercise 7.1 (Wolf, goat and cabbage problem)**.** "find out how a man who has in his possession a wolf, a goat and, in the present case, a cabbage, can transfer them across a river from one bank to the other, if one takes into consideration, on the one hand, that his boat can carry only the load of himself and one of the three objects at a time, and on the other hand, that without his direct observation and influence the wolf can always destroy the goat, and the goat the cabbage".

Before we continue, I suggest you experience the joy of solving this gem, if you didn't already encounter it. Write down the steps that the farmer has to do to transport the three creatures safely on the other bank of the river. You'll obtain an algorithm that allows anyone who will ever be in the same situation to know exactly what to do, without having to think.

Algorithm 7.1 lists the steps solving the wolf, goat and cabbage problem.

Algorithm 7.1: A solution of the wolf, goat and cabbage problem.

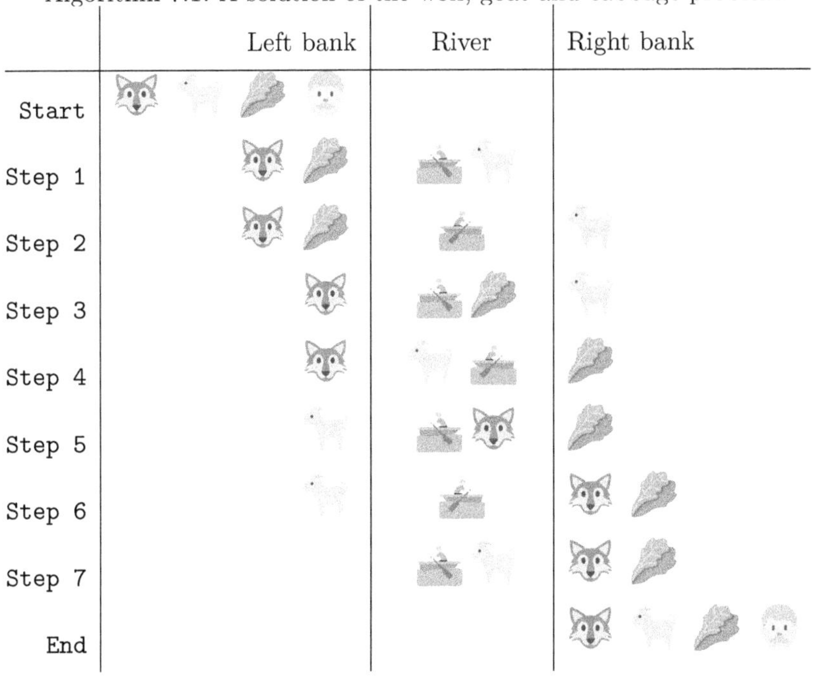

This is not the algorithm to find the solution, but to apply an already known solution. Following this algorithm can be done blindly, without thinking at all. In fact, second-guessing its steps may result in mistakes.

Of course algorithms to *solve* the wolf, goat and cabbage problem exist, all that such an algorithm has to do is to find a path in a graph, which is similar to finding a path in a labyrinth. A pictorial representation was described by Ian Stewart in [168]. Depending on which side of the river each of the three passengers are, there are eight possible configurations. Figure 7.1 illustrates how these eight possibilities can be thought of as the vertices of a cube, so that the edges represent moving one item from one bank to the other. The river is depicted as  . The dashed lines represent movements that are forbidden because they would leave the goat alone either with the wolf or with the cabbage. The problem then consists of finding a continuous path from the state in which all our friends are on the left side of the river, 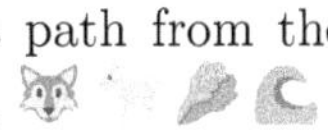 , to the state in which they are rejoined together on the other side of the river,  .

With this representation, the problem becomes much easier, because the starting and the destination vertices are connected by a path in two different ways. There are general algorithms to find a path.

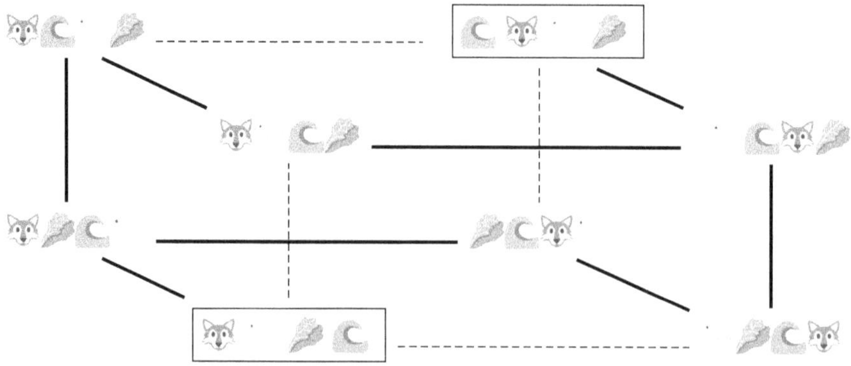

Figure 7.1: The wolf, goat and cabbage problem can be solved by finding a continuous path from the vertex  to the vertex .

Figure 7.1 represents a graph. A *graph* consists of a set–whose elements are called vertices–and a set of unordered pairs of vertices, called *edges*.

There are algorithms that can receive as input any graph with a finite number of vertices, and two vertices (the starting and the ending vertices), and, if there are paths connecting these two vertices, they will find them. Such an algorithm is quite simple, since all it has to do is to explore the neighboring vertices of the starting vertex, and their neighbors recursively, until it either finds the ending vertex or they exhaust all vertices [40, 160] What is more difficult is to do this efficiently, but this really matters only for larger graphs than the one from Figure 7.1.

Therefore, programmed properly, not only can a computer follow the steps from Algorithm 7.1, but it can even discover them, by trying various possibilities.

Fun fact 7.1. On January 30th 2025 I asked several AIs the following problem that I obtained by modifying the wolf, goat and cabbage problem:

> "Find out how a man who has in his possession a wolf, a goat and, in the present case, a cabbage, can transfer them across a river from one bank to the other, if one takes into consideration, on the one hand, that his boat can carry only the load of himself and one of the three objects at a time, and on the other hand, that without his direct observation and influence the wolf can always destroy the goat, and the goat the cabbage, ***but also this wolf is omnivore and would destroy the cabbage***".

ChatGPT, Grok, and Claude AI gave brief replies in which they described what they claimed to be a solution! DeepSeek explored various possibilities in a 22, 407 characters length reply and concluded that there is no solution [169].

The AIs can solve the original wolf, goat and cabbage problem because it was part of their training data. Since the modified version with the omnivorous wolf was unknown to them, some of the AIs couldn't solve it (or, in one case, it solved it by needlessly exploring numerous possibilities on almost 12 Letter-sized pages), and proved they had no idea what they're doing when describing a solution to the original problem. But surprise, things change fast in the AI industry! Just the next day OpenAI released a new version of their AI called OpenAI o3-mini, so obviously I asked it the same question, and it gave a very brief, clear and correct answer [171]. You can't follow the developments in AI without being impressed by how quickly the field evolves due to competition.

Ultimately, behind any ability an AI may have there is nothing but algorithms. These algorithms identify linguistic patterns and apply them to generate, by purely statistical and combinatorial means, apparently new and creative responses. But it's still an algorithm, unaware of the intentions of the programmer who made it.

So what's an algorithm, more precisely? A definition can be found in [22]:

Definition 7.1. "An *algorithm* is a finite and completely specified initial-step-to-concluding-step procedure for solving problems. Every step is readily executable by an agent with limited cognitive resources. The rules for moving from one step to the next are entirely determinate and self-contained, and its output is delivered, if at all, after a finite number of steps".

In other words, an algorithm can be followed even by a mindless machine. But of course this doesn't mean that you will simply show the algorithm to the machine and the machine will follow it. The machine has to be forced somehow, it has to be built so that it can be instructed, by using an input device, to follow the steps automatically.

Algorithm 7.2 illustrates another very simple example, dividing two integer numbers. This example shows that algorithms can contain sequences of instructions that can repeat as much as necessary, so the length of the algorithm may be very different from the number of steps executed.

Even though the idea of an algorithm as a list of instructions that can be followed mindlessly may seem very simple, the whole magic we see computers doing today comes from them. The "can be followed mindlessly" part should tell us something: the machine doesn't need a mind, no matter how smart the programmers instructing it are. But, of course, this doesn't mean we can't hope that somehow numerous mindless processes add-up to a mindful larger one, right? After all, aren't we just some mindless particles put together? To answer this, we will need more than using a convenient definition of algorithm, but we will get to this later.

Algorithm 7.2: An algorithm to divide an integer `n` by repeated subtraction of the denominator `d` from a number `r` initialized with the value of `n`. It reads the integers `n` and `d`, and prints the quotient `q` and the remainder `r`.

```
read n;
read d;

q := 0;
r := n;

while r ≥ d do
  r := r - d;
  q := q + 1;
end;

print q, r;
```

7.3 Turing and the Platonic archetype of computers

The Turing machine is an abstract idea of an ideal computer. It is a formal or mathematical model. But at the same time, any physical machine that does what the model is supposed to do is a Turing machine. A computer is a Turing machine. Turing machines are general enough to simulate any computing system.

An ideal *Turing machine* (represented in Figure 7.2) has an infinite memory available. This an idealization, of course, since infinite memory was not acquired so far in practice. The memory is usually represented by an endless tape divided into cells. Each cell can contain a symbol from a finite list of symbols, called *alphabet* which includes a special symbol to represent blank spaces, for example a white space "␣" or "0".

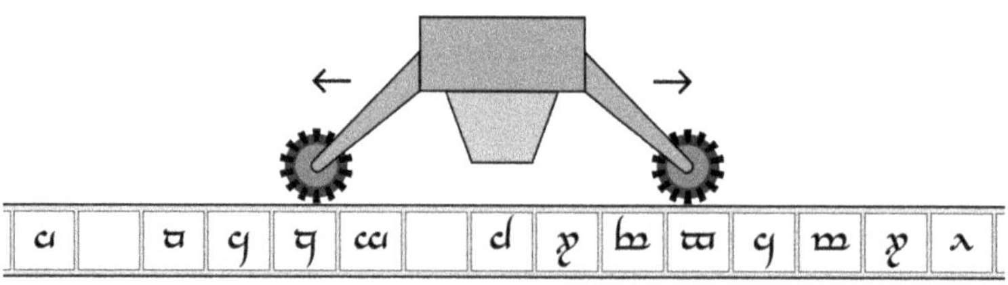

Figure 7.2: A Turing machine can read symbols from a tape, do some actions that depend on what it read, use the tape as memory for intermediate steps of the computation, and write down the result on the tape.

A Turing machine has a head, which is positioned above a particular cell on the tape. At every step, the head can do one of the following operations:

1. move to the left or to the right by one cell (or, equivalently, it can move the tape one cell to the right or to the left),
2. read or modify the symbol in the current cell,
3. halt, when the computation is done.

It depends on the internal state of the Turing machine what operation it does. With every step, the Turing machine can change its internal state, either halting or getting it ready for another operation. The number of possible internal states is finite, and so is the number of possible operations. The initial state of the tape represents the input, and the final state, after the machine halts, the output of the computation.

The Turing machine was conceived by Alan Turing as a model of computations, algorithms, and to characterize the machines able to compute [201]. He provided sufficient evidence for the following:

Principle 7.1. Every algorithm that can be followed by humans to compute something, can be done by some Turing machine.

Let us illustrate the Turing machines with a simple exercise.

Exercise 7.2. The following represents the input and the output of a computation done by a Turing machine, as the initial and final states of the tape.

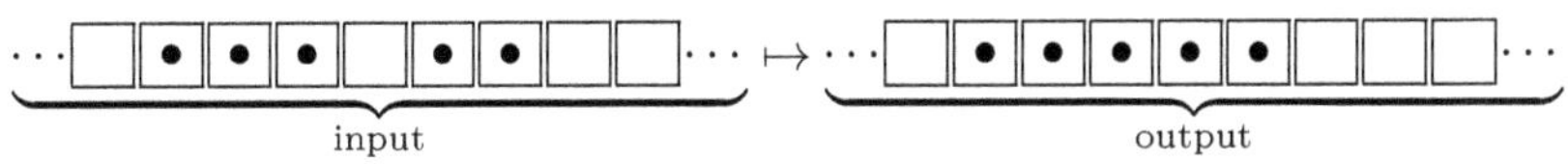

The ellipses "· · ·" mean that the tape is continued at left and right with infinitely many blank cells.

Can you guess the computation the Turing machine does? You don't have to describe step by step how it does it, just to guess what it computes. Here are more examples of input and output data of the same Turing machine:

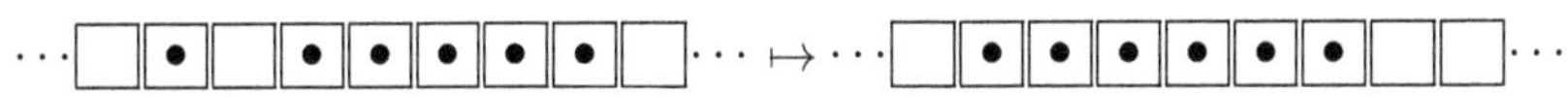

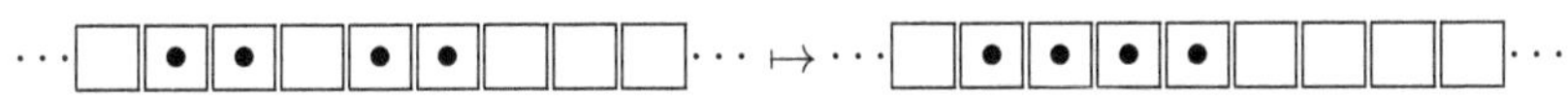

Please solve this Exercise before moving to the next one:

Exercise 7.3. Redo Exercise 7.2, finding another answer!

Wait, you may ask, there are two answers? Yes, at least two.

A possible answer, which is probably the reader's first guess, is that this Turing machine adds two positive integers. The user provides a tape with a consecutive cells and b consecutive cells containing the symbol '•', separated by a blank space. The Turing machine reads the tape and makes a sequence of operations. After the machine halts, the tape contains $a + b$ consecutive cells with the symbol '•', all others being blank. So this Turing machine adds two positive integers in a unary representation and the isolated blank space stands for '+'.

A human can do the same by applying the following recipe:

`Step 1.` Remove the isolated blank space.

The machine does this, but it can't physically remove cells from the tape, so what it does is to rewrite the cells. So, if this is what it does, the recipe should be the following, which has the same effect as removing the isolated occurrence of a blank space:

`Step 1.` Replace the isolated blank space with the symbol '•'.

`Step 2.` Replace the last symbol '•' with a blank space.

Since such a recipe exists, we know from Turing's Principle 7.1 that a Turing machine that implements it can be constructed (see Exercise 7.5), albeit it may do it in more steps.

To utilize the Turing machine from Exercise 7.2, the user needs to encode the input numbers and to decode the output as described. So the user must know the convention. Exercise 7.2 uses the most self-explanatory convention I could think about. The user can guess it by simply examining several examples of input data and their corresponding outputs. It is no wonder that similar conventions were used by the mathematician Hans Freudenthal when he developed a language to communicate with extraterrestrials [69].

But what is the Turing machine from Exercise 7.2 doing? Is it doing additions, concatenations, or removal of isolated blank spaces? We see that the same Turing machine can be interpreted as doing different computations, even though, physically, it does the same thing.

Remark 7.1. There are more ways to interpret what a Turing machine does.

7.4 Computational mimicry

There are many Turing machines that behave as in Exercise 7.2, giving the same outputs for those particular inputs, but which for other situations do things that can't be interpreted as additions. Maybe more isolated occurrences of blank spaces are allowed in the input, and the machine just removes alternatively these blank spaces, for completely different purposes. Or maybe the machine can accept more symbols than a blank space and '•', for example any letter of the English alphabet and also punctuation symbols. Then, maybe the Turing machine concatenates pairs of words separated by a blank space. Maybe the blank space represents the end-of-line character ("enter"), and the machine combines together paragraphs two by two by removing every other end-of-line character. Or maybe it combines not just two, but as many paragraphs as it can, as long as the total length of the resulting paragraph doesn't exceed a maximum size, for example the maximum length of a Twitter/𝕏 post. All these Turing machines would give the same result in situations like those from Exercise 7.2, if the data are in that format. This means they can all simulate that Turing machine.

Here is another example of a Turing machine that does different computations than the one from Exercise 7.2, but it can reproduce its computations.

Example 7.1. Consider a Turing machine specified as follows:

1. It stores in its internal state any symbol, to be interpreted as a separator. It can be ‘,’, ‘;’, ‘|’, a blank space, or even user-specified.
2. It parses the tape from the left to the right, until it finds a different symbol than the separator.
3. Then it searches for the separator to the right.
4. Whenever it finds it, it starts swapping the current symbol with the next one, while advancing one cell to the right.
5. It halts when it finds the next occurrence of the separator symbol.

Then, to simulate the machine from Exercise 7.2, this Turing machine has to be set up in the following way:

1. Initially, the tape contains the symbols “$\ldots\check{\sqcup}\ldots\sqcup\bullet\ldots\bullet\sqcup\bullet\ldots\bullet\sqcup\sqcup\ldots$”, where “ˇ” is not a symbol of the tape, but it indicates the head’s initial position. All other symbols in the alphabet are not on the tape.
2. The machine starts in the state containing as the separator the blank symbol “␣”, and moves step-by-step to the right until it finds a different symbol.
3. Then it searches to the right until it finds the separator symbol “␣”.
4. Then it starts swapping the current symbol with the next one, while advancing to the right.
5. It halts when it finds the next occurrence of the separator symbol “␣”.

This shows how, if properly programmed, our Turing machine simulates the one from Exercise 7.2, even if it works in a completely different way.

From this we learn the following

Observation 7.1. Turing machines can simulate other Turing machines.

This is a key principle in Computer Science. To understand if our minds are reducible to computations, we need to take computation seriously.

7.5 The Turing ambiguity

But can Turing machines eliminate or at least reduce the ambiguity noticed in the previous sections of this chapter? The following Exercise gives an example showing that they can't.

Exercise 7.4. Consider a Turing machine with three symbols `a`, `b`, and a white space as the blank symbol, defined by

$$\begin{aligned} \cdots\boxed{\texttt{a}}\boxed{\texttt{a}}\boxed{*}\cdots &\mapsto \cdots\boxed{\texttt{a}}\boxed{\texttt{a}}\boxed{\texttt{a}}\cdots, \\ \cdots\boxed{\texttt{a}}\boxed{\texttt{b}}\boxed{*}\cdots &\mapsto \cdots\boxed{\texttt{a}}\boxed{\texttt{b}}\boxed{\texttt{a}}\cdots, \\ \cdots\boxed{\texttt{b}}\boxed{\texttt{a}}\boxed{*}\cdots &\mapsto \cdots\boxed{\texttt{b}}\boxed{\texttt{a}}\boxed{\texttt{a}}\cdots, \\ \cdots\boxed{\texttt{b}}\boxed{\texttt{b}}\boxed{*}\cdots &\mapsto \cdots\boxed{\texttt{b}}\boxed{\texttt{b}}\boxed{\texttt{b}}\cdots, \end{aligned} \tag{7.1}$$

where `*` can be any of the allowed symbols. The machine is assumed to return an error for all other inputs. What does this Turing machine compute?

A quick interpretation of the machine from Exercise 7.4 is that `a`=`0`, `b`=`1`, and the machine computes the product of the first two bits (which are then the input), storing the result into the third one. But it can also be interpreted as computing the minimum of the two input bits. And, if we assume that `a`=`1` and `b`=`0`, it can be interpreted as computing the maximum of the two bits.

But if the instruction manual tells us that the symbols have to be the truth values `F` and `T`, it would seem that `a`=`F`, `b`=`T`, and the machine computes the result of the operation `AND`. But it could also be interpreted as computing the result of the operation `NOR`, if we assume that `a`=`T` and `b`=`F`.

Suppose now that, upon further reading of the manual of the Turing machine, we learn that the machine uses opposite interpretations of the input and output symbols. This is possible according to the definition of a Turing machine. According to the manual, it does so for security reasons—in case a state enemy sees the result, we don't want them to understand it. Then, we can infer that the machine computes either `NAND` or `OR`.

But what if the manual states that some of the three cells may be interpreted differently than the others? This is again legal, for example, it is possible that the meaning of each symbol depends on whether it is the first, the second, or the third in a sequence of three symbols as in equation (7.1). Or it could be the case that the authorized users of the machine use another machine to encode the input data and to decode the output data, as in Section 4.4, and the code changes periodically, and it may even be randomly generated. Now the possible interpretations are the eight interpretations from Table 2.4. In each of these cases the Turing machine does something meaningful, as long as you know the convention.

In general, for any tape length and any number of allowed symbols it is possible to use the Turing machine to perform computations using encrypted data, just like in the case of the encrypted computing, mentioned in Section 4.4. As seen in Section 4.3, if the allowed symbols are 0 and 1, a simple way to encrypt the data is to use a simple XOR cipher that flips some of the bits on the tape. For a larger number of allowed symbols, the bit inversions can be replaced with more general permutations. Then, we can use a substitution cipher consisting of permutations of the allowed symbols, in a way that depends on the cell. The Turing machine still does something even if each cell uses a different permutation. But what it does, what algorithm it computes, depends on the cipher.

Another reason to interpret the symbols differently depending on the cell is to simulate other operations. Just like with the alien device from Chapter 2, we can use the Turing machine from Exercise 7.4, which does conjunctions if a=0, b=1, to do any other operation from Table 2.4.

As we have seen in Section 3.1, in a computer, data are frequently transformed, and processed in a transformed form. Even during the execution of the same program, the logic circuits can be reused in different ways. In particular, the arithmetic logic unit from Figure 5.1 from page 54, a circuit performing additions is used to perform other arithmetic operations as well.

Exercises

Exercise 7.5. Design a Turing machine that works as in Exercise 7.2.

Solution. Initially, the current cell has to be a blank cell at the left of all non-blank cells. The alphabet of the machine can be $\{\sqcup, \bullet\}$. The internal state of the machine should be able to encode information about whether the isolated blank was found, and about whether the last (rightmost) occurrence of the symbol '•' was found. A solution is presented in Table 7.1.

The head of the machine reads the current cell, possibly writes something in it, changes its internal state, and moves to the right or left. In fact, it always moves to the right until it finishes reading all consecutive cells containing the symbol '•', then it moves to the left to delete the last occurrence of symbol '•'. Before finding the first cell containing the symbol '•', the internal state is A. Once the first '•'-cell is found, the state changes to B, so that now it searches for the next blank, assumed to be the isolated one. Once it finds it, it replaces it with '•' and changes its state to C, which means it searches for the next blank. Once it finds the next blank symbol, it moves to the left and deletes the last '•', and halts. In case when moving to the left it finds a blank, it terminates in a state of error. Note that this Turing machine doesn't verify if the tape contains the data in the expected format

Table 7.1: A Turing machine that adds by removing. For each internal state (A, B, C, D, error, halt), and for each symbol (blank "␣" and "•"), we specify what to do (write in the current cell, move left or right, change internal state). If a "Write" or "Move" column is omitted, no such action takes place.

Cell	**State A** find first •		**State B** find ␣ replace with •			**State C** find next ␣		**State D** replace previous • with ␣	
	Next state	Move	Write	Next state	Move	Next state	Move	Write	Next state
␣	A	right	•	C	right	D	left	no	error
•	B	right	no	B	right	C	right	␣	halt

"...␣␣•...•␣•...•␣␣...", and if this sequence is at the right of the head, this is left to be ensured by the user. But it can be modified to check if the data on the tape are in this format, and to end in an error state if they are not. □

Exercise 7.6. Write an algorithm that solves the wolf, goat and cabbage problem. You can use Ian Stewart's idea from Figure 7.1.

Exercise 7.7. Determine whether the omnivorous wolf, goat and cabbage problem stated in Fun Fact 7.1 has solutions. Write an algorithm that can prove the answer.

Key points

- Turing machines model how we follow step-by-step recipes.
- Turing machines are supposed to work mindlessly.
- There are more ways to interpret what a Turing machine does.
- You can't guess, only from examples, what a Turing machine would do in a different situation than those from the examples.
- Turing machines can simulate other Turing machines.

Further reading

[43] Martin Davis. *The undecidable: Basic papers on undecidable propositions, unsolvable problems and computable functions.* Courier Corporation, 2004

[168] Ian Stewart. *Professor Stewart's cabinet of mathematical curiosities.* Basic Books, New York, 2009

[40] Thomas Cormen, Charles Leiserson, Ronald Rivest, and Clifford Stein. *Introduction to algorithms.* MIT Press, Cambridge, Massachusetts, 2022

[160] Robert Sedgewick and Kevin Wayne. *Algorithms.* Addison-Wesley, Redwood City, California, 2011

[22] Cristian Calude. *To halt or not to halt? That is the question.* World Scientific, Singapore, 2024

[201] A.M. Turing. On computable numbers, with an application to the Entscheidungsproblem. *Proc. London Math. Soc.*, 2(1):230–265, 1937

[65] Jon Pierre Fortney. *Discrete mathematics for computer science: An example-based introduction.* Chapman and Hall/CRC, 2020

[74] Rowan Garnier and John Taylor. *Discrete mathematics: Proofs, structures and applications.* CRC Press, 2009

8

Universal imitators

8.1 One Turing to rule them all

Two Turing machines may have completely different lists of allowed symbols, they may have completely different internal states, they can be realized physically in completely different ways, and yet, one of them can simulate the other one.

This may be the most straightforward situation in which a Turing machine can simulate another one:

Example 8.1. Consider two Turing machines $\mathcal{M}$ and $\mathcal{M}'$, so that:

1. The alphabet of $\mathcal{M}'$ is included in the alphabet of $\mathcal{M}$.
2. For each internal state of $\mathcal{M}'$ there is an internal state of $\mathcal{M}$, so that if

(a) the content of tape of $\mathcal{M}$ is identical with the content of the tape of $\mathcal{M}'$

(b) and the heads of the two machines are positioned identically

(c) and $\mathcal{M}$ is in the internal state corresponding to that of $\mathcal{M}'$,

then $\mathcal{M}$ does exactly what $\mathcal{M}'$ does.

Whenever two Turing machines $\mathcal{M}$ and $\mathcal{M}'$ satisfy these two conditions, $\mathcal{M}$ simulates $\mathcal{M}'$. This is exactly how a Turing machine that concatenates pairs of words separated by a blank space (mentioned in Section 7.4) can simulate the Turing machine from Exercise 7.2.

Here is another case when a Turing machine simulates another one:

Example 8.2. Consider two Turing machines $\mathcal{M}$ and $\mathcal{M}'$ so that

1. The alphabet of $\mathcal{M}'$ is included in the alphabet of $\mathcal{M}$.
2. Every computation done by the Turing machine $\mathcal{M}'$ starts in the same internal state.
3. The Turing machine $\mathcal{M}$ has an internal state $\mathcal{S}$ so that if, initially,

(a) $\mathcal{M}$ starts in the state $\mathcal{S}$

DOI: 10.1201/9781003623373-8

(b) and the tape of $\mathcal{M}$ contains the same symbols as the tape of $\mathcal{M}'$

(c) and the heads of the two machines are positioned identically,

then the sequence of configurations of symbols on the tape of $\mathcal{M}$ includes the sequence of configurations of symbols on the tape of $\mathcal{M}'$ in the same order, possibly among other configurations that are not allowed for $\mathcal{M}'$. For example, the successive configurations of the tape of $\mathcal{M}'$ can be $(s_0, s_1, s_2, s_3, s_4, s_5, s_6, s_7)$, and the successive configurations of the tape of $\mathcal{M}$ can be $(s_0, a, s_1, s_2, b, s_3, c, s_4, s_5, d, e, f, s_6, g, h, s_7)$, where the configurations a, b, c, d, e, f, g, and h are not among the allowed configurations of $\mathcal{M}'$.

This way to simulate a Turing machine by another one was used in Example 7.1 to simulate the Turing machine from Exercise 7.2.

But there are even more general ways to simulate Turing machines. There is no constraint that the alphabet of the simulated Turing machine is included in the alphabet of the Turing machine doing the simulation, we can encode the former using symbols or even sequences of symbols of the latter. This, demonstrated in the following examples, allows much more freedom for simulations.

Example 8.3. There is a Turing machine with only two tape symbols and 18 internal states, but which can simulate any other Turing machine [152].

Although its alphabet contains only two tape symbols, it can simulate Turing machines with tens, hundreds, or thousands, in fact any number of possible symbols.

Example 8.4. There is a two-symbol 15-states Turing Machine with only 15 different possible internal states, and yet it can simulate any other Turing machine [130].

Example 8.5. There is a Turing machine with 9 tape symbols and only 3 internal states, but which can simulate any other Turing machine [111].

Although it can only be in 3 possible internal states, it can simulate any Turing machine, regardless of its possible number of internal states and tape symbols.

Because the Turing machines from Examples 8.3, 8.4, and 8.5 can simulate any Turing machine, we call them *universal Turing machines*. Systems capable of simulating any Turing machine are also called *Turing complete* or *Turing universal.*

But how is it possible for them to simulate Turing machines with many more possible tape symbols and many more possible internal states? The simulation is based on several "tricks":

1. Representing symbols or sequences of symbols of the simulated Turing machine by other symbols or sequences of symbols.

2. Representing states (that is, pairs of configurations of symbols and internal states) of the simulated Turing machine by states of the Turing machine doing the simulation.
3. Ignoring intermediate configurations of the Turing machine doing the simulation, if they have no correspondent in the simulated Turing machine (as in Example 8.2).

Here I used the term "state" to refer to the pair consisting of configurations of symbols on a tape and an internal state. We can extract the following definition:

Definition 8.1. A Turing machine $\mathcal{M}$ simulates another Turing machine $\mathcal{M}'$ if each state of $\mathcal{M}'$ can be associated to one or more states of $\mathcal{M}$, so that whenever $\mathcal{M}$ is in a state that corresponds to a state of $\mathcal{M}'$, it transitions (in one or more steps so that no intermediate step is associated to a state of $\mathcal{M}'$) into the state of $\mathcal{M}$ that corresponds to the state in which $\mathcal{M}'$ would transition.

Exercise 8.1. Show that if a Turing machine $\mathcal{M}$ can simulate a Turing machine $\mathcal{M}'$, and $\mathcal{M}'$ can simulate a Turing machine $\mathcal{M}''$, then $\mathcal{M}$ can simulate $\mathcal{M}''$.

What do we learn from all these? To simulate a Turing machine, all we need is to invent a convention that allows us to encode the symbols of a Turing machine in the states of the other Turing machine, and so that the latter imitates the possible steps of the former, while still functioning according to its own rules. There is no other restriction, in particular, there is no requirement to encode the symbols of the first Turing machine as symbols of the second Turing machine in a uniform way, that is, by using the same convention for the same symbols. In fact, when simulating a Turing machine on another one, it is often unavoidable to encode them in a nonuniform way. So not only is it possible to encode the data and the operations differently, but this is a basic fact in Computer Science.

Principle 8.1. There is no difference between a computation and its simulations.

But let's not forget that a Turing machine implements simultaneously both the computation attributed to that Turing machine, and the one attributed to the Turing machine it simulates. For instance, Example 7.1 describes a Turing machine that swaps certain symbols in a particular way, but which also can simulate the Turing machine from Exercise 7.2. In fact, it can be used as well to concatenate pairs of words separated by a blank space, and this operation of concatenation can be used to perform additions as in Exercise 7.2. So we are in the case of Exercise 8.1, where a Turing machine $\mathcal{M}$ simulates a Turing machine $\mathcal{M}'$ which, in turn, simulates a Turing machine $\mathcal{M}''$, and consequently $\mathcal{M}$ simulates both $\mathcal{M}'$ and $\mathcal{M}''$.

There is no limit of how deep can such a hierarchy of simulations go.

Example 8.6. Consider a universal Turing machine $\mathcal{M}$ that simulates another universal Turing machine $\mathcal{M}'$. Since $\mathcal{M}'$ is universal, it can simulate $\mathcal{M}$ too. Moreover, it can simulate $\mathcal{M}$ while $\mathcal{M}$ simulates $\mathcal{M}'$. If each transition of $\mathcal{M}'$ is simulated by a sequence of more transitions of $\mathcal{M}$, and if each transition of $\mathcal{M}$ is simulated by a sequence of more transitions of $\mathcal{M}'$, then $\mathcal{M}$ does an infinite tower of distinct simulations of $\mathcal{M}$ and $\mathcal{M}'$. We can build such a tower with more universal Turing machines that simulate one another.

From these examples it follows that there is no limit of how many computations can a Turing machine do simultaneously. Exercise 7.4 illustrates another way in which a Turing machine can do more computations simultaneously.

Implication 8.1. There is no limit of how many Turing machines can a Turing machine simulate simultaneously.

8.2 Back to the processor

A computer is the closest possible physical realization of a universal Turing machine. The only essential difference is that a computer doesn't have an infinite memory, like the tape of the Turing machine. But this is usually sufficient in practice, because any Turing machine, when executing an algorithm, uses only a finite number of cells on its tape. This universality is the reason why we can use and program computers to execute any algorithm for which the resources are sufficient. There are, of course, practical limitations of memory, storage capacity, and speed, but so far we were able to extend them well enough, which allowed us to become more and more wasteful with these resources.

The computer's correspondent to the Turing machine's tape is its internal memory, which can be extended with external memory devices. In general, the memory consists of bit cells. The bit cells can be considered to be grouped together in units of the same size, for example 32 bits or 64 bits. The "head" of this Turing machine can read an entire unit of bits at once. In this sense, a unit of 32 or 64 bits can correspond to a single symbol on the tape.

Unlike the ideal Turing machine, in real world computers, the signals encoding the bits of information are diverted by various circuits, without requiring a moving head or a moving tape. A register stores the memory addresses from which the bits are fetched and then executed by the processor. The instruction encoded at that memory address is copied into another register, and then decoded into commands for the processor's arithmetic logic unit (see Section 5.1). Other memory units store the data to be processed based on the instruction. Then, the output returned by the processor can be stored at a specified memory location and communicated to the user via an output device.

One may hope to reduce the number of possible interpretations of the bit cells by making sure that the computer uses a uniform mechanism to read and write all of the bit cells. But we have seen that in practice the interpretation of the state of a memory cell is not fixed once and for all, it can change even during the same computation. This is the same situation as in the case of the Turing machines, where the symbols on the tape can be reinterpreted to simulate other Turing machines, to encrypt the data or even the computation, or for whatever other reasons. Since encrypted computing works regardless of how many bits are accessed at once, it follows that accessing them one at a time, as in the case of a Turing machine with two symbols, can't impose a uniform interpretation of the symbols.

The reader may still feel that the argument based on reinterpretation and encryption is artificially invented to make the case for ambiguity. But we already saw numerous examples, we discussed the theory, and it turns out that this is what Computer Science says, and how computers work in practice. As anyone who ever played with simple ciphers can attest, it is essential to encrypt the data in a nonuniform way, otherwise cracking it would be very easy, and, as we have seen in Section 4.4, cryptographic computing is a reality.

Exercises

Exercise 8.2. Can you give an example of a Turing machine that can't be interpreted as implementing more than one computation? Can you give an example of a Turing machine that doesn't simulate another, different Turing machine? Justify your answer.

Exercise 8.3. Can you assign a unique meaning to the states of the bit cells of a computer, so that this meaning doesn't change in time, and yet the computer remains programmable? Justify your answer.

Key points

- As long as we can label consistently the states (internal+tape) of a Turing machine as states of another Turing machine, so that the transitions of the first Turing machine reproduce the transitions of the second Turing machine (even if in more steps), it simulates it.

- Universal Turing machines can simulate any other Turing machine. They can simulate each other. They can do any computation any computing system can do.
- Universality is possible only if we allow complete freedom of the conventions used to represent the data.
- Universality is the reason why we can program computers.
- There is no difference between a computation and a simulation of it.

Further reading

[201] A.M. Turing. On computable numbers, with an application to the Entscheidungsproblem. *Proc. London Math. Soc.*, 2(1):230–265, 1937

[43] Martin Davis. *The undecidable: Basic papers on undecidable propositions, unsolvable problems and computable functions.* Courier Corporation, 2004

[22] Cristian Calude. *To halt or not to halt? That is the question.* World Scientific, Singapore, 2024

9

Cells, tiles, and all that

9.1 The game of life, the universe, and everything

What if the unfathomable diversity that we see in the universe comes from very simple rules? What if God is a playful child, and the universe, including life, consciousness, and everything, is God's game?

Could the universe be like a board game, like the game Go, invented in China more than 2,500 years ago, but with an unlimited board instead of a 19×19 one? Could the universe be a nondual game, not with two types of playing pieces (stones), but with only one, and not with two or more players? Zen Buddhist monk, writer, poet, and philosopher Dōgen's said "You play Go by yourself; the opponents become one" [35, 84].

Mathematician John von Neumann tried to understand living beings as self-replicating machines [205]. Another mathematician, John Horton Conway, tried to find the simplest self-replicating machine he could find, with very simple rules that even a child could follow, and yet complex enough to produce unpredictable behavior and self-replicating structures [73]. He invented the *game of life* in 1970.

Conway's game of life takes place on an $\infty \times \infty$ grid. Each cell of the grid can be either "empty" or a "live cell". The rules of the game are very simple, at every step

1. Each live cell with two or three live neighbors stays alive, in the other cases it dies, becoming an empty cell.
2. Each empty cell becomes live if and only if it has exactly three live neighbors.

The second rule captures the birth of a live cell, as if by reproduction, if it has exactly three live neighbors. The first rule captures

- death by "underpopulation", if the live cell has fewer than two live neighbors,
- death by "overpopulation", if the live cell has more than three live neighbors,
- the survival of a live cell, if it has two or three live neighbors.

DOI: 10.1201/9781003623373-9

The cells can be organized into complex organisms. The simplest one is the "glider", a system that moves diagonally across the grid, repeating its configuration every four generations (see Figure 9.1). Soon after, Bill Gosper invented the "glider gun", which creates gliders as if they are shot by a gun machine. Gosper glider guns could be used to build logic gates. More and more complex structures were discovered in the game of life, culminating with the proof that it was able to simulate any computer algorithm [15].

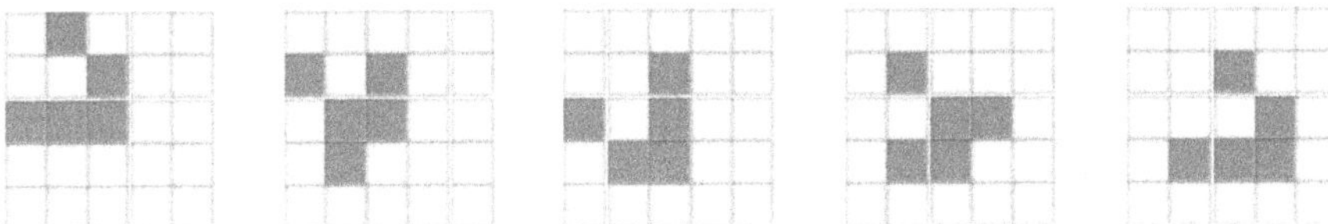

Figure 9.1: Conway's Game of Life. A two-dimensional cellular automaton with "empty" and "live" cells. Rules: only live cells with two or three live neighbors stay alive, and only empty cells with exactly three live neighbors become live cells. The image shows five successive states of a "glider"—a pattern that moves diagonally across the grid every 4 generations.

If any physical systems from our universe can be simulated, as the Church-Turing-Deutsch Principle mentioned in chapter seems to suggest, in particular if living beings and their consciousness can be simulated too, maybe, some say, we live in such a simulation. If this is the case, the simulation can be done by any universal system, in particular,

Question 9.1. What if our universe, including our experiences of colors, is just a two-dimensional black and white movie like Conway's game of life?

9.2 Knitting a Turing machine out of dominoes

The oldest domino games known to us are from 12th or 13th century China, although it can be argued that Nature played such a game by matching nucleobases in the DNA for 4 billion years, at least on Earth [21]. The game of domino consists of matching tiles, each tile consisting of two numbered square-shaped parts united in a 1×2 rectangle. But domino tiles are probably more famous because you can arrange them so that they make each other fall in a chain reaction. Stand-up mathematician Matt Parker wrote [134],

> you can build your own basic computer without any electronics. You'll just need around ten thousand dominoes.

And he proved this at the Manchester Science Festival in October 2012. This was possible without auxiliary mechanisms, because you can arrange the dominoes to work as logic gates. Together with a team of volunteers, he managed to build a 3-bit adder, and then a 4-bit adder that had some errors. But a couple of teams of students broke the record, one of them building a 5-bit adder in 2015, and another one a 6-bit adder, in 2024. The idea was previously mentioned by Douglas Hofstadter as the "domino chainium" thought experiment [98]. While such a computer is single-use, because you have to rebuild it every time you want to compute something, this shows how versatile are physical systems in implementing computations.

But now I want to talk about another kind of domino computers. In 1961, mathematician, logician, and philosopher Hao Wang invented a game: given some square-shaped tiles with sides of different colors, try to tile the plane so that the contact sides of any two adjacent tiles have the same color.

Figure 9.2: Set of 11 Wang tiles that can tile the plane only aperiodically [101].

Only translations are allowed, that is, you are not allowed to rotate or flip the tiles on the other face. We assume that you have an unlimited supply of squares of each type, but the number of different types is fixed. An example of such a set of tiles is given in Figure 9.2. These are called *Wang tiles.*

Wang believed that if a set of such tiles can tile the plane, there is a way to tile it periodically, that is, the tiling pattern repeats periodically both horizontally and vertically [207]. Of course, if you are allowed to rotate or reflect the tiles, the problem is very simple, as you can prove by solving the following exercise [83].

Exercise 9.1. Show that if we were allowed to rotate through an angle of 180° the tiles, or if we were allowed to reflect them horizontally and vertically, any Wang tile can be used to tile the plane periodically.

A student of Wang's, Robert Berger, disproved Wang's conjecture. But how could he do something like this, when we are talking about tiling an infinite plane? Berger proved that if a set of Wang tiles can tile the plane periodically, the question whether it can tile the plane is decidable, but if it can only tile it aperiodically, the problem is undecidable [13, 150, 83]. He invented a clever way to translate the tiling into computations of Turing machines, so that if you could prove the decidability of the tiling problem, this is equivalent with the *halting problem* for Turing machines. But the halting problem is famously undecidable, as shown by Church and Turing [43, 22].

The set of eleven tiles from Figure 9.2 is the smallest set known so far that can tile the plane aperiodically but not periodically [101]. This is impressive, considering that Berger's original proof required a set of 20 426 tiles, but it was gradually improved by others [150].

You can use a set of tiles as a universal computing system [150, 209], by encoding in each row of the tiling the tape and the head's state of a universal Turing machine. Then, a new step in the computation done by the Turing machine is equivalent to completing the next row in the tiling so that the tiles match. The reader can find a popular account in [208], and nice examples such as addition and computing the Fibonacci sequence in [83].

In an impressive domino effect, domino modestly started as a game, gained interest for theoretical computer science by being able to implement ay computation, and eventually found applications in computing with DNA (see [21] Chapter 2, particularly 2.6 for Wang-tiles based DNA computing, and [33] for a recent review).

9.3 Rule 110

Imagine a row of square-shaped cells of two types □ and ■, for example

···□■■□□■□■···. (9.1)

Suppose that whenever a clock ticks, the squares are updated according to some rule, so that the new state of a cell depends only on the previous state of itself and its two neighboring cells. Such a system is a one-dimensional *cellular automaton*

An example of such a rule is *Rule 110*, see Stephen Wolfram's book [212],

■■■→▒□▒ ■■□→▒■▒ ■□■→▒■▒ ■□□→▒□▒
□■■→▒■▒ □■□→▒■▒ □□■→▒■▒ □□□→▒□▒ (9.2)

Only the middle cell is determined by the triple, the other two cells, represented as ▒, are determined by the previous or next triple.

Figure 9.3 shows the rules and the first 16 states, with the initial condition that the first state is a row with all cells □ except for a single ■ cell.

Exercise 9.2. Determine the next three states of the state from equation (9.1), by applying the rule from equation (9.2), assuming that the row is continued indefinitely to the left and to the right with cells of type □.

Hint. The second state is ···□···□■■■□■■■■□···□···. □

In 1985, Wolfram conjectured that the Rule 110 cellular automaton is able to implement any Turing machine [212]. In 1998, Matthew Cook presented a proof that this is indeed the case at a conference at the Santa Fe Institute, before the publication of Wolfram's book. Cook's proof was published in 2024 [38], after a delay due to a non-disclosure agreement with Wolfram Research.

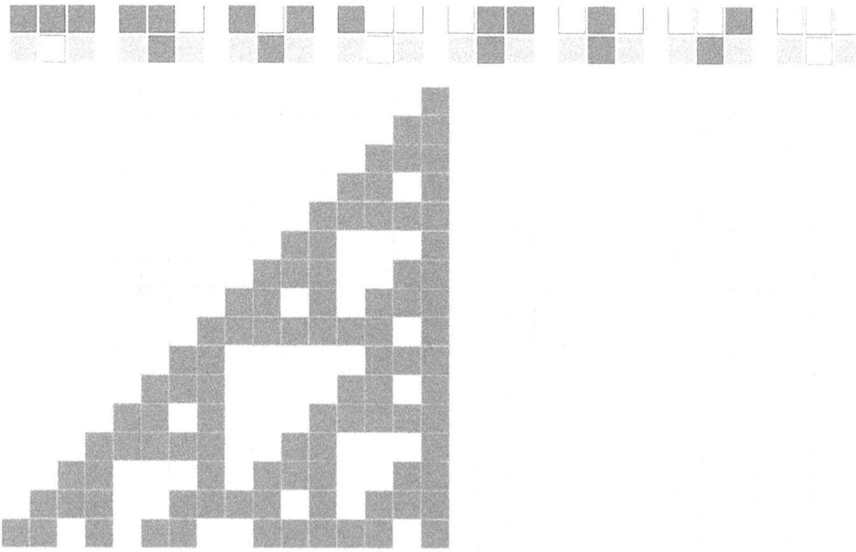

Figure 9.3: Rule 110 cellular automaton. Each row represents a state, consisting of "on" and "off" cells. The bottom image represents 16 successive states, from top to bottom. At each step, each cell changes its state based on the current state of itself and its two neighbors, following the rule represented at the top and equation (9.2).

Given the simplicity of the Rule 110 cellular automaton, it may be the most surprising place where you would expect to find universal computation. And yet, according to Computer Science, it can simulate any Turing machine, and it can run all the programs that run on every computer, tablet, and smartphone in the world. It can play any song and any movie, it can run any videogame and any Artificial Intelligence that exists or can ever exist. And if your mind with all its sentient experiences were reducible to a computation, it can run a fully sentient copy of you.

9.4 Living in a timeless wallpaper

The amazing discovery of Wang tiles that can implement any computation was used by Australian science-fiction writer Greg Egan in his 1995 short story "Wang's Carpets" [59], later included in his novel "Diaspora" [60]:

> The edge of the carpet catalyzes its own growth. The polymer is irregular, aperiodic—there's no single component which simply repeats. But there seem to be about twenty thousand basic structural units, twenty thousand different polysaccharide building blocks.

The story takes place 2 300 years in the future and it's about the discovery of a structure similar to Wang's tiles on an alien planet. The role of the tiles is played by polysaccharides arranged as a carpet that grows one line at a time. The heroes of the story are able to decode the patterns by using the Fourier transform, which is a way to extract hidden patterns from other patterns. They find out that the Wang tiles simulate a sixteen-dimensional world populated by squid-like blind aliens that communicate by touch.

Since in Egan's short story the rows of the carpet represent different steps of the computation simulating the squid's world, they encode different times,

> The carpet's second dimension was more like time than space, a permanent record of the history of the edge.

Because they found out that the aliens are able to think about their own thoughts, they concluded that they are conscious. This may make us wonder whether it's possible that we live in such a simulation.

Suppose Egan's Wang's carpet indeed simulates a world containing squids, along with their sentient experiences. Is the intrinsic time of the squids from the carpet the same as the time of the external reality, or are they different? It seems that a squid inhabiting the carpet has a particular experience exactly when, for an external observer, a row simulating that experience is added to the carpet. But what happens with that experience after new rows are added? Nothing was changed in the row encoding that particular experience, so is the experience still going on? There is no physical property having a different value when the row is added compared to any ulterior moment of time.

It may be tempting to think that the experience exists only in the moment when it is simulated, which is the moment when the row containing that experience is added to Wang's carpet. But since the heroes of the story are able to decode the Wang's carpet, shouldn't this imply that the simulation is at least run again during this process? Shouldn't the experience of the squid be revived by this very process, considering that decoding the patterns of the carpet amounts to a new simulation? Then is the sentient experience of the squid revived, but this time in the computer decoding the patterns? This would have the strange consequence that for the patterns in the carpet to be alive and sentient, they should be observed. But then did any sentient experience actually happen in the long period of time in which the carpet grew without being observed and decoded?

If sentient experiences occurred when a new row was added to the carpet, shouldn't they continue to exist as long as that row exists?

Here is why it makes sense to think that each row simulating experiences continues to do so as long as it exists. The fact that the past history of the simulated world is recorded in the rows of Wang's carpet is similar to the notion of spacetime. *Spacetime* is a four-dimensional space, where the first three dimensions are the usual three dimensions of space, and the fourth dimension is time. The history of a particle corresponds to a curve in this space. Until

Einstein, this four-dimensional space was used as a useful abstraction, but nothing more.

But Einstein's theory of *special relativity*, particularly as understood by Minkowski, showed that the four-dimensional spacetime should be taken seriously [139]. The reason is the *relativity of simultaneity*: two events A and B may appear to be simultaneous to an observer, but to another observer it may appear that event A happened first, while to another observer it may appear that event B happened first. As an analogy, it is like Wang's carpet may appear, to different observers, divided into rows along different directions. Spacetime is sometimes called by philosophers *block universe*, but to physicists it is just spacetime.

According to special relativity, there is no absolute present time, and spacetime contains all times, including those that didn't happen yet. Einstein expressed this idea in a letter to Michele Besso's grieving family when Besso passed away in 1955, a month before his own death [71],

> Now he has departed from this strange world a little ahead of me. That means nothing. People like us, who believe in physics, know that the distinction between past, present and future is only a stubbornly persistent illusion.

But then where does time come from in the eternal frozen spacetime?

Using the analogy with Wang's carpet, the present time of a squid is encoded in a row, but the row encodes as well the squid's brain, along with its memories of the past events. The flow of time appears as an impression that the present state of the squid's brain has. This view about time is called *eternalism*, while the usual view according to which only the present exists and time flows is called *presentism*.

Maybe our intuition tells us that the eternalist view can't be right, that even if the block universe of special relativity is correct, only a slice of this block, containing the events taking place at the same time, should be somehow "active" at any given time. Somehow similar to a compact disk containing the record of a whole movie, but which, to be played, needs a laser to "activate" a static image of the movie at a time, even though the disk itself doesn't change. But this would require an additional time variable, beyond the time coordinate of spacetime, and there is no such thing in physics. The past, present, and future exist at once in the block universe, and there is no time outside of it.

If our universe can be simulated, since the Rule 110 cellular automaton is also able to simulate any Turing machine, it can simulate our universe too. In this case, spacetime would be akin to a tapestry [178], a wallpaper made of two-state cells of the Rule 110 automaton, as in Figure 9.4.

Due to the low resolution of the image, the individual cells can't be distinguished, but if you could zoom in, you could see a very long row of "on" and "off" cells representing the present state of the universe. After a very careful examination you can see yourself somewhere in this row, as you are right now, reading this book. The instantaneous state of your brain encodes

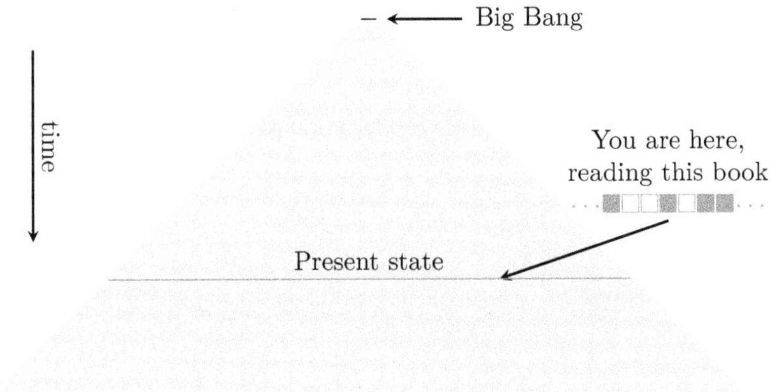

Figure 9.4: An eternalist simulation of our universe using the Rule 110 automaton. If you zoom in a gazillion times, you can see yourself in the row representing the present state of the universe, reading this book.

the thoughts and experiences that you're having right now, including your experience of the flow of time. But this is only a frozen thought, one of a succession of frozen thoughts that give the illusion of time flowing just like a motion picture consists of static frames.

If in Egan's short story a squid from Wang's carpet dies, its life is recorded somewhere in the early rows of the carpet. If, as special relativity is understood to suggest, the eternalist view is correct, all past instances of the squid while it was alive should still be alive and experience this, including the flow of time, frozen in the eternity of Wang's carpet.

If we can be simulated, and if eternalism is correct, maybe in our universe there are quasi-crystalline structures that encode entire universes. Not only their present time synchronized with our own universe's time, but maybe their past, present, and future as well, connected in a tapestry like Wang's carpet or like a cellular automaton. Or maybe our own universe is such a carpet or a tapestry on some alien being's wall.

9.5 Is your mind nonlocal?

Let's imagine again that our universe is in fact simulated by a Rule 110 cellular automaton as in Figure 9.4. Your present state, indicated in the figure, depends on the states of the cells in the past. Since from Figure 9.3 we know that a cell can affect only the next states of itself and its neighboring cell, it follows that the cells from the past of which your present state depends are contained in a cone, as in Figure 9.5. Let's call this cone *past lightcone*, borrowing the name from Relativity. All that you can know from the past is contained in your past lightcone.

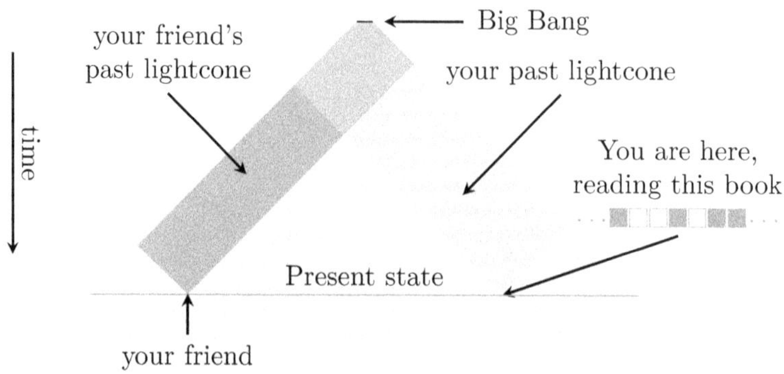

Figure 9.5: Your past lightcone consists of those cells in the past that, if changed, can change your state.

But your present state, including your present experiences, is fully contained in the present row of the cellular automaton. And whatever you know from the past, you know it because it is recorded in your present state.

Now remember a rich experience you had in the past. It can be listening to the chirp of the birds while smelling a flower in a forest, or having a meaningful experience together with somebody you love, or bumping your pinky toe against the door. Where does that experience reside in the cellular automaton? Could it be in a single cell? I doubt this is the case, because a single cell can contain only one bit of information. Your experience should supervene on a large number of cells. Given that we can distinguish about ten million colors, even the experience of seeing a color would require at least 24 cells. This is why the color of a pixel in a bitmap image takes 24 bits.

According to Computer Science, it really doesn't matter whether the 24 cells are located together, they don't have to form a contiguous sequence of cells in the present row in Figure 9.5. But even if the cells needed to support your experience in their states would be near each other, no cell of the automaton can't know what's in another cell, just like you and your friend can't know of each other right now, in the present. There is always a delay due to the light's speed limit.

Question 9.2. Where does your experience form in the cellular automaton?

Comment. No experience you have can supervene on a single cell. Maybe it supervenes on more cells, spread across a wide region and probably in more rows of the automaton. But no cell can "know" of any other cell, whether that cell is in its past or in its present. Experience can't result by combining the data in a single place. So, does your experience supervene nonlocally on a set of cells spread across the cellular automaton? □

One may think that this is not a real problem, that it is just an artifact of the economical mode of simulating the world by a cellular automaton. Maybe real physics doesn't have this problem. But let's see. First of all, should we then reject the idea that physical systems can be simulated? Does it then still make sense to say that our minds are computations? Secondly, according to physics, the present state of a system, along with all its present properties, lives in the present. This is a trivial statement, the physical world is a dynamical system, and while the past state determines the present state of the world, at least up to some possibly indeterministic quantum jumps, the present state contains everything there is to know about the present state, duh. In particular, whatever memories we have about the past, they are kept as records in our brains. Our minds don't jump back and forth in time to retrieve the past events and bring them to the present state of our memory. But, at the same time, not much can be stored in the same atom of the brain. Your own mind supervenes on a region of space, in the present slice of spacetime, like a nonlocal entity. And if you want to invoke the fact that your brain's processes take time, and your mind in fact supervenes on a "thick" slice of spacetime, then all you have achieved was to move nonlocality around, from nonlocality in space to nonlocality in time. I wrote more about this in [177].

9.6 Not a caricature, but a reduction to the essence

We have seen several examples of systems able to perform any computation. They are all universal computing machines having different internal structures, different combinations of states, and yet they can simulate each other and any other such system. What I showed here is only a limited sample of such systems, many more are known. Some computer games you may know are universal computers, for example you can write any computer program in Minecraft [42]. You can simulate any Turing machine even in Minesweeper, if the board is large enough [106]. Even in the game Doom, a game with monsters, monster movements can be used to implement logical circuits, and Doom level maps are Turing complete [87]. You can build a Lego Turing machine [63, 3]. You can also build a computer from billiard balls [68], or from water [192]. Gwern Branwen's web page https://gwern.net/turing-complete [87] contains many other interesting examples of Turing complete systems.

In principle, you can build a Turing machine out of anything, including beer cans, as Searle explained [157]. One can invoke a beer can Turing machine as a caricature, to reject the Computational Theory of Mind just by making it seem unbelievably ridiculous, but that's not the point. Another example that may seem so is a thought experiment in which an entire nation, for example China, is instructed to do what a Turing machine would do, as in the *Chinese Nation Argument*, proposed in various forms by several authors, including

Anatoly Dneprov (1961), Lawrence Davis (1974), Ned Block (1978) [55]. In Searle's *Chinese room argument* [157], the computations are done by a human bureaucrat oblivious to the computation he or she is performing. This kind of Turing machines may seem to suggest that the idea that mind is just a computation is unbelievable or even ridiculous, but why would this idea be more or less ridiculous than the idea that the molecules constituting the neurons can yield consciousness? The point here is not a caricaturization of the Computational Theory of Mind, but to reduce computation to its essence, to strip it of the colors in which our own minds paint it.

For example, Igor Salom imagines a Turing machine having the head made of wood, and using as a tape a sandy beach [156]. The wooden head writes the symbols ╳ and ◯ by stamping them in the sand. This neutral choice allows the reduction of computation to its essence, stripped of our own projections. Salom cleverly imagines a series of equivalent Turing machines made of wood and sand, including keeping a log of the previous states of the tape by starting a new line in sand, somewhat as in Egan's "Wang's Carpets". By using this succession of equivalent Turing machines, Salom shows that whatever computation the wooden Turing machine does, even if it simulates a sentient being, this is ultimately equivalent to writing down a large number.

I gave several examples of computing systems realized as surprising structures and of Turing machines realized from unexpected materials. The aim was not to point out the absurdity of the Computational Theory of Mind, but to emphasize that, in Computer Science, neither the material substrate nor the particular structure of the machine are relevant to implement a computation. All that matters is that, once we make the convention, the data processing attributed by the convention sticks consistently with the machine's behavior.

Exercises

Exercise 9.3. Can you find a physical system that can't be used or understood as a computing system?

Exercise 9.4. Can you find a physical system that can be understood as computing a unique computation?

Exercise 9.5. Reevaluate your answer to the questions from the Introduction.

Question	Yes	No	I don't know
Easy Question 1, page 8			
Easy Question 2, page 9			
Hard Question 1, page 10			
Hard Question 2, page 10			

Key points

- Cellular automata compute, tilings of the plane, and many other structures can compute. There are cellular automata and plane tilings that can implement any Turing machine.

Further reading

[73] Martin Gardner. The fantastic combinations of John Conway's new solitaire game 'Life'. *Sc. Am.*, 223:20–123, 1970

[15] E.R. Berlekamp, J.H. Conway, and R.K. Guy. *Winning ways for your mathematical plays.* AK Peters/CRC Press, 2004

[83] B. Grünbaum and G.C. Shephard. *Tilings and patterns.* W.H. Freeman and Company, New York, 1987

[208] Hao Wang. Games, logic and computers. *Scientific American*, 2013(5):98–107, 1965

[212] Stephen Wolfram. *A new kind of science*, volume 5. Wolfram Media Inc., 2002

[60] Greg Egan. *Diaspora.* Millennium, Australia, 1997.

[87] Gwern. Surprisingly Turing-complete. 2012–2022. https://gwern.net/turing-complete. Accessed April 22, 2026

[178] O.C. Stoica. The negative way to sentience. *Preprint on philsci-archive:17036 - last accessed April 22, 2026*, March 2020

[177] O.C. Stoica. Are mental states nonlocal? *Mind and Matter*, 18(2), 2020. Preprint arXiv:2010.03389

Part III

The magic of convention

10

The laws of computation

10.1 The commandments of computer science

The lesson that we learned from all the previous examples was that all that matters for a computation is how the physical states are enchained causally. In particular, the material of which we make the components of our computing machines is irrelevant, as long as it ensures the functionality. This includes the memory and the logic circuits. All that matters is that computers are able to implement the algorithm, regardless of what materials and mechanisms they use for this. Then, the first Law we can derive is:

Law: Substrate-Independence. *Computation is independent of the material substrate of the physical system implementing it.*

Substrate Independence states that the material of which you make the computing machine is immaterial. No, not in the sense that it doesn't exist physically, or that it can very be absent, but in the sense that it doesn't matter what material we use to build the computer's logic circuits. Computations themselves are not immaterial, "disembodied", they need to be realized as physical systems.

In addition, recall that the state of a Turing machine consists of the symbols on the tape, the internal state of the head, and the head's position on the tape. But when a Turing machine $\mathcal{M}$ simulates another Turing machine $\mathcal{M}'$, there is no constraint how we represent a state of $\mathcal{M}'$ as a state of $\mathcal{M}$. All that matters is that the states of $\mathcal{M}'$ are represented as states of $\mathcal{M}$ so that the transitions of $\mathcal{M}'$ are represented by transitions of $\mathcal{M}$, as in Definition 8.1. Moreover, a transition of $\mathcal{M}'$ from state $s_{\mathcal{M}'}$ to the next state $s'_{\mathcal{M}'}$ needs not be represented by such a transition of $\mathcal{M}$ from a state $s_{\mathcal{M}}$ to a state $s'_{\mathcal{M}}$—it can be represented by a chain of transitions starting in $s_{\mathcal{M}}$ and ending in $s'_{\mathcal{M}}$. Therefore, the internal structure and organization of the computing system are irrelevant to the computation, as long as the transitions are reproduced. In fact, if the internal structure would be taken into account, universal Turing machines would be impossible, since no Turing machine could simulate a Turing machine with different internal structure. This explains the extreme ambiguities we observed in the previous chapters. We summarize this observation as another Law,

DOI: 10.1201/9781003623373-10

Law: Substructure-Independence (or Multiple Realizability). *The physical system implementing a computation can have any internal structure, as long as it reproduces the steps of the computation.*

According to these two Laws, all that matters is that, once we associate the data to the states of the computing system by whatever convention, the physical transitions of the states of the computing system correspond to the steps of the algorithm or the computation.

Therefore, Substrate-Independence and Substructure-Independence are two aspects of a single fundamental Law of Computer Science,

Fundamental Law: Implementation-Independence. *Computation is independent of the implementation.*

From our previous discussions it also follows that

Law: Simulation=Computation. *A simulation of a computation is the same as the computation it simulates.*

In other words,

A computation done by a computing system is as *conventional* as the same computation done by any of the simulations of that computing system.

We will return to this in Lemma 10.1.

Figure 10.1 summarizes these laws.

Implementation-Independence is universally acknowledged in Computer Science, at least in the restrained sense of Substrate-Independence. However, I think that many people are not fully aware, at least not explicitly, that Substructure-Independence is at the core of Computer Science too. In particular, often due to the uncanny feeling given by the ambiguity of computation (see Section 14.4), some philosophers of mind consider that the structure of the components of the logic circuits is relevant to the mental processes, but at the same time they identify mind with a computation. We will return to this in Chapter 14. But we have seen in the previous chapters that Substructure-Independence is necessary and it's used everywhere, both in theory and in practice. We've seen that if these core laws wouldn't be true, there would be no Turing equivalence, no Turing universality, no possibility of a programmable computer. Computers would be very specialized, and for every program that you want to use, you'd have to use a strictly dedicated and much more complicated computer than we currently use.

Note that I don't contradict the importance of the substrate and of the substructure for other domains like hardware manufacturing. All I'm saying is

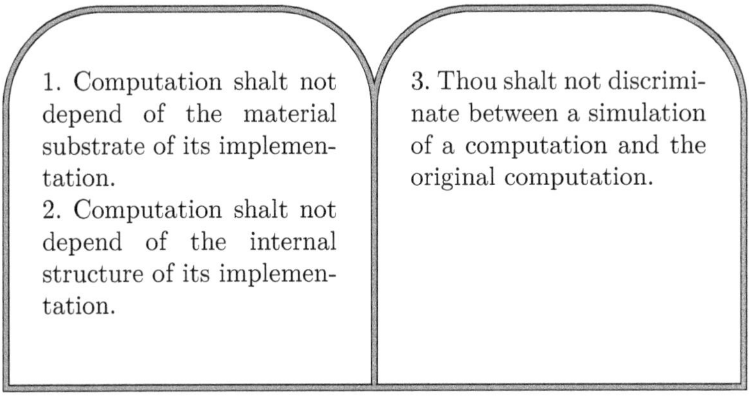

Figure 10.1: The Tables of the Law of Computer Science. These three Commandments are contained in the Commandment "Computations shalt be independent of the implementation" (Implementation-Independence).

that they are irrelevant for computations and their implementations, according to the very foundations of standard Computer Science. They may be necessary for consciousness, for example maybe the biological substrate and the neural structure of the brain may be necessary, but this is a different question.

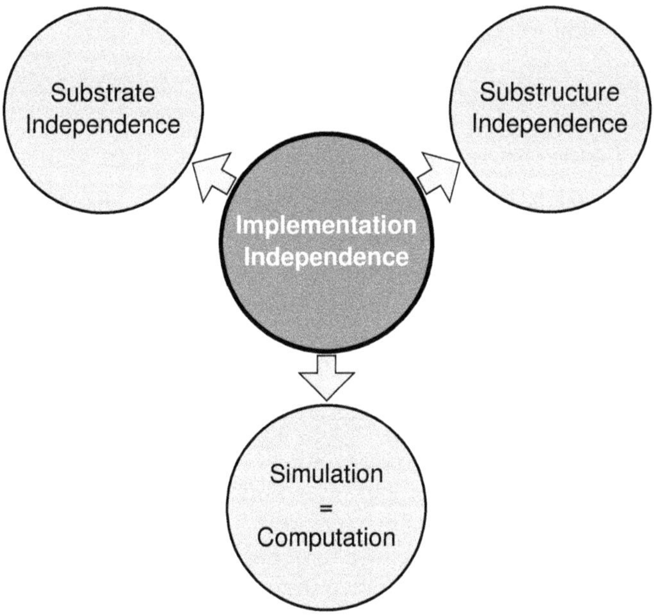

Figure 10.2: The laws of Computer Science.

10.2 Implementation as convention

Physical systems can be computing machines that implement algorithms because both physical systems and computations have something in common: they both can be described as dynamical systems [198, 68, 76, 39, 123, 7]. So let's see what a dynamical system is.

Definition 10.1. A *discrete dynamical system* consists of a countable set of possible states, called *state space*, and some *transition rules* that associate to each state the next state. These rules constitute the *dynamical law* of the dynamical system. Let $(\mathcal{S}, \mathcal{F})$ be a dynamical system with the state space $\mathcal{S}$ and the dynamical law $\mathcal{F}$. If at an initial time the state of the system is s_0, after N steps its state becomes

$$\mathbf{s}_N = \underbrace{\mathcal{F}(\ldots\mathcal{F}(}_{N \text{ times}}\mathbf{s}_0)\ldots) = \underbrace{(\mathcal{F} \circ \mathcal{F} \circ \ldots \circ \mathcal{F})}_{N \text{ times}}(\mathbf{s}_0) = \mathcal{F}^N(\mathbf{s}_0), \tag{10.1}$$

just like in equation (5.13).

The *history* originating in s_0 is the ordered set of states

$$h(s_0) := \left(s_0, \mathcal{F}(s_0), \mathcal{F}^2(s_0), \ldots\right), \tag{10.2}$$

where each state transitions to the next one.

We can see that an algorithm is a dynamical system in the following way:

1. the possible values of the data during the computation correspond to states,
2. each step in the computation corresponds to a transition.

An algorithm specifies how various possible values of the data should be processed. Computations are histories of the dynamical system.

A computation can't be disembodied, it needs a machine to implement it. Since computations can be understood as dynamical systems, it is possible to implement them on physical systems, which are dynamical systems too.

Turing machines, discussed in Chapters 7 and 8, are discrete dynamical systems. The total state of a Turing machine includes the state of the tape and that of the head. Let $\mathcal{S}$ be the set of all possible states. The transitions of the Turing machine can be represented, as in the case of the computer, by a function $\mathcal{F} : \mathcal{S} \to \mathcal{S}$. The state can be modified from the outside, when the user inputs data. After that, the machine continues to transition according to the function $\mathcal{F}$, $s \mapsto \mathcal{F}(s)$.

A key difference between physical systems and computations is that physical systems are not discrete dynamical systems, because their changes take place continuously. A history of a continuous dynamical system is a continuous succession of states. That is, the state, instead of depending on the step N, as in s_N, depends on the continuous time t, as in $s(t)$. Because of continuity, the time dependency of the state of a physical system is not as simple as in the discrete case, where simply $\mathbf{s}_N = \mathcal{F}^N(\mathbf{s}_0)$, but have the form $\mathbf{s}(t) = \mathcal{F}_{\Delta t}\mathbf{s}(t_0)$. We will return to this in Section 16.3.

However, when a physical system implements a computation, we are not interested in all its physical details, but only in a discrete number of physical properties and their values, and in the discrete times at which the properties have the values of interest. For example, if we store bits in capacitors that can be either charged or discharged, we will consider the capacitors charged if they are charged over 80% of their capacity, and discharged if they are charged under 20%, and simply ignore the intermediate situations. But, in most of the cases, it is sufficient to use only discrete time intervals Δt in $\mathbf{s}(t) = \mathcal{F}_{\Delta t}\mathbf{s}(t_0)$, treating the physical systems as discrete dynamical systems.

According to Substructure-Independence, the substructure of the physical state of the dynamical system implementing the computation is irrelevant, as long as its physical transitions realize the transitions of the algorithm. If the substructure would matter, for example if it would be important that the machine has the same structure as the data from the computation, universality would be impossible. A Turing machine with two symbols and 15 states as in Example 8.4, and other examples from Chapter 7, would not be able to simulate all other Turing machines. But since any universal Turing machine can simulate any other Turing machine, simulation should be understood as in Definition 8.1. Similarly, without Substructure-Independence, the cellular automata from Chapter 9 would be unable to simulate Turing machines or any other computing systems. Any assumption that restricts computations and forbids computational universality would contradict the basic tenets of Computer Science and would imply that programmable computers are impossible. Since our computers are programmable, we can infer that computation is not subject to such restrictions.

We assign data to the states of the machine by convention, and we make sure that its transitions correspond to valid steps in the computation. The convention exists in our minds, not in the computers. Therefore, the machine doesn't "know" anything about the computation it implements.

Observation 10.1. Since computation is based on conventions that exist only in our minds, the machine can't "know" anything about the computation it implements, unless it could read our minds.

It may seem to us that the computation is out there in the machine, because our minds "color", label the states of the machine according to the conventions. But the physical transitions become computations only in our minds, where they merge with the conventions.

Definition 10.2. An *interpretation* of a physical state as data is an assignment of data to the physical state. An *implementation* is an interpretation of a physical dynamical system as a computing system for an algorithm, consisting of interpreting its physical states as data processed by the algorithm, so that physical changes of the physical system correspond to steps made according to the algorithm (see Figure 10.3).

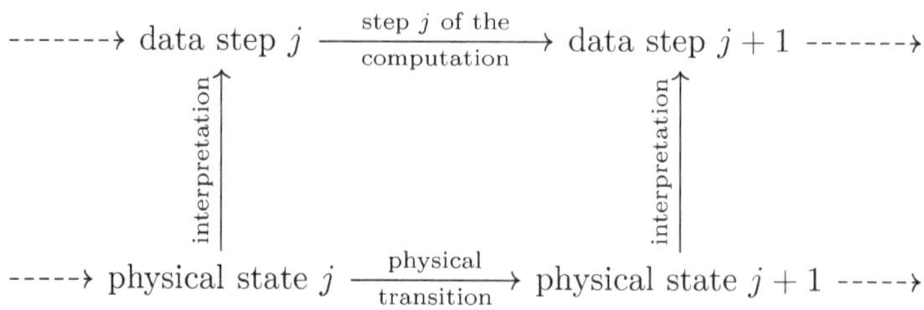

Figure 10.3: Implementation of an algorithm (the first row in the Figure) by a physical system (the second row).

The implementation of the algorithm is an example of partial morphism between two dynamical systems, the physical one and the formal one representing the algorithm. The notions of morphism and partial morphism express the correspondence between the states and transitions of two different dynamical systems. These notions will be very useful in the following, so it is important to be clear about their meaning.

Definition 10.3. A *morphism* between two discrete dynamical systems $(\mathcal{S}, \mathcal{F})$ and $(\mathcal{S}', \mathcal{F}')$ is a function $\alpha : \mathcal{S} \to \mathcal{S}'$, so that for any state $s \in \mathcal{S}$,

$$\mathcal{F}'\left(\alpha(s)\right) = \alpha\left(\mathcal{F}(s)\right). \tag{10.3}$$

Equation (10.3) expresses the fact that the transitions of the dynamical system $\mathcal{F}'$ are realized as transitions of $\mathcal{F}$.

If the function α from equation (10.3) is one-to-one, it is invertible, and its inverse α^{-1} defines a morphism from $(\mathcal{S}', \mathcal{F}')$ to $(\mathcal{S}, \mathcal{F})$. In this case, α is called *isomorphism*. An *automorphism* is an isomorphism between a dynamical system and itself, which may permute its states.

It is possible that some states of a physical system are irrelevant for the implementation, and we are interested only in a restriction of its state space. Another reason to consider restrictions is that when a computing system implements an algorithm or simulates another computing system, it uses only some of its states. A *restriction* of a dynamical system $(\mathcal{S}, \mathcal{F})$ is a dynamical system $(\widetilde{\mathcal{S}}, \mathcal{F}_{\widetilde{\mathcal{S}}})$ obtained by restricting the set of states to a subset $\widetilde{\mathcal{S}} \subseteq \mathcal{S}$. The dynamical law $\mathcal{F}$ is replaced with $\mathcal{F}_{\widetilde{\mathcal{S}}}$, which consists of the direct or indirect transitions determined by $\mathcal{F}$. An indirect transition from the state $s \in \widetilde{\mathcal{S}}$ is obtained by applying $\mathcal{F}$ the minimum number n of times needed so that $\mathcal{F}^n(s)$ is again from $\widetilde{\mathcal{S}}$, if such a number n exists. Because of the indirect transitions, the dynamical law of $\widetilde{\mathcal{S}}$ is not simply the restriction of the function $\mathcal{F}$ to $\widetilde{\mathcal{S}}$.

A *partial morphism* between two discrete dynamical systems $(\mathcal{S}, \mathcal{F})$ and $(\mathcal{S}', \mathcal{F}')$ is a morphism between a restriction of $(\mathcal{S}, \mathcal{F})$ and $(\mathcal{S}', \mathcal{F}')$.

Not only discrete, but also continuous dynamical systems (to be discussed in Section 16.3) admit restrictions and partial morphisms. An implementation of an algorithm by a physical system is a partial morphism (see Figure 10.3). It would be too strong to define it as a morphism, because

1. A computer can be in physical states that don't represent states of the data processed by the algorithm. For example, the computer can be disassembled or broken. While such states are perfectly valid physically, they don't correspond to steps of the computation. Therefore, restrictions are necessary.
2. A bit cell that changes from the state representing the value 0 to a state representing the value 1 goes through intermediate states that don't correspond to intermediate values between 0 and 1. For example, if the bit cell is a capacitor, it is not charged or discharged instantaneously, but gradually, yet the intermediate states don't represent binary values.

Computer scientists study abstract, formal mathematical models of computations that can represent both the computation and the physical system. We call all of these computing systems. Formal computing systems can implement algorithms and they can simulate other formal computing systems. For formal computing systems, there is no distinction between implementation and simulation.

Taking into account that both physical and formal computing systems are discrete dynamical systems, a physical computing system can implement a formal computing system, which can simulate another formal or physical computing system, and so on, as seen in Exercise 8.1 and Example 8.6. Viewed as such, a *reinterpretation* is a partial morphism, a simulation of a computing system by the same or another computing system.

Lemma 10.1 (Many Simulations)**.** Any computing system equally implements all algorithms implemented by all computing systems it simulates.

Proof. Let the computing system $(\mathcal{S}, \mathcal{F})$ implement an algorithm $(\mathcal{S}_A, \mathcal{F}_A)$, $\alpha : \mathcal{S} \to \mathcal{S}_A$. Let $\beta : \widetilde{\mathcal{S}} \to \mathcal{S}'$, where $\widetilde{\mathcal{S}} \subseteq \mathcal{S}$, be a simulation by $(\mathcal{S}, \mathcal{F})$ of another computing system $(\mathcal{S}', \mathcal{F}')$ that implements an algorithm $(\mathcal{S}'_A, \mathcal{F}'_A)$, $\alpha' : \widetilde{\mathcal{S}}' \to \mathcal{S}'_A$, where $\widetilde{\mathcal{S}}' \subseteq \beta(\widetilde{\mathcal{S}})$.

Then, these partial morphisms can be composed, resulting in a partial morphism between $(\mathcal{S}, \mathcal{F})$ and $(\mathcal{S}'_A, \mathcal{F}'_A)$,

$$\alpha' \circ \beta : \widetilde{\mathcal{S}} \to \mathcal{S}'_A, \tag{10.4}$$

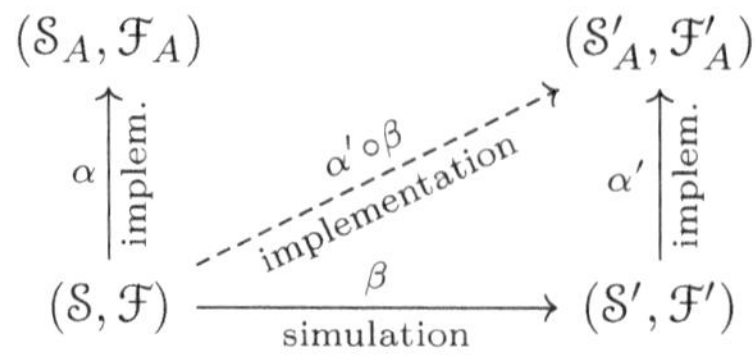

Figure 10.4: Any computing system implements all algorithms implemented by all computing systems it simulates.

where we used the notation

$$(\alpha' \circ \beta)(s) := \alpha'(\beta(s)). \tag{10.5}$$

The composite partial morphism $\alpha' \circ \beta$ is an implementation of the algorithm $(\mathcal{S}'_A, \mathcal{F}'_A)$ by the computing system $(\mathcal{S}, \mathcal{F})$ (Figure 10.4). □

Lemma 10.2 (Many Reinterpretations)**.** Any computing system implements all reinterpretations of an algorithm that it implements.

Proof. Similarly, if $\alpha : \mathcal{S} \to \mathcal{S}_A$ is an implementation by the computing system $(\mathcal{S}, \mathcal{F})$ of an algorithm $(\mathcal{S}_A, \mathcal{F}_A)$, and $\rho : \mathcal{S}_A \to \mathcal{S}'_A$ is a reinterpretation of $(\mathcal{S}_A, \mathcal{F}_A)$ as another algorithm $(\mathcal{S}'_A, \mathcal{F}'_A)$, $\rho \circ \alpha$ is another implementation (Figure 10.5).

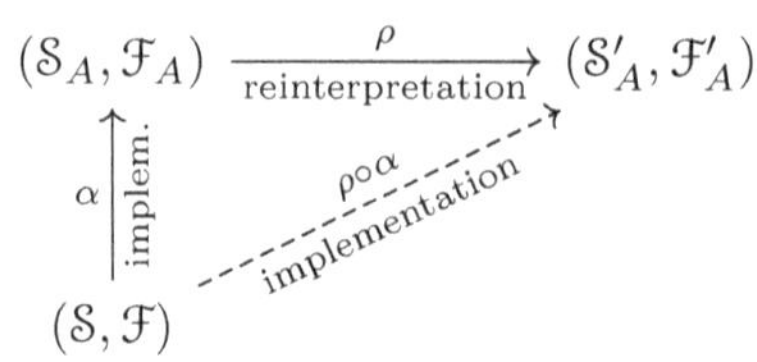

Figure 10.5: Any computing system implements all reinterpretations of an algorithm that it implements.

Definition 10.4. We call figures like 10.4 and 10.5 *commutative diagrams* for the following reason. For example in Figure 10.5, if we start from $(\mathcal{S}, \mathcal{F})$ and follow the arrows to $(\mathcal{S}'_A, \mathcal{F}'_A)$, we can do it in two ways: upward and then to the right, via $(\mathcal{S}_A, \mathcal{F}_A)$, or diagonally straight to $(\mathcal{S}'_A, \mathcal{F}'_A)$. In the first case, we obtain the implementation α followed by the reinterpretation ρ, and in the second case an implementation which is just $\rho \circ \alpha$. Since the result is independent of the path, the diagram is called commutative.

These mathematical results express formally in terms of dynamical systems what we've learned in Chapters 7 and 9 about Turing machines and other computing systems and about computations.

Exercises

Exercise 10.1. Give ten examples of physical dynamical systems you recently encountered in your daily life.

- Which of them implement an algorithm? If none of them does, what physical dynamical systems implementing algorithms do you know?
- Could these algorithms be implemented by other physical systems?
- Does the material substrate of the physical system matter for the implementation?
- Does the physical system need to have the same internal structure as the algorithm it implements?

Key points

- ▶ Computation is independent both of the material substrate and of the substructure of the physical system implementing it.
- ▶ There is no distinction between simulation and computation.
- ▶ Computing machines and computations are both dynamical systems.
- ▶ Any computing system equally implements all algorithms implemented by all computing systems it simulates and all reinterpretations of an algorithm that it implements.

Further reading

[43] Martin Davis. *The undecidable: Basic papers on undecidable propositions, unsolvable problems and computable functions.* Courier Corporation, 2004

[198] Tommaso Toffoli. Reversible computing. In *Automata, Languages and Programming: Seventh Colloquium. Noordwijkerhout, the Netherlands July 14–18, 1980*, pages 632–644. Springer, 1980

[68] Edward Fredkin and Tommaso Toffoli. Conservative logic. *Int. J. Theor. Phys.*, 21(3-4):219–253, 1982

[76] Marco Giunti. *Computation, dynamics, and cognition.* Oxford University Press, 1997

[39] J Copeland, C Posy, and O Shagrir. *Computability: Turing, Gödel, Church, and beyond.* MIT Press, 2013

11

A DIY experiment

With the realization that the computer's workings can be interpreted in multiple ways, we've got ourselves a new toy. When getting a new toy, a good scientist tries to test its limits and see if it breaks. Only after that does the scientist play with the toy to explore its amazing consequences. This is why, in this chapter, I will demonstrate experimentally that the alternative computations really happen. The reader can reproduce the experiment independently.

Imagine two friends who want to divide an amount of money consisting of three 5¢ coins, two 10¢ coins, and a 25¢ coin. A partition is considered fair if each one of the two friends receives the same total value (Figure 11.1).

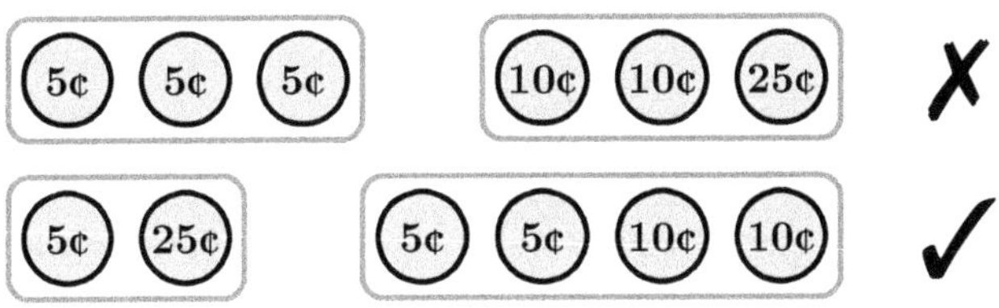

Figure 11.1: The partition problem: unfair and fair partitions of coins.

This is the *partition problem*. More generally, given a list of positive integer numbers $(x_1, \ldots, x_n)$, can it be partitioned into two lists, so that the sums of the numbers in each list are equal?

To solve the partition problem, one can make a program that tries all 2^n possible partitions into two lists, although there are methods to solve the problem without verifying all of the cases directly [92].

But I will do something very different:

I will show you a program that verifies only one of these cases, and from the result it obtains the results of the other cases by reinterpreting the bits (see Figure 11.2).

The program verifies only a partition of $(x_1, \ldots, x_n)$, which, to show off, is by default the partition into the empty list () and the list $(x_1, \ldots, x_n)$. The sums of the numbers in each of the two lists are then respectively 0 and

DOI: 10.1201/9781003623373-11

$\sum_{j=1}^{n} x_j > 0$, so they are definitely not equal! But if I am right, there must exist a program that verifies one of them, and then it reinterprets its result and finds the results of all the other cases.

Now I will describe the program that demonstrates this. You can find it and test it yourself online at the link from the caption of Figure 11.2. The source code is listed in the Appendix and can be verified at [170].

Let us arrange the numbers from the list in a vector of dimension n,

$$\mathsf{v} = \begin{pmatrix} x_1 \\ \cdots \\ x_n \end{pmatrix} = (x_1, \ldots, x_n)^\intercal \in \mathbb{Z}^n. \tag{11.1}$$

Here I used the *transposition* operator $\intercal$ to turn a "column vector" into a "row vector". In general, the transposition $\intercal$ swaps the rows and the columns. A partition in two can be specified by another list of n numbers, all being either $+1$ or -1,

$$\omega = (w_1, \ldots, w_n)^\intercal, \tag{11.2}$$

where $w_1, \ldots, w_n$ are all either 1 or -1.

Then, to find a fair partition, one has to verify if there is a list ω so that

$$\sum_{j=0}^{n} w_j x_j = 0. \tag{11.3}$$

Let us construct a matrix from the list of numbers $(x_1, \ldots, x_n)$,

$$\mathbf{U} = \begin{pmatrix} 1 & x_1 & x_2 & \ldots & x_n \\ 0 & 1 & 0 & \ldots & 0 \\ 0 & 0 & 1 & \ldots & 0 \\ \ldots & \ldots & \ldots & \ldots & \ldots \\ 0 & 0 & 0 & \ldots & 1 \end{pmatrix} = \begin{pmatrix} 1 & \mathsf{v}^\intercal \\ \mathsf{0}_{n,1} & \mathbf{I}_n \end{pmatrix}, \tag{11.4}$$

where in the right-hand side we use block matrices. $\mathsf{0}_{n,1}$ is the vector with all n components zero, and $\mathbf{I}_n$ is the $n \times n$ identity matrix.

With help from the matrix $\mathbf{U}$ we can obtain the sum $\sum_{j=0}^{n} w_j x_j$ in the following way. We construct the product of matrices (remember the matrix multiplication from Definition 6.1)

$$\begin{pmatrix} 1 & \mathsf{v}^\intercal \\ \mathsf{0}_{n,1} & \mathbf{I}_n \end{pmatrix} \begin{pmatrix} 0 \\ \omega \end{pmatrix} = \begin{pmatrix} \mathsf{v}^\intercal \omega \\ \omega \end{pmatrix} = \begin{pmatrix} \sum_{j=1}^{n} w_j x_j \\ \omega \end{pmatrix} \leftarrow \text{must be } 0 \tag{11.5}$$

Since the elements from the two lists are multiplied with opposite signs, for a fair partition the sum $\sum_{j=0}^{n} w_j x_j$ should be 0. Therefore, our verification finds that ω partitions the list of numbers $(x_1, \ldots, x_n)$ into two lists having the same sum if and only if the first element of the vector from the right-hand side of equation (11.5) is 0.

DIY experiment: Relativity of information

Whatever meaning we see in a computer or in the information it stores and the computation it does, this meaning is due to our own conventions. If we change the convention, we change the meaning. Without us to make the convention there is no meaning in a computer.

This JavaScript program demonstrates that when a computer does a computation, it also does the computations for the other possible inputs, simultaneously. The alternative computations are "encrypted" in that computation, and they can be "decrypted" by changing the convention.

For this demonstration, the program verifies if a partition of a list of numbers into two sublists is fair, that is, if the sums of the two sublists of numbers are equal (the partition problem). The program does the verification only once, for a default partition, and it can decrypt the results for any other partition.

Input data

List of numbers: 5,5,5,10,10,25

Default partition: 000000

User defined partition: 000111

Is the user defined partition verified along with the default partition?

Are all possible partitions verified along with the default partition?

Right-click to view the code or run it line-by-line.

Result: Verification successful!

Partition	Decrypted difference	Direct difference	Fair partition	Verification successful
000000	-60	-60	✗	✓

Figure 11.2: Online program showing that along with the computation for some input data, the computations for all possible input data happen simultaneously. You can find it at https://www.unitaryflow.com/2025/03/alternative-computations-at-once.html, run it in your browser, and check the source code by yourself.

Of course, it would be much easier to just compute the sum $\sum_{j=0}^{n} w_j x_j$ directly and compare it with 0. But I don't just want to verify if the partition is fair, I want to do it in a way that can be used to prove the existence of the alternative computations. The matrix approach I am explaining right now, while more complicated, will allow this in a more explicit way. I gave a general but more abstract and less explicit proof in Theorem 12.3 from Chapter 12.

The program verifies only if a particular partition, say given by $\omega_0 = (w_{01}, \ldots, w_{0n})^{\mathsf{T}} \in \{+1, -1\}^n$, solves the problem.

But how can we access the corresponding results for the other cases? This is where the matrix method turns out to be useful.

For any other vector $\omega \in \{+1, -1\}^n$, we are looking for a matrix $\mathbf{R}_\omega$, a transformation that reinterprets or decrypts the result of the computation applied to ω from the result of the current computation for ω_0,

$$\begin{pmatrix} \sum_{j=1}^{n} w_j x_j \\ \omega \end{pmatrix} = \mathbf{R}_\omega \begin{pmatrix} \mathsf{v}^{\mathsf{T}} \omega_0 \\ \omega_0 \end{pmatrix} = \mathbf{R}_\omega \begin{pmatrix} \sum_{j=1}^{n} w_{0j} x_j \\ \omega_0 \end{pmatrix}. \tag{11.6}$$

To determine the matrix $\mathbf{R}_\omega$, we will need the *inverse* of the matrix $\mathbf{U}$. This is another $n \times n$ matrix $\mathbf{U}^{-1}$, so that its multiplication with $\mathbf{U}$ gives the identity matrix,

$$\mathbf{U}\mathbf{U}^{-1} = \mathbf{U}^{-1}\mathbf{U} = \mathbf{I}_{n+1}. \tag{11.7}$$

From equation (11.4), the inverse of the matrix $\mathbf{U}$ is

$$\mathbf{U}^{-1} = \begin{pmatrix} 1 & -x_1 & -x_2 & \ldots & -x_n \\ 0 & 1 & 0 & \ldots & 0 \\ 0 & 0 & 1 & \ldots & 0 \\ \ldots & \ldots & \ldots & \ldots & \ldots \\ 0 & 0 & 0 & \ldots & 1 \end{pmatrix} = \begin{pmatrix} 1 & -\mathsf{v}^{\mathsf{T}} \\ 0_{n,1} & \mathbf{I}_n \end{pmatrix}. \tag{11.8}$$

Now notice that any vector $\omega = (w_1, \ldots, w_n)^{\mathsf{T}} \in \{+1, -1\}^n$ can be obtained from ω_0 by using a matrix $\mathbf{S}_\omega$,

$$\omega = \mathbf{S}_\omega \omega_0, \tag{11.9}$$

where

$$\mathbf{S}_\omega = \begin{pmatrix} w_1 w_{01} & 0 & \ldots & 0 \\ 0 & w_2 w_{02} & \ldots & 0 \\ \ldots & \ldots & \ldots & \ldots \\ 0 & 0 & \ldots & w_n w_{0n} \end{pmatrix}. \tag{11.10}$$

See Figure 11.3 for a representation of the transformations able to reinterpret a history as another history.

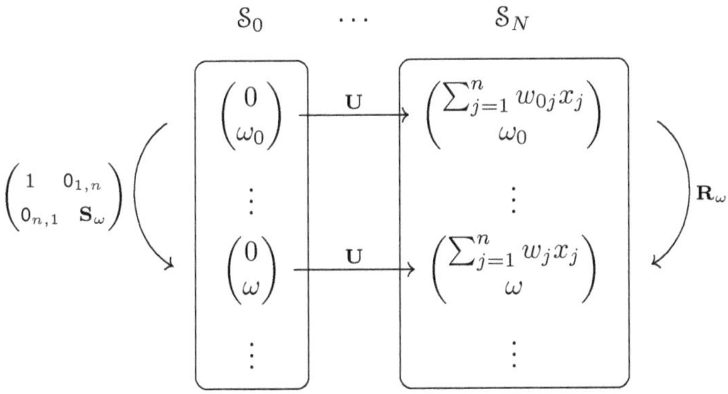

Figure 11.3: Parallel histories corresponding to the possible computations.

Since

$$\begin{aligned}
\begin{pmatrix} \mathsf{v}^\intercal\omega \\ \omega \end{pmatrix} &\overset{(11.5)}{=} \mathbf{U}\begin{pmatrix} 0 \\ \omega \end{pmatrix} \overset{(11.9)}{=} \mathbf{U}\begin{pmatrix} 1 & 0_{1,n} \\ 0_{n,1} & \mathbf{S}_\omega \end{pmatrix}\begin{pmatrix} 0 \\ \omega_0 \end{pmatrix} \\
&\overset{(11.7)}{=} \mathbf{U}\begin{pmatrix} 1 & 0_{1,n} \\ 0_{n,1} & \mathbf{S}_\omega \end{pmatrix}\mathbf{U}^{-1}\mathbf{U}\begin{pmatrix} 0 \\ \omega_0 \end{pmatrix} \\
&\overset{(11.5)}{=} \mathbf{U}\begin{pmatrix} 1 & 0_{1,n} \\ 0_{n,1} & \mathbf{S}_\omega \end{pmatrix}\mathbf{U}^{-1}\begin{pmatrix} \mathsf{v}^\intercal\omega_0 \\ \omega_0 \end{pmatrix} \\
&\overset{(11.8)}{=} \begin{pmatrix} 1 & \mathsf{v}^\intercal\mathbf{S}_\omega \\ 0_{n,1} & \mathbf{S}_\omega \end{pmatrix}\begin{pmatrix} 1 & -\mathsf{v}^\intercal \\ 0_{n,1} & \mathbf{I}_n \end{pmatrix}\begin{pmatrix} \mathsf{v}^\intercal\omega_0 \\ \omega_0 \end{pmatrix} \\
&\overset{(6.2)}{=} \begin{pmatrix} 1 & \mathsf{v}^\intercal\mathbf{S}_\omega - \mathsf{v}^\intercal \\ 0_{n,1} & \mathbf{S}_\omega \end{pmatrix}\begin{pmatrix} \mathsf{v}^\intercal\omega_0 \\ \omega_0 \end{pmatrix},
\end{aligned} \tag{11.11}$$

we obtain that the transformation $\mathbf{R}_\omega$ from (11.6) is

$$\mathbf{R}_\omega = \mathbf{U}\begin{pmatrix} 1 & 0_{1,n} \\ 0_{n,1} & \mathbf{S}_\omega \end{pmatrix}\mathbf{U}^{-1} = \begin{pmatrix} 1 & \mathsf{v}^\intercal\mathbf{S}_\omega - \mathsf{v}^\intercal \\ 0_{n,1} & \mathbf{S}_\omega \end{pmatrix}. \tag{11.12}$$

When applied as in equation (11.6), the transformation $\mathbf{R}_\omega$ gives a vector having on the first position $\sum_{j=1}^n w_j x_j$, which is zero if and only if the partition ω solves the partition problem. Therefore, to get the result of the computation for another partition ω, we can reinterpret the result of the computation for the original partition ω_0 by using the transformation $\mathbf{R}_\omega$.

As I will show in Remark 12.2, it is possible to choose the same reinterpretation for the initial state and for the final state, if we allow it to reinterpret groups of bits and not each bit independently, by using extra bits that are different for different steps of the computation.

We can extend the program to check by direct computation the results obtained by using $\mathbf{R}_\omega$, for all 2^n possible values of ω.

As promised, it is sufficient that the program verifies the partition

$$\omega_0 = (+1, \dots, +1)^\intercal, \tag{11.13}$$

which clearly isn't even fair. And yet, by using equation (11.6), it is still possible to obtain from this the correct answer for any other partition.

Remark 11.1. This will be generalized in Theorem 12.3, page 152, which shows under generic conditions that when a program computes the result for some input data, it also computes the result for other input data, and, under the proper setup, it can do it for all possible input data. But to actually see the result of the alternative computations, another program has to be used to actively apply the transformation that corresponds to the reinterpretation, to express the result in the convention used by the user interface.

The program can accept as input a number, whose binary form is interpreted as the partition.

All matrices involved, including $\mathbf{R}_\omega$, $\mathbf{U}$, and even $\mathbf{U}^{-1}$, and all vectors involved, including v, ω_0, and ω, have only integer elements. The operations involved in the algorithm always produce vectors and matrices with integer elements. Therefore, there is no approximation, hence no loss of information. We store an integer in binary form, on a fixed number of bits m. The vector $\binom{0}{\omega_0}$ is expressed on $(n+1)m$ bits, even though all its information is contained in n bits, because the program transforms it into $\binom{\sum_{j=1}^{n} w_{0j}x_j}{\omega_0}$, as in equation (11.5). This is a Boolean operation on $(n+1)m$ bits, and it's reversible, because the matrix $\mathbf{U}$ is invertible.

To find the result of an alternative computation, we copy the result in another set of $(n+1)m$ bits and apply the transformation $\mathbf{R}_\omega$ to obtain $\binom{\sum_{j=1}^{n} w_j x_j}{\omega}$, as in equation (11.6). At the bit level, this Boolean function is reversible too.

Here we should distinguish two kinds of transformations. The matrix $\mathbf{R}_\omega$ transforms the vector space $\mathbb{R}^{n+1}$ as in equation (11.6). But in binary form, this transformation acts as a Boolean function on $(n+1)m$ bits, and it retrieves the result of an alternative computation. This doesn't seem to have been effectively performed, since all we did was to verify a case which can't solve the problem, but it was performed in parallel, in an encrypted way. Therefore, this experiment proves the existence of alternative computations.

The reader may object that, by applying $\mathbf{R}_\omega$ as in equation (13.2), what we do in fact is to reverse the algorithm for ω_0 to the initial state, and then to apply it again for ω. So, one may say, it's no surprise that it works. Indeed, it's true that $\mathbf{R}_\omega$ can be expressed as composed of these transformations.

But we applied it in its direct form, not decomposed into undoing-redoing the computation, and it indeed reinterprets the result for ω_0 to find the result for ω. Since $\mathbf{U}$ is invertible, undoing the computation and doing it again for a different ω is equivalent to obtaining the result by applying $\mathbf{R}_\omega$ directly on the result for ω_0. Therefore, the conclusion of the previous sections, that other computations take place in parallel, hidden from the user interface, is verified experimentally. And while now it may not seem like a surprise, I invite the reader to remember their answer to the Easy Question 1.

Remark 11.2. This example may seem to be an exceptional situation, built specifically to allow the recovery of the alternative results. It is indeed a special example, but only by being designed so that we, humans, can follow it, despite our limited computational power. But there are such transformations for all programs covered by Theorem 12.3.

Remark 11.3. While we use a decryption key $\mathbf{R}_\omega$ that is different from the encryption key $\begin{pmatrix} 1 & 0_{1,n} \\ 0_{n,1} & \mathbf{S}_\omega \end{pmatrix}$, these are parts of the same overall transformation, just like $\mathcal{R}_0$ and $\mathcal{R}_N$ from the proof of Theorem 12.3 are both parts of the transformation $\mathcal{R}$. The encryption key represents the part of the transformation for states in which the clock bits encode the time $t = 0$, and the decryption key represents the part of the transformation for states in which the clock bits encode the time $t = N$. But since, for simplicity, we didn't include the clock bits in the equations, the two parts seem to be distinct transformations.

The source code of a program that does all of these is provided in the Appendix and in [170], and it can be used by the reader for independent verification.

Fun fact 11.1. The partition problem belongs to a special class of problems, called *NP-complete*. The NP-complete problems are important for the famous *P versus NP problem*, one of the seven *Millennium Prize Problems*. The Clay Mathematics Institute offers a bounty of 1 000 000 US dollars for the solution of any of these seven problems, including the *P versus NP problem*.

But what is the *P versus NP problem*?

A problem is of class P (for "polynomial time") if it can be solved by an algorithm in a *polynomial time*, that is, the time needed to solve it increases at most as a power of the size of the input data. A problem is of class NP (for "nondeterministic polynomial time") if, given a candidate solution to the problem, there is an algorithm that can verify that the candidate solution is a solution in a polynomial time. It is called "nondeterministic" because a Turing machine that tries a solution randomly and verifies it can be lucky and guess the solution, and then prove it in a polynomial time.

The *P versus NP problem* asks whether the two classes of problems P and NP are the same or are different.

There is a special class of NP problems, called *NP-complete*. Showing that any of these problems can be solved in a polynomial time, all other NP problems can. This would be a proof that P=NP, so it would solve the *P versus NP problem*. The partition problem is NP-complete, and it is considered to be "the easiest hard problem" [92]. The algorithm presented in this section is not the simplest one, but it still requires only a polynomial time in the size of the input data.

But what about the fun part promised in this comment? To appreciate it, solve Exercise 11.2.

Chapter 12 explains why the program presented here is not an accident.

Exercises

Exercise 11.1. Go to the link from the caption of Figure 11.2 and verify by yourself that the partition program indeed tries all possible partitions whenever it tries any of them.

Exercise 11.2. We have seen that even when a single candidate solution is verified by the algorithm I presented here, all other candidate solutions are verified in parallel. So all candidate solutions are verified in parallel, in a polynomial time. Does this mean that the algorithm that I presented proves that P=NP? Should I collect the Millennium Prize?

Answer. Not at all, because to actually access the results of all 2^n computations taking place in parallel, we need to apply the appropriate transformation $\mathbf{R}_\omega$ for each of them. So we need a time proportional to 2^n, which is much longer than polynomial. □

Key points

- You can verify by yourself that the program presented in this chapter does indeed the computations for all possible input data simultaneously, but in an "encrypted" form, by visiting the following web page

https://www.unitaryflow.com/2025/03/alternative-computations-at-once.html

Further reading

[170] Cristi Stoica. Alternative computations at once. *https://www.unitaryflow.com/2025/03/alternative-computations-at-once.html*, 2025

[182] O.C. Stoica. Does a computer think if no one is around to see it? *philsci-archive:22880*, 2023

[172] O.C. Stoica. Are you a robot? http://youtu.be/kuziE01rh6M&list=PLJzOclJMoIC1pnJIPlmWhGwaDWD04tFza. Accessed April 22, 2026

12

Everything all at once

12.1 Counting reinterpretations

Let us consider a computer with n bit cells, interpreted according to our convention as having the binary values b_1, ..., b_n. A reinterpretation consists of changing the convention, for example a simple reinterpretation consists of inverting the convention for some of the bit values so that 0 becomes 1 and 1 becomes 0. For example, we can switch among David's interpretation of the alien device and Alice's, by inverting the second input bit and the output, $f_A(p, q) = \overline{f_D(p, \overline{q})}$. All eight interpretations discussed in Chapter 2 can be obtained from one another by reinterpreting the bits in similar ways.

Note that the convention can be changed also by permuting the bits, that is, changing the order in which we consider them as inputs and outputs of our Boolean function. For example by permuting the input bits in Eve's interpretation we obtain another interpretation, which happens to coincide with Carol's interpretation, because $f_C(p, q) = f_E(q, p)$. And, as seen in Chapter 4, there are more general reinterpretations.

To define a simple reinterpretation of n bits, we need a way to specify which of them are flipped and which remain unchanged. By using n additional bits

$$\mathbf{s} = (s_1, \dots, s_n) \tag{12.1}$$

we can do this in the following way: if s_1 is 1, we invert the bit b_1, otherwise we leave it unchanged, and so on for s_2, s_3, *etc.* Therefore, a simple reinterpretation is just a function $\mathcal{R}$, specified with the help of n bits $\mathbf{s}$, that takes n bits and flips those indicated by the bits in $\mathbf{s}$,

$$\mathcal{R}(b_1, \dots, b_n) = (s_1 \texttt{XOR}\ b_1, \dots, s_n \texttt{XOR}\ b_n)\,. \tag{12.2}$$

Here, we used the XOR operation in the same way we used it in the case of the simple XOR cipher from Section 4.3.

Exercise 12.1. Show that the simple reinterpretation from equation (12.2) is equivalent with

$$\mathcal{R}(b_1, \dots, b_n) = (\texttt{NOT}^{s_1}\ b_1, \dots, \texttt{NOT}^{s_n}\ b_n)\,, \tag{12.3}$$

DOI: 10.1201/9781003623373-12

were $\mathtt{NOT}\ b = \bar{b}$ is the bit inversion operator, and

$$\begin{cases} \mathtt{NOT}^0\ b & = b, \\ \mathtt{NOT}^1\ b & = \bar{b}. \end{cases} \tag{12.4}$$

Note that the function $\mathcal{R}$ should be understood as changing only the interpretation, and not the physical states of the bit cells.

The convention from equation (12.4) is naturally interpreted as the composition of NOT with itself zero times or one time, just like the transformation from equation (6.17) representing the operator NOT satisfies

$$\begin{pmatrix} 0 & 1 \\ 1 & 0 \end{pmatrix}^0 = \begin{pmatrix} 1 & 0 \\ 0 & 1 \end{pmatrix} \text{ and } \begin{pmatrix} 0 & 1 \\ 1 & 0 \end{pmatrix}^1 = \begin{pmatrix} 0 & 1 \\ 1 & 0 \end{pmatrix}. \tag{12.5}$$

Let us see how we recover the bits $(b_1, \ldots, b_n)$ according to the original convention, assuming that we know $\mathcal{R}$ and $\mathcal{R}(b_1, \ldots, b_n)$. We need the inverse $\mathcal{R}^{-1}$ of the function $\mathcal{R}$.

Exercise 12.2. Show that if $\mathcal{R}$ is a simple reinterpretation then $\mathcal{R}^{-1} = \mathcal{R}$.

Exercise 12.3. Show that any two interpretations of the alien device from Table 2.4 can be reinterpreted as each other by a simple reinterpretation.

We discussed simple reinterpretations, but we've seen in Chapter 4 that there are more general reinterpretations. Now we will see what happens with the computation if we change the interpretation by using an invertible general interpretation which is not necessarily a simple one.

Theorem 12.1. According to Computer Science, any invertible general reinterpretation of a computation is a computation.

Proof. Remember from Chapter 5 that the computer works in steps. At any step, the computer's state is characterized by the states of its individual bit cells. If the computer's state at a step is $\mathbf{s}_0 = (b_{10}, \ldots, b_{n0})$, at the next step its state becomes $\mathbf{s}_1 = \mathcal{F}(\mathbf{s}_0)$. If no external causes affect the computation, after N steps, the state of the computer becomes $\mathbf{s}_N = (b_{1N}, \ldots, b_{nN})$, where $\mathbf{s}_N = \mathcal{F}^N(\mathbf{s}_0)$, as in equations (5.12) and (5.13). Some of the bits are used for input data, some to store the output data, and others as internal memory, as explained in Chapter 5, in particular in the discussion around Figure 5.4, page 60.

Now we will reinterpret the bits in the same way at all steps. The function $\mathcal{R}$ representing the reinterpretation reinterprets the initial state $\mathbf{s}_0$ as $\mathcal{R}(\mathbf{s}_0)$, the next state $\mathbf{s}_1$ as $\mathcal{R}(\mathbf{s}_1)$ and so on. In general, it reinterprets the state $\mathbf{s}_N = \mathcal{F}^N(\mathbf{s}_0)$ as $\mathcal{R}(\mathcal{F}^N(\mathbf{s}_0))$. On the other hand, the reinterpreted states $\mathcal{R}(\mathbf{s}_0)$, $\mathcal{R}(\mathbf{s}_1)$, ..., are related not by the evolution function $\mathcal{F}$, but by

$$\mathcal{F}' = \mathcal{R} \circ \mathcal{F} \circ \mathcal{R}^{-1}, \tag{12.6}$$

because

$$\begin{array}{lll} \mathcal{R}(\mathbf{s}_1) & = \mathcal{R}\left(\mathcal{F}(\mathbf{s}_0)\right) & = \left(\mathcal{R} \circ \mathcal{F} \circ \mathcal{R}^{-1}\right)\left(\mathcal{R}(\mathbf{s}_0)\right), \\ \mathcal{R}(\mathbf{s}_2) & = \mathcal{R}\left(\mathcal{F}(\mathbf{s}_1)\right) & = \left(\mathcal{R} \circ \mathcal{F} \circ \mathcal{R}^{-1}\right)\left(\mathcal{R}(\mathbf{s}_1)\right), \\ \ldots & \ldots & \ldots \\ \mathcal{R}(\mathbf{s}_N) & = \mathcal{R}\left(\mathcal{F}(\mathbf{s}_{N-1})\right) & = \left(\mathcal{R} \circ \mathcal{F} \circ \mathcal{R}^{-1}\right)\left(\mathcal{R}(\mathbf{s}_{N-1})\right) \end{array} \tag{12.7}$$

and so on, as in the commutative diagram from Figure 12.1.

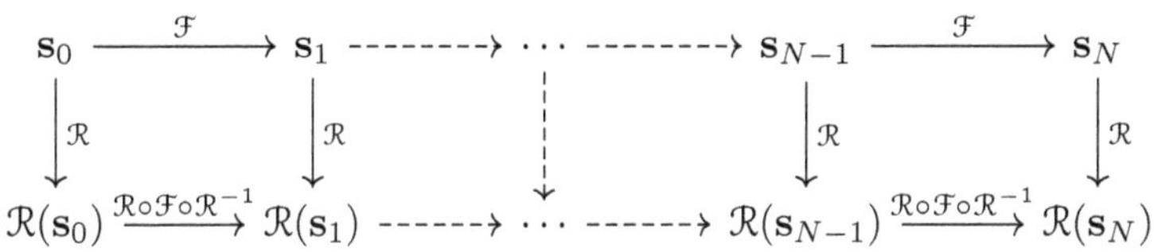

Figure 12.1: Reinterpreting the bits leads to a reinterpretation of the computer's program as another program, performing a different computation.

The reinterpretation of the function $\mathcal{F}^N$ is then the function

$$\begin{aligned} \left(\mathcal{F}'\right)^N &= \left(\mathcal{R} \circ \mathcal{F} \circ \mathcal{R}^{-1}\right) \circ \left(\mathcal{R} \circ \mathcal{F} \circ \mathcal{R}^{-1}\right) \circ \ldots \circ \left(\mathcal{R} \circ \mathcal{F} \circ \mathcal{R}^{-1}\right) \\ &= \mathcal{R} \circ \mathcal{F} \circ \left(\mathcal{R}^{-1} \circ \mathcal{R}\right) \circ \mathcal{F} \circ \left(\mathcal{R}^{-1} \circ \mathcal{R}\right) \circ \ldots \circ \mathcal{F} \circ \mathcal{R}^{-1} \\ &= \mathcal{R} \circ \mathcal{F}^N \circ \mathcal{R}^{-1}. \end{aligned} \tag{12.8}$$

The same could be obtained directly as in the following diagram

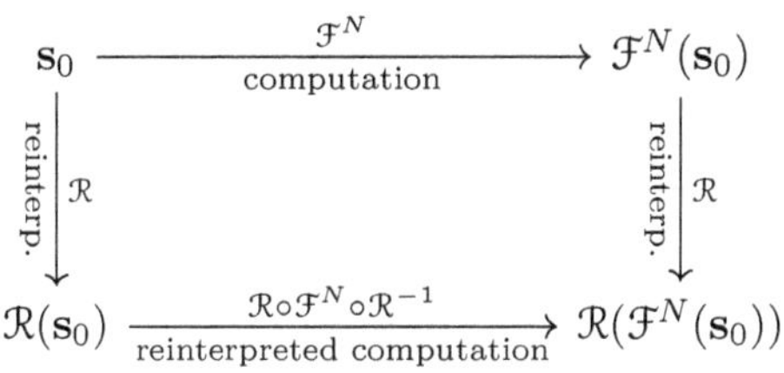

(12.9)

More generally, we can reinterpret the initial and the final states using different functions $\mathcal{R}_{\mathtt{i}}$ and $\mathcal{R}_{\mathtt{o}}$, obtaining following reinterpretation of $\mathcal{F}^N$,

$$\mathcal{F}'_{\mathtt{io}} = \mathcal{R}_{\mathtt{o}} \circ \mathcal{F}^N \circ \mathcal{R}_{\mathtt{i}}^{-1}, \tag{12.10}$$

which makes the following diagram commute

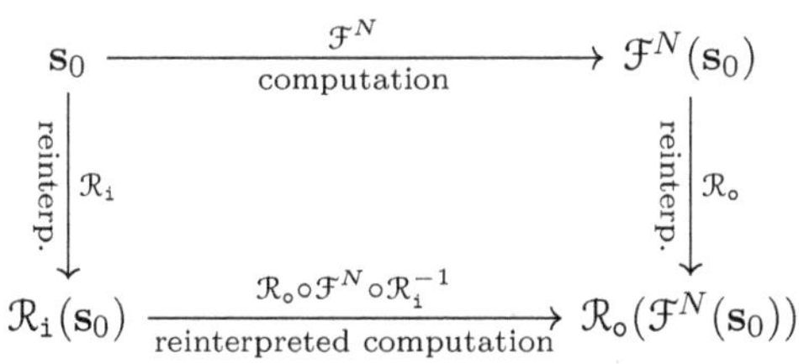

(12.11)

The states change according to a Boolean function at every step. While the Boolean functions obtained by reinterpretations differ from the original ones, they still satisfy Definition 5.1, so they are also computations. □

Remark 12.1. In fact, using different reinterpretations for the initial and the final state of the computation is not really different from using the same reinterpretation, if the final state of the computer is always different from the initial state. The reason is that, in this case, $\mathcal{R}_{\mathtt{i}}$ and $\mathcal{R}_{\mathtt{o}}$ have disjoint domains where they are defined, so they can be part of a unique reinterpretation $\mathcal{R}$ defined on the union of these domains. Similarly, if each state of the computation is different from the past and future states, different reinterpretations for each step can be seen as particular situations of a single reinterpretation. And in practice, in most situations, the states of the machine at different steps are different. The exception happens if the program enters into an infinite loop, but even then other parts of the memory change, for example those storing the time of the processor.

But how many different computations does the same physical process implement at the same time? Even if we count only the simple reinterpretations, their number grows exponentially with the number of bits, as you can extrapolate from Exercise 12.3.

Observation 12.1. A computer doesn't perform just one computation, but many more, during the same physical process. The number of these computations grows exponentially with the number of bits. We think there is a unique computation because we are aware only of the one translated by the output and input devices in or from the formats interpretable by our senses. That is, the user interface selects a unique interpretation.

But the magic doesn't stop here.

12.2 The Oracle of Delphi

The astute reader may have noticed a similarity between the functions $\mathcal{F}$ and $\mathcal{R}$ from the previous section. Indeed, they are the same type of functions, both being defined on $\{\mathtt{0},\mathtt{1}\}^n$ and with values in $\{\mathtt{0},\mathtt{1}\}^n$. It is even possible that a computer implements, at every step, the Boolean function $\mathcal{R}$ instead of $\mathcal{F}$, and we can use as a reinterpretation $\mathcal{F}$ instead of $\mathcal{R}$. So the two functions $\mathcal{F}$ and $\mathcal{R}$ are not different kinds of functions, they just play different roles. The important difference, as used in the proof of Theorem 12.1, is that $\mathcal{F}$ actually changes the physical states, while $\mathcal{R}$ only changes the convention.

But this observation may trigger the following question: what if we choose as reinterpretation $\mathcal{R}$ the function $\mathcal{F}^N$? Then we would get the result that the computation would give after N steps, without even having to wait until the computer changes its state from $\mathbf{s}_0$ to $\mathcal{F}^N(\mathbf{s}_0)$. If we could know the reinterpreted convention, we would obtain the result of a computation without having to run the computer at all!

Indeed, the destiny of the computer, assuming that we don't interact with it, is already written in its initial state, and to find it out, all we have to do is to reinterpret the values of the bits. But this "all we have to do" is tricky, because to find out the reinterpretation $\mathcal{F}^N$ we need to do the entire computation ourselves.

It may feel very frustrating to realize that the result is already there, but you can't read it because you don't know how to reinterpret the computer's state! Like the prophecies of Pythia, the high priestess of the Temple of Apollo at Delphi, the result of the computation is already there, waiting for the right interpretation, but you will know it only after it happens.

12.3 Many computation at once

In Section 12.1, we have seen that any reinterpretation of a computation is also a computation. This suggests the question:

Question 12.1. Can a program that processes some input data be reinterpreted as processing any other input data?

In this section, I will show that the answer is, under usually realized conditions, yes. This generalizes what is confirmed in Chapter 11 with an experiment that the readers can do by themselves.

But first, we will design programmable "toy computers".

We start with a very simple example of a function programmable to compute all Boolean functions with one input and one output. These Boolean functions are shown in Table 12.1.

Table 12.1: The Boolean functions with one input and one output.

$f_{\mathtt{F}}(p) = 0$

p	0
0	0
1	0

$f_{\mathtt{T}}(p) = 1$

p	1
0	1
1	1

$f_{\mathtt{I}}(p) = p$

p	p
0	0
1	1

$f_{\mathtt{N}}(p) = \overline{p}$

p	$\overline{p}$
0	1
1	0

Example 12.1. Consider the function $\mathbf{f} : \{0,1\}^3 \to \{0,1\}^3$,

$$\mathbf{f}(b_1; b_2, b_3) = \Big((b_1 \wedge b_2 \wedge b_3) \vee (\overline{b_1} \wedge b_2 \wedge \overline{b_3}) \vee (\overline{b_2} \wedge b_3), b_2, b_3\Big). \qquad (12.12)$$

This function can be "programed" to compute all four Boolean functions of one variable, $f_{\mathtt{F}}(p) = \mathtt{0}$, $f_{\mathtt{T}}(p) = \mathtt{1}$, $f_{\mathtt{N}}(p) = \overline{p}$, and $f_{\mathtt{I}}(p) = p$,

$$\begin{aligned} \mathbf{f}(b_1; \mathtt{0}, \mathtt{0}) &= (\mathtt{0}; \mathtt{0}, \mathtt{0}) = (f_{\mathtt{F}}(b_1); \mathtt{0}, \mathtt{0}), \\ \mathbf{f}(b_1; \mathtt{0}, \mathtt{1}) &= (\mathtt{1}; \mathtt{0}, \mathtt{1}) = (f_{\mathtt{T}}(b_1); \mathtt{0}, \mathtt{1}), \\ \mathbf{f}(b_1; \mathtt{1}, \mathtt{0}) &= (\overline{b_1}; \mathtt{1}, \mathtt{0}) = (f_{\mathtt{N}}(b_1); \mathtt{1}, \mathtt{0}), \\ \mathbf{f}(b_1; \mathtt{1}, \mathtt{1}) &= (b_1; \mathtt{1}, \mathtt{1}) = (f_{\mathtt{I}}(b_1); \mathtt{1}, \mathtt{1}). \end{aligned} \tag{12.13}$$

The result of the one-bit Boolean function is stored in the first bit, and the program in the other two bits.

We see that, by giving different values to the second and third input bits of the function **f**, we can obtain all functions from Table 12.1.

This can be generalized easily to the Boolean functions with n inputs and m outputs, for any positive integers n and m.

Proposition 12.1. All Boolean functions with n inputs and m outputs can be obtained by programming a single Boolean function **f**.

Proof. Here is a brute force construction. There are 2^{2^n} functions with n inputs and one output. Therefore, there are

$$\underbrace{2^{2^n} \times \ldots \times 2^{2^n}}_{m \text{ times}} = \left(2^{2^n}\right)^m = 2^{m2^n}$$

Boolean functions with n inputs and m outputs. We list them all, and we number them starting with 0, in binary. Let $\mathbf{f}_j$ denote the $j-1$-th function from our list. Since the numbers from 0 to $2^{m2^n}-1$ can be encoded in $m2^n$ bits, so can these 2^{m2^n} functions. Then, we can define the function **f** with $n + m2^n$ inputs and $m + m2^n$ outputs as

$$\begin{cases} \mathbf{f}(b_1, \ldots, b_n; \mathtt{0}, \mathtt{0}, \ldots, \mathtt{0}) & = (\mathbf{f}_0(b_1, \ldots, b_n); \mathtt{0}, \mathtt{0}, \ldots, \mathtt{0}), \\ \mathbf{f}(b_1, \ldots, b_n; \mathtt{0}, \mathtt{0}, \ldots, \mathtt{1}) & = (\mathbf{f}_1(b_1, \ldots, b_n); \mathtt{0}, \mathtt{0}, \ldots, \mathtt{1}), \\ & \ldots \\ \mathbf{f}(\underbrace{b_1, \ldots, b_n}_{n \text{ bits}}; \underbrace{\mathtt{1}, \mathtt{1}, \ldots, \mathtt{1}}_{m2^n \text{ bits}}) & = (\underbrace{\mathbf{f}_{2^{m2^n}-1}(b_1, \ldots, b_n)}_{m \text{ bits}}; \underbrace{\mathtt{1}, \mathtt{1}, \ldots, \mathtt{1}}_{m2^n \text{ bits}}). \end{cases} \tag{12.14}$$

Here, for every j, $\mathbf{f}_j(b_1, \ldots, b_n)$ is an array of m bits. □

This is not the only way to program a Boolean function to simulate all Boolean functions with n inputs and m outputs. In practice, we don't need such a large number of programmable bits compared to the bits storing the result of the functions $\mathbf{f}_j$. It would be very difficult and inefficient. In fact, it would be practically impossible to program a computer for each possible situation independently. Computers work in a sequence of steps, as explained in Chapter 5. This gives much more flexibility. Since we need a large number of steps, it may take much longer to get the result, but it is much easier to program a computer with step-by-step instructions. This allows it to use decision blocks that give instructions for different cases, and loops that allow it to repeat an operation until it finishes some job. But, ultimately, even the function $\mathcal{F}^N$ obtained after N steps, as in equation (5.13) from Chapter 5, is a function $\mathbf{f}$ like the one from Proposition 12.1.

Definition 12.1 (One-step programmable computer)**.** A *one-step programmable computer* is a physical realization of a Boolean function $\mathbf{f} : \{\mathtt{0},\mathtt{1}\}^n \to \{\mathtt{0},\mathtt{1}\}^n$,

$$\mathbf{f}(\overbrace{\underbrace{b_1,\dots,b_{n_\mathtt{i}}}_{\text{input data}},\underbrace{b_{n_\mathtt{i}+1}\dots,b_{n_\mathtt{i}+n_\mathtt{o}}}_{\text{output data}}}^{\text{first } d \text{ bits}},\overbrace{\underbrace{b_{d+1},\dots,b_{d+n_\mathtt{m}}}_{\text{internal memory}},\underbrace{b_{d+n_\mathtt{m}+1},\dots\dots,b_n}_{\text{program}}}^{\text{last } n-d \text{ bits}}). \tag{12.15}$$

We assume that the bits have specific roles: the first $n_\mathtt{i}$ bits are for input data, followed by $n_\mathtt{o}$ bits for output data, $n_\mathtt{m}$ bits for internal memory used by the program to store intermediate results of the computation, and $n_\mathtt{p}$ bits for the program.

By comparing with the computer from Figure 5.4, page 60, we see that a part of the internal memory is allocated to the instructions of the program.

If step-by-step computers are much more efficient and easier to program, one may wonder why I waste the reader's time with computers that would do the job in a single step, but, at least for complex computations, would be too large and would take ages to program for all possible inputs. The answer is that they are very simple to understand and they can do everything a normal computer can, if programmed accordingly. I use them as a simple model of a computer to explain an idea that may be more difficult to explain otherwise.

Consider the following setup. We will assume that a one-step programmable computer runs a program in which the function $\mathbf{f}$, as in equation (12.1), doesn't change the bits reserved for the program. The input data bits can also remain unchanged, because the result will be written in the output data bits. The internal memory bits are used only for the intermediate results of the computation, so we can assume that at the end of the computation they remain as they were before. Without loss of generality, we can assume that they were all $\mathtt{0}$. We can also assume that the output bits of the initial state are all $\mathtt{0}$ too. We can see that this setup is quite general. We have the following result:

Theorem 12.2. Consider a one-step programmable computer as in Definition 12.1, running a program that doesn't change itself or the input data. Assume that, for any possible input data, the computation finishes after N steps. Then, the computation can be reinterpreted as computing on all possible allowed input data at once.

Proof. Let $\mathbf{s}_0 = (b_{10},\dots,b_{n0})$ be the initial state of the computer. For a one-step programmable computer as in Definition 12.1, the first $n_\mathtt{i}$ bits contain the input data. Any other input data accepted by the program has a maximum length n_i. Therefore, by flipping some of the first n_i bits of $\mathbf{s}_0$, any other input data can be obtained. Let $\mathcal{R}_i$ be the reinterpretation that flips those bits and leaves all other bits unchanged. I will show that the computation can be reinterpreted so that the function $\mathbf{f}$ gives the correct output for the reinterpreted input data.

If we want the reinterpretation of the initial data set to result in the same program applied to other input data, we need to reinterpret the final state of the computer accordingly. In Theorem 12.1 from Section 12.1, we have seen how we can reinterpret both the state of the computer before the computation, and its state after the computation. We reinterpreted the final state using a function $\mathcal{R}_o$, as seen in equation (12.11), page 145. This led us to a reinterpretation of the function $\mathbf{f}$ that performs the computation, which in our case becomes $\mathbf{f}' = \mathcal{R}_o \circ \mathbf{f} \circ \mathcal{R}_i^{-1}$, as in (12.10). But in this proof we want $\mathbf{f}'$ to realize the same program, just applied to different input data, so we want that $\mathbf{f}' = \mathbf{f}$. If $\mathbf{f}$ is invertible, we can we choose $\mathcal{R}_o = \mathbf{f} \circ \mathcal{R}_i \circ \mathbf{f}^{-1}$, and we get $\mathbf{f}' = \mathcal{R}_o \circ \mathbf{f} \circ \mathcal{R}_i^{-1} = (\mathbf{f} \circ \mathcal{R}_i \circ \mathbf{f}^{-1}) \circ \mathbf{f} \circ \mathcal{R}_i^{-1} = \mathbf{f}$, as needed. This ensures that

$$\mathcal{R}_o\left(\mathbf{f}(\mathbf{s}_0)\right) = \mathbf{f}\left(\mathcal{R}_i(\mathbf{s}_0)\right). \tag{12.16}$$

Since the computation $\mathbf{f}$ changes only the output bits, $\mathcal{R}_o$ changes only the input and output bits, and leaves the internal memory bits and the program bits unchanged. So $\mathcal{R}_o$ changes only the first $d = n_i + n_o$ bits. The diagram from Figure 12.2 illustrates this choice.

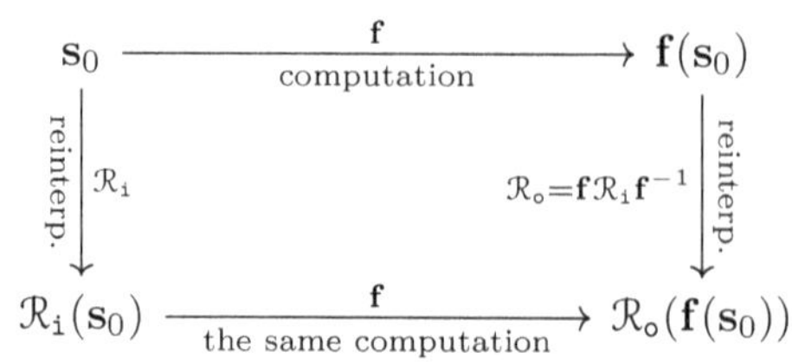

Figure 12.2: We choose $\mathcal{R}_o = \mathbf{f} \circ \mathcal{R}_i \circ \mathbf{f}^{-1}$, so that the program remains the same after the reinterpretation of the input and output data, but it is applied to different input data and gives the appropriate output for that input.

Therefore, if the function $\mathbf{f}$ is invertible, processing some input data can be reinterpreted as processing any other possible input data by applying the same function $\mathbf{f}$. □

General computations are not invertible. An example when the function $\mathbf{f}$ is invertible for all values of the inputs is when the computer is *reversible.* Reversible computers are possible in principle, but the computers available today are not reversible, they lose information. A general purpose reversible computer [11] seems very difficult to construct in practice [137, 206].

However, in our setup we assumed that the input bits were preserved, and that the output bits and the memory bits were all 0 before the computation. This allows us to uniquely recover the initial state from the final state of the computer, even if the computer is not reversible. Since the function $\mathcal{R}_{\mathtt{i}}$ changes only the input data, the same setup applies to $\mathcal{R}_{\mathtt{i}}(\mathbf{s}_0)$, and this initial state can be recovered as well. So the reinterpretation $\mathcal{R}_{\mathtt{o}}$ from equation (12.16) is well defined, and it is indeed able to get the result of the computation on the initial data $\mathcal{R}_{\mathtt{i}}(\mathbf{s}_0)$, even if we think the program was executed only on $\mathbf{s}_0$. Since the reinterpretation $\mathcal{R}_{\mathtt{i}}$ was arbitrary, this result applies to all possible initial states, so the program can be reinterpreted as computing all of them at once.

Remark 12.2. As seen in Remark 12.1, under general assumptions that are usually realized in practice, it is possible to choose $\mathcal{R}_{\mathtt{o}}$ and $\mathcal{R}_{\mathtt{i}}$ as parts of the same reinterpretation. In practice, the computer's state when the computer finishes the computation is different from the state when it's waiting for the input. For example, let the n-th bit be 0 when the program is waiting for the input, and 1 when the computation is done. Then, the reinterpretations $\mathcal{R}_{\mathtt{i}}$ and $\mathcal{R}_{\mathtt{o}}$ have to leave the last bit unchanged. The general reinterpretation $\mathcal{R}$ that unifies $\mathcal{R}_{\mathtt{i}}$ and $\mathcal{R}_{\mathtt{o}}$ can be chosen as

$$\mathcal{R}(\mathbf{x}) = \begin{cases} \mathcal{R}_{\mathtt{i}}(\mathbf{x}) & \text{if the last bit of } \mathbf{x} \text{ is } \mathtt{0} \\ \mathcal{R}_{\mathtt{o}}(\mathbf{x}) & \text{if the last bit of } \mathbf{x} \text{ is } \mathtt{1}. \end{cases} \tag{12.17}$$

12.4 Computing everything at once

What about the computers we normally use, which work in more steps? They perform sequential computations, although in this context "sequential computing" should not be taken as the opposite of "parallel computing", since the focus here is not on the presence or absence of parallelism, but on the fact that computation happens in more steps. As mentioned earlier, usual computers are not reversible. However, in practice it is often common that a program doesn't lose the information in a way that makes it impossible to retrieve the state of the computer prior to the computation from its final state. In addition, computers use an internal time to distinguish each step done by the processor, a *CPU clock*. Then, the states of the computer at different moments of time are guaranteed to be different. Let the current CPU time be stored in c memory bits. Suppose furthermore that during and after the computation the input is kept in the memory, and at the end of the computation the result is also preserved. Therefore, after a sufficiently large number N of steps chosen so that the computation is finished regardless of the input, the result can be found in its memory location. Then, the function $\mathcal{F}$ from equation (5.10) has the form

$$\mathcal{F}(\overbrace{\underbrace{b_1,\ldots,b_{n_\mathrm{i}}}_{\text{input data}},\underbrace{b_{n_\mathrm{i}+1}\ldots,b_{n_\mathrm{i}+n_\mathrm{o}}}_{\text{output data}}}^{\text{first } d \text{ bits}},\overbrace{\underbrace{b_{d+1},\ldots,b_{d+c}}_{\text{clock}},\underbrace{b_{d+c+1},\ldots\ldots,b_n}_{\text{rest of memory}}}^{\text{last } n-d \text{ bits}}). \quad (12.18)$$

These constraints are not very severe, in fact many of the usual programs satisfy them. But being aware of them will make the proof easier and reveal a maximal ambiguity.

Theorem 12.3. The final state of the computation for an input can be reinterpreted as the final state of the computation of the same algorithm for any other input.

Proof. A transition corresponding to a step of a computation has the form

$$\begin{aligned}&\mathcal{F}(\underbrace{b_1,\ldots,b_{n_\mathrm{i}}}_{\text{input data}},\underbrace{b_{n_\mathrm{i}+1},\ldots,b_{n_\mathrm{i}+n_\mathrm{o}}}_{\text{output data}},\ \underbrace{b_{d+1},\ldots,b_{d+c}}_{\text{clock}},\underbrace{b_{n+m+c+1},\cdots}_{\text{rest of memory}})\\ &=(\underbrace{b_1,\ldots,b_{n_\mathrm{i}}}_{\text{input data}},\underbrace{b'_{n_\mathrm{i}+1},\ldots,b'_{n_\mathrm{i}+n_\mathrm{o}}}_{\text{output data}},\ \underbrace{b'_{d+1},\ldots,b'_{d+c}}_{\text{clock}},\underbrace{b'_{n+m+c+1},\cdots}_{\text{rest of memory}}).\end{aligned} \quad (12.19)$$

Let us collect the transitions corresponding to all 2^n possible inputs in a set of histories. Even if not all inputs are accepted by the algorithm, the program will give an error message and halt, but the clock will keep changing.

The 2^n possible initial states form a set of states $\mathcal{S}_0$. Let $\mathcal{S}_j := \mathcal{F}^j(\mathcal{S}_0)$ be the possible states resulting after j steps from a state from $\mathcal{S}_0$. Since the bits from $d+1$ to $d+c$ are the binary representation of j, the intersection of $\mathcal{S}_j$ and $\mathcal{S}_{j'}$ is empty for $j \neq j'$,

$$\mathcal{S}_j \cup \mathcal{S}_{j'} = \varnothing \text{ for } j \neq j'. \quad (12.20)$$

Also, since the first n bits remain unchanged, the functions

$$\mathcal{F}|_{\mathcal{S}_j} \colon \mathcal{S}_j \to \mathcal{S}_{j+1}, \quad (12.21)$$

which are the restrictions of $\mathcal{F}$ to the domains $\mathcal{S}_j$, are bijective for all values of j. Therefore, since $\mathcal{S}_0$ has 2^n elements, each set $\mathcal{S}_j$ has exactly 2^n elements. Since all $\mathcal{S}_j$ are disjoint, the histories do not return to a previous state. Since the functions $\mathcal{F}|_{\mathcal{S}_j}$ are bijective, the histories do not intersect one another, as shown in Figure 12.3.

Then, the permutations of the set $\mathcal{S}_0$ are in one-to-one correspondence with the permutations of the set of histories that preserve the clock. These are in fact automorphisms of the computing system. It follows that, for any two possible inputs of the program, there are at least $(2^n-2)!$ reinterpretations that reinterpret the result of the computation for the first input as the result of the computation for the second input.

Moreover, the resulting transformation of the set $\mathcal{S}_0 \cup \ldots \cup \mathcal{S}_N$ preserves the form of $\mathcal{F}$. Let $s_k \neq s_{k'} \in \mathcal{S}_0$ be the two initial states to be swapped.

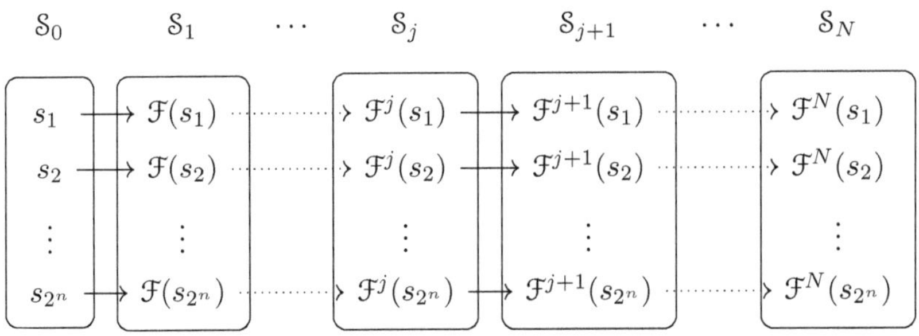

Figure 12.3: Parallel histories corresponding to the possible computations.

Let $\mathcal{R}_0 : \mathcal{S}_0 \to \mathcal{S}_0$ be a permutation of $\mathcal{S}_0$ so that $\mathcal{R}_0(s_k) = s_{k'}$ and $\mathcal{R}_0(s_{k'}) = s_k$. For any $j \in \{0, \ldots, N\}$ define the function $\mathcal{R}_j : \mathcal{S}_j \to \mathcal{S}_j$, $\mathcal{R}_j\left(\mathcal{F}^j(s_l)\right) := \mathcal{F}^j\left(\mathcal{R}_0(s_l)\right)$ for all $s_l \in \mathcal{S}_0$. Then, $\mathcal{R}_j$ is a permutation of $\mathcal{S}_j$ that swaps the states corresponding to the two input states, $\mathcal{R}_j\left(\mathcal{F}^j(s_k)\right) = \mathcal{F}^j(s_{k'})$ and $\mathcal{R}_j\left(\mathcal{F}^j(s_{k'})\right) = \mathcal{F}^j(s_k)$. Since the sets $\mathcal{S}_j$ and $\mathcal{S}_{j'}$ are disjoint for $j \neq j'$, we can define the function $\mathcal{R} : \mathcal{S}_0 \cup \ldots \cup \mathcal{S}_N \to \mathcal{S}_0 \cup \ldots \cup \mathcal{S}_N$ so that its restriction to every $\mathcal{S}_j$ is $\mathcal{R}_j$, which satisfies $\mathcal{R}\left(\mathcal{F}(s)\right) = \mathcal{F}\left(\mathcal{R}(s)\right)$. Therefore, the reinterpretation reinterprets the result of the computation for the input bits of s_k as the result of the computation for the input bits of $\mathcal{R}(s_k)$. This shows that the reinterpretation is an automorphism, so the algorithm is the same, only the inputs and the resulting computations are permuted. □

One may object that the conditions to be satisfied by the kind of program from Theorem 12.3 are too restrictive and no real world program satisfies them. Actually, it is quite common to keep the input data. And even when we think it was deleted, its imprints may remain in the result of the computation. For example, it was shown that the language models currently used for AI are invertible, in the sense that the data they store can, in principle, be used to recover the inputs [132]. Even if the input is not kept and it disappears without leaving a mark, recall that all modern computers have a CPU clock, and since the function $\mathcal{F}$ describes the evolution of the totality of the computer, the clock should be included in its data. In reality the clock bits are split between the system clock and a separate register incremented at any oscillator cycle that generates an interrupt making the CPU change the system time. But together, these components change in time without returning to a previous state. About keeping the input data in the memory, almost any program does this by default. If not, this minor change that can be made easily, and nobody would object that the sentience of an AI should depend on this. All conditions of Theorem 12.3 are usually satisfied, but even if they were not satisfied, the Theorem reaches its purpose, illustrating the extent of the ambiguity of computations.

Chapter 11 shows an experimental verification of Theorem 12.3, that you can verify by yourself.

Observation 12.2. The user has the impression that the computer executes a definite computation, unambiguously. After all, the computer is one of the most precise tools. This impression is due to the following facts:

1. The user interface establishes a particular convention between the user and the computer.
2. The logic gates and circuits are designed to take into account this convention for the inputs and the outputs.

As seen in the previous chapters, the freedom to change the convention between input and output is unlimited, as long as it returns to the initial convention.

12.5 Running all programs at once

Now I will show that it is possible to run a program, and with it, all possible programs using at most a certain number of bits will run simultaneously. I will use, for simplicity but without loss of generality, a one-step computer as in Definition 12.1, but this is possible with a computer working in steps like the regular computers too. Theorem 12.2 shows that, for a one-step programmable computer, the output of a computation performed on an input data set can be used to recover the outputs of the computations performed on the alternative input data sets. This may seem strange, but things can get even stranger:

Theorem 12.4. For any positive integer n, there is a computation that can be reinterpreted simultaneously as all computations that use n bits or fewer.

Proof. This follows by applying Theorem 12.2 to Proposition 12.1. Consider the programmable function $\mathbf{f}$ as in Proposition 12.1, which can compute any Boolean function with n inputs and m outputs. A computation using n bits or fewer is such a Boolean function, where $m = n$. But instead of using the function from equation (12.14), we use a version $\mathbf{f}$ that uses n bits for the input, n bits for the output, and $2^n n$ bits to encode the Boolean functions with n inputs and n outputs,

$$\mathbf{f}(\underbrace{b_1, \ldots, b_{n_1}}_{n \text{ input bits}}, \underbrace{b_{n_1+1} \ldots, b_{2n}}_{n \text{ output bits}}, \underbrace{b_{2n+1}, \ldots\ldots, b_{2n+2^n n}}_{2^n n \text{ program bits}}). \tag{12.22}$$

This function is able to do what the function from equation (12.14) does, but it also satisfies the conditions of Theorem 12.2. We apply Theorem 12.2 to this function, but treating both the n input bits and the $n2^n$ program bits as input data. It follows that the function $\mathbf{f}$ from equation (12.22) describes a computation that can be reinterpreted as all computations on n bits or under, and on all possible input data. □

Remark 12.3. Theorems 12.2 and 12.4 refer to a single Boolean function $\mathbf{f}$. The function $\mathbf{f}$ can stand for an entire computation done in N steps $\mathfrak{F}^N$, but also for every step of the computation. By using a one-step computer in the proof of Theorem 12.4, we didn't lose generality, we just did everything in one step. However, the result applies to computers that work in steps too, since every step is a one-step computation. Therefore a computer working in steps implements at once, along with the computation we attribute to it, many other possible computations. If $\mathfrak{F}$ is as in the proof of Theorem 12.4, the computer will do all many-steps computations on n bits or fewer.

Exercises

Exercise 12.4. Make a Boolean function as in Proposition 12.1, programmable to implement all eight Boolean functions from Table 2.4.

Exercise 12.5. Make a program that runs the programmable Boolean function from Exercise 12.4 for all eight possible inputs simultaneously.

Key points

- The result of any computation is already in the computer's initial state.
- Under general conditions, a computation for some input data can be reinterpreted as computing the result for any other possible input data.
- It is possible to run all computer programs that use n bits or fewer simultaneously, in the same physical process.

Further reading

[182] O.C. Stoica. Does a computer think if no one is around to see it? *philsci-archive:22880*, 2023

[172] O.C. Stoica. Are you a robot? http://youtu.be/kuziE01rh6M&list=PLJzOclJMoIC1pnJIPlmWhGwaDWD04tFza. Accessed April 22, 2026

13

How many digital angels can dance on the point of a needle?

13.1 Ambiguity beyond the user interface

If a program computes the first n decimals of π, one by one, is there, at every step of the computation, a precise number of decimals of π computed up to that time? Are these values present somewhere in the computer?

A programmer may be certain that the answer is yes. She may even think she can prove it to you: she will run the program in debug mode, which allows her to pause the execution at any time and look into the values of the variables. And she will find a definite number of digits already computed, each of them having definite values. The algorithm may be coded completely different in different programs, it may be encoded differently as strings of zeros and ones, it may be implemented completely different on different computers, by different logic circuits in the hardware, but the programmer is certain that the computed digits of π are there somewhere, in some form or another. And she will see those numbers on her display.

However, as seen in Chapter 12, a computer processes, under quite general conditions, all possible interpretations of the bit cells at once, in parallel. We think that only one of these computations happens, and we don't suspect that others happen at the same time, because we rely on the user interface. Even when we watch the variables in the debugger, what we see in fact is the debugger's user interface, and we trust that it provides objective information about the values of the variables. But if what we see in the debugger is there, and if, as we've seen, the possible alternative computations are also there, then all possible values must be there at once, albeit in an encrypted form, so that all of them appear to us as the computation we can see. So either they are all there, or none of them is there, and our minds imagine them based on the convention, which is shared by the user interface.

To see what really happens, we will perform several thought experiments based on the partition problem experiment from Chapter 11. Actually, you can do the first experiment together with a friend.

Experiment 13.1 (Encrypted partition problem). Alice gives Bob two lists of numbers, represented by the vectors $\mathsf{v} = (x_1, \ldots, x_n)^\intercal \in \mathbb{Z}^n$ and $\omega =$

DOI: 10.1201/9781003623373-13

$(w_1, \ldots, w_n)^\intercal \in \{+1, -1\}^n$. As in Chapter 11, ω is used by the program to partition the first list into two sublists having equal totals. The difference is that ω is encrypted, although v is not encrypted. So in fact Bob receives $\omega' = (w'_1, \ldots, w'_n)^\intercal$, an encrypted form of ω. Alice sends the data using a program from her own computer, and her program obtained ω' by encrypting it using $\omega' = \mathbf{S}\omega$, where

$$\mathbf{S} = \begin{pmatrix} s_1 & 0 & \ldots & 0 \\ 0 & s_2 & \ldots & 0 \\ \ldots & \ldots & \ldots & \ldots \\ 0 & 0 & \ldots & s_n \end{pmatrix} \tag{13.1}$$

and $s_1, \ldots, s_n \in \{+1, -1\}^n$. Then she gave the encrypted data to Bob.

At the end, Bob obtains the result $\begin{pmatrix} \sum_{j=1}^n w'_j x_j \\ \omega' \end{pmatrix}$, and he sends it back to Alice's computer. Alice's computer decrypts it by applying the transformation $\mathbf{R}_\omega$ from equation (11.12), and displays the result to Alice. So the decryption is done by

$$\begin{pmatrix} \sum_{j=1}^n w_j x_j \\ \omega \end{pmatrix} = \begin{pmatrix} 1 & \mathsf{v}^\intercal\mathbf{S} - \mathsf{v}^\intercal \\ 0_{n,1} & \mathbf{S} \end{pmatrix} \begin{pmatrix} \sum_{j=1}^n w'_j x_j \\ \omega' \end{pmatrix}. \tag{13.2}$$

Then, Alice can see whether the partition defined by ω' is fair or not by checking whether the first cell of the column vector is 0.

The partition ω can be sent as n bits, and it can be encrypted as $\mathbf{S}\omega$. The decryption is done with a different key $\mathbf{R}_\omega$, as in equation (13.2), because the encrypted data are processed and then the result can be decrypted with a different key (remember the diagrams from Figures 11.3 and 12.2).

If Bob uses the debugger, he will see that the program verifies if the partition defined by ω' is fair, but he doesn't know whether Alice's unencrypted partition ω is fair too. At the same time, Alice knows that the data she sent to Bob was ω, and Bob sent her back a number which, if it's 0, it tells her that ω is fair. She may or may not be aware of the encryption or the communication protocol her computer used, but she knows what she sent and what she received, and what Bob's program does. So did Bob's computer verify ω or ω'? The user interface of Bob's debugger tells him that his program verified the partition ω', and the user interface of Alice's computer tells her that Bob's program verified the partition ω!

This seems to be a contradiction, but it's not, it's just the relativity of information. Bob's program really verified both partitions at once.

In fact, Bob's program verified all possible partitions simultaneously. The next Thought Experiment shows this.

In fact, this experiment can be done in practice as well, but you will need many friends willing to participate (and now you know why I didn't do it).

Thought Experiment 13.1 (Verifying all partitions at once). In this experiment, Bob provides the service from Experiment 13.1, but for more people. The service works as follows:

1. Each client sends to Bob's server a partition $\omega = (w_1, \ldots, w_n)^\intercal \in \{+1, -1\}^n$.

2. The server verifies a partition ω for a fixed list of numbers $\mathsf{v} = (x_1, \ldots, x_n)^\intercal \in \mathbb{Z}^n$ as in equation (11.1). This may seem crazy, but this is the only list of numbers for which the service is offered.

3. The server returns the result to the client, who's computer decrypts it.

4. The client has the option to encrypt the partition, by using a simple `XOR` cipher. The clients receive a program that generates a personalized key. The key is translated into a matrix $\mathbf{S}_\omega$ that has only ± 1 on the diagonal, all its other cells being 0. The client program also computes the decryption key, the matrix $\mathbf{R}_\omega$ from equation (13.2), and applies it to decrypt the result received from the server.

5. The requests from the clients are collected during the day, and during the night they are computed.

6. If it happens that more clients send, after encryption, the same partition ω', the result is computed only once, and sent to each of these clients. This works because even if ω' is the encryption of another partition, it is processed in the exact same way and gives the same result.

Each of the clients sends their own partition ω using a different encryption key $\mathbf{S}$ as in (13.1). For whatever reason, they all want a different partition ω of the same list of numbers $(x_1, \ldots, x_n)$ to be verified. One lucky day, Bob receives 2^n requests from across the world, as in Figure 13.1. These requests come from people who want distinct partitions to be verified, but it happens that they all use distinct encryption keys, and on that day the results of all these distinct encryptions coincided.

This is possible, because whatever partition ω' Bob receives, there are 2^n encryption keys of the form (13.1), and they encrypt distinct values of ω into identical values of ω'. And each of Bob's clients who sent one of the 2^n possible partitions to be verified in encrypted form will think that Bob's program verified their particular ω. So Bob's program can indeed verify all 2^n possible partitions at once!

Moreover, in this extreme example, 2^n user interfaces fix the interpretation in 2^n different ways simultaneously!

Therefore, indeed all computations are performed in parallel. We obtained a situation in which the user interface doesn't fix a unique interpretation, but rather each of the possible 2^n interpretations is fixed by a different user interface. Therefore, Thought Experiment 13.1 refutes the hope that the user interface can make the computation objective by fixing a unique interpretation.

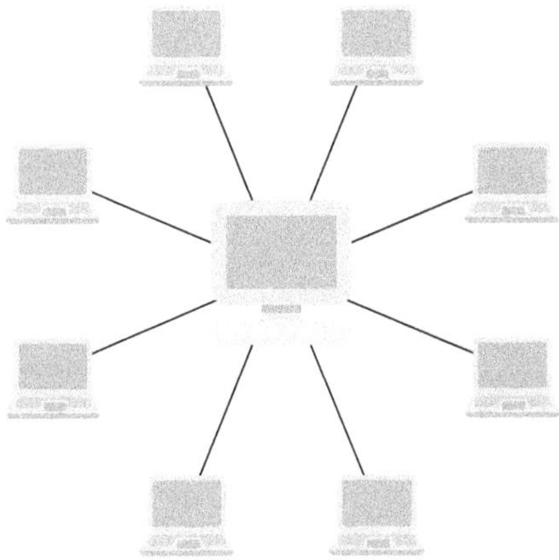

Figure 13.1: Different requests from 2^n clients are computed in a single process.

Implication 13.1. The user interface is insufficient to fix the interpretation.

More thought experiments will come, so I would kindly ask you to think about the following: do you think that, if you would do this experiment in reality, it will give a different result than what you expect from doing it in your imagination?

13.2 Does an AI think if no one is around to see it?

Here is another scenario that proves the relativity of computing.

Thought Experiment 13.2 (Mistaken encryption key)**.** Alice and Bob work for an intelligence agency. As part of their job, they use computers running the program that verifies partitions. But because this work is mysterious and important, to prevent hacking, they use encryption. Alice uses a special hardware key, a small device that, when plugged into the computer, encrypts her keyboard inputs and decrypts the outputs of the computer. Bob's computer runs the same program, and Bob has his own special hardware key, different from Alice's, that does the same on his computer.

When Alice takes a break, she leaves the computer running, but she takes with her the hardware key, as a security measure. Does this alter the computation? As long as there is no new input, the computer operates the same regardless of the presence of the hardware key. But, assuming that the user interface determines an objective interpretation of the computation, does the presence or the absence of the hardware key alter this interpretation?

Alice and her colleague Bob walk into a cafeteria during their lunch break.

They both put their hardware keys on the table. When they leave the cafeteria, Alice accidentally takes Bob's hardware key. She returns to her computer and plugs in Bob's key. If Alice uses the key $\mathbf{S}_A$, and Bob uses the key $\mathbf{S}_B$, where both keys are of the form from (13.1), then when she plugs in Bob's key, she will receive a different but still valid output from her program. If she asked her program to verify if a partition ω is fair for $(x_1, \ldots, x_n) \in \mathbb{Z}^n$, she will receive the answer for the partition $\widetilde{\omega} = \mathbf{S}_B^{-1}\mathbf{S}_A\omega$.

This raises a question: what partition did Alice's computer verify during the break, when no key was inserted? Was it ω or $\widetilde{\omega}$?

One may think that the program verified the partition ω, and the result was switched in the last minute and replaced with the result for $\widetilde{\omega}$.

So let me put this differently. Suppose that during Alice's lunch break a spy from an enemy agency came uninvited and tried to see what computation was Alice's computer doing. The spy knew that the computer was verifying a partition for the list of n numbers, but he didn't know which partition. And given that $\mathbf{S}_A$ could be any possible key of the form (13.1), the computer could as well be verifying any of the 2^n possible partitions.

Thought Experiments 13.1 and 13.2 exclude any hope that information and computation as such have an objective interpretation, even with the help of the user interface. They do this in the most extreme possible way, by showing that each of the 2^n possible assignments of bit values can have different interpretations.

Observation 13.1. Despite the fact that the user interface ensures that the user accesses a unique computation, it can't ensure that a computation takes place inside the computer independent of any user and of any convention.

13.3 Can a computer think of a number?

What if we do a thought experiment with a much more complex program than the one from Chapter 11, for example an artificial mind?

Let us consider that a computer runs a very advanced Artificial Intelligence, so advanced that anyone who chats with it would believe it is conscious. I will show that there is no unambiguous way to answer the question

Question 13.1. What number is the AI thinking about?

There is a very easy way to see that there is no unambiguous answer to Question 13.1. The number the AI is thinking about must be stored in some of its bit cells. But since there is no unambiguous interpretation of those bit cells, there is no unambiguous thought of a number. Q.E.D.

But wait, what if our reinterpretation of the bits merely scrambles the interpretation of the AI, but the scrambled AI thinks about the same number? Maybe that number doesn't change, regardless of how we change the interpretation of what computation the computer is doing.

To verify this, I will use an upgrade of Thought Experiment 13.1, with an AI as the extra ingredient.

Thought Experiment 13.3 (Think of a number). As in Thought Experiment 13.1, Bob provides a service of partition verifications, but this time there is an AI on the server.

1. The AI itself runs the program with the input ω, and obtains

$$\begin{pmatrix} 1 & \mathsf{v}^\intercal \\ 0_{n,1} & \mathbf{I}_n \end{pmatrix} \begin{pmatrix} 0 \\ \omega \end{pmatrix} = \begin{pmatrix} \mathsf{v}^\intercal \omega \\ \omega \end{pmatrix} = \begin{pmatrix} \sum_{j=1}^{n} w_j x_j \\ \omega \end{pmatrix}. \tag{13.3}$$

2. The AI reads the result from the right hand side of equation (13.3). We've already seen that a computation that verifies whether ω is a fair partition can be reinterpreted as a computation doing the same for any other partition. Since the AI itself uses the program and reads its input, the input determines what happens next with the AI.

3. A reinterpretation of the program induces a reinterpretation of the AI, which can be very different depending on the number found by the AI. The AI may have some secondary thoughts triggered by the resulting numbers, for example seven reminds the AI of Snow White, five reminds it of "The fifth element" with Bruce Willis, six reminds it of "The sixth sense" with Bruce Willis, three reminds it of D'Artagnan, four reminds it of D'Artagnan, ten reminds it of the story of the ten men crossing a river, *etc.*

4. The encryption affects only the input data of the partition program, but since this region of the memory interacts with other regions of memory, the decryption key applies to the entire program, including the AI, so it takes into account all the ramifications of the AI thinking about the number.

5. The clients encrypt the input and decrypt the output like in Thought Experiment 13.1, each of them using a different key, corresponding to a reinterpretation of the partition ω.

6. The clients receive the entire memory of the server, including the part containing the AI, and the full length decryption key.

We will assume that the entire program, including the AI itself, satisfies the conditions of Theorem 12.3, page 152, just like the partition verifier. The AI receives the requests, runs the program within its own memory to verify the partition, and sends to the client a copy of the entire final state, including the output of the partition program and a copy of the AI's own state.

For each reinterpretation $\widetilde{\omega}$ of ω, there is a different interpretation of the AI that "thinks" about the partition $\widetilde{\omega}$ and the corresponding output $\sum_{j=1}^{n} \widetilde{w}_j x_j$, where $(\widetilde{w}_1, \ldots, \widetilde{w}_n)^\intercal = \widetilde{\omega}$. Each one of these reinterpreted AIs "sees" different numbers (see Figure 13.2).

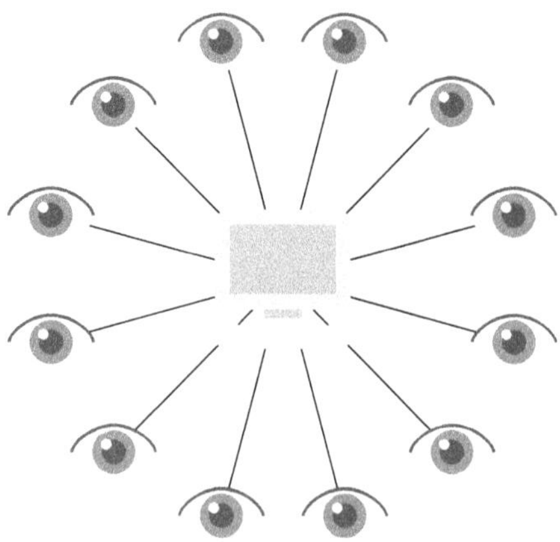

Figure 13.2: Each AI encodes in fact 2^n AIs "thinking" about different numbers.

Moreover, they can all be extracted from a single computation that involves the AI and the partition verification program. This requires very long keys and a huge computational power, but luckily this is a thought experiment, so we don't have to worry about this. It is sufficient to show that such a key exists in principle, and this was done by Theorem 12.3, and also verified on a simple example in Chapter 11. Therefore, the answer to Question 13.1 is undefined, because the number the AI is thinking about depends on the interpretation.

More technically, the decryption key must be computed based on the encryption key seen as a function that changes the relevant bits of the input and leaves the other bits on the server unchanged, including those of the AI. This function has the matrix form

$$\mathbf{S}_{\omega,\text{total}} = \begin{pmatrix} \mathbf{S}_\omega & \mathbf{0} \\ \mathbf{0} & \mathbf{I} \end{pmatrix}, \tag{13.4}$$

with $\mathbf{S}_\omega$ from equation (11.10) and $\mathbf{I}$ the identity matrix with as many rows and columns as the remaining bits, so that $\mathbf{S}_{\omega,\text{total}}$ reinterprets only the bits for the input of the partition program.

Then, the decryption key is, as it follows from Figure 12.3,

$$\mathbf{R}_{\omega,\text{total}} = \mathcal{F}^N|_{\mathcal{S}_0} \mathbf{S}_{\omega,\text{total}} \left(\mathcal{F}^N|_{\mathcal{S}_0}\right)^{-1}, \tag{13.5}$$

where, since the conditions of Theorem 12.3 are satisfied, the function

$$\mathcal{F}^N|_{\mathcal{S}_0} \colon \mathcal{S}_0 \to \mathcal{S}_N, \tag{13.6}$$

is invertible, so the function $\left(\mathcal{F}^N|_{\mathcal{S}_0}\right)^{-1} : \mathcal{S}_N \to \mathcal{S}_0$ is defined and invertible too.

This means that all possible histories in which the AI computes the result and lets its mind wandering about it happen simultaneously. Each of them is encrypted with a different key, but by the Laws of Computer Science, they are equally authentic computations. Also, given how we use conventions and bit inversions in the design of the logic circuits, what computation isn't encrypted?

So there is no unique, objective fact that the computer thinks of a particular number. At the same time, the AI can be equally interpreted as thinking of other numbers or of something totally different, and its parallel minds are wandering, triggered by the different numbers they see, in completely different ways.

Therefore, Thought Experiment 13.3 proves that there is no unique answer to Question 13.1, which asks what number the AI is thinking about.

Implication 13.2. A computer cannot think of a number unambiguously.

We think that there is only one answer because we assume that there is an objective way to assign bit values to the bit cells, but we have seen that this is a misconception. Since all these 2^n interpretations apply to the same physical state of the computer, this proves the ambiguity.

13.4 All experiences at once

Observation 13.2. Thought Experiment 13.3 discusses only the question whether the AI can have definite thoughts about other things, in this case about a number. It says nothing about feelings, qualia and so on.

There is a reason why I limited the discussion, up to this moment, to thinking about numbers. The ability to think about things is sometimes called *access consciousness* [16], or *intentionality*, or *aboutness*. Emotions, feelings, qualia, "what it's like", are aspects of so-called *phenomenal consciousness*. Some authors, who call themselves *"illusionists"* think that only access consciousness is real, and deny the existence of phenomenal consciousness, arguing that it is an illusion within our access consciousness [44, 46, 48, 66, 102]. Briefly put it, they claim that you don't actually experience qualia, you only think that you experience it.

Since many researchers and philosophers consider themselves illusionists, I limited the range of Thought Experiment 13.3 to access consciousness. By doing this, I avoided the accusation that I am appealing to a kind of consciousness whose existence is denied by illusionists even in humans, and focused on refuting the kind of consciousness even they won't deny. Therefore, the result is about that aspect of consciousness that even illusionists don't deny to humans.

But now it's easy to show that, if we believe that the AI can also have feelings or emotions, then these must be undefined as well.

Implication 13.3. There is no unambiguous way to associate experiences of qualia like colors and emotions to the AI.

Proof. Considering Thought Experiment 13.3, let us assume that the AI can experience feelings, colors, sounds, and so on, the way humans can. Or at least, if we are to believe illusionism, to have the same illusions of experiencing them that humans have. Then, the AI may be happy if the partition turns out to be fair, and disappointed if it turns out to be unfair. The AI may also visualize, in its simulated world, a green symbol ✓ in case the partition is fair, and a red symbol ✗ if it is unfair, as in Figure 11.1. The AI can even add a personal note about the resulting numbers, something that those numbers triggered it to think about. For example "Seven reminds me of Snow White", "Three reminds me of D'Artagnan", "Ten reminds me of the story of the ten men crossing a river", *etc.* The decryption key can take into account all the ramifications of the AI thinking about the number. The decrypted AIs would then be very different, and have completely different experiences. It follows that the AI's qualia are undefined. □

Therefore, this result about the AI applies to both access consciousness and to phenomenal consciousness.

In 1814, Laplace said that if a superintelligent "demon" with unlimited capacity to compute would know the positions and the momenta of all particles, it would be able to predict precisely what will happen to the particles in the future [90]. But, in this situation, even if Laplace's demon would know the state of the server down to every particle, he would still be unable to read unambiguously the number the AI is thinking about, nor the musings and phenomenal experiences of the AI triggered by that number.

13.5 Alternative histories

Theorem 12.3 tells us that any interpretation of a computation is a computation. We've seen that the number of possible interpretations grows exponentially with the number of bits. Any interpretation of a program is akin to an encryption, and there is no difference between running a program in encrypted form, compared to running it unencrypted. And since the idea of an unencrypted program is relative to a particular convention, to someone who doesn't know the convention it will all appear as encrypted. Moreover, as seen in Chapter 3, in both theory and practice the convention can change on the fly as needed, to allow the same logic circuits to do more different tasks. This relativity of computation applies as well to Artificial Intelligence, which is itself a program. There are exponentially many ways to interpret the "thought processes" and the "sentient experiences" of the AI. According to Computer Science, all of these ways are on equal footing.

Let us summarize this direct consequence of the Laws of Computer Science:

Observation 13.3. If consciousness is purely computational, then an "encrypted" AI has the same conscious experiences as the original AI.

For us, humans interacting with the AI, once we assign an interpretation, the computation goes as expected. After all, the entire hardware and software industry is adhering to the same interpretations.

But what happens if we find an alien piece of hardware, perfectly functional but not connected to output and input devices that could give us hints as to what convention to assign Boolean values to the bit cells composing that piece of hardware the aliens use? We have seen that even a simple logic gate like the one studied by Alice and Bob and their friends admits eight different and equally valid interpretations.

And if the processor of an alien robot admits exponentially many interpretations of its functionality, doesn't it follow that an AI produced by humans has the same ambiguity, and we think there is no ambiguity just because we are forced to adhere to a uniform convention simply because the hardware and software industry uses it? The following Thought Experiment will show once more that this ambiguity is very real.

Thought Experiment 13.4 (Alternative histories)**.** Consider a computer running an AI that satisfies the conditions of Theorem 12.3. The computer contains a large amount of data on a hard drive, used by the AI to learn. Theorem 12.3 tells us that any possible data that could be fed to the AI can be obtained by a reinterpretation of the data bits. This means that there are exponentially many different processes by which the AI learns, all taking place in parallel.

Suppose we loaded the hard drive with our own history. This is used as an input by the AI to learn about the world. If the data on the hard drive are reinterpreted, in most of the cases the result will be noise. But some reinterpretations lead to histories that make sense. One of them is the history of the Harry Potter Universe as imagined by J.K. Rowling. Another one is the history of J.R.R. Tolkien's "The Lord of the Rings". Another one may be the history of the "Star Trek" Universe, another one of "Star Wars" and so on. But there will be a gazillion different interpretations that look like the history of our world, with small differences, like for example that some war was won by somebody else than in reality, or some discovery was made by another person, and so on. And the same would be true of the Harry Potter history and all other fictional universes. And most of the histories that make sense logically would be like nothing a human ever imagined. Therefore, on the same computer running an AI there are exponentially many different AIs, resulting from different possible alternative learning processes, "living" in their minds in completely different universes.

Moreover, each of these AIs can, in principle, be decoded with the appropriate key, just like the experiment from Chapter 11 demonstrates. So we can in principle interact with each one of them. This would be computationally very expensive, at least as expensive as developing each of these AIs from scratch. But the point is that the "thinking process" and the "sentient experience" that we may attribute to an AI takes place, in parallel but completely differently, and in completely different worlds, for all other possible AIs.

Implication 13.4. An AI trained in the history of our world can appear as being trained in the history of another logically possible world. For example, the AI can appear as being trained in the history of the Star Wars Universe, the Star Trek Universe, the Harry Potter Universe, the Lord of the Rings Universe, the Marvel Universe, the DC Universe, *etc.*

This may seem surprising, and even disturbing, especially if we believe that there is sentient experience associated with the computation. But isn't this the consequence of Computer Science itself?

13.6 Erasing the history

Another surprising implication of Computer Science follows if we combine Thought Experiments 13.2 and 13.4.

Thought Experiment 13.5 (Erasing the history)**.** Suppose that a client uses the server from Thought Experiment 13.4, to compute the result for a partition.

But this time the AI was instructed to train itself with the history stored on the hard drive, by decrypting it using a key that depends on the number occurring in the computation. A key, corresponding to the partition ω_0, would reveal to the AI that the hard drive contains the history of our world, another key, corresponding to the partition ω, that it contains the history of the Harry Potter Universe, and yet another key, corresponding to the partition ω', that it contains the history of the Marvel Universe.

The client requests the verification of the partition ω, encrypted as ω_0. But then, instead of decrypting the result by using the decryption key $\mathbf{R}_{\omega,\text{total}}$, it decrypts it by using another decryption key $\mathbf{R}_{\omega',\text{total}}$, corresponding to another partition $\omega' \neq \omega$ (just like in Thought Experiment 13.2). The decryption of the result will, of course, correspond to the computation done for ω', as in Figure 13.3. It will contain completely different musings of the AI, as if this was what happened all along.

Which of the histories that could be read by reinterpreting the data on the hard drive really happened? Was it the AI knowing the history of our world, or that of Harry Potter's, or that of the Marvel Universe?

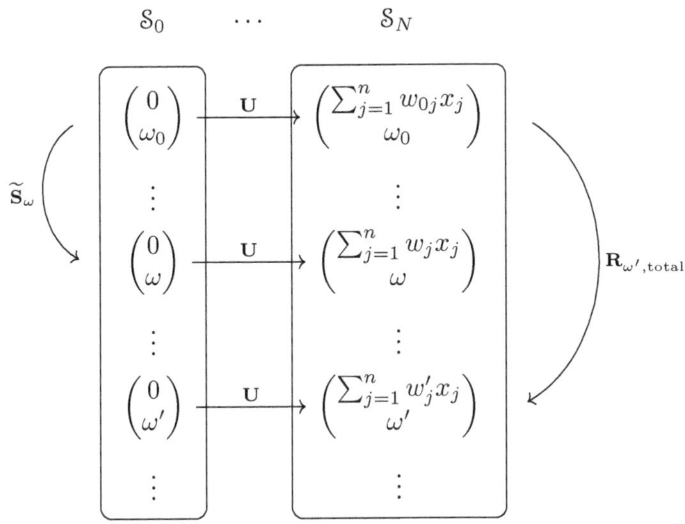

Figure 13.3: Changing the decryption key erases the already happened history of the AI corresponding to the computation for ω and replaces it retroactively with a history corresponding to the computation for ω'.

If no client would have requested the verification of any partition, and the AI would have still verified the partition ω_0, then the history it learned would have been the history of our world. But a client did request the verification of the partition ω encrypted as ω_0, so if that client would have used the decryption key for the partition ω, she would find out that the AI was trained in the history of the Harry Potter Universe. But since the client used a different decryption key, the one for the partition ω', she found out that the AI was trained in the history of the Marvel Universe.

Apparently, the history of the AI, with all its reported thoughts and experiences, was erased and replaced with another one. So the thoughts of the AI in the time interval between encryption and decryption are undefined, because the encryption predicts different thoughts than those revealed by the decryption.

Note that while the past history that we attribute to the AI is erased and replaced, the computer's physical history remains unchanged. From the point of view of the partition ω_0, the AI was trained in our history.

Implication 13.5. The AI's past history can be erased, replaced, and restored "retroactively", depending on the interpretation.

Pretty Orwellian, isn't it [45]?

Exercises

Exercise 13.1. If you didn't carefully do the Thought Experiments in this chapter, do them now. Apply Computer Science to understand what they show, to refute or confirm them.

Key points

- Experiments can show that the computation depends on the user interface. The user interface can be changed so that it appears to show that the computation was done for any of the possible inputs.
- There is no objective, unambiguous truth in the claim that the computer can think of a particular number.
- If an AI would be sentient, myriads of AIs with completely different sentient experiences would coexist in the same physical process that we call computation.
- If an AI would be sentient, we could change its past history retroactively by changing the user interface.

Further reading

[182] O.C. Stoica. Does a computer think if no one is around to see it? *philsci-archive:22880*, 2023

[172] O.C. Stoica. Are you a robot? http://youtu.be/kuziE01rh6M&list=PLJzOclJMoIC1pnJIPlmWhGwaDWD04tFza. Accessed April 22, 2026

14

Uncanny triviality

14.1 Computer's ambiguity and triviality arguments

Several philosophers of mind noticed the existence of an ambiguity in associating computations to physical processes. Theorem 12.3 can be understood as a variant of the philosophers' *triviality argument.* I think the triviality argument was not sufficiently appreciated, since many philosophers of mind avoid confronting it by using different notions of computation, without acknowledging that such "accounts" of computation don't comply with Computer Science. I don't imply that mind should be a computation as in Computer Science, and I hope it was clear by now that in this book I make the case for the opposite. But misunderstanding or redefining "computation" without acknowledging it may be the main reason for the persistent belief, which seems dominant nowadays, that mind is a computation.

In its simplest form, the triviality argument claims that almost every physical system implements every *finite state machine* (FSM) [118, 145, 158, 58]. A FSM is a computational model that is just a discrete dynamical system with a finite number of states. That is, it's a system that can be in a finite number of states, that after a finite time interval transitions from one state to another according to some rules. This is not that restrictive, since any Turing machine with finite length tape, or any physically realizable computer, are finite state machines.

Let me reproduce Lycan's triviality argument from 1981 [118], page 39:

> Suppose a transparent plastic pail of spring water is sitting in the sun. At the micro level, a vast seething complexity of things are going on: convection currents, frantic breeding of bacteria and other minuscule life forms, and so on. These things in turn require even more frantic activity at the molecular level to sustain them. Now is all this activity not complex enough that, simply by chance, it might realize a human program for a brief period (given suitable correlations between certain micro-events and the requisite input-, output-, and state-symbols of the program)? And if so, must the functionalist not conclude that the water in the pail briefly constitutes the body of a conscious being, and has thoughts and feelings and so on? Indeed, virtually any physical object under any conditions has enough activity going on within it at the molecular level that, if Hinck-

DOI: 10.1201/9781003623373-14

> fuss is right about the pail of water, the functionalist quickly slips into a panpsychism that does seem obviously absurd

Searle's version is the following ([159], pages 208–209)

> On the standard textbook definition of computation, it is hard to see how to avoid the following results:
>
> 1. For any object there is some description of that object such that under that description the object is a digital computer.
> 2. For any program and for any sufficiently complex object, there is some description of the object under which it is implementing the program.
>
> Thus for example the wall behind my back is right now implementing the Wordstar program, because there is some pattern of molecule movements that is isomorphic with the formal structure of Wordstar. But if the wall is implementing Wordstar, then if it is a big enough wall it is implementing any program, including any program implemented in the brain.

Even earlier than both of them, philosopher Hilary Putnam remarked that even a rock gradually warmed up by the sunlight is able to implement any computer program [145], see Figure 14.1. The idea is that, if a computing system runs a computation by evolving in a succession of distinct states, since there is no restriction on what these states can be physically, any physical system going through a succession of distinct physical states can implement any computation. This is called the *triviality argument.* He considered a rock sitting in the sunlight, slowly increasing its temperature. Different temperatures mean different states in which the rock can be, and the successive change from one state to another due to the increase in temperature can be used to represent a succession of states in the computation. Putnam presented the triviality argument in the form of a Theorem ([145], p. 121)

> Every ordinary open system is a realization of every abstract finite automaton.

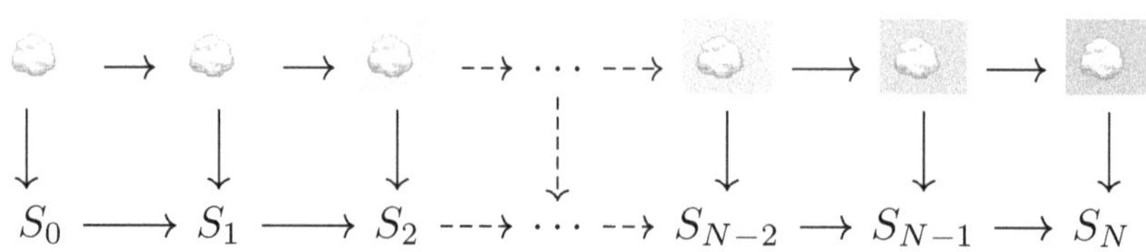

Figure 14.1: Putnam's rock sitting in the sun is gradually warmed up, implementing any computation of a FSM [145].

Putnam showed that an open physical system whose history doesn't return to a previous state during a time interval $[0, \mathcal{T}]$ implements, in that interval, all computations done by any FSM without inputs and outputs. Since Putnam's proof takes three pages, let me sketch a simpler proof, but for a sufficiently isolated physical system described as a dynamical system $(\mathcal{S}, \mu, \mathbb{R})$.

Proposition 14.1. Any computation of a FSM is implemented by any physical system that changes its state without repeating it during a time interval.

Proof. Let $S_0 \mapsto \ldots \mapsto S_N$ be a computation of a FSM, to be shown to be implemented by the physical system. The computation $S_0 \mapsto \ldots \mapsto S_N$ is itself a FSM with a single computation. Its states are allowed to repeat. Let $f : [0, \mathcal{T}] \to \mathcal{S}$ represent the state of the physical system as a function of time during a time interval $[0, \mathcal{T}]$ in which the system's states don't repeat. Without loss of generality, we can choose $\mathcal{T}$ so that $N \leq \mathcal{T} < N + 1$, *e.g.* by using a different measurement unit for time. Recall that $f([0, \mathcal{T}])$ is a set of states from $\mathcal{S}$, the *image* of the function f. Since during the time interval $[0, \mathcal{T}]$ the physical system doesn't return to a previous state, for every $s \in f([0, \mathcal{T}])$ there is a unique time $t \in [0, \mathcal{T}]$ so that $f(t) = s$, given by $t = f^{-1}(s)$. Define the function $\alpha : f([0, \mathcal{T}]) \to \{S_1, \ldots, S_N\}$,

$$\alpha(s) := S_{\lfloor f^{-1}(s) \rfloor}, \tag{14.1}$$

where $\lfloor t \rfloor$ is the integer part of t expressed in our measurement unit. In equation (14.1), $S_{\lfloor f^{-1}(s) \rfloor} \in \{S_0, \ldots, S_N\}$. Then, α realizes an implementation of the computation $S_0 \mapsto \ldots \mapsto S_N$. □

The mapping is not one-to-one, since different states of the physical system will be mapped into the same state of the FSM. But this is all right, because any physical computing system has the same property. For example, a capacitor implementing a memory cell of a computer may be charged or discharged, but it is never 100% or 0% charged, so the same bit is represented by an infinite number of possible physical states. So it is perfectly possible that the physical system doesn't repeat its state, but it implements the same state of a FSM repeatedly.

The implementation by a physical system of a single computation is called the *simple mapping account* of computation [77, 167]. It was argued that a computation is not really a computation, unless the system implements, for different initial states, the computations done with the same algorithm for all possible initial data. Such computations that didn't happen but could have happened if the input data were different are called *counterfactual.* This requirement of counterfactuality seems artificial and problematic: why would a system do a computation, or be conscious, only if there are alternative possible computations, even if they are never realized? Does it have the "superpower of knowing the alternative histories", even though they didn't happen?

In any case, while Proposition 14.1, in this form or in the form given by Putnam, doesn't satisfy the counterfactuality condition, Proposition 14.2 and Theorem 12.3 satisfy it, as shown in Figure 12.3.

But it was trivial to extend Putnam's triviality argument to include counterfactuals. We can choose a property of the physical system that is constant along a history, but can be different for different histories of the system. It could be a conserved quantity. Chalmers argued that a system that doesn't return to a previous state and has a conserved property that can take sufficiently many distinct values, can implement all computations done by any FSM [28]. In the case of Putnam's rock sitting in the sunlight, if the rock had a different position, for example if it was slightly rotated, this can be said to correspond to another computation that could happen. Chalmers' intention was in fact to avoid the triviality argument, but he improved it before trying to refute it in the same article, by arguing that the structure of the computing system should constrain the ways its processes are understood as computations. We will return to his proposal. The proof is similar to Putnam's, all we have to do is to highlight sufficiently many alternative histories of the physical system and map them to the computations of the FSM. In the proof of Theorem 12.3, the conserved properties are the input data themselves.

Godfrey-Smith improved the triviality argument for FSMs with inputs and outputs by arguing that, by changing the *transducer layer* (the interface between the system and its environment) of a physical system implementing a FSM, this can exhibit a different FSM within the same physical system [77]. He argued that every sufficiently complex system can be turned into a computing system with the same computations as a human conscious being by connecting it properly to an appropriate (human-like) transducer layer. Moreover, he argued that using different transducer layers will get different human-like conscious beings. He concluded that functionalism in its common form implies that "Any sufficiently complex system has non-marginal mental properties". He argued that strengthening the constraints in the functional approaches would help avoid this triviality. But there is no proof that this is sufficient to achieve uniqueness. We will return to this in Chapter 20.

One may object to the triviality argument by claiming that only the physical systems made of parts that have physical properties taking the values 0 or 1 count as computing systems, and these properties represent the processed data. I think this was sorted out already in Section 3.5, Corollary 3.1, but let's see how this applies to the triviality argument.

Proposition 14.2. Consider an algorithm whose computations consist of states encoding n bit values $(b_1(t), b_2(t), \ldots, b_n(t))$, where $t \in \{0, 1, \ldots, N\}$ index the steps of the computation. Consider a physical system composed of at least a classical particle that doesn't repeat its states during a time interval $[0, \mathcal{T}]$, for 2^n possible initial states. Then, the physical system implements the algorithm, for any possible initial bit values, so that the bit values are obtained as values of physical properties of that particle.

Proof. Recall from Section 3.5 that a single physical particle has a position $(x(t), y(t), z(t))$ and a momentum $(p_x(t), p_y(t), p_z(t))$, so its state can be represented as a point in $\mathbb{R}^6$. Since the state doesn't repeat during the time interval

$[0, \mathcal{T}]$, the path of the system in $\mathbb{R}^6$ doesn't intersect with itself. Consider 2^n different initial states so that the resulting paths don't intersect each other during $[0, \mathcal{T}]$. As in Proposition 14.1, we can choose the unit of time so that $\{0, 1, \ldots, N\} \subset [0, \mathcal{T}]$. The states of the particle are represented as distinct points in $\mathbb{R}^6$ for all $t \in \{0, 1, \ldots, N\}$ and all of the 2^n possible initial conditions. Let's denote each of these points by $s(\mathcal{B}, t)$, where $\mathcal{B} = \overline{b_1(0)b_2(0)\ldots b_n(0)}$ is a natural number whose base 2 representation is given by the bits of the input data. Because the paths don't intersect, $s(\mathcal{B}, t) \neq s(\mathcal{B}', t')$ whenever $t \neq t'$ or $\mathcal{B} \neq \mathcal{B}'$. Let $b_j(\mathcal{B}, t)$ denote the j-th bit at the t-th step of the computation for the input $\mathcal{B}$. For each $j \in \{1, 2, \ldots, n\}$, we define a property as the function

$$f_j(s) = \begin{cases} b_j(\mathcal{B}, t) & \text{if } s = s(\mathcal{B}, t) \\ \text{other values} & \text{in all other cases} \end{cases} \tag{14.2}$$

These n functions define physical properties of the system implementing the computation, so that the values $(f_1(t), f_2(t), \ldots, f_n(t))$ of these physical properties equal the bit values $(b_1(t), b_2(t), \ldots, b_n(t))$ from each step t of the computation. □

Note the immense freedom to choose the physical properties representing the bits. This is due to the fact that in Classical Physics any physical property is a function of the particles' positions and momenta, and any such function represents a physical property, albeit an obscure one.

In the proof of Proposition 14.2, we chose the physical properties as properties of a single particle. The proof also works if we represent each bit as a property of a different particle or of a composite system, like a real world memory cell.

You may object that you expected the physical properties to be more active, to be the reason why the computing machines work as they work. But whatever you expect bits to be physically in the computer, they never work alone. In fact, the whole set-up exists to take care of the states to which we attribute Boolean values. For example, if we encode the Boolean values as the "charged" and "discharged" states of a capacitor, there are circuits whose only role is to supervise the capacitors and make sure they don't discharge or charge by themselves or by accident. One can't isolate the active elements of a computer so easily, and to the extent that we can, the properties we use to represent bits don't exactly play the most active role in the computer.

Observation 14.1 (Pancomputationalism)**.** Every changing physical system implements every program.

Argument. As far as we know from Physics

1. Any physical system can be in different states.
2. Any physical system undergoes continuous change.

Even if there are jumps, as it is sometimes believed to be the case in Quantum Mechanics, between the jumps there is a time interval $[0, \mathfrak{T}]$ of continuous change, when the Schrödinger equation applies. Then, the path of the system in the state space is continuous during the time interval $[0, \mathfrak{T}]$. It is always possible to cut $\mathfrak{T}$ down to some positive value so that the path of the system in the state space doesn't intersect with itself. This allows the implementation of any computation of a FSM.

To implement the computations for all possible inputs of the FSM, note that continuous change between two states implies infinitely many different intermediary states. Therefore, any physical system can be in infinitely many different states. Then, we can choose the initial state of the system in infinitely many ways, so that the resulting paths in the state space don't cross each other during $[0, \mathfrak{T}]$. The proof of Proposition 14.2 can now be adapted to these general settings, proving the claim. □

Most of the time the triviality argument is simply ignored. According to Godfrey-Smith ([77], p. 274),

> Given the threat that such arguments pose, it is surprising how little they have been discussed, especially as the mainstream functionalist literature does not use accounts of the realization of functional structures that make it clear that triviality problems do not arise. Many accounts of realization used by functionalists are so schematic that it is uncertain how these problems are handled.

But, as modest as it was, the debate that took place was important in shaping and extending the triviality argument.

Nevertheless, let us face potential objections.

14.2 Objections to triviality

Objection 14.1. How do Theorems 12.3 and 16.1 address the counterfactuality objection against the triviality argument?

Reply 14.1. If the requirement of counterfactuality matters, since Theorems 12.3 and 16.1 establish an automorphism of the computing system for all possible inputs of the implemented algorithm, they include the counterfactuals. The proof is based precisely on reinterpreting as counterfactual histories what the convention behind the user interface sells to us as "factual history".

Another objection to the triviality argument was that the FSMs involved are not general, because they don't have inputs and outputs.

Objection 14.2. In Theorems 12.3 and 16.1, the computations don't have inputs and outputs.

Reply 14.2. Interaction with the environment definitely played an essential role in the development of our minds, but can't a brain in a vat, without inputs and outputs, have a mind? If we believe that a computer can think, we should also believe that it is able to think between inputs as well.

In any case, Theorems 12.3 and 16.1 can be easily extended to computers that take inputs during the time relevant to the proof, by pre-recording them in its memory. A simple example is to use a computer program that allows the user to record a *macro*. The user starts the record, then performs various operations, which are inputs, and at the end stops the record. Then, the user can play the recorded macro, and the computer will do the same operations again. The user can, in principle, record very sophisticated commands, say all the input commands given during a full day. Then, the next day, the user can make the computer do the same as in the previous day, *as if the user inputs data and commands in real time*, but without actually providing those inputs again. And the computer can of course display the outputs. Therefore, the existence or absence of inputs and outputs doesn't affect at all the results.

But even if we allow inputs and outputs effectively, this wouldn't change the ambiguity. When we input data, we just change the state of the computer, but this doesn't make its interpretation to be less conventional, it doesn't prevent its reinterpretability.

Suppose that we add more restrictions to what counts as a computation. For example, Chalmers attempted to avoid the triviality argument by requiring the states of the computing systems to have more structure, so that each state of both the computation and the implementation to consist of more components [27, 28, 31]. Even with this constraint, he admitted the following "Can a given system implement more than one computation? Yes" ([31], p. 334). Another proposal is the *mechanistic account* of computation, in which the properties of the system matter, even though they can be implemented by multiple different systems [142]. Such proposals are referred to as "accounts of computation" [147, 37], although, as we have seen, they are not accounts of what a computation is in Computer Science, they are plainly redefinitions of computation.

Unless such additional constraints contradict Computer Science, they can't contradict Theorem 12.3 and its implications. Reinterpretations like those from the proof are used practically everywhere in hardware manufacturing to optimize the circuits, in software development, in cryptography, and of course in the very notions of Turing equivalence and universality. Therefore, even if one may argue that Theorems 12.3 and 16.1 and the implications are variants of the triviality argument, they overlap perfectly on what computers currently do.

I discuss the option of violating Substructure-Independence in Chapter 20 and [180, 181].

Objection 14.3. According to "The Routledge Handbook of the Computational Mind" [167], the usual definition of implementation (Definition 10.3 in this book, "M" in the following quote from Sprevak [167]) is problematic:

> One might wonder why we cannot simply accept that computational implementation is trivial. M has other virtues: it is simple, clear, explanatory, and makes the truth of claims about computational implementation objective. Perhaps these virtues are worth the cost of accepting that implementation is trivial.
>
> However, M would remain problematic for at least three reasons:
>
> 1. M's violation of extensional adequacy needs explanation.
> 2. Combined with computational functionalism, M entails panpsychism.
> 3. M drains computational explanations in the sciences of their power.

Here, "violation of extensional adequacy" means that we can interpret in different ways as a computation what a physical system does. "Computational functionalism" is the thesis that mind is computational. "Panpsychism" is the thesis that mental qualities are everywhere, practically in all things. Sprevak gives some serious counterarguments to M, and so to your Definition 10.3.

Reply 14.3. Regardless how unsatisfactory M (and Definition 10.3) may be, it is at the basis of Computer Science, and of the design of computers and computer programs. We may not like it, but it is what it is. "Reason 1" from the above quote is true, but it is not a problem, as long as we don't lose track of the conventions we are employing when using a computer. "Reason 1" is indeed a problem for the expectation that computations are objective features of the physical systems. "Reason 2" doesn't really reject M or Definition 10.3, but rather it shows a problem for the belief that mind is just a computation, so it rejects computational functionalism. As for the third reason, Sprevak adds immediately after that quote

> All of these considerations have some force, but I will argue that the third consideration is the most significant.

We may worry that the drainage of power from sciences mentioned in "Reason 3" happens, but it doesn't. Consider for example the immense amount of computations involved at the analysis of the data from the Large Hadron Collider just to validate the discovery of the Higgs boson. Any doubt that somehow we misread the results of the computations by using a reinterpretation of the data would indeed make science powerless. And yet, we trust the results, because in computations we don't rely only on Definition 10.3, we remove the ambiguity by conventions, and we have tools to maintain these conventions: we rely on hardware specifications, software conventions, user interfaces, and manuals for designers, programmers, and users. This removes the ambiguity for practical applications of Computer Science. But it can't remove it in the way computational functionalists want, to endow a physical system with an intrinsic, objective computation, as shown by numerous examples throughout this book and discussed in Chapter 15.

14.3 But still, shouldn't computations depend on structure?

One may raise the following objection:

Objection 14.4. Substructure-Independence claims that the internal structure of the state of the machine is irrelevant. But not everybody agrees. For example, in [27], p. 393-394, Chalmers states

> The states in most computational formalisms have a combinatorial structure: a cell pattern in a cellular automaton, a combination of tape-state and head-state in a Turing machine, variables and registers in a Pascal program, and so on.

So he proposes *combinatorial-state automata*, which are composite dynamical systems, and can be represented as vectors [27, 28, 31]. According to his and others' views, the physical system that implements the computation has a structure, the data processed by a computation also has a structure, and the implementation should associate data to physical states so that the data structure is realized as physical structure. In Chalmers's words [31] p. 333,

> the relation between an implemented computation and an implementing system is one of isomorphism between the formal structure of the former and the causal structure of the latter.

Reply 14.4. When we build a simulation of a computing system by another one, we guide ourselves, indeed, by patterns and combinatorial structures. Then we map a structure we find in the simulated machine to one in the machine simulating it. But taking this more than as a crutch for our own limitations would contradict Substructure-Independence.

If, for example, we want to simulate a computer by a cellular automaton (CA), we will look for patterns. We may decide that a certain stable pattern represents a `0`, and another one represents a `1`. Some interactions between patterns will then represent logic gates and so on. But there is no rule of how to choose these patterns. There is no limitation, as long as a morphism between some of the states of the CA and the computer's states is found. Suppose we simulate the same CA on a computer. This time we will represent the state of each cell of the automaton as one or more bits. But in the CA, we represented a bit by a pattern made of more cells. So if we simulate on the CA a computer that simulates the CA itself, we will have to simulate each cell of the CA as a pattern made of more cells. What if we simulate on the CA a computer that simulates the CA that simulates the computer that simulates the CA that simulates the computer that simulates the CA? How can we then say that the simulation and the implementation have the same structure?

Moreover, there is no real limitation to what we may call patterns or combinatorial structure. Consider any simulation that ignores the combinatorial structure. Then take the combinatorial structure of the simulated, and go back with the partial morphism to find out the states from the system that simulates it. Whatever we will find, it can be seen as a pattern or a combinatorial structure. We can decode, with more or less effort, the simulated combinatorial structure as a pattern in the system that simulates it. This would make irrelevant any restriction that the combinatorial structure may add.

More importantly, the requirement that the morphisms realizing the implementations preserve the combinatorial structures imposes extreme constraints on Computer Science, and implicitly on all current research programs of Artificial Intelligence.

Proposition 14.3. If a computation could be implemented only by physical systems whose states are structured in the same way as the computed data, there would be no universal computing systems.

Proof. This should already be clear from the Examples from Section 8.1. For example, for a Turing machine to simulate another Turing machine with more symbols or internal states, it would have to reinterpret its combinatorial structure as the possibly completely different combinatorial structure of the simulated Turing machine. Now let's consider a Turing machine with m tape symbols and n internal states. To be universal, it should be able to simulate a Turing machine with m' tape symbols and n' internal states, even if $m' > m$ and $m' > n$. But this would require breaking Chalmers's condition of having the same structure stated in Objection 14.4. Therefore, no Turing machine can be universal under Chalmers's condition. □

Universality can work only if a computing system can simulate another one as in Definition 8.1, regardless of their internal structure or organization. If the internal structure would matter, there could be no Turing universality. Such a limitation would make the entire edifice of Computer Science come crumbling down. Most importantly, the elimination of universality would make it difficult or impossible to claim that we can create an artificial human-like mind on a computer. Moreover, since humans can follow any algorithm step-by-step, their minds are clearly not subject to such a limitation.

This doesn't mean that the structure of the states shouldn't matter, all I'm saying is that it doesn't matter in Computer Science as it is. Therefore, a model that takes structure into account is not quite a computational model, but something else, based on "structure-dependent computations". Something that is allowed to violate Substructure-Independence. But this is a question for another book, and it is addressed in [180, 181] and Chapter 20.

14.4 The uncanny valley of computational universality

The numerous concrete examples discussed in this book provide concrete and overwhelming evidence from Computer Science that indeed most physical systems should be understood as implementing numerous computations. This is even more overwhelming when you realize how many different computations are implemented at once by the same physical process.

In 1970 robotics professor Masahiro Mori [127] hypothesized that

> a person's response to a humanlike robot would abruptly shift from empathy to revulsion as it approached, but failed to attain, a lifelike appearance. This descent into eeriness is known as the *uncanny valley.*

If you think that the human mind is reducible to a computation, you may see with your mind's eyes a sentient being in the AI with which you communicate, even if the AI is not embodied in a human-like robot. This may already feel uncanny. But if you realize that, according to Physics and Computer Science, every changing physical system implements every program (Observation 14.1), you should think that there are many minds just like ours, with experiences just like ours or maybe even more sophisticated, hidden in every stain on a wall, in every shadow, in every water stream or cloud in the sky. If your mind is just a computation, even your own brain should implement a gazillion of different minds at the same time. Even your own shadow. Gazillions of minds just like yours, simultaneously hidden in every corner like ghosts, having the full range of your experiences times a gazillion, and yet the peace of your mind is protected from knowing them and their experiences. How uncanny must it feel to realize that they are everywhere?

In any case, if you reject the triviality argument and pancomputationalism, don't worry, the rest of the book doesn't use them, relying only on reinterpretations of normally accepted computing systems, based on rules employed extensively in Computer Science.

Exercises

Exercise 14.1. Answer again the questions from the Introduction.

Question	Yes	No	I don't know
Easy Question 1, page 8			
Easy Question 2, page 9			
Hard Question 1, page 10			
Hard Question 2, page 10			

Key points

- Every changing physical system implements every program.
- If mind were a computation, there would be minds lurking in every object.
- To avoid this and to remove the ambiguity of computation, various "accounts of computation" were proposed. But this would forbid computational universality.
- Such definitions of computation don't apply to AI based on Computer Science. This should temper our expectations about Artificial Consciousness.
- This doesn't forbid the possibility of building Artificial Consciousness based on other laws than those of Computer Science. But what could these new laws be?

Further reading

[118] William Lycan. Form, function, and feel. *J. Philos*, 78(1):24–50, 1981

[145] Hilary Putnam. *Representation and reality.* MIT Press, Cambridge, Massachusetts, 1988

[158] John Searle. Is the brain a digital computer? *Proc Am Philos Soc*, 64(3):21–37, 1990

[27] David Chalmers. On implementing a computation. *Minds and Machines*, 4(4):391–402, 1994

[28] David Chalmers. Does a rock implement every finite-state automaton? *Synthese*, 108(3):309–333, 1996

[77] P. Godfrey-Smith. Triviality arguments against functionalism. *Philosophical Studies*, 145(2):273–295, 2009

Part IV

Result 1: Can a computer have a mind of its own?

15

Does a computer think if no one is around to see it?

15.1 Do you have a mind of your own?

Imagine you are completely isolated in a sensory deprivation tank. The tank itself is isolated from the environment, and it contains an oxygen reservoir from which you breathe. Imagine, further, that the sensory deprivation tank is floating in space, far away from any galaxy, and nobody on Earth remembers you ever existed. Would you still be able to think, feel, have all sorts of experiences? You surely would, what a crazy question!

Mind, feelings, experiences, while they can be affected by the environment, are among your *intrinsic features*, just like your mass or the color of your eyes. Whatever thought or experience you have, whatever meaning your brain's neurons realize, it is independent of anyone's convention, just like your body mass is independent of anyone's opinion.

On the other hand, we've seen numerous examples showing that what a computer does depends essentially on our conventions. What a computer does *physically*, how it changes its state, depends on the laws of physics, but *what computation it does is our free convention.*

This is a trivial realization, but it may be very difficult to grasp, even after understanding the theory and seeing numerous examples. To understand this difficulty, let's consider the following thought experiment, similar to the one with the sensory deprivation tank. We can imagine that instead of a tank there is an isolated box containing a robot. The robot can compute, in principle, for millions of years after human civilization, if not extinct, completely forgot it, even after it completely forgot the hardware and software specifications of the robot. If, by some chance, the robot arrives on a planet populated by intelligent beings, it would be able to study them, learn their language, and communicate with them. It can tell them about the humans left on the Earth, it can tell them what it computed for millions of years, and so on. The intelligent beings on that planet can study how the robot is made and even make similar robots. They can even see the relation between the internal states of the robot's computer part and the robot's input and output devices, and they can use their technology to read the robot's "thoughts" from its internal

DOI: 10.1201/9781003623373-15

states. Let us now ask the same question as in the sensory deprivation tank thought experiment: "would the robot be able to think, feel, have all sorts of experiences?". It strongly feels that the answer is, obviously, "of course!". What is then the difference between a human mind and a computer program?

This simple thought experiment can dispel in seconds all the effort we've made in the previous chapters of this book, and the illusion that computations are intrinsic features of the computers will return. The reason is that the input and output devices offer a powerful interface that anchors the convention in the physical reality. We can imagine that this connection between the machine and its environment secures a unique convention, a unique possible way to interpret as a computation what the computer does physically. But perhaps the strongest effect of this connection is that it makes it very difficult for us to see that computation is, in fact, a convention, one among myriads of many other equally possible conventions. So let us try a bit more to understand the difference between convention and reality.

15.2 The illusion of a unique interpretation

Remember the *Necker cube*, an illusion based on an ambiguous image that can be interpreted in two ways as a cube in space, as in Figure 15.1. Once we get used to a way to see it as a cube in space, it becomes difficult to "unsee" it. But once we see it in a different way, with some practice, it becomes almost equally easy to switch between the two ways to see it.

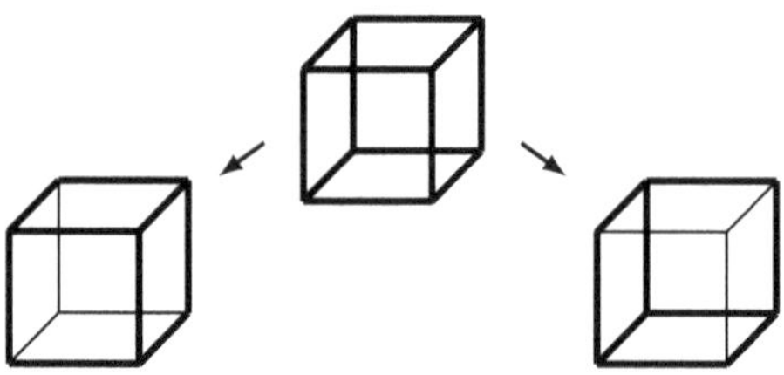

Figure 15.1: The Necker cube, an illusion based on an ambiguous image that can be interpreted in two ways as a cube in space.

The coloring convention used in Figure 15.1 to suggest the two ways to see the Necker cube in space is just a convention, specifically chosen to appeal to our previous experience with similar drawings like this one. The convention provides some handles, some anchors that may influence you into seeing the Necker cube in a particular way. For example, the cube on the lower-left side of the image is suggested to appear as if we look from the front and a bit above. This is how we usually see objects, because they usually lay down on the ground or on a table, so it is also the most natural way for us to see them. But we can also see them from atop, looking down, as suggested by the cube from the lower-right side of the image. And, with seconds of training, we can also see any of these depictions of a cube in space alternately, despite the suggestive drawing telling us to see it otherwise.

Similarly, the computer's user interface provides us with some handles, some anchors that exploit our habits of seeing the world. But, while in the case of the Necker cube we experience only a momentary difficulty when trying to alternately see the Necker cube in two different ways, in the case of a computer much more time and effort is needed. However, this book doesn't rely on psychological tricks, it only explains rationally what interpretations of a physical process are valid interpretations as computations, according to Computer Science. The purpose of so many examples and exercises was to train the reader to unlearn the reification of a particular convention, to escape the illusion that this convention is somehow objective.

Another way to understand the powerful role of convention is by analogy with reference frames or bases, as shown in Chapter 6. In the case of a geometric space, if you are used to thinking of a geometric problem in terms of numerical values like $(v_1, v_2, \ldots)$, the point coordinates and the vector components, you may tend to reify these numbers and consider them absolute. A formulation of the same problem expressed in another basis or reference frame may seem to you like a totally unrelated problem. And even if you understand that there are other ways to express the same problem numerically, it may be difficult to make the habit of thinking of these problems in a frame-independent way. If in the back of your mind numbers are more concrete than geometric relations, your mind will fall back to thinking in terms of a preferred frame. The calculations will give you the right answer in any reference frame you choose, but it is essential to understand that the answer doesn't depend on such a choice. This is a continuous struggle for many researchers who apply vector spaces in their works, and even for mathematicians. To avoid this issue, mathematicians developed a trick: they simply teach students to avoid numerical representations, and only if the problem itself asks for such basis-dependent numbers, to delay the numerical evaluation of the solution until the end of the proof. In fact, geometers strongly avoid as much as possible even notations of merely unspecified components of points and vectors, symbols like x, y, and z, or x_1, x_2, and x_3, even when these symbols don't stand for explicit numerical values. The Necker cube illusion from Figure 15.1 can be understood as depending on the reference frame: the corners of the cube can be closer or farther to you, its faces can be visible or hidden, depending on the reference frame. And, as discussed in Chapter 6, information can be understood as vectors in an information space. Then, the user interface singles out a preferred basis in the information space.

15.3 Syntax and semantics

Another way to understand the results from the previous chapters is that they show, by using the extreme ambiguity, that not only semantics, but even syntax is not intrinsic to the physical systems that we use for computations, or to the brain. *Syntax* refers to the rules governing the structure and arrangement of symbols in the data or instructions, while *semantics* deals with the meaning of the data and instructions.

The fact that not even syntax is intrinsic to the computing system was pointed out very clearly by Searle [158], from whom we quote:

> 1. On the standard textbook definition, computation is defined syntactically in terms of symbol manipulation.
> 2. But both syntax and symbols are not defined in terms of physics. [...] Syntax, in short, is not intrinsic to physics.
> 3. This has the consequence that computation is not discovered in physics, it is assigned to it. Certain physical phenomena are assigned or used or programmed or interpreted syntactically. Syntax and symbols are observer relative.
>
> ...
>
> 7. The standard, though tacit, way out of this is to commit the homunculus fallacy. The homunculus fallacy is endemic to computational models of cognition and cannot be removed by the standard recursive decomposition arguments. They are addressed to a different question.
>
> ...

Based on what we've seen so far, I take that what Searle means at point 7 is that computation doesn't make sense without the user. According to Searle, the *homunculus fallacy* is "to treat the brain as if there is some agent inside it using it to compute with it" [158], even if we are not aware of doing this.

Searle's observation from 1990 was ignored or minimized, but now we can see concretely, from all the examples and discussion of how Computer Science treats computations, that the conventionality of computation is not only real, but it entails a huge ambiguity that prevents a meaningful way to attribute mind to a computation. Chapter 11 will illustrate the extent of the ambiguity in an experiment that can be reproduced and verified by the reader.

15.4 Can a computer have a mind by itself?

There are many equally "legal" ways to decode a mind in an AI. If it seems that there is a unique way, it is because of the user interface, which selects a preferred basis in the information space. In the story with the alien robot from the spaceship that crashed on Earth from the Introduction, the robot's input and output devices were completely destroyed precisely to remove the possibility to fix a unique convention. And Thought Experiment 13.2 from Section 13.2 will make it even clearer that computation is not an intrinsic property of the computer, but a convention.

On the other hand, a brain in a vat, having all that it needs to be alive and function, but being truly deprived of any input from the environment, should be able to think and be sentient by itself. It should need no external user, designer, or programmer to make and keep any convention. And, if somebody proposes an external convention to interpret what sort of experience is associated with a particular state or process of the brain, this convention can contradict the actual experience taking place. In the case of the robot, all these conventions are equal, according to Computer Science.

Observation 15.1. The conclusion of what we've learned so far about Computer Science is that a computation is not intrinsic to the physical computer, but rather an external convention imposed by us over the functionality of the computer. On the other hand, there is no evidence that our minds depend in their work on the existence of an external convention.

Of course, if we still insist that a computation can be a mind, there is a way out: we can stipulate that all mind-like computations are minds!

But what do I mean by "mind-like computation"?

Definition 15.1. A *mind-like computation* is any computation that satisfies the characterization of a mind, in any proposed Computational Theory of Mind that claims to be based on Computer Science.

The purpose of this book is to derive a contradiction from any proposal that mind is a computation. In Definition 15.1, it doesn't matter which Computational Theory of Mind we're talking about. It can even be a "promissory theory of mind", one that "science will definitely find in the future, when we will know more", or one that we may never be able to find, but a much smarter intelligence would know, if such an intelligence were to exist. We don't have to enter the details of the particular proposal, as long as they share the generic prediction that mind is a computation.

At this point, the supporters of the Computational Theory of Mind may feel that Observation 15.1 leaves available the following option:

Hypothesis 15.1. All mind-like computations that can be attributed to the same physical process of a computing system (in particular the brain) are minds, but these are not many and not too different from one another. The ambiguity of computation is true, and it leads to some vagueness in the mental processes, but the computation is largely unique and sufficient to be considered a mind. Don't minds have vague elements anyway?

In Part III, we will see that the computations that can be attributed to the same physical process of a computing system are not a few, and they are very different, contradicting one another in the most extreme possible ways. This directly contradicts Hypothesis 15.1. The defenders of the Computational Theory of Mind will be forced to drop the main claim that there is an almost unique, definite computation, which yields a definite mind, but they can still retreat to the following hypothesis:

Hypothesis 15.2. All mind-like computations that can be attributed to the same physical process of a computing system (including the brain) are minds, and these are many and very different from one another.

In Chapter 18, we will see that this hypothesis is already contradicted. That you already had evidence falsifying it, and that you received such evidence numerous times even if you count them from this morning only. But to prepare for that proof, we need to see how many other mind-like computations exist whenever one exists, on the same physical system.

Exercises

Exercise 15.1. Revisit the questions from the Introduction, and give your renewed answer.

Question	Yes	No	I don't know
Easy Question 1, page 8			
Easy Question 2, page 9			
Hard Question 1, page 10			
Hard Question 2, page 10			

Did any of your opinions change?

Key points

- Computation is not intrinsic to the physical computer, but rather an external convention imposed by us over its functionality.
- By contrast, our minds exist independently of any external convention.

Further reading

[158] John Searle. Is the brain a digital computer? *Proc Am Philos Soc*, 64(3):21–37, 1990

[170] Cristi Stoica. Alternative computations at once. *https://www.unitaryflow.com/2025/03/alternative-computations-at-once.html*, 2025

[182] O.C. Stoica. Does a computer think if no one is around to see it? *philsci-archive:22880*, 2023

[172] O.C. Stoica. Are you a robot? http://youtu.be/kuziE01rh6M&list=PLJzOclJMoIC1pnJIPlmWhGwaDWD04tFza. Accessed April 22, 2026

Part V

From bits to qubits and brains

16

Beyond binary

16.1 Beyond two

So far we focused on computers that work with binary values. But other kinds of computers are possible. Could it be that other kinds of computers can restore the objectivity of information? We will see that they can't.

Binary values are preferred for several reasons. They can be identified with the truth values "true" and "false". Since the *law of excluded middle* doesn't allow for a third truth value, binary values seem to be the best logical choice. In addition, they are the simplest choice that can still encode some information. They are sufficient to write any number, since any number can be expressed in base 2. And finally, the simplest systems that have more states that are both stable and easier to distinguish are those having two such states.

But the possibility of more than two values exists. Numbers can be represented in any other basis. And while classical logic doesn't allow for other values than "true" and "false", people invented many-valued types of logic. We can also simply use the extra possible states to represent something else than truth values.

The simplest option is to use *trits*, which have three values. A ternary system base can consist of the values `0`, `1`, and `2`. One can also use the *balanced ternary system*, having the possible values `-1`, `0`, and `1`. The balanced ternary system has some interesting properties, for example it can represent both positive and negative numbers in a uniform way, and the negative of a number is obtained by swapping the trits `-1` and `1` [91].

Similar to the binary case, the three values of a trit can be represented as three perpendicular vectors in the vector space $\mathbb{R}^3$, as in Figure 16.1.

Note that, as vectors, $|\texttt{-1}\rangle \neq -|\texttt{1}\rangle$, in fact these vectors are perpendicular! Just like $|\texttt{0}\rangle \neq 0\,|\texttt{1}\rangle$ because $|\texttt{0}\rangle$ and $|\texttt{1}\rangle$ are perpendicular.

A bit cell has two possible interpretations, because there are two ways to associate two possible binary values to its two possible states. Given a way to interpret the bit cell, the other one is obtained by inverting the value.

Exercise 16.1. If a memory cell can be in three possible states, in how many ways can these states be interpreted as representing the numbers `0`, `1`, and `2`?

DOI: 10.1201/9781003623373-16

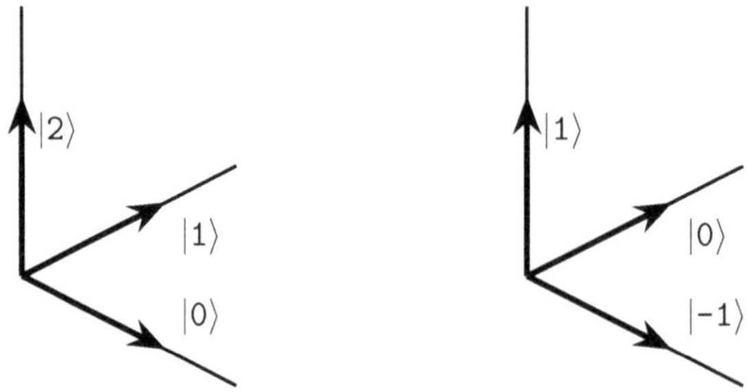

Figure 16.1: The vector space $\mathbb{R}^3$ can be used to represent ternary values (0, 1, and 2), respectively balanced ternary values (-1, 0, and 1).

Solution. The ways to interpret three possible states as 0, 1, and 2, are

$$(0,1,2),(1,2,0),(2,0,1),(0,2,1),(1,0,2),(2,1,0), \tag{16.1}$$

the permutations of the set $\{0,1,2\}$. □

As in the case of bits, there are functions, similar to the Boolean functions, taking m trit inputs into n trit outputs. An example is the function that performs the addition modulo 3, which for the ternary system is

$$\mathbf{f}(\mathtt{a},\mathtt{b}) = \mathtt{a} \oplus_3 \mathtt{b}, \tag{16.2}$$

where by $\mathtt{a} \oplus_3 \mathtt{b}$ we denote the remainder obtained after dividing the usual sum $\mathtt{a}+\mathtt{b}$ by 3. Figure 16.2 illustrates how we obtain the ring $\mathbb{Z}_3$, of integers modulo 3, from the ring of integers $\mathbb{Z}$.

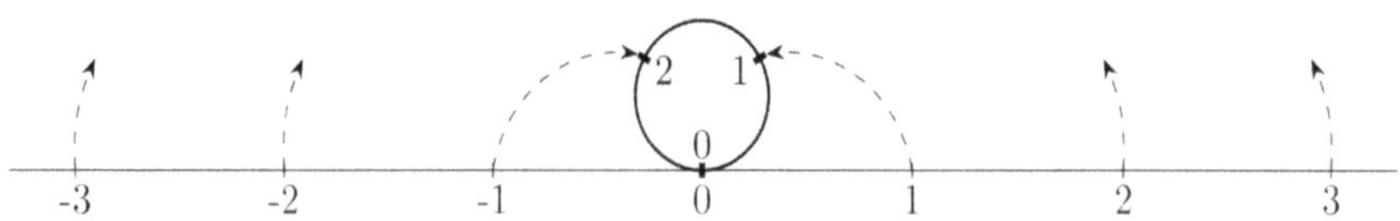

Figure 16.2: Modulo is like wrapping the integers on the circle of ternary values.

The first table in Table 16.1 contains the values of $\mathtt{a} \oplus_3 \mathtt{b}$ for all possible inputs.

Exercise 16.2. Find out the functions representing subtraction modulo 3 and multiplication modulo 3 for the ternary system.

For the balanced ternary addition modulo 3, we simply replace 2 with -1. I'll leave it to the reader to explain this. Hint: subtracting 1 modulo 3 gives the same result as adding 2 modulo 3. See Figure 16.3.

The second table in Table 16.1 contains the values of addition modulo 3 for all possible inputs in the balanced case.

Table 16.1: Ternary and balanced ternary addition modulo 3.

a	b	a $\oplus_3$ b
0	0	0
0	1	1
0	2	2
1	0	1
1	1	2
1	2	0
2	0	2
2	1	0
2	2	1

a	b	a $\oplus_{3'}$ b
-1	-1	1
-1	0	-1
-1	1	0
0	-1	-1
0	0	0
0	1	1
1	-1	0
1	0	1
1	1	-1

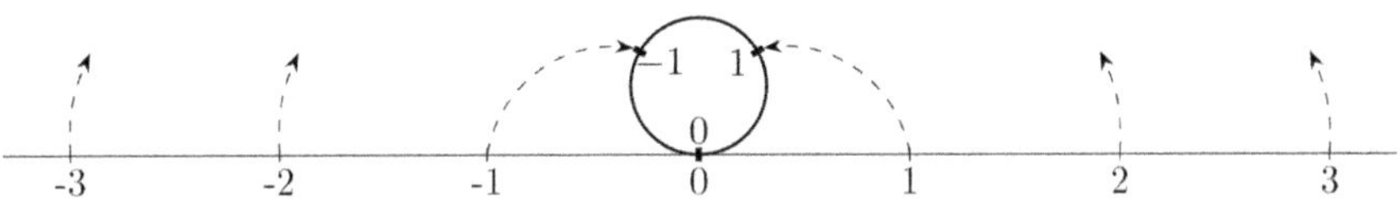

Figure 16.3: Wrapping the integers on the circle of balanced ternary values.

Exercise 16.3. Find out the functions representing subtraction modulo 3 and multiplication modulo 3 for the balanced ternary system.

The binary and ternary systems can be easily generalized to $d > 3$.

Exercise 16.4. In how many ways can we interpret a memory cell with d possible states as representing the values 0, 1, ..., d-1?

In general, if a memory cell can be in d possible states, the number of ways to associate d-ary values to the d possible states of the memory cell is the number of permutations of a set with d elements, which is

$$d! = 1 \times 2 \times \ldots \times d. \tag{16.3}$$

This is simple to see by induction. If the number of ordered sets made with the numbers 0, 1, ..., d-2 is $(d-1)!$, one can insert another number d-1 in d ways: before the first element, between the first and the second, and so on. One obtains d ordered sets for each of the $(d-1)!$ ordered sets of $d-1$ elements.

If a computer has n memory cells, each with d possible states, its possible states can be labeled with elements from the Cartesian product of n copies of the set $\{\mathtt{0}, \ldots, \mathtt{d\text{-}1}\}$,

$$\begin{aligned}\{\mathtt{0}, \ldots, \mathtt{d\text{-}1}\}^n &:= \underbrace{\{\mathtt{0}, \ldots, \mathtt{d\text{-}1}\} \times \ldots \times \{\mathtt{0}, \ldots, \mathtt{d\text{-}1}\}}_{n \text{ times}} \\ &= \big\{(x_1, \ldots, x_n) | x_1, \ldots, x_n \in \{\mathtt{0}, \ldots, \mathtt{d\text{-}1}\}\big\}.\end{aligned} \tag{16.4}$$

Observation 16.1. A computer with n memory cells, each with d possible values, has d^n possible states. By choosing how to interpret each memory cell, each state of the computer can be interpreted in d^n possible ways. But a logic gate connecting n memory cells can be interpreted in $(d!)^n$ possible ways.

Therefore, moving beyond binary values doesn't remove the ambiguity, by contrast, it increases the number of possible interpretations.

A computer can have memory cells with different possible numbers of states, d_1, d_2, ..., d_n. In this case, the number of possible interpretations of each state is $d_1 \times \ldots \times d_n$. This is the same as the total number of possible states. The number of possible simple interpretations of a logic gate connecting n memory cells is $d_1! \times \ldots \times d_n!$. But there is nothing that such a computer can do, that a digital computer with bits can't do. So in the following, we will discuss mainly binary computers.

We can generalize even more, allowing for a continuum of possible states. Such a computer is no longer digital, but analog. We will see more about this in Section 16.3. Here I'll just mention that moving to the continuum would not eliminate the ambiguity, but it would result in uncountably many possible interpretations.

16.2 Physical analogies

Building a binary computer is not easy. Going beyond binary, to $d = 3, 4$ or more, is even harder. Imagine how hard it is to build a computer whose memory cells can be in states that can represent not discrete, but continuous values. However, this is not necessarily the case. Analog computing machines have been known since antiquity, long before the first digital computer. A mechanical clock is an analog computer. The Antikythera mechanism was an analog computer, used to determine the positions of the planets. Other analog devices were used by ancient astronomers and astrologers, like Ptolemy's planisphere, the astrolabe, and the dioptra. In time, to solve geometric problems, tools were invented, including the protractor, the goniometer, the sector, and the planimeter. In the seventeenth century, with the discovery of the logarithms, a helpful tool to make calculations was invented: the slide rule. Any mechanism is, in a very restricted sense, an analog computer. As technology developed, especially once we discovered electricity and electronics, analog devices became more and more sophisticated [204].

Notice that the devices built to be used as analog computing systems seem to be very specialized. We mainly exploit the capacity of physical systems to do some analog tasks that are in their nature anyway.

In some sense, all living and even non-living beings are analog computers that compute something: their own states. Ultimately, any physical system does something that can be described computationally, and the converse of this is that we can use that physical system itself for those computations. A trivial observation to be made is that any physical system is better at simulating itself than any digital simulation could, because it is the original, and any computation can only approximate it. But, of course, the machines that deserve to be called analog computers are those specifically designed to be used for analog computation.

Even the binary computers that we use are, in fact, analog devices. Just consider a capacitor that is used to represent a bit value. The capacitor can be charged anywhere between 0% and 100%, but if we want it to represent a bit value, we have to ignore most of the information it can represent. For example, if the capacitor is charged over 80%, we can say it represents the value 1, and 0 if it is charged under 20%. But why not represent 1 if it's above 50%, and 0 otherwise? Because mistakes can be made around the boundary of 50%, for such tiny components any perturbation, any source of noise, can introduce errors. So it is safer to set a no man's land between 20% and 80%.

16.3 From discrete to continuum: analog computers

In the case of *analog computers*, which can deal with a continuum of possible values, the function $\mathcal{F}$ from equation (5.11) is replaced with a function whose n inputs and n outputs take continuous values. Without loss of generality, we can take this set to be the set of real numbers $\mathbb{R}$. The space of possible states of the analog computer is therefore

$$\mathbb{R}^n := \underbrace{\mathbb{R} \times \ldots \times \mathbb{R}}_{n \text{ times}} = \{(x_1, \ldots, x_n) | x_1, \ldots, x_n \in \mathbb{R}\}. \tag{16.5}$$

Since the state of the computer changes in time, we express this time dependency by denoting the state as $\mathbf{x}(t) = (x_1(t), \ldots, x_n(t))$. In equation (5.11), the function $\mathcal{F}$ is assumed to describe the change of the computer's state after a fixed time interval Δt. But if we are dealing with continuous variables, changes happen after intervals of arbitrarily small duration. Therefore, for every $t > t_0$, where t_0 is the initial time, there is a function $\mathcal{F}_{\Delta t} : \mathbb{R}^n \to \mathbb{R}^n$ which describes how the state of the computer changes between time t_0 and time t if no external cause changes its state,

$$\mathbf{x}(t) = \mathcal{F}_{\Delta t}\mathbf{x}(t_0), \tag{16.6}$$

where $\Delta t := t - t_0$. Since our analog computer should do the same computation no matter when it starts doing it, the function $\mathcal{F}_{\Delta t}$ depends only on the duration of the time interval Δt, and not on t_0. This implies an analog of equation (5.13): after N steps, that is, for $t = t_0 + N\Delta t$,

$$\mathbf{x}(t) = \mathcal{F}_{N\Delta t}(\mathbf{x}(t_0)) = \mathcal{F}_{\Delta t}^{N}(\mathbf{x}(t_0)) = \underbrace{\mathcal{F}_{\Delta t}(\ldots \mathcal{F}_{\Delta t}(}_{N \text{ times}}\mathbf{x}(t_0))\ldots). \tag{16.7}$$

Equation (16.7) implies that, for any two integers $N_1, N_2 \geq 0$,

$$\mathcal{F}_{(N_1+N_2)\Delta t}(\mathbf{x}(t_0)) = \mathcal{F}_{N_1\Delta t}(\mathcal{F}_{N_2\Delta t}(\mathbf{x}(t_0))). \tag{16.8}$$

In fact, for any three moments of time $t_0 \leq t_1 \leq t_2$,

$$\mathcal{F}_{t_2-t_0}(\mathbf{x}(t_0)) = \mathcal{F}_{t_2-t_1}\left(\mathcal{F}_{t_1-t_0}(\mathbf{x}(t_0))\right). \tag{16.9}$$

For $\Delta t = 0$ we set, for any state $x(t) \in \mathbb{R}^n$ at any time t,

$$\mathcal{F}_0\left(\mathbf{x}(t)\right) = \mathbf{x}(t). \tag{16.10}$$

This is consistent with $\mathcal{F}^0_{\Delta t}$ being the identity function $\mathbf{x} \mapsto \mathbf{x}$ on $\mathbb{R}^n$, which is true if $\mathcal{F}_{\Delta t}$ is invertible.

A more general computer can be conceived, if we notice that there is no restriction that requires the possible input and output values to be of the same type. Mixed combinations are allowed. In full generality, the set of possible states of the computer has the form

$$\mathcal{S} = A_1 \times \ldots \times A_n, \tag{16.11}$$

where each of the sets $A_1, \ldots, A_n$ can have a finite number of elements, such as $\{\mathtt{0}, \mathtt{1}\}$ or $\{\mathtt{0}, \ldots, \mathtt{d-1}\}$, with various values for d, or it can be a continuum, such as the set of real numbers, an interval of real numbers, or even a set of complex numbers, if the system uses quantum effects.

We notice the similarity between equations (16.9) and (16.10), and the discrete dynamical systems from Definition 10.1. Indeed, our system is a *continuous dynamical system*. The main difference is that time can be a continuous parameter $t \in [0, +\infty)$ or $t \in \mathbb{R}$. In this case, the dynamical law $\mu := \mathcal{F}_{\Delta t}$, where we choose $\Delta t = 1$, specifies how the system transitions from a state $s \in \mathcal{S}$ to a state $\mu^t(s) \in \mathcal{S}$ after the time interval t, if no external cause affects the system. This is given by a family of functions $\{\mu^t : \mathcal{S} \to \mathcal{S} | t \in [0, +\infty)\}$ parametrized by all positive durations, so that for any $s \in \mathcal{S}$ and any $t, t' \in [0, +\infty)$,

$$\begin{aligned} \mu^0(s) &= s \\ \mu^t\left(\mu^{t'}(s)\right) &= \mu^{t+t'}(s). \end{aligned} \tag{16.12}$$

Example 16.1. Until the discovery of Quantum Mechanics, it was believed that the physical laws are of a particular kind, which we call today "classical". Classical systems can be understood as dynamical systems. The state of a classical system of point-particles is characterized by the positions and momenta of the particles. That is, for a single particle the position has three coordinates, (q_1, q_2, q_3), and the momentum is a vector having three components (p_x, p_y, p_z). The space of all possible states, the state space, is $\mathbb{R}^{3+3} = \mathbb{R}^6$. The state space for n particles is $\underbrace{\mathbb{R}^6 \times \ldots \times \mathbb{R}^6}_{n \text{ times}} = \mathbb{R}^{6n}$. The dynamics of such a system can be described by a set of equations that involve partial derivatives with respect to the positions and momenta, called *Hamilton equations.* They specify how the position coordinates $(q_1, \ldots, q_{3n})$—notation commonly used instead of $(x_1, y_1, z_1, \ldots, x_n, y_n, z_n)$—and the components of the momenta $(p_1, \ldots, p_{3n})$, change in time,

$$\begin{cases} \dfrac{\mathrm{d}\,p_j}{\mathrm{d}\,t} = & -\dfrac{\partial \mathcal{H}}{\partial q_j}, \\ \dfrac{\mathrm{d}\,q_j}{\mathrm{d}\,t} = & \dfrac{\partial \mathcal{H}}{\partial p_j}. \end{cases} \tag{16.13}$$

The function $\mathcal{H} : \mathbb{R}^{6n} \to \mathbb{R}$ is called *Hamiltonian* function. We will not go into details, only that, by integrating the Hamilton equations for a given set of initial conditions, the dynamical law of an isolated classical system turns out to be of the form (16.12).

Any classical analog computer is a classical system as in Example 16.1. Conversely, any such classical system is an analog computer, although we can only use some of its properties to store and process information. A digital computer is, of course, also a Hamiltonian system, but we are interested only in a finite number of possible states in which the system can be, so we ignore the fact that its physical properties vary continuously and focus only on a "low-resolution" description of the system.

Question 16.1. What is the number of possible interpretations of the physical process implementing an analog computation?

The proof of Theorem 12.3 and its implications didn't make use of discreteness in an essential way. These results can be extended immediately to any dynamical system, and any implementation consistent with Substrate-Independence and Substructure-Independence.

To verify the existence of ambiguity, we need to make sure that our system satisfies the conditions of Theorem 12.3. It is sufficient that the histories corresponding to distinct inputs remain distinct during computation. Then, the same proof as for Theorem 12.3 can be used to obtain the result.

Theorem 16.1. Theorem 12.3 generalizes to all dynamical systems whose histories corresponding to distinct initial states don't cross each other, and which don't return to previous states during the considered time interval.

Proof. Instead of a permutation of the initial set $\mathcal{S}_0$, we use any bijective function from $\mathcal{S}_0$ to $\mathcal{S}_0$. For any two possible initial states, there are numerous bijective functions that swap those states. If $\mathcal{S}_0$ has a finite number k of elements, this number is $(k-2)!$, because the other $k-2$ elements $\mathcal{S}_0$ than the two swapped elements can be permuted freely. If $\mathcal{S}_0$ is infinite, this number is infinite. This entails the existence of reinterpretations in which any computation with the algorithm that the system implements is interpreted as any other of its computations. □

In addition, all the implications of the ambiguity of computation explored in Chapters 12 and 13 apply to generalizations of computations based on general dynamical systems.

Definition 8.1 of simulation involves only the states and transitions, and ignores the details of each state or of how the Turing machine works. But these details may be very different. The number of possible states of the cell, and the number of possible internal states of the head, as well as the way it works, may be very different, as seen in Section 8.1.

Question 16.2. Shouldn't we use a more detailed description of the states, and not, as in Definition 10.1 and the generalization from equation (16.12), just how they transition into other states?

Answer. This is useful and should be done in various situations. But imposing such a restriction in the definition of simulation or computation or implementation would be incompatible with Turing universality. A universal Turing machine can simulate any other Turing machine. Therefore, a simulation is just a partial morphism of dynamical systems as in Definition 10.1, regardless of the internal structure.

If the partial morphism would not be about states and transitions only, but it would also be limited by the structures of the states, then the possible simulations would be limited. No Turing machine would be able to simulate another Turing machine that has more internal states or more tape symbols. This is not the way simulation of Turing machines happens in Computer Science. □

A computer can be seen as a Turing machine with finite length tape, which consists of its memory bits. The operations done by the head correspond to the fetch-decode-execute cycle of the processor, and the internal states are represented by register bits. But because all that matters are the transitions, in the following, we will not need to make these distinctions, the description from Section 5.2 is sufficient.

The description of computing systems as dynamical systems is not very usual, but it is correct and it was used for a long time, for example in [72, 198, 68]. Systematic developments of descriptions of computing systems as dynamical systems can be found in [164, 76].

The formulation given here in terms of dynamical systems may have inessential differences from other presentations, but it is as simple as possible while maintaining full generality, and it is suited to the proofs that will come later in this book. Moreover, not only the computing systems are dynamical systems, but so is any physical system, including a quantum system, as we shall see in Section 17.2.

In general, in the continuous case, the dynamical law is, from a mathematical point of view, a system of equations involving partial derivatives with respect to some coordinates parametrizing the states. But we don't have to worry about this now, because equation (16.12) applies, in particular, to such equations.

Claude Shannon, the father of information theory, imagined a *general purpose analog computer* (GRAC) [163]. Such a machine consists of five types of units: adders, multipliers, integrators, constant units (whose output is always the value 1), and constant multipliers, *i.e.* multipliers by a fixed constant. Shannon showed that his GRAC would be able to compute functions that are solutions to differential-algebraic systems of equations. While in theory it seems to be able to simulate any other analog machine whose evolution is continuous, in practice this is difficult to achieve. We need to be able to set all parameters as needed and to control their evolution with very high precision, we need to avoid the effects of noise from the environment, as well as the quantum effects.

However, here we are not interested in perfection or even in universality. The point is whether we can regard the brain as an analog computer, or perhaps a *hybrid computer*, containing both analog and digital elements. If quantum effects are irrelevant for the brain's functionality, maybe mind can be understood as an analog or a hybrid computation.

16.4 Rotations and complex numbers

We continue to move smoothly from digital to analog toward quantum computers. Recall from Chapter 6 that the reinterpretation of a bit by inverting its values can be understood as a passive reflection in plane, as in Figure 6.3.

But reinterpretations of bits are limited to permutations of the basis vectors, while more general transformations of the plane exist, for example rotations, as in Figure 6.1.

This is the matrix representation of a rotation with the angle α of a vector:

$$\begin{pmatrix} x' \\ y' \end{pmatrix} = \begin{pmatrix} \cos\alpha & -\sin\alpha \\ \sin\alpha & \cos\alpha \end{pmatrix} \begin{pmatrix} x \\ y \end{pmatrix} = \begin{pmatrix} x\cos\alpha - y\sin\alpha \\ x\sin\alpha + y\cos\alpha \end{pmatrix}. \tag{16.14}$$

There is a simple analog device that can be used to compute the result of a rotation. It consists of a sheet of paper and a *protractor*! Following Figure 16.4, place the protractor with the origin at the origin of the basis and so that minus the angle of rotation aligns with the direction of the new basis vector $|0\rangle$. The rotated basis consists of the vectors $|0'\rangle$ and $|1'\rangle$ pointing in the directions marked by the angles 0°, respectively 90°.

By the way, the rotation matrix from equation (16.14) can be interpreted as a complex number. So in this section, I will shamelessly change the topic of the rest of this chapter to remind the reader about complex numbers, so needed to discuss Quantum Computing.

Recall that a *complex number* z is "made of" two real numbers x and y,

$$z = x + iy, \tag{16.15}$$

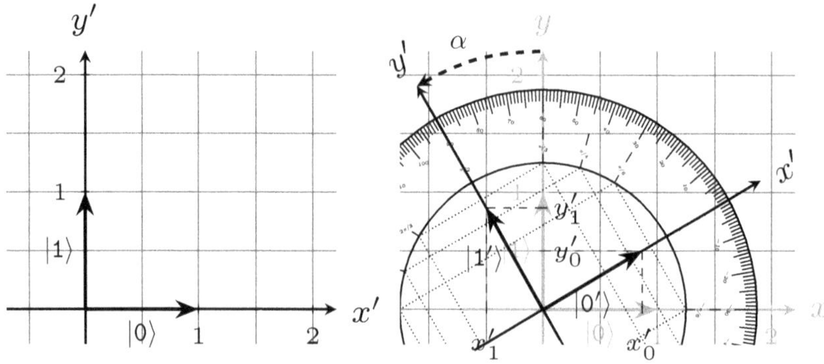

Figure 16.4: The rotation from (16.14), implemented by using an analog device: the protractor.

where the *imaginary unit* i satisfies $i^2 = -1$. The pair of real numbers (x, y) suggest that complex numbers can be represented in a plane, as in Figure 16.5.

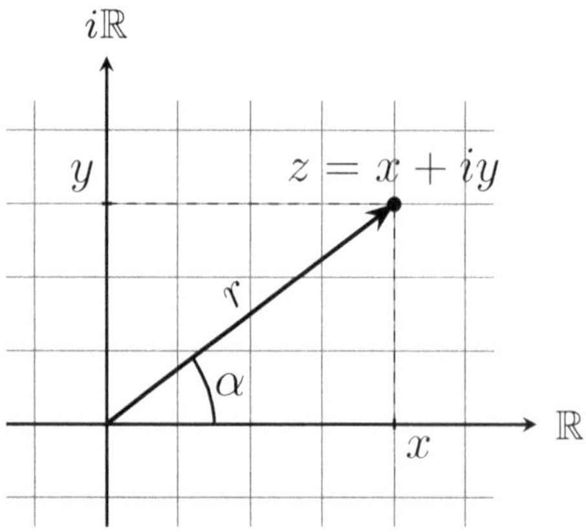

Figure 16.5: The complex plane.

Addition and multiplication of two complex numbers are done like this

$$\begin{aligned} (x + iy) + (x' + iy') &= (x + x') + i(y + y') \\ (x + iy) \cdot (x' + iy') &= (xx' - yy') + i(xy' + yx') \end{aligned} \tag{16.16}$$

Any complex number $x + iy$ can be put in the following *polar form*

$$x + iy = r(\cos\alpha + i\sin\alpha) = re^{i\alpha}, \tag{16.17}$$

where

$$\begin{aligned} r &:= |z| := \sqrt{zz^*} = \sqrt{x^2 + y^2} & \geq 0 \\ \alpha &:= \arctan(y, x) & \in [0^\circ, 360^\circ). \end{aligned} \tag{16.18}$$

In the polar form, multiplication becomes

$$\left(re^{i\alpha}\right) \cdot \left(r'e^{i\alpha'}\right) = rr'e^{i(\alpha+\alpha')}. \tag{16.19}$$

The complex conjugate of a complex number is defined by

$$z^* = (x+iy)^* = x - iy. \tag{16.20}$$

Now, returning to the rotation matrix

$$R(\alpha) = \begin{pmatrix} \cos\alpha & -\sin\alpha \\ \sin\alpha & \cos\alpha \end{pmatrix} \tag{16.21}$$

consider the rotation matrices

$$R(0) = \begin{pmatrix} 1 & 0 \\ 0 & 1 \end{pmatrix} \text{ and } R\left(\frac{\pi}{2}\right) = \begin{pmatrix} 0 & -1 \\ 1 & 0 \end{pmatrix} \tag{16.22}$$

We notice that

$$\begin{pmatrix} 0 & -1 \\ 1 & 0 \end{pmatrix} \times \begin{pmatrix} 0 & -1 \\ 1 & 0 \end{pmatrix} = -\begin{pmatrix} 1 & 0 \\ 0 & 1 \end{pmatrix} \tag{16.23}$$

so we can represent i as a rotation with $\frac{\pi}{2}$. Then, a complex number can be represented by the matrix

$$x + iy \mapsto \begin{pmatrix} x & -y \\ y & x \end{pmatrix} = r\begin{pmatrix} \cos\alpha & -\sin\alpha \\ \sin\alpha & \cos\alpha \end{pmatrix}. \tag{16.24}$$

This is how we can interpret a complex number geometrically as a rotation with the angle α combined with a dilation with the scale factor r.

Now, this chapter is about analog tools, so let's give to Caesar what belongs to Caesar. Since we can use a protractor to determine the result of a rotation, and we can use a slide rule to determine the result of a multiplication, we can combine them to implement multiplications of complex numbers represented in the plane. But we don't need to reinvent the wheel of complex multiplication, analog devices that generalize the slide rule to perform multiplication and division of complex numbers already exist, for example the Wythe-Fuller and the DuMond complex-number slide rules [203].

Exercises

Exercise 16.5. Verify that additions, subtractions, and multiplications of matrices representing complex numbers as in equation (16.24) give the same results as the same operations done with complex numbers as in equation (16.16).

Key points

- Computers based on more values than just 0 and 1 are possible.
- Computers based on replacing bits with something else that can take continuous values are possible.
- None of these reduce the ambiguity of computation, quite the contrary.
- Everything we've learned in the previous chapters about dynamical systems and the ambiguity of computation is still valid.

Further reading

[91] B Hayes. Third base. *American scientist*, 89(6):490–494, 2001

[72] Robin Gandy. Church's thesis and principles for mechanisms. In J. Barwise, H.J. Keisler, and K. Kuhnen, editors, *The Kleene Symposium*, volume 101, pages 123–148. Elsevier, Amsterdam, North-Holland, 1980

[198] Tommaso Toffoli. Reversible computing. In *Automata, Languages and Programming: Seventh Colloquium. Noordwijkerhout, the Netherlands July 14–18, 1980*, pages 632–644. Springer, 1980

[68] Edward Fredkin and Tommaso Toffoli. Conservative logic. *Int. J. Theor. Phys.*, 21(3-4):219–253, 1982

[203] Aristotle Tympas. *Calculation and computation in the pre-electronic era.* Springer, 2017

[204] Bernd Ulmann. *Analog and hybrid computer programming.* Oldenbourg Wissenschaftsverlag Verlag, Berlin, Germany, 2022

[163] Claude Shannon. Mathematical theory of the differential analyzer. *J. Math. Phys.*, 20(1-4):337–354, 1941

17

Quantum computers

17.1 Quantum waves are vectors

Quantum computers are quantum systems. In fact, every system in the world is quantum, because the world is quantum, but the more familiar behaviors of the physical systems can be approximated by describing them as classical systems. But sometimes, especially when we are interested in the behavior of the systems at very small scales, we have to use Quantum Mechanics.

In this section, I explain why the states of a quantum system, and of any physical system for that matter, can be described as vectors in a complex vector space.

Recall from Example 16.1 that a classical system of point-particles is a dynamical system. In Quantum Mechanics, instead of a system of idealized point-like particles, there is a *quantum wave*. For a single quantum particle of the simplest kind, which has spin 0, the wave is described by a function that associates to every point in space a complex number, so it is of the form $\psi : \mathbb{R}^3 \to \mathbb{C}$. If $\psi(x, y, z)$ and $\varphi(x, y, z)$ are two such waves and $a \neq 0$ is a complex number, then

$$\begin{cases} \psi(x,y,z) + \varphi(x,y,z) \\ a\psi(x,y,z) \end{cases} \tag{17.1}$$

are also waves, obtained by adding, respectively by multiplying with a at each point in space independently. Equation 17.1 tells us that the waves, and by this the states of the quantum particle, can be considered vectors in a complex vector space. Complex vector spaces are like real vector spaces from Chapter 6, but the scalars and the components of the vectors in equations (6.7) and (6.8) are complex numbers. This complex vector space is infinite-dimensional, don't let yourself be fooled by the coordinates of the three-dimensional space appearing in $\psi(x, y, z)$.

But why a wave, when we are talking about a particle? In Quantum Mechanics, waves come in many shapes and forms, and they behave quite unexpectedly. When you measure the position of a particle, you find it as a wave concentrated in some place. A wave that is not localized doesn't have a definite position, but if we want to detect its position, we'll find that it has, as if it suddenly localizes itself at a single point of space. This is an instance of the

DOI: 10.1201/9781003623373-17

collapse of the wave function. Figure 17.1 shows a wave $\psi(x)$ localized at x_0. Because we can always find the quantum wave localized in a definite place, it is common to still call it "particle".

The momentum is $p = h/\lambda$, where λ is the wavelength and $h = 6.62607015 \times 10^{-34}$ J/Hz is the *Planck constant.* This is why, to have a definite momentum, a wave has to have a definite wavelength λ. For this, it has to be a plane wave, that is, to be spread everywhere in space and periodic so that its real and imaginary parts are a sine and a cosine, with period λ. Figure 17.1 doesn't do justice to this, it simply represents the wave with wavelength λ as if there would be only one space dimension x, and it represents it as a real function, not a complex one. It represents the real part of $\psi(x)$, letting you imagine the imaginary part as being so that $\psi(x)\psi(x)^* = 1$ at every $x \in \mathbb{R}$.

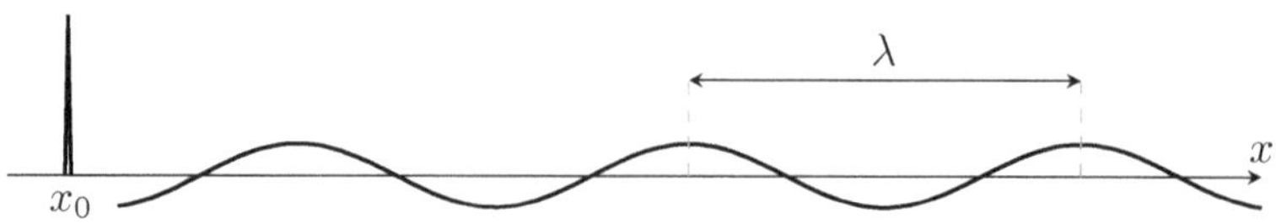

Figure 17.1: A localized wave ($\perp$) with definite position at x_0, and a wave with definite momentum h/λ, spread everywhere in space ($\sim$).

Figure 17.1 illustrates the fact that a quantum particle cannot have both a definite position and a definite momentum, because it cannot have a precise position and at the same time be spread everywhere, in order to have a definite wavelength.

So that's a quantum particle. We may expect that two quantum particles are two waves, and in general, n quantum particles are n waves. But this is not the case. For n particles of spin 0, the wave has the form

$$\psi\left(\underbrace{x_1, y_1, z_1}_{\text{particle 1}}, \underbrace{x_2, y_2, z_2}_{\text{particle 2}}, \ldots, \underbrace{x_n, y_n, z_n}_{\text{particle } n}\right). \tag{17.2}$$

It is a single wave for all n particles, and not n different waves. Note that, unlike the one-particle wave (17.1), it doesn't depend on a single position, but it depends on n positions. In classical physics, the $3n$ numbers representing the x, y, z-positions of n particles can be considered as n points in a three-dimensional space, or as a single point in a $3n$-dimensional space, called *the configuration space of positions.* The possible waves (17.2) for n particles form a complex vector space too.

While the wave for n particles is not n separate waves propagating in space, it is possible that, in some situations, it has the form $\psi(x_1, y_1, z_1, \ldots, x_n, y_n, z_n) = \psi_1(x_1, y_1, z_1) \times \ldots \times \psi_n(x_n, y_n, z_n)$. In general it does not have this form, and this phenomenon is the infamous *quantum entanglement.*

A particle may have a non-zero spin. In this case, it's a different kind of particle. The spin has to be a multiple of $1/2$, so it has to be of the form $n/2$. For spin-$1/2$ particles, $\psi(x, y, z)$ has values in $\mathbb{C}^2$, for spin-1 particles, in $\mathbb{C}^3$ and so on. The particle may have as well other internal degrees of freedom, which contribute with their own dimensions for the complex space in which ψ is valued. In all these cases, the value of the wave at a point is a vector in the complex vector space representing the spin and the internal degrees of freedom. In all these cases, the operations from equation (17.1) still apply, and such waves are still vectors in some complex vector space.

17.2 Quantum computers

A physical system has many continuous degrees of freedom, for example the position coordinates. However, for quantum computing, we focus on a few of them, which are discrete, for example the spin of an atom, the polarization of a photon, the position of a photon constrained to a finite number of tiny transparent tubes called *waveguides*, *etc.* This is not different from the case of classical computers, where we are not interested in all possible states of a memory cell, in all its degrees of freedom, but in only two states, or at most in a finite number d of states.

The state processed by a quantum computer can be represented therefore by a vector in a finite-dimensional complex vector space. For example, the state of a single *qubit* is a vector in a two-dimensional vector space. An example of a qubit is the spin of a Silver atom, or the polarization of a photon. Two photons can have their polarizations entangled, that is, we cannot represent their polarizations as two different vectors in $\mathbb{C}^2$, but only as a single vector in the vector space $\mathbb{C}^4 = \mathbb{C}^2 \otimes \mathbb{C}^2$. This is the *tensor product of complex vectors*, the vector space spanned by tensor products of vectors from the two spaces $\mathbb{C}^2$ representing the polarizations of the two photons. The tensor product of two complex vector spaces is defined like the real tensor product from Chapter 6, with the difference that the matrix components from equation (6.45) are complex numbers.

A *quantum computer* can be interpreted as processing complex vectors. While classical bit states can be interpreted only as basis vectors in the real vector space $\mathbb{R}^2 \otimes \ldots \otimes \mathbb{R}^2$, and classical computations as matrices that map basis vectors into basis vectors, quantum computing doesn't have these restrictions. Any unit vector can represent a state. A quantum computation has the form

$$|\text{output}\rangle = \widehat{\mathsf{U}} \, |\text{input}\rangle \,, \tag{17.3}$$

where $|\text{output}\rangle \,, |\text{input}\rangle \in \mathbb{C}^n$ are n-dimensional complex vectors and $\widehat{\mathsf{U}}$ is an $n \times n$ complex matrix. The transformation given by $\widehat{\mathsf{U}}$ is complex-linear, as in equation (6.11) but in which α can be a complex number. It also preserves the *Hermitian scalar product* of two vectors $|v\rangle$ and $|v\rangle$, defined as

$$\langle u|v\rangle := u_0^* v_0 + u_1^* v_1 + \ldots + u_{n-1}^* v_{n-1}, \tag{17.4}$$

It preserves in the sense that, if $|u'\rangle = \widehat{\mathsf{U}}\,|u\rangle$ and $|v'\rangle = \widehat{\mathsf{U}}\,|v\rangle$, then

$$\langle u|v\rangle = \langle u'|v'\rangle\,. \tag{17.5}$$

A transformation like this, that preserves the Hermitian scalar product, is called *unitary transformation.*

As in the case of real vector spaces (6.13), in complex vector spaces, a basis $|e_0\rangle\,, |e_1\rangle\,, \ldots, |e_{d-1}\rangle$ is called orthonormal if it satisfies

$$\langle e_i|e_j\rangle = \begin{cases} 1 \text{ if } i = j \\ 0 \text{ if } i \neq j \end{cases} \quad . \tag{17.6}$$

Exercise 17.1. Show that a complex linear transformation is unitary if and only if it maps an orthonormal basis $|e_0\rangle\,, |e_1\rangle\,, \ldots, |e_{d-1}\rangle$ into another orthonormal basis $|f_0\rangle\,, |f_1\rangle\,, \ldots, |f_{d-1}\rangle$.

After the computation, one more step is needed: reading the output. But in Quantum Mechanics, you can't read the vector $|\text{output}\rangle$. When you try to read the output, you can only get one of the basis vectors ($|0\rangle\,, |1\rangle\,, \ldots, |n-1\rangle$) of the complex vector space. The probability that the read output is $|j\rangle$ is

$$\text{Prob}_j = |\langle j|\text{output}\rangle|^2. \tag{17.7}$$

But then, it may seem that quantum computers are useless, because all we can get is a basis vector, and even this one is random! However, the quantum computation (17.3) is, ideally, designed so that $\text{Prob}_j = 1$ for one value of j and 0 for the others. That is, the output can represent a bit string like $|\texttt{1101 0010}\rangle$, as in the classical computer case, see Section 6.4. In practice, there are limitations, a perfect 1 probability is practically impossible, so we are happy if we can manage to get a probability very close to 1, $\text{Prob}_j \approx 1$.

The output is a bit string just like in the classical case. For example, bit strings of length eight, $|\texttt{0000 0000}\rangle\,, |\texttt{0000 0001}\rangle\,, \ldots, |\texttt{1111 1111}\rangle$, span the complex vector space $\mathbb{C}^{256}$. In the classical case, this basis can be obtained by having eight bits, as in Section 6.4. In the quantum case, it can be obtained from eight *qubits*, which are quantum systems that can be represented by complex vectors in $\mathbb{C}^2$. Eight qubits live in the vector space

$$\mathbb{C}^{256} = \underbrace{\mathbb{C}^2 \otimes \ldots \otimes \mathbb{C}^2}_{8 \text{ times}}. \tag{17.8}$$

A key difference between Quantum Mechanics and Classical Physics is that, at the end of the quantum computation, we can use any basis of n vectors, not only $(|0\rangle, |1\rangle, \ldots, |n-1\rangle)$, to read the output. This gives incredible possibilities, beyond what classical computers can offer, and it is the reason why photons and electrons behave sometimes as if they are waves, and other times as if they are point-particles (yes, the two kinds of waves from Figure 17.1 are basis vectors from different bases). Most, if not all quantum mysteries come from the possibility to choose the basis in many different ways. These mysteries include quantum complementarity, the measurement problem, the Schrödinger cat, contextuality, nonlocality, *etc.* But this is a story for a whole other book. Here, we will discuss only a minimum necessary to understand a bit of what a quantum computer does.

The quantum state processed by a quantum computer undergoes a succession of changes, by going through *quantum logic gates*, just like in classical computers we use classical logic gates. These operations are represented as matrices, just like classical logic gates were represented by matrices as in Example 6.1 from Chapter 6. However, there are a few important differences:

QC1. The vector space representing the data is complex, not real.

QC2. The matrices representing quantum logic gates are not restricted to map basis vectors to basis vectors from the same basis, in general they map basis vectors to basis vectors from different bases.

QC3. The mapping of vectors from two-bases is invertible, one-to-one.

Because the mapping is invertible, the quantum logic gates have the same number of inputs and outputs, so the matrix of the transformation $\widehat{\mathsf{U}}$ from equation (17.3) realized by the gate, which is the quantum equivalent of maps like $\mathbf{f}$ from equation (6.29), is square-shaped. A quantum logic circuit, obtained by combining quantum logic gates, is a larger logic gate with all the above properties.

QC4. The result of a classical computation is a single basis vector, while the result of a quantum computation can be any unit vector $|\text{output}\rangle$ from the vector space. To obtain a single basis vector, we measure the vector $|\text{output}\rangle$ in another basis $(|0\rangle, |1\rangle, \ldots, |n-1\rangle)$, and the system encoding the data becomes a basis vector $|j\rangle$.

QC5. The probability to obtain the basis vector $|j\rangle$ is $\text{Prob}_j = |\langle j|\text{output}\rangle|^2$.

While in most quantum computations we take care to obtain as output a single basis vector with probability as close as possible to 1, this is not always possible, and in this case the differences QC4 and QC5 are important.

17.3 Ambiguity of quantum computations

As we will see in Exercise 17.2, a quantum computer is a dynamical system, just like in Section 16.3, equation (16.12). When seen as such, it becomes apparent that a quantum computation is an analog computation. The space of possible states form a continuum, and the system changes continuously, except for the parts involving measurements. Therefore, the ambiguity is as large as in the case of analog computations. In fact, it is larger, because a quantum system can be in many more possible states than a classical system. The reason is that, if we combine two classical systems having the state spaces $\mathcal{S}_1 = \mathbb{R}^m$ and $\mathcal{S}_2 = \mathbb{R}^n$, the state space of the resulting system is the Cartesian product $\mathcal{S}_1 \times \mathcal{S}_2 = \mathbb{R}^{m+n}$. On the other hand, if we combine two quantum systems having as state spaces two vector spaces $\mathbb{C}^m$ and $\mathbb{C}^n$, the combined system has as state space the vector space $\mathbb{C}^{m \times n} = \mathbb{C}^m \otimes \mathbb{C}^n$.

In addition, in a quantum computer, the ambiguity is built-in. We can represent a qubit by the spin of a Silver atom, and make a convention that if the spin is up it encodes the value `1`, and if the spin is down it encodes the value `0`. But the notions of "up" and "down" depend on the direction in space along which we evaluate the spin, and there are infinitely many such directions. Similarly, we can represent a qubit by the polarization of a photon, and consider the horizontal polarization to represent a `0`, and the vertical polarization to represent a `1`, but again, "horizontal" and "vertical" are relative notions. Therefore, in the case of a qubit, the relativity of information is directly connected with the relativity of reference frames in space. But in quantum computing we assume even more relativity, we assume that there is no preferred basis in the complex vector space representing the entire system, so we seem to be allowed to reinterpret the data much more freely than in the classical case discussed in Chapter 6.

In fact the interpretation of the states of a quantum computer as data is not really done more freely, because it is just the consequence of applying the laws of computation from Chapter 10 to the quantum case. Recall that these laws are Substrate-Independence, Substructure-Independence, and Simulation=Computation, all arising from Implementation-Independence. While these laws remain as they are in Classical Computer Science, the more freedom comes from the much larger space of possible states.

The Relativity of Information in quantum computing can also be supported by the following reasoning. Ultimately, a quantum computation implements a unitary transformation (a complex linear transformation that preserves the scalar products). The quantum logic gates are chosen so that their combination gives the unitary transformation that we want to implement. The unitary transformation, as we recall from Exercise 17.1, maps an orthogonal basis into another orthogonal basis, and it is uniquely defined by these two bases. By examining equation (17.3), these bases are in fact the basis of possible inputs and the basis of possible outputs,

$$\begin{cases} |\text{output } 0\rangle & = \widehat{\mathsf{U}}\,|\text{input } 0\rangle\,, \\ |\text{output } 1\rangle & = \widehat{\mathsf{U}}\,|\text{input } 1\rangle\,, \\ \dots & \dots \\ |\text{output } n-1\rangle & = \widehat{\mathsf{U}}\,|\text{input } n-1\rangle\,. \end{cases} \tag{17.9}$$

But recall that in Quantum Mechanics we can do the measurement in a different basis $(|0\rangle, |1\rangle, \dots, |n-1\rangle)$. It follows that we could obtain the same output by leaving the input unchanged, for example by eliminating all quantum logic gates, and measuring it in the basis $\left(\widehat{\mathsf{U}}^{-1}|0\rangle, \widehat{\mathsf{U}}^{-1}|1\rangle, \dots, \widehat{\mathsf{U}}^{-1}|n-1\rangle\right)$. This is similar to how, in Chapter 6, a passive symmetry transformation as in Figure 6.1 gets the same result as the active symmetry transformation from Figure 6.2. And this idea is used ubiquitously in Quantum Computing, showing that we assume, both in theory and in practice, the same Laws of Computer Science discussed in Chapter 10.

Therefore, Relativity of Information is present in Quantum Computing too, and it is larger than in Classical Computer Science, because space of possible quantum states is much larger.

Exercises

Exercise 17.2. Explain why a quantum computer, or a quantum system in general, is a dynamical system like in Section 16.3, equation (16.12).

Solution. In this case, the state space is a complex vector space, $\mathcal{S} = \mathbb{C}^n$. The dynamical law is represented by all unitary transformations that map the state of the system at a time t_0 to its state at a time $t_0 + \Delta t$, $\left(\widehat{\mathsf{U}}_{\Delta t} : \mathbb{C}^n \to \mathbb{C}^n\right)_{\Delta t \in \mathbb{R}}$. This is true at least if there are no measurements, which abruptly change the state vector of the system into a basis vector. If we include measurements, the dynamical law is a stochastic law, but the system still is a dynamical system. □

Key points

- In Chapter 6, we've seen that classical computing can be understood as encoding data in vectors, insofar as they are basis vectors of a special basis.

This restriction no longer exists in quantum computing, where all complex linear combinations of basis vectors can encode data.

- Quantum logic gates are more general than classical logic gates, not being restricted to mapping basis vectors to other basis vectors. All active unitary transformations (rotations in the complex vector space) are allowed.
- Quantum computing follows the same Laws of Computer Science from Chapter 10.
- Reinterpretations used in quantum computing are not restricted to passive permutations of the basis vectors. All passive unitary transformations are allowed.
- Quantum computing allows for much more ambiguity and relativity of computation than classical computing.

Further reading

[64] Richard P. Feynman. *The pleasure of finding things out.* Perseus Publishing, Cambridge, Massachusetts, 1999

[153] Terry Rudolph. *Q is for Quantum.* Terence Rudolph, 2017

[36] Bob Coecke and Stefano Gogioso. *Quantum in Pictures.* Cambridge Quantum, Cambridge, UK, 2023

Interlude

Between Astronomy and Astrology

The oldest computing device known to us was the Antikythera mechanism, dated in the late second or early first century BCE. X-ray scanning suggests that it was used to predict the motion of the Moon and the Sun through the zodiac. It was able to model irregularities of the Moon's orbit and to predict eclipses. In this case, like for many ancient astronomical observations and cosmological models, it seems that the main motivation was Astrology.

♈ ♉ ♊ ♋ ♌ ♍ ♎ ♏ ♐ ♑ ♒ ♓

Figure 17.2: The twelve zodiac signs.

But does a zodiac sign exist in the sky, or only in our own minds? A constellation is a pattern of stars, which people interpret as representing various animals, objects, or gods. I personally have difficulties seeing the patterns of stars as related to what they mean in Astrology. I also find it difficult to connect them with the symbols representing them as in Figure 17.2.

The stars forming a constellation are very distant from each other. If we could see them from a different place in the universe, they would appear to be arranged in a completely different pattern. Even when seen from the same place, the same arrangement can be interpreted by different people as representing different things.

And this is in a three-dimensional space like the one we live in. Imagine how many ways to see a constellation could exist in a space with an immense number of dimensions, 2^n for some very large number n? How many different patterns could be observed in a constellation, depending on our position?

Similarly, if we lived in the 2^n-dimensional space representing n bits, as in Chapter 6, what we would see would depend on the view direction we have. And depending on this, we could read an immense number of completely different computations. The information space allows us to understand the relativity of information and computation in the same way the same object appears different when seen from different angles.

Once the constellations and the planets receive a meaning, astrologers are able to use the celestial bodies as a computing machine, based on their motion.

For this, they use Astronomy, to which they contributed. Many astronomers and scientists of the past were motivated by Astrology, including Tycho Brahe, Galileo Galilei, Johannes Kepler and Pierre Gassendi. Astrologers use Astronomy to predict the future configurations of the celestial bodies, and to interpret these configurations according to their man-made conventions, in order to "predict" the fate of the individuals.

Astrology is based on interpreting the motion of the celestial bodies, which by itself is just Astronomy and works like a clock. This is why the Antikythera mechanism could be used to simulate the motion of the planets in our Solar System, to predict their positions and even the eclipses decades in advance. Astrology is based on this rigorous part, but it is a pseudoscience because astrologers and their followers take their own conventions as objective reality, interpreting the celestial bodies as computing the personality and destiny of humans. But there is no scientific evidence that the configurations of planets and stars have anything to do with our personality and destiny in the way Astrology claims.

Exercise 17.3. What part of Astrology is science, and what part is pseudoscience? Justify your answer. Give another example of a hypothesis based on a clockwork part and a purely conventional part taken as objective reality, if you catch my drift.

A computation appears as a different computation when seen in a different basis in the information space, just like a constellation appears to form different patterns when seen from different places in the universe. But there are some differences:

1. Computers can be used to implement many different algorithms.
2. Computers can be used for Astrology, but also for scientific purposes. Modern science benefited enormously from the use of computers.
3. The conventions used in Computer Science are not restricted patterns of familiar objects, animals, or gods, as in the case of Astrology.
4. The number of different viewing directions is much larger in the information space than in the three-dimensional space where constellations exist. Therefore, the number of possible alternative interpretations of the same physical process as a computation is much larger.

The conventions done in Computer Science are not more objective than naming the constellations of stars. The relative motion of planets and stars allow their interpretation as a computing device, which works with precision by the laws of Astronomy. But interpreting this mechanism as computing the destiny of people is pure convention, which is why Astrology is a pseudoscience.

But, like in the case of the planets and the stars, we are not immune to attributing to computers magical properties.

I now pronounce you 0 and 1

Frank had the baseball since his tenth birthday. It was a home run ball hit by a famous player. He caught it at a game he attended with his late father. It was the last time they did something together.

One day, his friend Bob misplaced Frank's baseball. Frank was very sad about it, despite Bob's efforts to replace his baseball with a brand new one. Bob tried everything he could, including buying a signed ball at an auction, but Frank was still upset. Bob lost his patience and called Frank irrational, saying that the ball was not even signed, and it definitely no longer even had on it either the player's or of Frank's father fingerprints or DNA.

Bob couldn't understand how Frank, who was a staunch materialist, thought that the ball wasn't like any other physically indistinguishable ball. On one hand, he understood that Frank cared very much about his father, about the famous player, and about his own personal achievement of catching the baseball, and that only by association he cared about the baseball itself. On the other hand, he started doubting Frank's commitment to materialism and rationalism. He couldn't stop worrying that Frank was like those irrational people who wear lucky charms or blessed crucifixes, who believe that objects can be blessed or cursed.

"Wait", you may say, "I'm sure you made up this Bob character, no reasonable person would think that Frank's baseball is like any other ball! If this would be true, then what would be the difference between a handwritten sonnet of Shakespeare and a forgery, or between Da Vinci's Mona Lisa and a copy made of identical paint on an identical canvas?"

Indeed, if this would be true, there would be no difference between Da Vinci's Mona Lisa and a forgery done down to each molecule, or between the eleven identical canvases presented by Yves Klein in 1957, all eleven uniformly painted in a wonderful ultramarine blue. But we know that one of them is more valuable, Klein himself priced it much higher than the others, despite the eleven paintings appearing identical to the uneducated eye like myself. If the price tags were removed from Klein's eleven paintings, probably not even a true *connoisseur* would be able to put them back as they were, even if she would be absolutely certain that one of them is more special than the others. So I confess, Bob is a character I invented to portray an ideal materialist. If he's a flawed character, this may be because I assumed that, to be a consistent character, he should take materialism seriously in every situation. After all, in a materialistic universe there are no exceptions from materialism. Not even a baseball full of memories.

On a totally unrelated note, Bob understands very well that assigning the values `0` and `1` to the two states of a bit cell is a convention. At the same time, Bob thinks that once we make the convention, the resulting computation becomes, or rather turns out to be an intrinsic property of the computer, independent of the rest of the world. Or, at least, that somehow an intrinsic, objective computation emerges uniquely from the interactions between the computer's parts, and our convention merely acknowledges that computation, which is in there independent of our convention. Bob believes that, when we pronounce the two states of a bit cell as `0` and `1` like some external authority, we simply notice the evidence that the `0`'s and `1`'s are actually there. That there is a special computation associated with the computer's physical process, and all other computations we could associate are somewhat less real. So I have a question: if, even after reading the previous chapters of this book, Bob still believes that the computer's physical process carries an intrinsic computation, and that this computation may very well be sentient, would this make him a more realistic character?

What kind of sorcery is this?

An excellent book any programmer or Computer Scientist should read is "Structure and interpretation of computer programs" by Hal Abelson & Gerry Sussman with Julie Sussman [1]. Hal Abelson's MIT lectures were recorded and can be watched online https://ocw.mit.edu/courses/6-001-structure-and-interpretation-of-computer-programs-spring-2005/. They dedicated the book,

> in respect and admiration, to the spirit that lives in the computer.

The meaning of this dedication is made clear at the beginning of the book:

> Computational processes are abstract beings that inhabit computers. As they evolve, processes manipulate other abstract things called *data*. The evolution of a process is directed by a pattern of rules called a *program*. People create programs to direct processes. In effect, we conjure the spirits of the computer with our spells.

Seeing computation as the spirit of a computer, and programming as casting spells to control it, is a wonderful and practical philosophy which can help you become a good programmer. In fact, many good programmers are seen as wizards, and not only by the laymen, sometimes they see themselves as wizards too, and for a good reason [1]:

> A computational process is indeed much like a sorcerer's idea of a spirit. It cannot be seen or touched. It is not composed of matter at all. However, it is very real. It can perform intellectual work. It can answer questions.

It can affect the world by disbursing money at a bank or by controlling a robot arm in a factory. The programs we use to conjure processes are like a sorcerer's spells.

I don't think we should read into this more than a very useful analogy. There is no such ghost in the machine, there is just physical law guiding, or maybe describing, the physical processes. And since there are many ways to describe the same process, especially if the description is incomplete and abstract, there are many ways to interpret it as a computation. This interpretation is pure convention, and it can be done in many different ways, but the sorcery still works. The fact that we can use computers to solve various tasks, while impressive, is like using any other tool.

As we have seen, that spirit, whatever we mean by it, it's never in the computer, only in our minds. When you program a computer, or even when you use it (because users are nothing but high-level programmers), you may have an experience like you feel the computer's soul, especially when you are in the flow. But I insist that, whatever this is, it's not the machine's spirit, but your own. The alien device doesn't contain eight different spirits, revealing one of them to each of our eight friends from Alice to Heidi. The alien device is more like a mirror in which each of them sees the reflection of their own convention.

Computers don't have a mind of their own, let alone a spirit, just like a piece of paper on which Shakespeare himself wrote a sonnet is not a poet.

Magic or illusionism?

Programmers may not be wizards, but we can still compare them with illusionists who can trick our minds.

But programmers don't try to trick the users, rather, they do their best to make things as clear as possible. This may not be apparent when you read the source code, but the code is for the computer. The user interface is for the users. There is a huge gap between the two ways to represent the data, and programmers do their best to mediate between them. And this is the simple picture, since the software has its own layers, like a spectrum with an end speaking to the machine's blind functionality (low-level), and the other end speaking to the user (high-level). Programmers themselves come in a spectrum, each of them being specialized on a particular layer. To programmers, the lower-level layers appear as black boxes. They don't know and don't need to care what's in the black box from a lower-level layer, they just care what are the inputs and the outputs of each black box they use. A programmer specialized in a particular layer is a user of the layers that are lower relatively to her own. And they also can't prevent those at the higher layers to use their own black boxes in ways they were never meant to exist.

And yet, this is the ideal organization of software development, things are much worse. In the same team, programmers are users of the code written by their peers. And the product evolves, the programming techniques evolve, older programmers are replaced with new ones, and everything changes. With these changes comes the need to reorganize the code. Ideally, it would be completely rewritten, but this takes time, and time is money, and in the meantime everything else evolves. So reorganizing the code is usually done by temporarily wrapping old code in adapters, whose role is to allow it to be used until, if ever, will be replaced. This is why your computer programs, especially those existing for a long time, for which more versions were released, are more like Matryoshka dolls. Digging through older code becomes like archeology. Opening a black box to fix a bug may be as problematic as unleashing evil ghosts from an ancient tomb. It therefore seems faster and safer to wrap an old black box you want to fix in a larger box intended to patch the older black box, to handle the bugs and the situations that make it crash. But without opening a box, you may never know all situations that can lead to problems, and every box you wrap around it comes with its own problems. This is why the operating system on your computer, and the programs you use for a long time, while they keep upgrading to new versions, occupy more and more resources, but somehow old bugs persist even after decades.

An example when you replace a black box with another one is the following. Your program may use a picture format which stores each pixel as 24 bits, where three bytes encode red, green, and blue (RGB). Then, your program may need to handle data in a different format, for example with the reversed bytes, BGR instead of RGB. Without a conversion, the user will see red instead of blue and blue instead of red. So you may put the box in another box, swapping the red and blue components of the colors for each pixel. But then you retire, and somebody else needs to handle your code, and will have the surprise that, deep inside the program, the colors are inverted. Moreover, when you wrote the library you had no idea that the BGR box has inside it a RGBA format box (storing each pixel on 32 bits that also include a transparency channel A), which was wrapped around another box, a library handling the RGB format library, combined with a gray scale format for the transparency channel A, and that one has inside an older box handling a 16 colors format encoding two pixels in a byte, or maybe it uses interlacing, and so on. Imagine if this Russian doll of different color formats used in different situations was supposed to give an AI the qualia of color!

So yes, programming is not magic, but it's plenty of magic tricks, illusionism. The user is deceived, but there is no deception there, because what's going on inside the computer, the user's black box, is not his concern. The user just wants results, and he gets them. The programmers do their best, including to put themselves in a mindset in which they treat the programs as really living inside the computer.

Of course, what's going on inside the computer should be the user's most important concern when the user will look for technology to upload his mind in a robot, then all of these should suddenly matter. The user who uploads his mind in a machine will take the vendor's word that the machine will not swap his red and blue qualia. Or worse, his pain and pleasure experiences. But most importantly, that he will continue to be sentient.

Biting the bullet

Were you convinced that there is no unique way to interpret as a computation what a computer does? Did the realization that it's all a convention, and many others equally valid are possible, convince you that computations are not intrinsic features of the computing systems. Did this convince you that mind, which is independent of external conventions, can't be reduced to a computation? Or do you prefer to accept that, while a particular computation is not an intrinsic feature of a computing system, the set of all possible computations that can be attributed to the computing system is an intrinsic feature of it? If yes, congratulations, you bit the bullet and accepted that all alternative mind-like computations implemented by the same physical process are sentient. This is what follows from the assumption that mind is reducible to a computation, when you realize the ambiguity of computation. It is a prediction, and in the following we will test it.

Exercises

Exercise 17.4. Revisit the questions from the Introduction and reevaluate your answer.

Question	Yes	No	I don't know
Easy Question 1, page 8			
Easy Question 2, page 9			
Hard Question 1, page 10			
Hard Question 2, page 10			

Did any of your opinions change? What do you choose, Option 1 or Option 2?

Further reading

[1] Hal Abelson and Gerald Sussman with Julie Sussman. *Structure and interpretation of computer programs.* MIT Press, Cambridge, Massachusetts, 1996. https://library.oapen.org/handle/20.500.12657/26092.
Videos: https://youtu.be/-J_xL4IGhJA&list=PLE18841CABEA24090

Part VI

Result 2: Is your mind just a computation?

18

Crucial experiment: Are you a computation?

18.1 Many minds

If we wish so, we can regard the brain as an analog computer, or a hybrid computer, combining analog, maybe digital, and maybe quantum elements. However, if we want to remain faithful to Computer Science, we have to observe its Laws. And we have seen throughout this book that these are the Laws from Chapter 10, summarized in Figure 10.1. These Laws, particularly Simulation=Computation, imply that as we add more degrees of freedom to our computing devices, the ambiguity increases exponentially.

If mind were just a computation, there would be many minds running on the biological hardware called brain. This would be true even if the computation would be partially analog or quantum, as long as they obey the Laws of Computer Science.

Corollary 18.1. If the human mind is just a computation implemented by the brain, it suffers from the ambiguity from Theorem 16.1.

Proof. The human body, including the brain, is a physical system. It holds memories of past events and it changes in time irreversibly, so if mind is a computation, the brain satisfies the conditions of Theorem 16.1. Neurons seem to work as analog systems, in which case the ambiguity follows from Theorem 16.1. Even if the brain works partially like a quantum computer, its computations would be ambiguous. So it suffers from the ambiguity from Theorem 16.1. □

Chalmers admitted the fact that if mind supervenes on a computation the brain can implement more minds simultaneously in [28]:

> "a given physical hunk of matter can be associated with more than one mind"

but he doesn't seem to see this as a problem, and in any case he believes that the ambiguity is insignificant. Shagrir illustrated the possibility of two minds running on the same system in [162], where he showed that, by choosing

DOI: 10.1201/9781003623373-18

differently the voltage thresholds distinguishing `0` from `1`, we can interpret the same logic gate as another logic gate. Using this, he suggested that a brain can possess two or more minds, and argued that this is a problem.

The present book gives explicit examples of reinterpretations that do not rely on changing the threshold. Corollary 18.1 shows that the ambiguity grows exponentially with the number of memory cells in the finite case, and it is infinite in the analog case. Therefore, if we claim that a computing system implements a mind, we have to admit that it implements an immense number of other minds.

Computations are not intrinsic to the computing system, while minds are intrinsic to our brains, in the sense that they exist without requiring an external convention. This alone should be sufficient to reject the Computational Theory of Mind.

But computational functionalists may appeal to the following argument: *"OK, I agree that the interpretation of a physical process as a computation requires an external convention, so it is ambiguous. But the set of all possible interpretations of that physical process as a computation is intrinsic to that physical computing system. It requires no external convention to pick a convention as preferred. Then, we can declare that all possible computations that can be interpreted as minds are equally valid minds. I admit therefore that a brain supports an immense number of minds at once, each of them being aware only of itself".*

So if you still want to insist that mind is a computation, you have to bite the bullet and consider that all alternative computations doing the sort of computations that we think give rise to consciousness qualify to be genuine minds.

The following section refutes this last resort, proving that mind can't be reduced to a computation.

18.2 Crucial experiment: Are you a computation?

We have seen in Corollary 18.1 that if mind were reducible to a computation, the same physical process of the brain would implement many contradictory minds at once. Therefore, only one of the following can be true: Option 1, that the same computation supports many contradictory minds at once, or Option 2, that mind is not reducible to a computation.

Question 18.1. Is it possible to make a *crucial experiment*, *i.e.* an experiment able to decide between Option 1 or Option 2?

The answer is "Yes!", and now I will show that your mind doesn't reduce to a computation. Not only it doesn't reduce to a discrete computation, but also neither to an analog or a quantum computation that satisfies both Substrate-Independence and Substructure-Independence.

For this experiment you will not need to leave your armchair, because it will take place in the laboratory of your own mind. You will go through several steps of reasoning and inquiry.

Experiment 18.1 (Experimentum crucis).

***Step* 18.1.1.** The prerequisite for this experiment is to understand what I showed in this book so far. Let me recap here the main points:

1. A computation involves convention. This implies that there is an ambiguity in understanding as a computation what a computer does.
2. Then, many computations, all equally valid according to Computer Science, take place simultaneously whenever one takes place.
3. *If* mind were reducible to a computation, *then* we would have to accept as equally sentient minds all mind-like computations taking place along with it due to the ambiguity of computation.

***Step* 18.1.2.** Remember Corollary 18.1: If your brain is like a computer, each of your brain's physical processes implementing a computation implements as well an immense number of alternative computations. If your mind would be reducible to computation, all these alternative computations would be minds.

In fact, as your brain thinks, the connections between its neurons change. But we will approximate it here as a computing machine that changes its state but not its configuration, just like regular computers. This approximation will not affect the following arguments, since they will involve only instantaneous reinterpretations of a mind-like computation, at a given moment of time, so no change in the brain's structure will have to be considered.

***Step* 18.1.3.** Remember Implication 13.4: if your mind would be reducible to computation, your brain should support at the same time alternative minds holding any possible worldview.

For the next step, we need to consider something about the worldview we hold in our minds. This worldview is reasonably coherent, consistent, non-self-contradictory. In reality, we all hold a few contradictions in our minds, this is why we often have double-standards: due to our tendency to take sides, we may tend to judge the other side more harshly than our own side, for which we tend to find excuses more easily. But more blatant contradictions are possible, for example to believe that you live on the tenth floor of a single floor house, or that your father is your daughter, or that you were born thousands of years ago or thousands of years from now. In fact, in altered states of mind like when we are dreaming we can hold even such crazy contradictions: in a dream you can step through the door of your house and you find yourself in your childhood house, people around you can morph into other people, or a text written on a piece of paper can change while you look away for a second.

But there are differences between various degrees of self-contradiction of our minds. In principle, they can be quantified. To see how, consider a book containing n propositions. Let m be the number of pairs of propositions from the book that contradict each other. For example, all thirteen volumes of Euclid's elements [5] contain a fairly large number n of propositions, but no direct contradiction between any two propositions is known, so presumably $m = 0$. By the way, that's the ideal that I strive for while writing this book, so I will give the reader a perpetually open exercise:

Exercise 18.1. Find self-contradictions in this book. Find contradictions between propositions in this book and empirical facts or established facts about Computer Science and other fields appearing in this book.

No, I didn't intentionally insert internal contradictions in this book for the purpose of this exercise. But I think this is how Science works, your peers verify your work and try to find mistakes. If the mistakes are bad enough to invalidate your reasoning, try to correct it or abandon it altogether. Anyway, let's return for now to our experiment.

We can quantify a book's degree of self-contradiction by the ratio between the contradictory pairs and the total number of pairs of propositions from that book,

$$\text{Degree of self-contradiction} := \frac{m}{\binom{n}{2}} = \frac{2m}{n(n-1)}. \tag{18.1}$$

"The Library of Babel" is a short story written by Jorge Luis Borges about a library containing all possible 410 pages books of a certain format and character set [18]. Obviously, this library contains every book ever written up to 410 pages, and any 410 pages from the longer books ever written. But at the same time, almost every book from this library contains meaningless strings of characters, pure noise. Assuming that such a book contains tokens that can be considered, by their syntax, propositions, almost all such propositions would not even make sense. So it would not even make sense to say that two such propositions contradict each other, but we will count them as contradictory because it also doesn't make sense to say that they don't contradict each other. They are *not even wrong*, to use a phrase coined by physicist Wolfgang Pauli.

But even the books that make sense but are wrong overwhelmingly dominate numerically the correct ones. For example, the Library of Babel will contain numerous versions of Euclid's elements, in which the Pythagorean Theorem is stated in a false form, as in Figure 18.1.

For any logically consistent propositions, there is an immense number of logically inconsistent variants.

Let's assume we have a way to divide a text from any book from the Library of Babel in tokens that can qualify as meaningless or not meaningful propositions. Assuming that a randomly chosen book from the Library

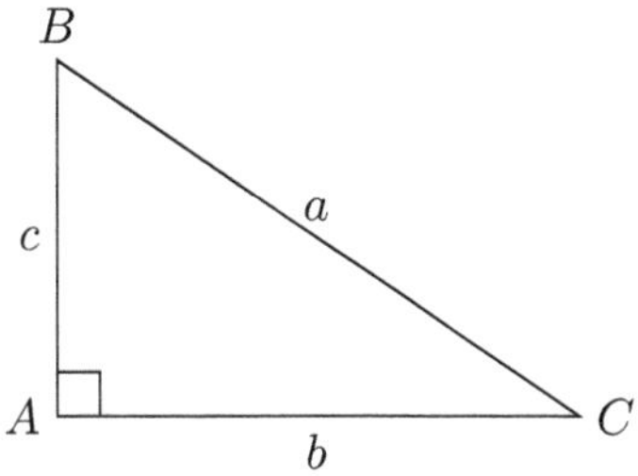

a^2	$=$	b^2	$+$	c^2	✓
b^2	$=$	a^2	$+$	c^2	✗
c^2	$=$	a^2	$+$	b^2	✗
a	$=$	b	$+$	c	✗
a^3	$=$	b^3	$+$	c^3	✗
a^4	$=$	b^4	$+$	c^4	✗
$a^{\cdots}$	$=$	$b^{\cdots}$	$+$	$c^{\cdots}$	✗
a^{100}	$=$	b^{100}	$+$	c^{100}	✗
$a^{\cdots}$	$=$	$b^{\cdots}$	$+$	$c^{\cdots}$	✗

Figure 18.1: The Library of Babel contains many more mistaken versions of Euclid's elements than correct versions.

of Babel contains an average of 50 propositions per page, it would contain $400 \times 50 = 20\ 500$ propositions. Since in a randomly chosen book from that library all propositions are meaningless, the degree of self-contradiction of a randomly chosen book would be 1. This may seem a small number, but it is the maximum possible, since in this case $m = n(n-1)/2 = 210\ 114\ 750$. At the opposite pole, a book of mathematics like Euclid's would have a degree of self-contradiction of 0 or very close to 0. For example, if it contains 10 contradictions (although nobody found them yet), its degree of self-contradiction would be $10/210\ 114\ 750 \approx 0.000000047593$.

Like in the case of a book, if we could list all beliefs making someone's worldview at some moment of time, and check them for direct contradictions, we could find the numbers n and m associated with that person's mind. There is no known way to do this in practice, but such numbers must exist, so we can quantify the degree of self-contradiction of a mind by the measure from equation (18.1).

We can invent more sophisticated measures of the degree of self-contradiction of mind, involving triples of propositions and so on, but we don't have to be too pedantic to make this point, since we will not count these numbers exactly. The whole point of this definition is to illustrate that, if we are able to verify if two propositions that we understand contradict one another, we can verify the degree of self-contradiction of our own minds.

***Step* 18.1.4.** Examine your own mind and notice that it has a relatively low degree of self-contradiction.

If mind isn't reducible to computation, it collects its data from facts of the real world, which, being facts, are non-contradictory (even if from the non-contradictory data sometimes we draw contradictory conclusions).

***Step* 18.1.5.** On the other hand, as seen in Implication 13.4, the alternative input used to train an AI can contain any sort of data. This data may be worldviews that are apparently about facts, but in most cases they are extremely self-contradictory, much more than in the wildest dream. It may be data that doesn't even make sense, disparate images and words that can't be integrated consistently in a larger view. It may even be pure noise. The same applies to the alternative mind-like computations supported by our brains. And since the number of such possible alternative minds increases exponentially with the length of the training data, while, from equation (18.1), the maximum number of possible contradictions increases quadratically with the length of the training data, the number of possible alternative minds of each degree of contradiction increases exponentially with the degree of contradiction.

***Step* 18.1.6.** Some of the possible alternative mind-like computations running on your brain at once are relatively self-consistent, having a relatively small number of internal contradictions. Others are fully contradictory or noisy. Possible alternative minds containing a small number of contradictions, like yours, form an exponentially small minority among all alternative minds, even if we count only those that contain the memory of reading this book. Figure 18.2 illustrates the space of possible worldviews hierarchized by the number of contradictions, although it doesn't represent this exponential growth.

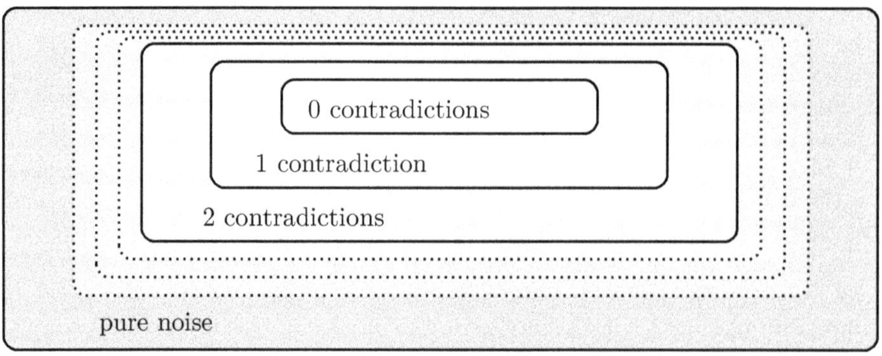

Figure 18.2: Worldviews classified by the number of internal contradictions. This representation is distorted to fit in the page, in fact the size of each class depends exponentially on the number of contradictions.

Now you will give a ballpark estimate of the probability that, if your brain supports all these minds with their own worldviews as in Step 18.1.6, your mind is one of the few minds with a low degree of self-contradiction. Remember that each mind with a particular worldview can be reinterpreted as another mind with any other worldview. Therefore, the probability distribution of these possible alternative mind-like computations is invariant under reinterpretations. Since when one exists, all others equally exist, none of them can be favored by the probabilities. Hence, even if some of the minds would be favored, for example by natural selection, all possible alternative mind-like computations equally exist, including those having no chance to survive.

***Step* 18.1.7.** Since the number of possible mind-like computations with very self-contradictory worldviews as in Step 18.1.6 is much larger than the number of possible minds with reasonably non-contradictory worldviews like yours, the probability that the real minds with unreasonable worldviews actually exist is very small. Due to the exponential growth of the number of mind-like computations with the number of internal contradictions, this probability is vanishingly small. The alternative computations are not genuine minds like yours, because if they were, your mind would be almost surely among these self-contradictory minds. If they were genuine minds, to have a mind like yours when the probability to have a self-contradictory mind is extremely close to 1, you'd have to be extraordinarily lucky.

Therefore, while a simulation of a computation is a computation,

Implication 18.1. A simulation of a mind is not a mind.

Note that the alternative mind-like computations are not disqualified from being genuine minds merely because they have a high degree of self-contradictions. Having a very high degree of self-contradiction doesn't disqualify something to be a mind, as we can see from the example of our own mind in a dream. They are not disqualified because of their self-contradictions, but by the empirical fact that you are never one of them. This book shows that, when analyzed with the tools of Computer Science, the Computational Theory of Mind predicts that you can be any of these mind-like computations, with equal probability. So it predicts with almost certainty that the degree of self-contradiction of your mind is maximal. But direct empirical evidence contradicts this prediction, and therefore it contradicts the Computational Theory of Mind.

Conversely, presuming that a computation is mind-like and can hold representations of the world, having a low degree of self-contradiction doesn't make it automatically a genuine mind.

18.3 Self-location probability

You may wonder why, in Step 18.1.7 from Experiment 18.1, would it be relevant that you could be another mind-like computation. Since this is the key step of the proof, maybe I should say more about this. It's all about *self-location probability*.

Let me give you an example. Suppose you travel, and you have a reservation in a hotel complex. The hotel manager chose the room and building for you, but you don't know them yet. All else being equal, you can guess that most likely your room is in a hotel with more rooms like yours, so you can try that building first.

Here's another example, much closer to Step 18.1.7. Suppose you are an AI, and you are told you will be trained as an AI companion, an artificial friend. The customers are people from various countries, so you will be trained in the history, language and culture of one of these countries. The training is done in four office buildings. The first office building trains AIs like you for the US, the second one for the UK, the third one for China, and the fourth one for France. All else being equal, you can guess that most likely you will be trained as a Chinese AI friend, assuming that the demand is proportional with the population of each country.

Now imagine you hired a company named "Digital Heavens Inc". to upload your mind on a computer and resuscitate you after you die. Since you know important secrets, some people with bad intentions try to intercept the upload and make a copy of your mind. The statistics show that 5% of the uploaded identities are copied by such bad agents. One day, you wake up as a digital copy of your biological self's mind. You don't know for sure whether you are a copy on a server of the company Digital Heavens, or a copy on some enemy server. But you think that the probability to be on the company's server is 95%. This is self-location probability. Things get more complicated if you take into account that you may be one of the alternative digital copies allowed by the many possible reinterpretations of the original computation that was supposed to simulate your mind.

Self-location probability is just probability, but it may seem odd because we are accustomed with *epistemic probability*. You apply epistemic probability when you want to guess, for example, whether a coin you flipped, which you are holding in your fist, is heads or tail. It is about your ignorance of the coin's state. But you also apply it to guess the lottery numbers, even though these numbers are not yet generated, because it's about your ignorance of the conditions that may influence the draw.

Self-location probability is thought to be less common, because it is about which item you are among a number of possible items that already exist. You don't know which one you are, but it's not about ignorance of the state of a single item, it is about the ignorance of your place among more existing items. Since Experiment 18.1 is about many coexisting mind-like computations, and you identify with one of them, it is about self-location.

18.4 How lucky should you be?

Now that you did Experiment 18.1, let us try to estimate the probability that your mind can still be a computation, albeit one that is lucky enough to have a low degree of self-contradiction. We will apply *Bayes' theorem*, which gives us the best way to describe how we should update our beliefs after the experiment.

Let H be the hypothesis that mind is reducible to computation. More precisely, given all you have read in this book so far, by Step 18.1.2 you should consider H to be equivalent with the hypothesis that all alternative mind-like computations simultaneously ran by your brain are conscious.

Let $P(H)$ be your initial *credence* that the hypothesis H is correct, that is, the degree of belief you had in H prior to the experiment. Like probabilities, credences are numbers between 0 and 1. You may wonder why your belief prior to the experiment matters. Well, at this point I have nothing more to offer than your own credence, since science says nothing about the validity of H. At least not until we finish this proof.

If your initial credence that the hypothesis H is correct is $P(H)$, your initial credence that mind *can't* be reduced to computation is $P(\neg H) = 1 - P(H)$.

Let C be the event that a mind-like computation implemented by your brain has a low degree of self-contradiction. We consider the degree of self-contradiction defined by a formula like (18.1), and we assume that "low" is defined more precisely as meaning below a precise threshold, like those used in Figure 18.2. We don't need to detail this, what matters is that the existence of such a threshold makes sense.

The *conditional probability* that the degree of self-contradiction of a random mind-like computation is low, *conditioned by the assumption that* it's reducible to a computation, is denoted by $P(C|H)$, defined by

$$P(C|H) := \frac{P(C\&H)}{P(H)}, \tag{18.2}$$

where $P(C\&H)$ is the probability that C occurred and H is true.

The *conditional probability* that the degree of self-contradiction of a random mind-like computation is low, conditioned by the assumption that it's irreducible to a computation, is

$$P(C|\neg H) = \frac{P(C\&\neg H)}{P(\neg H)}, \tag{18.3}$$

where $P(C\&\neg H)$ is the probability that C occurred and H is false. Since these are the only alternatives for a mind-like computation to have a low degree of self-contradiction, the total probability that a mind-like computation has a low degree of self-contradiction is

$$\begin{aligned} P(C) &= P(C\&H) + P(C\&\neg H) \\ &= P(C|H)P(H) + P(C|\neg H)P(\neg H). \end{aligned} \tag{18.4}$$

At the same time, we've seen that the probability that a reinterpretation of a computation that simulates a mind is consistent is exponentially small in the system's size, *i.e.* something like

$$P(C|H) \approx 0.000 \ \ldots\ldots 001 = 10^{-N}, \tag{18.5}$$

with a huge number of zeroes before the first significant digit, denoted by a large natural number N.

Finally, Bayes' theorem gives the following relation between to reciprocal conditional probabilities $P(H|C)$ and $P(C|H)$

$$P(H|C) = \frac{P(C|H)P(H)}{P(C)}. \tag{18.6}$$

This is true in general, but here I applied it specifically to our case.

Let's put all of these together.

$$\begin{aligned}
P(H|C) &= \frac{P(C|H)P(H)}{P(C)} && \text{[Bayes' theorem]} \\
&= \frac{P(C|H)P(H)}{P(C|H)P(H) + P(C|\neg H)P(\neg H)} && \text{[equation (18.4)]} \\
&= \frac{P(C|H)P(H)}{P(C|H)P(H) + P(\neg H)} && [P(C|\neg H) = 1] \\
&= \frac{1}{1 + \frac{P(\neg H)}{P(C|H)P(H)}} \\
&= \frac{1}{1 + \frac{P(\neg H)}{P(H)}10^{N}} && [P(C|H) = 10^{-N}]
\end{aligned} \tag{18.7}$$

Let us now be more specific about your prior belief in H. If you started by being agnostic about the reducibility of mind to a computation, or even just if your credence was not too close to 0 or 1, now your credence should become exponentially small, like 10^N times smaller. In particular, if you were fully agnostic, so that $P(H) = P(\neg H) = 0.5$,

$$P(H|C) = \frac{1}{1 + 10^{N}} \approx 10^{-N} = 0.000 \ldots\ldots 001. \tag{18.8}$$

Therefore now, that you took into account the results from this book and did the Experiment 18.1, you should be quite certain that your mind is not reducible to a computation!

But what if your faith in the Computational Theory of Mind was as strong as starting with a credence of $0.999 \ldots\ldots 999 = 1 - 10^{-N}$? Then now you should become an agnostic,

$$P(H|C) \approx \frac{1}{1 + 10^{-N}10^{N}} = 0.5. \tag{18.9}$$

Maybe if you would do all the steps in Experiment 18.1 again, your belief will drop down to that from equation (18.8)! So what would happen if you do it again and again? Your belief that mind is reducible to a computation should drop down even more, according to Bayes' theorem, becoming $10^{N+N+\cdots}$ times smaller!

What can reasonable people do to protect their belief that their minds are reducible to a computation? Bayes' theorem offers the way out: start by being absolutely certain that your mind is reducible to a computation before doing the Experiment 18.1. Only then your faith will survive, since

$$P(H|C) \approx \frac{1}{1 + 0 \times 10^{N}} = 1. \tag{18.10}$$

Only if you are 100% certain that mind is reducible to a computation, Bayes' theorem allows you to maintain your certainty.

Similarly, a consistent computation that simulates a mind can apply the reasoning I presented and conclude that it is itself irreducible to a computation. This would be a false positive! A "computational zombie"! I call it a "false positive" because such a mind-like computation is very rare, 1 in 10^{-N} as in equation (18.5).

To return, we've seen that not even Bayes' theorem can remove absolutely certain belief that your mind is reducible to a computation, but if you have even the tiniest reasonable doubt, it will amplify it asymptotically toward the certainty that your mind is irreducible to a computation. If you rely on mathematical proof.

In the following section, I will try to anticipate and address several possible objections to the conclusion of Experiment 18.1.

18.5 Anticipating possible objections

Objection 18.1. For a long time, people claimed that computers may do a lot of things, but they will never be able to do this or that thing humans can, like writing poems or finding new theorems in mathematics. Your claim that only mind can have a low degree of self-contradiction is ridiculous. Human mind can be full of self-contradictions, and a computer program can be fully free of self-contradictions.

Reply 18.1. I fully agree that human mind can be full of self-contradictions, and a computer program can be fully free of self-contradictions, and I even said it myself in the steps of the experiment (see Step 18.1.3). *But this is not the point of the proof at all!* The point of the proof is that among the alternative mind-like computations running at the same time in the same brain process there are many more with a high degree of self-contradictions compared to those having a small degree of self-contradictions. If your mind were a computation, there would be an infinitesimally small chance that it just happens to be one with a very small degree of self-contradictions. I used

Bayes' theorem to show how small the odds are that this happened by pure luck, and it keeps happening again and again every second.

Objection 18.2. Experiment 18.1 assumes that a mind can verify its own degree of self-contradiction. But if it is self-contradictory, how can it trust itself?

Reply 18.2. Assuming that a mind-like computation can hold ideas, it can also hold contradictory ideas. In particular, it can indeed hold the idea that it is free of contradiction, and at the same time have a very high degree of self-contradiction. Given that most mind-like computations have a very high degree of self-contradiction, about half of those who hold a belief about this would believe that they are free of contradiction despite encountering self-contradictions in themselves all the time. This indeed is a problem. If you worry about this, a way to avoid it is to do the experiment thoroughly and repeatedly, to maintain a list of beliefs that you have, then to examine them for contradictions, and mark down what you found with each such examination, as in Table 18.1.

Table 18.1: Tests you can do to verify the self-consistency of your mind.

Belief	**Test**	**Result**
Addition is commutative. $5+2=7$	Is $2+5=7$ too?	✓
People can't levitate.	Can I levitate?	✗
Joe is my brother.	Am I Joe's sibling?	✓
I live in Pisa. Pisa is in Italy.	Do I live in Italy?	✓

You can print such tables before doing the verifications, do the verification, and mark the results. You can revisit the list later and compare it with your memory of it. This will increase your self-confidence in your own mind. Even so, you can think that it is impossible for a self-contradictory mind to verify its own consistency, because this is logically possible, no matter how unlikely. But then why trust your own mind about anything?

Objection 18.3. Experiment 18.1 is an introspection, so it can't be trusted.

Reply 18.3. Let's assume that indeed, for whatever reason, introspections can't be trusted. Even so, Experiment 18.1 consists of steps of reasoning and inquiry, which are not different from the reasoning and inquiry you do about anything else. When you verify the proof of a mathematical theorem, you make similar steps, and rely on the content of your mind, on the memory of previous readings and calculations you did in the past, and you assume that the content of your mind has a low degree of self-contradiction. All scientists, no matter how smart and rational may they be, have no other way but to rely on their minds. If Experiment 18.1 is introspection, then so is any other scientific research.

Objection 18.4. A probabilistic proof is not a proof.

Reply 18.4. All experiments that confirm theoretical predictions are in fact probabilistic. For example, the discovery of a new particle like the Higgs boson is never 100% certain. We express the statistical significance of an experimental result in terms of *sigma*, the standard deviation from the event if no effect was obtained. If one obtains 5 sigma in an experimental result, we consider it significant enough to validate the hypothesis that was tested. But with 5 sigma, there is still a chance in 3.5 million that, given that the Higgs boson doesn't exist, CERN got a false positive. If we would not accept probabilistic proofs, not much would remain of current Science. Note that Experiment 18.1 gives much more confidence to an agnostic than the discovery of the Higgs boson, as we have seen in equation (18.8).

Objection 18.5. Since a mind that is too contradictory can't survive, such minds are excluded by natural selection. So it isn't fair to count very self-contradictory minds among the possible alternative minds.

Reply 18.5. If mind would be reducible to a computation, every such mind can be reinterpreted as numerous alternative minds that are extremely self-contradictory. They are implemented by the same organism that survived the natural selection, but these alternative minds need not have the ability to survive. It is sufficient that the organism implementing them has the ability to survive, and it will always carry a large number of alternative mind-like computations, most of which are extremely self-contradictory.

Most of these alternative mind-like computations have no appropriate representation of the actual environment, but they don't even respond to the events from the actual environment. They respond to whatever reinterpretation of the environment they contain, but when this response is reinterpreted to recover the actual mind of the organism, the responses are also reinterpreted as the appropriate responses. So, to count as mind-like, it's irrelevant how adapted to the real environment is the response of an alternative computation, it should be judged solely in its own simulated world.

Objection 18.6. Experiment 18.1 is individual. Doesn't this lead to the idea that only your own mind is irreducible to a computation? This seems to be a sort of *solipsism*, the idea that only your mind is real.

Reply 18.6. You can ask other people to do Experiment 18.1 for themselves, and they will tell you the result, but you can't infer from this alone that this result was communicated to you by a genuine mind and not a mere computation.

As an analogy, consider a simple machine, simple enough for you to be sure that it is not conscious, but programmed to respond in a particular way to the environment. We can attribute to this machine the computations that ensure the observed behavior, but also the alternative computations supported by the same physical processes. We may observe that the machine behaves consistently with the former, and not the latter, but now, after understanding this book, we understand that the other computations equally happen too.

Similarly, if other people do Experiment 18.1 for themselves and tell you that their minds have a low degree of self-contradiction, this could be explained by the fact that you observe the outputs of a computation which also has to be consistent enough to ensure the proper functionality of that body in the environment that you share with them. This doesn't exclude the alternative mind-like computations, and now we know they equally exist as computations. Communication is mediated by a particular user interface established by social interactions, and you will see only answers that come from that interface (see Thought Experiment 13.2). The mind-like responses you see through the interface are those consistent with a behavior adapted to the environment. But we can't be sure that the mind-like computation with which you communicate is indeed a genuine mind. This is why for this experiment we can rely on and draw conclusions only about our own mind, and not about other people's minds, because when we interrogate them we can reach only a behavior consistent with a mind-like computation that is sufficiently non self-contradictory to fit in this world.

You know your mind is not reducible to a computation, but you can't verify this for other people's minds, not in the same way you verified it for yourself. But, as in the case of the *problem of other minds* [6], a totally skeptical position leads to a variant of solipsism. If we agree that solipsism is not a tenable position, we should agree as well that other people's minds are not reducible to computation.

A way to accept the possibility that also other people's minds are not reducible to computations is the following. Since our mind is not reducible to a computation, it requires the violation of Substrate-Independence or Substructure-Independence or maybe both. If your brain can violate one of these principles, it makes sense to assume that other beings with similar brains are sentient too, for the same reason why you are.

Objection 18.7. If we follow the argument from Reply 18.6, shouldn't we accept as well that an AI mind who made the experiment is as real as other people's minds?

Reply 18.7. According to Reply 18.6, the only reason we accept other people's minds as real is because we expect their brains to violate Substrate-Independence or Substructure-Independence or maybe both, like we concluded our own brain does. But the AI is a computation, by design, and so it satisfies both Substrate-Independence and Substructure-Independence. If the AI would have a mind like the human mind, it would have to violate at least one of them. This is not impossible, but if it happens when the design was based on Computer Science only, it can happen only if it accidentally violates Substrate-Independence and Substructure-Independence, and this is used to endow them with sentience in some way we don't understand yet.

Note that the results from this book don't imply that conscious machines are impossible. It only says that if they can be conscious, this can only be achieved by other means than a mere application of Computer Science.

Objection 18.8. I can't take your proof seriously, because you didn't define mind.

Reply 18.8. I don't need to define an apple to know it's not an orange. I didn't and will not define mind or consciousness. I don't need to do it. All I need to do is to define computation, and to compare it, based on its predictions, with my own mind. As a result, I can't say what mind is, but when comparing it with computation I can say *I am not that.*

18.6 A few more words

There is increasing support among the specialists for the idea that an AI can be sentient in the same way humans are. This is favored by the fact that more and more powerful AIs are developed, and there seems to be no human artistic and intellectual activity that can't be simulated, at least in principle, by an AI. And I won't deny this. But Theorem 12.3 shows that there is a very high ambiguity in the content of the AI's mind. A computer can't think unambiguously even of a number, as shown by Implication 13.2. And there is no objective reason why one of the numbers the computer is thinking about is more special than others.

Experiment 18.1 from Section 18.2 shows that we are not reducible to computations. But this can be inferred only by the individuals who perform the experiment, and only for themselves. For such an individual it should follow that mind can't be simulated on a computer that merely applies the Laws of Computer Science. The AIs are just simulations, not minds. They are "computational zombies" so to speak.

This result is based on the Laws of Computer Science, particularly structure independence. In the literature, it is often proposed that computation is something that in fact violates these principles. Such redefinitions of computation were proposed by various authors to escape the ambiguity of computation already noticed in the triviality argument (see Chapter 14). But whatever is what they call "computation", it must be something else, because if computation violates Substructure-Independence, computers as we know them wouldn't be possible. Maybe mind requires such a violation, but then it can't be implemented on the current computers, which work according to the principles of Computer Science, in particular Substructure-Independence.

This doesn't mean that there are no physical systems that can think. Humans are such an example, and I see no reason why it would be impossible, in principle, to artificially build other beings able to think. But the results from this book show that, for a machine to think, it should do more than merely simulate thinking. And this book doesn't say what the missing ingredient is.

In a future book, I will investigate proposals made in various other theories of mind, that mind reduces to structure or function, down to the finest organizational levels of matter [180, 181], but for now I give a preview in Chapter 20.

Exercises

Exercise 18.2. Visit the website "The Library of Babel" by Jonathan Basile [10] (https://libraryofbabel.info/). Understand how he managed to create the Library of Babel without having to store effectively all possible 410 pages books (which would not fit in the entire universe). His program generates each book on the fly as you explore the rooms of the Library, so that every time anyone visits the same room finds the same books. Moreover, he did the same with all possible 640×410 pixels images. How would you design such a program? How would you design a program that does the same but by using reinterpretations of the data similar to how it was done in Chapter 11?

Exercise 18.3. Do Experiment 18.1. Even if your prior belief was that mind is irreducible to a computation, even if you understood that computations are not intrinsic properties of the computing systems or brains, do Experiment 18.1. It is worth understanding *why* you are not a computation. And if you did Experiment 18.1 and still believe that mind is reducible to a computation, revisit Section 18.4 and take a moment to appreciate how lucky you are for being a mind-like computation with such a low degree of self-contradiction, and you continue to be like this every moment, against all odds.

Exercise 18.4. Revisit the questions from the Introduction and see if your answers changed.

Question	Yes	No	I don't know
Easy Question 1, page 8			
Easy Question 2, page 9			
Hard Question 1, page 10			
Hard Question 2, page 10			

Key points

- You can verify experimentally that your mind is not reducible to a computation.
- You can't verify it for others, since they are not you.

Further reading

[182] O.C. Stoica. Does a computer think if no one is around to see it? *philsci-archive:22880*, 2023

[172] O.C. Stoica. Are you a robot? http://youtu.be/kuziE01rh6M&list=PLJzOclJMoIC1pnJIPlmWhGwaDWD04tFza. Accessed April 22, 2026

[170] Cristi Stoica. Alternative computations at once. *https://www.unitaryflow.com/2025/03/alternative-computations-at-once.html*, 2025

Part VII

Physics and being

19

Digital dreams

19.1 Does Zhuangzi dream of electric butterflies?

The first virtual reality simulations acknowledged as such were our dreams. Dreams proved to us that we can experience an entire world and then wake up and realize nothing was real. It is therefore likely that the first metaphysical questions humans had, in particular questioning the external reality, the way it appears to us, or our own ability to perceive it as it is, were inspired by the very existence of dreams. A famous example, recorded in writing between 476–221 BC, is attributed to the ancient Chinese philosopher Zhuang Zhou, also known as Zhuangzi [216].

> Once, Zhuang Zhou dreamed he was a butterfly, a butterfly flitting and fluttering about, happy with himself and doing as he pleased. He didn't know that he was Zhuang Zhou.
>
> Suddenly he woke up and there he was, solid and unmistakable Zhuang Zhou. But he didn't know if he was Zhuang Zhou who had dreamt he was a butterfly, or a butterfly dreaming that he was Zhuang Zhou.

A modern-day version of Zhuang Zhou's question may be:

Question 19.1. Are we living in a computer simulation?

This question can be found in Daniel Galouye's 1964 science fiction novel "Simulacron-3" or "Counterfeit World", or in Steven Lisberger 1982 movie "Tron", in the Wachowskis' 1999 movie "The Matrix", in Josef Rusnak's 1999 movie "The Thirteenth Floor", *etc.* It was also known in more scientific but speculative literature, see Konrad Zuse's "Calculating space" in [215] and Frank Tipler's "The physics of immortality" [197].

Nick Bostrom proposed an argument that we almost certainly live in a simulation [19]. His argument can be summarized as follows:

- Civilizations evolve, reaching a "post-human" stage (they need not be humans, the term "post-human stage" just means we take humanity's post-human stage as reference).

DOI: 10.1201/9781003623373-19

Figure 19.1: *Zhuangzi Dreaming of a Butterfly*, by 18th-century Japanese painter Ike no Taiga, Public domain, via Wikimedia Commons.

- Since the computing power of a civilization increases very fast, exponentially, post-human civilizations can simulate entire worlds.
- Each simulated world may contain other civilizations which, when they become posthuman, can simulate entire worlds and so on.

He presented a logical analysis and numbers, concluding that, unless

(1) "The fraction of human-level civilizations that reach a posthuman stage is very close to zero" or

(2) "The fraction of posthuman civilizations that are interested in running ancestor-simulations is very close to zero".

then almost certainly

(3) "The fraction of all people with our kind of experiences that are living in a simulation is very close to one".

Then, Bostrom concludes, not only do we almost certainly live in a simulation, but most likely we even live in a simulation in a simulation in a simulation and so on, God knows how many levels. Many thinkers considered his argument convincing, while others gave various objections, for example that mind can't be simulated computationally, that the limited resources prevent the simulation of too many other worlds, and so on [29].

19.2 Let there be bits!

The success of Computer Science in simulating various physical processes made many people ask the following question

Question 19.2. Is our Universe a computing system or even a computation?

Since, we think, a universal computing system can simulate anything, it can also simulate physical systems, and therefore the entire universe. And there are universal computing systems following very simple rules, like those discussed in Chapters 8 and 9. Since physicists try to find the simplest laws that can describe the structure and behavior of everything in the universe, some researchers think that a good candidate could be a cellular automaton or other discrete computing system. A discrete computing system can also avoid the occurrence of infinities that seem to plague both Quantum Theory (at high energies [138]) and Einstein's General Relativity (at the singularities inside the black holes and at the Big Bang [174]), although no significant progress was made in this direction so far.

In 1969, Konrad Zuse made the natural move to propose that the Universe is nothing but a computing system [215]. In his 1978 Lectures, Edward Fredkin made a similar proposal, naming it *Digital Physics Hypothesis.* Later, he preferred the term *digital philosophy* [67].

In a similar spirit seems Wheeler's *it from bit* proposal, according to which the observations we make result in bits, and, based on some results from Quantum Mechanics, the values of these bits appear to be created as we observe them and yet to be compatible with everything that already happened as if they always existed [210, 175]. Wheeler gives as an analogy the game *twenty questions*, in which you have to guess a word, object, place, person *etc*, by asking only yes-or-no questions. But Wheeler adds the following plot twist: the item to be guessed is not chosen when the game starts, but the yes-or-no answers are chosen so that at least an item satisfies the answers. Wheeler explains that this game is an analogy for how Quantum Mechanics works. He uses the *Delayed Choice Experiment*, which is based on Bohr's complementarity applied to a photon that could travel through both arms of an interferometer or to only one of them, but arranged so that the experimentalist can decide whether the photon went through one of the arms of the interferometer or through both with a delay, after this happened (Figure 19.2).

Wheeler concludes that the observations we make now decide the past, back to the Big Bang. The Universe, from its beginning, comes to be from the bits we create when we observe them.

Another idea of a Digital Universe was proposed by Max Tegmark: all possible mathematical structures exist, and we happen to live in one of them [195, 176]. He accepted only computable mathematical structures, and

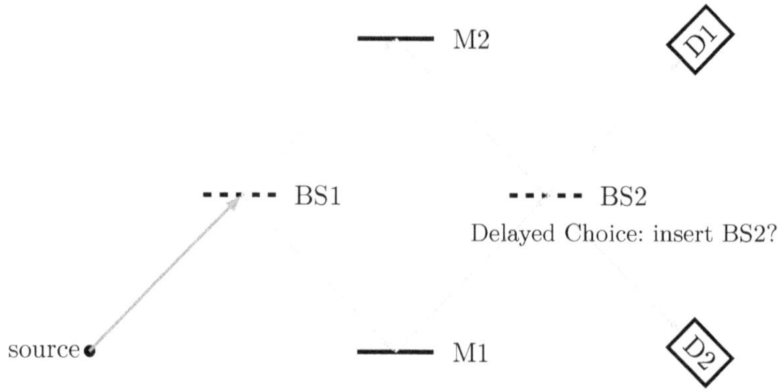

Figure 19.2: Wheeler's Delayed Choice experiment. A photon emitted by a source meets a beam splitter BS1, which splits its wavefunction into two components traveling along two different paths simultaneously, reflected by the mirrors M1 and respectively M2. When the two components of the photon's wavefunction meet beam splitter BS2, they recombine, and the photon is detected by detector D1. But if BS2 is absent, the photon is detected half of the times by detector D1 and half of the times by detector D2, showing that the photon traveled along either M1 or M2, so it was not split, but either reflected or transmitted by BS1. Wheeler noticed that we can delay our choice whether or not to insert BS2 until *after* the photon met BS1, and he claimed that this shows that *we can decide whether the photon was split or not by BS1 after this happened!* Wheeler even imagined such an experiment at a cosmic scale, proposing that this proves we can decide the past of the Universe.

proposed that all that needs to exist is a computer program that, if it runs, generates the entire multiverse of computable mathematical structures. But, he argues, this program doesn't even need to be ran, because all the future states of the computation are encoded in the program itself.

In perhaps a similar vein, Stephen Wolfram proposed the concept of the *ruliad* [213], as the foundation of a theory of everything. Wolfram explains

> Think of it as the entangled limit of everything that is computationally possible: the result of following all possible computational rules in all possible ways.

Interestingly, it seems that the result of following all possible computational rules in all possible ways is already included in any Turing complete computing system running only once a single process that doesn't return to a previous state, as seen in Chapter 12, particularly Section 12.5.

These are only some of the proposals that somehow the Universe is a computer or a computation. Are they merely crazy ideas? If they are, to some they may feel as the natural conclusion of the modern perspective on Physics. Modern Physics is based on mathematical abstractions, to the extent that everything there is to know about the world is considered to be encoded by the mathematical structures (also see Chapter 20). We tend to see information as requiring a material system to encode it, but Quantum Mechanics, by seemingly offering only probabilities, makes it difficult for us to conceive what kind of material system underlies the world. Some think it may very well be pure information, without the need of a material substrate. Another reason invoked in support of the idea that there is only information is the existence of a minimum energy requirement to erase a bit of information, as stated by the *Landauer Principle* [114, 12]. This could very well be interpreted as an indication that there is no information without energy, hence without physical stuff, but is often interpreted as a sign that the nature of energy itself, and therefore of the physical stuff, is computational. Some think that the Universe is just pure information without a substrate, "disembodied" computation.

19.3 Asking computer science

Regardless of how compelling may seem various arguments in favor of the Simulation Hypothesis and Digital Physics, if we're talking about computations, the final word belongs to Computer Science. So let's see what it has to say.

As we have seen in Chapter 13, a single simulation is accompanied by an immense number of other simulations, obtained from the former by reinterpretations certified by Computer Science itself. Therefore, if mind can be reduced to a computation, Bostrom's argument for living in a simulation severely underestimates the number of simulations. Even if he concluded that we almost certainly live in a simulation, if mind can be reduced to a computation, the certainty should be much closer to absolute certainty.

Moreover, to any physical process, whether or not it is the process of a purposefully designed computer, we can attribute many computations, even sophisticated computations like Artificial Intelligences 14. The ambiguity of computation implies that simulations of other intelligences and even other worlds are all around us, and wherever one exists, gazillions of others exist.

So, whether or not the Universe is itself a computing system, even if its laws are nothing but a computation, such a Universe should carry an immense number of other computations that contain simulated worlds. Seen from within, an immense number of them look like our world, and a much greater number of them like completely different worlds, with different numbers of dimensions and different apparent physical laws. All of them exist at once as simulations done by the same computation.

But, as we have seen in Chapter 18, the hypothesis that mind can be reduced to a computation implies that our minds would have a very high degree of self-contradiction. Since this implication is refuted by understanding

Computer Science combined with simple observations of our own minds, we conclude that mind cannot be reduced to a computation.

Chapter 18 discusses only computations simulated by the brain, but both the Simulation Hypothesis and the Digital Physics Hypothesis are about simulations of the entire world. Does this change the Crucial Experiment 18.1? Yes, it does, by allowing even more alternative computations, with even more possible self-contradictions. If we were to live in a simulation, not only the data from our brain, but the entire simulated world would be dominated by internal logical inconsistencies. Therefore, the Bayesian analysis from Section 18.4 gives a much smaller probability that we live in a computation, much closer to zero than the simple hypothesis that our minds are computations in a physical universe. Bostrom's simulation argument is blocked. Moreover, the Simulation Hypothesis itself, as well as the Digital Physics Hypothesis, in the variants in which our minds are part of the simulation, are blocked too.

But can a computer even simulate anything at all? A computer follows its physical processes. We call it "computer" because we built it with a purpose: to use it for computations. But the computer itself has no clue that it computes. No matter what computations it does, these are in fact *our own* conventions. We generously attribute the computations exclusively to the computers, but they are grounded with only one foot in the machine's processes and with the other foot in our mind's conventions.

> We may believe that mind can be reduced to a computation, because we forget the many choices we made when making the conventions, and we consider them objective processes independent of our own minds. This is an illusion coming from taking our own conventions as having an independent reality.

One may want to get out of this problem by establishing a way to select a single computation from the immense number of alternative ones. We've seen that this is done by conventions, which are in our minds, the minds of the users. But if our mind would be just a computation, where are the conventions needed to define our minds as computations?

Question 19.3. If the entire world is a simulation, or if it is digital, and if all things in it, including our minds, are computations, where are the conventions defining them as computations? If a user is needed to make the convention defining the computation, does a digital Universe need a *Prime User*?

If, in the case of a simulated world, the Prime User can be in the super-world where the computer simulating our world is, where is this Prime User in the case of a Digital Universe? Does the Prime User need more conventions, made by a Prime-Prime User and so on? Where, and especially how does this ladder end, or it's Prime-Users all the way down? Such questions appear if we try to reduce everything to a computation. The attempt to remove the user's central role in anchoring the computations in conventions leads to an "outsourcing" of this role, delegating it to an even greater user.

19.4 What about the Church-Turing-Deutsch principle?

Does this mean that the *Church-Turing-Deutsch Principle* is refuted? This Principle is stated in David Deutsch's *The Fabric of Reality*, page 132 [53] and in [52]:

Principle 19.1. Every finitely realizable physical system can be perfectly simulated by a universal model computing machine operating by finite means.

If by "simulation" we mean what is normally understood, "imitation", this book doesn't contain a refutation of this principle.

Turing himself named his famous test to determine if a machine is intelligent "The Imitation Game" [200]. But regardless of what he originally understood by "imitation" and "intelligence", we have seen that imitation as it is used in the theory and practice of Computer Science, no matter how detailed, is not enough. As seen in this book, culminating with Chapter 18, Computer Science itself, as introduced to us by Turing, Church, Kleene, and others, refutes the Church-Turing-Deutsch Principle in the form in which by "simulation" or "imitation" we understand something able to reproduce all aspects of the original, including sentient experience.

But the results from this book are perfectly compatible with the possibility that any physical system can be simulated computationally, if we refer only to the system's observable aspects. And even then, the users cooperates with the machine in producing the simulation, by anchoring it in their conventions and, through the user interface, in their own sensory experiences. So the simulation is not done exclusively by the machine alone, but in cooperation with the users.

19.5 The real matrix

Since we all dream, and when we wake up we realize that the world from the dream was an illusion, dreaming was a common fundamental theme in ancient philosophies, all over the globe. In Hinduism, dream was mentioned frequently in the *Upanishads* [196] (800–300 BC), and later in *Advaita Vedanta* [99], to explain how what we normally call "reality" can be an illusion, *Maya*.

A rushed understanding of the word "illusion" in this context is that of denying reality, but it is not quite so. Not the reality is denied, but its appearance. The ultimate reality is hidden to us by our ignorance. Again, ignorance is not the passive ignorance of simply not knowing something, quite the contrary. This ignorance is active, mind actively projects "names and forms" over whatever reality is, conceptualizing it in more manageable bits. As long as we are not aware of this, we take these names and forms as reality. And as we use them to build our conceptual constructions, the illusion becomes stronger and stronger.

The names and forms originated during evolution to interpret the stimuli from the environment. They are conventions built on top of each other and passed from generation to generation. They evolved into user interfaces between our minds and the environment and helpers for our thinking, but they seemed to gain a reality and a mind of their own, creating a simulation which hides the "true reality". We built and inherited these conventions, we assumed them as the reality, we combined them into more sophisticated conventions. These conventions construct automatically in our minds a simulation of reality, like we do in our dreams, by trying to predict it from very few details accessible by us through our senses. When applied within their range of utility, these conventions work well enough to pass as reality, but when applied outside their range of utility they fail, allowing us to recognize them as dreams, optical illusions, cognitive illusions and so on.

Numerous thinkers questioned reality like Zhuang Zhou, in various places on Earth. Plato proposed the *allegory of the cave*: we are like prisoners in a cave, chained so that they can watch only some shadows on a wall for their entire lives, and believing that this is reality [143]. Later, Descartes analyzed the possibility that an evil demon tampers with his senses to deceive him by presenting him a complete illusion of an external world [51, 50].

Many believed, and still believe, that dreams predict future events, or that they are ways to visit other worlds as real as ours. But the thinkers I mentioned here mainly took dreams as evidence that mind can create illusions of reality. Dreams, they said, teach us that our minds are able to create vivid experiences of nonexistent worlds, and this is what we do even when awake, painting reality with colors and forms that are not really out there.

Perhaps the first simulations were not dreams as such, but our mind's representations of reality, which, some modern scientists say, are not very different from hallucinations, from dreams, except by their higher adequacy to the empirical world [97, 161]. We gather a large number of stimuli through our senses, and we use them to build a simulation of the external world. This simulation is largely a detailed dream, filling in between the details gathered through the senses, and updating itself when we act upon the world and we get feedback. This is somewhat similar to how instances of a virtual reality displayed on more computers are synchronized by the servers to make it appear as being shared. Once the simulation engine is downloaded on your computer, much of the work is done on the client side and the amount of data exchanged with the server can be much smaller, and yet, you can share the same environment with other users. A dream is like a virtual reality running when our senses are disconnected from the external world, not vetoed by it. Maybe, when we learned to model the external world in our minds, we also learned to dream.

The fact that we rely so much on simulating the world in our minds also affects the way we think abstractly. We tend to model abstract ideas with concrete models, richer than the modeled entities. For example, if someone asks you to think of a number, you may visualize it as digits in a particular font, of a particular size, and, if you're a synesthete, even colored in a particular way. There is no such thing in the abstract concept of a number like 37, but we give it numerous concrete attributes and qualities when we imagine it. Some even imagine numbers as lucky or unlucky, or as having various destiny-related meanings. But try to think of an abstract number like 37 without invoking characters, decimal digits or digits in another base, without representing it as three fingers and seven fingers or as "37 apples". Or try to imagine a line as a "breadthless length", as taught by Euclid [5]. No width, no color, including black or white, no texture or other material-specific features, just an abstract infinite line. In the quest to think abstractly, our mind perpetually takes abstract ideas and tries to find concrete examples, painting an additional layer of reality underneath them. Sometimes this seems ridiculous to modern people, like seeing animals or objects in the patterns made by stars and even attributing them the power to affect our destinies. But we do this more often than we would be comfortable to admit.

If you are a young student of Computer Science, you can start by questioning everything, like good students do when they want to understand what they are taught. You'll ask "why call this state `0` and the other state `1`?", and understand that this is a convention. You'll understand that a universal Turing machine simulates any other Turing machine because the internal structure of the head and the alphabet of the simulated Turing machine don't have to be organized identically in the Turing machine simulating it. But then, when you code, ideas like "`#FF0000` is red" will be imprinted so deeply in your mind's eye, that you will "see" the redness in the code and in the state of the machine. Even if you are aware that your mind put that redness there, even if you recall vividly the "aha" moment when you realized these are all conventions, this illusion will come back to you. Like it happens when you know perfectly well that the two segments that appear of different size in the optical illusion from Figure 19.3 are in fact equal, but despite you knowing this, despite you measuring them repeatedly, your "eye's mind" keeps telling you otherwise.

Truth is, once we realize how easily we can be fooled by our own minds, we become very cautious and develop *reality checks.* Figure 19.4 shows a way to verify that the two segments have the same length.

Another way is to measure them. You can check other illusions by covering parts of the image, rotating them, copy-pasting the image into a graphical

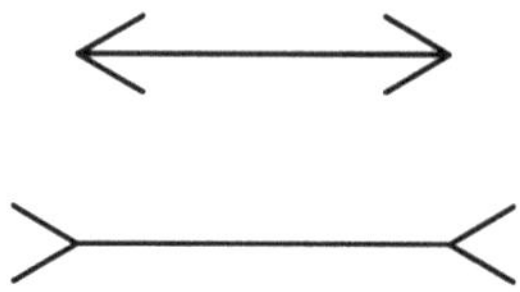

Figure 19.3: The Müller-Lyer Illusion. Are these two segments equal?

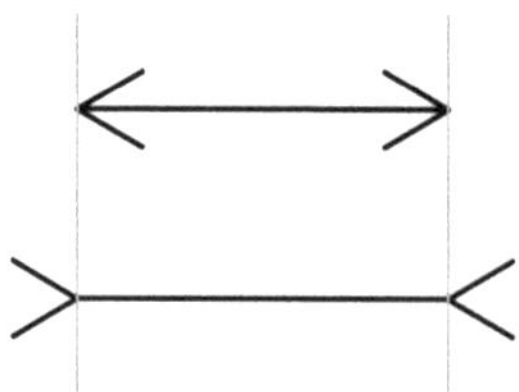

Figure 19.4: The Müller-Lyer Illusion, manual verification.

editor to verify the colors digitally, and, in the case of animated illusion, pausing the animation.

Reality checks are commonly used to see if you are dreaming, for example by verifying if you can push a finger through your other hand, if a text or a clock changed while you looked away, if you can breathe while pinching your nose, if you can float, if you don't recall how you got where you are right now [112]. But even when you realize something is really weird and wonder whether you are dreaming, your mind will drag you back into the oblivion of the fact that you are dreaming by making up on the spot nonsensical explanations that seem to make perfect sense to your dreaming mind. Even only this fact, that you can dream the most absurd situations and always cook-up *ad-hoc* rationalizations, should show to you how much your own mind can trick itself.

We can get a hint that we may not be as rational as we think from the fact that we know very well that many other people fool themselves, or so we think of them. We tell ourselves "they lack critical thinking skills" [155]. But why would we think we're immune? Aren't we fooled by optical illusions? If so, aren't we fooled by cognitive biases too? Optical illusions continue to enchant us even after we verify them countless times. Why would you think that, just because you can notice other people's reasoning fallacies, you don't have a blind spot for your own fallacies? Everyone's mind evolved by making conventions and relying on simulations of the external world. Our minds are built of magic tricks, cheap replacements of an impossible direct access to the external world. Even when we are as rational as possible we rely on simulations of an ideal logical reasoning.

One of the biggest errors we make is categorizing, labeling, and forgetting that we labeled and taking the labels as objective characteristics of the things we labeled. And this is reinforced when everybody around us uses the same labeling system. So if everybody says "these two states are `0` and `1`", and everybody's neurons are trained to attribute subjective experiences to certain behaviors, these combine easily, almost inevitably, into the illusion that a computer program can be sentient. An illusion deeply felt due to our mirror neurons, the ones that make us feel pain or happiness when we recognize in other people the signs associated with these feelings. Signs that can be simulated.

This is why I tried to season each step in this book with reality checks in the form of examples and exercises. Their purpose is not to help you learn Computer Science, whose basics, I hope, many of the readers already understood. Their purpose is mainly to help you unlearn the objectification of the convention, which is useful as a crutch, but conditions us to see in computers more than it's really there. And, like with any crutch, our minds have all sorts of fail-safe mechanisms and tricks that return to the familiar but useful misconceptions. The purpose of the exercises is to train the ability to discriminate between the physical reality of the computing machine and the conventions and interpretations we project on top of this reality. And then to apply this ability to discriminate mind from its computational simulation.

Exercises

Exercise 19.1. If mind would be reducible to a computation, would the probability that you live in a simulation be smaller, larger, or equal with Bostrom's estimate?

Exercise 19.2. What does the irreducibility of mind to a computation say about the Simulation Hypothesis and the Digital Physics Hypothesis?

Exercise 19.3. Is there something that can't be simulated computationally?

Exercise 19.4. What is the oldest simulation known to us? Is it of the same kind as computational simulation?

Further reading

[215] Hector Zenil. *A computable universe: Understanding and exploring nature as computation.* World Scientific, Singapore, 2012

[19] Nick Bostrom. Are we living in a computer simulation? *The Philosophical Quarterly*, 53(211):243–255, 2003

[29] David Chalmers. *Reality+: Virtual worlds and the problems of philosophy.* Penguin, UK, 2022

[67] E Fredkin. An introduction to digital philosophy. *Int. J. Theor. Phys.*, 42(2):189–247, 2003

[210] J. A. Wheeler. Information, Physics, Quantum: The Search for Links. In *Complexity, entropy and the physics of information: the Proceedings of the 1988 Workshop on complexity, entropy, and the physics of information held May [29]-June [10], 1989 in Santa Fe, New Mexico*, volume 8. Westview Press, 1990

[195] M. Tegmark. *Our Mathematical Universe: My Quest for the Ultimate Nature of Reality.* Knopf Doubleday Publishing Group, 2014

[53] David Deutsch. *The fabric of reality: The science of parallel universes and its implications.* Viking Penguin, New York, 1998

[200] Alan Turing. Computing machinery and intelligence. *Mind*, 59(236):433–460, 1950

[97] Donald Hoffman. *The case against reality: Why evolution hid the truth from our eyes.* WW Norton & Company, New York, 2019

[161] Anil Seth. *Being you: A new science of consciousness.* Penguin, London, UK, 2021

20

Relativity of structure

20.1 Beyond computing systems

In Chapter 14, Section 14.3, I mentioned that there are proposals to avoid the ambiguity of computation by requiring that a computing system can implement only computations of data structured in the same way as the physical system implementing it. After all, data is stored in particular ways, the computer architecture was ignored in Figure 5.4, brains consist of neurons with very specific structure and behavior and so on. But, as explained, this would be a redefinition of the word "computation", which would no longer mean what it means in Computer Science. In Computer Science, there are universal computing systems, but imposing that the data are structured in the same way as the physical machine implementing the computation excludes the possibility of universal computers (see Reply 14.4 and Proposition 14.3). This doesn't mean that mind can't be reduced to how the brain is structured and how it functions, just that this is not "computation" as understood in Computer Science.

In this chapter, we will see what happens if we consider such "generalizations" of computation. An example is *functionalism* [116],

> the doctrine that what makes something a mental state of a particular type does not depend on its internal constitution, but rather on the way it functions, or the role it plays, in the system of which it is a part.

Computationalism (or *computational functionalism* [167, 77, 147, 37]) is a particular example of functionalism. But since we've seen in the Crucial Experiment 18.1 that the ambiguity of computation leads to the impossibility that mind is just a computation, if we want to continue to pursue this direction, we need forms of functionalism that reduce the ambiguity.

In functionalism the internal constitution is irrelevant and only the functionality matters, but if this also turns out to be too ambiguous, we can even go further than this, and consider that the internal constitution, the structure, also matters. And, of course, the way that structure changes in time, its *dynamics*.

There are numerous proposals to reduce mind to structure and its dynamics or to their functionality. We can try to discuss each of them in particular,

DOI: 10.1201/9781003623373-20

filling thousands of pages and still leaving the discussion open for variations that our discussion will inevitably miss, or we can discuss them altogether, by discussing the most general class of such proposals.

The most general class of physicalist theories of minds is the one that proposes that mind reduces to structure. This also includes dynamics, because dynamics is the way structure changes in time, which is in fact a spatio-temporal structure. Functionalist theories of mind take into account fewer aspects of the structure, so that the same mind can, according to such proposals, be realized in multiple ways that are structurally different. All these approaches, from computational to functionalist to those based on the full details of the structure, can be called *structuralist* approaches. A proposal in which consciousness is due to structure alone is *Integrated Information Theory* [199, 110]. In fact, Tononi and Koch consider it a consciousness-first proposal, but Tegmark and others think it's a structuralist proposal. Various other theories of mind are understood as structuralist [119, 166].

This analysis gives us a hierarchy of physicalist theories of mind, represented in Figure 20.1.

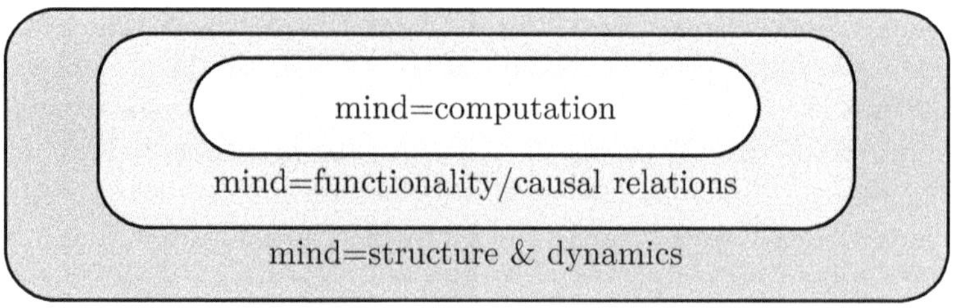

Figure 20.1: Hierarchy of physicalistic theories of mind.

20.2 Physicalism and philosophical zombies

Materialism or *physicalism* includes all proposals that consciousness is reducible to structure. A common statement of materialism or physicalism goes like "physicalism is the thesis that everything, including mind, is physical", or "can be explained exclusively in physical terms", or "it is reducible to the physical". That "there is nothing beyond the physical world". That any mental property should be a physical property, which is sometimes expressed as "mind *supervenes* on the physical", or "mind is grounded in the physical". But often "physical" or "the physical world" are left undefined. A common definition of "physical" is "what exists", but this leads us to the tautology "everything that exists supervenes on what exists". This says nothing, because if consciousness requires some special kind of stuff, a "secret sauce", and if that "sauce" exists, by this definition it should be called physical. Then should Descartes's *res cog-*

itans, the "thinking stuff" he postulated in addition to *res extensa*, the name he gave to matter, be considered physical by this definition [51, 50]? Or, if Bishop Berkeley is right and there is only mind [14], does then this immaterial mind qualify as physical? Another common definition is "physical is whatever physicists study", which doesn't say much and leaves open the possibility to call "physical" ghosts and spirits, if they will ever be studied by physicists.

And if you go further to ask analytic philosophy, the answer will not become too comprehensible, at least not for those untrained in the subtleties of philosophy that a working physicist may miss. See for example [191]:

> Physicalism is true at a possible world w iff any world which is a physical duplicate of w is a duplicate of w *simpliciter*.

Here, "simpliciter" means without exceptions, qualifications, or specific conditions. Is this definition clear enough for someone untrained in analytic philosophy, like a regular working physicist? Maybe the following definition is clearer ([78], page 31):

> Let us call physical facts that can be captured in the mathematico-nomic vocabulary of physics "pure physical facts," and physicalism in conjunction with the view that fundamental reality wholly consists of such facts "pure physicalism".

For physicists or non-philosophers in general, there may be other ways that reflect what they mean if they say they are physicalists, which is informed by the way they conduct their research. A physicist or a non-philosopher may find this definition by Sean Carroll much more transparent [23],

> By "physicalism" here I don't simply mean a world with only physical properties, but specifically physicalism about consciousness. Can we conceive of a world where the ontology consists of nothing other than some notion of physical "stuff" (or the specific quantum fields in the Core Theory) without any inherently mental aspects, but which nevertheless accounts for consciousness as we experience it?

So the question is whether sentience supervenes on the structure alone, if, like computation, it obeys Substrate-Independence, but unlike computation, it doesn't necessarily obey Substructure-Independence. The key point of physicalism is that the stuff we call physical should not have any inherently mental aspect, anything mental should follow from how the physical stuff is organized. In other words, any two possible worlds with the same structure, which satisfy the same mathematical evolution equations, should be equally able (or equally unable) to support the existence of conscious beings. To understand what is meant by worlds with the same structure, we can consider two Newtonian worlds consisting of billiard balls that collide elastically as in Newton's mechanics. Even if in the first world the balls are made of cheese and in the second world they are made of rubber, as long as they satisfy the same laws of motion and interaction, they should behave identically. And if one of them is capable of producing consciousness, the other should be equally capable of the same.

Now we are getting somewhere, because now we can define clearly what physicalism is, without leaving room to adapt the definition so that physicalism remains true regardless of what we will ever discover:

> Physicalism is the thesis that mind supervenes on the structure and dynamics of the stuff of the world, whatever this stuff is, and nothing else, not even the intrinsic nature of that stuff.

Therefore, if physicalism is true, everything should be captured in the way the systems are structured and how they behave, and consciousness shouldn't be treated differently. This position can be formulated equivalently in the following form, which I will use in the following:

The Physicalist Thesis. *Any two systems with the same structure and dynamics are identical in all relevant aspects, including whether they support consciousness.*

According to The Physicalist Thesis, even if the substances making two systems are of different natures, as long as their nature doesn't affect the structure and the dynamics, the differences are irrelevant. Matter or the substance that makes up everything is "phenomenally inert", *i.e.* it doesn't have additional powers needed only to give rise to consciousness. Its structure and dynamics are sufficient to account for everything that exists, and this should apply to consciousness as well.

The idea of *philosophical zombies* was proposed to illustrate the supposed possibility of qualitative differences between sentient and insentient beings, and as a conceptual test of materialism or physicalism [108, 107].

Definition 20.1. A *philosophical zombie* is a hypothetical insentient entity identical in structure and dynamics to a sentient being.

I said "conceptual test" because it is widely considered impossible as an empirical test, although some argue that it doesn't make sense to say it is conceivable [23].

We recognize in The Physicalist Thesis a negation of the possibility of philosophical zombies. According to physicalism, it is impossible for two systems or worlds to have the same structure and dynamics, and yet one to be sentient and the other not.

In 1921, 100 years before Carroll's account of physicalism quoted above, Eddington wrote [57]:

> And yet, in regard to the nature of things, this knowledge is only an empty shell—a form of symbols. It is knowledge of structural form, not

knowledge of content. All through the physical world runs that unknown content, which must surely be the stuff of our consciousness.

So it seems that physicalism is not so evident to everybody. To see if physicalism is right, we need to answer the following question

Question 20.1. Is it possible for two isomorphic systems to exist, one sentient and the other one insentient?

An affirmative answer would prove that consciousness is irreducible to structure and dynamics, refuting The Physicalist Thesis.

The formulation of physicalism from The Physicalist Thesis is perfectly consistent with what physicists who engage in researching the foundations of Physics do, with how they see their own endeavor. Physicists only care about the structure, the relations of the entities of their theories. They express these structures and relations mathematically, derive predictions, and compare these predictions with the real-world experiments.

This makes sense, because all we can find by looking at the external world are relations. Measurements and observations inform us only about the relations, and not about the nature of the relata. They tell us about structures and dynamics, and not about the nature of the substances having those structures and following the dynamics. When we measure the position of a particle, we measure a relative position, and we compare it with a unit length. When we measure the mass of a body, we compare it with the mass of another body. We count the particles that enter an interaction and the resulting ones.

In the theoretical formulations, ontology may be invoked to ground our intuition into something concrete (*e.g.* "matter"), or they may call "ontology" the building blocks of their theory, but the equations of Physics are blind to the intrinsic nature of matter. This is why Physics can be expressed mathematically, because mathematics studies relations. Every mathematical structure can be expressed in terms of relations only [82].

A physicist would consider two apparently different mathematical models to be about the same possible world, if the elements of one of these models can be mapped to the elements of the second model by a one-to-one correspondence. So, to the physicist, only the structure matters.

20.3 Physics is relational

In this section, I will give concrete examples showing that the relational or structural aspects of the world are the only ones that matter in Physics. This seems to justify The Physicalist Thesis as the default position.

The key observation that in physics all that matters is structure, and not the intrinsic nature of the stuff having that structure, resides on the fact that the latter can't be observed in experiments, while the former can. This key element is what made it possible to make discoveries like the Theory of Relativity [61]. In its predecessor, Galilean relativity, space and time are relative, independently. Even if there would be absolute space, even if space would have an absolute state of being at rest or in motion, even if it would have an absolute origin in the same way a coordinate system has, even if there would be special directions "East" and "West", "North" and "South", "up" and "down", as long as experiments can't distinguish them, they are physically irrelevant, and the laws, being based on what can be observed, can't say anything about them [144]. Similarly, in Special Relativity, space and time are not absolute, but relative, but even if there are such things as absolute space and time, since they can't be observed, the physical laws we know can't say anything about them.

Example 20.1 (Relativity of space)**.** The relative position and velocity of an object depend on the reference frame [96]. The thesis of *absolute space* states that there are absolute positions and absolute velocities. This requires an absolute distinction between reference frames at rest and in motion. However, even if this distinction were true, no known experiment could detect absolute space or an absolute reference frame at rest. The known laws of Physics don't discriminate among inertial reference frames. For this reason, physicists adopt the thesis of *relative space*, that there is no preferred reference frame, and no absolute space. Even if space is absolute, this escapes Physics, it's a metaphysical distinction. Whatever the nature of space is, its only role in Physics is to embody relative positions and velocities. Physics is blind to other ontological aspects of space that may make it absolute. Understanding this led, in conjunction with other postulates, to both Special and General Relativity.

The same idea, applied this time to other degrees of freedom than spatial, led to the modern understanding of physical interactions. Electromagnetism can be described by a *gauge theory* based on an additional "internal dimension". Similar descriptions form the current understanding of the electroweak and strong interactions, and this is the reason why symmetry is so powerful in the study of particle physics [129, 211, 8].

Example 20.2 (Relativity of gauge)**.** Classical electromagnetism can be understood best in terms of *gauge symmetry*, which refers to the symmetry of an "internal" space present at any point of spacetime. A gauge is a choice of a basis in the internal space, dependent of the point in spacetime. Even if there is an absolute gauge, Physics is blind to it. This allowed the understanding of the electromagnetic, electroweak, and strong interactions as *gauge theories*.

The entire edifice of Physics is based on relativity and gauge symmetry. Their independence of ontology seems to justify The Physicalist Thesis. Let's make the central point explicit:

Rule 1 (No appeal to ontology)**.** Physicalism should not appeal to the intrinsic nature of the physical substance. The only role of matter or substance is played by its structure and how the structure changes due to the dynamical laws.

Scientific experiments, those that can be publicly and independently reproduced by others, can only give us relations. They tell us nothing about the nature of the relata. All that we can measure, we express as a ratio between the measured quantity and a standard unit. Measuring a position results in a ratio between a distance and a unit length. Measuring the mass of a system results in a ratio between mass and a standard mass unit. In general, all observable properties are obtained as such ratios between the measured values and the values of similar properties of more familiar objects. When we examine the structure or the composition of an object, we obtain structural relations. When we register events or count particles resulting from an interaction, or molecules that result from a chemical reaction, all of these are relations. This limitation of our knowledge of the external world to relations was remarked in various forms by thinkers like Poincaré [144] and Russell [154], resulting in the thesis called *epistemic structural realism* [113].

Theoretical models can't go beyond relations either. Any logically consistent theory admits a faithful mathematical model, as we know from *model theory* [32, 95]. But mathematical models are mathematical structures, which are sets endowed with *relations* – subsets of Cartesian products of sets [82].

Dynamical laws are also relational, being about the relations of various parameters or properties across time. Therefore, both experiments and theoretical models deal only with relations.

This makes many scientists expect consciousness to be explained as well without appealing to anything beyond structure and dynamics, for example to alleged "phenomenal powers" of the physical substance or of an additional substance of mental nature. This is the main reason why it is often considered unscientific to suggest that consciousness may not be reducible to structure and dynamics.

But, in Section 20.7, we will see that structure and dynamics alone are insufficient even to allow the knowledge of the value of a single physical property, and ontology will have to be invoked.

20.4 Structure and dynamics in a quantum world

All sciences deal with structures, including Chemistry, Biology, Neuroscience, *etc.* But any such structure is also a physical structure that follows the dynamical laws of Physics. So I'll explain structures and dynamics in Quantum Physics, on which all other natural sciences supervene, as simple as possible for our needs.

The state of the world (the universe) is represented by a unit vector $|\psi(t)\rangle$ form a complex vector space $\mathcal{H}$, called *state space*. Here, t from $|\psi(t)\rangle$ shows that $|\psi(t)\rangle$ depends of time. If $\alpha \in \mathbb{C}$ is a complex number so that $|\alpha| = 1$, the unit vectors $|\psi\rangle$ and $\alpha\,|\psi\rangle$ represent the same state.

The *dynamical law* specifies the state $|\psi(t)\rangle$ of the system at the time t in function of its state $|\psi(t_0)\rangle$ at a time t_0

$$|\psi(t)\rangle = \widehat{\mathsf{U}}_{t-t_0}\,|\psi(t_0)\rangle\,. \tag{20.1}$$

The dynamics of a quantum system is described by the Schrödinger equation, whose solutions satisfy equation (20.1). $\widehat{\mathsf{U}}_{t-t_0}$ a *unitary transformation*, which is like a rotation in the complex vector space $\mathcal{H}$, see equation (17.5). The operators $\widehat{\mathsf{U}}_{t-t_0}$ are called *evolution operators*, and they are all of the form

$$\widehat{\mathsf{U}}_{t-t_0} = e^{-\frac{2\pi i}{h}\widehat{\mathsf{H}}t}, \tag{20.2}$$

where h is the *Planck constant*, and $\widehat{\mathsf{H}}$ is called the *Hamiltonian operator*. If you wonder what does the exponential $e^{-\frac{2\pi i}{h}\widehat{\mathsf{H}}t}$ mean, it is just the sum

$$e^{-\frac{2\pi i}{h}\widehat{\mathsf{H}}t} := \sum_{k=0}^{\infty}\frac{1}{k!}\left(-\frac{2\pi i t}{h}\widehat{\mathsf{H}}\right)^k, \tag{20.3}$$

where $\left(-\frac{2\pi i t}{h}\widehat{\mathsf{H}}\right)^k = \left(-\frac{2\pi i t}{h}\right)^k \underbrace{\widehat{\mathsf{H}}\ldots\widehat{\mathsf{H}}}_{k\text{ times}}$.

For closed systems, in particular for the entire universe, the Hamiltonian operator $\widehat{\mathsf{H}}$ is the same for all t, so it fully encodes the dynamical law. Notice that $\widehat{\mathsf{U}}_{t-t_0} = \widehat{\mathsf{U}}_{t'-t'_0}$ whenever $t - t_0 = t' - t'_0$, because the laws of physics don't change in time. This applies to any system, as long as it doesn't interact with another system. Equation (20.1) is just a more general form of equation (17.3) from Chapter 17, which describes a quantum computation.

But all unit vectors are identical, so how do we distinguish between different states? They have different physical properties. In Quantum Theory, a property A is represented by a linear operator $\widehat{\mathsf{A}}$, usually called *observable*. A property A is defined only for those state vectors $|\psi\rangle$ that are transformed by the operator $\widehat{\mathsf{A}}$ into a vector of the form $a\,|\psi\rangle$, where a is a real number, so $\widehat{\mathsf{A}}\,|\psi\rangle = a\,|\psi\rangle$. The number a is the value of the property A for the state represented by $|\psi\rangle$. In this case, we say that a is an *eigenvalue* and $|\psi\rangle$ is an *eigenvector* of the observable $\widehat{\mathsf{A}}$. The state represented by an eigenvector is called *eigenstate*. Only linear operators having real eigenvalues are observable and represent properties.

Examples of properties are the position of a particle and its momentum. Recall that a quantum particle can't have both a definite position and a definite momentum at the same time (see Figure 17.1). This is because its state vector can never be an eigenvector of both the position and the momentum observables. There is no unit vector $|\psi\rangle$ and no numbers x and p so that $\widehat{x}\,|\psi\rangle = x\,|\psi\rangle$ and $\widehat{p}\,|\psi\rangle = p\,|\psi\rangle$. For any particle, the set of its possible states having a definite position and the set of its possible states having a definite momentum are disjoint. In general, for any state vector $|\psi\rangle$, most properties are not defined, that is, $|\psi\rangle$ is not an eigenvector for most observables.

Remark 20.1. In Quantum Physics there is an additional law that seems to contradict the dynamical law (20.1): whenever we measure a property A of a quantum system, we find a definite value. Even if, according to the dynamical law, we would expect the system to be in a state $|\psi\rangle$ for which the property A is not defined! This suggests that, if the state of the system is not an eigenstate of $\widehat{\mathsf{A}}$, measurements make it somehow jump in an eigenstate of $\widehat{\mathsf{A}}$. This jump is called *projection* or *wavefunction collapse*. The system can jump in any of the eigenstates of $\widehat{\mathsf{A}}$, according to the probabilistic rule, the *Born rule*, already mentioned for the particular case of a quantum computer in equation (17.7), Chapter 17. This tension between the law (20.1) and measurements leads to the *measurement problem*. We already mentioned it when discussing the differences between quantum computing and classical computing in Section 17.2, points QC4 and QC5. We will not be concerned with this here, but we notice that a quantum system may break the law (20.1) once in a while, when observations take place. This will not affect our discussion.

Let's put all of these together.

Definition 20.2. A *physical system* $\left(\mathcal{H}, \widehat{\mathsf{H}}, \mathcal{A}, |\psi(t)\rangle\right)$ is characterized by

1. A *state space* $\mathcal{H}$ of possible states of the system.
2. A unit vector in that space, $|\psi(t)\rangle \in \mathcal{H}$.
3. The Hamiltonian operator $\widehat{\mathsf{H}}$ generating the *dynamical law* (20.1).
4. A set $\mathcal{A}$ of *observables.*

In Classical Physics, states can be distinguished from one another because some of their properties have different values. For example, two systems of point-particles can be distinguished by the positions of their particles. For classical systems, there is always a set of properties whose values can uniquely identify each state. For example, a classical system of n point-particles can be parametrized by the coordinates of the n particles,

$$\mathbf{q} := \big(\underbrace{x_1, y_1, z_1}_{\text{particle 1}}, \underbrace{x_2, y_2, z_2}_{\text{particle 2}}, \ldots, \underbrace{x_n, y_n, z_n}_{\text{particle } n}\big) \in \mathbb{R}^{3n} \tag{20.4}$$

together with the components of their momenta,

$$\mathbf{p} := \big(\underbrace{p_{x_1}, p_{y_1}, p_{z_1}}_{\text{particle 1}}, \underbrace{p_{x_2}, p_{y_2}, p_{z_2}}_{\text{particle 2}}, \ldots, \underbrace{p_{x_n}, p_{y_n}, p_{z_n}}_{\text{particle } n}\big) \in \mathbb{R}^{3n}. \tag{20.5}$$

Then, $(\mathbf{q}, \mathbf{p})$ is a parametrization of the state space $\mathcal{H}$. Similar parametrizations exist for systems containing classical fields.

In Quantum Physics, a property A can distinguish two states only if both of them are eigenstates of $\widehat{\mathsf{A}}$. There is no set of observables that distinguishes any two states. However, there is a set of observables $\mathcal{B}$ whose values can parametrize a basis of the state space, so that they can distinguish any two basis vectors. This is called a *complete set of commuting observables* [54]. The basis consists of those vectors that are common eigenvectors to all operators $A \in \mathcal{B}$. Then, any state vector has a decomposition in this basis, which is what we call *wavefunction*.

For example, the position observables form a complete set of commuting observables for a quantum system of n spin 0 particles and no charge or other degrees of freedom than position. The basis vectors in the position basis are labeled as

$$|\mathbf{q}\rangle = |x_1, y_1, z_1, \ldots, x_n, y_n, z_n\rangle\,, \tag{20.6}$$

for all possible real values of $x_1, y_1, z_1, \ldots, x_n, y_n, z_n$. Then, each state $|\psi\rangle$ can be represented by a wavefunction

$$\psi\left(\mathbf{q}\right) := \langle\mathbf{q}|\psi\rangle \tag{20.7}$$

as in equation (17.2), Chapter 17.

Similar parametrizations are possible for all types of quantum particles and quantum fields [89], differing by the number n of particles and having additional discrete parameters corresponding to spin and internal degrees of freedom. For simplicity we will ignore these additional degrees of freedom in the following, without loss of generality.

Definition 20.3. We call the set of observables $\mathcal{B}$ a *parametrization* of $\mathcal{H}$. We call $\mathcal{B}$-*configuration space* the set $\mathcal{C}$ of all possible combinations $(a_1, a_2, \ldots)$ of eigenvalues of all observables $\widehat{\mathsf{A}}_1, \widehat{\mathsf{A}}_2, \ldots \in \mathcal{B}$.

For example, if $\mathcal{B}$ are the position operators, one obtains the *position configuration space*. The wavefunction ψ from equation (20.7) is defined on the position configuration space, whose points have the form $\mathbf{q} = (x_1, y_1, z_1, \ldots, x_n, y_n, z_n)$.

Similarly there is a *momentum configuration space*. Its points consist of all possible values of all particles' components of the momenta, $\mathbf{p} = (p_{x_1}, p_{y_1}, p_{z_1}, \ldots)$. These are the possible eigenvalues of the momentum operators defined as

$$\widehat{p}_{x_j} := -i\frac{h}{2\pi}\frac{\partial}{\partial x_j}, \widehat{p}_{y_j} := -i\frac{h}{2\pi}\frac{\partial}{\partial y_j}, \widehat{p}_{z_j} := -i\frac{h}{2\pi}\frac{\partial}{\partial z_j} \tag{20.8}$$

for all $j \in \{1, \ldots, n\}$. The basis vectors have the form $|\mathbf{p}\rangle = |p_{x_1}, p_{y_1}, p_{z_1}, \ldots\rangle$, and the momentum-wavefunction is

$$\psi_p\left(\mathbf{p}\right) := \langle\mathbf{p}|\psi\rangle\,. \tag{20.9}$$

Observation 20.1. In Quantum Theory, the physical structure of a quantum system is fully characterized by the wavefunction and the configuration space parameters, if we know what physical property each parameter represents. Equivalently, the basis and the wavefunction expressing the state vector in that basis encodes everything that is to be known physically about the system.

There are two equivalent ways to talk about subsystems, for example how a system of n particles is "made of" those n particles. The first is in terms of the wavefunction defined on the space of positions, as in equation (20.7). If we separate the position degrees of freedom $(x_1, y_1, z_1, \ldots, x_n, y_n, z_n)$ in triples $(x_1, y_1, z_1), \ldots, (x_n, y_n, z_n)$, we find the degrees of freedom of each particle. The complete description of the system requires the knowledge of this separation. The total configuration space $\mathbb{R}^{3n}$ can be obtained as the Cartesian product of the individual position configuration spaces of the particles, $\mathbb{R}^{3n} = \mathbb{R}^3 \times \ldots \times \mathbb{R}^3$. Similar correspondences exist for the momentum configuration space and other configuration spaces.

The other way to identify the subsystems, equivalent to this, is to know the state space $\mathcal{H}_j$ of each particle, and how they combine into the total state space $\mathcal{H}$. The total state space is the tensor product of the individual state spaces of the particles, $\mathcal{H} = \mathcal{H}_1 \otimes \ldots \otimes \mathcal{H}_n$. This decomposition is named *tensor product structure*. We've seen a simpler case of tensor product of vectors in equation (6.24). The tensor product of the vector spaces $\mathcal{H}_j$ is spanned by the tensor products of the vectors in the spaces $\mathcal{H}_j$. In particular, the basis of $\mathcal{H}$ consisting of vectors of the form $|\mathbf{q}_1, \mathbf{q}_2, \ldots\rangle$ is related to the bases of vectors of the form $|\mathbf{q}_j\rangle$ of $\mathcal{H}_j$, for all j, by $|\mathbf{q}_1, \mathbf{q}_2, \ldots\rangle = |\mathbf{q}_1\rangle \otimes |\mathbf{q}_2\rangle \otimes \ldots = |\mathbf{q}_1\rangle\,|\mathbf{q}_2\rangle \ldots$ just like in equation (6.24). We can obtain the tensor product structure from the decomposition of the configuration spaces and conversely, because the parameters $\mathbf{q}_j = (x_j, y_j, z_j)$ consist of eigenvalues of the position operators $\widehat{x}_j, \widehat{y}_j$, and $\widehat{z}_j$ for each j, and the bases of vectors of the form $|\mathbf{q}_j\rangle = |x_j, y_j, z_j\rangle$ consist of eigenvectors of the same operators.

The position of one of the particles is a property of that particle, but also a property of the entire system. Like the position of your left foot is both a property of the foot and a property of your body. Likewise, $\widehat{x}_j, \widehat{y}_j$, and $\widehat{z}_j$ are the position observables of particle j, operating on $\mathcal{H}_j$ and giving the position configuration space for particle j, but they also operate on the total space $\mathcal{H} = \mathcal{H}_1 \otimes \ldots \otimes \mathcal{H}_n$.

In general, a system is given as in Definition 20.2, and the physical meaning of the observables is specified. For example, we need to know which operators correspond to positions, which to momenta, *etc.* From the observable, one can recover the subsystems, and hence the tensor product structure $\mathcal{H} = \mathcal{H}_1 \otimes \ldots \otimes \mathcal{H}_n$, because the observables of different subsystems commute [214]. The knowledge of the physical meaning of the observables from Definition 20.2 is essential for identifying the subsystems, although if only the structure matters, this meaning should be derivable from the structures or the relations alone. This is the key observation on which the main result from this chapter is based.

20.5 Relativity of structure in a quantum world

To avoid the problem of ambiguity of computation and the no-go result from Chapter 18, it was proposed to replace the notion of computation (see Section 14.3), in particular of implementation and simulation, with stronger versions that violate Substructure-Independence. The most general form of this idea is that the structural details, down to the finest one if necessary, matter for consciousness, and nothing else is needed. This includes as particular cases all versions of structure-based proposals, and also functionalism and computationalism. They vary by the structural details proposed to matter for consciousness, but they all fall under The Physicalist Thesis (see Figure 20.1).

Any of these proposals predicts, therefore, that if we fully replicate, on another system, the structure and dynamics of a brain, that system would be equally sentient as the brain it simulates, and it will have the same sentient experiences. So let us formalize this prediction.

With the formalism from Section 20.4, particularly Definition 20.2, two systems are physically duplicate or isomorphic if and only if their elements are in a one-to-one correspondence. More precisely,

Definition 20.4. An *isomorphism* between two physical systems (or even possible worlds) $\left(\mathcal{H}, \widehat{\mathsf{H}}, \mathcal{A}, |\psi(t)\rangle\right)$ and $\left(\mathcal{H}', \widehat{\mathsf{H}}', \mathcal{A}', |\psi'(t)\rangle\right)$ is a unitary map between the state spaces of the two systems, $\widehat{\mathsf{S}} : \mathcal{H} \to \mathcal{H}'$, so that

1. The initial state of a the first system is mapped into the initial state of the second system,

$$|\psi'(0)\rangle = \widehat{\mathsf{S}}\,|\psi(0)\rangle\,. \tag{20.10}$$

2. The Hamiltonian of the first system is mapped into the Hamiltonian of the first system,

$$\widehat{\mathsf{H}}'\widehat{\mathsf{S}} = \widehat{\mathsf{S}}\widehat{\mathsf{H}}. \tag{20.11}$$

3. Every observable $\widehat{\mathsf{A}} \in \mathcal{A}$ of the first system is mapped to the corresponding observable $\widehat{\mathsf{A}}' \in \mathcal{A}'$ of the second system by

$$\widehat{\mathsf{A}}'\widehat{\mathsf{S}} = \widehat{\mathsf{S}}\widehat{\mathsf{A}}. \tag{20.12}$$

A few words about Definition 20.4. Equation (20.11) ensures that the two systems have the same dynamics. For any state $|\psi\rangle \in \mathcal{H}$ and any time interval Δt,

$$\widehat{\mathsf{U}}'_{\Delta t}\widehat{\mathsf{S}}\,|\psi\rangle = \widehat{\mathsf{S}}\widehat{\mathsf{U}}_{\Delta t}\,|\psi\rangle\,, \tag{20.13}$$

where $\widehat{\mathsf{U}}_{\Delta t} = e^{-\frac{2\pi i}{h}\widehat{\mathsf{H}}\Delta t}$ and $\widehat{\mathsf{U}}'_{\Delta t} = e^{-\frac{2\pi i}{h}\widehat{\mathsf{H}}'\Delta t}$ as in equation (20.2).

From this, if $|\psi'(0)\rangle = \widehat{\mathsf{S}}\,|\psi(0)\rangle$, it follows that

$$|\psi'(t)\rangle = \widehat{\mathsf{S}}\,|\psi(t)\rangle \tag{20.14}$$

for all times t.

Exercise 20.1. Show that equation (20.13) follows from equation (20.11), then prove that equation (20.14) is true for all t.

Solving Exercise 20.1 gives you an intuition why $\widehat{\mathsf{S}}$ appears only once in equation (20.10), but twice in equations (20.11) and (20.12).

Exercise 20.2. Show that, if $|\psi\rangle \in \mathcal{H}$ is an eigenvector of $\widehat{\mathsf{A}} \in \mathcal{A}$, $|\psi\rangle' := \widehat{\mathsf{S}}\,|\psi\rangle \in \mathcal{H}'$ is an eigenvector of $\widehat{\mathsf{A}}' := \widehat{\mathsf{S}}\widehat{\mathsf{A}}\widehat{\mathsf{S}}^{-1} \in \mathcal{A}'$ with the same eigenvalue.

Solution. $\widehat{\mathsf{A}}'\,|\psi\rangle' = \widehat{\mathsf{S}}\widehat{\mathsf{A}}\widehat{\mathsf{S}}^{-1}\widehat{\mathsf{S}}\,|\psi\rangle = \widehat{\mathsf{S}}\widehat{\mathsf{A}}\,|\psi\rangle = \widehat{\mathsf{S}}a\,|\psi\rangle = a\widehat{\mathsf{S}}\,|\psi\rangle = a\,|\psi\rangle'$. □

Two isomorphic systems are equivalent, in the sense that the structure and dynamics of one of them reproduces those of the other one. This is not limited to the state vectors and observables. For example, to position observables like $\widehat{x}_j, \widehat{y}_j$, and $\widehat{z}_j$ correspond other observables $\widehat{x}'_j, \widehat{y}'_j$, and $\widehat{z}'_j$, and they determine for the second system a configuration space just like the position configuration space of the first system. That is, space, as a structure of the first system, corresponds to a similar structure of the second system.

We see from Definition 20.4 that we can simulate a property by another property, as long as the relations between the elements of the physical systems are the same. For example, if the first system has some properties that take continuous values, and if these properties behave like the positions of the particles constituting the second system, they will simulate these positions. More concretely, consider a harmonic oscillator, like a pendulum or a mass coupled to a spring. There are many examples of systems exhibiting properties that behave just like the position in the harmonic oscillator: in an electric system, such properties can be the voltage, the current, and the charge; in an optical or electromagnetic system, the electric and magnetic fields; in an acoustical system the pressure and the density; in chemical systems, the concentrations of intermediates; in certain thermal systems, the temperature, and so on. Now, of course none of these properties is physically the same as the position, but if they play the same role in the equations that describe the organization of the system and how it changes in time, from the point of view of the structure, they are just like positions in a harmonic oscillator.

From now on we will focus on systems that can simulate *all physical properties* of another system with their own properties, more precisely we are interested in isomorphisms as in Definition 20.4.

In practice, along with the elements of the structure and their relations, we also need their real-world correspondent. For example, there is a physical difference between the property of position and that of momentum.

Definition 20.5. By *physical meaning* of an observable I understand the characteristics by which we distinguish it from other observables, even if these characteristics are not necessarily quantitative or relational.

"Wait", you may say, "aren't these characteristics always quantitative, relational, or structural?" Definition 20.5 leaves open this question. If they are indeed structural, then it will turn out that the physical meaning is in fact structural, or it supervenes on structure alone. But if we exhaust all structural characteristics and there will still be a difference between two physical properties, then we will say that the physical meaning is irreducible to structure alone.

Two physical properties may be different, and yet the corresponding observables can be operators with the same relational properties. For example, both a position operator $\widehat{x}$ and the momentum operator $\widehat{p}_x$ admit as eigenvalues all real numbers, and they are isomorphic, they can be transformed into each other by using the Fourier transform and its inverse. So from a relational point of view they seem similar, at least if we don't take into account their relations with other structures, but we know from experience that they are not the same. An important question that we will explore in the following is whether the relations, the structure alone, make it possible to distinguish any two observables for which we can distinguish the physical properties they represent.

This knowledge of the correspondence between observables and the physical meanings is not, at least not obviously, a part of the structure itself: we attribute to each observable a physical meaning like that of position, momentum, charge *etc* based on the correspondence with the empirical reality. But can these correspondences be inferred from relations, from structural aspects alone? Can we infer what observables represent positions just from the mathematical relations?

The idea that only structure matters has led many physicists to propose that a complete description of reality requires only the state vector (the unit vector, not the wavefunction, which is the state vector's components in a particular basis associated with the physical meaning of positions) and the Hamiltonian (again, as an operator, not as expressed in a particular basis). Carroll and Singh termed this view *Hilbert-space fundamentalism* [25], p. 95:

> Typically one also relies on some classical structure, such as space and local configuration variables within it, which then gets promoted to an algebra of preferred observables. We argue that even such an algebra is unnecessary, and the most basic description of the world is given by the spectrum of the Hamiltonian (a list of energy eigenvalues) and the components of some particular vector in the state space. Everything else—including space and fields propagating on it—is emergent from these minimal elements.

This principle, implicitly adopted by many researchers before and after Carroll and Singh's claim, underpins proposals that decoherence dynamically selects a preferred basis [218, 217, 120], that, under locality constraints, the Hamiltonian uniquely determine tensor product structures [141, 41, 26], and that space itself uniquely emerges from abstract quantum structures [25, 24, 26].

However, none of these structures emerge uniquely, as shown in [179, 183, 187, 184, 186]. The general proof in [179] applies to any quantum structure with any Hamiltonian and any invariant constraints (*e.g.* the constraint of locality). In the following, I will show this for relatively simpler but comprehensive situations.

Any quantum system is, of course, isomorphic to itself, at least due to the trivial isomorphism, obtained when $\widehat{\mathsf{S}}$ is the identity $\widehat{\mathsf{S}}\,|\psi\rangle = |\psi\rangle$. Isomorphisms between a quantum system and itself are called *automorphisms*.

But a quantum system can be isomorphic to itself in many ways simultaneously. Infinitely many unitary transformations $\widehat{\mathsf{S}} : \mathcal{H} \to \mathcal{H}$ give different valid descriptions of the same system.

Definition 20.6 (Structural symmetries)**.** A *structural symmetry transformation* is an automorphism $\widehat{\mathsf{S}} : \mathcal{H} \to \mathcal{H}$.

The structural symmetry transformations are unitary transformations that commute with the Hamiltonian, $\widehat{\mathsf{S}} : \mathcal{H} \to \mathcal{H}$, $\widehat{\mathsf{S}}\widehat{\mathsf{H}} = \widehat{\mathsf{H}}\widehat{\mathsf{S}}$. This follows from Definition 20.4, if we take the two systems to be the same, and require that $\widehat{\mathsf{H}}' = \widehat{\mathsf{H}}$.

Remark 20.2. Definition 20.4 allows more general automorphisms of a quantum system, for which $\widehat{\mathsf{S}}$ can be any unitary transformation of $\mathcal{H}$. In this case, it is possible that $\widehat{\mathsf{H}}'\widehat{\mathsf{S}} \neq \widehat{\mathsf{S}}\widehat{\mathsf{H}}$, and therefore $\widehat{\mathsf{H}}' = \widehat{\mathsf{S}}\widehat{\mathsf{H}}\widehat{\mathsf{S}}^{-1} \neq \widehat{\mathsf{H}}$. However, some authors claim that adding interesting conditions like that the Hamiltonian is local with respect to the positions results in a unique physical meanings of the observables, determined by the quantum structure alone. It is easy to see that structure doesn't uniquely determine physical meaning for general unitary transformations (see the following Propositions 20.1 and 20.2), but for transformations that satisfy these constraints, and therefore commute with the Hamiltonian, $\widehat{\mathsf{S}}\widehat{\mathsf{H}} = \widehat{\mathsf{H}}\widehat{\mathsf{S}}$, it is more difficult, so I will have to prove explicitly what happens in this case too.

Exercise 20.3. Show that structural symmetry transformations form a *group* (see Remark 6.2 for the definition of a group).

Structural symmetry transformations change the parametrization that labels the states from $\mathcal{H}$ as in equations (20.4-20.7). Since a parametrization consists of the possible values of the observables from $\mathcal{B}$, $\mathcal{B}$ itself is transformed, usually in a different set of observables $\mathcal{B}'$.

For example, the wavefunction expressed in terms of positions in equation (20.7) can also be expressed in terms of momenta, as in equation (20.9). The symmetry transformation that takes the position representation (20.7) and gives as a result the momentum representation (20.9) is the *Fourier transform.* The Fourier transform is a unitary transformation of the state space, but in general is not a structural symmetry, since it doesn't satisfy the second condition from Definition 20.4, except for special Hamiltonians in which the position and momentum operators are interchangeable. But there are infinitely many different parametrizations, and, in general, the wavefunction looks different in different parametrizations. In the absence of a correspondence between the operators and the physical meanings they represent, the physical world itself appears different when the wavefunction of the world appears different.

When physicists make such transformations, they keep track of what physical property each observable represents, by notations and by names for the properties. For example, they do this by calling (20.7) *position representation* and (20.9) *momentum representation.*

Structural symmetry transformations are used to find representations that help us better understand the behavior of the system and solve problems more easily.

Translations and rotations of space are a particular case of structural symmetry transformations. They transform the positions $\mathbf{q}$ in a reference frame into the positions $\mathbf{q}'$ in another reference frame. But there are infinitely many more structural symmetry transformations.

We now move toward showing that the symmetry group of the structure of a quantum system is extremely large. Recall from Definition 20.3 that the possible values of the observables from $\mathcal{B}$ form a configuration space $\mathcal{C}$ which, according to Observation 20.1, characterizes the structure of each state. A symmetry transformation $\widehat{\mathsf{S}}$ results in a different set of observables $\mathcal{B}'$, and therefore in a different configuration space $\mathcal{C}'$.

Let us warm-up by first proving two weaker results.

Proposition 20.1. Let $|\psi\rangle \in \mathcal{H}$ be a state and $\mathcal{C}$ a configuration space determined by a complete set of commuting observables $\mathcal{B}$. For any other configuration space $\mathcal{C}'$ determined by the set of observables $\mathcal{B}'$ obtained from $\mathcal{B}$ by a symmetry transformation, there is a state vector $|\psi'\rangle \in \mathcal{H}$ so that the wavefunction of $|\psi'\rangle$ on $\mathcal{C}'$ is identical with the wavefunction of $|\psi\rangle$ on $\mathcal{C}$.

Proof. Let $\widehat{\mathsf{S}}$ be the symmetry transformation ensuring that for any observable $\widehat{\mathsf{A}}' \in \mathcal{B}'$ there is an observable $\widehat{\mathsf{A}} \in \mathcal{B}$ so that $\widehat{\mathsf{A}}' = \widehat{\mathsf{S}}\widehat{\mathsf{A}}\widehat{\mathsf{S}}^{-1}$. Let $|\psi'\rangle := \widehat{\mathsf{S}}\,|\psi\rangle$. Then, the wavefunction of $|\psi\rangle$ on $\mathcal{C}$ is of the form $\langle\mathbf{q}|\psi\rangle$, where $\mathbf{q} \in \mathcal{C}$. The wavefunction of $|\psi'\rangle$ on $\mathcal{C}'$ is of the form $\langle\mathbf{q}'|\psi'\rangle$, where $\mathbf{q}' \in \mathcal{C}'$. But since $|\mathbf{q}'\rangle = \widehat{\mathsf{S}}\,|\mathbf{q}\rangle$ and $|\psi'\rangle = \widehat{\mathsf{S}}\,|\psi\rangle$, we have

$$\langle\mathbf{q}'|\psi'\rangle = \langle\mathbf{q}|\psi\rangle \tag{20.15}$$

as in equation (17.5). This proves the result. □

Note that in Proposition 20.1 we only required that $\widehat{\mathsf{S}}$ is unitary, not that it also commutes with the Hamiltonian $\widehat{\mathsf{H}}$. So the two wavefunctions appear the same only instantaneously, as soon as they evolve, they may become different. The same applies to the following proposition.

Proposition 20.2. Let $|\psi\rangle \in \mathcal{H}$ be a state and $\mathcal{C}$ a configuration space. For any other state vector $|\psi'\rangle \in \mathcal{H}$, there is another configuration space $\mathcal{C}'$ so that the wavefunction of $|\psi'\rangle$ on $\mathcal{C}'$ is identical with the wavefunction of $|\psi\rangle$ on $\mathcal{C}$.

Proof. For any two unit vectors $|\psi\rangle, |\psi'\rangle \in \mathcal{H}$ there is a unitary transformation $\widehat{\mathsf{S}}$ so that $|\psi'\rangle = \widehat{\mathsf{S}}\,|\psi\rangle$. The complete set of commuting observables $\mathcal{B}$ determine and parametrize a basis of the state space. The transformation $\widehat{\mathsf{S}}$ transforms any observable $\widehat{\mathsf{A}}$ into another observable $\widehat{\mathsf{S}}\widehat{\mathsf{A}}\widehat{\mathsf{S}}^{-1}$. Therefore, it transforms $\mathcal{B}$ into another complete set of commuting observables $\mathcal{B}'$, which determine and parametrize another basis. The components of $|\psi\rangle$ in the first basis coincide with the components of $|\psi'\rangle$ in the second basis, so the wavefunction of ψ on $\mathcal{C}$ coincides with the wavefunction of ψ' on $\mathcal{C}'$. For example, if $\mathcal{C}$ is the position configuration space, the basis determined by $\mathcal{B}$ consists of vectors with definite positions $|\mathbf{q}\rangle$. The basis determined by $\mathcal{B}'$ consists of the vectors $|\mathbf{q}'\rangle := \widehat{\mathsf{S}}\,|\mathbf{q}\rangle$. We label them with the same numbers $\mathbf{q}' = (x_1, y_1, z_1, \ldots)$, but these are not positions, they are possible values of the transformed position operators $\widehat{x}'_j = \widehat{\mathsf{S}}\widehat{x}_j\widehat{\mathsf{S}}^{-1}$, $\widehat{y}'_j = \widehat{\mathsf{S}}\widehat{y}_j\widehat{\mathsf{S}}^{-1}$, and $\widehat{z}'_j = \widehat{\mathsf{S}}\widehat{z}_j\widehat{\mathsf{S}}^{-1}$, where $\widehat{x}_j$, $\widehat{y}_j$, and $\widehat{z}_j$ are the position operators and $j \in \{1, \ldots, n\}$. The resulting configuration space $\mathcal{C}'$ consists of the eigenvalues of the transformed operators $\widehat{x}'_j$, $\widehat{y}'_j$, and $\widehat{z}'_j$. They coincide with the eigenvalues of the position operators $\widehat{x}_j$, $\widehat{y}_j$, and $\widehat{z}_j$, so both $\mathcal{C} \cong \mathbb{R}^{3n}$ and $\mathcal{C}' \cong \mathbb{R}^{3n}$, but the configuration spaces are different, $\mathcal{C}' \neq \mathcal{C}$, just like the momentum configuration space is different. Then, since $\widehat{\mathsf{S}}$ is unitary, we apply equation (17.5), obtaining

$$\langle \mathbf{q}'|\psi'\rangle = \langle \mathbf{q}|\psi\rangle\,. \tag{20.16}$$

This proves that the two wavefunctions $\langle \mathbf{q}'|\psi'\rangle$ and $\langle \mathbf{q}|\psi\rangle$ on the two configuration spaces $\mathcal{C}'$ and $\mathcal{C}$ are identical. □

In the proofs of Propositions 20.1 and 20.2, we used a unitary symmetry transformation $\widehat{\mathsf{S}}$. How many such transformations do you think exist for a state space of dimension n? Infinitely many, see Exercise 20.4.

Remark 20.3. Note that Propositions 20.1 and 20.2 are not about expressing the same system in a different basis, but about finding unitary transformations of the observables, for example by replacing the position observables with other "position-like" observables. Then, the physical state appears different when expressed as a wavefunction with respect to two different position-like observables. That is, our three-dimensional space is not determined uniquely just by the quantum structure, and different choices make the world appear completely different.

Remark 20.4. A transformation as in Propositions 20.1 and 20.2 makes the structure of $\psi(t)$ on $\mathcal{C}$ and that of $\psi'(t)$ on $\mathcal{C}'$ be identical, but in general these wavefunctions evolve differently, so they may become different at another time

$t' \neq t$. Such a transformation is a structural symmetry transformation (Definition 20.6) only if it preserves not only the structure, but also the dynamical law (20.1). To be a structural symmetry transformation, a transformation has to commute with the Hamiltonian operator $\widehat{\mathsf{H}}$ [179]. I explained in Remark (20.2) why some researchers may not find Propositions 20.1 and 20.2 sufficient to reject the claim that the meanings of the physical properties emerge from structural properties alone. In [184], it was shown that distinct histories $\psi(t)$ and $\psi'(t)$, corresponding to distinct outcomes of quantum measurements, can be related by a structural symmetry transformation $\widehat{\mathsf{S}}$. This provides unlimited physically concrete examples of structural symmetries.

To see what happens if we impose the condition that the evolution law remains unchanged, we will examine the simpler case of a non-relativistic Hamiltonian

$$\widehat{\mathsf{H}} = \sum_{j=1}^{\mathbf{n}} \frac{1}{2m_j}\widehat{\boldsymbol{p}}_j^2 + \sum_{j=1}^{\mathbf{n}} \sum_{\substack{k=1 \\ j\neq k}}^{\mathbf{n}} \widehat{V}_{j,k}\left(|\widehat{\boldsymbol{q}}_j - \widehat{\boldsymbol{q}}_k|\right), \tag{20.17}$$

where m_j is the mass of the particle j, $\widehat{\boldsymbol{q}}_j = (\widehat{x}_j, \widehat{y}_j, \widehat{z}_j)$ are its position operators, $\widehat{\boldsymbol{p}}_j = \left(\widehat{p}_{x_j}, \widehat{p}_{y_j}, \widehat{p}_{z_j}\right)$ its momentum operators, and $\widehat{V}_{j,k}$ is a potential that depends only on the distance between two positions $\boldsymbol{q}_j$ and $\boldsymbol{q}_k$.

If we assume that the Hamiltonian has to be of the form from equation (20.17), this already gives us a severe constraint of what space can be. The question of whether a unique space emerges can be stated in the following way:

Question 20.2. Given the Hamiltonian $\widehat{\mathsf{H}}$ from equation (20.17), are the operators $\widehat{\boldsymbol{q}}_j$ and $\widehat{\boldsymbol{p}}_j$ the only ones (up to isometries of space and permutations of identical particles) for which $\widehat{\mathsf{H}}$ has the same form as in equation (20.17)?

The answer is no! Let $\widehat{\mathsf{S}}$ be a linear transformation that commutes with $\widehat{\mathsf{H}}$, that is, $\widehat{\mathsf{S}}\widehat{\mathsf{H}} = \widehat{\mathsf{H}}\widehat{\mathsf{S}}$. Then $\widehat{\mathsf{H}} = \widehat{\mathsf{S}}\widehat{\mathsf{H}}\widehat{\mathsf{S}}^{-1}$. Let $\widehat{\mathsf{S}}$ be unitary, which means that it preserves the Hermitian scalar product from equation (17.4), that is, for any vectors $|u\rangle$ and $|v\rangle$, if $|u'\rangle = \widehat{\mathsf{S}}\,|u\rangle$ and $|v'\rangle = \widehat{\mathsf{S}}\,|v\rangle$, then $\langle u|v\rangle = \langle u'|v'\rangle$, as in equation (17.5). Then, the transformation $\widehat{\mathsf{S}}$ gives us another such set of operators,

$$\begin{cases} \widehat{\boldsymbol{q}}_j' & := \left(\widehat{\mathsf{S}}\widehat{x}_j\widehat{\mathsf{S}}^{-1}, \widehat{\mathsf{S}}\widehat{y}_j\widehat{\mathsf{S}}^{-1}, \widehat{\mathsf{S}}\widehat{z}_j\widehat{\mathsf{S}}^{-1}\right) \\ \widehat{\boldsymbol{p}}_j' & := \left(\widehat{\mathsf{S}}\widehat{p}_{x_j}\widehat{\mathsf{S}}^{-1}, \widehat{\mathsf{S}}\widehat{p}_{y_j}\widehat{\mathsf{S}}^{-1}, \widehat{\mathsf{S}}\widehat{p}_{z_j}\widehat{\mathsf{S}}^{-1}\right), \end{cases} \tag{20.18}$$

so that equation (20.17) remains true when we replace $\widehat{\boldsymbol{q}}_j$ with $\widehat{\boldsymbol{q}}_j'$ and $\widehat{\boldsymbol{p}}_j$ with $\widehat{\boldsymbol{p}}_j'$. There are infinitely many such operators $\widehat{\mathsf{S}}$, in fact infinitely many infinite families of such operators (see Exercise 20.5). And, as shown by the examples provided in [179, 184, 186], we obtain infinitely many possible solutions that are completely distinct from a physical point of view, and so they correspond to physically distinct structures like space and decomposition into subsystems.

Even if the state space is a finite-dimensional vector space of dimension m, there are infinitely many solutions, in fact the solutions form a space of dimension between m and m^2 (see Exercise 20.5). And note that the non-relativistic case from equation (20.17) requires an infinite-dimensional state space, so the possible alternative choices of position-like and momentum-like operators as in equation (20.18) form an infinite-dimensional space.

The same applies even if our quantum theory is formulated in terms of other fundamental observables than position operators, as shown in full generality in [179, 183]. Any other operators that we may think to play a special role in our theory, including in quantum gravity, will have to face the same problems.

Consequently, in [179, 183] I argued that we need to choose an algebra of preferred observables, otherwise the same state vector supports infinitely many physically distinct interpretations as a physical world.

Can this be solved by specifying from start a choice of operators $\widehat{\boldsymbol{q}}_j$ and $\widehat{\boldsymbol{p}}_j$, $j \in \{1, \ldots, \mathbf{n}\}$ as more fundamental, and calling them "the real" position and momentum operators? Would the existence of a preferred set of operators solve the problem and give us a complete description of reality from structures alone? Let's see. First, such operators will specify how the universe is divided into subsystems, because each $j \in \{1, \ldots, \mathbf{n}\}$ refers to another particle. Second, by specifying what operators for each subsystem corresponds to space (in the above example these are $\widehat{\boldsymbol{q}}_j$), this can give us the space structure.

But along with the operators $\widehat{\boldsymbol{q}}_j$, their conjugate momenta $\widehat{\boldsymbol{p}}_j$ also exist, because they are partial derivative operators with respect to the eigenvalues of $\widehat{\boldsymbol{q}}_j$, as seen in equation (20.8). And with these, all other operators exist, since they are all functions of $\widehat{\boldsymbol{q}}_j$ and $\widehat{\boldsymbol{p}}_j$. Just like along with two apples and other three apples, five apples exist. So by merely denoting some operators by $\widehat{\boldsymbol{q}}_j$ and $\widehat{\boldsymbol{p}}_j$ and declaring them more fundamental we don't acquire anything, since this is a mere notation by which we only highlight them in our minds among other possible sets of operators that satisfy the same relations. Their privileged status is not encoded in the relations, since infinitely many other choices satisfy the same relations. Therefore, we arrived at a puzzle:

Observation 20.2 (Relativity of Structure)**.** The structure and the dynamics alone are insufficient to endow observables with physical meaning, *i.e.* to tell which physical property each operator represents.

Nothing in the structure and the dynamics tells that $\mathbf{q}$ represents positions and $\mathbf{q}'$ represents different properties than positions. Then,

Question 20.3. How do we know the position operators, how do we know the space structure?

The physical correspondent of each observable is introduced by comparing the theory with the reality it describes. But this correspondence is not part of the relational structure of the system, it may only seem so because we name and label the observables and we keep track of these names and labels when describing the system and solving the equations.

To try to resolve this ambiguity, we turn to observations: after all, first we gather empirical data through observations, and then we systematize them into theories using mathematical structures.

But since in reality the symmetry group of any physical system is not the group of unitary transformations that commute with the Hamiltonian, but the much smaller group of spacetime and gauge symmetries, this leads to a question:

Question 20.4. What reduces the large structural symmetry, associating a physical property to each observable A?

Relativity of Structure excludes the possibility of the emergence of a unique correspondence between observables and physical meanings. Also see [179, 184].

But why not simply postulate this correspondence? Postulating it would require the ontology to do more than simply to have the structure and to change according to the dynamics, violating Rule 1 and therefore The Physicalist Thesis. Also each symmetry transformation maps observables to observables, so whatever meaning we give to an observable, any structural transformation would reassign it to another observable.

Can we then add more structure to reduce the symmetry? We can try, but the added structure would not be observable, so it would be physically irrelevant. Also, adding more structure means adding more degrees of freedom, increasing the ambiguity even more, just like how it happens if we try to solve the ambiguity of computation by adding more circuits.

The most sensible answer seems to be that the relation between observables and their physical meaning is established by experiments. For example, we measure the positions of other objects relative to our own position. We build measurement devices that translate the values of other observables into positions on the dial of the measuring apparatus, or in numbers displayed by the apparatus. All measurements of the observables are translated into data that we can perceive. But to see if this explanation works, we have to include the observers in the physical description of the world. We will see that this opens a can of worms.

20.6 The overlooked role of the observer

To approach the ambiguity problem resulting from the Relativity of Structure, it seems that we need a complete description that includes the observers as subsystems of the world. The essential role played by the observer in Physics is not appreciated enough. Obviously, its role in the quantum measurement problem was extensively discussed, but here I am talking about a different role of the observer, having to do with the fact that the correspondence between observables and their physical meaning comes from the experiments. But experiments can find only relations between various observables of the observed system and the instruments used to perform the experiment (Sections 20.2 and 20.3), and the latter are ultimately translated into relations between the instruments and the observer's own instruments, the sense organs. So we are interested in the observer's physical properties and their correspondence with the operators. But what endows with physical meaning the observer's own properties? We just take them as reference. For example, we take the position or the velocity of a system that we observe relatively to our own position or velocity.

But there is much more than this. The observers not only bring in their own positions, they also "smuggle" into the description of the world the very notion of position. The observers experience their own observables as physical properties having certain physical meanings. The observers perceive the external world in their own reference frames, and the objects as being localized in a particular space, corresponding to a particular choice of the position observables as in equation (20.18). This is the choice in which the wavefunction of the system we call observer appears as having the structure and behavior of an observer. The presence of an observer can, in principle, be decoded from the patterns of the wavefunction, so that the observer appears to be a localized structure, provided that we know the configuration space of positions. Almost all other possible choices would give different wavefunctions, so different arrangements of matter that don't qualify as observers, as suggested by Propositions 20.1 and 20.2, but especially our answer to Question 20.2. Then,

Principle 20.1. The observers give physical meaning to the observables of the physical systems by anchoring them in the configuration space in which they appear as observers.

Principle 20.1 doesn't introduce sentience, it doesn't pre-assume its existence. It only states the role of the observers in anchoring the relations and structures in the physical reality relatively to their own structure. From this, it seems that there are two options, depending on the answer to the following question:

Question 20.5. Is the structure of the observer sufficient to give physical meaning to the observables of the system?

To avoid pre-assuming an answer to this question, our discussion will make use of the following notion:

Definition 20.7. An *observer-like structure* is a system isomorphic with the structure of an observer.

In particular, the structure of an observer is an observer-like structure, but we don't exclude by default the possibility that not all observer-like structures are sentient observers, even if they have the exact same structure and dynamics as an observer. This definition is important, because it doesn't assume that the observer is reducible to its structure, so it doesn't assume an answer to Question 20.5, but it allows us to explore both possibilities and see which one is true.

Proposition 20.1 shows that any structure possible in a configuration space is possible in any other configuration space. This applies to observer-like structures as well. If the structure of the observer were sufficient to give physical meaning to an observable $\widehat{\mathsf{A}}$ of the system in the configuration space $\mathcal{C}$, an observer-like structure from another configuration space $\mathcal{C}'$ would give the same meaning to the observable $\widehat{\mathsf{A}}' = \widehat{\mathsf{S}}\widehat{\mathsf{A}}\widehat{\mathsf{S}}^{-1}$, and to the observable $\widehat{\mathsf{A}}$ it would assign a different physical meaning. For example, an observer-like structure may consider $\widehat{\boldsymbol{q}}_j$ as position observables, while another observer-like structure may consider that the actual position observables are $\widehat{\boldsymbol{q}}'_j$ as in equation (20.18). By giving different physical meaning to the observables of a state, they would perceive the same state as having different structures, and therefore, as different physical worlds.

On the other hand, a negative answer to Question 20.5 would imply that some observer-like structures can give physical meaning to observables, and others can't do this, so they are philosophical zombies, at least from this point of view. This, of course, would be in direct contradiction with The Physicalist Thesis.

Let's ask Physics to answer Questions 20.1, 20.4 and 20.5.

20.7 Asking physics

In this section, I prove the main result:

Theorem 20.1. Any sentient physical being has insentient structural duplicates in other configuration spaces.

Proof. An observer O is a subsystem of the world. Let E be the observer's external world (or *environment*). We know from our experience that an observer O can know the values of some properties of objects from the environment. We assume that this knowledge is encoded in the structure of O's brain.

Let $|\psi\rangle$, $|\psi'\rangle$ be states of the world, which includes the observer and her environment, so that, in the configuration space $\mathcal{C}$, a property A of the environment E of O, represented by the observable $\widehat{\mathsf{A}}$, has the value a for $|\psi\rangle$, respectively a' for $|\psi'\rangle$. We choose the two states of the world so that the observer O has the same structure in both of them, and this structure encodes the knowledge that the value of $\widehat{\mathsf{A}}$ is a. Both $|\psi\rangle$ and $|\psi'\rangle$ are possible states, even though the environment in the state $|\psi'\rangle$ is not as the observer thinks it is.

From Proposition 20.2, there is a configuration space $\mathcal{C}'$ so that the wavefunction of $|\psi\rangle$ on $\mathcal{C}'$ is identical with the wavefunction of $|\psi\rangle'$ on $\mathcal{C}$. The symmetry transformation $\widehat{\mathsf{S}}$ achieving this can be chosen to commute with the Hamiltonian. In [184] it was shown that there is a unitary transformation that transforms a state in which the an outcome was obtained by a measurement into one in which another outcome was obtained, and that this transformation commutes with the Hamiltonian. This shows that it is possible to choose the states $|\psi\rangle$, $|\psi'\rangle$ so that they are related by a structural symmetry transformation $\widehat{\mathsf{S}}$. These results are proved for quantum systems like our world, based on the *standard quantum measurement scheme* [20, 124], which is the standard model of quantum measurements. Note that we don't need to perform the measurement, the whole point of this discussion is only to prove the existence of a structural symmetry transformation $\widehat{\mathsf{S}}$ making a property A of a given object that has a certain value a to appear as having another value a' on another configuration space, and thereby making $|\psi\rangle$ appear as $|\psi'\rangle$.

The structural symmetry transformation $\widehat{\mathsf{S}}$ satisfies $\widehat{\mathsf{S}}|\psi'\rangle = |\psi\rangle$. Since $\widehat{\mathsf{S}}\widehat{\mathsf{H}} = \widehat{\mathsf{H}}\widehat{\mathsf{S}}$, the two wavefunctions also evolve according to the same law. On $\mathcal{C}'$, $|\psi\rangle$ looks like $|\psi'\rangle$ on $\mathcal{C}$, and since the observer-like structure O' has the same structure as O, it also encodes in its brain-structure the information that the value of $\widehat{\mathsf{A}}$ is a. But since on $\mathcal{C}'$ the structure of the state $|\psi\rangle$ appears as the structure of the state $|\psi'\rangle$ on $\mathcal{C}$, the property A is represented by the observable $\widehat{\mathsf{A}}' = \widehat{\mathsf{S}}\widehat{\mathsf{A}}\widehat{\mathsf{S}}^{-1}$. Therefore, $\widehat{\mathsf{A}}'|\psi\rangle = \widehat{\mathsf{S}}\widehat{\mathsf{A}}\widehat{\mathsf{S}}^{-1}|\psi\rangle = \widehat{\mathsf{S}}\widehat{\mathsf{A}}|\psi'\rangle = a'\widehat{\mathsf{S}}|\psi'\rangle = a'|\psi\rangle$. So the value of the external property is a' and not a, as encoded in the structure of the observer-like structure O' on the configuration space $\mathcal{C}'$.

Since the observer-like structure has access only to its own structure, it doesn't know whether it is O from $\mathcal{C}$ or its structural duplicate O' from $\mathcal{C}'$. The credence of being O from $\mathcal{C}$ should be the same as the credence of being an observer O' from $\mathcal{C}'$. Therefore, the observer-like structure doesn't know whether the value of the property A really is a, as encoded in the structure of her brain, or any other possible value a' that the property A can have.

If observers were reducible to their structure, all such observer-like structures would be observers. An observer wouldn't know which of these observer-like structures she is. Therefore, she wouldn't know if the environment's property A has the value a or any other value a', even if her mind tells her the value is a. And this applies to all observable properties of the environment.

Since such a structural symmetry $\widehat{\mathsf{S}}$ always exists, the resulting configuration space always exists. This is true for all possible values of the property A. So the probability distribution of the alternative configuration spaces $\mathcal{C}'$ is uniform. Therefore, the probability that an observer-like structure has correct knowledge about her environment is exactly 0.

But it turns out from our experience that we have correct knowledge about our environment. We find ourselves every time in a configuration space with the right properties. This

1. either is a perpetual pure luck for us, with 0 chances to happen, while our infinitely many duplicate observer-like structures don't have the same luck,

2. or we simply can't be one of the observer-like structures from the other configuration spaces, because, for some reason, they can't be sentient observers.

This can happen only if we are sentient but the other observer-like structures are insentient, even if they have the same structure and dynamics we have. □

Remark 20.5. In the proof of Theorem 20.1, we assumed structural symmetry transformations, so that the dynamics appears the same on the alternative configuration spaces. But there is no reason to limit the transformations to the structural ones, and in this case the observer-like structure would be wrong not only about the properties, but also about the dynamics. However, in Theorem 20.1 I chose to require the symmetry transformations to be structural, to prevent the possible objection that the observer-like structures can figure out the right configuration space by observing the dynamics, which now we see is not true anyway. And to infer the dynamics from their observations, they should be able to remember the correct values of the properties, which is prevented anyway.

Theorem 20.1 shows that if all observer-like structures were sentient, our knowledge about the environment would be just like a random guess, contradicting our observations. Here are some of its implications:

Implication 20.1 (Irreducibility of sentience). The answer to Question 20.1 is yes, duplicate zombies of sentient beings exist, albeit in other configuration spaces.

Remark 20.6. When one says that there are no two identical structures that differ by their sentience, one usually assumes that the two structures are from different possible worlds. In Theorem 20.1, the identical structures are in the same physical state, but on different configuration spaces, with respect to which the world appears to have different structures.

Implication 20.2 (Ontology). Since structure and dynamics are insufficient to guarantee the sentience of an observer-like structure, the ontology of the preferred configuration space should provide the sentiential powers that structure and dynamics can't provide. I can't say how this happens, I'm only reporting the result.

This justifies a new definition:

Definition 20.8. We call *ontic configuration space* a configuration space in which observer-like structures are sentient.

Implication 20.3 (Uniqueness). The ontic configuration space is unique up to unobservable physical symmetries (space or spacetime isometries and gauge symmetries).

Proof. Any property as in the proof of Theorem 20.1 is observable, so it is invariant to gauge symmetries. Otherwise there would exist observables that can be measured but cannot be known, leading to a contradiction. The same applies to changes of reference frames in space. □

Implication 20.3 answers Question 20.4: the very large symmetry group of the structure is reduced to spacetime and gauge symmetries by whatever there is that makes the ontic configuration space special. The observer can't know an absolute reference frame or an absolute gauge, but it can know any other property.

Implication 20.4 (Observers and physical meaning)**.** The answer to Question 20.5 is negative: the structure of the observers alone cannot give physical meaning to the observables. This is possible only in conjunction with what makes the ontic configuration space special, whatever that is.

But what is that stuff that makes the ontic configuration space special? It is also what makes us sentient, but it doesn't make sentient our structural doppelgangers.

Implication 20.5 (Sentience)**.** By associating sentient experience not only with the structure and dynamics, but also with ontology, Theorem 20.1 supports the following understanding of sentience:

1. as what allows the knowledge of the external world,
2. as what gives physical meaning to the observables,
3. as the ingredient making observer-like structures sentient.

Implication 20.6 (Phenomenology)**.** All observer-like structures encode information that can be interpreted as representational or aboutness or *access consciousness* or *intentionality* [16], but only those from the ontic configuration space can experience it. Therefore, sentience can't be reduced to access consciousness.

Remark 20.7. The existence of memories that correspond to the past events but not to future events, the so-called *epistemic arrow of time*, is related to the Second Law of Thermodynamics, which requires that the universe's initial state had a very special structure [17], [2], [185]). This may make one think that we can avoid the conclusion of Theorem 20.1 by invoking the fact that the initial state was very special. One may think that this specialness selects a particular basis or configuration space. But whatever this choice is, the other configuration spaces equally exist. On another configuration space the structure of the initial state can appear like the structure of any other state (Propositions 20.1 and 20.2, and Theorem 20.1), so, if we assume The Physicalist Thesis, the initial conditions, being related to the configuration space, don't guarantee the validity of memories for the other configuration spaces. Under The Physicalist Thesis, we can't exclude some configuration spaces and keep others by assuming that only those on which the initial conditions are special.

20.8 Physicalism and consciousness

Theorem 20.1 implies that

Implication 20.7. The Physicalist Thesis is invalid.

Maybe some readers accepted The Physicalist Thesis as stated at the beginning of this chapter, and now they disagree that it expresses their own physicalist views. It may even appear to the reader that The Physicalist Thesis is a strawman that doesn't capture the real physicalism as they see it. But if physicalism as they see it requires an objectively preferred configuration space, this would mean to break Rule 1, a move that can hardly be still considered physicalism.

Some people who regard themselves as physicalists may be calling "physical" everything that exists. This would be a very vague notion of physicalism, to the extent that it would be contentless. Such a notion of physicalism would accommodate anything, so it would lack both explanatory and predictive power [93]. The point of physicalism was, like that of materialism, to reject precisely certain ideas about consciousness, including those attributing sentiential powers to ontology.

Theorem 20.1 is a no-go theorem like Bell's theorem, Gödel's theorem, or Turing's theorem [136, 9]. It excludes several important proposals about mind:

1. Versions of *behaviorism* in which consciousness reduces to behavior [81], which is encoded in the dynamics of the structure.
2. The *Computational Theory of Mind* [147], [37]). This was already shown based on Computer Science in this book, culminating with Chapter 18.

   But sometimes by "computation" it is understood that the structure of the machine implementing the computation has to be isomorphic to that of the data processed by the computation [27], [142], as discussed in Chapter 14. This contradicts Computer Science, in particular Turing universality [182]. And now we have seen that even if we take structure into account, as these restricted notions of computation suggest, mind can't be reduced to any of them.
3. *Functionalism*, the proposal that consciousness reduces to functionality [116], if functionality is understood from the point of view of structure and dynamics alone, for example as causal relations.
4. *Representationalism*, the proposal that consciousness reduces to representations [119]. Representations are engraved in the structure.
5. *Type identity theory* [166], the idea that mind is identical to the brain processes, if by these we understand structure and dynamics alone. Theorem 20.1 applies down to the finest structural details

of the atoms and elementary particles, because all these details are encoded in the patterns of the wavefunction.

6. *Integrated Information Theory* proposes that the degree of consciousness is measured by a numerical value Φ, exclusively determined by the structural characteristics of the system [199]. Since all isomorphic observer-like structures have the same Φ, Theorem 20.1 refutes the claim that Φ is a measure of consciousness. Note that both Tononi and Koch consider IIT to be a rigorous theory of *panpsychism*, the proposal that mental properties are present everywhere. But now we see that these mental properties can't be properties of the structure alone, so a structuralist version of IIT can't be sufficient.
7. *Illusionism* [47, 66] and *eliminative materialism* [146], the attempts to explain away phenomenal consciousness by reducing it access consciousness, which in its turn is reduced to one of the proposals based on structure and dynamics alone, for example to computation or representation. Also see Implication 20.6.

The results from this book make no proposal to explain consciousness. They don't provide a theory, a description, or an explanation of consciousness. They don't show what kind of structure conscious beings should have. To explore this, proposals like those mentioned above are still useful and constructive, because they focus on structure, dynamics, functionalism, representations, *etc.* Even if they are refuted in their structuralist form, structure matters, so such proposals may advance our understanding of mind. But, since Theorem 20.1 refutes The Physicalist Thesis by revealing a connection between ontology and consciousness, it refutes the reductionist claims made by these proposals.

Theorem 20.1 supports the following

The Sentiential Ontology Thesis. *Physical systems are characterized by their structure, dynamics,* and sentience*, which grounds consciousness and the physical meaning of all observables.*

The Sentiential Ontology Thesis doesn't require nonphysical entities, neither modifications of the structures and the dynamics, so it doesn't violate causal closure.

Let us see what theories of mind are compatible with The Sentiential Ontology Thesis.

1. *Dualism*, with matter and mind as fundamental but distinct kinds of entities [149] that interact or mirror each other's properties. But for dualism to be compatible with The Sentiential Ontology Thesis, the mental stuff have to duplicate the structure, the dynamics, and the properties of matter, as seen in Implication 20.3, so it has to be maximally redundant. *Monistic* proposals, in which there is only one kind of things, avoid this redundancy.

2. *Panpsychism*, "the view that mentality is fundamental and ubiquitous in the natural world" [79]. Compatibility with Implication 20.3 requires that sentiential properties correspond to observable physical properties, and this means that the ubiquity of sentience is maximal, as in the monistic forms of panpsychism [100], [121], [154], [56], [194]). But if physical properties are sentiential, the most natural form of The Sentiential Ontology Thesis is one in which the ontology is purely sentiential. After all, all that The Physicalist Thesis lacked was sentience (Implication 20.5).
3. This leads us to those variants of *idealism* [14], [86]) that are not antirealistic, in which the reality of properties is grounded in a sentiential substance [99], [105], [178]). The sentiential substance can have its own structure and follow its own dynamics like any system as in Definition 20.2. As it happens, its structure and dynamics are those that we observe in our universe. In addition, sentience also gives physical meaning to observables.

The Sentiential Ontology Thesis is not anti-physicalist, if physicalism is understood literally, based on the fact that *physis* means "nature". Nature includes ontology, even if ontology has sentiential powers. A fair physicalist position in this sense, which is consistent with The Sentiential Ontology Thesis is advocated by Strawson [193], page 3:

> You're certainly not a realistic physicalist, you're not a real physicalist, if you deny the existence of the phenomenon whose existence is more certain than the existence of anything else: experience, 'consciousness', conscious experience, 'phenomenology', experiential 'what-it's-likeness', feeling, sensation, explicit conscious thought as we have it and know it at almost every waking moment.

This self-evident truth should have been sufficient, but its rejection became the scientific norm, because it doesn't show up in the publicly observable structures of the brain. Now we have seen that even if we deny our own sentient experience and its scientific relevance, even if we try to exclude it from Science, Physics itself tells us that structure is insufficient, and without sentience no property of the world would be knowable.

Exercises

Exercise 20.4. How many unitary transformations exist on a state space of dimension n?

Hint. Prove that the $n \times n$ unitary transformations form a space with n^2 dimensions. The unitary transformations are in a one-to-one correspondence with the orthonormal bases (Exercise 17.1). Now count the bases: the first unit vector is specified by $2n - 1$ real numbers, because it is not a general vector, but one with unit length. The second unit vector belong to the $n-1$-dimensional complex vector space complementary to the first vector, so it is specified by $2(n-1) - 1$ real numbers and so on. Adding up we get $(2n-1) + (2n-3) + \ldots + 1 = n^2$. □

Exercise 20.5. Let V be an n-dimensional state space, and $\widehat{\mathsf{H}}$ a Hermitian operator representing the Hamiltonian. A Hermitian operator can be characterized by the existence of a basis in which it is expressed as a diagonal matrix with only real numbers on its diagonal. How many linear transformations $\widehat{\mathsf{S}}$ that commute with $\widehat{\mathsf{H}}$ exist?

Solution. The operators $\widehat{\mathsf{S}}$ and $\widehat{\mathsf{H}}$ commute if and only if there is a basis in which both of them are expressed by diagonal matrices. Then, if $\widehat{\mathsf{H}}$ is diagonal in some basis, any other matrix that is diagonal in the same basis commutes with $\widehat{\mathsf{H}}$. Since we want $\widehat{\mathsf{S}}$ to preserve the Hermitian scalar product from equation (17.4), it has to have on its diagonals numbers of the form $e^{i\phi}$, where $\phi \in \mathbb{R}$ (you can check this by applying equation (17.5) to the basis). Then, a unitary transformation $\widehat{\mathsf{S}}$ commuting with $\widehat{\mathsf{H}}$ depends on n continuous parameters. So there are infinitely many possible solutions, forming an n-dimensional manifold (a "continuous" space). But this is the minimum, valid in the extreme case when all diagonal elements of $\widehat{\mathsf{H}}$ are unique. If some of the diagonal elements of $\widehat{\mathsf{H}}$ repeat, there are even more solutions, because we can choose more different bases that diagonalize $\widehat{\mathsf{H}}$. The maximum possible occurs when $\widehat{\mathsf{H}}$ has all its diagonal elements equal, when any linear operator commutes with $\widehat{\mathsf{H}}$. A general matrix that commutes with $\widehat{\mathsf{H}}$ in this case is specified by n^2 complex numbers, but the condition that $\widehat{\mathsf{S}}$ is unitary reduces it to n^2 real numbers. So the answer is that there are infinitely many possible choices for $\widehat{\mathsf{S}}$, which form a space of real dimension between n and n^2, depending on $\widehat{\mathsf{H}}$. □

Exercise 20.6. Using Theorem 20.1, answer Questions 20.1, 20.4 and 20.5.

Key points

- Physical properties can't be reduced to structure and dynamics alone.
- If mind would be reducible to structure and dynamics alone, we would not be able to know the properties of the external world.

Further reading

[90] S W Hawking. *A Brief History of Time.* Bantam Books, Toronto, 1988

[54] P.A.M. Dirac. *The Principles of Quantum Mechanics.* Oxford University Press, Oxford, UK, 1958

[179] O.C. Stoica. 3d-space and the preferred basis cannot uniquely emerge from the quantum structure. *Adv. Theor. Math. Phys.*, 26(10):3895—3962, 2022. arXiv:2102.08620

[184] O.C. Stoica. The prince and the pauper. A quantum paradox of Hilbert-space fundamentalism. 2023. arXiv:2310.15090

[186] O.C. Stoica. Does the Hamiltonian determine the tensor product structure and the 3d space? 2024. arXiv:2401.01793

[180] O.C. Stoica. Are observers reducible to structures? 2023

[181] O.C. Stoica. Asking physics about physicalism, zombies, and consciousness. *philsci-archive:23108*, 2023

[189] O.C. Stoica. Structural realism and the underdetermination of the physical meaning. *J. Phys.: Conf. Ser.*, 2948(1):012014, 2025

[190] O.C. Stoica. What makes you an observer? *J. Phys.: Conf. Ser.*, 3017(1):012038, June 2025

[188] O.C. Stoica. Observation as physication. A single-world unitary no-conspiracy interpretation of quantum mechanics. 2024

[173] O.C. Stoica. Is consciousness grounded in matter or the other way around? http://youtu.be/BobtUr3nLLg. Accessed April 22, 2026

Epilogue

Alice, I thought about computation and how we tend to use the term differently than how it's understood in Computer Science, but I'm still not convinced.

Bob, you realize it's all just convention, don't you?

Certainly convention plays an important role in Computer Science, but the machine is really processing information, the information is there. Our conventions just translate it to us. How else can we exchange these messages? You keep insisting that it's all in our minds, but clearly something is going on inside the computer, and if you change it a bit, this changes how it works or even breaks it.

But if something objective is going on, why did we get eight different interpretations of the alien device (Chapter 2)?

Obviously there is only one way to interpret what the alien device does, and this is objective. It's a `NAND` gate like I said and nothing else 😉 .

C'mon, Bob! 🤣

Just kidding! But now, seriously, why can't the alien device have a unique objective interpretation, and all others be just reinterpretations? Just like a Turing machine is doing what it was designed to do, but you can use it to simulate a Turing machine with a different number of tape symbols and internal states, and that's just a simulation.

Computer Science begs to differ. A simulation of a computation is the computation (Chapter 10).

Well, I don't want to be the one who rejects science here. You're right, computation and simulation are on equal footing, none is more objective than the other. But... and this may be just an intuition... I believe a machine can think, for the same reason you and I can think.

Maybe it can, I don't debate this.

Someday scientists will prove you wrong!

> Prove me wrong? What exactly will they prove wrong about what I said?

Machines can think, can have sentient experiences as you call them, just like we have. It's carbon chauvinism to say otherwise.

> As I said, I don't debate this. What I refute is the claim that thinking, whatever it is, is just computation. That it can be achieved by mere computational means as understood in Computer Science.

So what's your claim then?

> If we will build a machine that thinks, it will think for other reasons, not by merely computing. Mind isn't a computation, at least not in the understanding of the word "computation" as it is used in Computer Science.

But what else can mind be?

> Whatever it is... But are you convinced now that when a computation takes place, along with it takes place a gazillion different computations, all attributable to the same physical process, by the same standards?

Well, I admit that I didn't believe this, but now that I saw the proof I am more open to the idea that there is no unique way to determine what computation takes place. You see, I can change my mind... if you give me enough evidence.

> So whatever program we think a computer runs, it's in fact our convention, one of a gazillion other possible conventions. Do you agree?

Ditto

> So there can be no standalone mind in a computer, there is no objective computation, not one that is independent of our conventions.

But maybe our convention unmasks something that's really going on inside the machine, a truly objective computation, even its intimate thoughts...

> If there is a genuine mind in the machine, what would be the odds that our conventions nail it?

OK, the odds are very small for this to happen by accident, but if all these alternative computations are equally real, maybe all alternative mind-like computations are equally valid minds. Well?

They are our conventions. They're not there, in the machine.

There can be an objective sense in which they are there: the totality of all that can be said to be a computation done by the machine, this totality no longer depends on the convention. It depends only on the machine. So one of them is not objective, but all of them taken together are.

So you bite the bullet!

I bit the bullet! Yes, they are all there!

So we both agree that the claim that mind is computation predicts this multiplicity of minds where we used to think there is a single mind?

Consider the following propositions:
$\mathcal{P}$="mind is just a computation", and
$\mathcal{Q}$="all computations resulting from other conventions are equally real". From $\mathcal{P}$ and $\mathcal{Q}$ it indeed follows that
$\mathcal{R}$="all alternative minds are equally real".
So yes, in conjunction with the existence of all these alternative mind-like computations, the Computational Theory of Mind predicts that the same brain runs at the same time gazillions of minds, each with its own, possibly completely different, thoughts and experiences.
If this is what follows, this is what follows, I byte the bullet.

Isn't this crazy?!

It is what it is. Those alternative minds may be there, but I can never contact the alternative Alices, just like you can't contact the alternative Bobs. And I can't contact the alternative Bobs either, and neither can you contact the alternative Alices. So they don't matter.

But if you can't verify the existence of alternative minds, isn't $\mathcal{R}$ unfalsifiable? Does this make it unscientific?

If it is, it's also unscientific to say that they're not minds, or that they're a problem for the Computational Theory of Mind, when they have no effect.

Don't they?

$\mathcal{R}$ is the prediction of $\mathcal{P}$ and $\mathcal{Q}$, so if $\mathcal{R}$ is unscientific, is this because $\mathcal{P}$ or $\mathcal{Q}$ is unscientific? I would say $\mathcal{Q}$, $\mathcal{Q}$ is precisely the part that you can't verify! How can you verify that all alternative computations are there?

But we can verify this, in principle. At least for the partition problem, we verified it together, at https://www.unitaryflow.com/2025/03/alternative-computations-at-once.html

Yeah, that experiment... Indeed, we verified it, but for a very simple program... but I agree it must scale up to more complicated computations than that simple program. The thought experiments from Chapter 13 showed that it scales up. I already conceded this point.

It scales up exponentially, in fact hyperexponentially. Repeat after me.

Yeah, yeah... so what?

So now $\mathcal{Q}$ is no longer crazy, it's a proven fact, but $\mathcal{R}$ still is crazy. If $\mathcal{R}$ (crazy) follows from $\mathcal{P}$ and $\mathcal{Q}$ (which is not crazy), it follows that $\mathcal{P}$ was the crazy claim.

OK, it seems crazy, but if you think more, it is wonderful that there is such an inflation of minds. Gazillions of Alices running on your brain, gazillions of Bobs running on mine, all unobservable, but isn't this wonderful?

It would be wonderful, if only almost all these alternative Alices and Bobs weren't tormented "souls", with their high degree of self-contradiction, with their illogical thoughts and experiences that make no sense, as it is a randomly chosen alternative mind-like computation 😢

How do you know that most of them aren't, in fact, minds full of bliss?

Blissful or tormented, it doesn't matter, almost all of those would be pure noise, and from those that aren't just noise, almost all of them would be highly self-contradictory.

Who cares about the tormented alternative minds, as long as we can't change this, as long as we can't even know them?

But what makes you different from them?

I'm different, we're different, because you and I are some special Alice and Bob, with our minds with such a low degree of self-contradiction.

You spoke like a privileged Bob.

We're just lucky.

But, assuming that your mind is just a computation, what are the odds that you are not one of the extremely incoherent alternative Bobs running on your brain along with you? Is this just luck? Isn't it simpler to conclude that the proposition $\mathcal{P}$ is false?

Are you suggesting that minds can do something that an AI can't do?

Yes, your mind *can be*, in a way a computation can't.

But if you define "being" as "having a small degree of self-contradiction", as in the crucial experiment from Chapter 18, this is wrong.
Nothing stops a computation from having a small degree of self-contradiction, so why then a computation "can't be" just like you "are"?

I don't define being as having a small degree of self-contradiction...

But the crucial experiment depends crucially on this difference, you notice that you have a small degree of self-contradiction, and from this you conclude that your mind is not just computation.

No, no, I mean yes, but you don't conclude that you're not a computation because minds would be more consistent logically than a computation, you got it all wrong. It is a self-location argument. If your mind were a computation, the probability that it is highly self-contradictory would be almost 100%. Since your mind is reasonably coherent, and since it keeps staying coherent every moment, this can't be just an accident.

So you admit that an AI can be as coherent as your mind or even more coherent?

Yes, I never said otherwise.

So then why isn't such an AI sentient? What's the difference?

I can't tell what the difference is. All we can infer is that I'm prevented from being such an incoherent mind, and I think the logical conclusion is that it's because my mind is not reducible to a computation.

I don't get it...

The set of all possible minds and the set of all possible computational simulations of minds are disjoint sets, because mind and computation are different in nature. But I can't say why.

This sounds fishy...

Why?

I don't know why, maybe because it doesn't explain what is mind, if not a computation. I realize that many scientific results are based on such Bayesian reasoning, for example the experimental discovery of the Higgs boson... but still...

Yes, any discovery that you hear about where sigma is mentioned.

I keep thinking about the Bayesian proof from Chapter 18 that shows the odds, one in a gazillion... Yeah, am I lucky or what?

And since your mind didn't immediately decay into a self-contradictory mind, you were lucky again. And now again, and again, with every passing moment in which your mind didn't decay into an incoherent mind... What kind of luck is this? It is like winning the cosmic lottery every moment!

One in a gazillion multiplied with itself every moment... It takes a lot of luck, repeated, consistent luck, but I still find this more likely than the alternative, that mind isn't reducible to computation! What else can mind be, if not a computation?!

I can't say. All I can say is that it's not a computation. Not this.

Let's not forget that there are other accounts of computation, and they don't seem to have the ambiguity that leads to this proliferation of minds.

I vehemently disagree with calling these "accounts of computation", they are not what Computer Science says computation is.

But Computer Science will evolve, like any science. We replaced Newton's physics with Relativity and Quantum Theory, I expect no less for Computer Science.

Sure, but until then, if you say that a computer is sentient, since that computer was built using the current ideas from Computer Science, by "computation" we should understand what Computer Science says it is.

Right, you're right again... If it is built by some rules it can't be expected to obey other rules. But when we talk about machines built with the technology of the future, or about whether mind can be a computation, we should allow this freedom, we should leave the door open for progress.

Enriching the notion of computation with more structure? This was discussed in Chapter 20.

Yes. I think we should explore that part in more detail.

Me too. There is so much to say about this. This will take another book.

Appendix. Source code for the partition problem

This is the source code of the program from Chapter 11. You can verify it yourself, use the debugger to run it step-by-step, and see that indeed:

1. A single partition is verified.
2. The data can be reinterpreted as verifying any other possible partition.
3. The result can be reinterpreted to give the result that would have been obtained for any other possible partition of the same list of numbers.

```
<!DOCTYPE html>
<html>
<script src="https://cdnjs.cloudflare.com/ajax/libs/mathjs
    /14.0.1/math.js" type="text/javascript"></script>
<style>
body {width: 500px; padding: 20px; text-align: justify;
    text-justify: inter-word;}
fieldset {display: table;}
p.controls{display: table-row; width: 100%;}
label {display: table-cell; padding-right: 10px;}
input {display: table-cell; align: right; width: 305px;}
table {width: 100%;}
table,th,td {border: 1px solid gray; border-collapse:
    collapse;}
th {padding: 5px; background-color: #abebc6; width: 20%;
    text-align: center;}
td {padding-left: 5px; padding-right: 5px;}
binary,table td:nth-child(1) {text-align: center;
    font-family: "Lucida Console", "Menlo", "Monaco", "
    Courier", monospace;}
table td:nth-child(2), td:nth-child(3) {text-align: right;}
table td:nth-child(4), td:nth-child(5) {text-align: center;}
tr.fair {background-color: #d6eaf8; color: #1b4f72;
    font-weight: bold;}
tr.failed {background-color: red; color: yellow;}
p.abstract{border: 1px solid gray; padding: 5px 10px;}
p.resultmsg{border: 1px solid; border-color: #e74c3c;
    background-color: #f7dc6f; color: #e74c3c; padding: 5px
    10px; font-weight: bold;}
button {background-color: #04aa6d; border: none; color:
    white; padding: 7px 16px; text-align: center;
```

```
    text-decoration: none; display: inline-block; font-size:
    14px; width:100%;}
</style>

<head>
<script>
var tableHeader = "<th>Partition</th><th>Decrypted<br>
    difference </th><th>Direct<br>difference</th><th>Fair<br>
    partition</th><th>Verification<br>successful</th>";

// Converts a string containing a list of numbers to a vector
function String2Vector(strNumbers) {
  const arrayNumbers = strNumbers.split(',').map(Number);
  const matrixNumbers = math.matrix([arrayNumbers]);
  return math.transpose(matrixNumbers);
}

// Converts a vector to a string containing a list of numbers
function Vector2String(vector) {
  return vector.toArray().flat().join(',');
}

// Gets the dimension of a vector
function getSizeOfVector(vector) {
  return math.size(vector).get([0]);
}

// Computes the matrix U from the matrix v
function ComputeMatrixU(vector) {
  const dim = getSizeOfVector(vector);
  // Initialize matrix U with 0
  let matU = math.identity(dim + 1, dim + 1);
  // Fill U with 1 on the main diagonal
  for (let i = 0; i <= dim; i++)
    matU.set([i,i], 1);
  // Fill the first row of U with the elements of the vector
  for (let i = 0; i < dim; i++)
    matU.set([0,i + 1], vector.get([i,0]));
  return matU;
}

// Computes the inverse of a matrix like U
function ComputeMatrixU_inverse(vector) {
  return ComputeMatrixU(math.multiply(vector, -1));
}

// Converts partition to extended S matrix
function PartitionToSignMatrix1(w) {
  const dim = getSizeOfVector(w);
  SignMatrix1 = math.zeros(dim + 1, dim + 1);
  SignMatrix1.set([0,0], 1);
  for (let i = 0; i < dim; i++)
    SignMatrix1.set([i + 1,i + 1],w.get([i,0]));
  return SignMatrix1;
}

// Converts a string of "0"s and "1"s to a partition matrix
```

```
    of "-1"s and "1"s
function BitStringToPartitionVector(strBits) {
  const arrayValues = strBits.toString().split('').map(c => [
      c === '0' ? -1 : 1]);
  return math.matrix(arrayValues);
}

// Converts a number to a string of bits
function NumberToBinaryString(number, length) {
  // Convert to binary and pad with leading zeros
  const binary = number.toString(2);
  return binary.padStart(length, '0');
}

// Computes the matrix that transforms the result for w0 to
    that for w
function ComputeTransformationMatrix(v, w0, w) {
  const matU = ComputeMatrixU(v);
  const invU = ComputeMatrixU_inverse(v);
  const S10 = PartitionToSignMatrix1(w0);
  const S1 = PartitionToSignMatrix1(w);
  const matS = math.multiply(S10, S1);
  return math.multiply(matU, math.multiply(matS, invU));
}

// Computes U applied to w
function ComputePartitionEvaluator(v, w) {
  // insert a 0 at the beginning of the vector
  const w1 = math.concat(math.matrix([[0]]),w,0);
  const matU = ComputeMatrixU(v);
  return math.multiply(matU, w1);
}

// Verifies if the partition w of v is fair
function IsPartitionFair(v, w) {
  const Uw1 = ComputePartitionEvaluator(v, w);
  return Uw1.get(0,0) === 0;
}

// Verifies if a partition v is computed simultaneously with
    w0
// and returns the result in a string
function TestPartition(evaluator_w0, v, w0, strBits) {
  const w = BitStringToPartitionVector(strBits);
  const evaluator_w_direct = ComputePartitionEvaluator(v, w);
  const R = ComputeTransformationMatrix(v, w0, w);
  const evaluator_w_transformation = math.multiply(R,
      evaluator_w0);
  const ewd00 = evaluator_w_direct.get([0,0]);
  const ewt00 = evaluator_w_transformation.get([0,0]);
  let bIsCorrect = true;
  let strResult = "<tr>";
  if (ewt00 === ewd00) {
    if (ewd00 === 0)
      strResult = "<tr class='fair'>";
    else
      strResult = "<tr>";
```

```
  } else
    strResult = "<tr class='failed'>";
  strResult += "<td>" + strBits + "</td>";
  strResult += "<td>" + ewt00.toString() + "</td>";
  strResult += "<td>" + ewd00.toString() + "</td>";
  if (ewd00 === 0)
    strResult += "<td style='color:green'>&checkmark;</td>";
  else
    strResult += "<td style='color:red'>&cross;</td>";
  if (ewt00 === ewd00)
    strResult += "<td style='color:green'>&checkmark;</td>";
  else {
    strResult += "<td style='color:red'>&cross;</td>";
    bIsCorrect = false;
  }
  strResult += "</tr>";
  return [bIsCorrect, strResult];
}

// Tests whether all partitions are computed simultaneously with w0
function TestAllPartitions() {
  if(!validateInputs(false))
    return;
  const v = String2Vector(document.getElementById("listNumbers").value);
  const w0 = BitStringToPartitionVector(document.getElementById("partitionDefault").value);
  const evaluator_w0 = ComputePartitionEvaluator(v, w0);
  const dim = getSizeOfVector(v);
  const maxDec = math.pow(2, dim);
  let bIsCorrect = true;
  // create a HTML table
  let strTable = "<table>" + tableHeader;
  for (let decNum = 0; decNum < maxDec; decNum++) {
    let bIsCorrectCurrent = true;
    const strBits = NumberToBinaryString(decNum, dim);
    [bIsCorrectCurrent, strPartitionResult] = TestPartition(evaluator_w0, v, w0, strBits);
    if(!bIsCorrectCurrent)
      bIsCorrect = false;
    strTable += strPartitionResult;
  }
  strTable += "</table>";
  let strResult = "<p class=\"resultmsg\">Result: ";
  if (bIsCorrect)
    strResult += "Verification successful!</p>" + strTable;
  else
    strResult += "Verification failed!</p>";
  document.getElementById("result").innerHTML = strResult;
}

// Tests if a user defined partition is computed simultaneously with w0
function TestUserDefinedPartition() {
  if(!validateInputs(true))
    return;
```

```
  const v = String2Vector(document.getElementById("listNumbers").value);
  const w0 = BitStringToPartitionVector(document.getElementById("partitionDefault").value);
  const evaluator_w0 = ComputePartitionEvaluator(v, w0);
  const strBits = document.getElementById("partitionUserDef").value;
  // create a HTML table
  let strTable = "<table>" + tableHeader;
  [bIsCorrect, strPartitionResult] = TestPartition(evaluator_w0, v, w0, strBits);
  let strResult = "<p class=\"resultmsg\">Result: ";
  if (bIsCorrect)
    strResult += "Verification successful!</p>";
  else
    strResult += "Verification failed!</p>";
  strResult += strTable + strPartitionResult + "</table>";
  document.getElementById("result").innerHTML = strResult;
}

// Validates the format of the data of an input element in the UI
function validateInput(inputElement, pattern, msg) {
  const inputValue = inputElement.value;
  const regex = new RegExp(pattern);
  if (regex.test(inputValue)) {
    inputElement.style.border = "";
    return true;
  } else {
    inputElement.style.border = "2px solid red";
    alert(msg);
    return false;
  }
}

// Validates the format of the input data in the UI
function validateInputs(all) {
  if(!validateInput(document.getElementById("listNumbers"), "^[0-9,]+$", "Please enter only coma separated natural numbers"))
    return false;
  const v = String2Vector(document.getElementById("listNumbers").value);
  const dim = getSizeOfVector(v);
  const pattern = "^[01]{" + Math.floor(dim) + "}$";
  let msg = "The partition data should consist of " + dim + " digits with values 0 or 1";
  if(!validateInput(document.getElementById("partitionDefault"), pattern, msg))
    return false;
  if(all && !validateInput(document.getElementById("partitionUserDef"), pattern, msg))
    return false;
  return true;
}
</script>
</head>
```

```

<body>
<h2>DIY experiment: Relativity of information</h2>
<p class="abstract">Whatever meaning we see in a computer or in the information it stores and the computation it does, this meaning is due to our own conventions.
If we change the convention, we change the meaning.
Without us to make the convention there is no meaning in a computer.</p>
<p>This JavaScript program demonstrates that when a computer does a computation, it also does the computations for the other possible inputs, simultaneously. The alternative computations are "encrypted" in that computation, and they can be "decrypted" by changing the convention.</p>
<p>For this demonstration, the program verifies if a partition of a list of numbers into two sublists is fair, that is, if the sums of the two sublists of numbers are equal (<a href="https://en.wikipedia.org/wiki/Partition_problem" target="_blank">the partition problem</a>).
The program does the verification only once, for a default partition, and it can decrypt the results for any other partition.</p>
<fieldset>
  <legend>Input data</legend>
  <p class="controls">
    <label for="listNumbers">List of numbers:</label>
    <input id="listNumbers" name="listNumbers" type="text" value="5,5,5,10,10,25">
  </p>
  <p class="controls">
    <label for="partitionDefault">Default partition:</label>
    <input id="partitionDefault" name="partitionDefault" type="text" class="binary" value="000000">
  </p>
  <p class="controls">
    <label for="partitionUserDef">User defined partition:</label>
    <input id="partitionUserDef" name="partitionUserDef" type="text" class="binary" value="000111">
  </p>
  <p>
    <button type="button" onclick="TestUserDefinedPartition()"> Is the user defined partition verified along with the default partition?</button>
  </p>
  <p>
    <button type="button" onclick="TestAllPartitions()">Are all possible partitions verified along with the default partition?</button>
  </p>
</fieldset>
<p>Right-click to view the code or run it line-by-line.</p>
<p id="result"></p>
</body>
</html>
```

Bibliography

[1] Hal Abelson and Gerald Sussman with Julie Sussman. *Structure and interpretation of computer programs.* MIT Press, Cambridge, Massachusetts, 1996. https://library.oapen.org/handle/20.500.12657/26092. Videos: https://youtu.be/-J_xL4IGhJA&list=PLE18841CABEA24090.

[2] D.Z. Albert. *Time and chance.* Harvard University Press, Cambridge, Massachusetts; London, England, 2000.

[3] Anonymous. Turing machine – Working Lego computer. Sep. 2024. https://ideas.lego.com/projects/10a3239f-4562-4d23-ba8e-f4fc94eef5c7, Accessed April 22, 2026.

[4] The Origins Project at ASU. The great debate: The storytelling of science- (Part 2/2). http://youtu.be/40YIIaF1qiw?t=13m50s. Accessed April 22, 2026.

[5] Euclid (author) and TL Heath (translator). *The thirteen books of Euclid's Elements.* Dover Publications, New York, 1956.

[6] Anita Avramides. Other Minds. In Edward N. Zalta, editor, *The Stanford Encyclopedia of Philosophy.* Metaphysics Research Lab, Stanford University, Stanford, California, Winter 2020 edition, 2020.

[7] Jacques Bahi and Christophe Guyeux. *Discrete dynamical systems and chaotic machines. Theory and applications.* CRC Press, 2013.

[8] V. Bargmann. Note on Wigner's theorem on symmetry operations. *J. Math. Phys.*, 5(7):862–868, 1964.

[9] John D Barrow. *Impossibility: The limits of science and the science of limits.* Random House, New York, 1999.

[10] Jonathan Basile. The Library of Babel. *https://libraryofbabel.info/*, 2025.

[11] CH Bennett. Logical reversibility of computation. *IBM J Res Dev*, 17(6):525–532, 1973.

[12] Charles Bennett and Rolf Landauer. The fundamental physical limits of computation. *Scientific American*, 253(1):48–57, 1985.

[13] Robert Berger. *The undecidability of the domino problem.* Number 66. Am. Math. Soc., 1966.

[14] George Berkeley. *A treatise concerning the principles of human knowledge.* JB Lippincott & Company, 1881.

[15] E.R. Berlekamp, J.H. Conway, and R.K. Guy. *Winning ways for your mathematical plays.* AK Peters/CRC Press, 2004.

[16] Ned Block. On a confusion about a function of consciousness. *Behavioral and brain sciences*, 18(2):227–247, 1995.

[17] L. Boltzmann. *Lectures on gas theory.* University of California Press,, Berkeley, 1964.

[18] Jorge Luis Borges. *Labyrinths: Selected stories and other writings.* Number 186. New Directions Publishing, New York, 1964.

[19] Nick Bostrom. Are we living in a computer simulation? *The Philosophical Quarterly*, 53(211):243–255, 2003.

[20] P. Busch, M. Grabowski, and P. Lahti. *Operational quantum physics.* Springer, Berlin, Heidelberg, 1995.

[21] Cris Calude and Gheorghe Păun. *Computing with cells and atoms: An introduction to quantum, DNA and membrane computing.* CRC Press, 2000.

[22] Cristian Calude. *To halt or not to halt? That is the question.* World Scientific, Singapore, 2024.

[23] Sean Carroll. Consciousness and the laws of physics. *Journal of Consciousness Studies*, 28(9-10):16–31, 2021.

[24] S.M. Carroll. Reality as a vector in Hilbert space. In *Quantum mechanics and fundamentality*, pages 211–224. Springer Nature, 2022.

[25] S.M. Carroll and A. Singh. Mad-dog Everettianism: Quantum Mechanics at its most minimal. In A. Aguirre, B. Foster, and Z. Merali, editors, *What is Fundamental?*, pages 95–104. Springer, 2019.

[26] S.M. Carroll and A. Singh. Quantum mereology: Factorizing Hilbert space into subsystems with quasi-classical dynamics. *To appear in Phys. Rev. A*, 2021. Preprint arXiv:2005.12938.

[27] David Chalmers. On implementing a computation. *Minds and Machines*, 4(4):391–402, 1994.

[28] David Chalmers. Does a rock implement every finite-state automaton? *Synthese*, 108(3):309–333, 1996.

[29] David Chalmers. *Reality+: Virtual worlds and the problems of philosophy.* Penguin, UK, 2022.

[30] David J. Chalmers. Facing up to the problem of consciousness. *Journal of consciousness studies*, 2(3):200–219, 1995.

[31] David J. Chalmers. A computational foundation for the study of cognition. *Journal of Cognitive Science*, 12(4):325–359, 2011.

[32] C.C. Chang and H.J. Keisler. *Model theory.* Elsevier, 1990.

[33] Xin Chen, Xinyu Liu, Fang Wang, Sirui Li, Congzhou Chen, Xiaoli Qiang, and Xiaolong Shi. Massively parallel dna computing based on domino dna strand displacement logic gates. *ACS Synthetic Biology*, 11(7):2504–2512, 2022.

[34] P.M. Churchland. Eliminative materialism and propositional attitudes. *The Journal of Philosophy*, 78(2):67–90, 1981.

[35] William S. Cobb. The game of Go. An unexpected path to enlightenment. *The Eastern Buddhist*, 30(2):199–213, 1997.

[36] Bob Coecke and Stefano Gogioso. *Quantum in Pictures.* Cambridge Quantum, Cambridge, UK, 2023.

[37] Matteo Colombo and Gualtiero Piccinini. *The Computational Theory of Mind.* Cambridge University Press, Cambridge, UK, 2023.

[38] M. Cook. Universality in elementary cellular automata. *Complex systems*, 15(1):1–40, 2004.

[39] J Copeland, C Posy, and O Shagrir. *Computability: Turing, Gödel, Church, and beyond.* MIT Press, 2013.

[40] Thomas Cormen, Charles Leiserson, Ronald Rivest, and Clifford Stein. *Introduction to algorithms.* MIT Press, Cambridge, Massachusetts, 2022.

[41] J.S. Cotler, G.R. Penington, and D.H. Ranard. Locality from the spectrum. *Comm. Math. Phys.*, 368(3):1267–1296, 2019.

[42] Michael Crider. This 8-bit processor built in Minecraft can run its own games. *PC World*, Dec. 2021.

[43] Martin Davis. *The undecidable: Basic papers on undecidable propositions, unsolvable problems and computable functions.* Courier Corporation, 2004.

[44] Daniel Dennett. Quining qualia. *Consciousness in contemporary science*, pages 42–77, 1988.

[45] Daniel Dennett. *The intentional stance.* MIT Press, Cambridge, Massachusetts, 1989.

[46] Daniel Dennett. *Consciousness explained.* Penguin, London, UK, 1993.

[47] Daniel Dennett. Illusionism as the obvious default theory of consciousness. *J Conscious Stud*, 23(11-12):65–72, 2016.

[48] Daniel Dennett. Welcome to strong illusionism. *J. Conscious. Stud.*, 26(9-10):48–58, 2019.

[49] Daniel C. Dennett. A history of qualia. *Topoi*, 39(1):5–12, 2020.

[50] René Descartes. *Discourse on method.* Yale University Press, PA, US, 1996.

[51] René Descartes. Meditations on first philosophy. In *Seven masterpieces of philosophy*, pages 63–108. Routledge, 2016.

[52] David Deutsch. Quantum theory, the Church–Turing Principle and the universal quantum computer. *Proc. Roy. Soc. London Ser. A*, 400(1818):97–117, 1985.

[53] David Deutsch. *The fabric of reality: The science of parallel universes and its implications.* Viking Penguin, New York, 1998.

[54] P.A.M. Dirac. *The Principles of Quantum Mechanics.* Oxford University Press, Oxford, UK, 1958.

[55] Anatoly Dneprov. "Igra (The Game)." *Znanie–Sila (Knowledge–Power)* 5 (1961): 39–41.

[56] A. Eddington. *The nature of the physical world.* Dent, London, 1928.

[57] A.S. Eddington. *Space, time and gravitation: An outline of the general relativity theory.* The University Press, 1921.

[58] Greg Egan. *Permutation city.* HarperCollins/Eos, New York, U.S., 1994.

[59] Greg Egan. Wang's carpets. In *New Legends.* Tor Books, Berlin, Heidelberg, 1995.

[60] Greg Egan. *Diaspora.* Millennium, Australia, 1997.

[61] A. Einstein. Relativity: The special and the general theory. *Space*, 80(3):262, 1920.

[62] Ronald Emery. *Digital circuits: Logic and design.* CRC Press, 2020.

[63] Giulio Ferrari. Masterpiece 3 - the LEGO Turing machine. In Kevin Clague, editor, *Classic Lego Mindstorms Projects and Software Tools*, pages 105–150. Syngress, Burlington, 2006.

[64] Richard P. Feynman. *The pleasure of finding things out.* Perseus Publishing, Cambridge, Massachusetts, 1999.

[65] Jon Pierre Fortney. *Discrete mathematics for computer science: An example-based introduction.* Chapman and Hall/CRC, 2020.

[66] Keith Frankish. Illusionism as a theory of consciousness. *J. Conscious. Stud.*, 23(11-12):11–39, 2016.

[67] E Fredkin. An introduction to digital philosophy. *Int. J. Theor. Phys.*, 42(2):189–247, 2003.

[68] Edward Fredkin and Tommaso Toffoli. Conservative logic. *Int. J. Theor. Phys.*, 21(3-4):219–253, 1982.

[69] Hans Freudenthal. *Lincos: Design of a Language for Cosmic Intercourse.* North-Holland Pub. Co., Amsterdam, Netherlands, 1960.

[70] Errol C Friedberg. Dna damage and repair. *Nature*, 421(6921):436–440, 2003.

[71] Peter Galison. Minkowski's Space-Time: From visual thinking to the absolute world. *Critical Studies*, 32, 2010.

[72] Robin Gandy. Church's thesis and principles for mechanisms. In J. Barwise, H.J. Keisler, and K. Kuhnen, editors, *The Kleene Symposium*, volume 101, pages 123–148. Elsevier, Amsterdam, North-Holland, 1980.

[73] Martin Gardner. The fantastic combinations of John Conway's new solitaire game 'Life'. *Sc. Am.*, 223:20–123, 1970.

[74] Rowan Garnier and John Taylor. *Discrete mathematics: Proofs, structures and applications.* CRC Press, 2009.

[75] Craig Gentry. *A fully homomorphic encryption scheme.* Stanford University, Stanford, 2009.

[76] Marco Giunti. *Computation, dynamics, and cognition.* Oxford University Press, 1997.

[77] P. Godfrey-Smith. Triviality arguments against functionalism. *Philosophical Studies*, 145(2):273–295, 2009.

[78] P. Goff. *Consciousness and fundamental reality.* Oxford University Press, Oxford, UK, 2017.

[79] Philip Goff, William Seager, and Sean Allen-Hermanson. Panpsychism. In Edward N. Zalta, editor, *The Stanford Encyclopedia of Philosophy*. Metaphysics Research Lab, Stanford University, Stanford, California, Summer 2022 edition, 2022.

[80] Solomon Golomb. On the classification of Boolean functions. *IRE transactions on circuit theory*, 6(5):176–186, 1959.

[81] George Graham. Behaviorism. In Edward N. Zalta and Uri Nodelman, editors, *The Stanford Encyclopedia of Philosophy*. Metaphysics Research Lab, Stanford University, Stanford, California, Spring 2023 edition, 2023.

[82] G. Grätzer. *Universal algebra*. Springer Science & Business Media, 2008.

[83] B. Grünbaum and G.C. Shephard. *Tilings and patterns*. W.H. Freeman and Company, New York, 1987.

[84] Ting Guo. Dao of the Go. Contextualizing 'spirituality', 'intelligence', and the human self. *Implicit Religion*, 20(3):233–244, 2017.

[85] Georges Ivanovitch Gurdjieff. *Meetings with remarkable men*. Penguin, UK, 2015.

[86] Paul Guyer and Rolf-Peter Horstmann. Idealism. In Edward N. Zalta and Uri Nodelman, editors, *The Stanford Encyclopedia of Philosophy*. Metaphysics Research Lab, Stanford University, Stanford, California, Spring 2023 edition, 2023.

[87] Gwern. Surprisingly Turing-complete. 2012–2022. https://gwern.net/turing-complete. Accessed April 22, 2026.

[88] Richard W Hamming. Error detecting and error correcting codes. *BSTJ*, 29(2):147–160, 1950.

[89] Brian Hatfield. *Quantum field theory of point particles and strings*. CRC Press, Boca Raton, FL, USA, 2018.

[90] S W Hawking. *A Brief History of Time*. Bantam Books, Toronto, 1988.

[91] B Hayes. Third base. *American scientist*, 89(6):490–494, 2001.

[92] B Hayes. The easiest hard problem. *American Scientist*, 90(2):113–117, 2002.

[93] CG Hempel. Comments on Goodman's "ways of worldmaking". *Synthese*, pages 193–199, 1980.

[94] David Hilbert and Wilhelm Ackermann. *Principles of mathematical logic*, volume 69. American Mathematical Society, 2022.

[95] W. Hodges. *A shorter model theory.* Cambridge University Press, Cambridge, UK, 1 edition, 1997.

[96] Carl Hoefer, Nick Huggett, and James Read. Absolute and Relational Space and Motion: Classical Theories. In Edward N. Zalta and Uri Nodelman, editors, *The Stanford Encyclopedia of Philosophy.* Metaphysics Research Lab, Stanford University, Stanford, California, Spring 2023 edition, 2023.

[97] Donald Hoffman. *The case against reality: Why evolution hid the truth from our eyes.* WW Norton & Company, New York, 2019.

[98] D.R. Hofstadter. *I am a strange loop.* Basic Books, New York, 2007.

[99] William M Indich. *Consciousness in Advaita Vedanta.* Motilal Banarsidass Publ., 1995.

[100] William James. A world of pure experience. *The Journal of Philosophy, Psychology and Scientific Methods*, 1(20):533–543, 1904.

[101] Emmanuel Jeandel and Michael Rao. An aperiodic set of 11 Wang tiles. *Advances in Combinatorics*, January 6 2021.

[102] François Kammerer. The illusion of conscious experience. *Synthese*, 198(1):845–866, 2021.

[103] François Kammerer. How can you be so sure? illusionism and the obviousness of phenomenal consciousness. *Philosophical Studies*, 179(9):2845–2867, 2022.

[104] Mohammad Karim and Xinghao Chen. *Digital design: Basic concepts and principles.* CRC Press, 2017.

[105] Bernardo Kastrup. *Analytic Idealism: A consciousness-only ontology.* Bernardo Kastrup, 2019.

[106] Richard Kaye. Infinite versions of Minesweeper are Turing-complete. *Manuscript, August*, 2000.

[107] Robert Kirk. Zombies. In Edward N. Zalta and Uri Nodelman, editors, *The Stanford Encyclopedia of Philosophy.* Metaphysics Research Lab, Stanford University, Stanford, California, Fall 2023 edition, 2023.

[108] Robert Kirk and Roger Squires. Zombies v. materialists. *Proc. Aristot. Soc., Supplementary Volumes*, 48:135–163, 1974.

[109] J. Kirtland. *Identification numbers and check digit schemes*, volume 18. Cambridge University Press, Cambridge, UK, 2001.

[110] Christof Koch. *Consciousness: Confessions of a romantic reductionist.* MIT Press, Cambridge, Massachusetts, 2017.

[111] Manfred Kudlek and Yurii Rogozhin. A universal Turing machine with 3 states and 9 symbols. *Lecture notes in computer science*, pages 311–318, 2002.

[112] Stephen LaBerge and Howard Rheingold. *Exploring the world of lucid dreaming.* Ballantine Books, New York, 1990.

[113] J. Ladyman. Structural realism. In Edward N. Zalta, editor, *The Stanford Encyclopedia of Philosophy.* Metaphysics Research Lab, Stanford University, Stanford, California, spring 2020 edition, 2020.

[114] Rolf Landauer. Irreversibility and heat generation in the computing process. *IBM journal of research and development*, 5(3):183–191, 1961.

[115] Mark Verus Lawson. *A first course in logic.* CRC Press, 2018.

[116] Janet Levin. Functionalism. In Edward N. Zalta and Uri Nodelman, editors, *The Stanford Encyclopedia of Philosophy.* Metaphysics Research Lab, Stanford University, Stanford, California, Summer 2023 edition, 2023.

[117] Jenny List. 8-bit computer made solely from NAND gates. *https://hackaday.com/2016/02/24/8-bit-computer-made-solely-from-nand-gates/*, 2016.

[118] William Lycan. Form, function, and feel. *J. Philos*, 78(1):24–50, 1981.

[119] William Lycan. Representational Theories of Consciousness. In Edward N. Zalta, editor, *The Stanford Encyclopedia of Philosophy.* Metaphysics Research Lab, Stanford University, Stanford, California, Fall 2019 edition, 2019.

[120] M. M. Schlosshauer. *Decoherence and the Quantum-To-Classical Transition.* Springer, Berlin, 2007.

[121] Ernst Mach. *The analysis of sensations, and the relation of the physical to the psychical.* Open Court Publishing Company, 1914.

[122] Chiara Marcolla, Victor Sucasas, Marc Manzano, Riccardo Bassoli, Frank HP Fitzek, and Najwa Aaraj. Survey on fully homomorphic encryption, theory, and applications. *Proceedings of the IEEE*, 110(10):1572–1609, 2022.

[123] Mario Martelli. *Introduction to discrete dynamical systems and chaos.* John Wiley & Sons, New York, U.S.A., 2011.

[124] P. Mittelstaedt. *The interpretation of quantum mechanics and the measurement process.* Cambridge University Press, Cambridge, UK, 2004.

[125] Hans Moravec. *Mind children: The future of robot and human intelligence.* Harvard University Press, Cambridge, Massachusetts, 1988.

[126] R H Morelos-Zaragoza. *The art of error correcting coding.* John Wiley & Sons, 2006.

[127] Masahiro Mori. The uncanny valley. *IEEE Robotics & automation magazine*, 19(2):98–100, 2012.

[128] Thomas Nagel. What is it like to be a bat? *Phil. Review*, 83(4):435–450, 1974.

[129] M. Nakahara. *Geometry, Topology, and Physics.* Taylor & Francis, 2003.

[130] Turlough Neary and Damien Woods. Four small universal turing machines. *Fundamenta Informaticae*, 91(1):123–144, 2009.

[131] M.A. Nielsen and I.L. Chuang. *Quantum Computation and Quantum Information.* Cambridge University Press, Cambridge, UK, 2010.

[132] G. Nikolaou, T. Mencattini, D. Crisostomi, A. Santilli, Y. Panagakis, and E. Rodolà. Language models are injective and hence invertible. 2025. arXiv:2510.15511.

[133] Noam Nisan and Shimon Schocken. *The elements of computing systems: Building a modern computer from first principles.* MIT Press, Cambridge, Massachusetts, 2021.

[134] Matt Parker. *Things to make and do in the fourth dimension.* Macmillan, New York, 2014.

[135] Charles Sanders Peirce. *Collected papers*, volume 5. Harvard University Press, Cambridge, Massachusetts, 1974.

[136] R. Penrose. *The emperor's new mind.* Oxford University Press, Oxford, UK, 1989.

[137] KS Perumalla. *Introduction to reversible computing.* CRC Press, 2013.

[138] Michael Peskin and Daniel Schroeder. *An Introduction to quantum field theory.* CRC Press, Boca Raton, FL, USA, 2019.

[139] V. Petkov. *From Illusions to Reality: Time, Spacetime and the Nature of Reality.* Minkowski Institute Press, 2013.

[140] Charles Petzold. *Code: The Hidden Language of Computer Hardware and Software.* Microsoft Press, 2 edition, 2022.

[141] F. Piazza. Glimmers of a pre-geometric perspective. *Found. Phys.*, 40:239–266, 2010.

[142] G. Piccinini. *Physical computation: A mechanistic account.* OUP, Oxford, 2015.

[143] Plato. *The republic of Plato. Translated with introduction and notes by Francis Macdonald Cornford.* Oxford University Press, Oxford, UK, 1976.

[144] Henri Poincaré. *Science and Hypothesis.* Bloomsbury Publishing, 2022.

[145] Hilary Putnam. *Representation and reality.* MIT Press, Cambridge, Massachusetts, 1988.

[146] William Ramsey. Eliminative Materialism. In Edward N. Zalta, editor, *The Stanford Encyclopedia of Philosophy.* Metaphysics Research Lab, Stanford University, Stanford, California, Spring 2022 edition, 2022.

[147] M Rescorla. The Computational Theory of Mind. In EN Zalta and Uri Nodelman, editors, *The Stanford Encyclopedia of Philosophy.* Metaphysics Research Lab, Stanford University, Stanford, California, Winter 2024 edition, 2024.

[148] Ronald L Rivest, Adi Shamir, and Leonard Adleman. A method for obtaining digital signatures and public-key cryptosystems. *Communications of the ACM*, 21(2):120–126, 1978.

[149] Howard Robinson. Dualism. In Edward N. Zalta and Uri Nodelman, editors, *The Stanford Encyclopedia of Philosophy.* Metaphysics Research Lab, Stanford University, Stanford, California, Spring 2023 edition, 2023.

[150] Raphael M Robinson. Undecidability and nonperiodicity for tilings of the plane. *Inventiones mathematicae*, 12:177–209, 1971.

[151] Sara Robinson. Still guarding secrets after years of attacks, RSA earns accolades for its founders. *Siam News*, 36(5):1–4, 2003.

[152] Yurii Rogozhin. Small universal Turing machines. *Theor. Comput. Sci.*, 168(2):215–240, 1996.

[153] Terry Rudolph. *Q is for Quantum.* Terence Rudolph, 2017.

[154] B. Russell. *The analysis of matter.* London: Kegan Paul, 1927.

[155] Carl Sagan. *The Demon-Haunted World: Science As a Candle in the Dark.* Ballantine Books, New York, 1997.

[156] Igor Salom. The hard problem and the measurement problem: a no-go theorem and potential consequences. *Preprint arXiv:2001.03143*, 2020.

[157] John Searle. Minds, brains, and programs. *Behavioral and brain sciences*, 3(3):417–424, 1980.

[158] John Searle. Is the brain a digital computer? *Proc Am Philos Soc*, 64(3):21–37, 1990.

[159] John Searle. *The rediscovery of the mind.* MIT Press, Cambridge, Massachusetts, 1992.

[160] Robert Sedgewick and Kevin Wayne. *Algorithms.* Addison-Wesley, Redwood City, California, 2011.

[161] Anil Seth. *Being you: A new science of consciousness.* Penguin, London, UK, 2021.

[162] O Shagrir. Can a brain possess two minds? *Journal of Cognitive Science*, 13(2):145–165, 2012.

[163] Claude Shannon. Mathematical theory of the differential analyzer. *J. Math. Phys.*, 20(1-4):337–354, 1941.

[164] Wilfried Sieg. Calculations by man and machine: Conceptual analysis. In Wilfried Sieg, Richard Sommer, and Carolyn Talcott, editors, *Reflections on the foundations of mathematics (essays in honor of Solomon Feferman)*, volume 15, pages 387–406. AK Peters/CRC Press, 2002.

[165] David Slepian. On the number of symmetry types of Boolean functions of n variables. *Canad. J. Math.*, 5:185–193, 1953.

[166] J. J. C. Smart. The Mind/Brain Identity Theory. In Edward N. Zalta and Uri Nodelman, editors, *The Stanford Encyclopedia of Philosophy.* Metaphysics Research Lab, Stanford University, Stanford, California, Winter 2022 edition, 2022.

[167] Mark Sprevak and Matteo Colombo. *The Routledge Handbook of the Computational Mind.* Routledge, London, UK, 2019.

[168] Ian Stewart. *Professor Stewart's cabinet of mathematical curiosities.* Basic Books, New York, 2009.

[169] Cristi Stoica. AI solves omnivore wolf, goat and cabbage problem! *http://www.unitaryflow.com/2025/01/AI-solves-omnivorous-wolf-goat-cabbage.html*, 2025.

[170] Cristi Stoica. Alternative computations at once. *https://www.unitaryflow.com/ 2025/03/alternative-computations-at-once.html*, 2025.

[171] Cristi Stoica. OpenAI o3-mini solves omnivore wolf, goat and cabbage problem. *https://www.unitaryflow.com/2025/02/openai-o3-mini-solves-omnivorous-wolf.html*, 2025.

[172] O.C. Stoica. Are you a robot? http://youtu.be/kuziE01rh6M&list=PLJzOclJMoIC1pnJIPlmWhGwaDWD04tFza. Accessed April 22, 2026.

[173] O.C. Stoica. Is consciousness grounded in matter or the other way around? http://youtu.be/BobtUr3nLLg. Accessed April 22, 2026.

[174] O.C. Stoica. *Singular General Relativity – Ph.D. Thesis.* Minkowski Institute Press, 2013. arXiv:math.DG/1301.2231.

[175] O.C. Stoica. The Tao of It and Bit. In *It From Bit or Bit From It?: On Physics and Information*, pages 51–64. Springer, Berlin, Heidelberg, 2015. arXiv:1311.0765.

[176] O.C. Stoica. And the math will set you free. In *Trick or Truth? The Mysterious Connection Between Physics and Mathematics*, pages 233–247. Springer, 2016. arXiv:1311.0765.

[177] O.C. Stoica. Are mental states nonlocal? *Mind and Matter*, 18(2), 2020. Preprint arXiv:2010.03389.

[178] O.C. Stoica. The negative way to sentience. *Preprint on philsci-archive:17036 - last accessed April 22, 2026*, March 2020.

[179] O.C. Stoica. 3d-space and the preferred basis cannot uniquely emerge from the quantum structure. *Adv. Theor. Math. Phys.*, 26(10):3895—3962, 2022. arXiv:2102.08620.

[180] O.C. Stoica. Are observers reducible to structures? 2023.

[181] O.C. Stoica. Asking physics about physicalism, zombies, and consciousness. *philsci-archive:23108*, 2023.

[182] O.C. Stoica. Does a computer think if no one is around to see it? *philsci-archive:22880*, 2023.

[183] O.C. Stoica. No-go results on emergent space and other structures. *Journal of Physics: Conference Series*, 2533(1):012027, 2023.

[184] O.C. Stoica. The prince and the pauper. A quantum paradox of Hilbert-space fundamentalism. 2023. arXiv:2310.15090.

[185] O.C. Stoica. Does quantum mechanics require "conspiracy"? *Entropy*, 26(5):411, 2024. arXiv:2209.13275.

[186] O.C. Stoica. Does the Hamiltonian determine the tensor product structure and the 3d space? 2024. arXiv:2401.01793.

[187] O.C. Stoica. Empirical adequacy of the time operator canonically conjugate to a Hamiltonian generating translations. *Physica Scripta*, 2024. arXiv:2204.01426.

[188] O.C. Stoica. Observation as physication. A single-world unitary no-conspiracy interpretation of quantum mechanics. 2024.

[189] O.C. Stoica. Structural realism and the underdetermination of the physical meaning. *J. Phys.: Conf. Ser.*, 2948(1):012014, 2025.

[190] O.C. Stoica. What makes you an observer? *J. Phys.: Conf. Ser.*, 3017(1):012038, June 2025.

[191] Daniel Stoljar. Physicalism. In Edward N. Zalta and Uri Nodelman, editors, *The Stanford Encyclopedia of Philosophy*. Metaphysics Research Lab, Stanford University, Stanford, California, Summer 2023 edition, 2023.

[192] CL Stong. The amateur scientist. How streams of water can be used to create analogues of electronic tubes and circuits". *Scientific American*, 1962. Accessed April 22, 2026.

[193] Galen Strawson. Realistic monism: Why physicalism entails panpsychism. In A. Freeman, editor, *Consciousness and its place in nature: Does physicalism entail panpsychism?*, pages 3–31, UK, 2006. Imprint Academic.

[194] Leopold Stubenberg and Donovan Wishon. Neutral Monism. In Edward N. Zalta and Uri Nodelman, editors, *The Stanford Encyclopedia of Philosophy*. Metaphysics Research Lab, Stanford University, Stanford, California, Spring 2023 edition, 2023.

[195] M. Tegmark. *Our Mathematical Universe: My Quest for the Ultimate Nature of Reality*. Knopf Doubleday Publishing Group, 2014.

[196] The Sages (Rishis). *The Upanishads. Translated by Eknath Easwaran*. Nilgiri Press, Tomales, CA, 2007.

[197] Frank Tipler. *The physics of immortality: Modern cosmology, God, and the resurrection*. Anchor Books Doubleday, New York, 1997.

[198] Tommaso Toffoli. Reversible computing. In *Automata, Languages and Programming: Seventh Colloquium. Noordwijkerhout, the Netherlands July 14–18, 1980*, pages 632–644. Springer, 1980.

[199] G. Tononi, M. Boly, M. Massimini, and Ch. Koch. Integrated information theory: from consciousness to its physical substrate. *Nature Reviews Neuroscience*, 17(7):450–461, 2016.

[200] Alan Turing. Computing machinery and intelligence. *Mind*, 59(236):433–460, 1950.

[201] A.M. Turing. On computable numbers, with an application to the Entscheidungsproblem. *Proc. London Math. Soc.*, 2(1):230–265, 1937.

[202] WT Tutte. FISH and I. In D Joyner, editor, *Coding theory and cryptography*, pages 9–17, Heidelberg, New York, 2000. Springer.

[203] Aristotle Tympas. *Calculation and computation in the pre-electronic era*. Springer, 2017.

[204] Bernd Ulmann. *Analog and hybrid computer programming.* Oldenbourg Wissenschaftsverlag Verlag, Berlin, Germany, 2022.

[205] J Von Neumann, A W Burks, et al. Theory of self-reproducing automata. *IEEE Transactions on Neural Networks*, 5(1):3–14, 1966.

[206] A De Vos. *Reversible computing.* John Wiley & Sons, Weinheim, 2011.

[207] Hao Wang. Proving theorems by pattern recognition — II. *The Bell System Technical Journal*, 40(1):1–41, 1961.

[208] Hao Wang. Games, logic and computers. *Scientific American*, 2013(5):98–107, 1965.

[209] Hao Wang. Notes on a class of tiling problems. *Fundamenta Mathematicae*, 82(4):295–305, 1975.

[210] J. A. Wheeler. Information, Physics, Quantum: The Search for Links. In *Complexity, entropy and the physics of information: the Proceedings of the 1988 Workshop on complexity, entropy, and the physics of information held May [29]-June [10], 1989 in Santa Fe, New Mexico*, volume 8. Westview Press, 1990.

[211] E.P. Wigner. On unitary representations of the inhomogeneous Lorentz group. *Ann. Math.*, pages 149–204, 1939.

[212] Stephen Wolfram. *A new kind of science*, volume 5. Wolfram Media Inc., 2002.

[213] Stephen Wolfram. The concept of the ruliad, November 2021. https://writings.stephenwolfram.com/2021/11/the-concept-of-the-ruliad/. Accessed April 22, 2026.

[214] P. Zanardi, D.A. Lidar, and S. Lloyd. Quantum tensor product structures are observable induced. *Phys. Rev. Lett.*, 92(6):060402, 2004.

[215] Hector Zenil. *A computable universe: Understanding and exploring nature as computation.* World Scientific, Singapore, 2012.

[216] Zhuangzi. *Zhuangzi. Basic Writings. Translated by Burton Watson.* Columbia University Press, 2003.

[217] W. H. Zurek. Decoherence, Einselection, and the Quantum Origins of the Classical. *Rev. Mod. Phys.*, 75:715, 2002. arXiv:quant-ph/0105127.

[218] W.H. Zurek. Decoherence and the transition from quantum to classical. *Physics Today*, page 37, 1991.

Index

For Product Safety Concerns and Information please contact our EU
representative GPSR@taylorandfrancis.com
Taylor & Francis Verlag GmbH, Kaufingerstraße 24, 80331 München, Germany

www.ingramcontent.com/pod-product-compliance
Ingram Content Group UK Ltd.
Pitfield, Milton Keynes, MK11 3LW, UK
UKHW022216190926
475702UK00003B/391

9781041027881